WORLD
ATLAS

WORLD ATLAS

Collins
An imprint of HarperCollins Publishers
Westerhill Road
Bishopbriggs
Glasgow G64 2QT

First Edition 2011

Printed in Thailand

British Library Cataloguing in Publication Data
A catalogue record for this book is available from the British Library

ISBN 978 0 00 789916 6
Imp 001

All mapping in this book is generated from Collins Bartholomew digital databases.
Collins Bartholomew, the UK's leading independent geographical information supplier,
can provide a digital, custom, and premium mapping service to a variety of markets.
For further information:
Tel: +44 (0) 141 306 3752
e-mail: collinsbartholomew@harpercollins.co.uk

or visit our website at: www.collinsbartholomew.com

Cover image: Planetary Visions
www.planetaryvisions.com

More mapping online at
www.collinsmaps.com

Collins
WORLD
ATLAS

CONTENTS

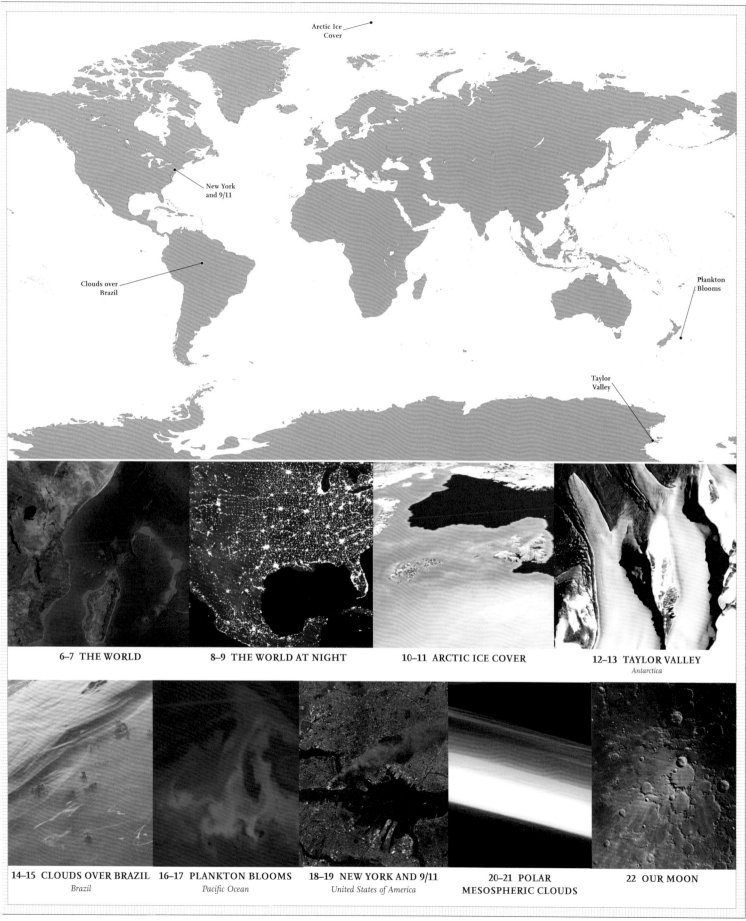

Arctic Ice
Cover

New York
and 9/11

Clouds over
Brazil

Plankton
Blooms

Taylor
Valley

6–7 THE WORLD

8–9 THE WORLD AT NIGHT

10–11 ARCTIC ICE COVER

12–13 TAYLOR VALLEY
Antarctica

14–15 CLOUDS OVER BRAZIL
Brazil

16–17 PLANKTON BLOOMS
Pacific Ocean

18–19 NEW YORK AND 9/11
United States of America

**20–21 POLAR
MESOSPHERIC CLOUDS**

22 OUR MOON

THE WORLD

Despite being summer in the northern hemisphere there is still snow and ice in the northern extremities of Canada, Scandinavia and Russia and the year-round ice sheet covering most of Greenland. Only snow on the southern end of the Andes in South America and on South Island, New Zealand give any indication of winter in the southern hemisphere.

Clearly visible through the tropics is the dark green belt of the rain forests of South America, central Africa and southern Asia. Also depicted in dark green extending across the subarctic areas of North America and Eurasia, are the coniferous forests of the taiga. Bordering these forest regions, a lighter green shows areas of grassland such as the prairies of North America, steppes of Eurasia and African savanna.

The deserts of the world appear in gold. The vast arid areas of the Sahara and Arabian Peninsula dominate the centre of the image and the Atacama in South America, Gobi in central Asia and deserts of the Australian interior are also easy to pick out.

Stretching approximately 16,000 kilometres (10,000 miles) in length, the Mid-Atlantic Ridge can be identified in light blue stretching from the north to south Atlantic.

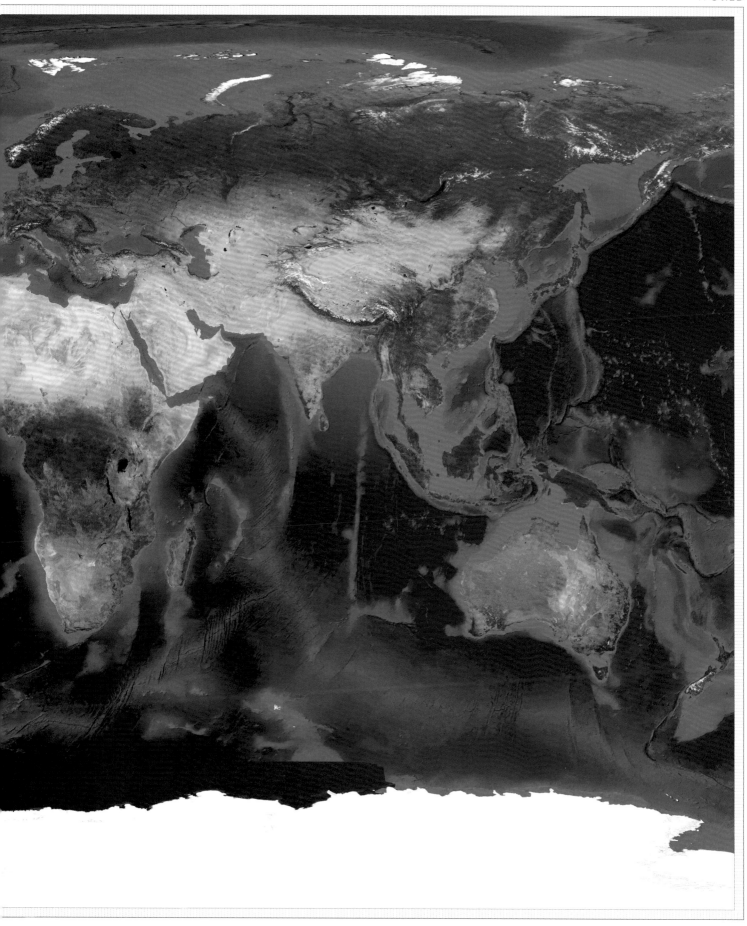

THE WORLD AT NIGHT

This striking image is a composite of hundreds of pictures taken in 1994–95 by the US Defense Meteorological Satellite Program (DMSP), which mapped the locations of night-time outdoor lights on the Earth's surface. By day, cities viewed from space blend into the countryside or appear as grey smudges, but at night their lights show up from space, meaning that even without any underlying map it would be possible to identify most continental outlines, some countries and even individual cities in some cases, from the distribution of light alone.

The location of major cities does not, however, show the whole picture as regards densest population areas. Although the image clearly shows that cities are concentrated in Western Europe, Japan, China, India and the United States (especially in the east), large areas of China and India which are in fact very densely populated do not stand out so well, because much of the population is distributed more evenly among rural areas and in many thousands of smaller towns.

The picture also reveals the extent to which big cities are often arranged in lines along major roads, railways and rivers, as well as by the coast.

The United Nations reported that world urbanisation crossed the 50 per cent mark by the middle of 2009 – the number of people living in urban areas (3.42 billion) just surpassed those living in rural areas (3.41 billion). The UN expects the world's urban population to increase to 6.3 billion by 2050, and virtually all of the expected population growth will be concentrated in the urban areas of the less developed regions. It would be interesting to compare any future map with this one.

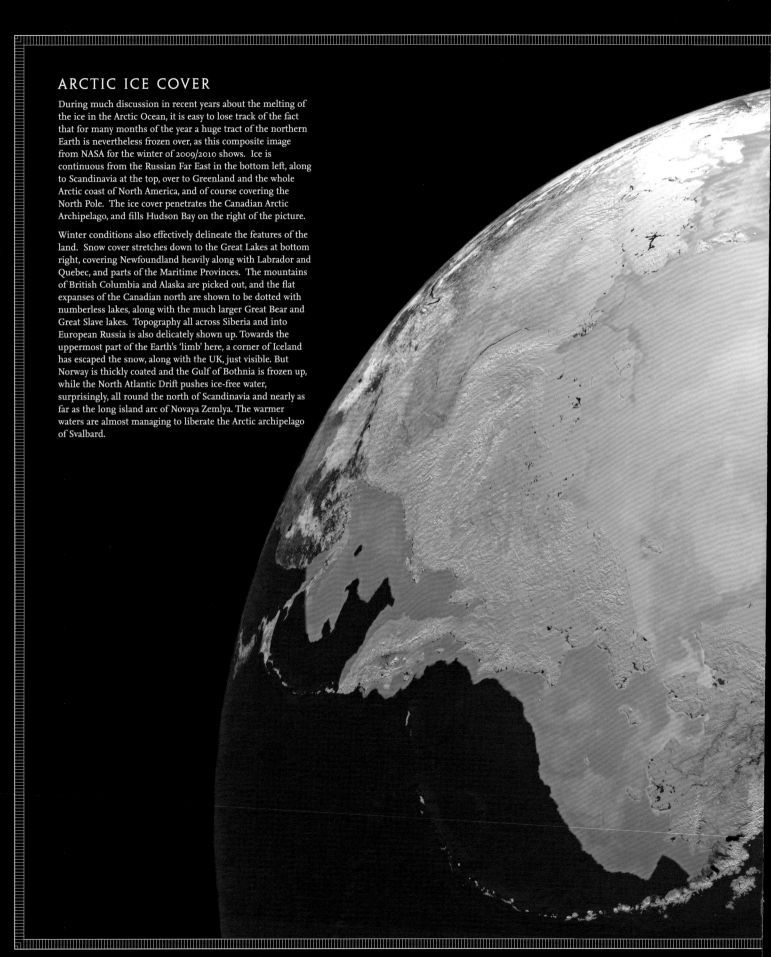

ARCTIC ICE COVER

During much discussion in recent years about the melting of
the ice in the Arctic Ocean, it is easy to lose track of the fact
that for many months of the year a huge tract of the northern
Earth is nevertheless frozen over, as this composite image
from NASA for the winter of 2009/2010 shows. Ice is
continuous from the Russian Far East in the bottom left, along
to Scandinavia at the top, over to Greenland and the whole
Arctic coast of North America, and of course covering the
North Pole. The ice cover penetrates the Canadian Arctic
Archipelago, and fills Hudson Bay on the right of the picture.

Winter conditions also effectively delineate the features of the
land. Snow cover stretches down to the Great Lakes at bottom
right, covering Newfoundland heavily along with Labrador and
Quebec, and parts of the Maritime Provinces. The mountains
of British Columbia and Alaska are picked out, and the flat
expanses of the Canadian north are shown to be dotted with
numberless lakes, along with the much larger Great Bear and
Great Slave lakes. Topography all across Siberia and into
European Russia is also delicately shown up. Towards the
uppermost part of the Earth's 'limb' here, a corner of Iceland
has escaped the snow, along with the UK, just visible. But
Norway is thickly coated and the Gulf of Bothnia is frozen up,
while the North Atlantic Drift pushes ice-free water,
surprisingly, all round the north of Scandinavia and nearly as
far as the long island arc of Novaya Zemlya. The warmer
waters are almost managing to liberate the Arctic archipelago
of Svalbard.

TAYLOR VALLEY ANTARCTICA

Antarctica may be known for ice and snow, but parts of it are kept snow free by cold dry winds. In this image we can see part of the area known as the Dry Valleys which lies between the Ross Sea and the East Antarctica Ice Sheet. At the bottom of the image is the Taylor Valley in which we can see several ice-covered lakes. The Taylor Valley lakes include Lake Bonney, which sits below the Taylor Glacier. This glacier-lake junction has an unusual feature as iron oxide seeps out of the Taylor Glacier leading to a red colouring to the ice and the name Blood Falls.

CLOUDS OVER BRAZIL

While at first sight this oblique satellite vista over a half-clouded and seemingly featureless landscape might challenge the interpreter to see what is really going on, closer inspection shows much atmospheric turmoil. The picture is of a part of the Amazon Basin in western Brazil, though that is not obvious from anything recognisable in this almost abstract image. The view is towards the Andes, which although huge mountains at ground level are not detectable under this amount of cloud cover and from this height. The painterly wriggles, caught here in the sunlight, are the river Madeira – one of the greatest tributaries of the Amazon itself, which runs somewhere off to the north (right). A vague impression of green hints at the still-extensive jungle occupying this central part of South America, but at the bottom of the picture a vast plume of smoke can be made out: it can only have come from the burning of yet more of the tropical forest for agriculture.

Dotting the less-clouded half of the picture are numerous apparently small pimple-like excrescences, which however are quite sizeable local thunderclouds: many of them probably gave rise to heavy storms on the day this photo was taken in 2009.

The more thickly clouded area however shows much bigger meteorological phenomena, including a number of more dramatic knot-like cloud formations, which are being driven upwards mainly by hot convection currents – though perhaps also by the unseen form of the ground underneath – to rise above the general level of the slowly swirling white. The Earth's 'limb' (its horizon edge) shows up across the far edge of the image as a hazy blue line.

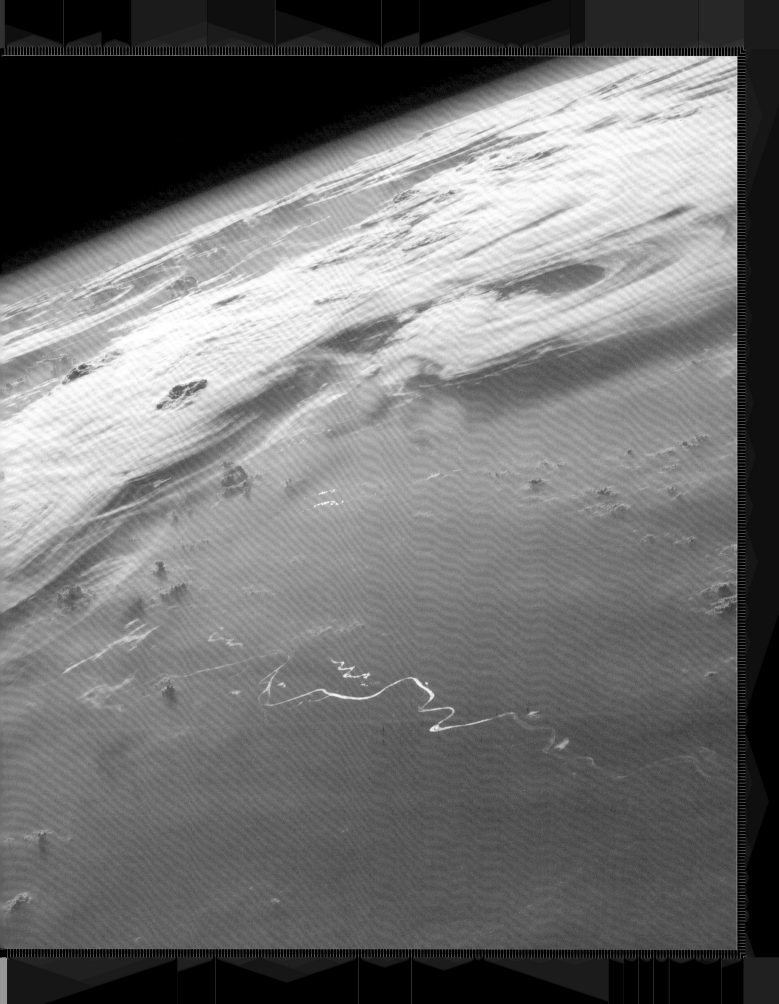

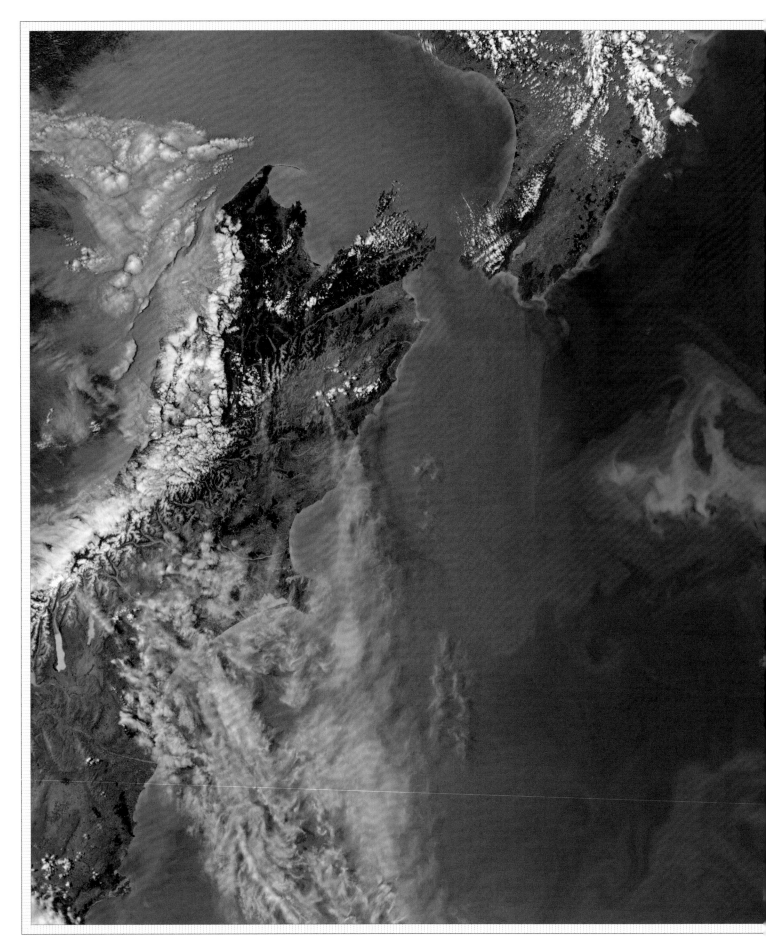

PLANKTON BLOOMS

The notion that such tiny organisms as those which make up the oceans' colossal population of plankton could produce something visible – and even rather dramatic – from space might seem counterintuitive, but here there is evidence of it in action, indeed in motion, in a colourful satellite image from NASA.

The location is easily pinpointed by the familiar shape of much of the North and South Islands of New Zealand, on the left-hand side (west), with the Cook Strait between them. Distinct from the expanses of very variable-textured cloud over some parts, snow also shows white on all the mountain tops of the Southern Alps, picking out the ridges in filigree. The angular island on the other side of the picture, which seems to be creating its own rippled cloud stream, is Chatham Island, also part of New Zealand but roughly 700 km (435 miles) from the mainland.

The open ocean area between the two is underlain by the Chatham Rise, and its topography relative to the deeper areas around it leads to the mixing of different waters and nutrients. Under favourable conditions this results in hugely extensive 'blooms' of phytoplankton, showing up as deep green against the deep blue of the rest of the ocean, a result of photosynthesis. The lighter, almost turquoise parts could well be caused by a particular type of plankton organism which is more light-reflective than the rest. The white areas show thin clouds which are floating over the middle of the swirl of plankton.

NEW YORK AND 9/11

At first sight the detailed satellite picture shown here is simply a good example of how effectively this now very well-known technology can be used to portray things very far below on the ground – in this case a densely populated urban and rural area with a clear and characteristic indented coastline, photographed from space on a clear day. The location might not be immediately familiar, but the picture is rotated at right angles compared with the usual view of north being at the top in such a map-like image. With that realisation, the outlines of Manhattan, the Hudson River, Staten Island, and the western end of Long Island become instantly familiar. The beaches along the south coast of Long Island, and also on the spit opposite, are prominent because of their pale colour. The outlines of docks, rivers, major industrial complexes, bridges and other features stand out, and there is the well-known rectangle of Central Park. It is only on a second look, perhaps, that the vast plume of smoke becomes apparent. Coordinated terrorist attacks against the USA on 11 September 2001, including the deliberate crashing of two passenger airliners into the Twin Towers of the World Trade Center in New York, killed nearly three thousand people – of whom nineteen were the hijackers but over four hundred were rescue workers. The fact that the resulting fire is obvious from space, polluting an otherwise peaceful image, underlines the sheer scale of the disaster in no uncertain terms.

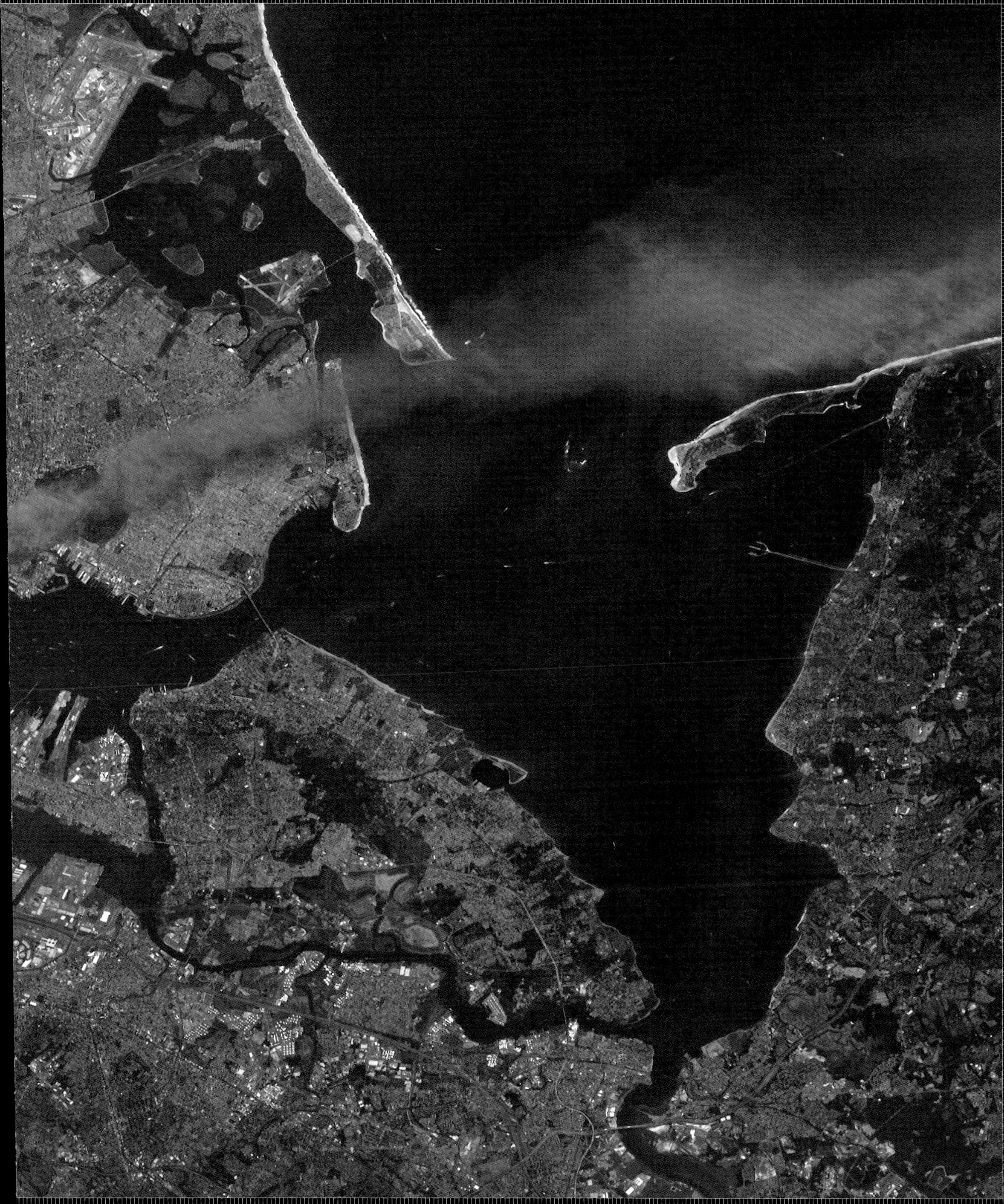

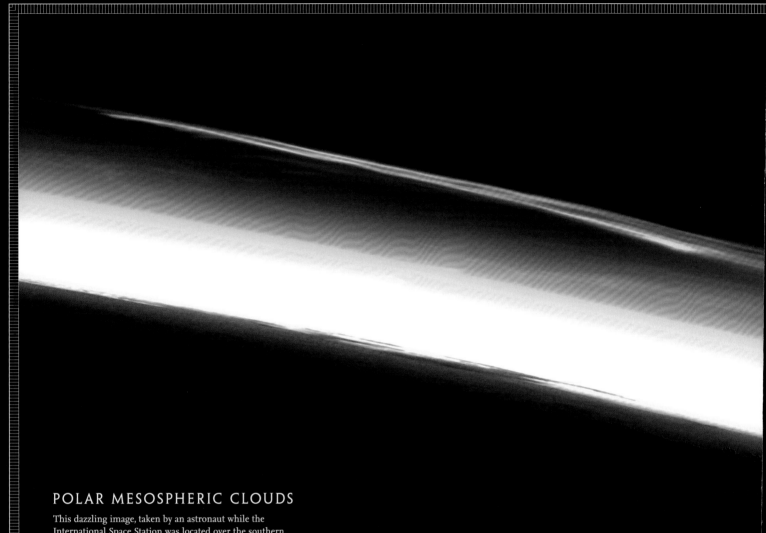

POLAR MESOSPHERIC CLOUDS

This dazzling image, taken by an astronaut while the International Space Station was located over the southern Atlantic Ocean in January 2010, shows what are known as 'polar mesospheric' clouds. These form over high latitudes (above 50° north or south) during summer months in the mesosphere, some 80 km (50 miles) above the surface of the Earth. The mesosphere is the third highest layer in our atmosphere, above the troposphere and stratosphere, and below the thermosphere (well above aviation levels). The aspects of polar mesospheric clouds that are occasionally visible from the ground are known as 'noctilucent' clouds (from the Latin for 'night-shining'). The clouds can only be seen if sunlight strikes them after sunset; they are most likely to be visible when the sun is just a few degrees below the horizon. Colours vary consistently from light blues in the upper regions through white or light orange layers and eventually reddish in the more strongly sunlit parts lower down.

These are the highest clouds in our atmosphere, and exactly why and how they form is still a matter of debate: if methane and perhaps water vapour from volcanic eruptions are critical ingredients, as has been suggested, that could explain why noctilucent clouds were only first sighted in 1885, two years after the Krakatoa eruption.

Though rare, these clouds have been increasing in frequency in recent decades – and also at lower latitudes – for reasons that are not yet known, though some scientists fear it is a sign of climate change.

OUR MOON

This finely-detailed image showing the Moon set against the black backdrop of space was made up from a composite of many taken (using a green filter) by the US spacecraft Galileo, which flew past the Moon in 1992 on its six-year journey to Jupiter. Close-up viewings from several manned landings – but also from cameras on passing spacecraft – have greatly enhanced our knowledge of the Earth's only satellite. The image's sharpness clarifies the huge number of meteorite craters of various sizes (some overlapping others), and the elevations of some of the larger circular crater walls are picked out by the angle of the sunlight.

The other main features of the Moon shown well here are the so-called Seas, or Maria, which are very dry and consist largely of vast, extremely ancient expanses of solidified lava: they acquired their still-used 'marine' designation from an early assumption that they might be bodies of water. The picturesque names of those shown here include the Sea of Tranquillity (Mare Tranquillitatis) at bottom left, the Sea of Serenity, Sea of Crises, and Sea of Rains. The Humboldt Sea, another area of volcanic activity, is the dark area located in the centre towards the zone that is in the shadow of the lunar night. Although almost all of one side of the Moon is never visible from Earth, it is incorrect to think of it as the 'dark side', since it is in daylight just as often as the visible side (when our side is in darkness).

To give an idea of the scale of the many geological features, the breadth of the Moon is over 1700 km (1056 miles).

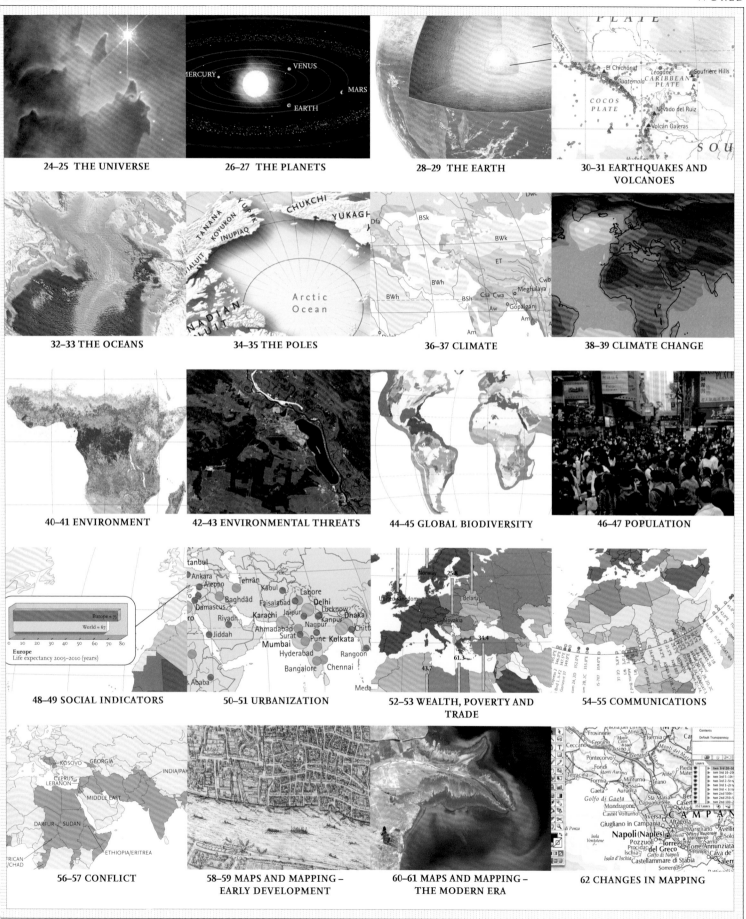

THE UNIVERSE

The nature and origin of the universe have inspired speculation and religious awe since people first looked into the sky, but scientific cosmology is only a century old. It began when Einstein's General Theory of Relativity and the discovery of the expansion of the universe inspired the 'Big Bang' theory of its origin in a single instant (now known to be 13.7 ± 0.28 billion years ago). This was the moment when space, time, matter and energy all came into existence. We now believe that the young universe was shaped by a process called Cosmic Inflation: 10^{-35} of a second after the Big Bang, a still-unknown field appears to have expanded it by at least 10^{26} times. Minute density fluctuations created 'seeds' of future galaxies. The field decayed into an inconceivably dense and hot 'quark-gluon plasma'. As the universe continued to expand and cool, protons and neutrons (baryons) formed. Later, protons and neutrons began fusing to produce helium and traces of other light nuclei.

The Eagle Nebula is a beautiful region where stars are forming in columns of dense gas and dust. Massive young, hot stars have heated the interstellar gas and blown away most of it, to reveal the famous 'pillars'. Denser regions within the pillars have collapsed under gravity to form a new generation of young stars, currently buried in the dust and visible only in infrared light. Rotation of their parent cloud causes most new (single) stars to form encircling discs of gas and dust from which planets will form.

The Hubble Deep Field comprises 342 separate images from the Hubble Telescope. It encapsulates much of the universe's history. The farthest objects, seen as they were only a billion years after the Big Bang, are mostly 'irregular' galaxies, small systems less organized than the few large galaxies in the image, which are 'nearby' in both distance and time. The large galaxies include spirals, such as the Milky Way and M101, and ellipticals. These probably formed through the merger of many of the small irregulars. In all, about 100 billion galaxies are 'observable', i.e. near enough for their light to have reached us since the Big Bang.

Some galaxies emit far more light than is accounted for by their stars. These 'active' galaxies derive their excess brightness from a huge central black hole. Most galaxies probably contain such holes – bodies so massive and dense that light cannot escape from them. The 'active' ones are those currently consuming matter. The most luminous are the Quasars or Quasi-Stellar Objects (QSOs), which can be seen at enormous distances – light from the farthest known examples was emitted when the universe was only one-tenth of its present age.

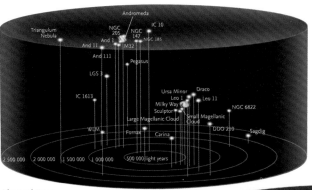

The Local Group

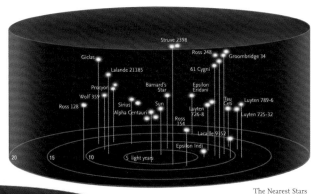

The Nearest Stars

The Milky Way

COMPOSITION OF THE UNIVERSE

Before the baryons formed, large quantities were created of a mysterious 'dark matter', composed of as yet unidentified, slow-moving, particles which interact almost exclusively by gravity, unlike baryonic matter which interacts with electromagnetic radiation (light, radio, x-rays, etc) Currently we can only detect dark matter by its gravitational effects which dominate the structure of the universe.

About 380 000 years after the Big Bang, the temperature fell low enough for electrons and protons to combine to form hydrogen. The opaque plasma filling the universe became transparent gas and the leftover radiation flowed freely. It is still detectable as the 'Cosmic Microwave Background Radiation' (CMBR), whose discovery in 1965 provided dramatic confirmation of the Big Bang scenario. In 1989 NASA's COBE satellite demonstrated that the CMBR carries an image of the structure of the universe at the time of its release. In 2003 the WMAP spacecraft showed that this structure is in accurate agreement with the predictions of inflation.

Dark matter had already begun gravitating to, and enhancing, the density peaks left over from inflation. Freed from the pressure of radiation, the newly-formed hydrogen was now also attracted by the gravity of these peaks. The concentrations of dark matter combined to form galaxies. Their attendant gas clouds merged, cooled and fragmented into smaller and smaller clouds, eventually condensing into stars. The galaxies themselves began to assemble into small groups and then large clusters.

Recently, observations of distant supernovae (exploding stars) showed that the expansion of the universe is speeding up. This is driven by the pressure of its third, largest and least understood component, the 'dark energy'. Studies of the CMBR and observations of galaxy distributions show that dark energy constitutes 73 per cent of the mass of the universe, dark matter 23 per cent and baryonic matter a mere 4 per cent.

The ultimate fate of the universe remains uncertain. If the dark energy pressure is constant, as seems likely, expansion will continue forever, but if its effect is increasing, expansion may accelerate until everything is torn apart in a 'big rip'.

THE LOCAL GROUP OF GALAXIES

Galaxies tend to reside in clusters, which in turn may form part of a supercluster. Our Milky Way is in a small cluster called The Local Group, on the periphery of the Local Supercluster, which is centred on the Virgo Cluster of galaxies. The Local Group is 5 million light years across and consists of two large spirals, the Milky Way and the Andromeda Galaxy (M31), two smaller spirals, M33 in Triangulum and the Large Magellanic Cloud, together with approximately thirty smaller irregular and spheroidal systems. Both the Milky Way and Andromeda have families of satellites, forming two separate subgroups. The most prominent Milky Way satellites are the Large and Small Magellanic clouds; the rest are inconspicuous dwarf spheroidal galaxies. Andromeda's four principal satellite galaxies are small ellipticals but it too has several dwarf spheroidal companions.

THE MILKY WAY

The Milky Way is visible on any clear night as a faint band of light stretching across the sky. It is our own home galaxy. It contains between 200 and 400 billion stars and is a 'barred' spiral. All spirals have flattened discs of stars and gas, surrounding central bulges of different sizes, enveloped by a thin, usually spherical, halo. Like those of other spirals, the disc of the Milky Way is composed of stars in roughly circular orbits around the centre, with ages ranging from twice that of the sun, itself part of the disc, down to just-formed newborns. The disc is about 100 000 light years across and 1 000 thick and contains nearly all the gas clouds where new stars form.

The barred, elongated, bulge is approximately 3 000 light years thick, 15 000 long and approximately half that in width. At its centre, in the constellation Sagittarius, is an inactive black hole of approximately three million solar masses. Older than those in the disc, bulge stars follow complex looping orbits, whose shapes give the bar its form. Vigorous star formation episodes, termed 'starbursts', sometimes occur in the centres of barred spirals. The Milky Way experienced such an event not long ago.

The galactic halo is a sphere approximately 200 000 light years across. Its thinly-spread stars are very old and mostly deficient in heavy elements, some by factors of thousands. The halo as a whole is not rotating. It contains about 200 globular star clusters, each of many thousand stars, and the remnants of several recently-cannibalized dwarf galaxies.

THE STARS – THE SUN'S NEAREST NEIGHBOURS

The first stars contained no elements heavier than helium and were probably much larger and hotter than those of subsequent generations. Like all except the very faintest stars, they obtained their energy from nuclear reactions in their cores. These reactions produced the heavier elements from hydrogen and helium. The stars' final explosions as supernovae dispersed these elements into the interstellar gas, ready for incorporation into the next stellar generation, of which some galactic halo stars may be examples. Heavy-element enrichment still continues with each new stellar generation.

A star's brightness increases very rapidly with its mass but its life-span decreases. Sirius A is two and a quarter times the mass of the Sun (and has that much more fuel) but it is twenty-two times as bright (so is burning it twenty-two times faster). It will live only approximately a billion years, a tenth as long as the Sun. The most massive stars, one hundred and ten times the mass of the sun, survive for much less than a million years. There are far fewer massive stars than small ones. Within fifteen light years of Earth there are fifty-three stars in thirty-eight solar systems. Only two are bigger, hotter and brighter than the Sun, three are similar to the Sun, five rather fainter and no less than forty are very faint 'red dwarfs'. Two are white dwarfs – tiny, very dense remains of stars once much brighter than the Sun but now thousands of times fainter.

The nearest star is Alpha Centauri (α Cen), a triple star four light years away. Here, two sun-like stars (A and B) orbiting close to one another are accompanied at a distance by the very faint red dwarf α Cen C, known as Proxima Centauri, currently the nearest star of all to the Sun. The brightest star in the sky is Sirius, fifth nearest, nine light years away. Its white dwarf companion, Sirius B, has the Sun's mass, but only five times the Earth's radius.

THE PLANETS

The nature and origin of our Solar System has been a subject of much debate. Early ideas of an Earth-centred system took many hundreds of years to be discarded in favour of Copernicus' heliocentric, or sun-centred model. More refined theories followed with Kepler's laws of orbital motion, and Newton's laws of gravity. The question of origin remained unanswered, and was regarded more as a philosophical matter.

The fact that the Sun and the planets rotate in the same direction suggests a common formation mechanism – that of a large collapsing cloud or nebula. It is now believed that this did happen, about 4 600 million years ago. The nebula consisted of predominantly hydrogen and helium, but with a small amount of heavier elements. Over time, the cloud collapsed to form a rotating disk around a dense core. As core collapse continued and pressure in the core increased, material was heated enough to allow the nuclear fusion of hydrogen. Meanwhile as the disk cooled, the heavier elements began to condense and agglomerate. Larger bodies grew rapidly by sweeping up much of the remaining smaller material. As the core began to shine, its radiation pushed back much of the nearby volatile disk material into the outer Solar System, where it condensed and accumulated on the more distant planetary cores. This left the Inner Planets as small rocky bodies, and produced the Gas Giants of the outer system. Bombardment of the planets by a decreasing number of small bodies continued for several hundred million years, causing the craters now seen on many of the planets and moons.

Periodic collisions with comets and other small bodies provided Earth with a large moon, and subsequently with an atmosphere and water. Alongside many other important factors, this has enabled our planet to become a very suitable environment for life to form and flourish.

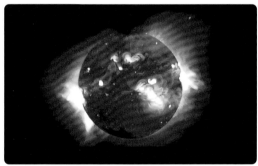

The Sun is a typical star and the closest one to Earth. It accounts for 99.85 per cent of the total mass contained within the Solar System, ensuring that it provides a dominating gravitational hold on its orbiting planets. The tremendous amount of heat and light produced by the Sun is the result of nuclear fusion reactions which occur in its core. In this process, hydrogen is converted into helium to produce a core temperature of roughly 15 million°C. Intense magnetic fields can induce cooling zones seen as dark sun spots on the Sun's surface. The Sun constantly emits a stream of charged particles which form the solar wind and cause auroral activity which can be seen on Earth.

THE SOLAR SYSTEM

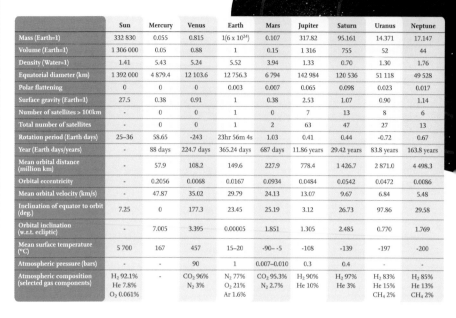

	Sun	Mercury	Venus	Earth	Mars	Jupiter	Saturn	Uranus	Neptune
Mass (Earth=1)	332 830	0.055	0.815	1(6 x 10²⁴)	0.107	317.82	95.161	14.371	17.147
Volume (Earth=1)	1 306 000	0.05	0.88	1	0.15	1 316	755	52	44
Density (Water=1)	1.41	5.43	5.24	5.52	3.94	1.33	0.70	1.30	1.76
Equatorial diameter (km)	1 392 000	4 879.4	12 103.6	12 756.3	6 794	142 984	120 536	51 118	49 528
Polar flattening	0	0	0	0.003	0.007	0.065	0.098	0.023	0.017
Surface gravity (Earth=1)	27.5	0.38	0.91	1	0.38	2.53	1.07	0.90	1.14
Number of satellites > 100km	-	0	0	1	0	7	13	8	6
Total number of satellites	-	0	0	1	2	63	47	27	13
Rotation period (Earth days)	25–36	58.65	-243	23hr 56m 4s	1.03	0.41	0.44	-0.72	0.67
Year (Earth days/years)	-	88 days	224.7 days	365.24 days	687 days	11.86 years	29.42 years	83.8 years	163.8 years
Mean orbital distance (million km)	-	57.9	108.2	149.6	227.9	778.4	1 426.7	2 871.0	4 498.3
Orbital eccentricity	-	0.2056	0.0068	0.0167	0.0934	0.0484	0.0542	0.0472	0.0086
Mean orbital velocity (km/s)	-	47.87	35.02	29.79	24.13	13.07	9.67	6.84	5.48
Inclination of equator to orbit (deg.)	7.25	0	177.3	23.45	25.19	3.12	26.73	97.86	29.58
Orbital inclination (w.r.t. ecliptic)	-	7.005	3.395	0.00005	1.851	1.305	2.485	0.770	1.769
Mean surface temperature (°C)	5 700	167	457	15–20	-90– -5	-108	-139	-197	-200
Atmospheric pressure (bars)	-	-	90	1	0.007–0.010	0.3	0.4	-	-
Atmospheric composition (selected gas components)	H_2 92.1% He 7.8% O_2 0.061%	-	CO_2 96% N_2 3%	N_2 77% O_2 21% Ar 1.6%	CO_2 95.3% N_2 2.7%	H_2 90% He 10%	H_2 97% He 3%	H_2 83% He 15% CH_4 2%	H_2 85% He 13% CH_4 2%

MERCURY

Mercury's long period of rotation, close proximity to the Sun, and minimal atmosphere make its surface an extremely hostile environment with temperatures ranging from 427 to minus 173°C between its day and night side. Mercury is similar to Earth's Moon in size and appearance; its cratered surface was first photographed in detail in the mid-1970s by the Mariner 10 space probe. However the internal structure differs from the Moon. Analysis of its magnetic field suggests that the core consists of molten iron, believed to be 40 per cent of the planet's volume. Mercury has a very eccentric orbit with its distance from the Sun varying from 46 to 70 million km.

VENUS

Venus' thick atmosphere of carbon dioxide and nitrogen creates not only a huge surface pressure of ninety times that on Earth but also a greenhouse effect producing temperatures in excess of 450°C. Traces of sulphur dioxide and water vapour form clouds of dilute sulphuric acid, making the atmosphere extremely corrosive. The thick clouds reflect almost all incident light and hide the surface from view. In 1990 use of radar imaging enabled the Magellan space probe to see through the cloud. Magellan mapped 98 per cent of the planet during three years to find a surface covered in craters, volcanoes, mountains and solidified lava flows. Venus is the brightest object in the sky after the Sun and Moon and is unusual in that its year is less than its rotation period.

SATURN

Although only slightly smaller than Jupiter, Saturn is a mere one-third of Jupiter's mass, and the least dense of all the planets – less dense than water. The low mass, combined with a fast rotation rate, leads to the planet's significant polar flattening. Saturn exhibits a striking ring system, more than twice the diameter of the planet. The rings consist of countless small rock and ice clumps which vary in size from a grain of sand to tens of metres in diameter. It is believed that the rings were formed from a stray moon coming too close to, and being ripped apart by Saturn. Distinct bands and gaps in the rings are the result of complex interactions between Saturn and its closer moons. Recent rare opportunities to view Saturn's rings edgeways have led to the discovery of at least 60 other moons.

URANUS

Uranus has many surprising features; the most prominent of these is the tilt of its rotation axis by over 90 degrees caused by a large collision in its early history. Like the other Gas Giants, Uranus is predominantly hydrogen and helium with a small proportion of methane and other gases. However, because Uranus is colder than Jupiter and Saturn, the methane forms ice crystals which give Uranus a featureless blue-green colour. The interior is also different from that expected. Instead of having a gaseous atmosphere above liquid and metallic hydrogen layers, Uranus has a super-dense gaseous atmosphere extending down to its core. Uranus' magnetic field is inclined at 60 degrees to the rotation axis, and is off centre by one-third of the planet's radius, which suggests that it is not generated by the core.

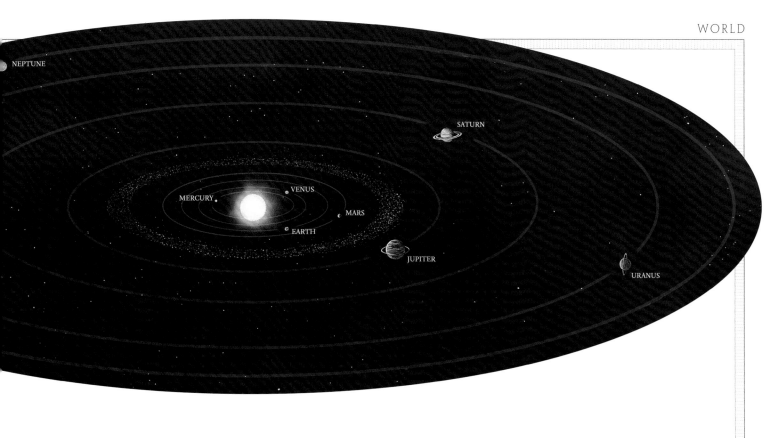

NEPTUNE

SATURN

MERCURY VENUS
MARS
EARTH

JUPITER

URANUS

EARTH

Earth is the largest and densest of the Inner Planets. Created some 4 500 million years ago, the core, rocky mantle and crust are similar in structure to Venus. The Earth's core is composed almost entirely of iron and oxygen compounds which exist in a molten state at temperatures of approximately 5 000°C. Earth is the only planet with vast quantities of life-sustaining water, with the oceans covering 70.8 per cent of its surface. The action of plate tectonics has created vast mountain ranges and is responsible for volcanic activity. The Moon is Earth's only natural satellite and with a diameter of over one quarter that of the Earth's, makes the Earth-Moon system a near double-planet.

MARS

Named after the Roman god of war because of its blood-red appearance, Mars is the last of the Inner Planets. The red colour comes from the high concentration of iron oxides on its surface. Mars has impressive surface features, including the highest known peak in the Solar System, Olympus Mons, an inactive volcano reaching a height of 23 km above the surrounding plains, and Valles Marineris, a 2 500 km long canyon four times as deep as the Grand Canyon. Mars has polar caps composed of water and carbon dioxide ice which partially evaporate during its summer. NASA's surface rovers Spirit and Opportunity, which landed in 2004, have provided clear evidence that water once flowed on Mars, increasing the likelihood that life once existed there.

JUPITER

Jupiter is by far the most massive of all the planets and is the dominant body in the Solar System after the Sun. It is the innermost of the Gas Giants. The dense surface atmosphere is predominantly hydrogen, with helium, water vapour, and methane. Below this is a layer of liquid hydrogen, then an even deeper layer of metallic hydrogen and possibly a small rocky core. Unlike solid bodies, Jupiter's rotation period is somewhat ill-defined, with equatorial regions rotating faster than the polar caps. This, combined with convection currents in lower layers, cause intense magnetic fields and rapidly varying surface features. Most notable of these is the Great Red Spot, a giant circular storm visible since the first telescopic observations of Jupiter, which shows no signs of abating.

NEPTUNE

Neptune has always been associated with Uranus because of its similar size, composition and appearance, but, unexpectedly, Neptune's atmosphere is more active than that of Uranus. This was shown by Voyager 2 in 1989 with the observation of the Great Dark Spot, Neptune's equivalent to Jupiter's Great Red Spot. Voyager 2 recorded the fastest winds ever seen in the Solar System, 2 000 km per hour, around the Dark Spot. This feature disappeared in 1994, but has been replaced by a similar storm in the northern polar cap. Like Uranus, Neptune has a magnetic field highly inclined to the planet's axis of rotation and off-centre by more than half of the planet's radius. The cause of this magnetic field is convection currents in conducting fluid layers outside the core.

PLUTO AND THE KUIPER BELT

Discovered in 1930, Pluto was long considered to be the 'ninth planet' but since 1992 many hundreds of similar objects have been found in a flattened disk beyond Neptune. Astronomers often call this region of trans-Neptunian bodies the 'Kuiper Belt'. As more and more Kuiper Belt Objects, some about the same size as Pluto and many having moons of their own, were discovered, a debate about Pluto's status erupted. Finally, in 2006 the International Astronomical Union decided to re-classify Pluto, and some of the larger Kuiper Belt Objects such as Eris and Sedna, as a new class of 'dwarf-planets'.

ASTEROIDS

Asteroids are small irregularly shaped rocky objects which orbit the Sun and which are remnants from the formation of the planets. The largest concentration of asteroids exists in a belt, 180 million km in width, which lies between the orbits of Mars and Jupiter. Over 100 000 asteroids are estimated to have diameters greater than 1 km and yet only a dozen or so are known to have diameters greater than 250 km. The entire mass of the asteroid belt is approximately one-thousandth of the Earth's mass. One-third of this mass is accounted for by Ceres, the largest asteroid known with a diameter of 913 km. Hundreds, possibly thousands of asteroids, of varying sizes, cross the Earth's orbit and on 13 April 2029 asteroid number 99942 Apophis will fly within 40 000 km of the Earth.

THE EARTH

Before the end of the 19th century, earth scientists had no way of discovering the composition of the interior of the Earth. Ideas about the internal structure were therefore based almost entirely on speculation. The only evidence related to phenomena apparent at the Earth's surface, but which seemed to arise from within. These consisted of earthquakes, volcanoes, and geysers. To early thinkers, earthquakes indicated that the Earth could not be made entirely of solid rock, but might contain underground caverns full of air. Geysers and springs also suggested that the interior of the Earth was partly, or largely, made up of water. On the other hand, volcanic eruptions seemed to indicate that fire existed underground. For a long time, debate continued between the neptunists who favoured a watery interior and the volcanists favouring a fiery one. With the development of instrumental seismology and worldwide seismic monitoring, starting around 1900, a more soundly based answer began to appear. Careful study of the time differences of different earthquake waves showed that features of the Earth's structure could be deduced by analysing the way in which waves travel through it. Boundaries between different layers within the Earth were identified by the way waves were reflected or refracted by them. It was also possible to tell which parts of the Earth's interior must be liquid, since some types of wave can only travel through solid regions. As a result, the basic internal structure of the Earth became known.

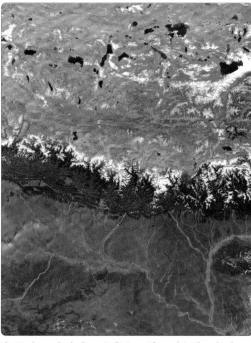

The Himalaya can be clearly seen in this image. They are being formed as the Indian continental plate to the south collides with the Asian plate to the north. This is an example of a continental destructive plate boundary.

PLATE TECTONICS

Over the course of geological time the Earth's crust has broken up into large fragments, which are known as lithospheric or tectonic plates. These plates are slowly moving relative to one another at rates of a few centimetres per year. This process – originally described as continental drift, a term coined by the meteorologist Alfred Wegener who first proposed the idea in the 1920s – is known as plate tectonics. The interaction of plates along their boundaries causes volcanic and seismic activity. The fact that the shapes of South America and Africa dovetail neatly into one another was noticed as early as the 17th century, and this has proved to be no coincidence.

THE EARTH'S INTERNAL STRUCTURE

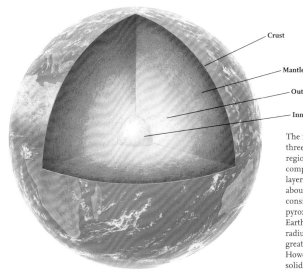

Crust

Mantle

Outer Core

Inner Core

The interior of the Earth can be divided into three principal regions. The outermost region is the crust which is extremely thin compared to the Earth as a whole. The next layer down is known as the mantle. This is about 2850 km thick and is believed to consist mostly of the minerals olivine, pyroxene and garnet. Below the mantle is the Earth's core, which is about 3470 km in radius, and is mainly made up of iron. The greater part of the core is completely liquid. However, there is an inner core which is solid, and about 1220 km in radius.

Mass	5.974×10^{21} tonnes
Total area	509 450 000 sq km / 196 698 645 sq miles
Land area	149 450 000 sq km / 57 702 645 sq miles
Water area	360 000 000 sq km / 138 996 000 sq miles
Volume	1 083 207 x 10⁶ cubic km / 259 911 x 10⁶ cubic miles
Equatorial diameter	12 756 km / 7 927 miles
Polar diameter	12 714 km / 7 901 miles
Equatorial circumference	40 075 km / 24 903 miles
Meridional circumference	40 008 km / 24 861 miles

PLATE TECTONICS

The Earth looked very different 200 million years ago. All the continents were at one time joined together in a great landmass called Pangaea.

By 100 million years ago Africa had split away from the Americas, Antarctica and Australia then broke away from Africa and subsequently from each other.

About 165 million years ago this super-continent began to break up.

Around 50 million years ago, North America and Europe separated, and India, which was formerly attached to Antarctica, moved northwards to collide with Asia.

TYPES OF PLATE BOUNDARY

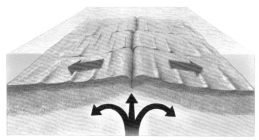

A constructive (or divergent) plate boundary occurs where two plates are moving away from each other, with new crust being formed along the ridge between them. One place where such a boundary occurs on land is in Iceland. Here the mid-Atlantic ridge creates a dramatic rift in the landscape at Thingvellir, the site of the old Icelandic parliament.

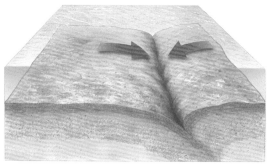

With a destructive (or convergent), boundary two plates are colliding. When an oceanic crust meets another piece of oceanic crust it sinks under it, creating a subduction zone (usually accompanied by a deep ocean trench) as it does so.

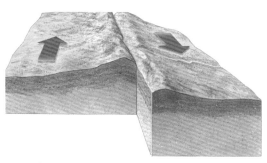

In some places, two plates slide past one another, with neither being destroyed. This is known as a conservative (or transform) boundary. The classic example is in California, where the Pacific Plate is sliding northwest relative to the North American Plate, along the line of the San Andreas Fault.

Occasionally, with a destructive (or convergent) boundary a continental crust meets another continental crust, and the two crumple up, one eventually being forced under the other. This is what is happening between India and Asia, with the Himalaya being formed as a result.

TECTONIC PLATE BOUNDARIES

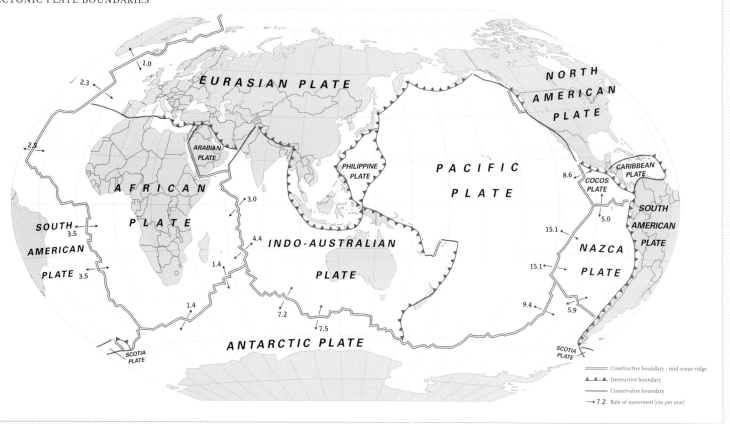

EURASIAN PLATE

NORTH AMERICAN PLATE

ARABIAN PLATE

PHILIPPINE PLATE

PACIFIC PLATE

CARIBBEAN PLATE

COCOS PLATE

AFRICAN PLATE

SOUTH AMERICAN PLATE

SOUTH AMERICAN PLATE

NAZCA PLATE

INDO-AUSTRALIAN PLATE

ANTARCTIC PLATE

SCOTIA PLATE

SCOTIA PLATE

1.0
2.3
2.5
3.5
3.5
1.4
3.0
4.4
1.4
7.2
7.5
8.6
5.0
15.1
15.1
9.4
5.9

═══ Constructive boundary - mid ocean ridge
▲▲▲ Destructive boundary
─── Conservative boundary
→ 7.2 Rate of movement (cm per year)

EARTHQUAKES AND VOLCANOES

Any map showing the distribution of earthquakes and volcanoes will inevitably look very similar to a map showing the boundaries of the tectonic plates. This is because both phenomena are largely controlled by the processes of plate tectonics. The vast majority of the world's earthquakes occur at plate boundaries as a result of one plate pushing past, or under, another. Even those earthquakes which occur away from plate margins are still mostly due to stresses in the rocks which result indirectly from plate movements.

TSUNAMIS

Earthquakes can sometimes give rise to another phenomenon which can cause even more destruction and loss of life – the tsunami. Tsunami is a Japanese word, meaning 'harbour wave', and is used today in preference to the expression 'tidal wave' (tides are not involved). When an earthquake occurs offshore, it may cause a sudden change in the shape of the ocean floor, as a result of submarine landslides or vertical fault movement. This causes a massive displacement of water, which in turn produces a powerful wave or series of waves, able to travel over huge distances.

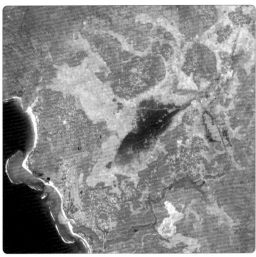

This satellite image of Lhoknga near the provincial capital of Banda Aceh, Sumatra was taken in January 2003 and shows lush and well-cultivated land, with woodland and several villages. The darker area in the centre is water. The coast has sandy beaches, some with barrier islands or reefs protecting them.

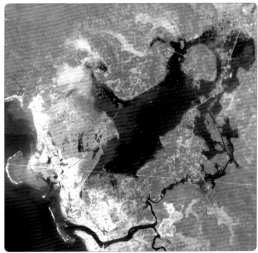

Three days after the tsunami of 26 December 2004 the extent of the destructive force of the waves can be seen. The coastal area has been stripped bare of vegetation and buildings. Inland, the low-lying areas are now filled with salt water and it is only the slightly higher level of the roads which keeps them visible.

DISTRIBUTION OF EARTHQUAKES AND VOLCANOES

- Deadliest earthquake
- Earthquake of magnitude >=7.5
- Earthquake of magnitude 5.5 – 7.5
- ▲ Major volcano
- ▲ Other volcano

DEADLIEST EARTHQUAKES 1900–2010

Year	Location	Deaths
1905	**Kangra**, India	19 000
1907	west of **Dushanbe**, Tajikistan	12 000
1908	**Messina**, Italy	110 000
1915	**Abruzzo**, Italy	35 000
1917	**Bali**, Indonesia	15 000
1920	**Ningxia Province**, China	200 000
1923	**Tōkyō**, Japan	142 807
1927	**Qinghai Province**, China	200 000
1932	**Gansu Province**, China	70 000
1933	**Sichuan Province**, China	10 000
1934	**Nepal/India**	10 700
1935	**Quetta**, Pakistan	30 000
1939	**Chillán**, Chile	28 000
1939	**Erzincan**, Turkey	32 700
1948	**Aşgabat**, Turkmenistan	19 800
1962	northwest **Iran**	12 225
1970	**Huánuco Province**, Peru	66 794
1974	**Yunnan** and **Sichuan Provinces**, China	20 000
1975	**Liaoning Province**, China	10 000
1976	central **Guatemala**	22 778
1976	**Tangshan**, Hebei Province, China	255 000
1978	**Khorāsān Province**, Iran	20 000
1980	**Chlef**, Algeria	11 000
1988	**Spitak**, Armenia	25 000
1990	**Manjil**, Iran	50 000
1999	**İzmit (Kocaeli)**, Turkey	17 000
2001	**Gujarat**, India	20 000
2003	**Bam**, Iran	26 271
2004	**Sumatra**, Indonesia/Indian Ocean	>225 000
2005	northwest **Pakistan**	74 648
2008	**Sichuan Province**, China	>60 000
2010	**Léogâne**, Haiti	222 570

RICHTER SCALE

The scale measures the energy released by an earthquake. The scale is logarithmic – a quake measuring 4 is 30 times more powerful than one measuring 3, and a quake measuring 6 is 27 000 times more powerful than one measuring 3.

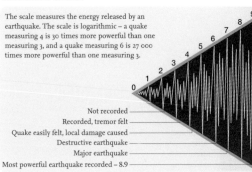

Not recorded
Recorded, tremor felt
Quake easily felt, local damage caused
Destructive earthquake
Major earthquake
Most powerful earthquake recorded – 8.9

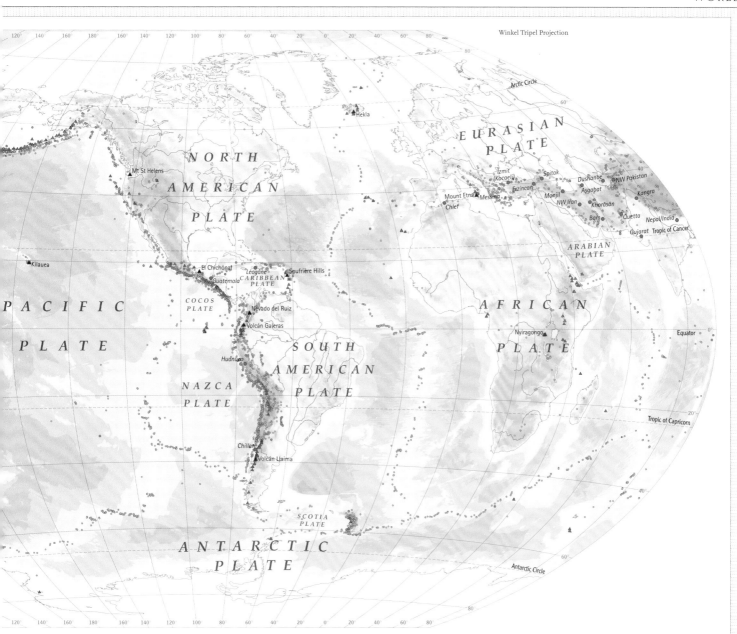

Winkel Tripel Projection

MAJOR VOLCANIC ERUPTIONS 1980–2010

Year	Volcano	Country
1980	Mt St Helens	USA
1982	El Chichónal	Mexico
1982	Gunung Galunggung	Indonesia
1983	Kilauea	Hawaii, USA
1983	Ō-yama	Japan
1985	Nevado del Ruiz	Colombia
1991	Mt Pinatubo	Philippines
1991	Unzen-dake	Japan
1993	Mayon	Philippines
1993	Volcán Galeras	Colombia
1994	Volcán Llaima	Chile
1994	Rabaul	Papua New Guinea
1997	Soufrière Hills	Montserrat
2000	Hekla	Iceland
2001	Mount Etna	Italy
2002	Nyiragongo	Democratic Republic of the Congo

Mount Bromo, Java, Indonesia, is one of the many active volcanoes that have formed around the edge of the Pacific Ocean.
It is unique in having seven eruptive centres in the caldera and is also a great location to see spectacular sunrises.

THE OCEANS

The oceans cover nearly three-quarters of the Earth's surface, and exert an extraordinary influence on the physical processes of the Earth and its atmosphere. The oceanic and atmospheric circulations, and the exchange of water between them, have a profound influence on our climate and therefore on human life. Any study of the Earth's climate relies upon a clear understanding of the role of the oceans and of the complex processes within them. The precise nature and effect of the processes varies geographically, but individual instances cannot be considered in isolation from the overall processes involved.

Methods of direct and indirect observation of the oceans, by sampling and through the application of satellite remote sensing, for example, have developed enormously over the last fifty years. These techniques have provided the amount and quality of data required to greatly develop our understanding of the oceans and their role in the Earth's climate. For example, we now appreciate that the ocean is changing in response to global warming – currents are changing, the ocean is warming and sea level is rising. These changes are manifest in both the upper ocean circulation driven by the wind and in a global circulation driven by regional differences in the temperature and salinity.

Until the advent of Earth-observation satellites in the late 1970s all ocean observations were made from ships. The first global survey of the oceans, their bathymetry and their physical and biological characteristics, was made by HMS *Challenger* between 1872 and 1876.

Throughout the 20th century, comprehensive descriptions of the distributions of temperature and salinity were made through numerous regional and global expeditions. Analysis of the temperature and salinity characteristics of a water sample allowed its origins to be determined, and enabled overall patterns of water circulation to be deduced.

Until the 1960s there was no means of directly measuring currents below the ocean surface. Parallel developments produced two solutions to this problem. In the USA, current-recording meters were designed which returned records of current speed and direction, and water temperature. In the UK, devices were produced which could be made to drift with the currents at a predetermined depth and which could be tracked from an attendant ship. Such floats can now be used globally, independent of ships.

Earth observation satellites have become increasingly important in observing the oceans. Radiometers allow sea surface temperatures to be monitored and radar altimeters permit ocean surface currents to be inferred from measurements of sea surface height. Such developments meant that by the early 1990s routine monitoring of ocean surface currents was possible. The combination of satellite altimetry and other observation methods has also allowed a detailed picture of the ocean floor to be established.

OCEAN CIRCULATION

Most of the Earth's incoming solar radiation is absorbed in the top few tens of metres of the ocean. Thus the upper ocean is warmed, the warming being greatest around the equator. Sea water has a high thermal capacity in comparison with the atmosphere or lithosphere and as a consequence, the ocean is an extremely effective store of thermal energy. Slow ocean currents play a major role in redistributing this heat around the globe and the oceans and their circulation are thus key elements in the climate system.

Global circulation consists of two parts: wind driven currents circulating in ocean-wide horizontal gyres; and a vertical thermohaline circulation where upper, warmer ocean water moves towards the poles and deep, cooler water moves towards the equator. Although conceptually we separate the wind driven and thermohaline circulations, in reality they are intimately connected by the exchange of energy – creating the global circulation known as the global ocean conveyor belt.

Ocean currents are influenced by winds, by density gradients and by the Earth's rotation. They are also constrained by the topography of the seafloor. Surface currents are usually strong, narrow, western-boundary currents flowing towards the poles. Some of these are well known, for example the Gulf Stream in the North Atlantic Ocean, the Kuroshio Current in the northwest Pacific, and the Brazil Current. These poleward flows are returned towards the equator in broad, slow, interior flows which complete a gyre in each hemisphere basin. Sea surface circulation is reflected in variations in sea surface height which can vary greatly across currents. For example, differences in sea surface height of over 1m are evident across the Kuroshio Current. At high latitudes, winter cooling produces high density water which sinks towards the ocean floor and flows towards the equator, being constrained by the sea floor topography. This fills the deep ocean basins with water at temperatures close to 0°C.

GLOBAL SEAFLOOR TOPOGRAPHY

The range of colours represents different depths of the ocean – from orange and yellow on the shallow continental shelves to dark blues in the deepest ocean trenches.

GLOBAL OCEAN CONVEYOR BELT

Circulation of light, warmer surface water (red) and deep, cooler water (blue).

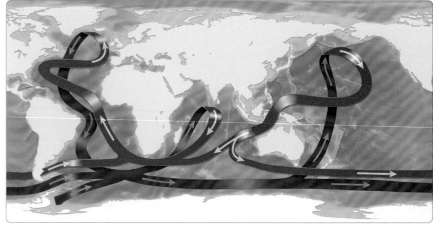

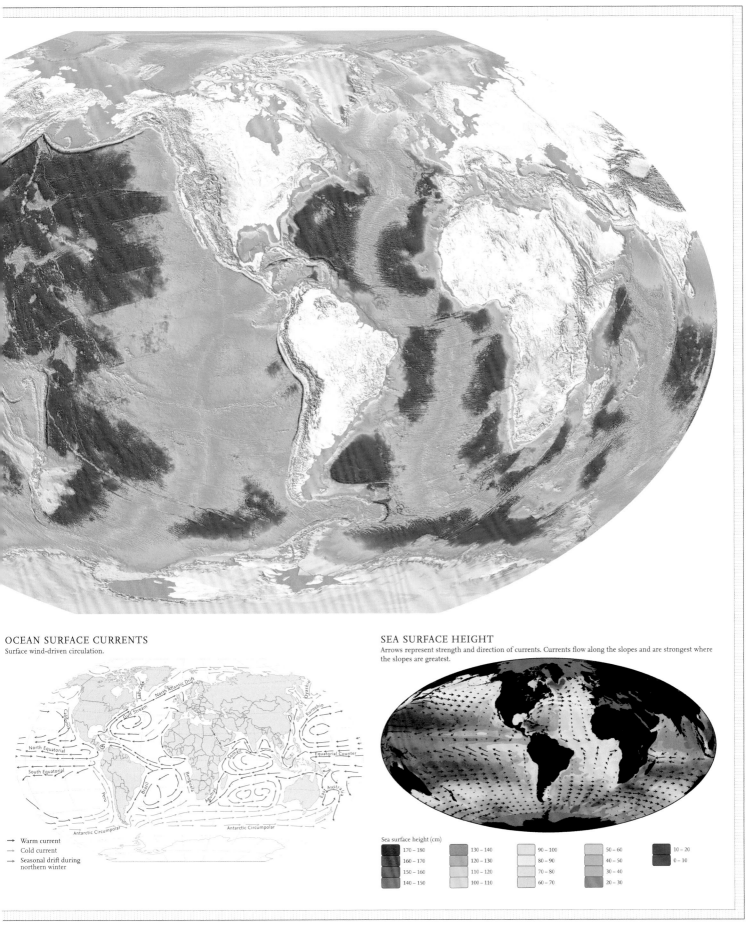

OCEAN SURFACE CURRENTS
Surface wind-driven circulation.

→ Warm current
→ Cold current
→ Seasonal drift during northern winter

SEA SURFACE HEIGHT
Arrows represent strength and direction of currents. Currents flow along the slopes and are strongest where the slopes are greatest.

Sea surface height (cm)

170 – 180	130 – 140	90 – 100	50 – 60	10 – 20
160 – 170	120 – 130	80 – 90	40 – 50	0 – 10
150 – 160	110 – 120	70 – 80	30 – 40	
140 – 150	100 – 110	60 – 70	20 – 30	

THE ARCTIC

The Arctic region is generally defined as the area including the Arctic Ocean – which lies entirely within the Arctic Circle – and the immediate hinterlands of those land areas adjacent to it. A large proportion of the ocean itself is permanently covered in sea ice, which in some places reaches a thickness of over 4 metres (13 feet). The extent of this ice varies seasonally and the impact of global warming on its overall extent is being closely monitored. It generates up to 50 000 icebergs per year. The ocean is almost landlocked, and is connected to the Pacific Ocean only by the narrow Bering Strait – an important shipping route for Russian merchant ships. Sharing similarly extreme climatic conditions to Antarctica, the main difference between the two polar regions is the habitation of the Arctic by numerous ethnic groups.

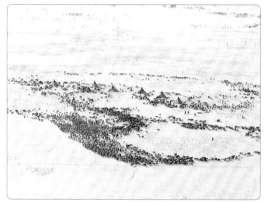

The nomadic lifestyle of the Nenets people is typical of many Arctic groups, but is becoming less common. The Nenets have long herded reindeer on both sides of the Ural Mountains and hunted seals and whales off the coasts of the Barents and Kara seas.

ANTARCTICA

While the Arctic region consists mainly of the Arctic Ocean, Antarctica is a huge landmass, covered by a permanent ice cap which reaches a maximum thickness of over four kilometres. Antarctica has no permanent population, unlike the Arctic regions of Europe, Asia and North America. The only minor settlements are research stations which serve as bases for scientific research. Such research, and the continent as a whole, is subject to the Antarctic Treaty of 1959 which does not recognize individual land claims and protects the continent in the interests of international scientific cooperation. There has been a significant rise over the last thirty years in tourism in Antarctica – an activity which itself demands close control to ensure the unique environment of the continent is not threatened.

Tourists aboard the cruise ship *Polar Circle* as it passes through the Weddell Sea. Most Antarctic tourism is ship-borne with tourists transported ashore for periods of up to three hours at a time. Most cruises depart from Ushuaia, Argentina, or Port Stanley, Falkland Islands.

ARCTIC SEA ICE EXTENTS

Although much of the Arctic Ocean is constantly frozen, there are wide variations in the amount of sea ice throughout the year, as shown by these satellite-generated images. The lightest areas show almost completely frozen sea which extends as far south as Hudson Bay, Canada in February. By September, most of this ice has melted and that remaining is thinner and less concentrated, as indicated by the red-pink areas. Observation of changes in the extent of the sea ice are important in monitoring climate change, and it is now clear that the Arctic ice is getting thinner, and is less extensive than in the past. The images indicate this sort of change, particularly with the total extent of ice in September 2004 being significantly less than in September 1980.

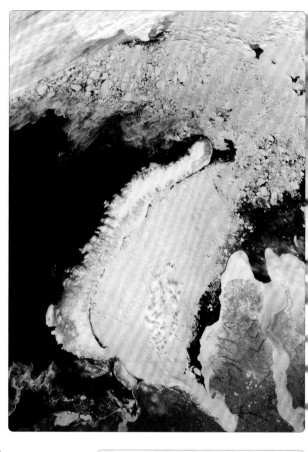

This satellite image shows the islands of Novaya Zemlya and a section of the northern coast of the Russian Federation. The warming influence of sea currents is evident in this image with the North Atlantic Drift, or Gulf Stream, being a major factor in the clear water of the Barents Sea to the left of the island. This contrasts with the ice-filled waters of the colder Kara Sea to the right of the island.

TOURISM IN ANTARCTICA

The Antarctic tourist 'industry' was born in 1969 when the Lindblad Explorer, the first purpose-built Antarctic tour ship began operating. Now, over 20 000 tourists visit the continent each year – a large increase from just over 8 000 ten years ago. The USA and Germany are the largest single contributors to the total number of visitors. The most popular destination is the Antarctic Peninsula, although visits are also possible to the Weddell Sea, Ross Sea and East Antarctica regions. Tourist activities can present a threat to the wildlife and delicate environment of the continent. Strict controls over visits are imposed by the Antarctic Treaty and also by the International Association of Antarctica Tour Operators (IAATO) which represents travel companies operating in the region.

TOP 10 TOURIST SITES IN ANTARCTICA 2003–2004

	Location	Visitors
1	Antarctic Peninsula Region	24 535
2	Cuverville Island	13 980
3	Goudier Island	12 496
4	Almirante Brown Base	12 233
5	Whalers Bay, Deception Island	11 928
6	Half Moon Island	10 871
7	Neko Harbor	9 627
8	Waterboat Point	8 129
9	Jougla Point, Douumer Island	7 913
10	Petermann Island	7 543

PEOPLES OF THE ARCTIC

The Arctic regions of Alaska, northern Canada, Greenland, and northern Scandinavia and Russian Federation contain the homelands of a diverse range of indigenous peoples. They are heavily dependent on the natural resources in the region, and recently, conflicts have arisen with governments eager to exploit these rich resources. There have also been moves towards greater autonomy for such groups. Most notably, in 1992 the Tungavik Federation of Nunavut and the government of Canada signed an agreement which addressed Inuit land claims and harvesting rights and established the new Canadian territory of Nunavut.

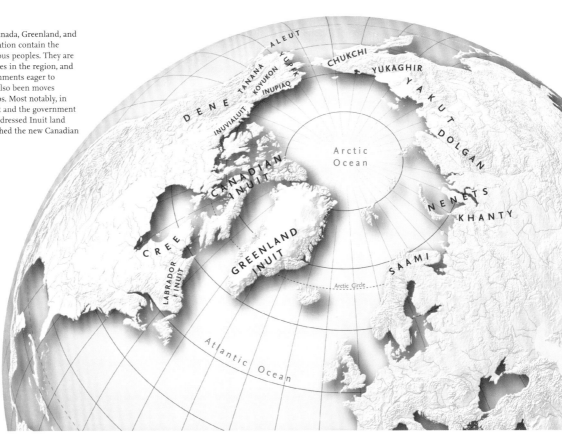

The main indigenous groups in the Arctic are shown on this map. These native peoples have subsisted for thousands of years on the resources of land and sea, as hunters, fishermen and reindeer herders.

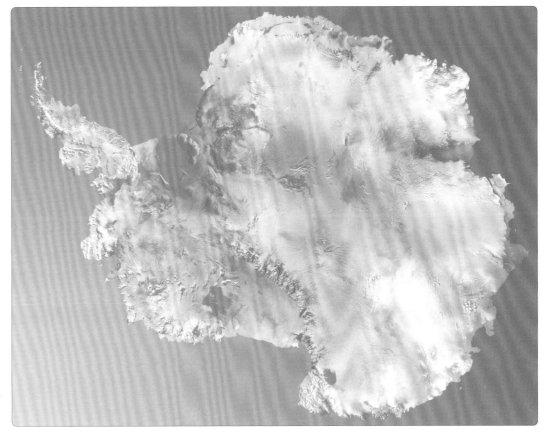

The unique beauty of Antarctica is evident in this image of the continent – a mosaic of twenty-five separate satellite images. The image is impressive in its depiction of the major physical features of the continent, including the Ronne Ice Shelf, including Berkner Island, and the Transantarctic Mountains.

CLIMATE

The climate classification shown on the main map is a simplified version of the system developed by W. Köppen. It is based on the relationship between temperature and precipitation data, and on vegetation characteristics. Extremes of climate, particularly tropical storms and tornadoes, are significant because of their destructive power. Increasing knowledge of these phenomena – particularly through the use of satellite imagery – will help in their prediction and will allow action to minimize their destructive effects.

TORNADOES

A tornado is a violent rotating column of air extending from a thunderstorm to the ground. The most violent tornadoes can cause massive destruction with wind speeds of 400 km per hr (249 miles per hr) or more. Although tornadoes occur in many parts of the world, they are found most frequently in the USA east of the Rocky Mountains and west of the Appalachian Mountains. They occur during the spring and summer months. In the USA in an average year 800 tornadoes are reported.

In April 2007 intense storms in northeast USA created a powerful tornado which touched down in southern Maryland destroying the historic centre of La Plata before moving east, flattening vegetation as it passed.

TROPICAL STORMS

Tropical storms have different names in different parts of the world: hurricanes in the north Atlantic and east Pacific; typhoons in the northwest Pacific; and cyclones in the Indian Ocean region. There are also many other local names for these often catastrophic events. Tropical storms are among the most powerful and destructive weather systems on Earth. Of the eighty to one hundred which develop annually over the tropical oceans, many make landfall and cause considerable damage to property and loss of life as a result of high winds and heavy rain.

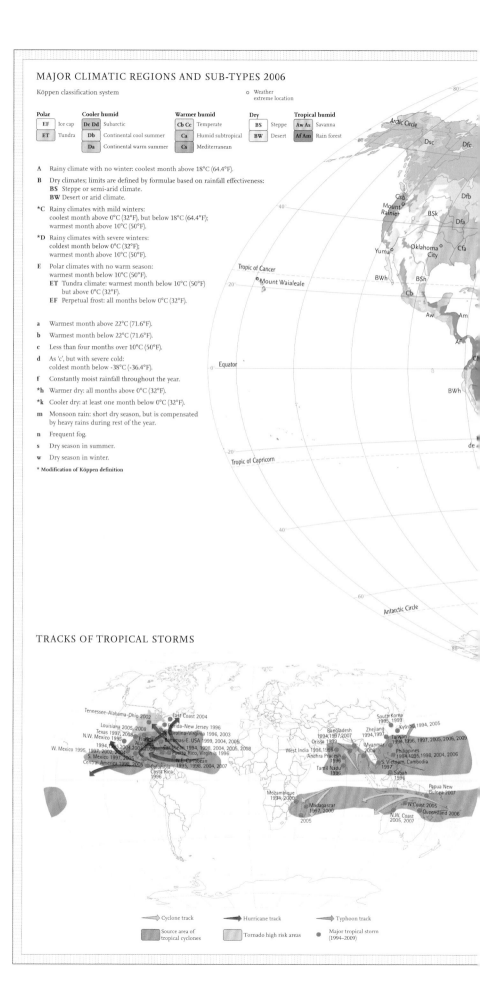

MAJOR CLIMATIC REGIONS AND SUB-TYPES 2006

Köppen classification system

o Weather extreme location

Polar		Cooler humid		Warmer humid		Dry		Tropical humid	
EF	Ice cap	De Dd	Subarctic	Cb Cc	Temperate	BS	Steppe	Aw As	Savanna
ET	Tundra	Db	Continental cool summer	Ca	Humid subtropical	BW	Desert	Af Am	Rain forest
		Da	Continental warm summer	Cs	Mediterranean				

A Rainy climate with no winter: coolest month above 18°C (64.4°F).

B Dry climates; limits are defined by formulae based on rainfall effectiveness:
  BS Steppe or semi-arid climate.
  BW Desert or arid climate.

*C Rainy climates with mild winters: coolest month above 0°C (32°F), but below 18°C (64.4°F); warmest month above 10°C (50°F).

*D Rainy climates with severe winters: coldest month below 0°C (32°F); warmest month above 10°C (50°F).

E Polar climates with no warm season: warmest month below 10°C (50°F).
  ET Tundra climate: warmest month below 10°C (50°F) but above 0°C (32°F).
  EF Perpetual frost: all months below 0°C (32°F).

a Warmest month above 22°C (71.6°F).

b Warmest month below 22°C (71.6°F).

c Less than four months over 10°C (50°F).

d As 'c', but with severe cold: coldest month below -38°C (-36.4°F).

f Constantly moist rainfall throughout the year.

*h Warmer dry: all months above 0°C (32°F).

*k Cooler dry: at least one month below 0°C (32°F).

m Monsoon rain: short dry season, but is compensated by heavy rains during rest of the year.

n Frequent fog.

s Dry season in summer.

w Dry season in winter.

* Modification of Köppen definition

TRACKS OF TROPICAL STORMS

→ Cyclone track   → Hurricane track   → Typhoon track

Source area of tropical cyclones   Tornado high risk areas   • Major tropical storm (1994–2009)

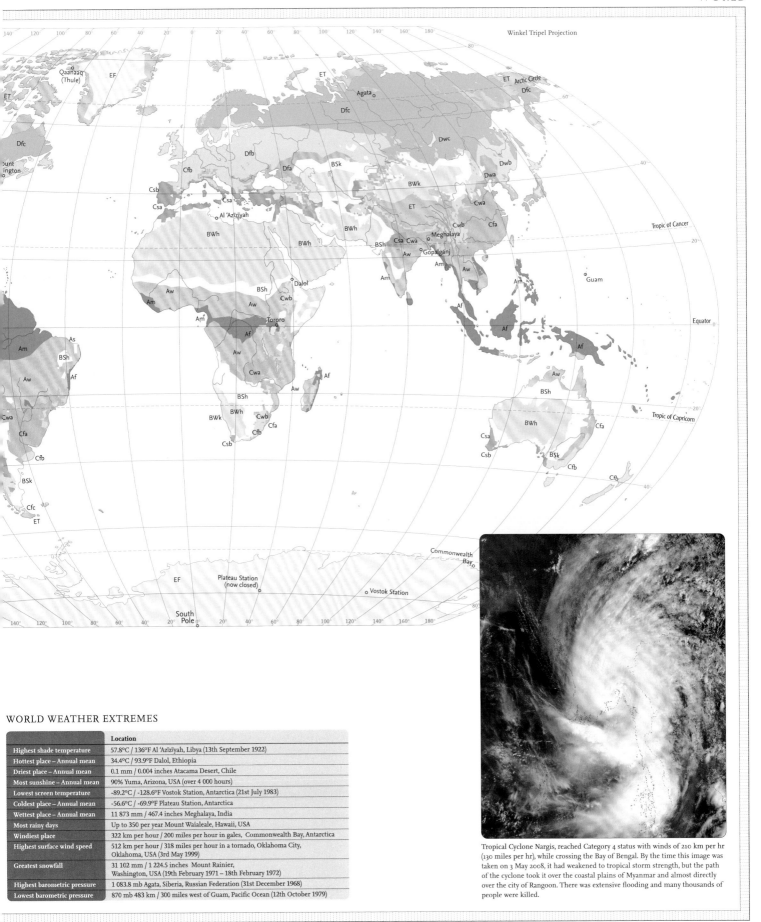

Winkel Tripel Projection

WORLD WEATHER EXTREMES

	Location
Highest shade temperature	57.8°C / 136°F Al 'Azīzīyah, Libya (13th September 1922)
Hottest place – Annual mean	34.4°C / 93.9°F Dalol, Ethiopia
Driest place – Annual mean	0.1 mm / 0.004 inches Atacama Desert, Chile
Most sunshine – Annual mean	90% Yuma, Arizona, USA (over 4 000 hours)
Lowest screen temperature	-89.2°C / -128.6°F Vostok Station, Antarctica (21st July 1983)
Coldest place – Annual mean	-56.6°C / -69.9°F Plateau Station, Antarctica
Wettest place – Annual mean	11 873 mm / 467.4 inches Meghalaya, India
Most rainy days	Up to 350 per year Mount Waialeale, Hawaii, USA
Windiest place	322 km per hour / 200 miles per hour in gales, Commonwealth Bay, Antarctica
Highest surface wind speed	512 km per hour / 318 miles per hour in a tornado, Oklahoma City, Oklahoma, USA (3rd May 1999)
Greatest snowfall	31 102 mm / 1 224.5 inches Mount Rainier, Washington, USA (19th February 1971 – 18th February 1972)
Highest barometric pressure	1 083.8 mb Agata, Siberia, Russian Federation (31st December 1968)
Lowest barometric pressure	870 mb 483 km / 300 miles west of Guam, Pacific Ocean (12th October 1979)

Tropical Cyclone Nargis, reached Category 4 status with winds of 210 km per hr (130 miles per hr), while crossing the Bay of Bengal. By the time this image was taken on 3 May 2008, it had weakened to tropical storm strength, but the path of the cyclone took it over the coastal plains of Myanmar and almost directly over the city of Rangoon. There was extensive flooding and many thousands of people were killed.

CLIMATE CHANGE

The global average temperature can be established for approximately the last 150 years from the worldwide network of weather stations on land and observations made on board ships. Twelve of the last fifteen years rank among the fifteen warmest years on record, so the world has been warmer over the last decade than at any time since measurements began. This warming is observed over the oceans as well as over land, suggesting that it is a truly global phenomenon and not a conglomeration of 'local' increases in temperature caused by some small-scale process such as the urban heat island effect.

OBSERVING CLIMATE CHANGE

Changes have also been seen in various areas of the climate system. Snow cover and mountain glaciers have shrunk, and some melting of the Greenland and Antarctic ice sheets has been measured. Global average sea level rose by approximately 17 cm through the 20th century, partly because of the additional water in the ocean basins resulting from the melting of ice on land, and partly because water expands when it heats up. Patterns of precipitation (rainfall and snowfall) have also changed, with parts of North and South America, Europe and northern and central Asia becoming wetter while the Sahel region of central Africa, southern Africa, the Mediterranean and southern Asia have become drier. Intense rainfall events have become more frequent. In Europe, Asia and North America, growing seasons have extended, with flowers emerging and trees coming into leaf several days earlier in the year than in the mid-twentieth century.

Male, the capital of the Maldives, is approximately 2 m above the sea, but its reclaimed land is lower leaving it very vulnerable to a sustained rise in sea level.

THE CAUSES OF CLIMATE CHANGE

Climate can change naturally, but over the last century the industrial and agricultural activities of humans have become additional causes of climate change. Changes in the concentration of 'greenhouse gases' can also result in climate change. The most important greenhouse gas is water vapour, followed by carbon dioxide. While many of these gases occur naturally in the atmosphere, humans are responsible for increasing the concentration of many of them through the burning of fossil fuels, deforestation and other industrial and agricultural processes. We have also introduced new greenhouse gases, the 'halocarbons' such as chlorofluorocarbons (CFCs) which have damaged the ozone layer in the stratosphere.

The McCarty Glacier in the Kenai Peninsula in Alaska is a tidewater glacier which has retreated around 16 km between 1909 (top) and 2004 (bottom).

PROJECTION OF GLOBAL TEMPERATURES 2090–2099
Based on IPCC scenario A1B. Change relative to 1980–1999.

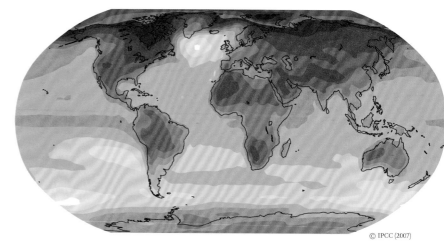

© IPCC (2007)

Change in average surface temperature (C°)

Faster warming is expected near the poles, as the melting snow and sea ice exposes the darker underlying land and ocean surfaces which then absorb more of the sun's radiation instead of reflecting it back to space in the way that brighter ice and snow do.

THREAT OF RISING SEA LEVEL

It has been suggested that further global warming of between 1.0 and 6.4 C° may occur by the end of the 21st century. Sea level is projected to rise by between 28 cm and 58 cm, threatening a number of coastal cities, low-lying deltas and small islands. Larger rises are predicted in some locations than others.

AREAS AT RISK OF SUBMERSION

○ Major cities

Coastal areas at greatest risk

Islands and archipelagos

Areas of low-lying islands

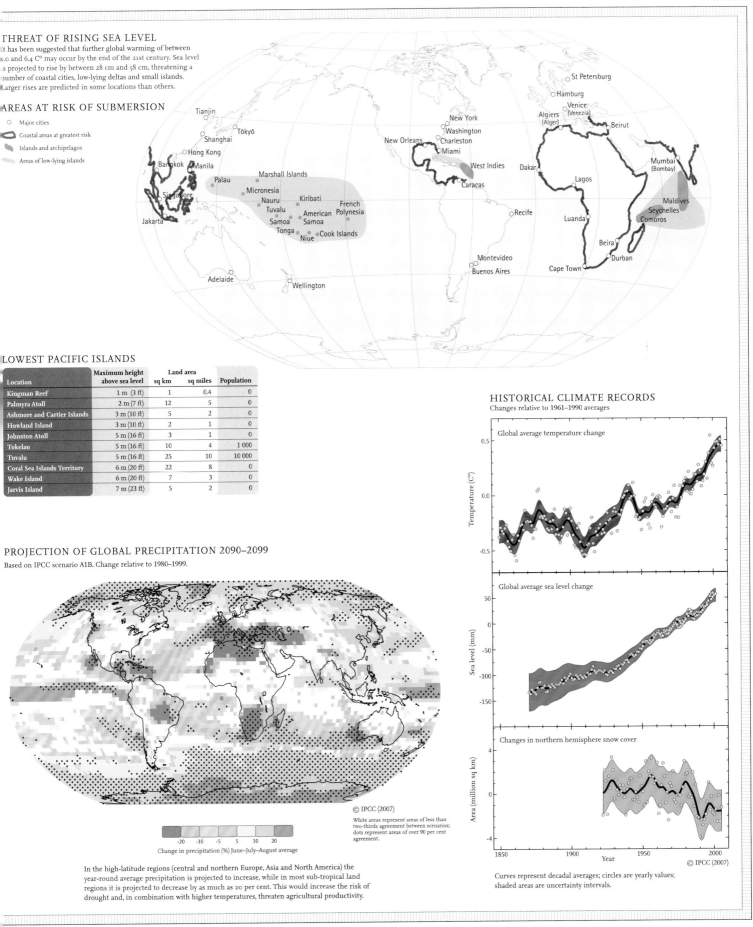

LOWEST PACIFIC ISLANDS

Location	Maximum height above sea level	Land area sq km	sq miles	Population
Kingman Reef	1 m (3 ft)	1	0.4	0
Palmyra Atoll	2 m (7 ft)	12	5	0
Ashmore and Cartier Islands	3 m (10 ft)	5	2	0
Howland Island	3 m (10 ft)	2	1	0
Johnston Atoll	5 m (16 ft)	3	1	0
Tokelau	5 m (16 ft)	10	4	1 000
Tuvalu	5 m (16 ft)	25	10	10 000
Coral Sea Islands Territory	6 m (20 ft)	22	8	0
Wake Island	6 m (20 ft)	7	3	0
Jarvis Island	7 m (23 ft)	5	2	0

PROJECTION OF GLOBAL PRECIPITATION 2090–2099

Based on IPCC scenario A1B. Change relative to 1980–1999.

© IPCC (2007)

White areas represent areas of less than two-thirds agreement between scenarios; dots represent areas of over 90 per cent agreement.

-20 -10 -5 5 10 20

Change in precipitation (%) June–July–August average

In the high-latitude regions (central and northern Europe, Asia and North America) the year-round average precipitation is projected to increase, while in most sub-tropical land regions it is projected to decrease by as much as 20 per cent. This would increase the risk of drought and, in combination with higher temperatures, threaten agricultural productivity.

HISTORICAL CLIMATE RECORDS

Changes relative to 1961–1990 averages

Global average temperature change

Global average sea level change

Changes in northern hemisphere snow cover

© IPCC (2007)

Curves represent decadal averages; circles are yearly values; shaded areas are uncertainty intervals.

ENVIRONMENT

Throughout history people have altered the natural environment, influencing landscapes, land cover, biodiversity, and the chemical composition of air, land, and water. The rate of change has accelerated dramatically since the industrial revolution, as a result of advances in technology, changing lifestyles and associated patterns of production and consumption, and the rapidly growing global population. As the human population has increased, so too has demand for the Earth's natural resources, leading in many areas to environmental degradation which has had significant impacts on people's lives in many parts of the world.

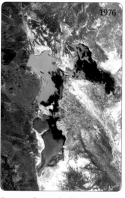

For many thousands of years the Hamoun wetlands have been a major source of food and shelter in the middle of vast arid plains in central Asia. From the mid 1990s however, the Helmand river was increasingly used for irrigation and diverted into dams leaving the area vulnerable to a prolonged drought. These false colour images of 1976 and 2001 show the extent of the devastation.

ENVIRONMENTAL CHANGE

Land cover has changed more over the past fifty years than at any time in human history. Much of this change has been due to the conversion of natural ecosystems to agricultural land to help meet demand for food production. Wetlands and other freshwater environments have been dramatically affected by changes in land cover and use. It is speculated that approximately one-third of all mangroves and half of all inland wetlands were converted during the 20th century. Fragmentation and the modification of river flow have resulted from the construction of dams and other structures along rivers, affecting almost 60 per cent of the large river systems in the world.

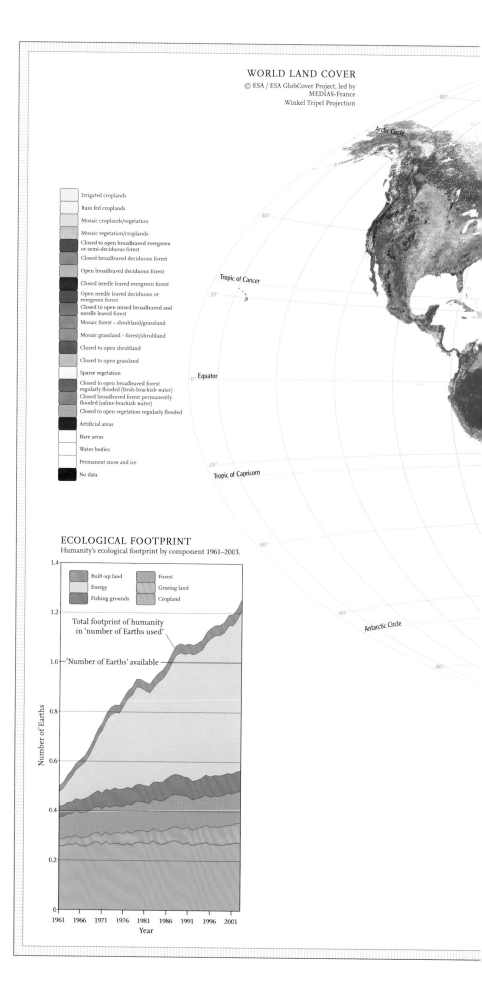

WORLD LAND COVER
© ESA / ESA GlobCover Project, led by
MEDIAS-France
Winkel Tripel Projection

- Irrigated croplands
- Rain fed croplands
- Mosaic croplands/vegetation
- Mosaic vegetation/croplands
- Closed to open broadleaved evergreen or semi-deciduous forest
- Closed broadleaved deciduous forest
- Open broadleaved deciduous forest
- Closed needle leaved evergreen forest
- Open needle leaved deciduous or evergreen forest
- Closed to open mixed broadleaved and needle leaved forest
- Mosaic forest – shrubland/grassland
- Mosaic grassland – forest/shrubland
- Closed to open shrubland
- Closed to open grassland
- Sparse vegetation
- Closed to open broadleaved forest regularly flooded (fresh-brackish water)
- Closed broadleaved forest permanently flooded (saline-brackish water)
- Closed to open vegetation regularly flooded
- Artificial areas
- Bare areas
- Water bodies
- Permanent snow and ice
- No data

ECOLOGICAL FOOTPRINT
Humanity's ecological footprint by component 1961–2003.

Legend:
- Built-up land
- Energy
- Fishing grounds
- Forest
- Grazing land
- Cropland

Total footprint of humanity in 'number of Earths used'

'Number of Earths' available

Number of Earths (y-axis): 0, 0.2, 0.4, 0.6, 0.8, 1.0, 1.2, 1.4

Year (x-axis): 1961, 1966, 1971, 1976, 1981, 1986, 1991, 1996, 2001

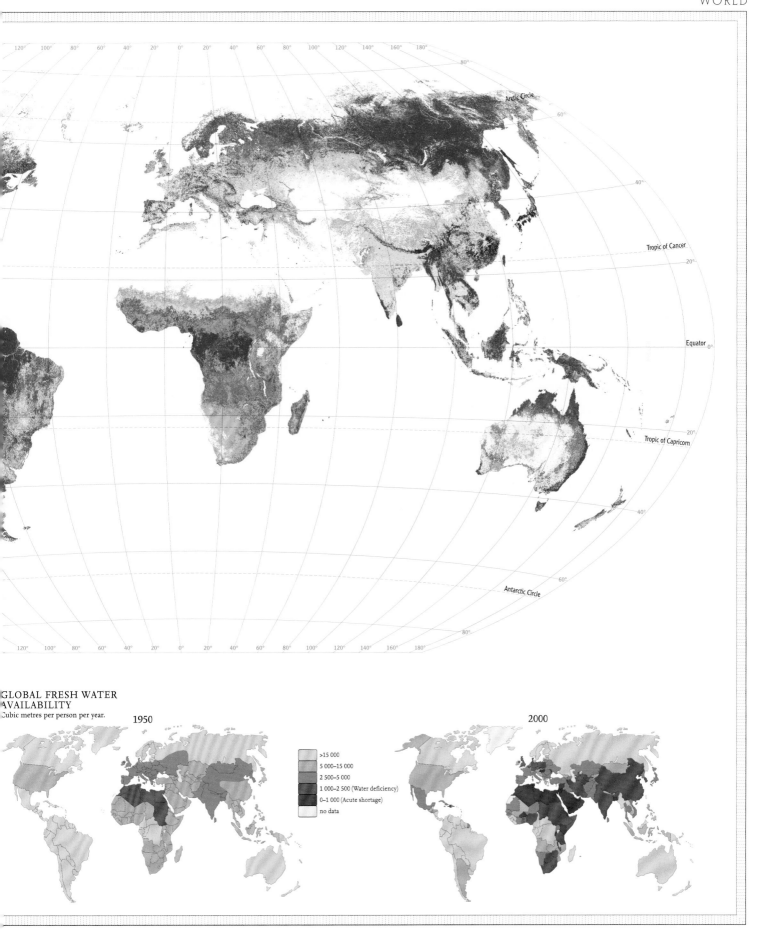

GLOBAL FRESH WATER
AVAILABILITY
Cubic metres per person per year.

1950

2000

>15 000
5 000–15 000
2 500–5 000
1 000–2 500 (Water deficiency)
0–1 000 (Acute shortage)
no data

ENVIRONMENTAL THREATS

The Earth has a rich and diverse environment which is under threat from both natural and man-induced forces. Forests and woodland form the predominant natural land cover with tropical rain forests – currently disappearing at alarming rates – believed to be home to the majority of animal and plant species. Grassland and scrub tend to have a lower natural species diversity but have suffered the most impact from man's intervention through conversion to agriculture, burning and the introduction of livestock. Wherever man interferes with existing biological and environmental processes degradation of that environment occurs to varying degrees. This interference also affects inland water and oceans where pollution, over-exploitation of marine resources and the need for fresh water has had major consequences on land and sea environments.

An oil spill in the Gulf of Mexico, one month after the Deepwater Horizon Oil Rig exploded and sank in April 2010. By the time it was finally capped on July 15, the estimated 5 million barrels of crude oil that had been released, made it the largest accidental oil spill in history. As with all major spills the effects on the local wildlife was catastrophic, and damage to the fishing and tourism industries of the area is expected to last for many years.

ENVIRONMENTAL CHANGE

Whenever natural resources are exploited by man, the environment is changed. Approximately half the area of post-glacial forest has been cleared or degraded, and the amount of old-growth forest continues to decline. Desertification caused by climate change and the impact of man can turn semi-arid/grasslands into arid desert. Regions bordering tropical deserts, such as the Sahel region south of the Sahara and regions around the Thar Desert in India, are most vulnerable to this process. Coral reefs are equally fragile environments, and many are under threat from coastal development, pollution and over-exploitation of marine resources.

Water resources in certain parts of the world are becoming increasingly scarce and competition for water is likely to become a common cause of conflict. The Aral Sea in central Asia was once the world's fourth largest lake but it now ranks less after shrinking by almost 40 000 square kilometres. This shrinkage has been due to climatic change and to the diversion, for farming purposes, of the major rivers which feed the lake. The change has had a devastating effect on the local fishing industry and the exposure of chemicals on the lake bed has caused health problems for the local population.

Deforestation and the creation of the Itaipu Dam on the Paraná river in Brazil have had a dramatic effect on the landscape and ecosystems of this part of South America. Some forest on the right of the images lies within Iguaçu National Park and has been protected from destruction.

Chernobyl, Ukraine 1986–1992. After the nuclear accident on 26 April 1986 the surrounding farmland was abandoned as a result of contamination. These areas have turned from bright red and white to grey.

ENVIRONMENTAL IMPACTS

Winkel Tripel Projection

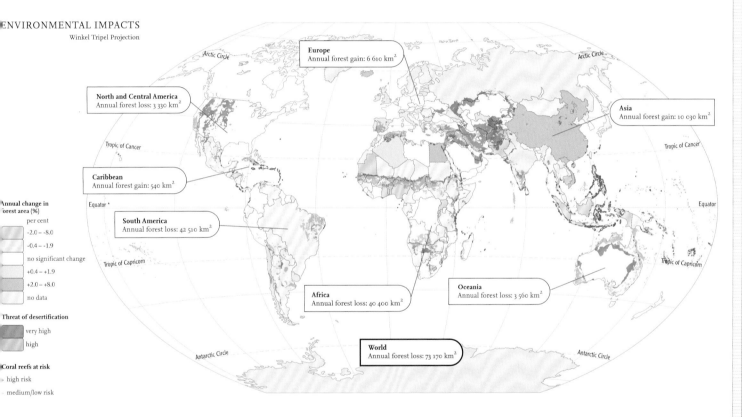

Europe
Annual forest gain: 6 610 km²

North and Central America
Annual forest loss: 3 330 km²

Asia
Annual forest gain: 10 030 km²

Caribbean
Annual forest gain: 540 km²

South America
Annual forest loss: 42 510 km²

Africa
Annual forest loss: 40 400 km²

Oceania
Annual forest loss: 3 560 km²

World
Annual forest loss: 73 170 km²

Annual change in forest area (%)

per cent
- -2.0 – -8.0
- -0.4 – -1.9
- no significant change
- +0.4 – +1.9
- +2.0 – +8.0
- no data

Threat of desertification
- very high
- high

Coral reefs at risk
- high risk
- medium/low risk

TOP 10 PROTECTED AREAS OF THE WORLD BY SIZE

Proportion of large marine ecosystems and terrestrial ecoregions under protection.

Rank	Protected area	Country	Size (sq km)	Designation
1	Northeast Greenland	Greenland	972 000	National Park
2	Rub' al-Khālī	Saudi Arabia	640 000	Wildlife Management Area
3	Phoenix Islands	Kiribati	410 500	Protected Area
4	Great Barrier Reef	Australia	344 400	Marine Park
5	Papahānaumokuākea Marine National Monument	United States	341 362	Coral Reef Ecosystem Reserve
6	Qiangtang	China	298 000	Nature Reserve
7	Macquarie Island	Australia	162 060	Marine Park
8	Sanjiangyuan	China	152 300	Nature Reserve
9	Galápagos	Ecuador	133 000	Marine Reserve
10	Northern Wildlife Management Zone	Saudi Arabia	100 875	Wildlife Management Area

Great Barrier Reef, Australia, the world's fourth largest protected area.

GLOBAL BIODIVERSITY

Biodiversity, derived from the term 'biological diversity', is the name given to the variety and processes of all life on Earth, including individual living organisms, their genes, and the habitats or ecosystems of which they are part, whether terrestrial, freshwater or marine. The diversity of life is not evenly distributed around the world, and based on the number of species in a location, or 'species richness', a general pattern emerges of considerably more biodiversity in the tropics than at higher latitudes.

To date approximately two million species have been identified and described. However, the total number of species on Earth is likely to be nearer 10–12 million, with most estimates ranging between 5 and 30 million. Much of this uncertainty relates to a lack of knowledge about the most species-rich groups, including invertebrates. By including bacteria, about which very little is known, the total estimate would increase still further.

LIVING PLANET INDEX

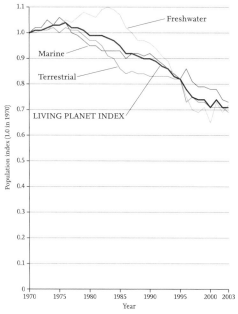

Trends in population of terrestrial, freshwater and marine species 1970–2003.

ECOSYSTEM SERVICES

	Examples
Provisioning services (ecosystem goods)	Food, fibre, fuel, genetic resources, biochemicals.
Regulating services	Pollination, seed dispersal, climate regulation, pest regulation, disease regulation, natural hazard protection, invasion resistance, erosion regulation, water purification.
Supporting services	Primary production, provision of habitat, nutrient cycling, soil formation and retention, production of atmospheric oxygen, water cycling.
Cultural services	Spiritual and religious values, education and inspiration, recreation and aesthetic values.

THE VALUE OF BIODIVERSITY

Genetic diversity provides the basis for living organisms to respond to natural selection and adapt to their environment. As such, genes play a role in the capacity of biodiversity to adapt to global change, such as through climate change or the emergence of novel diseases. Genetic diversity also provides many direct benefits to people, for example through its use in improving yield and disease resistance of crops and for developing medicines.

Ecosystems consist of living creatures interacting with one another and with the air, water, and soil around them. People and the millions of species with which they share the planet are all dependent on the health and functioning of the world's ecosystems. They provide the basic necessities of human life such as food, materials for shelter, and clean water. They also offer protection from natural disasters and disease, and contribute in many non-material ways to our well-being. These 'ecosystem services' also support and maintain the essential life processes of the planet, such as primary production and nutrient cycling.

Changes in biodiversity affect the functioning of ecosystems, and can leave them more vulnerable to disturbances, and less able to supply benefits to people through ecosystem services. An increasing number of studies show that managing ecosystems in a more sustainable way, for a wider range of ecosystem services, can yield greater total overall benefit than managing for a specific, even high-value, product such as timber.

TRENDS IN BIODIVERSITY

Biodiversity is declining globally, largely as a result of human activities. Over the past few hundred years species extinction rates have increased by as much as 1 000 times the natural rates of extinction. Between 10 and 50 per cent of well-studied groups of species (mammals, birds, amphibians, conifers, and cycads) are currently threatened with extinction, and there has been a consistent decline in populations of species, of about 40 per cent between 1970 and 2003. Exceptions to this general decline include a few species which have been protected through specific conservation measures, and those which thrive well in human-modified landscapes.

Virtually all of the planet's ecosystems have now been dramatically transformed through human actions. Although human impacts on biodiversity are not a recent phenomenon, changes have been occurring more rapidly in the past fifty years than at any time in human history. Global deforestation, for example, took place at an estimated average rate of over 350 sq km per day between 1990 and 2005. Between 1960 and 2000 reservoir storage capacity quadrupled, resulting in water stored behind large dams is now estimated to be three to six times the amount held by rivers. Approximately one-third of mangrove ecosystems have been removed, and up to 40 per cent of known coral reefs have been destroyed or degraded in the last few decades.

The pressures causing changes in, and loss of, biodiversity are diverse and numerous. Five main threats are commonly identified: habitat change, overexploitation, pollution (including that caused by excess nutrients from agriculture and industry), climate change, and the spread of invasive non-native species. Ultimately it is a combination of patterns of consumption and human population distribution which is underlying the threats placed on the planet's living resources.

CONSERVATION

Concern over the loss of biodiversity led to the creation, in 1992 of a global treaty, the Convention on Biological Diversity (CBD). In 2002, national governments, through the CBD and other forums, adopted a target to greatly reduce the rate of loss of biodiversity by 2010.

GLOBAL BIODIVERSITY

Diversity of terrestrial vertebrates and flowering plants.

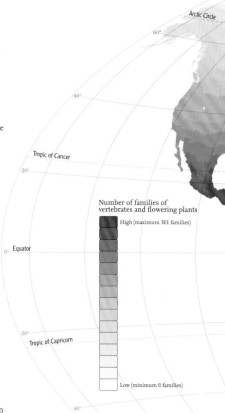

Number of families of vertebrates and flowering plants

High (maximum 301 families)

Low (minimum 0 families)

One of the best-known conservation tools is the establishment and management of Protected Areas. 1872 saw the world's first Protected Area at Yellowstone National Park, USA. Presently over 19 000 000 sq km (13 per cent of the world's land surface) is now included within over 107 000 designated Protected Areas worldwide. However, there is great variation in the degree to which different ecosystem types are protected. Protection of terrestrial ecosystems varies considerably, but all fare better than freshwater or marine ecosystems. Restoration activities are now common in many countries for wetlands, forests, grasslands, and coastal systems. However, restoration is generally far more costly than the conservation and sustainable use of the original ecosystem, and only in rare cases can this be fully restored.

Recently there has been an increasing emphasis on a more holistic approach to biodiversity conservation. This integrates management of land, water and living resources, promoting conservation and sustainable use in an equitable way, recognizing that people are an integral component of ecosystems. Successful implementation will be central to achieving dual goals of conservation and sustainable development.

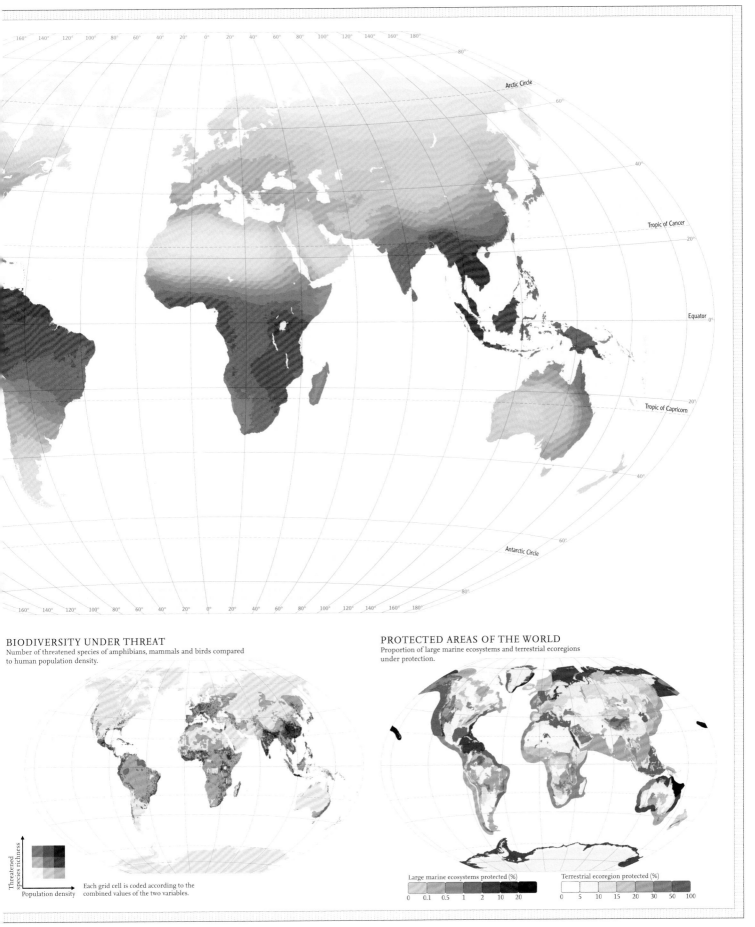

BIODIVERSITY UNDER THREAT
Number of threatened species of amphibians, mammals and birds compared
to human population density.

Threatened
species richness

Population density

Each grid cell is coded according to the
combined values of the two variables.

PROTECTED AREAS OF THE WORLD
Proportion of large marine ecosystems and terrestrial ecoregions
under protection.

Large marine ecosystems protected (%)

0   0.1   0.5   1   2   10   20

Terrestrial ecoregion protected (%)

0   5   10   15   20   30   50   100

POPULATION

World population is currently undergoing the biggest transformation that it has ever seen, but this process is impacting very unevenly. While overall numbers have been growing extremely rapidly since 1950, almost nine-tenths of the increase has taken place in the less developed regions, especially southern and eastern Asia, while Europe's population is now estimated to be in overall decline and ageing rapidly. India and China alone are responsible for over one-third of current growth, but most of the highest percentage rates of growth are to be found in Sub-Saharan Africa, where the demographic transition process is still at a relatively early stage.

Population growth in the 20th century was rapid and continued growth could carry the world's population past seven billion by 2015.

POPULATION DISTRIBUTION

People are distributed very unevenly over the face of the planet, even after allowing for the two-thirds that is covered by water. As shown on the main map, over a quarter of the land area is uninhabited or has extremely low population density, notably the polar regions, the Amazon basin and the dry deserts of Saharan Africa, southwest and central Asia, and Australia.

POPULATION GROWTH

Over the past half century world population has been growing faster than it has ever done before. While world population did not pass the one billion mark until 1804 and took another 123 years to reach two billion, it then added the third billion in 33 years, the fourth in 14 years and the fifth in 13 years, with the addition of the 6 billionth person being celebrated by the UN 12 years after this on 12 October 1999. The latest trends in population growth at country level emphasize the continuing contrast between the more and less developed regions. Annual growth rates of 1.5 per cent or more remain common in Latin America, Africa and southern Asia. A number of countries have rates in excess of 3.0 per cent, which if continued would lead to the doubling of population in 23 years or less. Ten countries account for 60 per cent of the world's current population growth, with India and China responsible for over half.

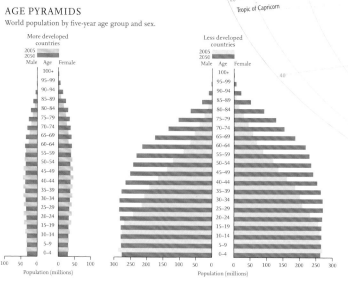

WORLD POPULATION DISTRIBUTION
Winkel Tripel Projection

TOP TWENTY COUNTRIES BY POPULATION AND POPULATION DENSITY 2007

Total population	Country	Rank	Country*	Inhabitants per sq mile	Inhabitants per sq km
1 313 437 000	China	1	Bangladesh	2 854	1 102
1 169 016 000	India	2	Taiwan	1 638	632
305 826 000	United States of America	3	South Korea	1 258	486
231 627 000	Indonesia	4	Netherlands	1 024	395
191 791 000	Brazil	5	India	988	381
163 902 000	Pakistan	6	Belgium	887	343
158 665 000	Bangladesh	7	Japan	877	339
148 093 000	Nigeria	8	Sri Lanka	762	294
142 499 000	Russian Federation	9	Philippines	759	293
127 967 000	Japan	10	Vietnam	687	265
106 535 000	Mexico	11	United Kingdom	646	249
87 960 000	Philippines	12	Germany	599	231
87 375 000	Vietnam	13	Pakistan	528	204
83 099 000	Ethiopia	14	North Korea	511	197
82 599 000	Germany	15	Italy	506	195
75 498 000	Egypt	16	Nepal	496	192
74 877 000	Turkey	17	Nigeria	415	160
71 208 000	Iran	18	China	355	137
63 884 000	Thailand	19	Czech Republic	335	129
62 636 000	Democratic Republic of the Congo	20	Uganda	332	128

*Only countries with a population of over 10 million are considered.

AGE PYRAMIDS
World population by five-year age group and sex.

More developed countries
2005
2050
Male Age Female

Less developed countries
2005
2050
Male Age Female

Population (millions)

KEY POPULATION STATISTICS FOR MAJOR REGIONS

	Population 2007 (millions)	Growth (per cent)	Infant mortality rate	Total fertility rate	Life expectancy (years)	% aged 60 and over 2005	% aged 60 and over 2050
World	6 671	1.2	49	2.6	67	10	22
More developed regions[1]	1 223	0.3	7	1.6	77	20	33
Less developed regions[2]	5 448	1.4	54	2.8	65	8	20
Africa	965	2.3	87	4.7	53	5	10
Asia	4 030	1.1	43	2.3	69	9	24
Europe[3]	731	0.0	8	1.5	75	21	35
Latin America and the Caribbean[4]	572	1.2	22	2.4	73	9	24
North America	339	1.0	6	2	79	17	27
Oceania	34	1.2	26	2.3	75	14	25

Except for population and % aged 60 and over figures, the data are annual averages projected for the period 2005–2010.

1. Europe, North America, Australia, New Zealand and Japan.
2. Africa, Asia (excluding Japan), Latin America and the Caribbean, and Oceania (excluding Australia and New Zealand).
3. Includes Russian Federation.
4. South America, Central America (including Mexico) and all Caribbean Islands.

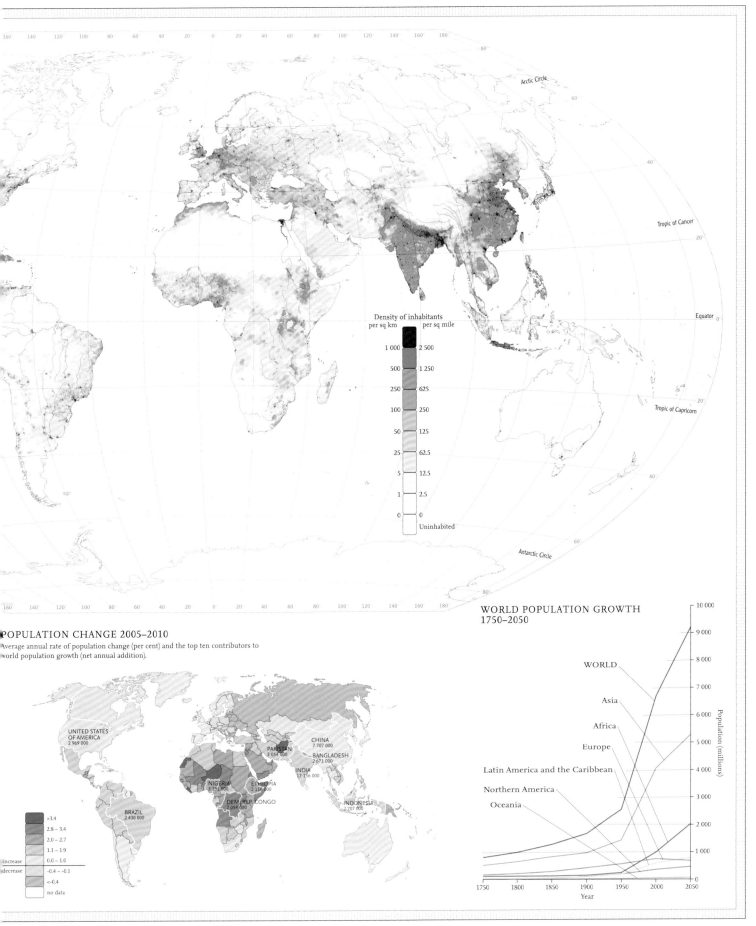

Density of inhabitants
per sq km   per sq mile

1 000	2 500
500	1 250
250	625
100	250
50	125
25	62.5
5	12.5
1	2.5
0	0
	Uninhabited

POPULATION CHANGE 2005–2010

Average annual rate of population change (per cent) and the top ten contributors to world population growth (net annual addition).

- UNITED STATES OF AMERICA 2 969 000
- CHINA 7 707 000
- PAKISTAN 3 054 000
- BANGLADESH 2 671 000
- INDIA 17 156 000
- NIGERIA 3 391 000
- ETHIOPIA 2 116 000
- DEM. REP. CONGO 2 054 000
- INDONESIA 2 707 000
- BRAZIL 2 430 000

	>3.4
	2.8 – 3.4
	2.0 – 2.7
	1.1 – 1.9
increase	0.0 – 1.0
decrease	-0.4 – -0.1
	<-0.4
	no data

WORLD POPULATION GROWTH 1750–2050

WORLD, Asia, Africa, Europe, Latin America and the Caribbean, Northern America, Oceania

Population (millions) — Year 1750–2050

SOCIAL INDICATORS

Countries are often judged on their level of economic development, but national and personal wealth are not the only measures of a country's status. Numerous other indicators can give a better picture of the overall level of development and standard of living achieved by a country. The availability and standard of health services, levels of educational provision and attainment, levels of nutrition, water supply, life expectancy and mortality rates are just some of the factors which can be measured to assess and compare countries.

While nations strive to improve their economies, and hopefully also to improve the standard of living of their citizens, the measurement of such indicators often exposes great discrepancies between the countries of the 'developed' world and those of the 'less developed' world. They also show great variations within continents and regions and at the same time can hide great inequalities within countries.

Children gather for class at a school on Carabane Island, Senegal. Many schools in deprived parts of the world rely on charity for their existence. This one is run by French NGOs and is supported by donations from tourists.

HEALTH AND EDUCATION

Perhaps the most important indicators used for measuring the level of national development are those relating to health and education. Both of these key areas are vital to the future development of a country, and if there are concerns in standards attained in either (or worse, in both) of these, then they may indicate fundamental problems within the country concerned. The ability to read and write (literacy) is seen as vital in educating people and encouraging development, while easy access to appropriate health services and specialists is an important requirement in maintaining satisfactory levels of basic health.

UNDER-FIVE MORTALITY RATE, 2006 AND
LIFE EXPECTANCY BY CONTINENT, 2005–2010

over 250
151 – 250
91 – 150
51 – 90
34 – 50
0 – 33
no data

Deaths of children under five per 1 000 live births

North America = 78
World = 67
North America
Life expectancy 2005–2010 (years)

Latin America and the Caribbean = 73
World = 67
Latin America and the Caribbean
Life expectancy 2005–2010 (years)

Arctic Circle
Tropic of Cancer
Equator
Tropic of Capricorn
Antarctic Circle

NORTH
AMERI

LITERACY RATE

Percentage of population age
15–24 with at least a basic abil
to read and write

over 95
86 – 95
66 – 85
41 – 65
0 – 40
no data

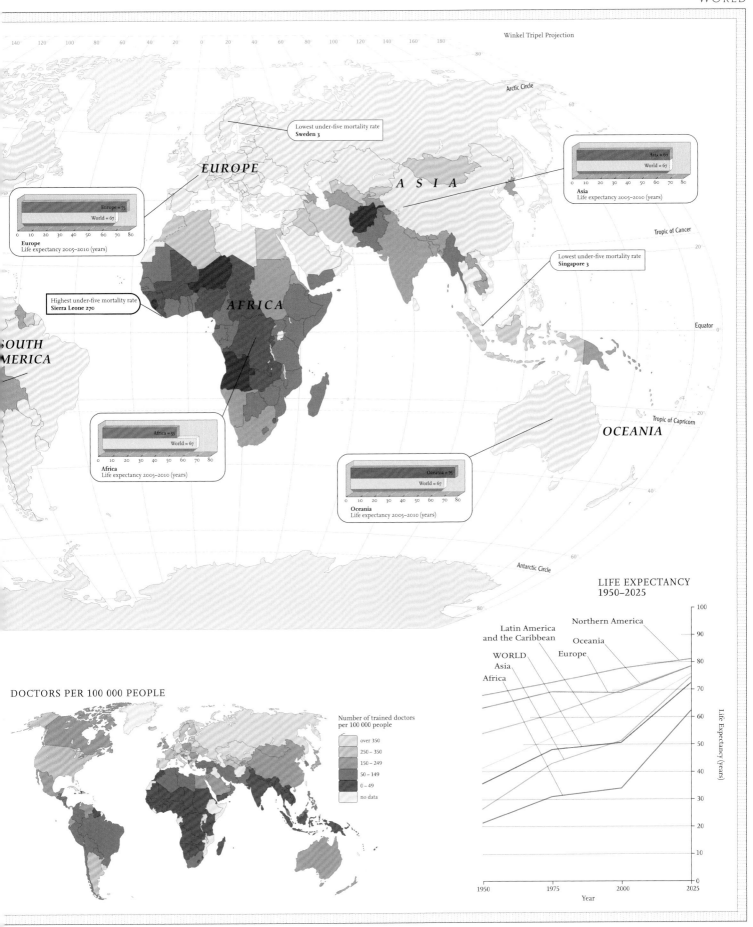

Winkel Tripel Projection

EUROPE

ASIA

AFRICA

SOUTH AMERICA

OCEANIA

Lowest under-five mortality rate
Sweden 3

Lowest under-five mortality rate
Singapore 3

Highest under-five mortality rate
Sierra Leone 270

Europe = 75
World = 67
0 10 20 30 40 50 60 70 80
Europe
Life expectancy 2005–2010 (years)

Asia = 67
World = 67
0 10 20 30 40 50 60 70 80
Asia
Life expectancy 2005–2010 (years)

Africa = 53
World = 67
0 10 20 30 40 50 60 70 80
Africa
Life expectancy 2005–2010 (years)

Oceania = 75
World = 67
0 10 20 30 40 50 60 70 80
Oceania
Life expectancy 2005–2010 (years)

Arctic Circle
Tropic of Cancer
Equator
Tropic of Capricorn
Antarctic Circle

DOCTORS PER 100 000 PEOPLE

Number of trained doctors
per 100 000 people

- over 350
- 250 – 350
- 150 – 249
- 50 – 149
- 0 – 49
- no data

LIFE EXPECTANCY 1950–2025

Latin America
and the Caribbean

Northern America

Oceania

WORLD

Europe

Asia

Africa

Life Expectancy (years)

100
90
80
70
60
50
40
30
20
10
0

1950   1975   2000   2025
Year

URBANIZATION

World population is urbanizing rapidly and, in this respect, 2008 was a momentous point in world history. In 2008, for the first time urban dwellers outnumber those living in traditionally rural areas. But the current level of urbanization varies greatly across the world, as too does its rate of increase. In the hundred years up to 1950 the greatest changes took place in Europe and North America. Relatively few large cities developed elsewhere and most of these were in coastal locations with good trading connections with the imperial and industrial nations. The main feature of the past half century has been the massive growth in the numbers of urban dwellers in the less developed regions.

Tōkyō is the largest city in the world and more than a quarter of the population of Japan live here. The city was established in 1603 and has been growing steadily ever since then.

TOWARDS AN URBANIZED WORLD

The annual rise in the percentage of the world's population living in cities has been accelerating steadily since the 1970s and it will be running at very high levels until at least 2030. As a result, by then, 3 in 5 people (59.9 per cent) will be urbanites compared to 35.9 per cent in 1970 and 50.8 per cent in 2010. In absolute terms, the global urban population more than doubled between 1970 and 2000, adding 1.5 billion to its 1970 total of 1.33 billion, and it is expected to grow by a further 2.07 billion by 2030. There is a broad contrast in the level of urbanization between the more and less developed regions, but also a great deal of variation within them. In the more developed regions as a whole, three-quarters of the population now live in urban areas.

THE GROWTH OF LARGE CITIES

Alongside the rise in the world's urban population has occurred a massive increase in the number and size of cities, especially of the very large cities or 'megacities'. In 1950, New York was the only agglomeration with over 10 million inhabitants, and there were still only three cities of this size by 1975 – New York, Tōkyō and Mexico City. By 2000, there were eighteen and there are expected to be twenty-two by 2015. Urban areas are also becoming more diffuse and polycentric, making the task of defining separate cities on the ground even more difficult.

WORLD'S LARGEST CITIES 2010

Figures are for the urban agglomeration, defined as the population contained within the contours of a contiguous territory inhabited at urban levels without regard to administrative boundaries. They incorporate the population within a city plus the suburban fringe lying outside of, but adjacent to, the city boundaries.

City	Country	Population
Tōkyō	Japan	35 467 000
Mumbai	India	20 036 000
São Paulo	Brazil	19 582 000
Mexico City	Mexico	19 485 000
New York	USA	19 388 000
Delhi	India	16 983 000
Shanghai	China	15 790 000
Kolkata	India	15 548 000
Dhaka	Bangladesh	14 625 000
Karachi	Pakistan	13 252 000
Buenos Aires	Argentina	13 067 000
Los Angeles	USA	12 738 000
Rio de Janeiro	Brazil	12 170 000
Cairo	Egypt	12 041 000
Manila	Philippines	11 799 000
Beijing	China	11 741 000
Ōsaka	Japan	11 305 000
Moscow	Russian Federation	10 967 000
Lagos	Nigeria	10 572 000
İstanbul	Turkey	10 546 000
Paris	France	9 856 000
Jakarta	Indonesia	9 703 000
Seoul	South Korea	9 554 000
Guangzhou	China	9 447 000
Chicago	USA	9 186 000
Kinshasa	Dem. Rep. Congo	9 052 000
London	United Kingdom	8 607 000
Bogotá	Colombia	8 416 000
Lima	Peru	8 375 000
Tehrān	Iran	8 221 000
Shenzhen	China	8 114 000
Chennai	India	7 545 000
Wuhan	China	7 542 000
Tianjin	China	7 468 000
Hong Kong	China	7 416 000
Bangalore	India	7 216 000
Lahore	Pakistan	7 201 000
Bangkok	Thailand	6 963 000
Hyderabad	India	6 749 000
Chongqing	China	6 690 000
Baghdād	Iraq	5 891 000

WORLD'S MAJOR CITIES

Urban agglomerations with over 2.5 million inhabitants.

- 2.5 million – 5 million
- 5 million – 10 million
- 10 million – 20 million
- over 20 million

LEVEL OF URBANIZATION

Percentage of total population living in urban areas 2005. The world's urban population is expected to reach 50 per cent of the total population during 2008.

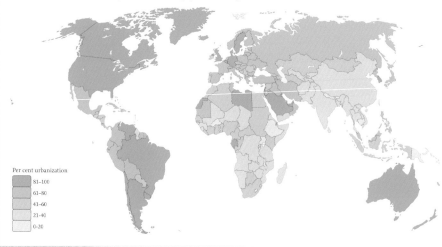

Per cent urbanization
- 81–100
- 61–80
- 41–60
- 21–40
- 0–20

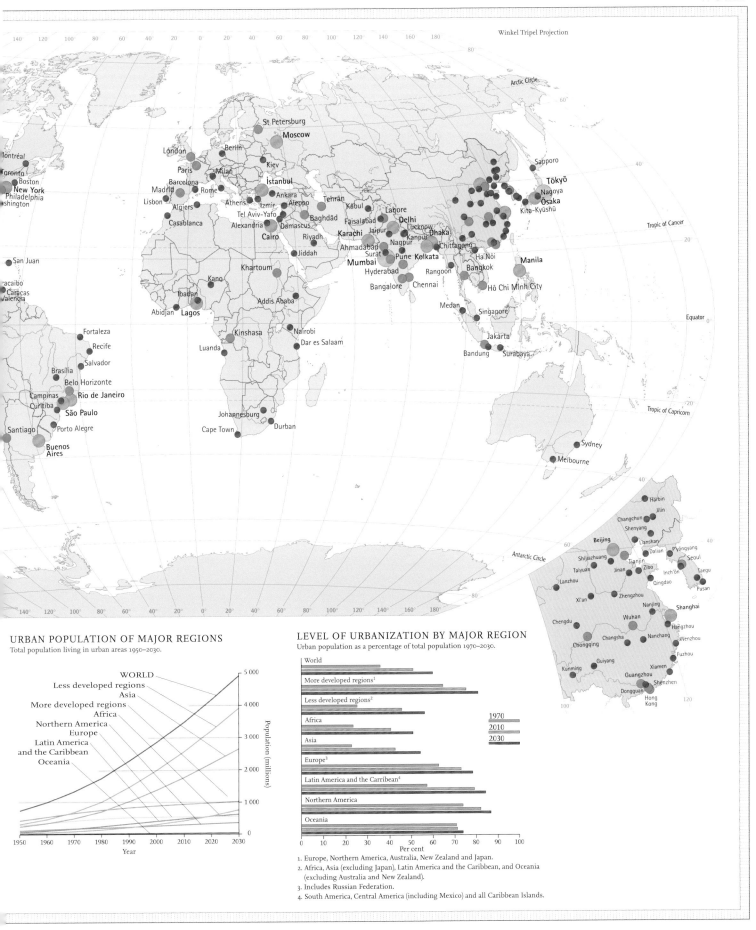

Winkel Tripel Projection

URBAN POPULATION OF MAJOR REGIONS

Total population living in urban areas 1950–2030.

WORLD
Less developed regions
Asia
More developed regions
Africa
Northern America
Europe
Latin America
and the Caribbean
Oceania

Population (millions)

5 000
4 000
3 000
2 000
1 000
0

1950 1960 1970 1980 1990 2000 2010 2020 2030
Year

LEVEL OF URBANIZATION BY MAJOR REGION

Urban population as a percentage of total population 1970–2030.

World
More developed regions[1]
Less developed regions[2]
Africa
Asia
Europe[3]
Latin America and the Carribean[4]
Northern America
Oceania

1970
2010
2030

0 10 20 30 40 50 60 70 80 90 100
Per cent

1. Europe, Northern America, Australia, New Zealand and Japan.
2. Africa, Asia (excluding Japan), Latin America and the Caribbean, and Oceania
   (excluding Australia and New Zealand).
3. Includes Russian Federation.
4. South America, Central America (including Mexico) and all Caribbean Islands.

WEALTH, POVERTY AND TRADE

The globalization of the economy is making the world appear a smaller place. However, this shrinkage is an uneven process. Countries are being included and excluded to differing degrees in the global economy. The world economy remains divided between the richer (core) and relatively poorer (peripheral) countries. A common method of defining these groups uses Gross National Income (GNI) per capita as a measure of average income in each country. The fates of core and peripheral countries are closely related. Economic success and prosperity for one country can often be at the expense of others. Some newly industrializing countries have attempted to grow fast enough to cross the divide between core and periphery. Economic inequalities exist between and within countries, as well as between and within social groups in countries. These inequalities are evident in terms of wealth, growth, and debt. Increasingly large and dominant transnational corporations are driving and, in turn, being driven by the process of globalization.

Poverty, hunger, and environmental degradation are problems experienced in areas such as this in Freetown, capital of Sierra Leone, one of the world's poorest countries.

TRADE, DEBT AND AID

Different countries and regions are participating in the global economy to different degrees. The value of merchandise exports, for instance, illustrates the extent to which countries are engaged in cross-border trading. Global trade is concentrated among the developed countries, in particular North America, the European Union, and the Asia-Pacific region. The USA, Germany, and Japan stand out as the world's largest exporters. Since exports earn hard currency, it is no coincidence that the weakest exporters are among the world's poorest countries, including Burundi and the Democratic Republic of the Congo in Africa. The developed countries with the higher values of exports are more closely integrated into the core of the global economy. The weak exporters remain reliant upon imports and stay on the periphery of the global trading system. Foreign direct investment (FDI) is another motor of the global economy. FDI inflows in 2004 were dominated by the developed countries, in particular western Europe, and, to a lesser degree, the Asia-Pacific region among the developing nations.

Globalization means the poorest countries find it particularly hard to develop and attract economic activity, resulting in an inability to repay loans or stimulate their own economies. Therefore their debts become greater and more loans are taken out to cover them. International efforts are ongoing in trying to suspend or write off some of these debts but meanwhile overseas aid is essential for the survival of some of the poorest countries.

INEQUALITIES IN WEALTH DISTRIBUTION

Gross National Income (GNI) per capita, 2005 and Gini Index (latest available figures).

Winkel Tripel Projection

The Gini Index reveals the degree of inequality in the internal distribution of income . When the figure is higher, national income is more concentrated in the hands of fewer people.

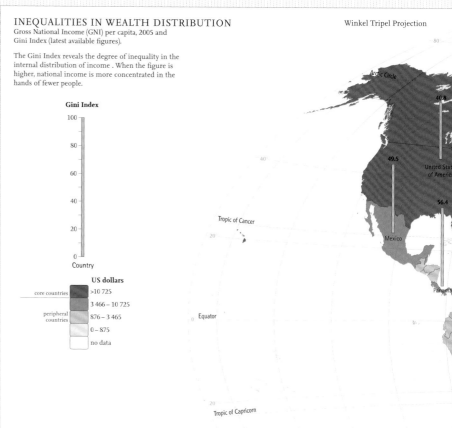

Gini Index

US dollars	
core countries	>10 725
	3 466 – 10 725
peripheral countries	876 – 3 465
	0 – 875
	no data

FOREIGN DIRECT INVESTMENT HOST ECONOMIES 2004

	Country	US$ (millions)
Developed countries	United States	106 831
	Luxembourg	78 678
	United Kingdom	72 561
	Australia	42 469
	Belgium	40 080
Developing countries	China	54 937
	Hong Kong	34 035
	Brazil	18 166
	Mexico	17 377
	Singapore	16 032

DEBT SERVICE RATIO

Debt as a percentage of GNI and top 5 total debt service, 2004.

	100 – 800
	70 – 99.9
	50 – 69.9
	30 – 49.9
	20 – 29.9
	0 – 19.9
	no data

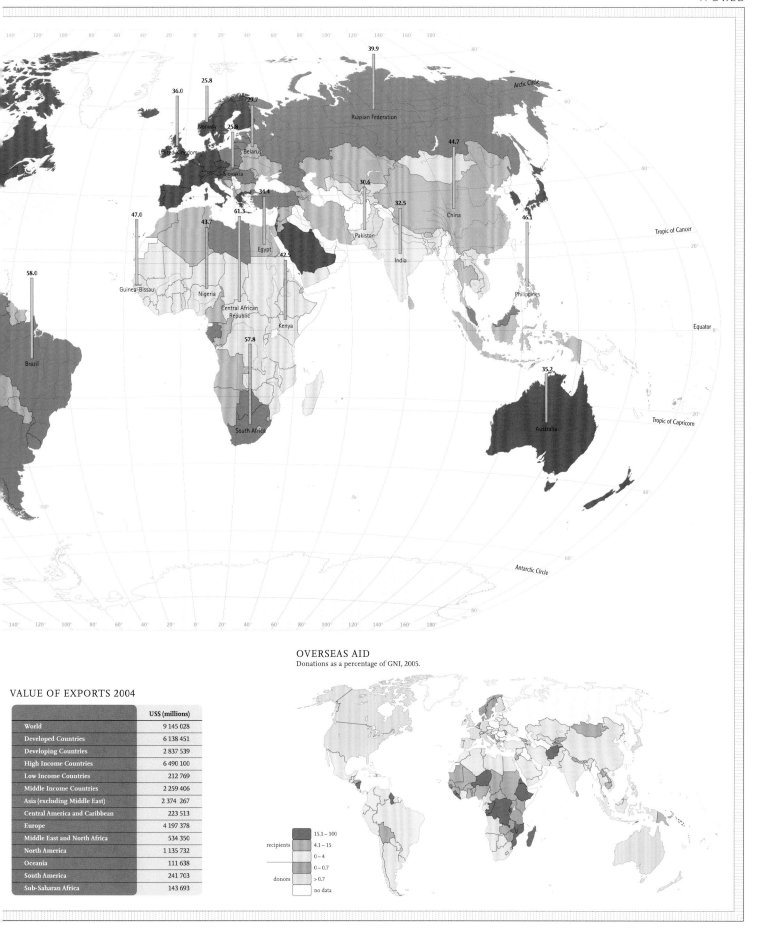

39.9 Russian Federation

25.8

36.0 Norway

29.7

25.8 United Kingdom

Belarus

Slovakia

44.7 China

34.4

30.6 Pakistan

32.5 India

46.1 Philippines

47.0 Guinea-Bissau

43.7 Nigeria

61.3

Egypt

42.5

Central African Republic

Kenya

58.0 Brazil

57.8 South Africa

35.2 Australia

Arctic Circle

Tropic of Cancer

Equator

Tropic of Capricorn

Antarctic Circle

OVERSEAS AID
Donations as a percentage of GNI, 2005.

recipients
- 15.1 – 100
- 4.1 – 15
- 0 – 4

donors
- 0 – 0.7
- > 0.7

no data

VALUE OF EXPORTS 2004

	US$ (millions)
World	9 145 028
Developed Countries	6 138 451
Developing Countries	2 837 539
High Income Countries	6 490 100
Low Income Countries	212 769
Middle Income Countries	2 259 406
Asia (excluding Middle East)	2 374 267
Central America and Caribbean	223 513
Europe	4 197 378
Middle East and North Africa	534 350
North America	1 135 732
Oceania	111 638
South America	241 703
Sub-Saharan Africa	143 693

COMMUNICATIONS

The rapid growth of the telecommunications industry over the last two decades, has contributed to the 'death of distance' by linking different parts of the world ever more cheaply and reliably due to improvements in technology. This process has meant that millions of virtual places, identified by telephone numbers, e-mail addresses, and World Wide Web sites, have become an essential part of the world's social and economic landscape. The huge demand for mobile and satellite telephones has contributed to satellite demand and to the building of ground stations. The parallel demand for electronic addresses has also triggered a building boom for international submarine cables as well as adding to the demand for satellites. Initially, most of these networks served an information belt running from western Europe across North America to eastern Asia, but now the rest of the world is gradually becoming connected.

INTERNET COMMUNICATIONS

Internet users have been increasing rapidly, especially in the last ten years. However, access levels vary, with approximately thirty countries still with less than 1 per cent internet penetration. In the G8 countries, with 15 per cent of the world's population, there are almost 50 per cent of total internet users while the entire continent of Africa, with over fifty countries, has fewer internet users than France. Constraints include the high costs of international bandwidth to developing countries if they have to pay for a link to a hub in a developed country. International bandwidth is a critical part of the infrastructure as it is the most important factor in the speed of access to websites in other countries.

SATELLITE COMMUNICATIONS

Communications satellites are important for person-to-person communication, including cellular telephones, and for broadcasting. Unlike submarine cables, which must connect at fixed points, satellites can transmit information between Earth stations located anywhere within a satellite's radio beam, or 'footprint'. Geostationary satellites, which orbit at 36 000 kilometres (22 370 miles) above the Earth may have footprints spanning over 1000 kilometres (620 miles), thus providing a broad service area for point-to-multi-point voice, video and data communications. The positions of communications satellites are critical to their use, and reflect the demand for such communications in each part of the world. While satellites are historically most important for international telephone calls they have since developed for the provision of television, radio and to provide broadband internet services.

Communications satellites are placed in 'geostationary' orbit above the equator. This means that they move at the same speed as the earth and remain fixed above a single point on the earth's surface. The Global Positioning System (GPS) – seen in use here in Antarctica for monitoring glacier movement – allows accurate position fixing and navigation. Originally developed by the US military, the signals from the satellites now serve hand-held personal and in-car navigation uses, as well as more sophisticated surveying and mapping applications.

WORLD COMMUNICATION EQUIPMENT 1993–2007

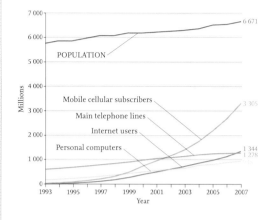

TOP BROADBAND ECONOMIES 2008
Countries with the highest broadband penetration rate – subscribers per 100 inhabitants

	Top Economies	Rate
1	Sweden	37.3
2	Denmark	36.8
3	Netherlands	35.0
4	Norway	34.0
5	Switzerland	33.0
6	Iceland	32.9
7	South Korea	32.0
8	Finland	30.6
9	Luxembourg	30.3
10	Canada	29.0
11	France	28.6
12	United Kingdom	28.3
13	Belgium	28.3
14	Germany	27.4
15	Hong Kong, China	26.8
16	USA	25.6
17	Macao, China	25.1
18	Australia	24.5
19	Malta	24.2
20	Estonia	23.9

INTERNATIONAL TELECOMMUNICATIONS INDICATORS BY REGION 2007

Main telephone lines

0.9% 2.4% 14.2% 8.0% 25.7% 48.8%

Legend:
- Africa
- North America
- Latin America and the Caribbean*
- Europe
- Asia
- Oceania

*Includes Mexico.

Mobile cellular subscribers

0.8% 8.2% 8.3% 11.4% 26.7% 44.6%

Internet users

1.1% 3.7% 18.3% 9.7% 24.7% 42.5%

INTERNET USERS AND CAPACITY

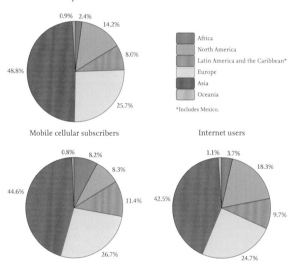

Total internet users 2008
Top ten countries

France 31 571 000

United States 220 000 000

United Kingdom 48 755 000

Germany 62 500 000

Russia 30 000 000

Japan 88 110 000

South Korea 37 475 800

China 298 000 000

France 31 571 000

India 81 000 000

Brazil 67 510 400

Internet users per 10 000 inhabitants 2008
- 4 000–9 999
- 2 000–3 999
- 700–1 999
- 200–699
- 0–199
- no data

INTERNATIONAL TELECOMMUNICATIONS TRAFFIC 2008

Winkel Tripel Projection

Telephone lines per
100 inhabitants 2008

- over 50.0
- 35.0 – 50.0
- 15.0 – 34.9
- 10.0 – 14.9
- 5.0 – 9.9
- 1.0 – 4.9
- 0 – 0.9
- no data

Total telephone
lines 2008

Europe
Total telephone lines
318 558 000

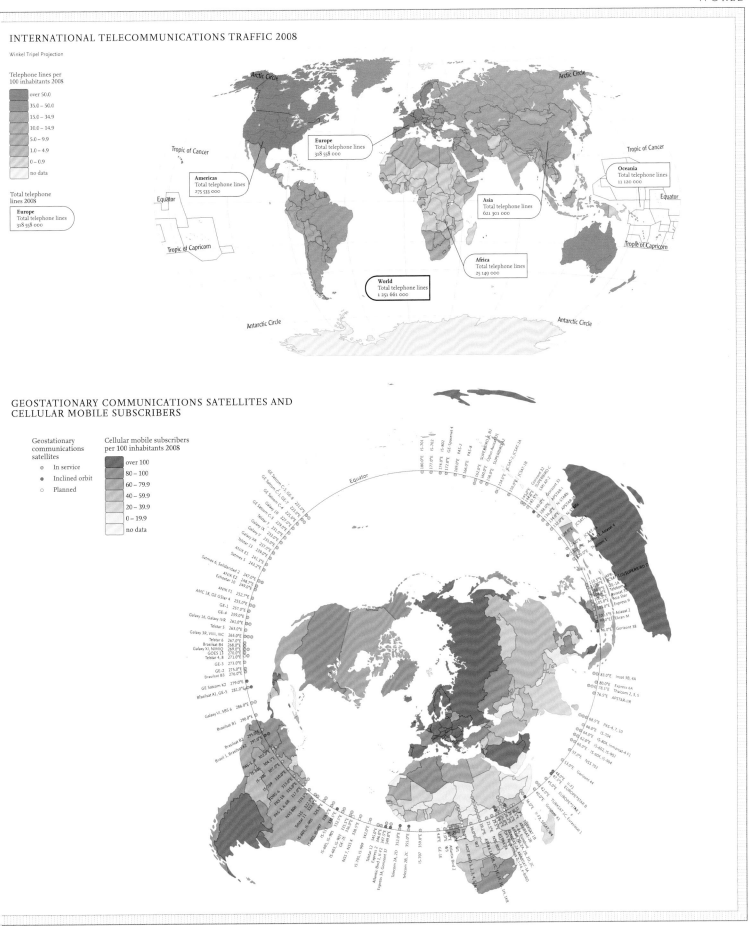

Europe
Total telephone lines
318 558 000

Americas
Total telephone lines
275 533 000

Asia
Total telephone lines
621 301 000

Oceania
Total telephone lines
11 120 000

Africa
Total telephone lines
25 149 000

World
Total telephone lines
1 251 661 000

GEOSTATIONARY COMMUNICATIONS SATELLITES AND CELLULAR MOBILE SUBSCRIBERS

Geostationary
communications
satellites

- ◉ In service
- ● Inclined orbit
- ○ Planned

Cellular mobile subscribers
per 100 inhabitants 2008

- over 100
- 80 – 100
- 60 – 79.9
- 40 – 59.9
- 20 – 39.9
- 0 – 19.9
- no data

CONFLICT

Geo-political issues shape the countries of the world and the current political situation in many parts of the world reflects a long history of armed conflict. Since the Second World War conflicts have been fairly localized, but there are numerous 'flash points' where factors such as territorial claims, ideology, religion, ethnicity and access to resources can cause friction between two or more countries. Such factors also lie behind the recent growth in global terrorism.

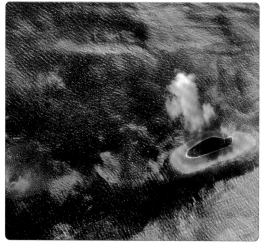

A small island and reef in the disputed Spratly Islands in the South China Sea.

MILITARY SPENDING

Military expenditure can take up a disproportionate amount of a country's wealth – Eritrea, with a Gross National Income (GNI) per capita of only US$190 spends twenty-four per cent of its total GDP on military activity. There is an encouraging trend towards wider international cooperation, mainly through the United Nations (UN) and the North Atlantic Treaty Organization (NATO), to prevent escalation of conflicts and on peacekeeping missions.

GLOBAL TERRORISM

Terrorism is defined by the United Nations as "All criminal acts directed against a State and intended or calculated to create a state of terror in the minds of particular persons or a group of persons or the general public". The world has become increasingly concerned about terrorism and the possibility that terrorists could acquire and use nuclear, chemical and biological weapons. One common form of terrorist attack is suicide bombing. Pioneered by Tamil secessionists in Sri Lanka, it has been widely used by Palestinian groups fighting against Israeli occupation of the West Bank and Gaza. In recent years it has also been used by the Al Qaida network in its attacks on the western world.

SPRATLY ISLANDS

The Spratly Islands in the South China Sea are an excellent example of how apparently insignificant pieces of land can become the source of conflict. Six countries claim ownership of some or all of these remote, tiny islands and reefs, the largest of which covers less than half a square kilometre.

The islands are strategically important – approximately a quarter of all the world's shipping trade passes through the area - and ownership of the group would mean access to 250 000 square kilometres of valuable fishing grounds and sea bed believed to be rich in oil and gas reserves. Five of the claimant countries have occupied individual islands to endorse their claims, although there appears little prospect of international agreement on ownership.

MAJOR TERRORIST INCIDENTS

Date	Location	Summary	Killed	Injured
December 1988	Lockerbie, Scotland	Airline bombing	270	5
March 1995	Tōkyō, Japan	Sarin gas attack on subway	12	5 510
April 1995	Oklahoma City, USA	Bomb in the Federal building	168	over 800
August 1998	Nairobi, Kenya and Dar es Salaam, Tanzania	US Embassy bombings	225	over 4 000
August 1998	Omagh, Northern Ireland	Town centre bombing	29	220
September 2001	New York and Washington D.C., USA	Airline hijacking and crashing	3 018	over 6 200
October 2002	Bali, Indonesia	Car bomb outside nightclub	202	over 200
October 2002	Moscow, Russian Federation	Theatre siege	170	over 600
March 2004	Bāghdad and Karbalā', Iraq	Suicide bombing of pilgrims	181	over 400
March 2004	Madrid, Spain	Train bombings	191	1 800
September 2004	Beslan, Russian Federation	School siege	385	over 700
July 2005	London, UK	Underground and bus bombings	56	700
July 2005	Sharm ash Shaykh, Egypt	Bombs at tourist sites	88	200
July 2006	Mumbai, India	Train bombings	209	700
August 2007	Qahtaniya, Iraq	Suicide bombing in town centres	796	over 1 500

TERRORIST INCIDENTS, 2000–2006

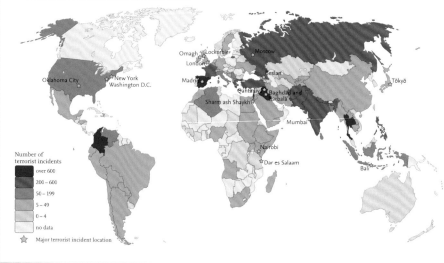

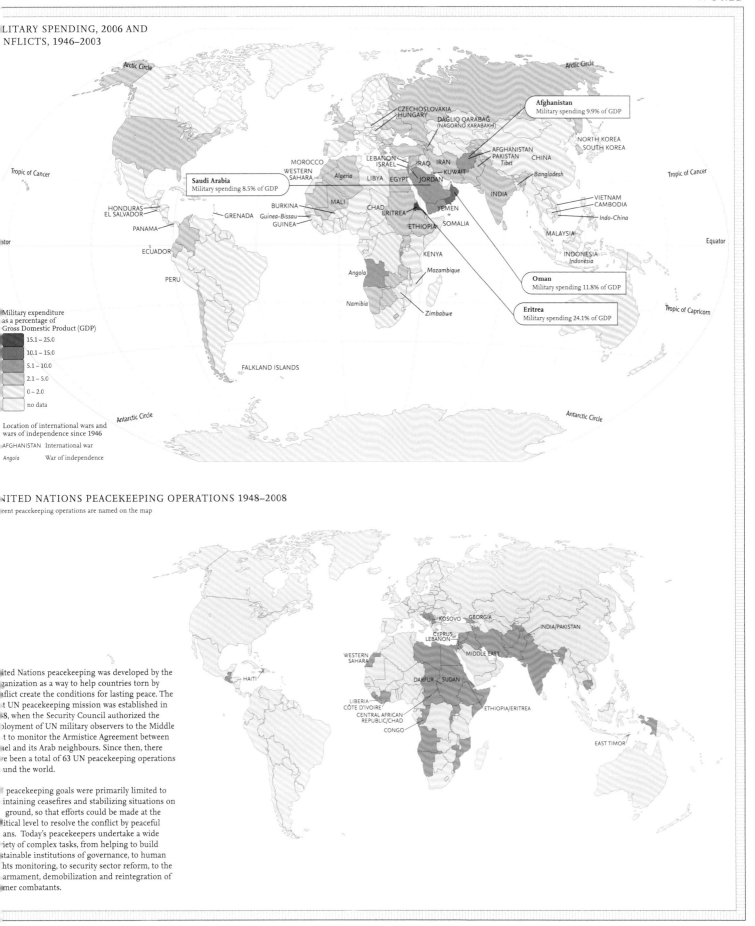

LITARY SPENDING, 2006 AND NFLICTS, 1946–2003

Afghanistan
Military spending 9.9% of GDP

Saudi Arabia
Military spending 8.5% of GDP

Oman
Military spending 11.8% of GDP

Eritrea
Military spending 24.1% of GDP

Military expenditure
as a percentage of
Gross Domestic Product (GDP)

	15.1 – 25.0
	10.1 – 15.0
	5.1 – 10.0
	2.1 – 5.0
	0 – 2.0
	no data

Location of international wars and
wars of independence since 1946

AFGHANISTAN   International war

Angola   War of independence

NITED NATIONS PEACEKEEPING OPERATIONS 1948–2008

rent peacekeeping operations are named on the map

ited Nations peacekeeping was developed by the
ganization as a way to help countries torn by
flict create the conditions for lasting peace. The
t UN peacekeeping mission was established in
8, when the Security Council authorized the
ployment of UN military observers to the Middle
t to monitor the Armistice Agreement between
ael and its Arab neighbours. Since then, there
ve been a total of 63 UN peacekeeping operations
und the world.

peacekeeping goals were primarily limited to
intaining ceasefires and stabilizing situations on
ground, so that efforts could be made at the
litical level to resolve the conflict by peaceful
ans. Today's peacekeepers undertake a wide
iety of complex tasks, from helping to build
stainable institutions of governance, to human
hts monitoring, to security sector reform, to the
armament, demobilization and reintegration of
mer combatants.

MAPS AND MAPPING –
EARLY DEVELOPMENT

Without knowledge of their spatial environments, for food, shelter and safety, our ancestors could not have survived. Their first 'maps' were probably instinctive and based on experience, to support personal navigation, and only later expanded to include gestures, speech and crude drawings. These simple expressions of our mapping instinct can still be employed today when we are challenged to explain a spatial problem or asked for directions. As most surviving artefacts are less than 10 000 years old, the 'cartography' of the previous million years must have been cognitive and mainly intangible. The tangible record of recent millennia confirms the continuing importance of mapping, through its reflection of people's ideas and knowledge of their world, their social and cultural environments and the growing complexity of the spatial challenges they faced, especially during recent centuries. Rather than evolving, maps appeared in various forms, in different parts of the world at different times and to meet different needs. Technical improvements also came in stages, often in response to contemporary advances in science and technology.

Through time, maps have displayed and stored geospatially-related information, real or imagined. As such they have expanded the scope for private thinking and have facilitated communication. The fact that most geospatial and map information is now stored digitally has not changed the fundamental uses of cartography, it just means that spatial data handling is now carried out more effectively. Maps have long been recognized as primarily communicative devices, but they have had equally significant roles in support of spatial data exploration and analysis. It is the latter two which have gained importance in recent decades as technologies have raised the potential of what is now often referred to as 'geovisualization'.

Map of the World. Carved on a Babylonian clay tablet, c.600 BC. Babylon is shown as a rectangle intersected by vertical lines representing the Euphrates river. Small circles show other cities and countries, and the world is encircled by an ocean – the 'Bitter River'. British Museum, Department of Western Asiatic Antiquities, London, UK.

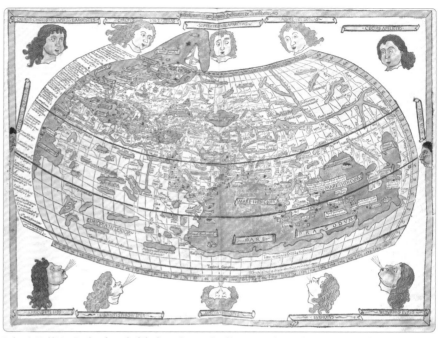

Ptolemaic World Map. Based on the work of Claudius Ptolemy, produced by Donis Nicolaus in Ulm, Germany, 1630. The map includes lines of latitude and longitude which give a sense of accuracy. The figures represent different wind directions. British Library, London, UK.

PREHISTORIC AND EARLY MAPPING IN EUROPE AND BEYOND

Map-like images have been discovered in the rock art and wall paintings of the late- and post-paleolithic periods in Europe and the Mediterranean, but the true beginnings of cartographic history are associated with the Babylonian and Egyptian civilizations during the final millennia BC. People in other world regions beyond Europe have also engaged in cartographic activities since prehistoric times, the traditional aspects of which are still echoed within some more contemporary indigenous communities. Recent studies of early Islamic and Asian societies as well as those in Africa, America, Australia, the Arctic and Pacific have revealed a fascinating diversity of cartographic heritage, although mapping traditions were often quite different from those of Europe. This is where factors such as culture and the nature of the environment are believed to have influenced whether people developed technical skills in graphic/cartographic expression or employed more ephemeral narrative forms. Surviving examples of early and traditional mapping are rare and difficult to interpret, but the limits of their coverage and use may indicate the beliefs and geographical knowledge of their creators. Representations of regions or 'worlds' beyond their immediate experience were more speculative, with cosmological and celestial themes.

Map of London. Extract from *Civitates Orbis Terrarum* by Georg Braun and Frans Hogenberg, 1572. St Paul's Cathedral is in the centre left, the Tower of London on the right and London Bridge in the lower centre. Guildhall Library, Corporation of London, UK.

CLASSICAL CIVILIZATION (GRAECO-ROMAN) 500 BC–AD 500

The Greeks employed topographical surveying methods in their colonial settlements, but their most outstanding contributions to cartography were theoretical rather than practical, especially with reference to the shape and size of the Earth. The Earth was once believed to be stationary, flat, surrounded by water, and even the centre of the universe. Belief in its spherical form arose from the ideas of the Greek philosopher Pythagoras (6th century BC) and, one century later, Aristotle's observations of how ships disappeared over the horizon. Important supporting evidence was also provided by astronomers noting the curved shadow cast by the Earth onto the Moon during an eclipse. However, experienced mariners such as the Phoenicians, using instinct and the observation of stars rising and setting as they sailed their trade routes, may already have been aware, for centuries, of the Earth as a sphere. The circumference of the globe was determined by Eratosthenes, the Greek mathematician and Librarian at Alexandria (c. 250 BC), to a value very close to that accepted today. Once knowledge of the Earth's shape and size was established, the next cartographic requirement was for a system to provide for geographical location, and once more the Greeks led the way. A graticule of meridians of longitude (stretching from pole to pole) and parallels of latitude (lines parallel to the Equator) is known to have existed in the 4th century BC, and later developed with the help of Eratosthenes, and especially Hipparchus of Rhodes who was the first to apply mathematical precision to geographical locations by their latitudes and longitudes.

Another challenge for cartography was how to depict a sphere on a plane surface. This cannot be done without distorting shapes and areas and compromises are inevitable. Transformations of the globe onto a flat surface, referred to as map projections, also had their earliest manifestations in Greek times (6th – 1st centuries BC). The written work of Claudius Ptolemy, another Greek mathematician, astronomer and geographer living in Alexandria in the 2nd century AD, contained some of the most detailed cartographic instructions. In his *Geographia* he describes projections of different types and provides information on the level of geographical knowledge of his time. This knowledge remained largely unchanged during the next thousand years. Geographia also included theoretical principles of cartography, lists of place names and computed coordinates of places and features but, as it may not have included cartographic illustrations, we must rely upon later maps, based on interpretations of Ptolemy's work, to help us imagine the world view of his time.

In some ways it could be said that the Romans took advantage of fundamental Greek ideas and developed more commonplace applications such as cadastral mapping, and maps for planning, engineering and travel. The *Tabula Peutingeriana* (Peutinger Table), is a 12th- or 13th-century copy of a 4th-century map showing roads, settlements and staging posts as an apparent aid to travel in the Roman Empire. The passing of that Empire gave way to the Arabic Byzantine Empire which may have inherited Roman knowledge and used maps, but little evidence remains.

MEDIEVAL AND EARLY MODERN PERIOD AD 500–AD 1400

The Medieval period was not rich cartographically. Maps from this time lack clear identity and were included by contemporary scholars within a broader category of diagrams and pictures. Although maps were not in regular use, some distinct cartographic traditions did continue, especially through mappae mundi (world maps) and 'portolan' charts. The former, appearing between the 7th and 13th centuries, had classical origins, often with a Christian perspective. They were usually oval or circular in shape, schematic in content, and centred on Jerusalem. Although unsuitable for navigation, these world maps had practical uses in a more cultural and philosophical sense, for illustrating principles in classical learning or as aids to teaching. Most were either scientific maps depicting the five climatic zones of the sphere, or 'T-O' maps of the known world of Roman and Medieval times. The latter category range in complexity from the Vatican map

by Isidore, Bishop of Seville, Spain in the 7th century, representing God's Creative Order, to the highly complex example, encyclopedic in content, attributed to Richard of Haldingham and Lafford (c. 1290), held in Hereford Cathedral, England. Another quite different product of this time was the Christian pictorial Madaba map (c. 550) in the form of a church floor mosaic discovered in Madaba, Jordan, the earliest known map of the Holy Land. Arabic cartography was revived in the 12th century when al-Idrisi was commissioned by the King of Sicily to produce a world map – a map whose influence continued into the 16th century.

Other quite different traditions in the later Medieval period gave rise to town plans, local, district and route maps and sea charts (portolan charts). The latter, designed primarily for navigation, were by far the most significant. Essentially products of the great maritime centres of northern Italy and Catalonia, eastern Spain, and produced on vellum, their origins remain obscure. They probably first appeared shortly before 1300, coinciding with the growth in seafaring activity and have been described as 'the first true charts in which medieval speculation and fantasy gave place to scientific cartography based on experiment and observation'. Providing impressive detail on coastlines, harbours and related navigational matters, and typically characterized by the depiction of rhumb lines (or loxodromes, lines of constant compass bearing) the charts appear to have been regularly updated as more information was acquired. Although the only surviving examples were for decorative purposes, there is no doubt that portolans represented a significant step in the development of cartography. Also, to meet the need to carry numerous maps on a voyage, some collections of portolans were combined as atlases. Route maps, for the use of pilgrims and merchants travelling overland, also developed during this period, exemplified by Matthew Paris's map of the route from London to Otranto, Italy produced around 1250 or the so-called Gough Map (1360) the oldest extant road map of Great Britain.

15TH AND 16TH CENTURIES

This was essentially the age of exploration and discovery, a period during which ships from Europe travelled the world seeking trade and commercial partners to satisfy the needs of new capitalism. It gave rise to an explosion of global knowledge and contributed to a veritable renaissance in cartography. Crucially, Ptolemy's *Geographia*, previously lost to European cartographic tradition, was re-introduced, and provided the baseline for further growth in mapmaking. The period saw a great development of world maps, the older traditions of the *mappae mundi* being gradually enriched and replaced by new geographical information and portolan-inspired coastlines, as in the great map by Fra Mauro. It was

not just that discoveries were mapped, the maps were the exciting products of exploration. The development of printing in the 15th century provided for one of the major surges in cartographic development. Italian city states, notably Rome and Venice, dominated the new European map trade from 1550 to 1570, and produced the earliest bound collections of maps of non-uniform size (the so-called 'Lafreri', or IATO – Italian, Assembled to Order – atlases). Later in the period, dominance in mapmaking passed to the Low Countries, giving rise to the Golden Age of Dutch cartography, exemplified by the first printed 'atlas' of map sheets in a uniform size and style produced by Abraham Ortelius in 1570 – the *Theatrum Orbis Terrarum*. Other particularly significant works of this period were Georg Braun and Frans Hogenberg's six-volume *Civitates Orbis Terrarum* containing 530 town plans and views, and Lucas Janszoon Waghenaer's collection of printed sea charts and sailing directions *Speculum nauticum*. The term 'atlas' was coined by Gerard Mercator the Flemish cartographer, and geographical colossus of the history of cartography, whose work included the famous world map (1569) on the projection which still bears his name and continues to be widely used.

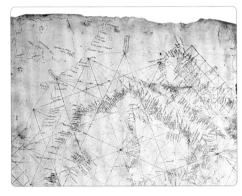

The Carte Pisane. The oldest surviving portolan chart, c. 1290. It shows most of Europe, with a remarkably detailed coastline of the Mediterranean Sea with Italy and Sicily in the centre. Bibliothèque Nationale, Paris, France.

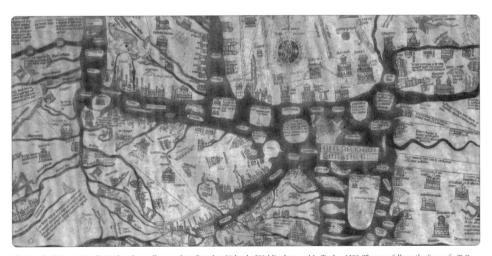

The Hereford Mappa Mundi. Produced on vellum, and attributed to Richard of Haldingham and Lafford, c. 1290. The map follows the form of a T-O map, centred on Jerusalem (top centre). It includes representations of the continents of Asia, Africa and Europe, separated by the Mediterranean Sea. Hereford Cathedral, Hereford, UK.

MAPS AND MAPPING –
THE MODERN ERA

The age of exploration and discovery, which had grown from the technologies and ideas of the Renaissance, produced a new, detailed and sophisticated picture of the world, much of which has since been confirmed as both extensive and accurate, despite the relatively primitive technology in use at the time. The last four centuries of the second millennium AD saw a rapid and massive increase in world population, urbanization and industrialization, and an associated growth in demand for products. They have also been characterized by an increasing recognition of the importance of mapping, and by developing technologies in the fields of surveying, navigation, printing, communications and computers. The historical importance of maps in the modern era lies not only in the information they contain, the manner in which they were produced, or their influences but also in their use across a whole range of activities – military, civilian, scientific, management, planning and education.

Swiss 1:50 000 official topographic map. Extract from Sheet 396 Grindelwald, published 1870 with revisions 1894 and 1899.
Glasgow University Library, Glasgow, UK.

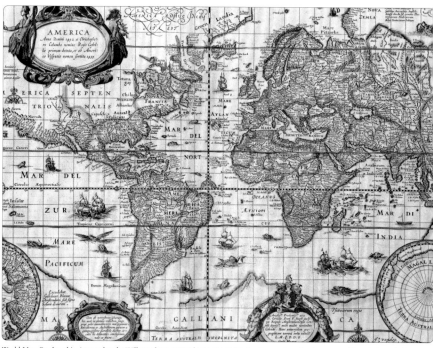

World Map. Produced in Amsterdam by Willem Blaeu, 1630. This is one of the finest examples of early maps on Mercator's projection. British Library, London, UK.

17TH AND 18TH CENTURIES

The earlier years of the 17th century were dominated by the vast cartographic output from the Low Countries, epitomized by the Blaeu publishing house and its competitors. Dutch map production benefited greatly from extensive voyaging, stimulated particularly by trading companies and war against Spain. But, by the end of that century the world centre for cartographic production had shifted from Amsterdam to Paris. France was one of the first countries (from the 1670s) to recognize the importance of establishing a national survey and mapping programme and led the way through the work of four generations of the Cassini family. They established the national survey of France well ahead of any other such surveys in western Europe, based on a systematic and scientific approach to trigonometrical surveying. Such projects were later developed more systematically to reflect national needs, often military, as in Great Britain where the Military Survey of Scotland (1746–1755) arose from the requirements of the army, and

the British Ordnance Survey (1791) began work in the south of England in recognition of the dangers of invasion by the French. The national Hydrographic Office was also established in 1795 to meet the needs of the Royal Navy.

Factors in the exploration and mapping of North America were the impetus given by fur-trading companies, notably the Hudson's Bay Company, the colonial dash into the continent and the American War of Independence (1775–1783). It was an age, too, when the exploration of Australia, Tasmania and New Zealand resulted in their appearance on world maps. The further development of road books, maps, atlases and itineraries in many European countries also continued throughout the period, including conveniently-folded 'saddle-bag' maps and mail-coach maps which emerged with the early post routes. This could be regarded as the beginnings of task-focused maps for the general public.

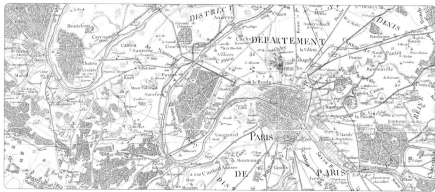

Carte de France. Detail from the first sheet – Sheet No. 1 Paris – by Cassini de Thury, 1736. Original scale 1:86 400.
National Library of Scotland, Edinburgh, UK.

Geological map of Britain. *A Delineation of Strata of England and Wales, with part of Scotland.* Produced by William Smith and published in 1815, this was the first geological map of Britain.
Natural History Museum, London, UK.

Landsat image of Huang He (Yellow River), China. Landsat Earth-observing satellites have been capturing images of the Earth since Landsat I was launched in 1972. Such imagery is an invaluable tool for assessing and mapping natural phenomena and for monitoring environmental change.

High resolution satellite image. Satellite images of 1 metre resolution, such as this one of Venice, Italy, can provide huge amounts of data for cartographers and planners. They can serve as source material for the compilation of large-scale maps, or may sometimes be used directly as a map base.

19TH CENTURY

During the 19th century the first person stepped onto Antarctica, the last continent to be discovered and explored, and the term 'cartography' was first used. Maps devoted to themed or special, more scientific subjects, began to appear, and some, such as the first geological map of Britain by William Smith, were huge illustrative undertakings. This map opened up a new science of the Earth and was one of the first uses of a map as a tool for spatial exploration and analysis in geoscience. Other special maps reflected scientific and social observation and investigation. One particularly significant example of thematic mapping was the *Physikalischer Atlas* of Heinrich Berghaus, published in two volumes in 1845 and 1848. Lithographic printing of maps, which was to have a profound influence on cartography and the availability of mapping, was developed in the early years of the century. It allowed the production of multiple copies very much more cheaply than earlier printing processes and developed to include the ability to print in colour. This stimulated a proliferation of maps for mass consumption, not least for educational purposes.

As the century progressed, factors such as exploration and emigration were reflected in extended coverage of maps and charts, for example in Australasia, South America, Africa, Arabia and Antarctica. Work on national surveys also proceeded and developed in style. One particularly notable achievement was the Great Trigonometrical Survey (GTS) of India which, while creating the survey network of the entire subcontinent, identified Everest as the highest mountain in the world and facilitated the creation of extensive and detailed topographic maps of the subcontinent. However, despite the considerable progress made in specific countries, less than 15 per cent of the world had been accurately mapped by the end of the century. A new genre of general atlases, such as *Stieler's Hand-Atlas* (from 1817) and the *Times Atlas of the World* (1895), began to appear, and the first modern national atlas, that of Finland, was published in 1899, typifying the growing use of maps to express national identity.

20TH AND 21ST CENTURIES

Geopolitics were instrumental in prompting the expansion of map and chart coverage throughout the 20th century. The application of new technology also forced the rate of change in a remarkable way, but, perhaps not surprisingly, the facilities for more precise re-measurement often confirmed rather than transformed the accuracy of a world map which had been painstakingly assembled together over many centuries by cartographers and explorers. Many countries now began to use their large-scale map coverage – which had been developing since the end of the 18th century – for the establishment of national spatial infrastructures. With increases in the accuracy of surveys, and with detailed horizontal and vertical control in place, mapping progressed, initially using ground surveying techniques, but later with aerial photography and photogrammetry. Colonial nations helped provide mapping of former colonies in Asia and Africa and this led to the gradual expansion of a global framework of topographic mapping. Similarly, especially through new data collection methods, global coverage of thematic topics such as soil, census and geophysical data also expanded rapidly.

The focus and nature of exploration and mapping extended steadily through the first half of the 20th century to embrace previously impenetrable domains such as continental interiors, polar regions and deep oceans, particularly through the use of aerial photography and submersible craft. The development of aviation and then satellite remote sensing, from the early 1970s, has offered new forms of imagery and measurement techniques, which have been particularly significant in recent cartographic developments. They allowed a new view of the Earth and spawned a new age in mapping. The introduction of the computer led to the production of digital maps and the rapid recoding of spatial data from paper to digital databases. This, in turn, supported the development of Geographical Information Systems (GIS), particularly from the 1990s which now allow users to select their own spatially referenced data and carry out exploratory and analytical manipulations to degrees of speed and complexity previously unimagined. The digital era has also changed the ways in which new spatially-related data are acquired. Even in the late 20th century optical instruments were still in use for topographic surveying but with new technologies such as GNSS (Global Navigation Satellite Systems) the first of which, NAVSTAR GPS (Global Positioning System), became universally available in the year 2000, there is now much greater potential for the rapid and precise measurement of position. While topographic base maps are still essential for many purposes, the growing need to map and monitor global environmental themes such as climate change, desertification, flooding and other hazards, have led to the development of advanced satellite imaging, including use of radar. Recent high-resolution (sub-metre) scanners on the Quick Bird and IKONOS satellites, are permitting these images to act as map substitutes for some tasks. With the replacement of analogue mapping by digital systems in recent decades, the storage, manipulation, transmission and visualization of all these data are becoming much simpler and more routine. The universal employment of GIS for virtually all spatially-related tasks is placing geographic data in great demand, not only for the production of accurate maps, but also for spatial data analysis and presentation within civilian, military and scientific contexts. The growth of the Internet and World-wide Web, especially since the 1990s, and GPS-enabled mobile technologies, have created almost utopian conditions for data access. High-speed and especially wireless links, mean that virtually any data can be accessed from anywhere at any time. Although the era of manually-created maps was drawing to a close, a new age of geospatial information, highly-customized maps and universal map use was just dawning which would pervade all aspects and levels of human activity.

CHANGES IN MAPPING

Although we retain our internal cognitive mapping abilities, the value of a pencil and paper (or a stick and some sand for our ancestors) to support the spatial thinking process is self evident, and was the genesis of the great developments in mapping we have seen. During the last two thousand years most fundamental theory and practical knowledge had been acquired. The great achievement of recent centuries was the introduction of printing which opened up markets and financial incentives to make high quality maps available to all. However, the introduction of computers in the mid-20th century has had a much greater impact. Not only has it transformed the production and use of maps but it has also changed the relationships between people, maps and spatial data forever.

Printed maps are still being provided by national and commercial agencies to satisfy established markets, but compilation, as in the case of this atlas is increasingly from digital databases, and their design and production increasingly uses Geographic Information System (GIS) and graphic software. Major reference databases now contain fundamental, often non-generalized information with greater potential to satisfy the more specific needs of narrower groups within the geospatial information community, generally via the Internet.

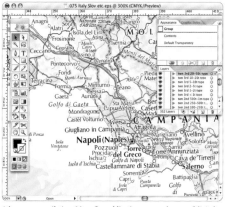

Atlas map compilation. Maps for publication now make use of digital geographic data and powerful graphics software to ensure high levels of accuracy and the highest standards of reproduction.

Mobile mapping. The latest in-car systems use Bluetooth technology to facilitate 'hands-free' navigation. Real-time traffic information is available and it is also possible for the user to load customized points of interest (POIs), such as the locations of speed cameras, to add to a pre-loaded POI database.

TOWARDS A NEW PARADIGM?

While cartographic production for established mass markets might now be diminishing, there is no doubt that mapping and the use of visualizations such as maps, aerial photography and satellite imagery are on the rise. With the Internet as the first destination of enquiry for many general and more specialized needs, a 'map', as noted by the International Cartographic Association (ICA), is no longer just a static image. Screen-based maps can offer dynamic and interactive facilities and, increasingly, are used as the interface to many other types of information available on the Internet. Examples include Multimap, Google Maps and Google Earth, the latter combining near photo-reality and map symbols, providing a global link for everyone.

Awareness of the possibilities for elaborate map design and more specialized spatial information is fuelling greater demand for detailed height data, for example from LIDAR (Light Image Detection and Ranging) technology, or Google's free modelling application Sketchup, to expand the 3-D capabilities of GIS and to allow the more authentic representation of landscape and buildings.

Much of this user base comprises government, scientific and major commercial groups who can access and, in some cases, request specialist data of very high quality. They include the military, merchant navies, utility companies and researchers. This has led to a powerful commercial response with geospatial companies competing to provide increasingly elaborate data sets and locational and navigational tools, for personal and in-vehicle use, employing what are called Location-based Services (LBS). Mobile phones, whose world-wide numbers have increased to over two billion units, offer perhaps the greatest opportunity for marketing geospatial information and maps. Existing map software can offer a wealth of possibilities including intelligent facilities which can anticipate, based on user 'profiles' built up from past behaviours and personal preferences, what an individual user might require in a particular location or how they might respond to a specific situation. With the promise of a new generation of feature-rich handsets with large screens, high resolution cameras and Internet connection, as well as integrated Global Positioning System (GPS) capability, digital compass and tilt sensors, phones will provide added access to data by merely pointing to a feature. Such extensions of the mapping domain could help 'transfer the usefulness, the intuitiveness and the excitement of geospatial mass-audience applications to the mobile domain' (Rainer Simon).

Increasingly mobile, non-professional, geospatially-aware communities already exist and include not just enthusiastic users but imaginative and innovative technical experts who are challenging many of the standard models of cartographic data acquisition and use. Instead of seeking and paying for official spatial data from official agencies, they are acquiring data directly, using GPS and their own software. One example, OpenStreetMap, is a project to create and provide free geographic data – particularly street maps – to anyone who wants them. Their belief, supported by the Open Source Initiative, is that legal (copyright) or technical restrictions on the use of many existing maps inhibit their use in creative, productive or unexpected ways. Within the project, anyone can capture and provide data, and anyone can freely use the data or the maps created from them – a true 'democratization' of the mapping process. Related to this is the use of what are called 'mashups' (a term derived from hip-hop music song-mixing), which are hybrid creations combining content from more than one source and encouraged through APIs (Application Program Interfaces) from the big companies. By using Google Maps, for example, with individually acquired georeferenced spatial data such as weather observations, house sales or even UFO sightings, a new and rapidly expanding world of democratic cartography has begun. Some are highly personal applications but corporate solutions have also been developed. One major airline has experimented with a Google Maps mashup to extend its own website to help passengers obtain more information about their destinations.

Unlike aerial and satellite images which contain, within their resolution characteristics, every detail recorded by their respective sensors, maps are unique symbolized representations showing only selected features. They are created to help users understand the geographical area or subject being portrayed and information is obtained primarily from visual inspection, map comparison or measurement. Their compilation and design was traditionally the responsibility of professional cartographers, but today, as explained, maps and map-like objects are being created by members of a much wider and non-professional community through use of GPS, GIS and related software and imagery. In the past, maps were used for both data storage and visualization. Once compiled, designed and printed they were normally sold and archived but, because of the time-lag introduced by elaborate production processes, and the need for standard specifications to satisfy broad user categories, they were often out-of-date or did not contain the information required for particular tasks. With the growth in the geospatial information market and the new cartographic user environment, a paradigm shift may be under way. Within this new paradigm the map reader, or user of a Web-based map product, becomes a rudimentary cartographer who can investigate a database using a map interface and then interactively apply selective processes to seek and compare information and examine spatial relationships in real-time, with the most recent data. This is quite unlike the relatively simple map-use process of the past. Rather than using a map it might, more correctly, be referred to as using cartography (in the same way as we 'use' mathematics). It is even possible that GPS/Internet cartography is reawakening and stimulating the dormant mapping instinct within us, in a way never possible before.

Unfortunately, the high standards of graphic representation implicit in the traditional paper map are much more difficult to incorporate automatically within new digital environments. Because of this, there is some concern that the role of skilled cartographers and the benefits of their specialist cartographic knowledge may be under threat. Attempts are being made within the profession to meet this challenge and to ensure that maps produced by, and provided through, the new technologies do not compromise standards of design, accuracy and relevance. Despite these upheavals, as history has revealed, new technology need not change completely how we do things. When we travel we still walk, use bicycles, motorcars or aircraft as circumstances demand. Thus the future can be interpreted as offering an increasingly wide spectrum of cartographic opportunities, sources and facilities for different uses – from traditional high quality publications produced by cartographic specialists, to exciting personal interactive experiences.

Throughout history, as the knowledge of the world around us has increased, so has the desire to map it. It was the development of geometry by the Greeks that first allowed accurate recording of world geography. However was only in the 15th and 16th centuries with the age of discovery and its resultant explosion in exploration, that led to greater geographical knowledge, allowing maps to be created that are easily recognisable as the world we know today.

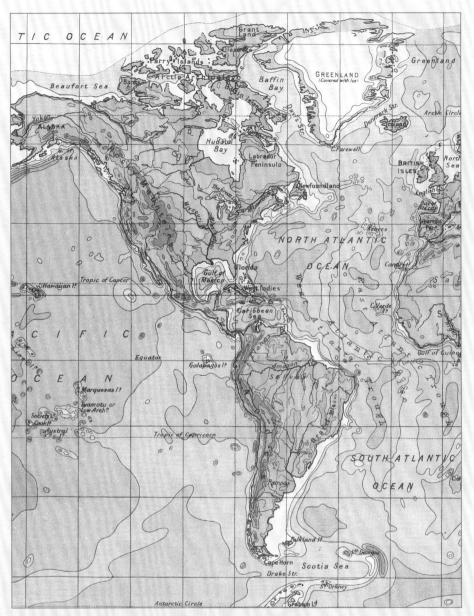

PHYSICAL CHART OF THE WORLD 1938

Extract from *The Oxford Preparatory Atlas*.

This chart from 1938 is an unusual physical representation of the world in that it shows not only land elevations but also sea depths relative to sea level.

Sonar measuring to compile bathymetric or depth charts was not used until after the Second World War (1939–45) and the measurements on this prewar map were taken using the centuries-old method of a sounding line: weighted ropes were dropped overboard and measurements taken as they touched the ocean bed. Despite the evident imprecision of the method, the oceanic features depicted on the chart are accurate and easily recognisable. In the graphic showing comparative heights and depths, the deepest part of the Pacific is recorded at 34 416 ft; the most accurate modern estimate has recorded a known depth of 36 201 ft, a difference of only 5 per cent.

Much of the basic survey work was carried out by the Royal Navy ship HMS Challenger between 1873 and 1876. The deepest point discovered by the Challenger scientists is marked at roughly 11°N, 142°E: Challenger Deep, in the Marianas Trench, still the deepest known point on Earth today.

The chart shows the features common to world physical maps: continents and islands; mountains and plains; rivers and lakes; and overall elevations above sea level. Although Europe was extensively mapped by the end of the nineteenth century, much of the rest of the world – most notably Africa, Asia and India – was not. The demands of empire speeded up the process, aided after the First World War (1914–18) by the development of aerial photography to supplement surveys.

BLAEU MAP 1630

Produced in Amsterdam by Willem Blaeu, 1630.

The early years of the seventeenth century were dominated by the vast cartographic output from the Low Countries, epitomized by the Blaeu publishing house. An example of one of their maps opposite from c.1630 can be seen opposite.

Until the late 1620s Jodocus Hondius II had published Mercator maps, with these dominating the European market. After Hondius' death the Blaeu house published a grand atlas called Theatrum Orbis Terrarum *or* Atlas Novus.

By the time of founder Willem Blaeu's death in 1638 they had only published two volumes of the work. It was completed in 1665, with eleven or twelve volumes depending on the language.

At the end of the seventeenth century Atlas Novus *by the Blaeu house was the most expensive book that money could buy.*

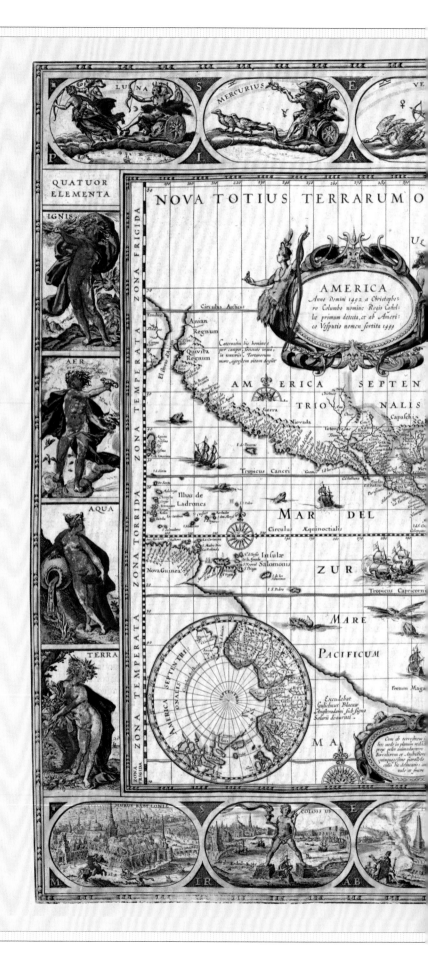

THE WORLD ON MERCATOR'S PROJECTION 1858

From the *Family Atlas of Physical, General and Classical Geography*.

The nineteenth century was the Age of Empire, when all the major European powers harboured imperial ambitions and used their commercial and military might to extend their influence in known parts of the world and open up new regions.

In the first half of the century, the process had been gradual. Britain had emerged as the pre-eminent overseas power, extending the boundaries of her established colonial possessions in North America, India and Australia and acquiring new footholds in Singapore (1819), Hong Kong (1842), and Natal (1843). Meanwhile, imperial rivals were weakened in the post-Napoleonic period. France, Spain and the Netherlands had all ceded colonial territory to Britain while Spain and Portugal were weakened by the loss of their Latin American colonies: Brazil seceded peacefully from Portugal in 1822, while the former Spanish colonies of Paraguay, Argentina (La Plata as recorded on the map), Chile, Colombia (New Granada), Venezuela, Ecuador, Peru, and Bolivia had fought their way to independence between 1811 and 1825. Mexico had secured its freedom from Spain in 1821 and two years later, Central America had seceded from it to create a federal republic which then further divided in 1839 into the independent states of Costa Rica, El Salvador, Guatemala, Honduras and Nicaragua (although interestingly, the cartographers have not recorded this).

In the second half of the century, the pace of imperial expansion increased markedly. By 1858, it is clear that Europeans had made few inroads into Africa; fifty years later, however, the map would show a multicoloured mosaic of colonial territories belonging to Britain, France, Portugal, and the newly unified nations of Germany and Italy. Asia was also a focus for European expansion, chiefly by the French, who secured control of Indo-China (1884–93) and by the British, who gained significant portions of the East Indies (1875–95). India also remained a focus of British interest. However, imperialism was not a solely European trait: Japan would acquire Formosa from China in 1895 and forcibly annex Korea in 1910, while the USA would secure the Philippines from Spain in 1898.

Other changes to this map during the second half of the century include the borders of the once-mighty Turkish or Ottoman Empire receding from the Balkans, north Africa and parts of the Persian Gulf. In North America, Russia abandoned its sole American colony, Alaska, which it would sell to the US Government in 1867 for $7.2 million. Elsewhere on the continent, the British colonies of North America were granted legislative autonomy under the Crown as part of a process begun by the establishment of the federal Dominion of Canada in 1867, while Britain's Australian possessions were already largely self-governing.

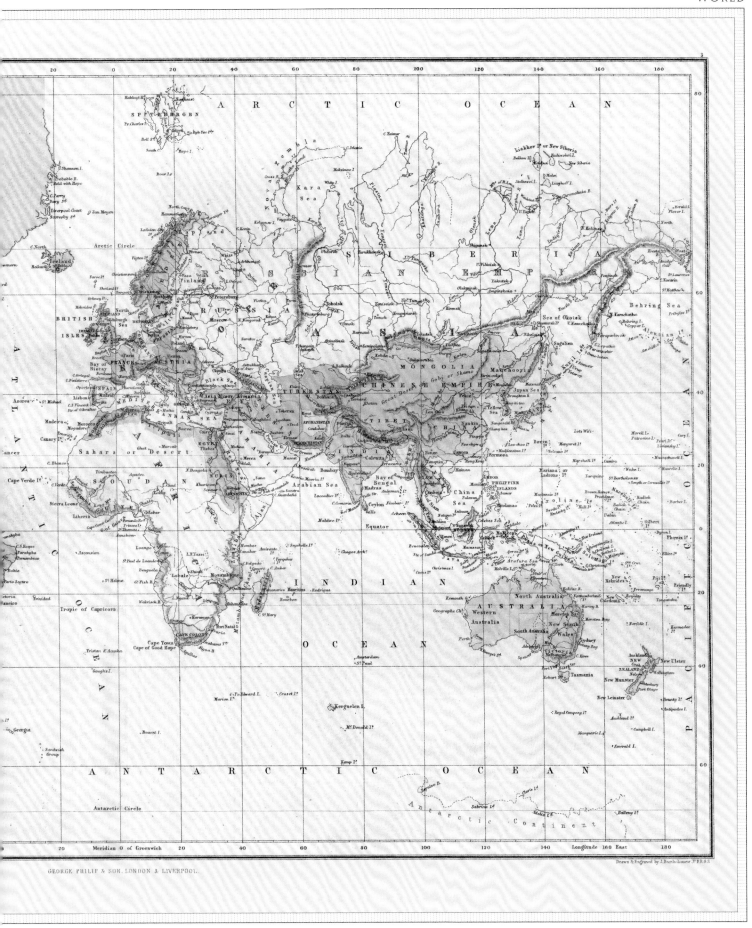

NORTH POLAR REGIONS AND SOUTH POLAR REGIONS 1890

From *The Citizen's Atlas*.

These maps of the polar regions allow a variety of interesting comparisons to be drawn about these extremes of the Earth and how they were being explored.

Far from being homogeneous ice masses, the northern and southern polar regions are physically very different. The North Pole is at the centre of the Arctic Ocean and is an almost landlocked body of water largely composed of drifting pack ice; the South Pole, by contrast, lies on a continental land mass. Reflecting this, the motivations of those who ventured into these unexplored regions were also different.

For many northern polar explorers, the intention was to find a navigable passage through the ice to open up a trade route to link the Atlantic and Pacific Oceans – the so-called Northwest Passage. During the nineteenth century several expeditions had ventured into the area and in 1851, British naval captain Sir Robert McClure was credited with the discovery of the Passage route, although it was not actually navigable by sea alone. Separate unsuccessful expeditions were also mounted during this period with the express purpose of reaching the North Pole itself. One of the most prominent of these is recorded on the map, that of the Norwegian Fridtjof Nansen. The closest point to the Pole that Nansen reached – 86°14' N, in April 1895 – was then the highest recorded latitude ever reached. The North Magnetic Pole had been first identified in 1831 by James Clark Ross on the Boothia Peninsula in the far north of Canada, and it can just be seen on the map at approximately 70°N 94°W.

Unlike the northern polar region, whose boundaries – Greenland and the North American and Eurasian continental masses – were mostly well mapped, the physical boundaries of the southern polar region were very poorly understood, as is evident from the map. The existence of Terra Australis Incognita – the unknown southern lands – had been assumed for centuries, but it was not until Cook's voyages in the 1770s that exploration of the region began in earnest. Sealers and whalers followed in his wake, but it was not until the 1820s that Antarctica was first actually sighted, probably by the Russian explorer, Bellingshausen. From the 1830s a series of national expeditions embarked for Antarctica: the French expedition of 1837–40 under Jules Dumont D'Urville; the United States Exploring Expedition of 1838–42 commanded by Charles Wilkes; and the British expedition of 1839–43 under James Clark Ross. The progress of these and other earlier explorations is plotted on the map, as are the varying attempts to find the South Magnetic Pole near Victoria Land. In spite of these efforts, it is obvious that the southern lands were still a largely unknown quantity when Scott, Shackleton, Amundsen and others began their drives to the Pole in the first decade of the new century.

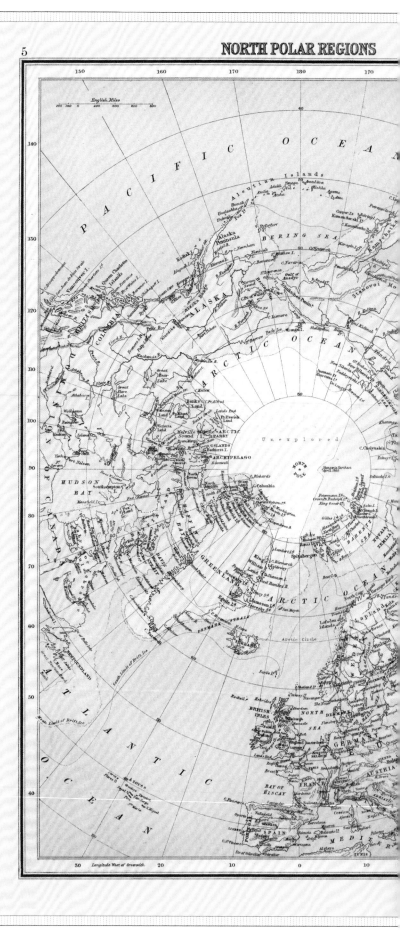

SOUTH POLAR REGIONS

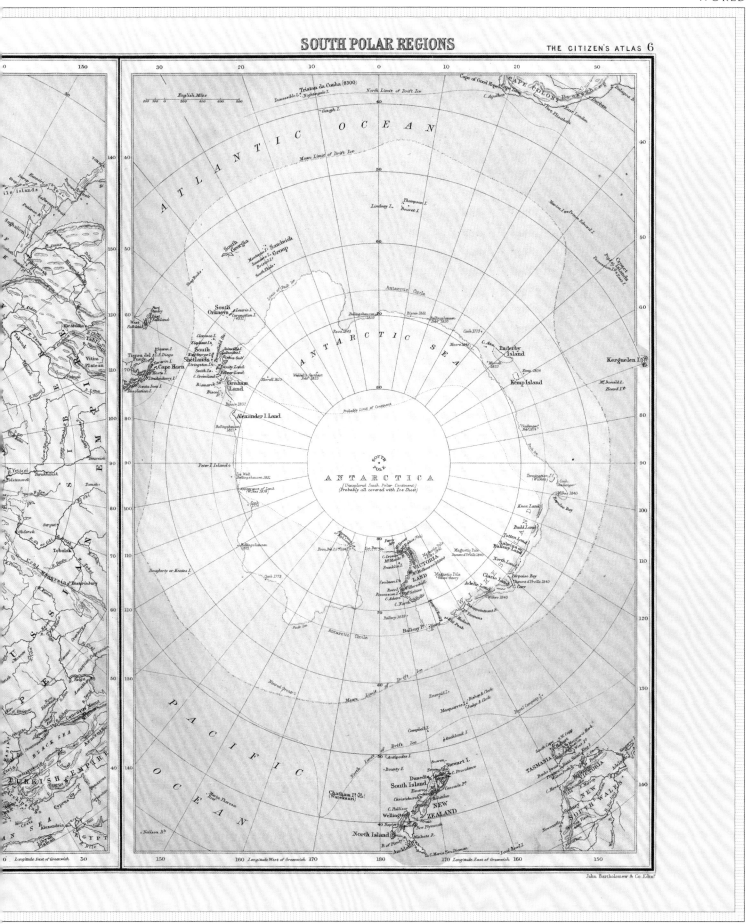

A T L A N T I C   O C E A N

Tristan da Cunha (8300)

North Limit of Drift Ice

Mean Limit of Drift Ice

A N T A R C T I C   S E A

Antarctic Circle

South Georgia

Sandwich Group

South
Orkneys

South
Shetlands

Graham
Land

Alexander I. Land

A N T A R C T I C A
(Unexplored South Polar Continent)
(Probably all covered with Ice Sheet)

SOUTH
POLE

Probable Limit of Continent

Enderby
Island

Kerguelen I.

Kemp Island

VICTORIA
LAND

Adélie Land

Knox Land

Budd Land

Totten Land

Balleny Land

North Land

Antarctic Circle

Mean Limit of Drift Ice

P A C I F I C
O C E A N

TASMANIA

NEW
SOUTH WALES

VICTORIA

NEW
ZEALAND

South Island

North Island

Dunedin

Christchurch

Wellington

Chatham Is.

Auckland I.

Campbell I.

Macquarrie I.

TURKISH EMPIRE

EGYPT

BLACK SEA

R U S S I A N   E M P I R E

Tobolsk

Tierra del
Fuego

Cape Horn

West
Falkland I.

Port
Stanley

John Bartholomew & Co. Edin.

OCEAN CURRENTS AND THE GREAT RIVER BASINS 1879

From the *Collins New Complete Atlas.*

This 1879 map shows the world's largest rivers and the main ocean currents as they were then known, with sea-depth measurements in fathoms, mostly for the Atlantic Ocean. Continental watersheds and the world's largest rivers are also shown, with the effect of showing the movement of water around the world.

Ocean currents were long misunderstood or unknown by mariners. The Portuguese explorers of the fifteenth century were regularly pushed off course by unexpected currents. The sixteenth-century Spanish explorer Ponce de León, who landed in Florida in 1513, noted the power of the Gulf Stream there. But observations and records for the most part remained uncollected and unanalysed, leaving sailors with no systematic charts of currents and winds. This situation continued until the mid-nineteenth century when, after extensive study of thousands of ships' logs, American naval officer and oceanographer Matthew Maury drew up the first detailed and reliable charts of ocean currents and winds. His book, The Physical Geography of the Sea, published in 1855, is one of the first-ever books on oceanography and is still the basis of the science today.

The map shows the main surface currents of the oceans as they had then been charted and named. The currents act like huge rivers in the seas, moving water around the world. They are caused primarily by wind and gravity, and their direction is affected by the rotation of the Earth. Surface currents generally affect the ocean to a depth of around 400 m (1 312 ft).

Currents function in effect as a circulatory system, regulating the climate by moving water from cooler regions into warmer ones and vice versa. An example is the California Current (here named the Mexican Current), which flows from the north Pacific and keeps the western coastal waters of the United States cooler than those of the east.

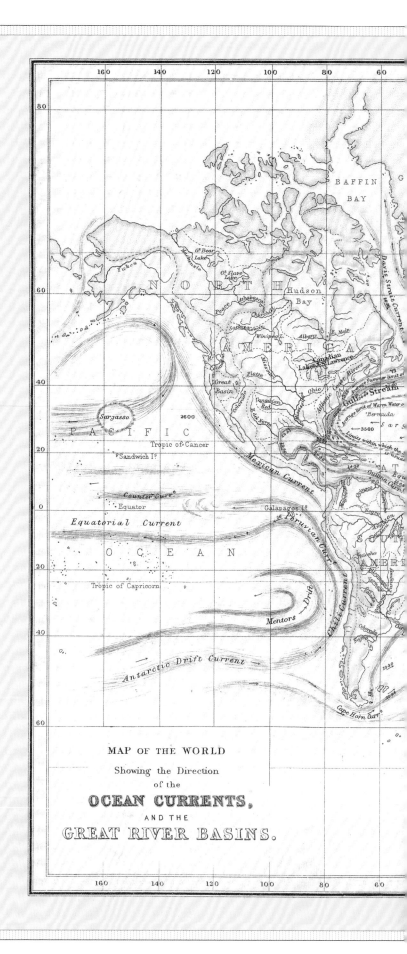

MAP OF THE WORLD

Showing the Direction
of the

OCEAN CURRENTS,

AND THE

GREAT RIVER BASINS.

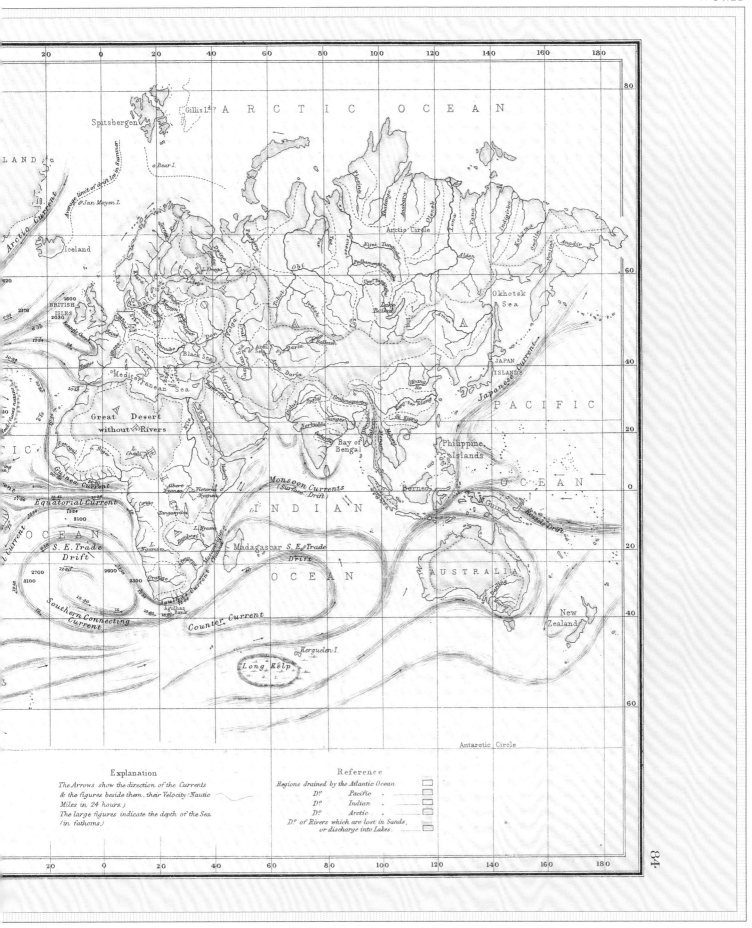

ARCTIC OCEAN

Spitsbergen · Gillis Ld.?

Bear I.

Average limit of drift Ice in Summer

Jan Mayen I.

Iceland

Arctic Current

A S I A

Arctic Circle

Okhotsk Sea

Lake Baikal

JAPAN ISLANDS

Japanese Current

PACIFIC

BRITISH ISLES

Black Sea

Mediterranean Sea

Great Desert without Rivers

Guinea Current

Equatorial Current

Aral Sea · L. Balkash

L. Chad

Albert Nyanza

Victoria Nyanza

L. Tanganyika

Monsoon Surface Currents Drift

Bay of Bengal

Philippine Islands

Borneo

N. Guinea

Rossels Drift

OCEAN

INDIAN

S. E. Trade Drift

Madagascar S. E. Trade Drift

OCEAN

AUSTRALIA

Southern Connecting Current

Agulhas Bank

Counter Current

Kerguelen I.

"Long Kelp"

New Zealand

Antarctic Circle

Explanation

The Arrows show the direction of the Currents
& the figures beside them, their Velocity (Nautic
Miles in 24 hours.)
The large figures indicate the depth of the Sea
(in fathoms.)

Reference

Regions drained by the Atlantic Ocean
  Dº   Pacific
  Dº   Indian
  Dº   Arctic
Dº of Rivers which are lost in Sands,
  or discharge into Lakes.

CONSTELLATIONS 1895

From *The Times Atlas*.

This two-part star map shows the relative positions of groups of stars, or constellations, over the northern and southern hemispheres. Star maps are drawn up from the viewpoint of Earth being at the centre of a celestial sphere, with all the features of the sky visible inside the sphere. Earth is tilted on its axis and on star maps the north celestial pole is orientated to Polaris which remains fixed in the sky. As Earth travels through space, the other stars seem to move from east to west while staying fixed in relation to one another.

As on terrestrial maps, latitude and longitude gridlines plot relative locations. The marked division into 360° units rings the outer edge in a dial along the celestial equator, the extent of the hemispherical viewpoint. The 0° point is set where the sun crosses the celestial equator into each hemisphere. The maps show the ecliptic, the apparent yearly progress of the sun through the sky, in an offset dotted line which becomes solid over each hemisphere at 180° and 360° when it crosses the celestial equator. Also depicted is the Milky Way, our solar system, appearing as a lighter trail across both hemispheres.

The configurations of stars depicted in star maps have been classified and named since ancient times: Ancient Greek astronomers named the constellations after their own mythology and common animals and objects and would have been familiar with the stars as they appeared on this 1895 map. There are eighty-eight recognised constellations.

The zodiac is made up of the twelve constellations through which the Sun seems to pass during the year and which form a belt 8–9° either side of the solar orbit.

Stars on the map are graded according to size, with a separate designation for nebulae, interstellar clouds of gases where stars may form, and variable stars of changeable luminosity.

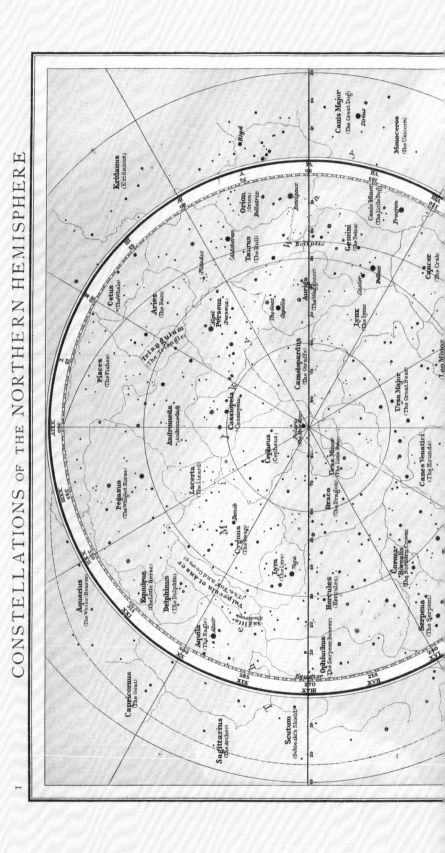

CONSTELLATIONS of THE NORTHERN HEMISPHERE

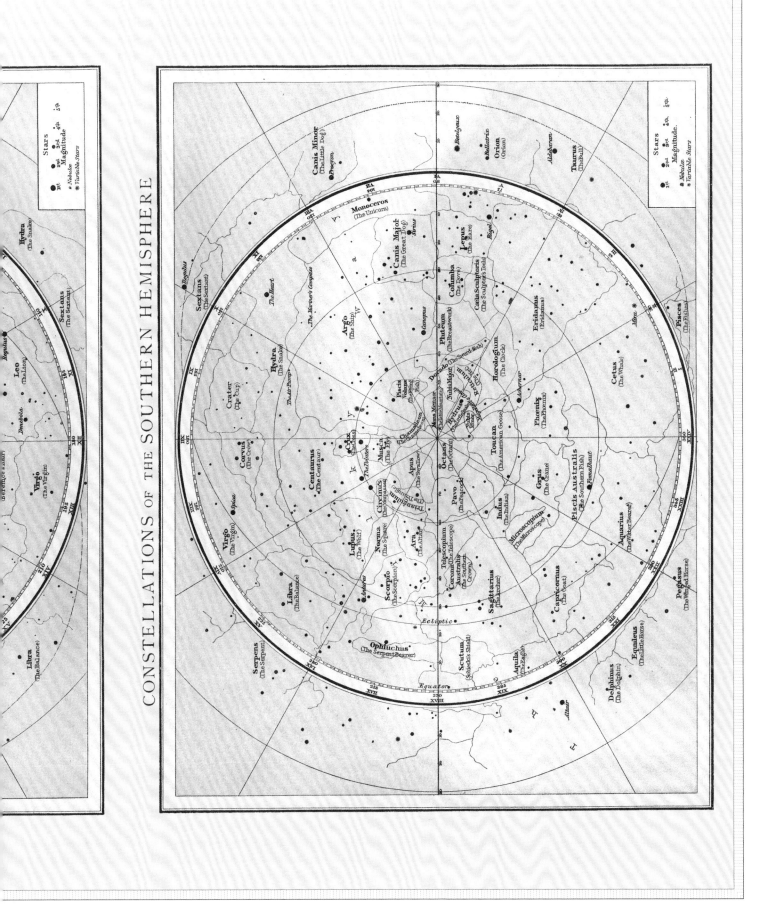

CONSTELLATIONS OF THE SOUTHERN HEMISPHERE

Stars
1st. 2nd 3rd. 4th. 5th.
Magnitude.
○ Nebulæ
✳ Variable Stars

Stars
1st. 2nd 3rd. 4th. 5th.
Magnitude.
● Nebulæ
✴ Variable Stars

Canis Minor
(The Little Dog)
Procyon

Monoceros
(The Unicorn)

Sextans
(The Sextant)

Canis Major
(The Great Dog)
Sirius

Lepus
(The Hare)
Rigel

Beteljeux
Bellatrix
Orion
(Orion)
Aldebaran
Taurus
(The Bull)

Argo
(The Ship)

Columba
(The Dove)
CœlaSculptoris
(The Sculptor's Tools)

Pisces
(The Fishes)

The Mariner's Compass

Hydra
(The Snake)

Phœnicum
(The Breastwork)

Eridanus
(Eridanus)

Mira

Cetus
(The Whale)

Crater
(The Cup)

Dorado
(The Sword Fish)

Horologium
(The Clock)

Corvus
(The Crow)

Centaurus
(The Centaur)

Crux
(The Cross)
The Pointers

Musca
(The Fly)

Chamæleon

Octans
(The Octant)

Toucan
(The American Goose)

Phœnix
(The Phœnix)

Grus
(The Crane)

Piscis Australis
(The Southern Fish)
Fomalhaut

Aquarius
(The Water Bearer)

Libra
(The Balance)

Virgo
(The Virgin)
Spica

Lupus
(The Wolf)
Norma
(The Square)
Ara
(The Altar)

Circinus
(The Compasses)

Triangulum

Apus

Pavo
(The Peacock)

Indus
(The Indian)

Microscopium
(The Microscope)

Capricornus
(The Goat)

Pegasus
(The Winged Horse)

Scorpio
(The Scorpion)
Antares

Telescopium
(The Telescope)

Corona
Australis
(The Southern
Crown)

Sagittarius
(The Archer)

Ecliptic

Serpens
(The Serpent)

Ophiuchus
(The Serpent Bearer)

Scutum
(Sobieski's Shield)

Aquila
(The Eagle)

Equuleus
(The Little Horse)

Delphinus
(The Dolphin)

Equator

Altair

Hydra
(The Snake)

Sextans
(The Sextant)

Leo
(The Lion)

Denebola

Virgo
(The Virgin)

Libra
(The Balance)

Regulus

Spica

POLITICAL MAP OF THE WORLD
1914

From the *International Reference Atlas of the World*.

This map shows the imperial divisions of the world at the onset of the First World War in 1914. European colonial empires had grown rapidly over the past century and by now the Great Powers of Europe had engrossed nine-tenths of Africa and much of Asia.

Prior to 1914, Europe had been run on balance-of-power politics, where a status quo was maintained between the major powers, often with unofficial agreements and alliances. However, the power system was changing and there was now less collaboration and more rivalry because empire powers wanted to preserve imperialism and control competitors (seen, for example, with the naval arms race between Britain and Germany). Imperial ambitions, shifting powers and rising tensions engulfed Europe.

The Balkans became a key area: this was the one region where the Habsburg empire of Austria-Hungary had a chance of maintaining its ascendancy. But, on 28 June 1914, the Archduke Franz Ferdinand, heir to the Habsburg throne, was assassinated in Sarajevo by a Serb nationalist, Gavrilo Princip. This incident threw Europe into turmoil. Austria-Hungary sought revenge, and invaded Serbia. German support for Austria and Russian support for Serbia gave way to a series of alliances and declarations of war involving global powers, and beginning the First World War.

Two major alliances emerged. The Allied (Entente) Powers consisted primarily of France, Britain, Russia and their associated empires and dependencies. They were later joined by, among others, Italy and, in 1917, the United States (the force of which would ultimately tip the balance). The Central Powers comprised Germany and Austria-Hungary and their empires, later joined by the Ottoman Empire and Bulgaria.

The war was expected to be short-lived, but four years of particularly bloody warfare later, millions of lives had been lost, both military and civilian. An armistice on 11 November 1918 between the Allied Powers (the victors) and Germany, and the Treaty of Versailles in 1919, finally brought an end to the conflict.

Following the Great War, the map would change completely, with the defeat of the German and Austro-Hungarian Empires and the collapse of the Russian Empire following the communist revolution. Territories in grey on this map belong to the German Empire, and would, five years later, be reapportioned to the victors in the war by the Treaty of Versailles: Tanganyika would go to Britain; Togoland and German Cameroon would be shared between France and Britain; German South West Africa would go to South Africa; the Pacific Islands to New Zealand; and New Guinea to Australia.

POLITICAL MAP OF THE WORLD
ON MERCATORS PROJECTION.
Steamship distances are given in Nautical Miles
Principal Railways shown thus

British Empire
United States
German Empire
Russian Empire
French Possessions
Portuguese Possessions
Dutch Possessions
Chinese Possessions

John Bartholomew & Co. Edinr

RIVERS AND MOUNTAINS
ILLUSTRATION 1852

From the *The College Atlas for Schools and Families*.

This unusual illustration is an early example of what today is better known as an infographic. Infographics use illustration to make complex or detailed data accessible and interesting.

It is easy to imagine the information on pages recording relative heights and lengths of the world's mountains and rivers, presented in dry and lengthy tabular format. Instead, the illustrator has cleverly designed a graphic around the central gutter of the book to combine comparative representations of the geographic features in the western and eastern hemispheres. Note that this division of hemispheres does not match the modern definition, dictated by the Prime Meridian at Greenwich, which itself was not formally settled until 1884. This explains, for example, the inclusion of the rivers Shannon and Ebro in the eastern hemisphere when they are, strictly speaking, in the west.

The representations of individual rivers and mountains are obviously not exact although some effort has gone into depicting river mouths, deltas and tributaries. Major settlements marked along the length of each river also help locate their courses and high-altitude plains are shown at their appropriate heights. The artist has also added some whimsical touches – smoke puffs identify active volcanoes and an Andean condor soars among the mountain peaks. There are also two tiny hot-air balloons: in the west, the balloon of French chemist and physicist Gay-Lussac who in 1804 reached 7 016 m (23 018 ft) while testing his theories of thermodynamics; and in the east, the balloon of Englishman Charles Green who in 1838 ascended to 8 274 m (27 146 ft).

The illustration shows the limits of knowledge of the physical world in the mid-nineteenthth century, omitting rivers in Asiatic Russia that are among the world's longest; similarly, no Australian rivers are featured. Furthermore, their relative lengths depicted here do not match what is now known following subsequent exploration and improvements in measuring techniques.

RIVERS.

EASTERN HEMISPHERE.

MOUNTAINS.

EASTERN HEMISPHERE.

London. Published by H.G.Collins. 22 Paternoster Row.

Drawn by C.J.W. Russell & Engraved by J.Archer Somerville London.

5

WORLD POLITICAL DIVISIONS
1936

From the *Advanced Atlas, Fifth Edition.*

The political situation of the world three years before the outbreak of the Second World War can be seen from this map. The power of empires had waned significantly after the First World War, and a number of treaties and pacts were signed between countries to safeguard against military attacks. Growing political and social conflict was leading to nationalist uprisings, while both communism and fascism were on the rise in Europe.

At the time this map was produced, General Franco and his nationalist troops had rebelled against the Spanish Republic. The resulting Spanish Civil War pitted Nationalists against Republicans. Republicans were supported mainly by secular and urban power bases such as Catalonia and the Basque Country, and also by peasants living in poverty under aristocratic landowners. The Nationalists, on the other hand, drew support mostly from the Catholic clergy and wealthier, conservative landowners. Their anti-communist stance also attracted international support from fascist Italy under Mussolini and Nazi Germany under Hitler. The last of the Republican forces surrendered on 1 April 1939, dissolving the Spanish Republic and leading to a dictatorship under Franco which was to last for many years to come.

On 25 November 1936, a pact was signed between Nazi Germany and the Empire of Japan, directed immediately against the Communist International (Comintern) but more subtly against the Soviet Union. The Anti-Comintern Pact would protect Germany and Japan's common interests, safeguarding them against Soviet attacks. Meanwhile, the Soviet Union was forging closer links with the countries of Western Europe.

On the African continent, Egypt had been granted independence from the British Empire in 1922, but fearing attack from Italy, Egypt signed the Anglo-Egyptian Treaty with the UK in 1936, under which the UK would have to supply and train Egypt's army and assist in its defence should war occur.

As can be seen from the shipping routes marked in blue on the inset map, it was impossible to transport goods between Europe and Asia without circumnavigating Africa one way or the other. Running between Port Said on the Mediterranean Sea and Suez on the Red Sea, the Suez Canal, which had been completed in 1869, was pivotal as it provided the shorter of the two routes. Military protection of this area was therefore vital, and it was for this reason that, although the UK withdrew its troops from the rest of Egypt as a result of the treaty, UK garrisons remained on the Suez Canal.

Worldwide, the scene was being set for a major conflict, which erupted in 1939 as the Second World War.

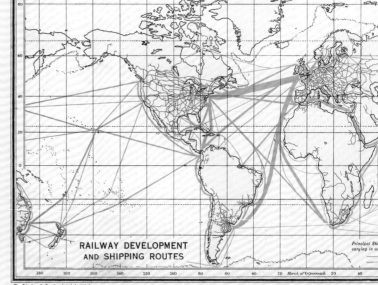

ORLD POLITICAL DIVISIONS

ED SINUSOIDAL
ea Projection
rtholomew

This is an arrangement of Sanson's Projection
re-centred on each continental mass
to give the least possible distortion.

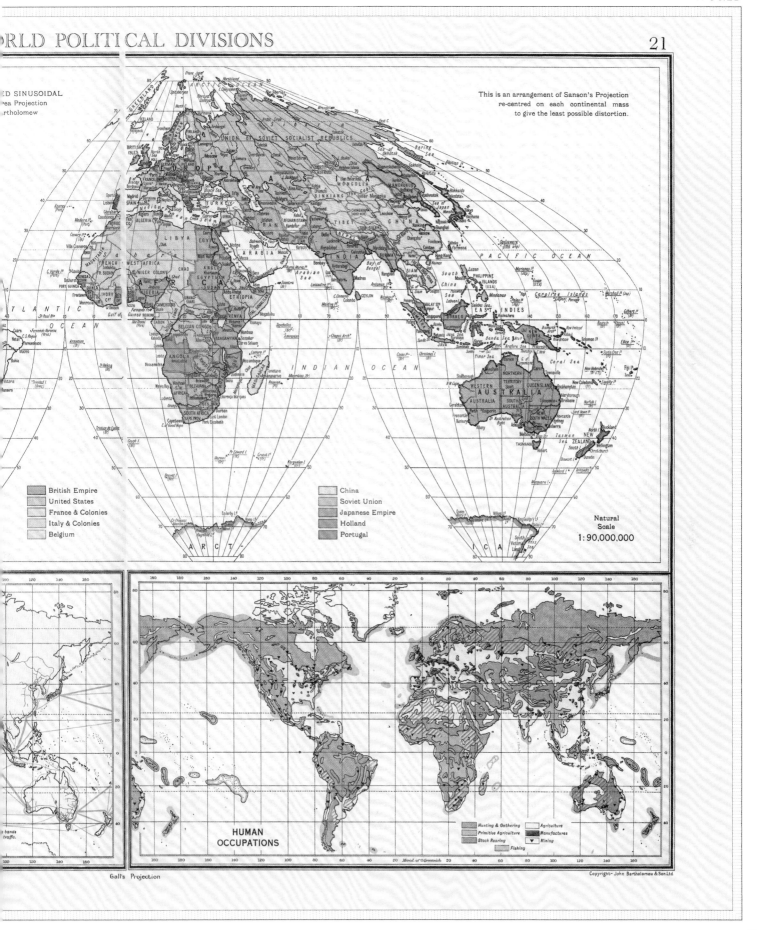

British Empire
United States
France & Colonies
Italy & Colonies
Belgium

China
Soviet Union
Japanese Empire
Holland
Portugal

Natural
Scale
1:90,000,000

HUMAN
OCCUPATIONS

Hunting & Gathering
Primitive Agriculture
Stock Rearing
Agriculture
Manufactures
Mining
Fishing

Gall's Projection

Copyright~ John Bartholomew & Son Ltd.

WORLD POWERS 1957

From the *Times Atlas of the World, Mid-Century Edition.*

The most striking feature of this map is its unusual viewpoint (or projection). Devised in 1948 by John Bartholomew of the famous cartographic dynasty, the Atlantis Projection abandons the common atlas convention of depicting maps that show the Arctic at the top and the Antarctic at the bottom, with the Atlantic in between. Here the projection is tilted and centred at 30°W 45°N to allow a focus on the world's oceans, in particular the Atlantic.

The use of the Atlantis Projection in this instance is particularly effective in conveying the combative nature of relations between the United States and the Soviet Union, the two superpowers which emerged to dominate the new world order following the Second World War. Like giant beasts poised to grapple, the major landmasses of the capitalist West and the communist East face each other across the Arctic and North Atlantic Oceans: this was an accurate reflection of the state of international politics at this time.

With the defeat of Fascism in 1945, any sense of unity and common purpose between the Soviet Union and the other Allied powers swiftly evaporated. This was soon replaced by a growing mutual distrust and outright hostility that was underpinned by the polarising effects of their respective political ideologies. Both power blocs possessed nuclear arsenals but were reluctant to confront each other in either nuclear or conventional warfare. The uneasy armed truce that emerged became known as the Cold War.

In spite of these geopolitical tensions, the United Nations Organization had been founded in 1947 as a vehicle for maintaining international peace and security and developing international economic and social cooperation. Ten years later, the UN had over eighty member nations, although their division into hostile armed camps did little to further the aims of the organization.

Both the USA and the Soviets sought to build economic, military and diplomatic alliances to support their particular strategic ambitions. In 1949, the USA established the North Atlantic Treaty Organization (NATO), formally allying itself to Western Europe in order to contain the spread of Communism there. Elsewhere in the world, in 1954–55, two similar alliances were formed to counter communist expansion – the South East Asian Treaty Organization (SEATO) in the Philippines and Indo-China, and the Baghdad Pact in the Middle East. The USSR and Communist China retaliated by providing military and economic support to anti-colonial or nationalist struggles in Africa, Asia and Latin America, while in 1955, the Soviets established the Warsaw Pact, their own military alliance among the communist countries of Eastern Europe.

Within a few short years of this particular map being drawn, significant colour changes would be required for a number of countries: Alaska would become a full member state of the USA (1959); Fidel Castro would establish a Marxist government on America's doorstep in Cuba (1959), and the process by which many African nations would shake off the last remnants of European colonialism would begin in earnest.

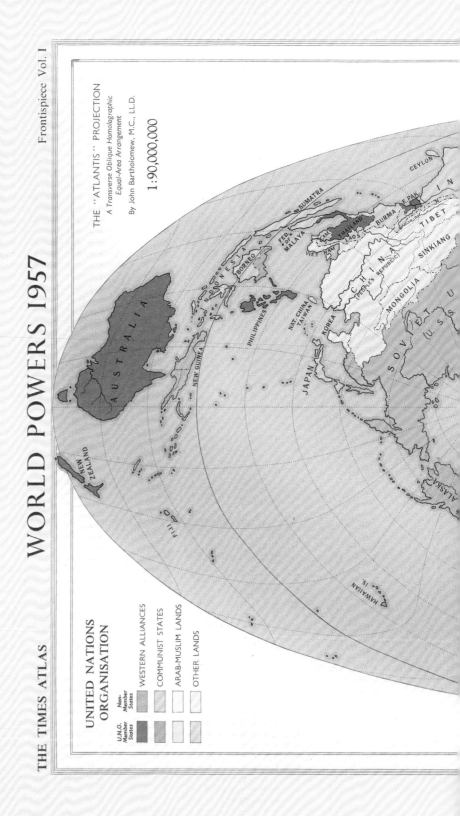

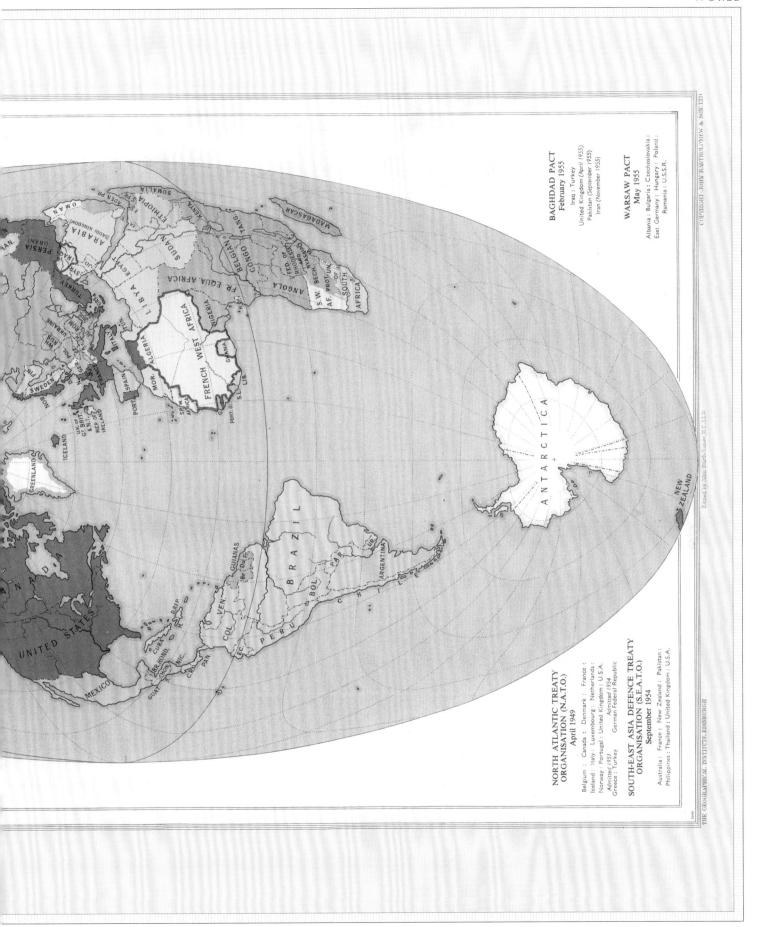

BAGHDAD PACT
February 1955

Iraq : Turkey
United Kingdom (April 1955)
Pakistan (September 1955)
Iran (November 1955)

WARSAW PACT
May 1955

Albania : Bulgaria : Czechoslovakia :
East Germany : Hungary : Poland :
Rumania : U.S.S.R.

**NORTH ATLANTIC TREATY
ORGANISATION (N.A.T.O.)**
April 1949

Belgium : Canada : Denmark : France :
Iceland : Italy : Luxembourg : Netherlands :
Norway : Portugal : United Kingdom : U.S.A.
Admitted 1951   Admitted 1954
Greece : Turkey   German Federal Republic

**SOUTH-EAST ASIA DEFENCE TREATY
ORGANISATION (S.E.A.T.O.)**
September 1954

Australia : France : New Zealand : Pakistan :
Philippines : Thailand : United Kingdom : U.S.A.

THE SOLAR SYSTEM AND
THE MOON 1895

From *The Times Atlas*.

This two-part illustration shows both Earth's place in our solar system and, in detail, the Moon, our nearest neighbour.

Our solar system comprises the Sun and those bodies – depicted here as planets, their satellites, comets and asteroids – that orbit it.

A great deal of detail has been packed into the map. Illustrations depict the Sun's appearance, including sunspots; eclipses of the Sun and the Moon on Earth; Moon phases as seen from Earth; Saturn as viewed from Earth; and Earth's orbit around the Sun, illustrating the changes of the seasons.

Also listed is the periodicity of comets' return to our solar system, and the larger asteroids and the planets are depicted in scale relative to one another. The size of the Sun is represented as the diameter (AB) of the central circle. Of the outer Jovian planets, only part of the orbit of Saturn appears within the central diagram at this scale.

Earth, Saturn and Jupiter are illustrated in relative distance to their moons. Beside each planet, and some of the asteroids, is shown its astronomical symbol e.g. Earth appears as a cross-quartered circle. Pluto, considered the ninth planet until its reclassification in 2006, was not discovered until 1930 and so does not appear.

The map of the Moon shows its near side which is always turned towards Earth. Contrary to conventional maps, south appears at the top and north at the bottom – this is the perspective seen through most astronomical telescopes.

Diagrams illustrate Moon features, the familiar pock-marked landscape of impact craters. The large crater of Posidonius is depicted individually, as are those near Hyginus. First discovered in 1877, these were a topic of heated debate at the time. Astronomers could not agree if they had simply been unnoticed, or if they were new and possibly volcanic in origin. Hyginus was the proposed landing site for the Apollo 19 mission cancelled in 1970.

The Sea of Tranquillity (labelled 'Mare Tranquilitatis') which appears in the lowerleft quadrant of this map, was the site of the first manned Moon landing by Apollo 11 in 1969.

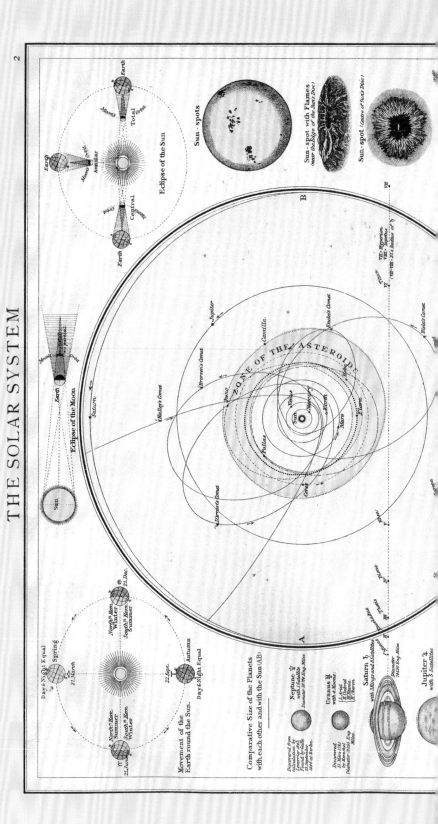

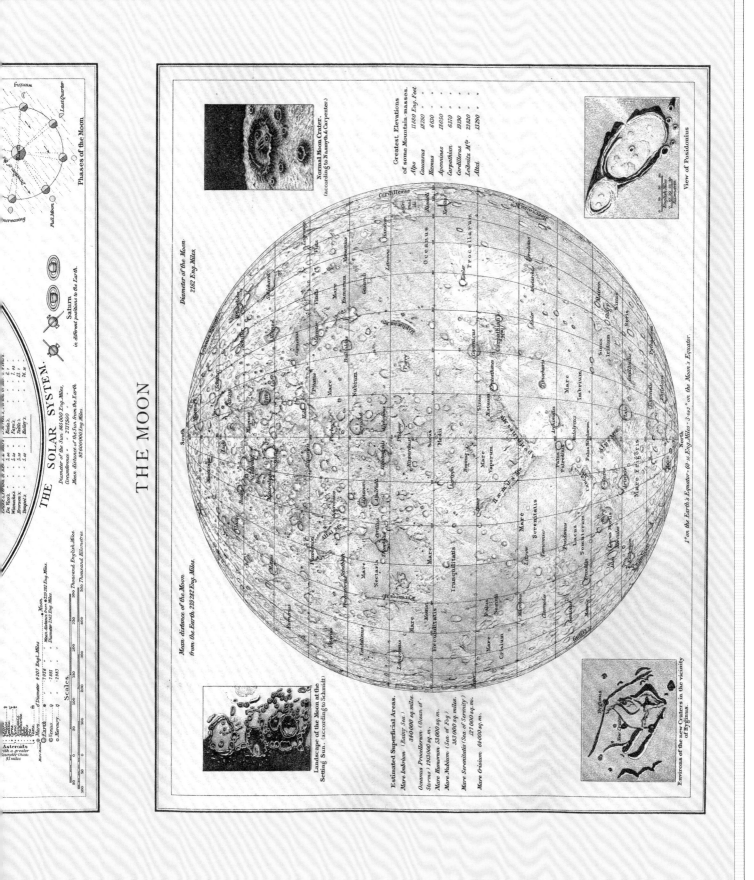

THE MOON

ROUTES OF COMMERCE 1950

From the *Advanced Atlas of Modern Geography*.

Just as the First World War had acted as a catalyst for massive change to the existing world order, so too the fallout from the Second World War brought significant political, territorial and economic upheaval across the globe. The interplay of these elements accounted for much of the tension in international relations for the remainder of the century. The rate of geopolitical change in the years after 1945 was so rapid that this map would soon be out-of-date.

The most significant development in world politics post-1945 was the emergence of the USA and USSR as hostile superpowers, and the ideological alignment of other nations with each respective camp. The armed stand-off which emerged between the two power blocs became known as the Cold War and lasted until the fall of Soviet communism in the early 1990s. Inevitably, Europe was the principal contact point between these conflicting ideologies.

For their part, the Soviets had extended their 1939 borders westwards towards Poland, incorporating Finland and the Baltic states en route. Moreover, they had created a buffer zone of satellite communist states in Eastern Europe to protect the motherland from further invasions from the west. From 1947, the USA sought to rebuild western Europe, economically and militarily, as a bulwark against the further spread of communism. Germany formed the boundary between these conflicting power bases, and in 1949, after several years of mounting tension, the country was formally partitioned between the occupying powers. The Soviet sector became East Germany (the GDR) and the Allies' sectors West Germany (the FDR). Interestingly, the map still records Germany as a single entity.

Beyond Europe, there were other flashpoints. The communist People's Republic of China had been established in 1949 after a lengthy civil war, and the following year, China invaded Tibet, over which it had always claimed authority – although this was and still is disputed. At about the same time, in neighbouring Korea, the first armed conflict of the Cold War began. Like the Great Powers of old, the superpowers intervened in a civil war, backing the respective forces of the communist North and the pro-western South, and creating a template for later conflict in Indo-China that would continue for decades.

Yet if the new emerging power blocs were to be the main source of future international tensions, issues from the past of the old imperial powers were also still to surface. As the map shows, in 1950, France, Britain, the Netherlands and Portugal still had a hold on their nineteenth-century colonies, particularly in Africa. In the following decade, each would gradually relinquish this control, peacefully in some cases and after bloody revolution in others. Britain's successor to empire, the Commonwealth of Nations, had dropped 'British' from its title in 1949 in acknowledgement of the shifting power balance in its relationship with its former colonies – though the map's legend has yet to catch up with this change.

Over page >>

ATLANTIC OCEAN 1879

From the *Collins New Complete Atlas*.

In 1879 ocean currents had been relatively recently charted, and are marked with their names and direction of flow. Long-distance shipping routes are shown and what is most striking about this map is that almost all converge on Britain.

While the map is undoubtedly drawn from a British perspective – the British Isles appear virtually in the centre – the mindset displayed here is not far from the reality. Britain in the 1870s was the richest and most dynamic nation in the world, at the head of an empire with the most extensive trading networks. The Royal Navy was the dominant maritime force and British technological supremacy meant that steam-powered steel ships maintained her position of superiority. The Scramble for Africa and its territories had not yet started and British trade vastly outweighed that of the European nations or of America.

ROUTES OF COMMERCE

25

Copyright- John Bartholomew & Son.Ltd.Edinburgh

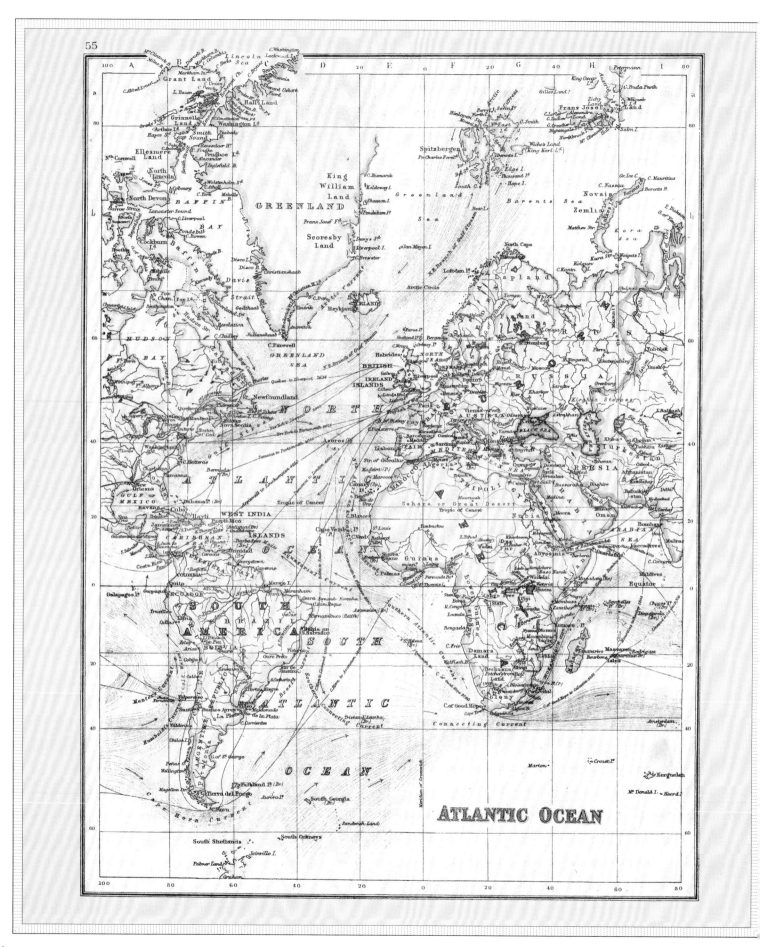

ATLANTIC OCEAN

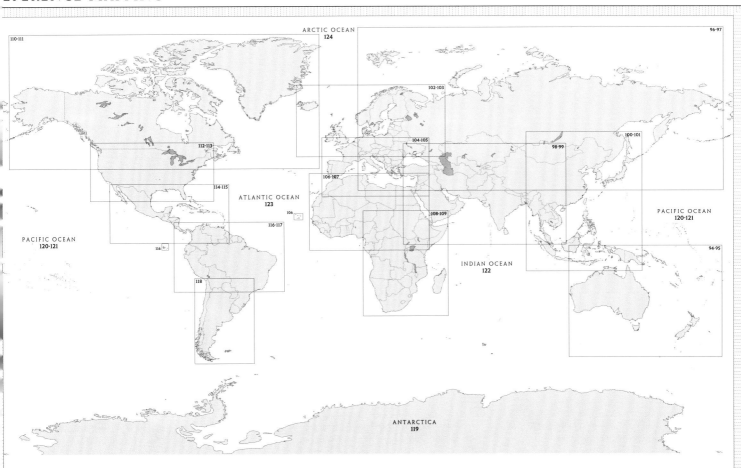

INTRODUCTION TO THE ATLAS AND MAP SYMBOLS

These pages explain the editorial policies followed for map pages in the atlas. The map symbols used on the maps are also explained here. The alphanumeric reference system used in the index is based on latitude and longitude, and the number and letter for each graticule square are shown within each map frame. The numbers of adjoining or overlapping plates are shown by arrows in the frame and accompanying numbers in the margin.

BOUNDARIES

The status of nations, their names and their boundaries, are shown in this atlas as they are at the time of going to press, as far as can be ascertained. The atlas includes any recent changes of status of nations and their boundaries. Where an international boundary symbol appears in the sea or ocean it does not necessarily infer a legal maritime boundary, but shows which islands belong to which country.

Where international boundaries are the subject of dispute it may be that no portrayal of them will meet with the approval of any of the countries involved. It is not seen as the function of this atlas to try to adjudicate between the rights and wrongs of political issues, and reference mapping at atlas scales is not the ideal medium for indicating the claims of many separatist and irredentist movements. However, every reasonable attempt is made to show where an active territorial dispute exists, and where there is an important difference between 'de facto' (existing in fact, on the ground) and 'de jure' (according to law) boundaries. This is done by the use of a different symbol where international boundaries are disputed, or where the alignment is unconfirmed, to that used for settled international boundaries. Ceasefire lines are also shown by a separate symbol. For clarity, disputed boundaries and areas are annotated where this is considered necessary. The atlas aims to take a strictly neutral viewpoint of all such cases, based on advice from expert consultants.

SCALE

In order to directly compare areas throughout the world it would be necessary to maintain a single map scale throughout the atlas. However, the desirability of mapping more densely populated and more significant areas of the world at larger, and therefore more detailed, scales means that a range of scales have been used. Scales for continental maps range from 1:17 500 000 to 1:32 000 000, depending on the size of the continental land mass being covered. Scales for regional maps are typically in the range 1:12 000 000 to 1:20 000 000, although smaller scales are used for remote areas. Mapping for most countries is at scales between 1:5 000 000 and 1:7 000 000.

MAP PROJECTIONS

The representation or 'projection' of the Earth into only two dimensions is a perennial problem for the cartographer. Distortions are inevitable and all map projections are compromises. Some projections seek to maintain correct area relationships (equal area projections), true distances and bearings from a point (equidistant projections) or correct angles and shapes (conformal projections). Others attempt to achieve a balance between these properties. The choice of projections used in this atlas has been made on an individual continental and regional basis. Projections used, and their individual parameters, have been defined to provide the best representation of the area mapped, to minimize distortion and to reduce scale errors as much as possible. The projection used is indicated at the bottom left of each map plate.

PLACE NAMES

The spelling of place names on maps has always been a matter of great complexity, because of the variety of the world's languages and the systems used to write them down. There is no standard way of spelling names or of converting them from one alphabet, or symbol set, to another. Instead, conventional ways of spelling have evolved in each of the world's major languages, and the results often differ significantly from the name as it is spelled in the original language.

In this atlas, local name forms are used where these are in the Roman alphabet, though for major cities and main physical features, conventional English names are given first. The local forms are those which are officially recognized by the government of the country concerned, usually as represented by its official mapping agency. This is a basic principle laid down by the United Kingdom government's Permanent Committee on Geographical Names (PCGN) and the equivalent United States Board on Geographic Names (BGN). Prominent English-language and historic names are not neglected, however. These, and significant superseded names and alternate spellings, are included in brackets on the maps where space permits, and are cross-referenced in the index.

Country names are shown in conventional English form and include any recent changes promulgated by national governments and adopted by the United Nations. The names of continents, oceans, seas and under-water features in international waters also appear in English throughout the atlas, as do those of other international features where such an English form exists and is in common use. International features are defined as features crossing one or more international boundary.

For languages in non-Roman alphabets or symbol sets, names need to be 'Romanized' through a process of transliteration (the conversion of characters or symbols from one alphabet into another) or transcription (conversion of names based on pronunciation). Different systems often exist for this process, but PCGN and its United States counterpart, the Board on Geographic Names (BGN), usually follow the same Romanization principles, and the general policy for this atlas is to follow their lead.

ABBREVIATIONS

Arch.	Archipelago		
B.	Bay		
	Bahia, Baía	Portuguese	bay
	Bahía	Spanish	bay
	Baie	French	bay
C.	Cape		
	Cabo	Portuguese, Spanish	cape, headland
	Cap	French	cape, headland
Co	Cerro	Spanish	hill, peak, summit
E.	East, Eastern		
Est.	Estrecho	Spanish	strait
G.	Gebel	Arabic	hill, mountain
Gt	Great		
I.	Island, Isle		
	Ilha	Portuguese	island
	Islas	Spanish	island
Is	Islands, Isles		

L.	Lake		
	Loch	(Scotland)	lake
	Lough	(Ireland)	lake
	Lac	French	lake
	Lago	Portuguese, Spanish	lake
M.	Mys	Russian	cape, point
Mt	Mount		
	Mont	French	hill, mountain
Mt.	Mountain		
Mte	Monte	Portuguese, Spanish	hill, mountain
Mts	Mountains		
	Monts	French	hills, mountains
N.	North, Northern		
O.	Ostrov	Russian	island
Pk	Puncak	Indonesian, Malay	hill, mountain
Pt	Point		
Pta	Punta	Italian, Spanish	cape, point
R.	River		

Ra.	Range		mountain range
S.	South, Southern		
	Salar, Salina, Salinas	Spanish	salt pan, salt pans
Sa	Serra	Portuguese,	mountain range
	Sierra	Spanish	mountain range
Sd	Sound		
S.E.	Southeast, Southeastern		
St	Saint		
	Sankt	German	Saint
	Sint	Dutch	Saint
Sta	Santa	Italian, Portuguese, Spanish	Saint
Ste	Sainte	French	Saint
Str.	Strait		
Tk	Teluk	Indonesian, Malay	bay, gulf
Tg	Tanjong, Tanjung	Indonesian, Malay	cape, point

RELIEF

Contour intervals used in layer-colouring for land height and sea depth on Physical maps

METRES FEET	
6000 / 19686	
5000 / 16404	
4000 / 13124	
3000 / 9843	
2000 / 6562	
1000 / 3281	
500 / 1640	
200 / 656	
0 / 0	
LAND BELOW SEA LEVEL	
200 / 656	
2000 / 6562	
3000 / 9843	
4000 / 13124	
5000 / 16404	
6000 / 19686	
7000 / 22967	
9000 / 29529	

1234 △ Summit Height in metres

123 • Ocean deep Depth in metres

LAND AND WATER FEATURES

—— River

----- Impermanent river/Wadi

------- Canal

·········· Flood dyke

——— Coral reef

——— Escarpment

| Dam/Barrage

≍ 123 Pass Height in metres

1234 ▲ Volcano Height in metres

ıı Waterfall

⌣ Oasis

Lake

Salt lake/Lagoon

Dry salt lake/Salt pan

Impermanent lake

Impermanent salt lake

Marsh

Sandy desert/Dunes

Rocky desert

Lava field

Ice cap/Glacier

CITIES AND TOWNS

Population	National Capital	Administrative Capital Shown for selected countries only	Other City or Town
over 10 million	**Tōkyō** ◉	**Karachi** ⊙	**New York** ⊙
5 million to 10 million	**Santiago** ◉	**Tianjin** ⊙	**Philadelphia** ⊙
1 million to 5 million	**Damascus** ◉	**Douala** ⊙	**Barranquilla** ⊙
500 000 to 1 million	**Bangui** ▣	**Bulawayo** ◎	**El Paso** ◎
100 000 to 500 000	Wellington □	Mansa ○	Mobile ○
50 000 to 100 000	Port of Spain □	Lubango ○	Zaraza ○
10 000 to 50 000	Malabo □	Chinhoyi ○	El Tigre ○
under 10 000	Roseau □	Ati ○	Soledad ○

STYLES OF LETTERING

Cities and towns are explained above

Country	**FRANCE**	Island	*Gran Canaria*
Overseas Territory/Dependency	**Guadeloupe**	Lake	*Lake Erie*
Disputed Territory	AKSAI CHIN	Mountain	*Mont Blanc*
Administrative name Shown for selected countries only	SCOTLAND	River	*Thames*
Area name	PATAGONIA	Region	*LAPPLAND*

TRANSPORT

═══ Motorway Shown on large-scale maps only

——— Main road

—— Other road

----- Track

—•••— Road tunnel

——— Main railway

——— Other railway

—•••— Railway tunnel

⊕ Main airport

✦ Regional airport

BOUNDARIES

International boundary

Disputed international boundary/ alignment unconfirmed

••••• Ceasefire line

Administrative boundary

MISCELLANEOUS SYMBOLS

-------- National park

············ Reserve

∿∿∿∿ Ancient wall

∴ Site of specific interest

Built-up area

WORLD PHYSICAL

The shapes of the continents and oceans have evolved over millions of years. Movement of the tectonic plates which make up the Earth's crust has created some of the best known land features. From the highest point Mount Everest to the deepest in the Mariana Trench is a height of almost 20 000 m /over 65 000 ft. Earthquakes, volcanoes, erosion, climatic variations and man's intervention all continue to affect the Earth's landscapes. Different landscapes reflect great variations in climate from deserts such as the Sahara, to the frozen ice cap of Antarctica.

FACTS

- The Pacific Ocean is larger than the continents' land areas combined.

- The average height of the Earth's land surface is 840 m (2755 ft) above sea level and 52 per cent of the land is below 500 m (1640 ft). Approximately 10 per cent of the surface is permanently covered by ice.

- The Ural Mountains define part of the boundary between Europe and Asia.

- The collision of two tectonic plates – the Indo-Australia and the Eurasian Plates – formed the Himalaya mountains. The mountains are still rising at a rate of approximately 5 mm (0.2 inch) a year.

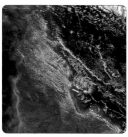

The Great Barrier Reef stretches for 2600 km (1616 miles) over an area of approximately 344 400 sq km (132 974 sq miles). The reef is located off the eastern coast of Queensland, Australia and can be seen from space.

The Kamchatka Peninsula in northeastern Asia is a mountainous landscape with numerous active volcanoes.

High sand dunes, sculpted by the wind, dwarf a desert oasis in the Sahara.

The flat featureless Great Plains of North America stretch from Saskatchewan, Canada in the north to Texas, USA in the south.

PHYSICAL EXTREMES

EARTH'S DIMENSIONS		HIGHEST MOUNTAINS	metres	fee
Mass	5.974 x 10²¹ tonnes	Mt Everest, China/Nepal	8 848	29 02
Volume	1 083 207 x 10⁶ cu km / 259 911 x 10⁶ cu miles	K2, China/Pakistan	8 611	28 25
Total area	509 450 000 sq km / 196 699 000 sq miles	Kangchenjunga, India/Nepal	8 586	28 16
Land area	149 450 000 sq km / 57 703 000 sq miles	Lhotse, China/Nepal	8 516	27 93
Water area	360 000 000 sq km / 138 996 000 sq miles	Makalu, China/Nepal	8 463	27 76
Water volume	1 389 500 x 10³ cu km / 333 405 x 10³ cu miles	Cho Oyu, China/Nepal	8 201	26 90
Equatorial diameter	12 756 km / 7 927 miles	Dhaulagiri, Nepal	8 167	26 79
Polar diameter	12 714 km / 7 901 miles	Manaslu, Nepal	8 163	26 78
Equatorial circumference	40 075 km / 24 903 miles	Nanga Parbat, Pakistan	8 126	26 66
Meridional circumference	40 008 km / 24 861 miles	Annapurna I, Nepal	8 091	26 54

Winkel Tripel Projection

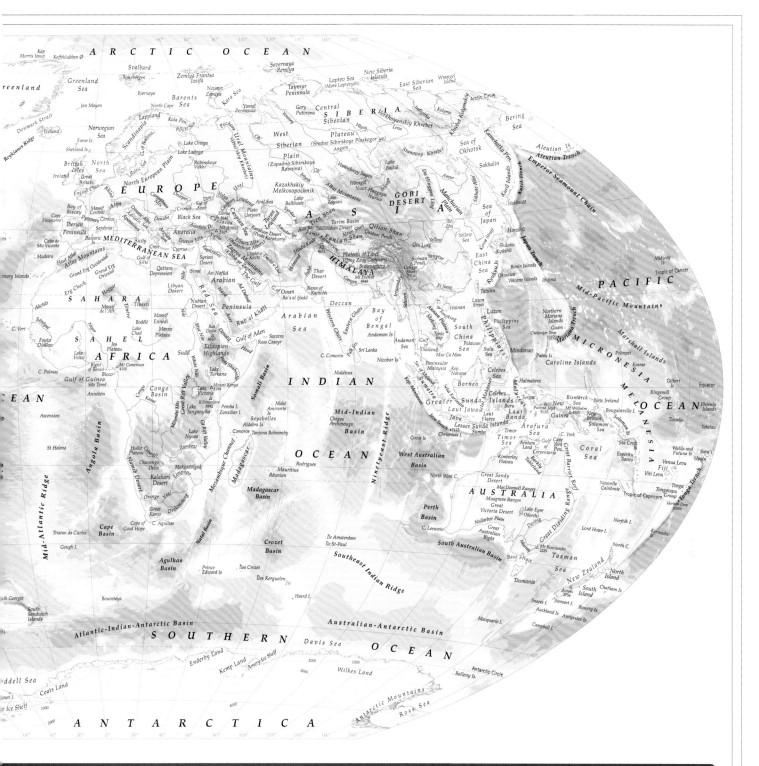

ONGEST RIVERS	km	miles	LARGEST ISLANDS	sq km	sq miles	LARGEST LAKES	sq km	sq miles	OCEANS AND SEAS	Area sq km	sq miles	Deepest point metres	feet
le, Africa	6 695	4 160	Greenland, North America	2 175 600	839 999	Caspian Sea, Asia/Europe	371 000	143 243	Pacific Ocean	166 241 000	64 186 000	10 920	35 826
nazon, South America	6 516	4 049	New Guinea, Oceania	808 510	312 166	Lake Superior, North America	82 100	31 699	Atlantic Ocean	86 557 000	33 420 000	8 605	28 231
ngtze, Asia	6 380	3 965	Borneo, Asia	745 561	287 861	Lake Victoria, Africa	68 870	26 591	Indian Ocean	73 427 000	28 350 000	7 125	23 376
ssissippi-Missouri, North America	5 969	3 709	Madagascar, Africa	587 040	266 656	Lake Huron, North America	59 600	23 012	Arctic Ocean	9 485 000	3 662 000	5 450	17 880
'-Irtysh, Asia	5 568	3 460	Baffin Island, North America	507 451	195 927	Lake Michigan, North America	57 800	22 317	South China Sea	2 590 000	1 000 000	5 514	18 090
nisey-Angara-Selenga, Asia	5 550	3 449	Sumatra, Asia	473 606	182 859	Lake Tanganyika, Africa	32 600	12 587	Caribbean Sea	2 512 000	970 000	7 680	25 197
llow, Asia	5 464	3 395	Honshū, Asia	227 414	87 805	Great Bear Lake, North America	31 328	12 096	Mediterranean Sea	2 510 000	969 000	5 121	16 801
ongo, Africa	4 667	2 900	Great Britain, Europe	218 476	84 354	Lake Baikal, Asia	30 500	11 776	Bering Sea	2 261 000	873 000	4 150	13 615
o de la Plata-Paraná, South America	4 500	2 796	Victoria Island, North America	217 291	83 896	Lake Nyasa, Africa	29 500	11 390	Bay of Bengal	2 172 000	839 000	4 500	14 764
tysh, Asia	4 440	2 759	Ellesmere Island, North America	196 236	75 767	Great Slave Lake, North America	28 568	11 030	Gulf of Mexico	1 544 000	596 000	3 504	11 496

WORLD POLITICAL

The present picture of the political world is the result of a long history of exploration, colonialism, conflict and negotiation. In 1950 there were eighty-two independent countries. Since then there has been a significant trend away from colonial influences and although many dependent territories still exist there are now 195 independent countries. The newest country is Kosovo which gained independence from Serbia in February 2008. The shapes of countries reflect a combination of natural features, such as mountain ranges, and political agreements. There are still areas of the world where boundaries are disputed or only temporarily settled as ceasefire lines.

FACTS

• The break up of the Soviet Union (or the U.S.S.R. – Union of Soviet Socialist Republics) in 1991 created fifteen new countries including the Russian Federation.

• The Maldives in the Indian Ocean consist of approximately 1200 low-lying islands, all under 2 m (6.5 ft) in height.

• The Commonwealth, first defined in 1926, has evolved from communities within the British Empire, to a free association of fifty-three member countries.

• Both China and the Russian Federation have borders with fourteen different countries.

THE UNITED NATIONS

The name "United Nations" was coined by United States President Franklin D. Roosevelt, and was first used in the "Declaration by United Nations" of 1 January 1942. The United Nations (UN) officially came into existence on 24 October 1945, when the United Nations Charter was ratified by China, France, the Soviet Union, the United Kingdom, the United States and a majority of other signatories. It was a successor to the League of Nations which had been unsuccessful in preventing the Second World War.

All *de facto* independent countries of the world, except Taiwan and Vatican City, are members – 192 in total. Kosovo is also not a member. The principal headquarters of the UN are in New York but other major agencies of the Organization are found in Geneva, The Hague, Vienna and other locations.

The United Nations building, New York, USA.

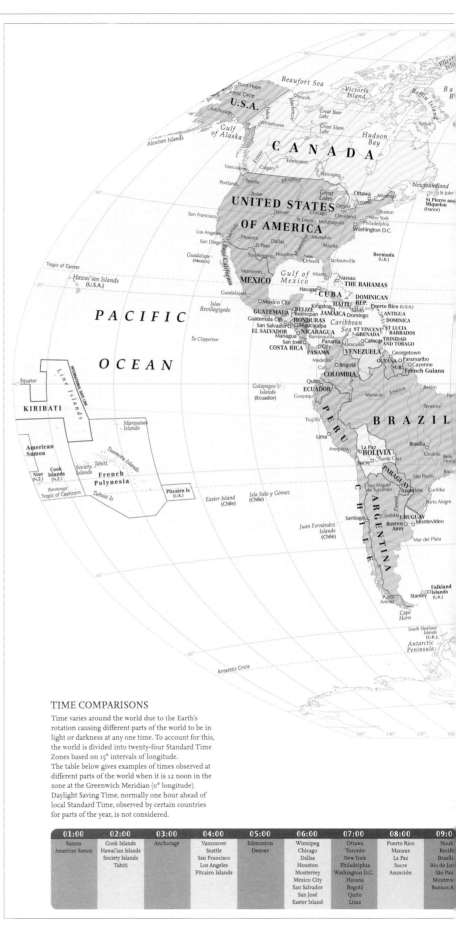

TIME COMPARISONS

Time varies around the world due to the Earth's rotation causing different parts of the world to be in light or darkness at any one time. To account for this, the world is divided into twenty-four Standard Time Zones based on 15° intervals of longitude.
The table below gives examples of times observed at different parts of the world when it is 12 noon in the zone at the Greenwich Meridian (0° longitude). Daylight Saving Time, normally one hour ahead of local Standard Time, observed by certain countries for parts of the year, is not considered.

01:00	02:00	03:00	04:00	05:00	06:00	07:00	08:00	09:0
Samoa	Cook Islands	Anchorage	Vancouver	Edmonton	Winnipeg	Ottawa	Puerto Rico	Nuuk
American Samoa	Hawai'ian Islands		Seattle	Denver	Chicago	Toronto	Manaus	Recife
	Society Islands		San Francisco		Dallas	New York	La Paz	Brasíli
	Tahiti		Los Angeles		Houston	Philadelphia	Sucre	Rio de Jan
			Pitcairn Islands		Monterrey	Washington D.C.	Asunción	São Pau
					Mexico City	Havana		Montevic
					San Salvador	Bogotá		Buenos A
					San José	Quito		
					Easter Island	Lima		

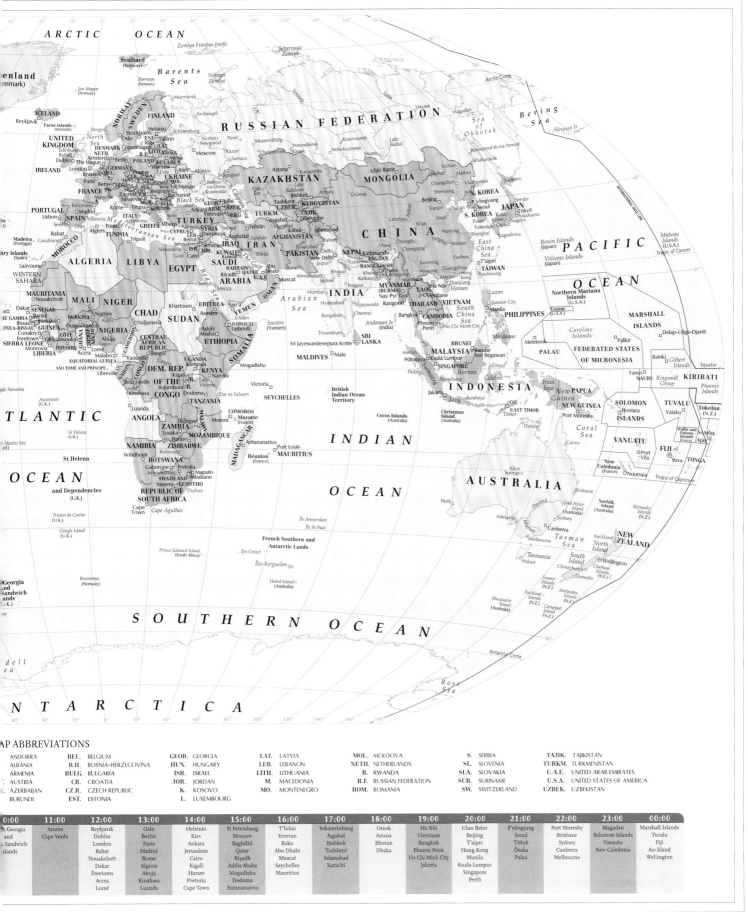

MAP ABBREVIATIONS

ANDORRA	BEL.	BELGIUM	GEOR.	GEORGIA	LAT.	LATVIA	MOL.	MOLDOVA
ALBANIA	B.H.	BOSNIA–HERZEGOVINA	HUN.	HUNGARY	LEB.	LEBANON	NETH.	NETHERLANDS
ARMENIA	BULG.	BULGARIA	ISR.	ISRAEL	LITH.	LITHUANIA	R.	RWANDA
AUSTRIA	CR.	CROATIA	JOR.	JORDAN	M.	MACEDONIA	R.F.	RUSSIAN FEDERATION
AZERBAIJAN	CZ.R.	CZECH REPUBLIC	K.	KOSOVO	MO.	MONTENEGRO	ROM.	ROMANIA
BURUNDI	EST.	ESTONIA	L.	LUXEMBOURG				

S.	SERBIA	TAJIK.	TAJIKISTAN
SL.	SLOVENIA	TURKM.	TURKMENISTAN
SLA.	SLOVAKIA	U.A.E.	UNITED ARAB EMIRATES
SUR.	SURINAME	U.S.A.	UNITED STATES OF AMERICA
SW.	SWITZERLAND	UZBEK.	UZBEKISTAN

10:00	11:00	12:00	13:00	14:00	15:00	16:00	17:00	18:00	19:00	20:00	21:00	22:00	23:00	00:00
South Georgia and South Sandwich Islands	Azores Cape Verde	Reykjavik Dublin London Rabat Nouakchott Dakar Freetown Accra Lomé	Oslo Berlin Paris Madrid Rome Algiers Abuja Kinshasa Luanda	Helsinki Kiev Ankara Jerusalem Cairo Kigali Harare Pretoria Cape Town	St Petersburg Moscow Baghdād Qatar Riyadh Addis Ababa Mogadishu Dodoma Antananarivo	T'bilisi Yerevan Baku Abu Dhabi Muscat Seychelles Mauritius	Yekaterinburg Aşgabat Bishkek Tashkent Islamabad Karachi	Omsk Astana Bhutan Dhaka	Ha Nôi Vientiane Bangkok Phnom Penh Ho Chi Minh City Jakarta	Ulan Bator Beijing T'aipei Hong Kong Manila Kuala Lumpur Singapore Perth	P'yŏngyang Seoul Tōkyō Ōsaka Palau	Port Moresby Brisbane Sydney Canberra Melbourne	Magadan Solomon Islands Vanuatu New Caledonia	Marshall Islands Tuvalu Fiji Au·kland Wellington

AUSTRALASIA AND SOUTHWEST PACIFIC

AUSTRALIA
Commonwealth of Australia

Area Sq Km	7 692 024	Languages	English, Italian, Greek
Area Sq Miles	2 969 907	Religions	Protestant, Roman Catholic, Orthodox
Population	20 743 000	Currency	Australian dollar
Capital	Canberra	Organizations	APEC, Comm., OECD, UN

Australia, the world's sixth largest country, occupies the smallest, flattest and driest continent. The western half of the continent is mostly arid plateaus, ridges and vast deserts. The central eastern area comprises the lowlands of river systems draining into Lake Eyre, while to the east is the Great Dividing Range, a belt of ridges and plateaus running from Queensland to Tasmania. Climatically, more than two-thirds of the country is arid or semi-arid. The north is tropical monsoon, the east subtropical, and the southwest and southeast temperate. The majority of Australia's highly urbanized population lives along the east, southeast and southwest coasts. Australia has vast mineral deposits and various sources of energy. It is among the world's leading producers of iron ore, bauxite, nickel, copper and uranium. It is a major producer of coal, and oil and natural gas are also being exploited. Although accounting for only five per cent of the workforce, agriculture continues to be an important sector of the economy, with food and agricultural raw materials making up most of Australia's export earnings. Fuel, ores and metals, and manufactured goods, account for the remainder of exports. Japan and the USA are Australia's main trading partners.

FIJI
Sovereign Democratic Republic of Fiji

Area Sq Km	18 330	Languages	English, Fijian, Hindi
Area Sq Miles	7 077	Religions	Christian, Hindu, Sunni Muslim
Population	839 000	Currency	Fiji dollar
Capital	Suva	Organizations	Comm., UN

The southwest Pacific republic of Fiji comprises two mountainous and volcanic islands, Vanua Levu and Viti Levu, and over three hundred smaller islands. The climate is tropical and the economy is based on agriculture (chiefly sugar, the main export), fishing, forestry, gold mining and tourism.

NEW ZEALAND

Area Sq Km	270 534	Languages	English, Maori
Area Sq Miles	104 454	Religions	Protestant, Roman Catholic
Population	4 179 000	Currency	New Zealand dollar
Capital	Wellington	Organizations	APEC, Comm., OECD, UN

New Zealand comprises two main islands separated by the narrow Cook Strait, and a number of smaller islands. North Island, where three-quarters of the population lives, has mountain ranges, broad fertile valleys and a central plateau with hot springs and active volcanoes. South Island is also mountainous, with the Southern Alps running its entire length. The only major lowland area is the Canterbury Plains in the centre-east. The climate is generally temperate, although South Island has colder winters. Farming is the mainstay of the economy. New Zealand is one of the world's leading producers of meat (beef, lamb and mutton), wool and dairy products; fruit and fish are also important. Hydroelectric and geothermal power provide much of the country's energy needs. Other industries produce timber, wood pulp, iron, aluminium, machinery and chemicals. Tourism is the fastest growing sector of the economy. The main trading partners are Australia, the USA and Japan.

PAPUA NEW GUINEA
Independent State of Papua New Guinea

Area Sq Km	462 840	Languages	English, Tok Pisin (Creole), local languages
Area Sq Miles	178 704		
Population	6 331 000	Religions	Protestant, Roman Catholic, traditional beliefs
Capital	Port Moresby		
		Currency	Kina
		Organizations	APEC, Comm., UN

Papua New Guinea occupies the eastern half of the island of New Guinea and includes many island groups. It has a forested and mountainous interior, bordered by swampy plains, and a tropical monsoon climate. Most of the workforce are farmers. Timber, copra, coffee and cocoa are important, but exports are dominated by minerals, chiefly gold and copper. The country depends on foreign aid. Australia, Japan and Singapore are the main trading partners.

VANUATU
Republic of Vanuatu

Area Sq Km	12 190	Languages	English, Bislama (Creole), French
Area Sq Miles	4 707	Religions	Protestant, Roman Catholic, traditional beliefs
Population	226 000		
Capital	Port Vila		
		Currency	Vatu
		Organizations	Comm., UN

Vanuatu occupies an archipelago of approximately eighty islands in the southwest Pacific. Many of the islands are mountainous, of volcanic origin and densely forested. The climate is tropical, with heavy rainfall. Half of the population lives on the main islands of Éfaté and Espíritu Santo, and the majority of people are employed in agriculture. Copra, beef, timber, vegetables, and cocoa are the main exports. Tourism is becoming important to the economy. Australia, Japan and Germany are the main trading partners.

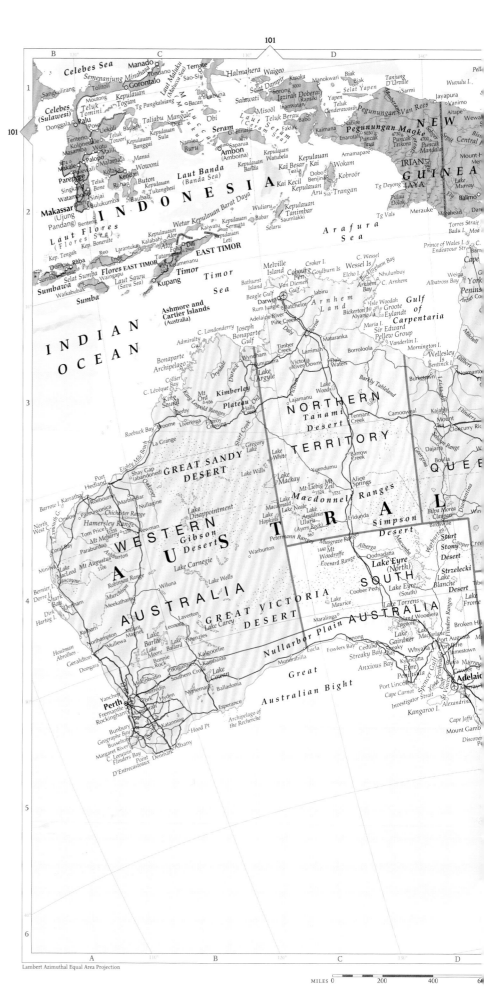

Lambert Azimuthal Equal Area Projection

MILES 0   200   400   60

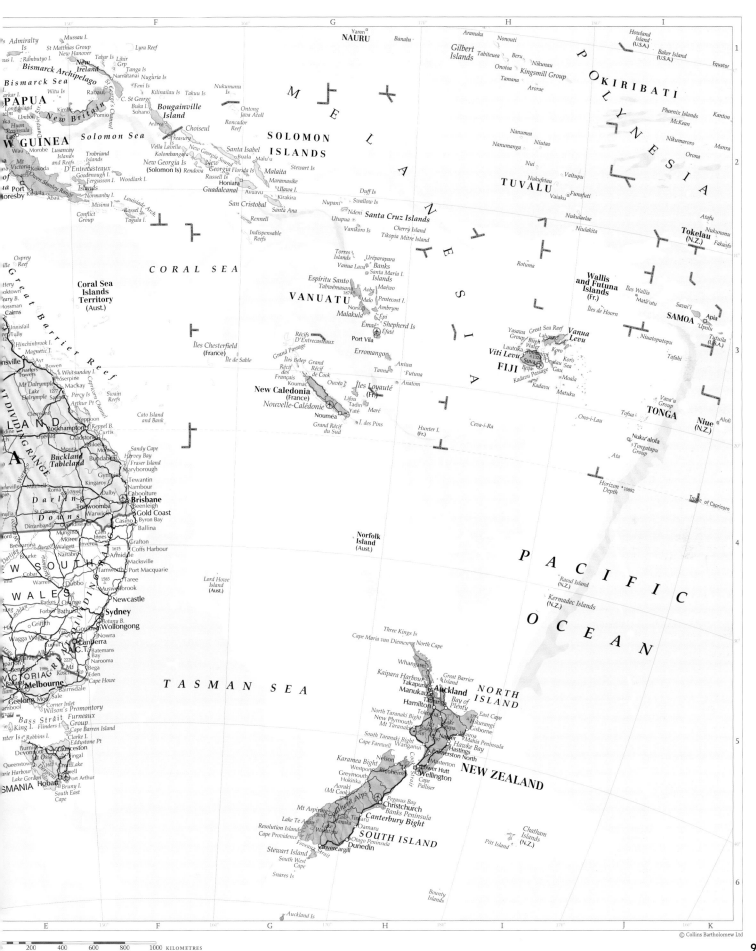

JAPAN

Area Sq Km	377 727	Languages	Japanese
Area Sq Miles	145 841	Religions	Shintoist, Buddhist, Christian
Population	127 967 000	Currency	Yen
Capital	Tōkyō	Organizations	APEC, OECD, UN

Japan lies in the Pacific Ocean off the coast of eastern Asia and consists of four main islands – Hokkaidō, Honshū, Shikoku and Kyūshū – and more than three thousand smaller islands in the surrounding Sea of Japan, East China Sea and Pacific Ocean. The central island of Honshū accounts for sixty per cent of the total land area and contains eighty per cent of the population. Behind the long and deeply indented coastline, nearly three-quarters of the country is mountainous and heavily forested. Japan has over sixty active volcanoes, and is subject to frequent earthquakes and typhoons. The climate is generally temperate maritime, with warm summers and mild winters, except in western Hokkaidō and northwest Honshū, where the winters are very cold with heavy snow. Only fourteen per cent of the land area is suitable for cultivation, and its few raw materials (coal, oil, natural gas, lead, zinc and copper) are insufficient for its industry. Most materials must be imported, including about ninety per cent of energy requirements. Yet Japan has the world's second largest industrial economy, with a range of modern heavy and light industries centred mainly around the major ports of Yokohama, Ōsaka and Tōkyō. It is the world's largest manufacturer of cars, motorcycles and merchant ships, and a major producer of steel, textiles, chemicals and cement. It is also a leading producer of many consumer durables, such as washing machines, and electronic equipment, chiefly office equipment and computers. Japan has a strong service sector, banking and finance being particularly important, and Tōkyō has one of the world's major stock exchanges. Owing to intensive agricultural production, Japan is seventy per cent self-sufficient in food. The main food crops are rice, barley, fruit, wheat and soya beans. Livestock rearing (chiefly cattle, pigs and chickens) and fishing are also important, and Japan has one of the largest fishing fleets in the world. A major trading nation, Japan has trade links with many countries in southeast Asia and in Europe, although its main trading partner is the USA.

MONGOLIA

Area Sq Km	1 565 000	Languages	Khalka (Mongolian), Kazakh, local languages
Area Sq Miles	604 250	Religions	Buddhist, Sunni Muslim
Population	2 629 000	Currency	Tugrik (tögrög)
Capital	Ulan Bator (Ulaanbaatar)	Organizations	UN

Mongolia is a landlocked country in eastern Asia between the Russian Federation and China. Much of it is high steppe land, with mountains and lakes in the west and north. In the south is the Gobi desert. Mongolia has long, cold winters and short, mild summers. A quarter of the population lives in the capital, Ulaanbaatar. Livestock breeding and agricultural processing are important. There are substantial mineral resources. Copper and textiles are the main exports. China and the Russian Federation are the main trading partners.

RUSSIAN FEDERATION

Area Sq Km	17 075 400	Languages	Russian, Tatar, Ukrainian, local languages
Area Sq Miles	6 592 849	Religions	Russian Orthodox, Sunni Muslim, Protestant
Population	142 499 000	Currency	Russian rouble
Capital	Moscow (Moskva)	Organizations	APEC, CIS, UN

The Russian Federation occupies much of eastern Europe and all of northern Asia, and is the world's largest country. It borders fourteen countries to the west and south and has long coastlines on the Arctic and Pacific Oceans to the north and east. European Russia lies west of the Ural Mountains. To the south the land rises to uplands and the Caucasus mountains on the border with Georgia and Azerbaijan. East of the Urals lies the flat West Siberian Plain and the Central Siberian Plateau. In the south-east is Lake Baikal, the world's deepest lake, and the Sayan ranges on the border with Kazakhstan and Mongolia. Eastern Siberia is rugged and mountainous, with many active volcanoes in the Kamchatka Peninsula. The country's major rivers are the Volga in the west and the Ob', Irtysh, Yenisey, Lena and Amur in Siberia. The climate and vegetation range between arctic tundra in the north and semi-arid steppe towards the Black and Caspian Sea coasts in the south. In general, the climate is continental with extreme temperatures. The majority of the population (the eighth largest in the world), and industry and agriculture are concentrated in European Russia. The economy is dependent on exploitation of raw materials and on heavy industry. Russia has a wealth of mineral resources, although they are often difficult to exploit because of climate and remote locations. It is one of the world's leading producers of petroleum, natural gas and coal as well as iron ore, nickel, copper, bauxite, and many precious and rare metals. Forests cover over forty per cent of the land area and supply an important timber, paper and pulp industry. Approximately eight per cent of the land is suitable for cultivation, but farming is generally inefficient and food, especially grains, must be imported. Fishing is important and Russia has a large fleet operating around the world. The transition to a market economy has been slow and difficult, with considerable underemployment. As well as mining and extractive industries there is a wide range of manufacturing industry, from steel mills to aircraft and space vehicles, shipbuilding, synthetic fabrics, plastics, cotton fabrics, consumer durables, chemicals and fertilizers. Exports include fuels, metals, machinery, chemicals and forest products. The most important trading partners include Germany, the USA and Belarus.

Conic Equidistant Projection

MILES 0   200   400   600

200 400 600 800 1000 1200 1400 KILOMETRES

© Collins Bartholomew Ltd

CHINA
People's Republic of China

Area Sq Km	9 584 492	Languages	Mandarin, Wu, Cantonese, Hsiang, regional languages
Area Sq Miles	3 700 593		
Population	1 313 437 000	Religions	Confucian, Taoist, Buddhist, Christian, Sunni Muslim
Capital	Beijing (Peking)		
		Currency	Yuan, Hong Kong dollar, Macao pataca
		Organizations	APEC, UN

China, the world's most populous and fourth largest country, occupies a large part of east Asia, borders fourteen states and has coastlines on the Yellow, East China and South China Seas. It has a huge variety of landscapes. The southwest contains the high Plateau of Tibet, flanked by the Himalaya and Kunlun Shan mountains. The north is mountainous with arid basins and extends from the Tien Shan and Altai Mountains and the vast Taklimakan Desert in the west to the plateau and Gobi Desert in the centre-east. Eastern China is predominantly lowland and is divided broadly into the basins of the Yellow River (Huang He) in the north, the Yangtze (Chang Jiang) in the centre and the Pearl River (Xi Jiang) in the southeast. Climatic conditions and vegetation are as diverse as the topography: much of the country experiences temperate conditions, while the southwest has an extreme mountain climate and the southeast enjoys a moist, warm subtropical climate. Nearly seventy per cent of China's huge population lives in rural areas, and agriculture employs around half of the working population. The main crops are rice, wheat, soya beans, peanuts, cotton, tobacco and hemp. China is rich in coal, oil and natural gas and has the world's largest potential in hydroelectric power. It is a major world producer of iron ore, molybdenum, copper, asbestos and gold. Economic reforms from the early 1980's led to an explosion in manufacturing development concentrated on the 'coastal economic open region'. The main exports are machinery, textiles, footwear, toys and sports goods. Japan and the USA are China's main trading partners.

INDIA
Republic of India

Area Sq Km	3 064 898	Languages	Hindi, English, many regional languages
Area Sq Miles	1 183 364		
Population	1 169 016 000	Religions	Hindu, Sunni Muslim, Shi'a Muslim, Sikh, Christian
Capital	New Delhi		
		Currency	Indian rupee
		Organizations	Comm., UN

The south Asian country of India occupies a peninsula that juts out into the Indian Ocean between the Arabian Sea and Bay of Bengal. The heart of the peninsula is the Deccan plateau, bordered on either side by ranges of hills, the western Ghats and the lower eastern Ghats, which fall away to narrow coastal plains. To the north is a broad plain, drained by the Indus, Ganges and Brahmaputra rivers and their tributaries. The plain is intensively farmed and is the most populous region. In the west is the Thar Desert. The mountains of the Himalaya form India's northern border, together with parts of the Karakoram and Hindu Kush ranges in the northwest. The climate shows marked seasonal variation: a hot season from March to June; a monsoon season from June to October; and a cold season from November to February. Rainfall ranges between very high in the northeast Assam region to negligible in the Thar Desert. Temperatures range from very cold in the Himalaya to tropical heat over much of the south. Over seventy per cent of the huge population – the second largest in the world – is rural, although Delhi, Mumbai (Bombay) and Kolkata (Calcutta) all rank among the ten largest cities in the world. Agriculture, forestry and fishing account for a quarter of national output and two-thirds of employment. Much of the farming is on a subsistence basis and involves mainly rice and wheat. India is a major world producer of tea, sugar, jute, cotton and tobacco. Livestock is reared mainly for dairy products and hides. There are major reserves of coal, reserves of oil and natural gas, and many minerals, including iron, manganese, bauxite, diamonds and gold. The manufacturing sector is large and diverse – mainly chemicals and chemical products, textiles, iron and steel, food products, electrical goods and transport equipment; software and pharmaceuticals are also important. All the main manufactured products are exported, together with diamonds and jewellery. The USA, Germany, Japan and the UK are the main trading partners.

SAUDI ARABIA
Kingdom of Saudi Arabia

Area Sq Km	2 200 000	Languages	Arabic
Area Sq Miles	849 425	Religions	Sunni Muslim, Shi'a Muslim
Population	24 735 000	Currency	Saudi Arabian riyal
Capital	Riyadh (Ar Riyāḍ)	Organizations	OPEC, UN

Saudi Arabia occupies most of the Arabian Peninsula in southwest Asia. The terrain is desert or semi-desert plateaus, which rise to mountains running parallel to the Red Sea in the west and slope down to plains in the southeast and along The Gulf in the east. Over eighty per cent of the population lives in urban areas. There are around four million foreign workers in Saudi Arabia, employed mainly in the oil and service industries. Summers are hot, winters are warm and rainfall is low. Saudi Arabia has the world's largest reserves of oil and significant natural gas reserves, both onshore and in The Gulf. Crude oil and refined products account for over ninety per cent of export earnings. Other industries and irrigated agriculture are being encouraged, but most food and raw materials are imported. Saudi Arabia has important banking and commercial interests. Japan and the USA are the main trading partners.

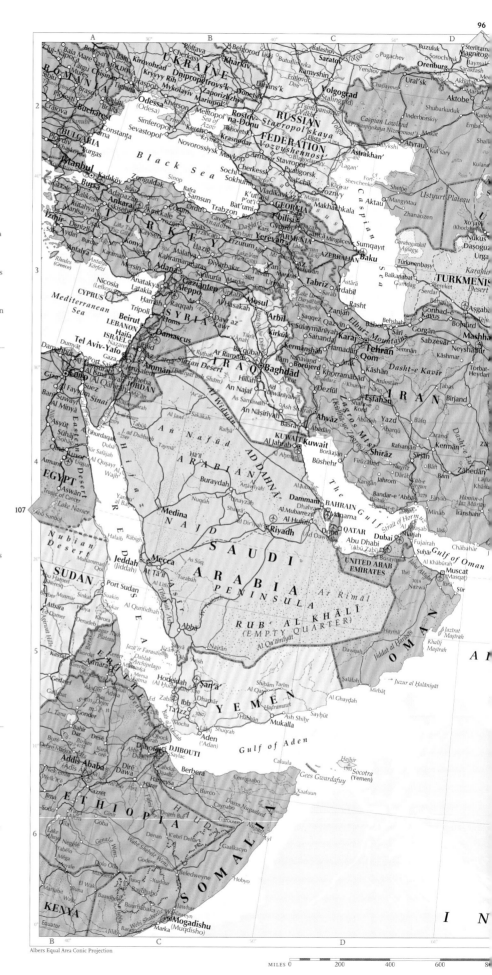

Albers Equal Area Conic Projection

MILES 0   200   400   600

Major labels

RUSSIAN FEDERATION · **KAZAKHSTAN** · **MONGOLIA** · **INNER MONGOLIA** · **GOBI DESERT** · **CHINA** · **XINJIANG** · **KYRGYZSTAN** · **TAJIKISTAN** · **AFGHANISTAN** · **PAKISTAN** · **KASHMIR** · **JAMMU AND KASHMIR** · **HIMALAYA** · **TIBET** · Plateau of Tibet (Qingzang Gaoyuan) · **NEPAL** · **BHUTAN** · **BANGLADESH** · **INDIA** · **MYANMAR (BURMA)** · **LAOS** · **THAILAND** · **VIETNAM** · **CAMBODIA** · **SRI LANKA** · **MALDIVES** · **MALAYSIA** · **INDONESIA**

Tien Shan · Tarim Basin (Tarim Pendi) · Taklimakan Desert · Kunlun Shan · Altun Shan · Qilian Shan · Qaidam Pendi · Tanggula Shan · Hindu Kush · Karakoram Range · Thar Desert · Deccan · Western Ghats · Eastern Ghats · Coromandel Coast · Malabar Coast

BAY OF BENGAL · **ANDAMAN SEA** · **INDIAN OCEAN** · Gulf of Thailand · Strait of Malacca · Mouths of the Ganges · Mouths of the Indus · Mouths of the Godavari · Mouths of the Krishna · Mouths of the Irrawaddy · Mouths of the Mekong

Andaman Islands (India) · Nicobar Islands (India) · Laccadive Islands (India) · Amindivi Islands · Mergui Archipelago · Ten Degree Channel · Nine Degree Channel · Eight Degree Channel

Selected cities
Barnaul · Astana (Akmola) · Almaty · Bishkek · Tashkent · Ulan Bator (Ulaanbaatar) · Beijing (Peking) · Tianjin · Shijiazhuang · Taiyuan · Xi'an · Lanzhou · Xining · Chengdu · Chongqing · Kunming · Wuhan · Changsha · Guangzhou · Guilin · Nanning · Karachi · Kabul · Peshawar · Srinagar · Islamabad · Lahore · Amritsar · Delhi · New Delhi · Jaipur · Lucknow · Kanpur · Kathmandu · Thimphu · Dhaka · Kolkata (Calcutta) · Chittagong · Mumbai (Bombay) · Pune · Hyderabad · Nagpur · Bangalore · Chennai (Madras) · Coimbatore · Cochin · Trivandrum · Colombo · Sri Jayewardenepura Kotte · Mandalay · Nay Pyi Taw · Rangoon (Yangon) · Bangkok · Krung Thep · Phnom Penh · Ho Chi Minh City · Hải Phòng · Hà Nội · Vientiane · Kuala Lumpur · Singapore · Medan

200 400 600 800 1000 1200 1400 KILOMETRES

INDONESIA
Republic of Indonesia

Area Sq Km	1 919 445	Languages	Indonesian, local languages
Area Sq Miles	741 102	Religions	Sunni Muslim, Protestant, Roman
Population	231 627 000		Catholic, Hindu, Buddhist
Capital	Jakarta	Currency	Rupiah
		Organizations	APEC, ASEAN, OPEC, UN

Indonesia, the largest and most populous country in southeast Asia, consists of over thirteen thousand islands extending between the Pacific and Indian Oceans. Sumatra, Java, Sulawesi (Celebes), Kalimantan (two-thirds of Borneo) and Papua (formerly Irian Jaya, western New Guinea) make up ninety per cent of the land area. Most of Indonesia is mountainous and covered with rainforest or mangrove swamps, and there are over three hundred volcanoes, many active. Two-thirds of the population lives in the lowland areas of the islands of Java and Madura. The climate is tropical monsoon. Agriculture is the largest sector of the economy and Indonesia is among the world's top producers of rice, palm oil, tea, coffee, rubber and tobacco. Many goods are produced, including textiles, clothing, cement, tin, fertilizers and vehicles. Main exports are oil, natural gas, timber products and clothing. Main trading partners are Japan, the USA and Singapore. Indonesia is a relatively poor country, and ethnic tensions and civil unrest often hinder economic development.

NORTH KOREA
Democratic People's Republic of Korea

Area Sq Km	120 538	Languages	Korean
Area Sq Miles	46 540	Religions	Traditional beliefs, Chondoist, Buddhist
Population	23 790 000	Currency	North Korean won
Capital	P'yŏngyang	Organizations	UN

Occupying the northern half of the Korean peninsula in eastern Asia, North Korea is a rugged and mountainous country. The principal lowlands and the main agricultural areas are the plains in the southwest. More than half the population lives in urban areas, mainly on the coastal plains. North Korea has a continental climate, with cold, dry winters and hot, wet summers. Approximately one-third of the workforce is involved in agriculture, mainly growing food crops on cooperative farms. Various minerals, notably iron ore, are mined and are the basis of the country's heavy industries. Exports include minerals (lead, magnesite and zinc) and metal products (chiefly iron and steel). The economy declined after 1991, when ties to the former USSR and eastern bloc collapsed, and there have been serious food shortages.

PHILIPPINES
Republic of the Philippines

Area Sq Km	300 000	Languages	English, Filipino, Tagalog, Cebuano,
Area Sq Miles	115 831		local languages
Population	87 960 000	Religions	Roman Catholic, Protestant,
Capital	Manila		Sunni Muslim, Aglipayan
		Currency	Philippine peso
		Organizations	APEC, ASEAN, UN

The Philippines, in southeast Asia, consists of over seven thousand islands and atolls lying between the South China Sea and the Pacific Ocean. The islands of Luzon and Mindanao account for two-thirds of the land area. They and nine other fairly large islands are mountainous and forested. There are active volcanoes, and earthquakes and tropical storms are common. Most of the population lives in the plains on the larger islands or on the coastal strips. The climate is hot and humid with heavy monsoonal rainfall. Rice, coconuts, sugar cane, pineapples and bananas are the main agricultural crops, and fishing is also important. Main exports are electronic equipment, machinery and transport equipment, garments and coconut products. Foreign aid and remittances from workers abroad are important to the economy, which faces problems of high population growth rate and high unemployment. The USA and Japan are the main trading partners.

SOUTH KOREA
Republic of Korea

Area Sq Km	99 274	Languages	Korean
Area Sq Miles	38 330	Religions	Buddhist, Protestant, Roman Catholic
Population	48 224 000	Currency	South Korean won
Capital	Seoul (Sŏul)	Organizations	APEC, OECD, UN

The state consists of the southern half of the Korean Peninsula in eastern Asia and many islands lying off the western and southern coasts in the Yellow Sea. The terrain is mountainous, although less rugged than that of North Korea. Population density is high and the country is highly urbanized; most of the population lives on the western coastal plains and in the river basins of the Han-gang in the northwest and the Naktong-gang in the southeast. The climate is continental, with hot, wet summers and dry, cold winters. Arable land is limited by the mountainous terrain, but because of intensive farming South Korea is nearly self-sufficient in food. Sericulture (silk) is important, as is fishing, which contributes to exports. South Korea has few mineral resources, except for coal and tungsten. It has achieved high economic growth based mainly on export manufacturing. The main manufactured goods are cars, electronic and electrical goods, ships, steel, chemicals and toys, as well as textiles, clothing, footwear and food products. The USA and Japan are the main trading partners.

Conic Equidistant Projection

MILES 0   200   400   600   80

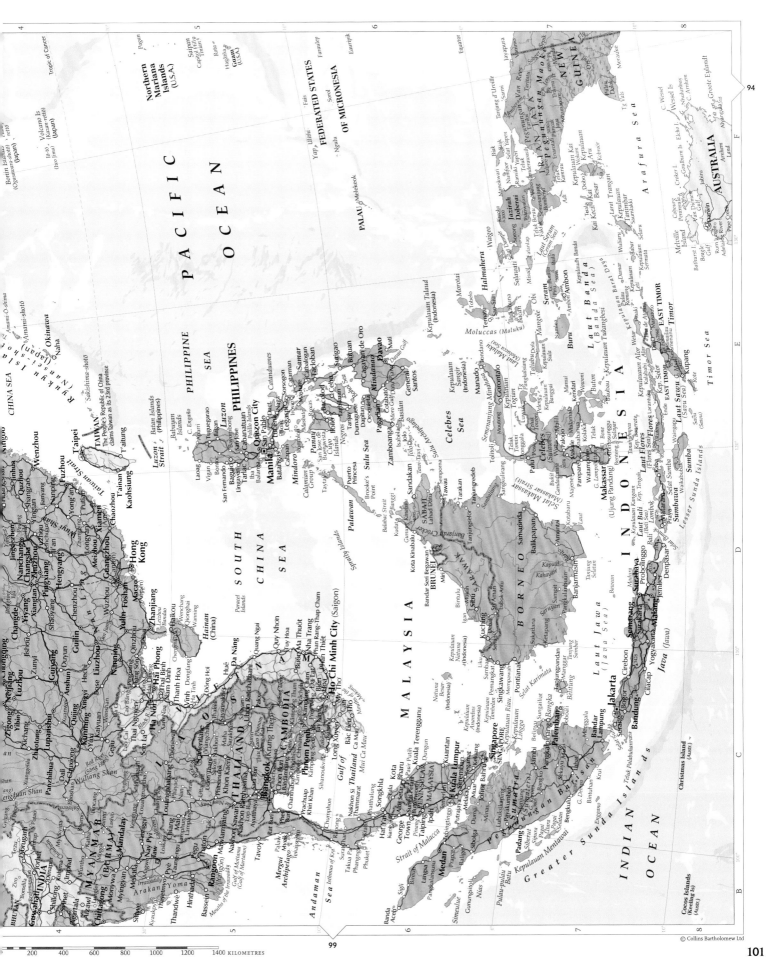

NORTHERN EUROPE

FINLAND

Republic of Finland

Area Sq Km	338 145	Languages	Finnish, Swedish
Area Sq Miles	130 559	Religions	Protestant, Greek Orthodox
Population	5 277 000	Currency	Euro
Capital	Helsinki (Helsingfors)	Organizations	EU, OECD, UN

Finland is in northern Europe, and nearly one-third of the country lies north of the Arctic Circle. Forests cover over seventy per cent of the land area, and ten per cent is covered by lakes. Summers are short and warm, and winters are long and severe, particularly in the north. Most of the population lives in the southern third of the country, along the coast or near the lakes. Timber is a major resource and there are important minerals, chiefly chromium. Main industries include metal working, electronics, paper and paper products, and chemicals. The main trading partners are Germany, Sweden and the UK.

GERMANY

Federal Republic of Germany

Area Sq Km	357 022	Languages	German, Turkish
Area Sq Miles	137 847	Religions	Protestant, Roman Catholic
Population	82 599 000	Currency	Euro
Capital	Berlin	Organizations	EU, NATO, OECD, UN

The central European state of Germany borders nine countries and has coastlines on the North and Baltic Seas. Behind the indented coastline, and covering about one-third of the country, is the north German plain, a region of fertile farmland and sandy heaths drained by the country's major rivers. The central highlands are a belt of forested hills and plateaus which stretch from the Eifel region in the west to the Erzgebirge mountains along the border with the Czech Republic. Farther south the land rises to the Swabian Alps (Schwäbische Alb), with the high rugged and forested Black Forest (Schwarzwald) in the southwest. In the far south the Bavarian Alps form the border with Austria. The climate is temperate, with continental conditions in eastern areas. The population is highly urbanized, with over eighty-five per cent living in cities and towns. With the exception of coal, lignite, potash and baryte, Germany lacks minerals and other industrial raw materials. It has a small agricultural base, although a few products (chiefly wines and beers) enjoy an international reputation. Germany is the world's third ranking economy after the USA and Japan. Its industries are amongst the world's most technologically advanced. Exports include machinery, vehicles and chemicals. The majority of trade is with other countries in the European Union, the USA and Japan.

SWEDEN

Kingdom of Sweden

Area Sq Km	449 964	Languages	Swedish
Area Sq Miles	173 732	Religions	Protestant, Roman Catholic
Population	9 119 000	Currency	Swedish krona
Capital	Stockholm	Organizations	EU, OECD, UN

Sweden occupies the eastern part of the Scandinavian peninsula in northern Europe and borders the Baltic Sea, the Gulf of Bothnia, and the Kattegat and Skagerrak, connecting with the North Sea. Forested mountains cover the northern half, part of which lies within the Arctic Circle. The southern part of the country is a lowland lake region where most of the population lives. Sweden has warm summers and cold winters, which are more severe in the north. Natural resources include coniferous forests, mineral deposits and water resources. Some dairy products, meat, cereals and vegetables are produced in the south. The forests supply timber for export and for the important pulp, paper and furniture industries. Sweden is an important producer of iron ore and copper. Zinc, lead, silver and gold are also mined. Machinery and transport equipment, chemicals, pulp and wood, and telecommunications equipment are the main exports. The majority of trade is with other European Union countries.

UNITED KINGDOM

United Kingdom of Great Britain and Northern Ireland

Area Sq Km	243 609	Languages	English, Welsh, Gaelic
Area Sq Miles	94 058	Religions	Protestant, Roman Catholic, Muslim
Population	60 769 000	Currency	Pound sterling
Capital	London	Organizations	Comm., EU, NATO, OECD, UN

The United Kingdom, in northwest Europe, occupies the island of Great Britain, part of Ireland, and many small adjacent islands. Great Britain comprises England, Scotland and Wales. England covers over half the land area and supports over four-fifths of the population, at its densest in the southeast. The English landscape is flat or rolling with some uplands, notably the Cheviot Hills on the Scottish border, the Pennines in the centre-north, and the hills of the Lake District in the northwest. Scotland consists of southern uplands, central lowlands, the Highlands (which include the UK's highest peak) and many islands. Wales is a land of hills, mountains and river valleys. Northern Ireland contains uplands, plains and the UK's largest lake, Lough Neagh. The climate of the UK is mild, wet and variable. There are few mineral deposits, but important energy resources. Agricultural activities involve sheep and cattle rearing, dairy farming, and crop and fruit growing in the east and southeast. Productivity is high, but approximately one-third of food is imported. The UK produces petroleum and natural gas from reserves in the North Sea and is self-sufficient in energy in net terms. Major manufactures are food and drinks, motor vehicles and parts, aerospace equipment, machinery, electronic and electrical equipment, and chemicals and chemical products. However, the economy is dominated by service industries, including banking, insurance, finance and business services. London, the capital, is one of the world's major financial centres. Tourism is also a major industry, with approximately twenty-five million visitors a year. International trade is also important, equivalent to one-third of national income. Over half of the UK's trade is with other European Union countries.

Conic Equidistant Projection

MILES 0   100   150   200   250   3

© Collins Bartholomew Ltd

SOUTHERN EUROPE AND THE MEDITERRANEAN

FRANCE
French Republic

Area Sq Km	543 965	Languages	French, Arabic
Area Sq Miles	210 026	Religions	Roman Catholic, Protestant, Sunni Muslim
Population	61 647 000		
Capital	Paris	Currency	Euro
		Organizations	EU, NATO, OECD, UN

France lies in western Europe and has coastlines on the Atlantic Ocean and the Mediterranean Sea. It includes the Mediterranean island of Corsica. Northern and western regions consist mostly of flat or rolling countryside, and include the major lowlands of the Paris basin, the Loire valley and the Aquitaine basin, drained by the Seine, Loire and Garonne river systems respectively. The centre-south is dominated by the hill region of the Massif Central. To the east are the Vosges and Jura mountains and the Alps. In the southwest, the Pyrenees form a natural border with Spain. The climate is temperate with warm summers and cool winters, although the Mediterranean coast has hot, dry summers and mild winters. Over seventy per cent of the population lives in towns, with almost a sixth of the population living in the Paris area. The French economy has a substantial and varied agricultural base. It is a major producer of both fresh and processed food. There are relatively few mineral resources; it has coal reserves, and some oil and natural gas, but it relies heavily on nuclear and hydroelectric power and imported fuels. France is one of the world's major industrial countries. Main industries include food processing, iron, steel and aluminium production, chemicals, cars, electronics and oil refining. The main exports are transport equipment, plastics and chemicals. Tourism is a major source of revenue and employment. Trade is predominantly with other European Union countries.

ITALY

Italian Republic

Area Sq Km	301 245	Languages	Italian
Area Sq Miles	116 311	Religions	Roman Catholic
Population	58 877 000	Currency	Euro
Capital	Rome (Roma)	Organizations	EU, NATO, OECD, UN

Most of the southern European state of Italy occupies a peninsula that juts out into the Mediterranean Sea. It includes the islands of Sicily and Sardinia and approximately seventy much smaller islands in the surrounding seas. Italy is mountainous, dominated by the Alps, which form its northern border, and the various ranges of the Apennines, which run almost the full length of the peninsula. Many of Italy's mountains are of volcanic origin, and its active volcanoes are Vesuvius, near Naples, Etna and Stromboli. The main lowland area, the Po river valley in the northeast, is the main agricultural and industrial area and is the most populous region. Italy has a Mediterranean climate, although the north experiences colder, wetter winters, with heavy snow in the Alps. Natural resources are limited, and only about twenty per cent of the land is suitable for cultivation. The economy is fairly diversified. Some oil, natural gas and coal are produced, but most fuels and minerals used by industry are imported. Agriculture is important, with cereals, vines, fruit and vegetables the main crops. Italy is the world's largest wine producer. The north is the centre of Italian industry, especially around Turin, Milan and Genoa. Leading manufactures include industrial and office equipment, domestic appliances, cars, textiles, clothing, leather goods, chemicals and metal products. There is a strong service sector, and with over twenty-five million visitors a year, tourism is a major employer and accounts for five per cent of the national income. Finance and banking are also important. Most trade is with other European Union countries.

SPAIN

Kingdom of Spain

Area Sq Km	504 782	Languages	Spanish, Castilian, Catalan, Galician, Basque
Area Sq Miles	194 897		
Population	44 279 000	Religions	Roman Catholic
Capital	Madrid	Currency	Euro
		Organizations	EU, NATO, OECD, UN

Spain occupies the greater part of the Iberian peninsula in southwest Europe, with coastlines on the Atlantic Ocean and Mediterranean Sea. It includes the Balearic Islands in the Mediterranean, the Canary Islands in the Atlantic, and two enclaves in north Africa (Ceuta and Melilla). Much of the mainland is a high plateau drained by the Douro (Duero), Tagus (Tajo) and Guadiana rivers. The plateau is interrupted by a low mountain range and bounded to the east and north also by mountains, including the Pyrenees, which form the border with France and Andorra. The main lowland areas are the Ebro basin in the northeast, the eastern coastal plains and the Guadalquivir basin in the southwest. Over three-quarters of the population lives in urban areas. The plateau experiences hot summers and cold winters. Conditions are cooler and wetter to the north, and warmer and drier to the south. Agriculture involves about ten per cent of the workforce, and fruit, vegetables and wine are exported. Fishing is an important industry, and Spain has a large fishing fleet. Mineral resources include lead, copper, mercury and fluorspar. Some oil is produced, but Spain has to import most energy needs. The economy is based mainly on manufacturing and services. The principal products are machinery, transport equipment, motor vehicles and food products, with a wide variety of other manufactured goods. With approximately fifty million visitors a year, tourism is a major industry. Banking and commerce are also important. Approximately seventy per cent of trade is with other European Union countries.

Conic Equidistant Projection

MILES 0   50   100   150   200   250   30

ALGERIA
People's Democratic Republic of Algeria

Area Sq Km	2 381 741	Languages	Arabic, French, Berber
Area Sq Miles	919 595	Religions	Sunni Muslim
Population	33 858 000	Currency	Algerian dinar
Capital	Algiers (Alger)	Organizations	OPEC, UN

Algeria, the second largest country in Africa, lies on the Mediterranean coast of northwest Africa and extends southwards to the Atlas Mountains and the dry sandstone plateau and desert of the Sahara. The climate ranges from Mediterranean on the coast to semi-arid and arid inland. The most populated areas are the coastal plains and the fertile northern slopes of the Atlas Mountains. Oil, natural gas and related products account for over ninety-five per cent of export earnings. Agriculture employs about a quarter of the workforce, producing mainly food crops. Algeria's main trading partners are Italy, France and the USA.

CAMEROON
Republic of Cameroon

Area Sq Km	475 442	Languages	French, English, Fang, Bamileke, local languages
Area Sq Miles	183 569		
Population	18 549 000	Religions	Roman Catholic, traditional beliefs, Sunni Muslim, Protestant
Capital	Yaoundé	Currency	CFA franc
		Organizations	Comm., UN

Cameroon is in west Africa, on the Gulf of Guinea. The coastal plains and southern and central plateaus are covered with tropical forest. Despite oil resources and favourable agricultural conditions Cameroon still faces problems of underdevelopment. Oil, timber and cocoa are the main exports. France is the main trading partner.

EGYPT
Arab Republic of Egypt

Area Sq Km	1 000 250	Languages	Arabic
Area Sq Miles	386 199	Religions	Sunni Muslim, Coptic Christian
Population	75 498 000	Currency	Egyptian pound
Capital	Cairo (Al Qāhirah)	Organizations	UN

Egypt, on the eastern Mediterranean coast of north Africa, is low-lying, with areas below sea level in the Qattara depression. It is a land of desert and semi-desert, except for the Nile valley, where ninety-nine per cent of Egyptians live. The Sinai peninsula in the northeast of the country forms the only land bridge between Africa and Asia. The summers are hot, the winters mild and rainfall is negligible. Less than four per cent of land (chiefly around the Nile floodplain and delta) is cultivated. Farming employs about one-third of the workforce; cotton is the main cash crop. Egypt imports over half its food needs. There are oil and natural gas reserves, although nearly a quarter of electricity comes from hydroelectric power. Main exports are oil and oil products, cotton, textiles and clothing.

LIBYA
Great Socialist People's Libyan Arab Jamahiriya

Area Sq Km	1 759 540	Languages	Arabic, Berber
Area Sq Miles	679 362	Religions	Sunni Muslim
Population	6 160 000	Currency	Libyan dinar
Capital	Tripoli (Ṭarābulus)	Organizations	OPEC, UN

Libya lies on the Mediterranean coast of north Africa. The desert plains and hills of the Sahara dominate the landscape and the climate is hot and dry. Most of the population lives in cities near the coast, where the climate is cooler with moderate rainfall. Farming and herding, chiefly in the northwest, are important but the main industry is oil. Libya is a major producer, and oil accounts for virtually all of its export earnings. Italy and Germany are the main trading partners.

SUDAN
Republic of the Sudan

Area Sq Km	2 505 813	Languages	Arabic, Dinka, Nubian, Beja, Nuer, local languages
Area Sq Miles	967 500		
Population	38 560 000	Religions	Sunni Muslim, traditional beliefs, Christian
Capital	Khartoum	Currency	Sudanese pound (Sudani)
		Organizations	UN

Africa's largest country, the Sudan is in the northeast of the continent, on the Red Sea. It lies within the upper Nile basin, much of which is arid plain but with swamps to the south. Mountains lie to the northeast, west and south. The climate is hot and arid with light summer rainfall, and droughts occur. Most people live along the Nile and are farmers and herders. Cotton, gum arabic, livestock and other agricultural products are exported. The government is working with foreign investors to develop oil resources, but civil war in the south and ethnic cleansing in Darfur continue to restrict the growth of the economy. Main trading partners are Saudi Arabia, China and Libya.

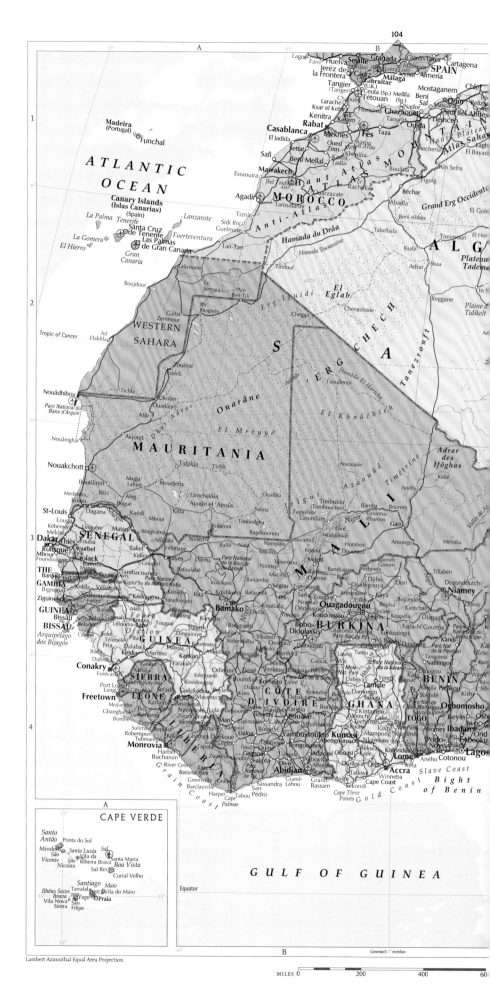

Lambert Azimuthal Equal Area Projection

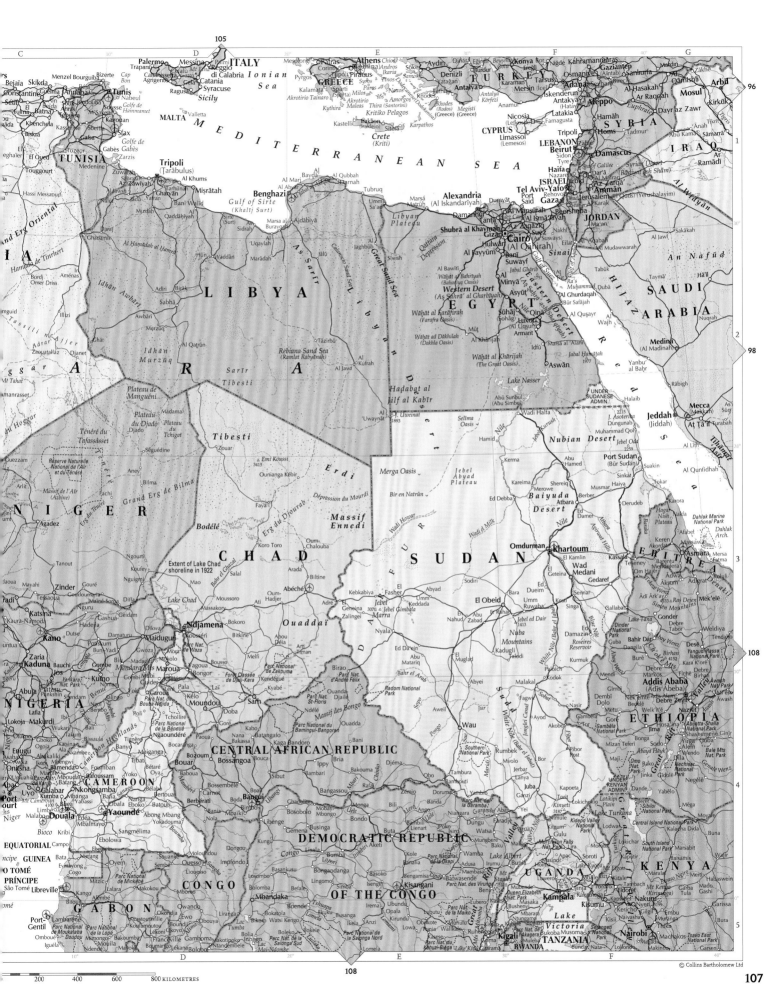

CONGO, DEMOCRATIC REPUBLIC OF THE

Area Sq Km	2 345 410	Languages	French, Lingala, Swahili, Kongo, local languages
Area Sq Miles	905 568		
Population	62 636 000	Religions	Christian, Sunni Muslim
Capital	Kinshasa	Currency	Congolese franc
		Organizations	SADC, UN

This central African state, formerly Zaire, consists of the basin of the Congo river flanked by plateaus, with high mountain ranges to the east and a short Atlantic coastline to the west. The climate is tropical, with rainforest close to the Equator and savanna to the north and south. Fertile land allows a range of food and cash crops to be grown, chiefly coffee. The country has vast mineral resources, with copper, cobalt and diamonds being the most important.

ETHIOPIA
Federal Democratic Republic of Ethiopia

Area Sq Km	1 133 880	Languages	Oromo, Amharic, Tigrinya, local languages
Area Sq Miles	437 794	Religions	Ethiopian Orthodox, Sunni Muslim, traditional beliefs
Population	83 099 000		
Capital	Addis Ababa (Ādīs Ābeba)	Currency	Birr
		Organizations	UN

A landlocked country in northeast Africa, Ethiopia comprises a mountainous region in the west which is traversed by the Great Rift Valley. The east is mostly arid plateau land. The highlands are warm with summer rainfall. Most people live in the central–northern area. In recent years civil war, conflict with Eritrea and poor infrastructure has hampered economic development. Subsistence farming is the main activity, although droughts have led to frequent famines. Coffee is the main export and there is some light industry. Ethiopia is one of the least developed countries in the world.

KENYA
Republic of Kenya

Area Sq Km	582 646	Languages	Swahili, English, local languages
Area Sq Miles	224 961	Religions	Christian, traditional beliefs
Population	37 538 000	Currency	Kenyan shilling
Capital	Nairobi	Organizations	Comm., UN

Kenya is in east Africa, on the Indian Ocean. Inland beyond the coastal plains the land rises to plateaus interrupted by volcanic mountains. The Great Rift Valley runs north-south to the west of the capital, Nairobi. Most of the population lives in the central area. Conditions are tropical on the coast, semi-desert in the north and savanna in the south. Hydroelectric power from the Upper Tana river provides most of the country's electricity. Agricultural products, mainly tea, coffee, fruit and vegetables, are the main exports. Light industry is important, and tourism, oil refining and re-exports for landlocked neighbours are major foreign exchange earners.

SOUTH AFRICA, REPUBLIC OF

Area Sq Km	1 219 090	Languages	Afrikaans, English, nine other official languages
Area Sq Miles	470 693		
Population	48 577 000	Religions	Protestant, Roman Catholic, Sunni Muslim, Hindu
Capital	Pretoria (Tshwane)/ Cape Town		
		Currency	Rand
		Organizations	Comm., SADC, UN

The Republic of South Africa occupies most of the southern part of Africa. It surrounds Lesotho and has a long coastline on the Atlantic and Indian Oceans. Much of the land is a vast plateau, covered with grassland or bush and drained by the Orange and Limpopo river systems. A fertile coastal plain rises to mountain ridges in the south and east, including Table Mountain near Cape Town and the Drakensberg range in the east. Gauteng is the most populous province, with Johannesburg and Pretoria its main cities. South Africa has warm summers and mild winters. Most of the country has the majority of its rainfall in summer, but the coast around Cape Town has winter rains. South Africa has the largest economy in Africa, although wealth is unevenly distributed and unemployment is very high. Agriculture employs approximately one-third of the workforce, and produce includes fruit, wine, wool and maize. The country is the world's leading producer of gold and chromium and an important producer of diamonds. Many other minerals are also mined. The main industries are mineral and food processing, chemicals, electrical equipment, textiles and motor vehicles. Financial services are also important.

ZIMBABWE
Republic of Zimbabwe

Area Sq Km	390 759	Languages	English, Shona, Ndebele
Area Sq Miles	150 873	Religions	Christian, traditional beliefs
Population	13 349 000	Currency	Zimbabwean dollar
Capital	Harare	Organizations	SADC, UN

Zimbabwe, a landlocked state in south-central Africa, consists of high plateaus flanked by the Zambezi river valley and Lake Kariba in the north and the Limpopo river in the south. Most of the population lives in the centre of the country. There are significant mineral resources, including gold, nickel, copper, asbestos, platinum and chromium. Agriculture is a major sector of the economy, with crops including tobacco, maize, sugar cane and cotton. Beef cattle are also important. Exports include tobacco, gold, ferroalloys, nickel and cotton. South Africa is the main trading partner. The economy has suffered recently through significant political unrest and instability.

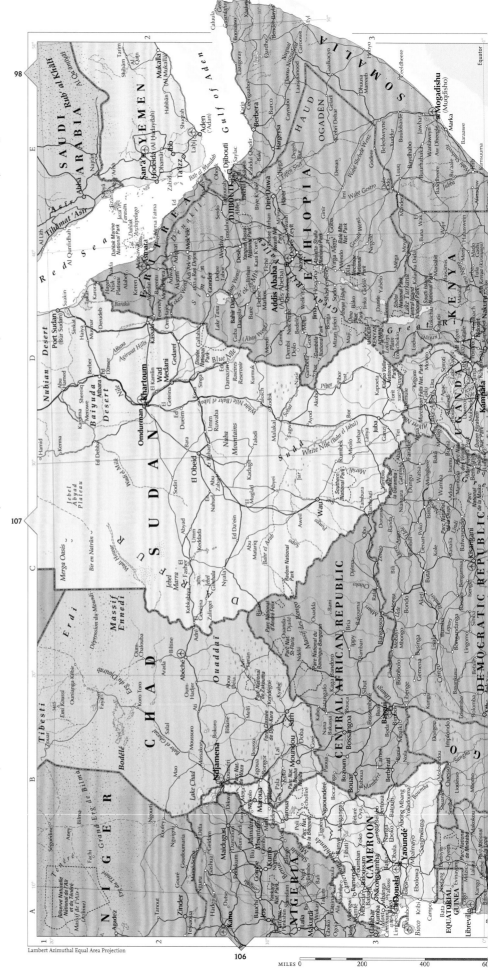

Lambert Azimuthal Equal Area Projection

MILES 0   200   400   60

© Collins Bartholomew Ltd

200   400   600   800   KILOMETRES

CANADA

 CANADA

Area Sq Km	9 984 670	Languages	English, French
Area Sq Miles	3 855 103	Religions	Roman Catholic, Protestant, Eastern Orthodox, Jewish
Population	32 876 000	Currency	Canadian dollar
Capital	Ottawa	Organizations	APEC, Comm., NATO, OECD, UN

The world's second largest country, Canada covers the northern two-fifths
of North America and has coastlines on the Atlantic, Arctic and Pacific
Oceans. In the west are the Coast Mountains, the Rocky Mountains and
interior plateaus. In the centre lie the fertile Prairies. Further east,
covering about half the total land area, is the Canadian Shield, a relatively
flat area of infertile lowlands around Hudson Bay, extending to Labrador
on the east coast. The Shield is bordered to the south by the fertile Great
Lakes-St Lawrence lowlands. In the far north climatic conditions are polar,
while the rest has a continental climate. Most Canadians live in the urban
areas of the Great Lakes-St Lawrence basin. Canada is rich in mineral and
energy resources. Only five per cent of land is arable. Canada is among the
world's leading producers of wheat, of wood from its vast coniferous
forests, and of fish and seafood from its Atlantic and Pacific fishing
grounds. It is a major producer of nickel, uranium, copper, iron ore, zinc
and other minerals, as well as oil and natural gas. Its abundant raw
materials are the basis for many manufacturing industries. Main exports
are machinery, motor vehicles, oil, timber, newsprint and paper, wood pulp
and wheat. Since the 1989 free trade agreement with the USA and the 1994
North America Free Trade Agreement, trade with the USA has grown and
now accounts for around seventy-five per cent of imports and around
eighty-five per cent of exports.

Greenland
Self-governing Danish Territory

Area Sq Km	2 175 600	Languages	Greenlandic, Danish
Area Sq Miles	840 004	Religions	Protestant
Population	58 000	Currency	Danish krone
Capital	Nuuk (Godthåb)		

Situated to the northeast of North America between the Atlantic and Arctic
Oceans, Greenland is the largest island in the world. It has a polar climate
and over eighty per cent of the land area is covered by permanent ice cap.
The economy is based on fishing and fish processing.

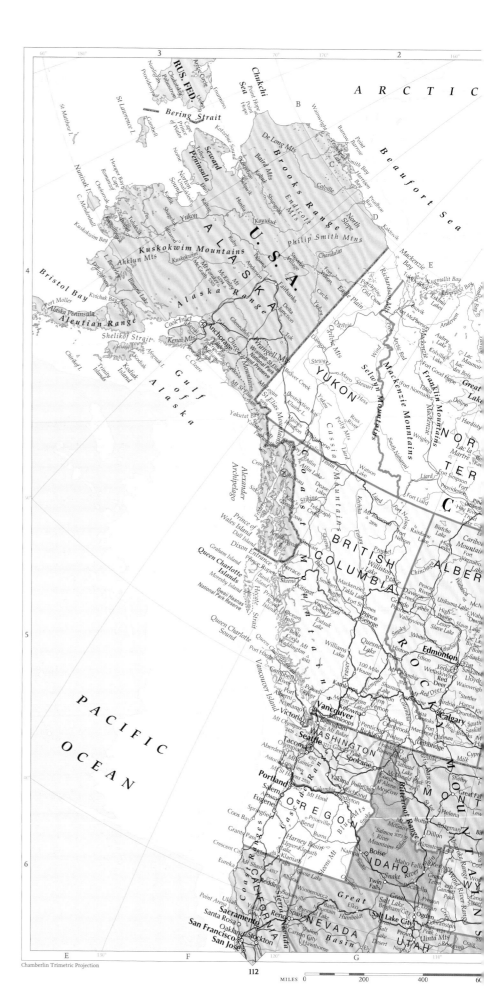

Chamberlin Trimetric Projection

MILES 0   200   400   60

© Collins Bartholomew Ltd

200   400   600   800   1000 KILOMETRES

UNITED STATES OF AMERICA

THE BAHAMAS

Commonwealth of the Bahamas

Area Sq Km	13 939	Languages	English, Creole
Area Sq Miles	5 382	Religions	Protestant, Roman Catholic
Population	331 000	Currency	Bahamian dollar
Capital	Nassau	Organizations	CARICOM, Comm., UN

The Bahamas, an archipelago made up of approximately seven hundred islands and over two thousand cays, lies to the northeast of Cuba and east of the Florida coast of the USA. Twenty-two islands are inhabited, and two-thirds of the population lives on the main island of New Providence. The climate is warm for much of the year, with heavy rainfall in the summer. Tourism is the islands' main industry. Offshore banking, insurance and ship registration are also major foreign exchange earners.

MEXICO

United Mexican States

Area Sq Km	1 972 545	Languages	Spanish, Amerindian languages
Area Sq Miles	761 604	Religions	Roman Catholic, Protestant
Population	106 535 000	Currency	Mexican peso
Capital	Mexico City	Organizations	APEC, OECD, UN

The largest country in Central America, Mexico extends south from the USA to Guatemala and Belize, and from the Pacific Ocean to the Gulf of Mexico. The greater part of the country is high plateau flanked by the western and eastern ranges of the Sierra Madre mountains. The principal lowland is the Yucatán peninsula in the southeast. The climate varies with latitude and altitude: hot and humid in the lowlands, warm on the plateau and cool with cold winters in the mountains. The north is arid, while the far south has heavy rainfall. Mexico City is the second largest conurbation in the world and the country's centre of trade and industry. Agriculture involves a fifth of the workforce; crops include grains, coffee, cotton and vegetables. Mexico is rich in minerals, including copper, zinc, lead, tin, sulphur, and silver. It is one of the world's largest producers of oil, from vast reserves in the Gulf of Mexico. The oil and petrochemical industries still dominate the economy, but a variety of manufactured goods are produced, including iron and steel, motor vehicles, textiles, chemicals and food and tobacco products. Tourism is growing in importance. Over three-quarters of all trade is with the USA.

UNITED STATES OF AMERICA
Federal Republic

Area Sq Km	9 826 635	Languages	English, Spanish
Area Sq Miles	3 794 085	Religions	Protestant, Roman Catholic, Sunni Muslim, Jewish
Population	305 826 000	Currency	United States dollar
Capital	Washington D.C.	Organizations	APEC, NATO, OECD, UN

The USA comprises forty-eight contiguous states in North America, bounded by Canada and Mexico, plus the states of Alaska, to the northwest of Canada, and Hawaii, in the north Pacific Ocean. The populous eastern states cover the Atlantic coastal plain (which includes the Florida peninsula and the Gulf of Mexico coast) and the Appalachian Mountains. The central states occupy a vast interior plain drained by the Mississippi-Missouri river system. To the west lie the Rocky Mountains, separated from the Pacific coastal ranges by intermontane plateaus. The Pacific coastal zone is also mountainous, and prone to earthquakes. Hawaii is a group of some twenty volcanic islands. Climatic conditions range between arctic in Alaska to desert in the intermontane plateaus. Most of the USA has a temperate climate, although the interior has continental conditions. There are abundant natural resources, including major reserves of minerals and energy resources. The USA has the largest and most technologically advanced economy in the world, based on manufacturing and services. Although agriculture accounts for approximately two per cent of national income, productivity is high and the USA is a net exporter of food, chiefly grains and fruit. Cotton is the major industrial crop. The USA produces iron ore, copper, lead, zinc, and many other minerals. It is a major producer of coal, petroleum and natural gas, although being the world's biggest energy user it imports significant quantities of petroleum and its products. Manufacturing is diverse. The main industries are petroleum, steel, motor vehicles, aerospace, telecommunications, electronics, food processing, chemicals and consumer goods. Tourism is a major foreign currency earner, with approximately forty-five million visitors a year. Other important service industries are banking and finance, Wall Street in New York being one of the world's major stock exchanges. Canada and Mexico are the main trading partners.

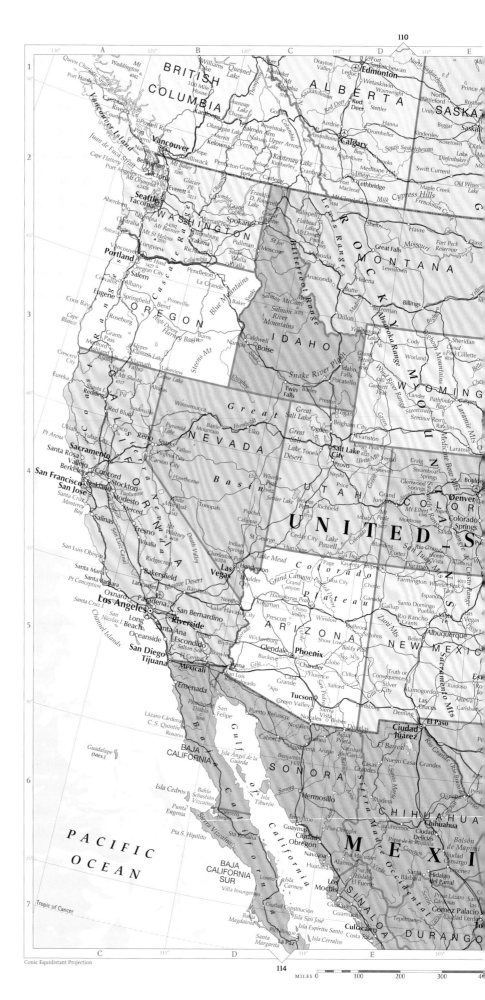

Conic Equidistant Projection

MILES 0   100   200   300   4

C A N A D A

MANITOBA

ONTARIO

QUÉBEC

NEW BRUNSWICK

MAINE

NORTH DAKOTA

SOUTH DAKOTA

MINNESOTA

WISCONSIN

MICHIGAN

VERMONT

NEW HAMPSHIRE

MASS.

NEBRASKA

IOWA

ILLINOIS

INDIANA

OHIO

PENNSYLVANIA

NEW YORK

CONN.

NEW JERSEY

KANSAS

MISSOURI

KENTUCKY

WEST VIRGINIA

VIRGINIA

MARYLAND

DEL.

TES OF AMERICA

OKLAHOMA

ARKANSAS

TENNESSEE

NORTH CAROLINA

SOUTH CAROLINA

GEORGIA

ALABAMA

MISSISSIPPI

TEXAS

LOUISIANA

FLORIDA

C O A S T A L   P L A I N

APPALACHIAN

Lake Winnipeg

Lake Superior

Lake Michigan

Lake Huron

Lake Erie

Lake Ontario

Lake Nipigon

James Bay

Winnipeg

Minneapolis

St Paul

Milwaukee

Chicago

Detroit

Cleveland

Toronto

Ottawa

Montréal

Québec

Boston

Providence

New York

Philadelphia

Baltimore

Washington D.C.

Richmond

Indianapolis

Cincinnati

Columbus

Pittsburgh

Buffalo

St Louis

Kansas City

Topeka

Wichita

Tulsa

Oklahoma City

Dallas

Fort Worth

Austin

San Antonio

Houston

Memphis

Little Rock

Nashville

Knoxville

Charlotte

Raleigh

Atlanta

Birmingham

Montgomery

Jackson

New Orleans

Baton Rouge

Shreveport

Corpus Christi

Monterrey

NUEVO LEÓN

TAMAULIPAS

COAHUILA

Jacksonville

Orlando

Tampa

St Petersburg

Miami

Fort Lauderdale

West Palm Beach

THE BAHAMAS

Nassau

Andros

ATLANTIC OCEAN

GULF OF MEXICO

Straits of Florida

Tropic of Cancer

100 200 300 400 500 600 KILOMETRES

© Collins Bartholomew Ltd

CENTRAL AMERICA AND THE CARIBBEAN

 ### BELIZE

Area Sq Km	22 965	**Languages**	English, Spanish, Mayan, Creole
Area Sq Miles	8 867	**Religions**	Roman Catholic, Protestant
Population	288 000	**Currency**	Belize dollar
Capital	Belmopan	**Organizations**	CARICOM, Comm., UN

Belize lies on the Caribbean coast of central America and includes numerous cays and a large barrier reef offshore. The coastal areas are flat and swampy. To the southwest are the Maya Mountains. Tropical jungle covers much of the country and the climate is humid tropical, but tempered by sea breezes. A third of the population lives in the capital. The economy is based primarily on agriculture, forestry and fishing, and exports include raw sugar, orange concentrate and bananas.

CUBA
Republic of Cuba

Area Sq Km	110 860	**Languages**	Spanish
Area Sq Miles	42 803	**Religions**	Roman Catholic, Protestant
Population	11 268 000	**Currency**	Cuban peso
Capital	Havana (La Habana)	**Organizations**	UN

The country comprises the island of Cuba (the largest island in the Caribbean), and many islets and cays. A fifth of Cubans live in and around Havana. Cuba is slowly recovering from the withdrawal of aid and subsidies from the former USSR. Sugar remains the basis of the economy, although tourism is developing and is, together with remittances from workers abroad, an important source of revenue.

DOMINICAN REPUBLIC

Area Sq Km	48 442	**Languages**	Spanish, Creole
Area Sq Miles	18 704	**Religions**	Roman Catholic, Protestant
Population	9 760 000	**Currency**	Dominican peso
Capital	Santo Domingo	**Organizations**	UN

The state occupies the eastern two-thirds of the Caribbean island of Hispaniola (the western third is Haiti). It has a series of mountain ranges, fertile valleys and a large coastal plain in the east. The climate is hot tropical, with heavy rainfall. Sugar, coffee and cocoa are the main cash crops. Nickel (the main export), and gold are mined, and there is some light industry. The USA is the main trading partner. Tourism is the main foreign exchange earner.

JAMAICA

Area Sq Km	10 991	**Languages**	English, Creole
Area Sq Miles	4 244	**Religions**	Protestant, Roman Catholic
Population	2 714 000	**Currency**	Jamaican dollar
Capital	Kingston	**Organizations**	CARICOM, Comm., UN

Jamaica, the third largest Caribbean island, has beaches and densely populated coastal plains traversed by hills and plateaus rising to the forested Blue Mountains in the east. The climate is tropical, but cooler and wetter on high ground. The economy is based on tourism, agriculture, mining and light manufacturing. Bauxite, aluminium oxide, sugar and bananas are the main exports. The USA is the main trading partner. Foreign aid is also significant.

NICARAGUA
Republic of Nicaragua

Area Sq Km	130 000	**Languages**	Spanish, Amerindian languages
Area Sq Miles	50 193	**Religions**	Roman Catholic, Protestant
Population	5 603 000	**Currency**	Córdoba
Capital	Managua	**Organizations**	UN

Nicaragua lies at the heart of Central America, with both Pacific and Caribbean coasts. Mountain ranges separate the east, which is largely rainforest, from the more developed western regions, which include Lake Nicaragua and some active volcanoes. The highest land is in the north. The climate is tropical. Nicaragua is one of the western hemisphere's poorest countries, and the economy is largely agricultural. Exports include coffee, seafood, cotton and bananas. The USA is the main trading partner. Nicaragua has a huge national debt, and relies heavily on foreign aid.

PANAMA
Republic of Panama

Area Sq Km	77 082	**Languages**	Spanish, English, Amerindian languages
Area Sq Miles	29 762		
Population	3 343 000	**Religions**	Roman Catholic, Protestant, Sunni Muslim
Capital	Panama City	**Currency**	Balboa
		Organizations	UN

Panama is the most southerly state in central America and has Pacific and Caribbean coasts. It is hilly, with mountains in the west and jungle near the Colombian border. The climate is tropical. Most of the population lives on the drier Pacific side. The economy is based mainly on services related to the Panama Canal: shipping, banking and tourism. Exports include bananas, shrimps, coffee, clothing and fish products. The USA is the main trading partner.

Lambert Azimuthal Equal Area Projection

MILES 0   200   4

SOUTH AMERICA NORTH

BOLIVIA
Republic of Bolivia

Area Sq Km	1 098 581	Languages	Spanish, Quechua, Aymara
Area Sq Miles	424 164	Religions	Roman Catholic, Protestant, Baha'i
Population	9 525 000	Currency	Boliviano
Capital	La Paz/Sucre	Organizations	UN

Bolivia is a landlocked state in central South America. Most Bolivians live on the high plateau within the Andes mountains. The lowlands range between dense rainforest in the northeast and semi-arid grasslands in the southeast. Bolivia is rich in minerals (zinc, tin and gold), and sales generate approximately half of export income. Natural gas, timber and soya beans are also exported. The USA is the main trading partner.

BRAZIL
Federative Republic of Brazil

Area Sq Km	8 514 879	Languages	Portuguese
Area Sq Miles	3 287 613	Religions	Roman Catholic, Protestant
Population	191 791 000	Currency	Real
Capital	Brasília	Organizations	UN

Brazil, in eastern South America, covers almost half of the continent, and is the world's fifth largest country. The northwest contains the vast basin of the Amazon, while the centre-west is largely a vast plateau of savanna and rock escarpments. The northeast is mostly semi-arid plateaus, while to the east and south are rugged mountains, fertile valleys and narrow, fertile coastal plains. The Amazon basin is hot, humid and wet; the rest of the country is cooler and drier, with seasonal variations. The northeast is drought-prone. Most Brazilians live in urban areas along the coast and on the central plateau. Brazil has well-developed agricultural, mining and service sectors, and the economy is larger than that of all other South American countries combined. Brazil is the world's biggest producer of coffee, and other agricultural crops include grains and sugar cane. Mineral production includes iron, aluminium and gold. Manufactured goods include food products, transport equipment, machinery and industrial chemicals. The main trading partners are the USA and Argentina. Despite its natural wealth, Brazil has a large external debt and a growing poverty gap.

COLOMBIA
Republic of Colombia

Area Sq Km	1 141 748	Languages	Spanish, Amerindian languages
Area Sq Miles	440 831	Religions	Roman Catholic, Protestant
Population	46 156 000	Currency	Colombian peso
Capital	Bogotá	Organizations	UN

A state in northwest South America, Colombia has coastlines on the Pacific Ocean and the Caribbean Sea. Behind coastal plains lie three ranges of the Andes mountains, separated by high valleys and plateaus where most Colombians live. To the southeast are grasslands and the forests of the Amazon. The climate is tropical, although temperatures vary with altitude. Only five per cent of land is cultivable. Coffee (Colombia is the world's second largest producer), sugar, bananas, cotton and flowers are exported. Coal, nickel, gold, silver, platinum and emeralds (Colombia is the world's largest producer) are mined. Oil and its products are the main export. Industries include the processing of minerals and crops. The main trade partner is the USA. Internal violence – both politically motivated and relating to Colombia's leading role in the international trade in illegal drugs – continues to hinder development.

ECUADOR
Republic of Ecuador

Area Sq Km	272 045	Languages	Spanish, Quechua, and other Amerindian languages
Area Sq Miles	105 037		
Population	13 341 000	Religions	Roman Catholic
Capital	Quito	Currency	United States dollar
		Organizations	OPEC, UN

Ecuador is in northwest South America, on the Pacific coast. It consists of a broad coastal plain, high mountain ranges in the Andes, and part of the forested upper Amazon basin to the east. The climate is tropical, moderated by altitude. Most people live on the coast or in the mountain valleys. Ecuador is one of South America's main oil producers, and mineral reserves include gold. Most of the workforce depends on agriculture. Petroleum, bananas, shrimps, coffee and cocoa are exported. The USA is the main trading partner.

PERU
Republic of Peru

Area Sq Km	1 285 216	Languages	Spanish, Quechua, Aymara
Area Sq Miles	496 225	Religions	Roman Catholic, Protestant
Population	27 903 000	Currency	Sol
Capital	Lima	Organizations	APEC, UN

Peru lies on the Pacific coast of South America. Most Peruvians live on the coastal strip and on the plateaus of the high Andes mountains. East of the Andes is the Amazon rainforest. The coast is temperate with low rainfall while the east is hot, humid and wet. Agriculture involves one-third of the workforce and fishing is also important. Agriculture and fishing have both been disrupted by the El Niño climatic effect in recent years. Sugar, cotton, coffee and, illegally, coca are the main cash crops. Copper and copper products, fishmeal, zinc products, coffee, petroleum and its products, and textiles are the main exports. The USA and the European Union are the main trading partners.

GALAPAGOS IS
(Ecuador)

Lambert Azimuthal Equal Area Projection

MILES 0   100   200   300

A T L A N T I C

O C E A N

Equator

Tropic of Capricorn

BRAZIL

GUYANA

SURINAME

French Guiana

PARAGUAY

ARGENTINA

Georgetown

Paramaribo

Cayenne

Manaus

Belém

São Luís

Fortaleza

Natal

João Pessoa

Recife

Maceió

Aracaju

Salvador

Brasília

Goiânia

Belo Horizonte

Vitória

Rio de Janeiro

São Paulo

Santos

Nova Iguaçu

Niterói

Campinas

Santo André

200 400 600 800 KILOMETRES

© Collins Bartholomew Ltd

SOUTH AMERICA SOUTH

ANTARCTICA

ARGENTINA
Argentine Republic

Area Sq Km	2 766 889	Languages	Spanish, Italian, Amerindian languages
Area Sq Miles	1 068 302		
Population	39 531 000	Religions	Roman Catholic, Protestant
Capital	Buenos Aires	Currency	Argentinian peso
		Organizations	UN

Argentina, the second largest state in South America, extends from Bolivia to Cape Horn and from the Andes mountains to the Atlantic Ocean. It has four geographical regions: subtropical forests and swampland in the northeast; temperate fertile plains or Pampas in the centre; the wooded foothills and valleys of the Andes in the west; and the cold, semi-arid plateaus of Patagonia in the south. The highest mountain in South America, Cerro Aconcagua, is in Argentina. Nearly ninety per cent of the population lives in towns and cities. The country is rich in natural resources including petroleum, natural gas, ores and precious metals. Agricultural products dominate exports, which also include motor vehicles and crude oil. Most trade is with Brazil and the USA.

CHILE
Republic of Chile

Area Sq Km	756 945	Languages	Spanish, Amerindian languages
Area Sq Miles	292 258	Religions	Roman Catholic, Protestant
Population	16 635 000	Currency	Chilean peso
Capital	Santiago	Organizations	APEC, UN

Chile lies along the Pacific coast of the southern half of South America. Between the Andes in the east and the lower coastal ranges is a central valley, with a mild climate, where most Chileans live. To the north is the arid Atacama Desert and to the south is cold, wet forested grassland. Chile has considerable mineral resources and is the world's leading exporter of copper. Nitrates, molybdenum, gold and iron ore are also mined. Agriculture (particularly viticulture), forestry and fishing are also important to the economy.

PARAGUAY
Republic of Paraguay

Area Sq Km	406 752	Languages	Spanish, Guaraní
Area Sq Miles	157 048	Religions	Roman Catholic, Protestant
Population	6 127 000	Currency	Guaraní
Capital	Asunción	Organizations	UN

Paraguay is a landlocked country in central South America, bordering Bolivia, Brazil and Argentina. The Paraguay river separates a sparsely populated western zone of marsh and flat alluvial plains from a more developed, hilly and forested region to the east and south. The climate is subtropical. Virtually all electricity is produced by hydroelectric plants, and surplus power is exported to Brazil and Argentina. The hydroelectric dam at Itaipú is one of the largest in the world. The mainstay of the economy is agriculture and related industries. Exports include cotton, soya bean and edible oil products, timber and meat. Brazil and Argentina are the main trading partners.

URUGUAY
Oriental Republic of Uruguay

Area Sq Km	176 215	Languages	Spanish
Area Sq Miles	68 037	Religions	Roman Catholic, Protestant, Jewish
Population	3 340 000	Currency	Uruguayan peso
Capital	Montevideo	Organizations	UN

Uruguay, on the Atlantic coast of central South America, is a low-lying land of prairies. The coast and the River Plate estuary in the south are fringed with lagoons and sand dunes. Almost half the population lives in the capital, Montevideo. Uruguay has warm summers and mild winters. The economy is based on cattle and sheep ranching, and the main industries produce food products, textiles and petroleum products. Meat, wool, hides, textiles and agricultural products are the main exports. Brazil and Argentina are the main trading partners.

Lambert Azimuthal Equal Area Projection

MILES 0   100   200   300   0   200   400   600 KILOMETRES

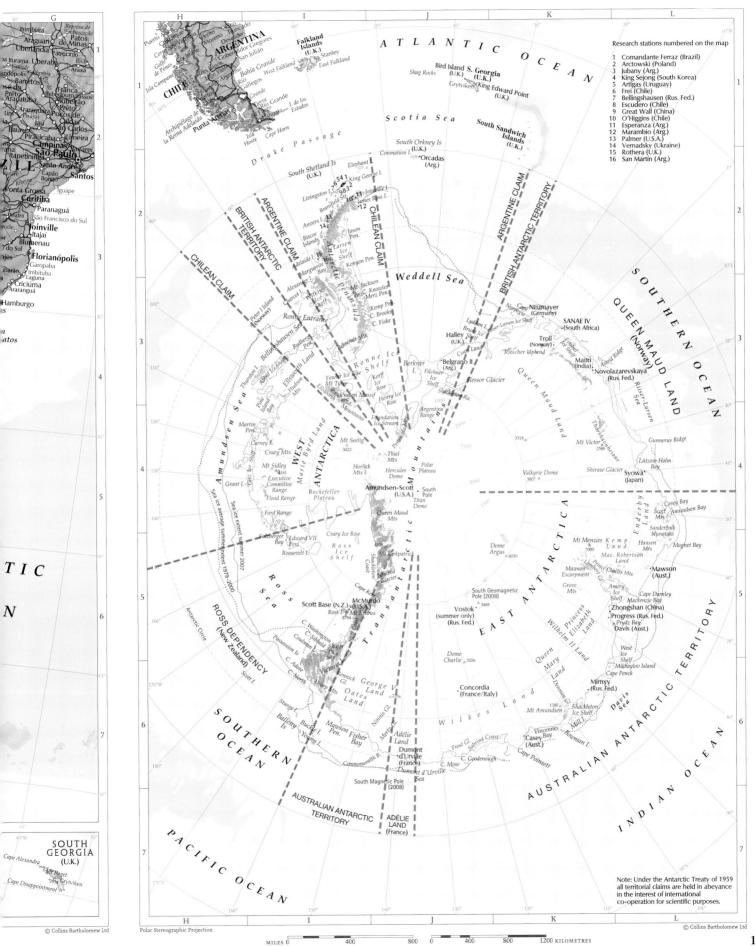

PACIFIC OCEAN

Stretching half way around the globe, the Pacific is the world's largest ocean and contains 45 per cent of the earth's water area. It is larger than the earth's continents combined and contains the earth's deepest point – Challenger Deep in the Mariana Trench 10 920 m (35 826 ft) deep. It includes hundreds of islands, including the main Pacific island groups of Polynesia (meaning many islands), Micronesia (small islands) and Melanesia (black islands). The ocean has an enormous effect on the world's climate, as a breeding ground for tropical storms and the source of the climatic phenomenon El Niño.

FACTS

- The Pacific was named by the 16th-century explorer Ferdinand Magellan after the calm waters he experienced there.

- The Panama Canal, 65 km (40 miles) long and opened in 1914, carries over 12 000 ships each year between the Pacific and Atlantic Oceans. It saves a journey of over 12 000 km (7457 miles) around the hazardous Cape Horn.

- The Pacific is estimated to contain over 315 million cu km (76 million cubic miles) of water and has an average depth of over 4000 m (13 123 ft).

- The countries adjoining the Pacific are often collectively referred to as the Pacific Rim.

TIME ZONES

The system of timekeeping throughout the world is based on twenty-four time zones, each stretching over fifteen degrees of longitude – the distance equivalent to a time difference of one hour. The prime, or Greenwich Meridian (zero degrees longitude), is the basis for Greenwich Mean Time (GMT), also known as Universal Coordinated Time (UTC), by which other time zones are measured.

This universal reference point was agreed by delegates from twenty-six countries at the International Meridian Conference in Washington D.C., in 1884. Prior to this, many separate central meridians were in use, for navigational and reference purposes, including London, Paris, Cadiz and Stockholm. Time zone boundaries can be altered to suit international or internal boundaries.

THE INTERNATIONAL DATE LINE

The International Date Line is an imaginary line passing down the Pacific Ocean at approximately 180 degrees west (or east) of Greenwich, across which the date changes by one day. To the left (west) of the line the date is always one day ahead of the right (east). If travelling eastwards across the line, travellers must move their calendars back one day.

The position and status of the line was agreed at the same conference at which Greenwich was adopted as the prime meridian. The line has no international legal status and countries near to it can choose which date they will observe. It was amended most recently so that Caroline Island, in the Pacific nation of Kiribati, would be the first land area to greet the year 2000. The island was renamed Millennium Island in recognition of this.

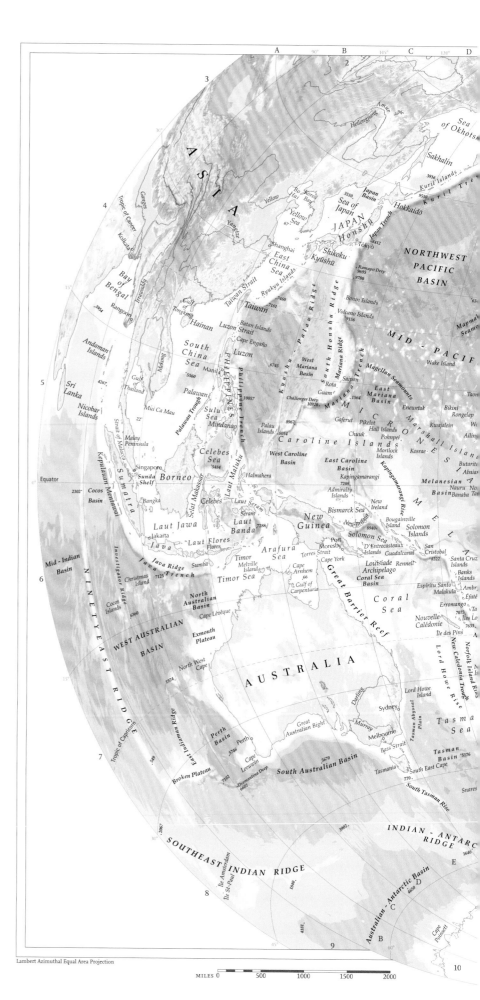

Lambert Azimuthal Equal Area Projection

MILES 0   500   1000   1500   2000

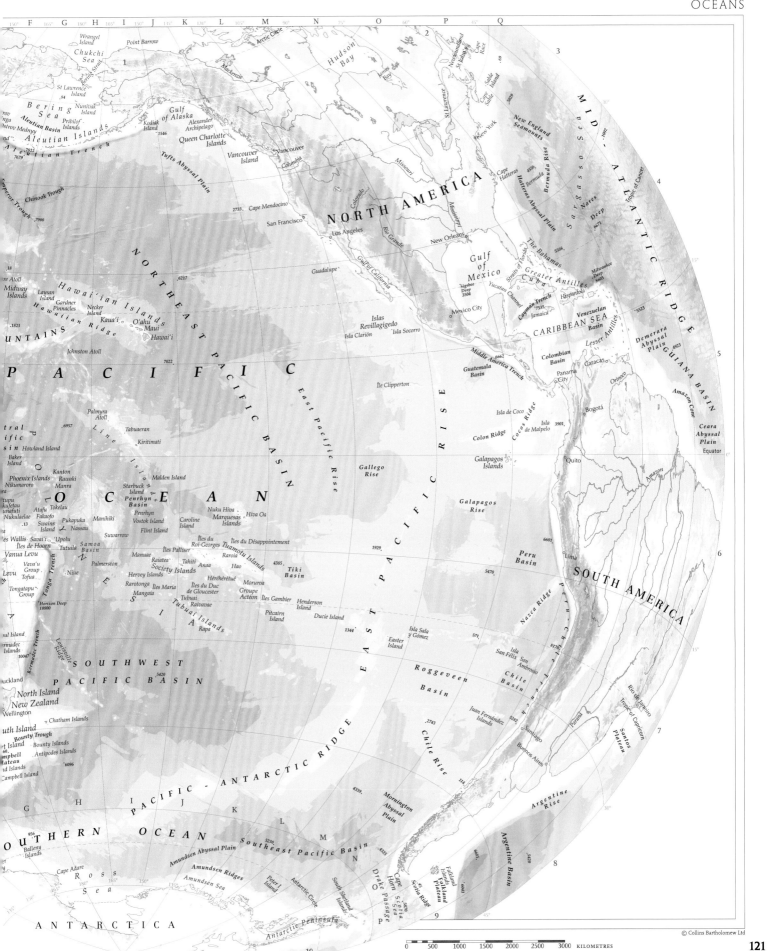

INDIAN OCEAN
ATLANTIC OCEAN

The Indian Ocean, which contains the Arabian Sea, the Bay of Bengal, the Red Sea and The Gulf, south of Cape Agulhas, the southernmost tip of Africa and also through the Suez Canal between the Mediterranean Sea and the Red Sea, joins the Atlantic Ocean. The Atlantic Ocean is the warmest and saltiest of the world's oceans. The Mediterranean Sea, the Gulf of Mexico, the Caribbean Sea and the Arctic Ocean are generally described as parts of the Atlantic. When combined together, these two oceans are still smaller than the Pacific.

FACTS

- The Mid-Atlantic ridge runs down the centre of the Atlantic. It marks the boundary between two of the Earth's tectonic plates and is an active volcanic zone which is pulling Europe and America apart at a rate of over 2 cm (almost one inch) per year.

- The major tsunami of December 2004 originated just off the coast of Sumatra and travelled the whole width of the Indian Ocean, hitting north Africa over six hours later.

- The North Atlantic Drift is an ocean current originating in the Gulf of Mexico. It carries warm water towards the Arctic Ocean and modifies the climate of northwest Europe.

OCEAN CONVEYOR BELT

All five of the world's oceans, Arctic, Atlantic, Indian, Pacific, and Southern are interlinked. Water is able to move freely creating one global ocean which covers more than 70 per cent of the earth's surface.

While surface winds drive ocean currents in the upper part of the ocean, the global Ocean Conveyor Belt, also know as the Thermohaline Circulation, moves water slowly thousands of metres below the surface.

As warm water moves north towards the Arctic it gradually cools. As sea ice forms, the remaining water becomes saltier and sinks. This initiates the circulation of the conveyor belt. However, this ocean circulation pattern could potentially be disrupted in the future. If increasing amounts of freshwater from melting glaciers and sea ice enter the ocean altering ocean salinity, this could have an impact on global climate.

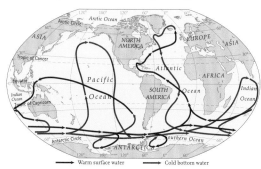

Ocean Conveyor Belt circulation

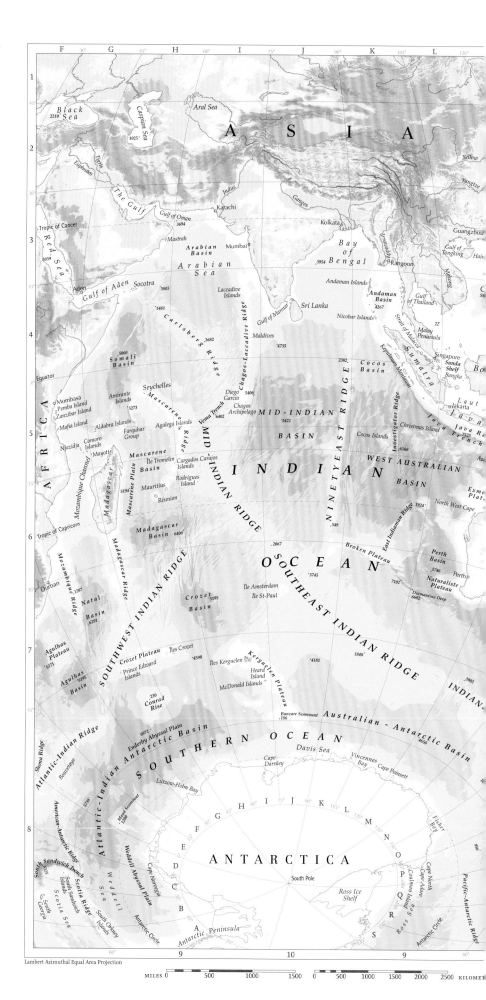

Lambert Azimuthal Equal Area Projection

MILES 0   500   1000   1500   0   500   1000   1500   2000   2500   KILOMET

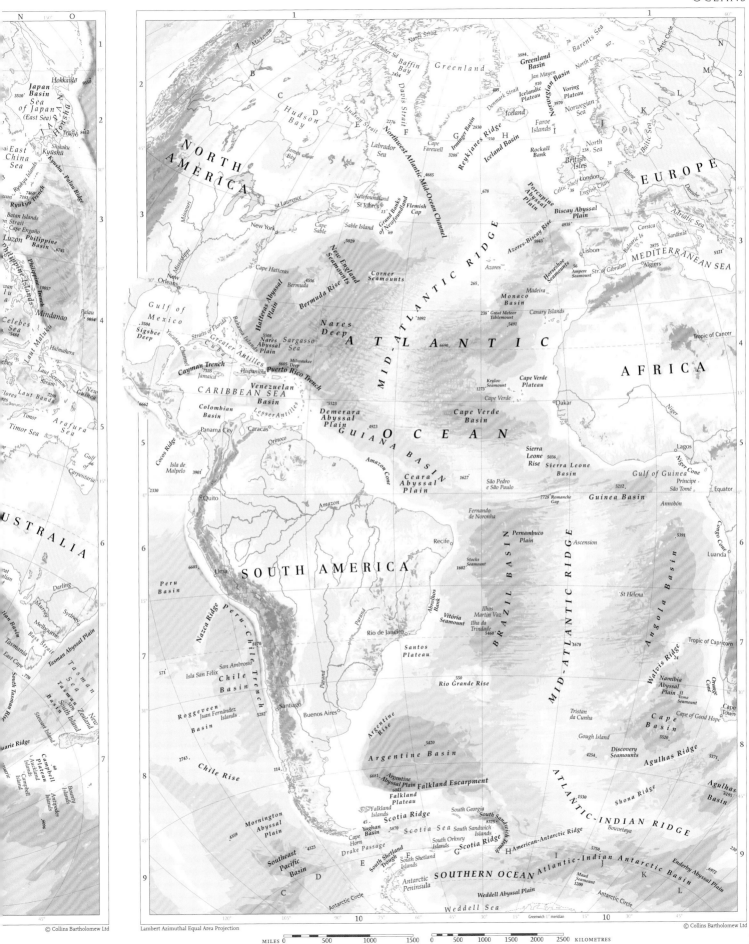

Lambert Azimuthal Equal Area Projection

MILES 0   500   1000   1500   0   500   1000   1500   2000   2500 KILOMETRES

ARCTIC OCEAN

Lying entirely within the Arctic Circle, a large proportion of the Arctic Ocean is permanently covered in sea ice, which in some places reaches a thickness of over 4 m (13 ft). It generates up to 50 000 icebergs per year. The ocean is almost landlocked, and is connected to the Pacific Ocean only by the narrow Bering Strait – an important shipping route for Russian merchant ships. Its main connection with the Atlantic Ocean is the Greenland Sea. It is the smallest and shallowest of the oceans, and is often considered to be an extension of the Atlantic Ocean.

FACTS

• Sea ice extent varies seasonally. For monitoring of sea ice go to www.nsidc.org

• Many features in the Arctic are named after early explorers, including the Englishman John Davis, the Dutchman Willem Barents, Vitus Bering from Denmark and the Norwegian Fridtjof Nansen.

• The North Pole is believed to have been first visited by the American Robert Peary in 1909. The Magnetic Pole – north on a compass – lies approximately 900 km (560 miles) to the south, towards Canada.

• Due to the number of major rivers flowing into it and its low evaporation rate, the Arctic is the least salty of all the oceans. For details on polar research visit www.spri.cam.ac.uk

Aerial view of melting sea ice floes in the Arctic Ocean.

The Arctic regions of Alaska, northern Canada, Greenland, northern Scandinavia and Russian Federation contain the homelands of a diverse range of indigenous peoples. They are heavily dependent on the natural resources in the region. Recently conflicts have arisen with governments eager to exploit these rich resources. Some countries bordering the Arctic Ocean have also initiated claims to the sea floor below the Arctic Ocean, and Canada and the USA are in dispute over the seasonal waterway known as the Northwest Passage.

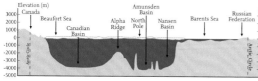

Cross-section of the Arctic Ocean from northwest Canada to northwest Russian Federation.

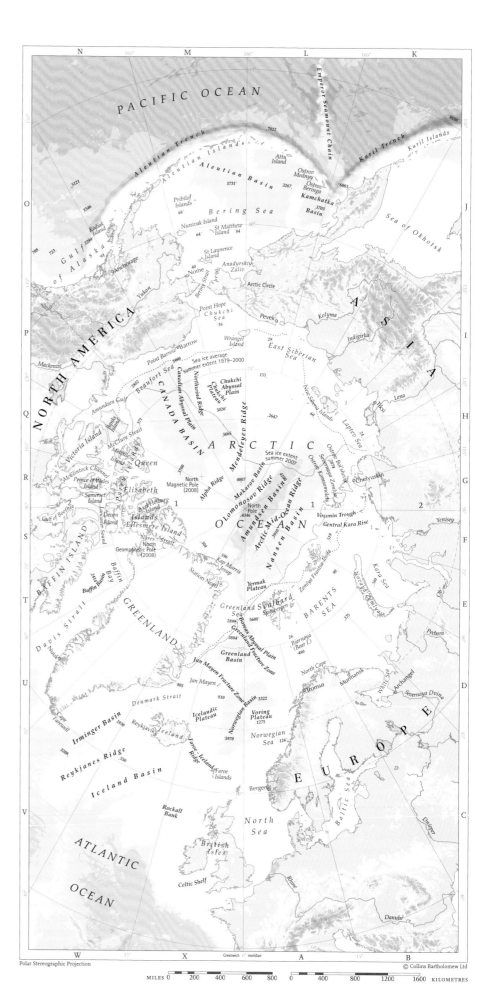

Polar Stereographic Projection

© Collins Bartholomew Ltd

AFGHANISTAN
Islamic Republic of Afghanistan

Area Sq Km	652 225	**Languages**	Dari, Pushtu, Uzbek, Turkmen
Area Sq Miles	251 825	**Religions**	Sunni Muslim, Shi'a Muslim
Population	27 145 000	**Currency**	Afghani
Capital	Kābul	**Organizations**	UN

A landlocked country in central Asia with central highlands bordered by plains in the north and southwest, and by the Hindu Kush mountains in the northeast. The climate is dry continental. Over the last twenty-five years war has disrupted the economy, which is highly dependent on farming and livestock rearing. Most trade is with the former USSR, Pakistan and Iran.

ALBANIA
Republic of Albania

Area Sq Km	28 748	**Languages**	Albanian, Greek
Area Sq Miles	11 100	**Religions**	Sunni Muslim, Albanian Orthodox, Roman Catholic
Population	3 190 000		
Capital	Tirana (Tiranë)	**Currency**	Lek
		Organizations	UN

Albania lies in the western Balkan Mountains in southeastern Europe, bordering the Adriatic Sea. It is mountainous, with coastal plains where half the population lives. The economy is based on agriculture and mining. Albania is one of the poorest countries in Europe and relies heavily on foreign aid.

American Samoa
United States Unincorporated Territory

Area Sq Km	197	**Languages**	Samoan, English
Area Sq Miles	76	**Religions**	Protestant, Roman Catholic
Population	67 000	**Currency**	United States dollar
Capital	Fagatogo		

Lying in the south Pacific Ocean, American Samoa consists of five main islands and two coral atolls. The largest island is Tutuila. Tuna and tuna products are the main exports, and the main trading partner is the USA.

ANDORRA
Principality of Andorra

Area Sq Km	465	**Languages**	Spanish, Catalan, French
Area Sq Miles	180	**Religions**	Roman Catholic
Population	75 000	**Currency**	Euro
Capital	Andorra la Vella	**Organizations**	UN

A landlocked state in southwest Europe, Andorra lies in the Pyrenees mountain range between France and Spain. It consists of deep valleys and gorges, surrounded by mountains. Tourism, encouraged by the development of ski resorts, is the mainstay of the economy. Banking is also an important economic activity.

ANGOLA
Republic of Angola

Area Sq Km	1 246 700	**Languages**	Portuguese, Bantu, local languages
Area Sq Miles	481 354	**Religions**	Roman Catholic, Protestant, traditional beliefs
Population	17 024 000		
Capital	Luanda	**Currency**	Kwanza
		Organizations	OPEC, SADC, UN

Angola lies on the Atlantic coast of south central Africa. Its small northern province, Cabinda, is separated from the rest of the country by part of the Democratic Republic of the Congo. Much of Angola is high plateau. In the west is a narrow coastal plain and in the southwest is desert. The climate is equatorial in the north but desert in the south. Over eighty per cent of the population relies on subsistence agriculture. Angola is rich in minerals (particularly diamonds), and oil accounts for approximately ninety per cent of export earnings. The USA, South Korea and Portugal are its main trading partners.

Anguilla
United Kingdom Overseas Territory

Area Sq Km	155	**Languages**	English
Area Sq Miles	60	**Religions**	Protestant, Roman Catholic
Population	13 000	**Currency**	East Caribbean dollar
Capital	The Valley		

Anguilla lies at the northern end of the Leeward Islands in the eastern Caribbean. Tourism and fishing form the basis of the economy.

ANTIGUA AND BARBUDA

Area Sq Km	442	**Languages**	English, Creole
Area Sq Miles	171	**Religions**	Protestant, Roman Catholic
Population	85 000	**Currency**	East Caribbean dollar
Capital	St John's	**Organizations**	CARICOM, Comm., UN

The state comprises the islands of Antigua, Barbuda and the tiny rocky outcrop of Redonda, in the Leeward Islands in the eastern Caribbean. Antigua, the largest and most populous island, is mainly hilly scrubland, with many beaches. The climate is tropical, and the economy relies heavily on tourism. Most trade is with other eastern Caribbean states and the USA.

ARMENIA
Republic of Armenia

Area Sq Km	29 800	**Languages**	Armenian, Azeri
Area Sq Miles	11 506	**Religions**	Armenian Orthodox
Population	3 002 000	**Currency**	Dram
Capital	Yerevan (Erevan)	**Organizations**	CIS, UN

A landlocked state in southwest Asia, Armenia lies in the south of the Lesser Caucasus mountains. It is a mountainous country with a continental climate. One-third of the population lives in the capital, Yerevan. Exports include diamonds, scrap metal and machinery. Many Armenians depend on remittances from abroad.

Aruba
Self-governing Netherlands Territory

Area Sq Km	193	**Languages**	Papiamento, Dutch, English
Area Sq Miles	75	**Religions**	Roman Catholic, Protestant
Population	104 000	**Currency**	Aruban florin
Capital	Oranjestad		

The most southwesterly of the islands in the Lesser Antilles in the Caribbean, Aruba lies just off the coast of Venezuela. Tourism, offshore finance and oil refining are the most important sectors of the economy. The USA is the main trading partner.

AUSTRIA
Republic of Austria

Area Sq Km	83 855	**Languages**	German, Croatian, Turkish
Area Sq Miles	32 377	**Religions**	Roman Catholic, Protestant
Population	8 361 000	**Currency**	Euro
Capital	Vienna (Wien)	**Organizations**	EU, OECD, UN

Two-thirds of Austria, a landlocked state in central Europe, lies within the Alps, with lower mountains to the north. The only lowlands are in the east. The Danube river valley in the northeast contains almost all the agricultural land and most of the population. Although the climate varies with altitude, in general summers are warm and winters cold with heavy snowfalls. Manufacturing industry and tourism are the most important sectors of the economy. Exports are dominated by manufactured goods. Germany is Austria's main trading partner.

AZERBAIJAN
Republic of Azerbaijan

Area Sq Km	86 600	**Languages**	Azeri, Armenian, Russian, Lezgian
Area Sq Miles	33 436	**Religions**	Shi'a Muslim, Sunni Muslim, Russian and Armenian Orthodox
Population	8 467 000		
Capital	Baku	**Currency**	Azerbaijani manat
		Organizations	CIS, UN

Azerbaijan lies to the southeast of the Caucasus mountains, on the Caspian Sea. Its region of Naxçıvan is separated from the rest of the country by part of Armenia. It has mountains in the northeast and west, valleys in the centre, and a low coastal plain. The climate is continental. It is rich in energy and mineral resources. Oil production, onshore and offshore, is the main industry and the basis of heavy industries. Agriculture is important, with cotton and tobacco the main cash crops.

BAHRAIN
Kingdom of Bahrain

Area Sq Km	691	**Languages**	Arabic, English
Area Sq Miles	267	**Religions**	Shi'a Muslim, Sunni Muslim, Christian
Population	753 000		
Capital	Manama	**Currency**	Bahraini dinar
		Organizations	UN

Bahrain consists of more than thirty islands lying in a bay in The Gulf, off the coasts of Saudi Arabia and Qatar. Bahrain Island, the largest island, is connected to other islands and to the mainland of Arabia by causeways. Oil production and processing are the main sectors of the economy.

BANGLADESH
People's Republic of Bangladesh

Area Sq Km	143 998	**Languages**	Bengali, English
Area Sq Miles	55 598	**Religions**	Sunni Muslim, Hindu
Population	158 665 000	**Currency**	Taka
Capital	Dhaka (Dacca)	**Organizations**	Comm., UN

The south Asian state of Bangladesh is in the northeast of the Indian subcontinent, on the Bay of Bengal. It consists almost entirely of the low-lying alluvial plains and deltas of the Ganges and Brahmaputra rivers. The southwest is swampy, with mangrove forests in the delta area. The north, northeast and southeast have low forested hills. Bangladesh is one of the world's most densely populated and least developed countries. The economy is based on agriculture, though the garment industry is the main export sector. Storms during the summer monsoon season often cause devastating flooding and crop destruction. The country relies on large-scale foreign aid and remittances from workers abroad.

BARBADOS

Area Sq Km	430	**Languages**	English, Creole
Area Sq Miles	166	**Religions**	Protestant, Roman Catholic
Population	294 000	**Currency**	Barbados dollar
Capital	Bridgetown	**Organizations**	CARICOM, Comm., UN

The most easterly of the Caribbean islands, Barbados is small and densely populated. It has a tropical climate and is subject to hurricanes. The economy is based on tourism, financial services, light industries and sugar production.

BELARUS
Republic of Belarus

Area Sq Km	207 600	**Languages**	Belorussian, Russian
Area Sq Miles	80 155	**Religions**	Belorussian Orthodox, Roman Catholic
Population	9 689 000		
Capital	Minsk	**Currency**	Belarus rouble
		Organizations	CIS, UN

Belarus, a landlocked state in eastern Europe, consists of low hills and plains, with many lakes, rivers and, in the south, extensive marshes. Forests cover approximately one-third of the country. It has a continental climate. Agriculture contributes one-third of national income, with beef cattle and grains as the major products. Manufacturing industries produce a range of items, from construction equipment to textiles. The Russian Federation and Ukraine are the main trading partners.

BELGIUM
Kingdom of Belgium

Area Sq Km	30 520	**Languages**	Dutch (Flemish), French (Walloon), German
Area Sq Miles	11 784		
Population	10 457 000	**Religions**	Roman Catholic, Protestant
Capital	Brussels (Bruxelles)	**Currency**	Euro
		Organizations	EU, NATO, OECD, UN

Belgium lies on the North Sea coast of western Europe. Beyond low sand dunes and a narrow belt of reclaimed land, fertile plains extend to the Sambre-Meuse river valley. The land rises to the forested Ardennes plateau in the southeast. Belgium has mild winters and cool summers. It is densely populated and has a highly urbanized population. With few mineral resources, Belgium imports raw materials for processing and manufacture. The agricultural sector is small, but provides for most food needs. A large services sector reflects Belgium's position as the home base for over eight hundred international institutions. The headquarters of the European Union are in the capital, Brussels.

BENIN
Republic of Benin

Area Sq Km	112 620	**Languages**	French, Fon, Yoruba, Adja, local languages
Area Sq Miles	43 483		
Population	9 033 000	**Religions**	Traditional beliefs, Roman Catholic, Sunni Muslim
Capital	Porto-Novo		
		Currency	CFA franc
		Organizations	UN

Benin is in west Africa, on the Gulf of Guinea. The climate is tropical in the north, equatorial in the south. The economy is based mainly on agriculture and transit trade. Agricultural products account for two-thirds of export earnings. Oil, produced offshore, is also a major export.

Bermuda
United Kingdom Overseas Territory

Area Sq Km	54	**Languages**	English
Area Sq Miles	21	**Religions**	Protestant, Roman Catholic
Population	65 000	**Currency**	Bermuda dollar
Capital	Hamilton		

In the Atlantic Ocean to the east of the USA, Bermuda comprises a group of small islands with a warm and humid climate. The economy is based on international business and tourism.

BHUTAN
Kingdom of Bhutan

Area Sq Km	46 620	**Languages**	Dzongkha, Nepali, Assamese
Area Sq Miles	18 000	**Religions**	Buddhist, Hindu
Population	658 000	**Currency**	Ngultrum, Indian rupee
Capital	Thimphu	**Organizations**	UN

Bhutan lies in the eastern Himalaya mountains, between China and India. It is mountainous in the north, with fertile valleys. The climate ranges between permanently cold in the far north and subtropical in the south. Most of the population is involved in livestock rearing and subsistence farming. Bhutan is the world's largest producer of cardamom. Tourism is an increasingly important foreign currency earner.

BOSNIA-HERZEGOVINA
Republic of Bosnia and Herzegovina

Area Sq Km	51 130	**Languages**	Bosnian, Serbian, Croatian
Area Sq Miles	19 741	**Religions**	Sunni Muslim, Serbian Orthodox, Roman Catholic, Protestant
Population	3 935 000		
Capital	Sarajevo	**Currency**	Marka
		Organizations	UN

Bosnia-Herzegovina lies in the western Balkan Mountains of southern Europe, on the Adriatic Sea. It is mountainous, with ridges running northwest- southeast. The main lowlands are around the Sava valley in the north. Summers are warm, but winters can be very cold. The economy relies heavily on overseas aid.

BOTSWANA
Republic of Botswana

Area Sq Km	581 370	**Languages**	English, Setswana, Shona, local languages
Area Sq Miles	224 468	**Religions**	Traditional beliefs, Protestant, Roman Catholic
Population	1 882 000	**Currency**	Pula
Capital	Gaborone	**Organizations**	Comm., SADC, UN

Botswana is a landlocked state in southern Africa. Over half of the country lies within the Kalahari Desert, with swamps to the north and salt-pans to the northeast. Most of the population lives near the eastern border. The climate is subtropical, but drought-prone. The economy was founded on cattle rearing, and although beef remains an important export, the economy is now based on mining. Diamonds account for seventy per cent of export earnings. Copper-nickel matte is also exported. Most trade is with other members of the Southern African Customs Union.

BRUNEI
Brunei Darussalam

Area Sq Km	5 765	**Languages**	Malay, English, Chinese
Area Sq Miles	2 226	**Religions**	Sunni Muslim, Buddhist, Christian
Population	390 000	**Currency**	Brunei dollar
Capital	Bandar Seri Begawan	**Organizations**	APEC, ASEAN, Comm., UN

The southeast Asian oil-rich state of Brunei lies on the northwest coast of the island of Borneo, on the South China Sea. Its two enclaves are surrounded by the Malaysian state of Sarawak. Tropical rainforest covers over two-thirds of the country. The economy is dominated by the oil and gas industries.

BULGARIA
Republic of Bulgaria

Area Sq Km	110 994	**Languages**	Bulgarian, Turkish, Romany, Macedonian
Area Sq Miles	42 855	**Religions**	Bulgarian Orthodox, Sunni Muslim
Population	7 639 000	**Currency**	Lev
Capital	Sofia (Sofiya)	**Organizations**	EU, NATO, UN

Bulgaria, in southern Europe, borders the western shore of the Black Sea. The Balkan Mountains separate the Danube plains in the north from the Rhodope Mountains and the lowlands in the south. The economy has a strong agricultural base. Manufacturing industries include machinery, consumer goods, chemicals and metals. Most trade is with the Russian Federation, Italy and Germany.

BURKINA
Democratic Republic of Burkina Faso

Area Sq Km	274 200	**Languages**	French, Moore (Mossi), Fulani, local languages
Area Sq Miles	105 869	**Religions**	Sunni Muslim, traditional beliefs, Roman Catholic
Population	14 784 000	**Currency**	CFA franc
Capital	Ouagadougou	**Organizations**	UN

Burkina, a landlocked country in west Africa, lies within the Sahara desert to the north and semi-arid savanna to the south. Rainfall is erratic, and droughts are common. Livestock rearing and farming are the main activities, and cotton, livestock, groundnuts and some minerals are exported. Burkina relies heavily on foreign aid, and is one of the poorest and least developed countries in the world.

BURUNDI
Republic of Burundi

Area Sq Km	27 835	**Languages**	Kirundi (Hutu, Tutsi), French
Area Sq Miles	10 747	**Religions**	Roman Catholic, traditional beliefs, Protestant
Population	8 508 000	**Currency**	Burundian franc
Capital	Bujumbura	**Organizations**	UN

The densely populated east African state of Burundi consists of high plateaus rising from the shores of Lake Tanganyika in the southwest. It has a tropical climate and depends on subsistence farming. Coffee is its main export, and its main trading partners are Germany and Belgium. The country has been badly affected by internal conflict since the early 1990s.

CAMBODIA
Kingdom of Cambodia

Area Sq Km	181 000	**Languages**	Khmer, Vietnamese
Area Sq Miles	69 884	**Religions**	Buddhist, Roman Catholic, Sunni Muslim
Population	14 444 000	**Currency**	Riel
Capital	Phnom Penh	**Organizations**	ASEAN, UN

Cambodia lies in southeast Asia on the Gulf of Thailand, and occupies the Mekong river basin, with the Tônlé Sap (Great Lake) at its centre. The climate is tropical monsoon. Forests cover half the country. Most of the population lives on the plains and is engaged in farming (chiefly rice growing), fishing and forestry. The economy is recovering slowly following the devastation of civil war in the 1970s.

CAPE VERDE
Republic of Cape Verde

Area Sq Km	4 033	**Languages**	Portuguese, Creole
Area Sq Miles	1 557	**Religions**	Roman Catholic, Protestant
Population	530 000	**Currency**	Cape Verde escudo
Capital	Praia	**Organizations**	UN

Cape Verde is a group of semi-arid volcanic islands lying off the coast of west Africa. The economy is based on fishing and subsistence farming but relies on emigrant workers' remittances and foreign aid.

Cayman Islands
United Kingdom Overseas Territory

Area Sq Km	259	**Languages**	English
Area Sq Miles	100	**Religions**	Protestant, Roman Catholic
Population	47 000	**Currency**	Cayman Islands dollar
Capital	George Town		

A group of islands in the Caribbean, northwest of Jamaica. There are three main islands: Grand Cayman, Little Cayman and Cayman Brac. The Cayman Islands are one of the world's major offshore financial centres. Tourism is also important to the economy.

CENTRAL AFRICAN REPUBLIC

Area Sq Km	622 436	**Languages**	French, Sango, Banda, Baya, local languages
Area Sq Miles	240 324	**Religions**	Protestant, Roman Catholic, traditional beliefs, Sunni Muslim
Population	4 343 000	**Currency**	CFA franc
Capital	Bangui	**Organizations**	UN

A landlocked country in central Africa, the Central African Republic is mainly savanna plateau, drained by the Ubangi and Chari river systems, with mountains to the east and west. The climate is tropical, with high rainfall. Most of the population lives in the south and west, and a majority of the workforce is involved in subsistence farming. Some cotton, coffee, tobacco and timber are exported, but diamonds account for around half of export earnings.

CHAD
Republic of Chad

Area Sq Km	1 284 000	**Languages**	Arabic, French, Sara, local languages
Area Sq Miles	495 755	**Religions**	Sunni Muslim, Roman Catholic, Protestant, traditional beliefs
Population	10 781 000	**Currency**	CFA franc
Capital	Ndjamena	**Organizations**	UN

Chad is a landlocked state of north-central Africa. It consists of plateaus, the Tibesti mountains in the north and the Lake Chad basin in the west. Climatic conditions range between desert in the north and tropical forest in the southwest. With few natural resources, Chad relies on subsistence farming, exports of raw cotton, and foreign aid. The main trading partners are France, Portugal and Cameroon.

Christmas Island
Australian External Territory

Area Sq Km	135	**Languages**	English
Area Sq Miles	52	**Religions**	Buddhist, Sunni Muslim, Protestant, Roman Catholic
Population	1 508		
Capital	The Settlement	**Currency**	Australian dollar

The island is situated in the east of the Indian Ocean, to the south of Indonesia. The economy was formerly based on phosphate extraction, although reserves are now nearly depleted. Tourism is developing and is a major employer.

Cocos Islands (Keeling Islands)
Australian External Territory

Area Sq Km	14	**Languages**	English
Area Sq Miles	5	**Religions**	Sunni Muslim, Christian
Population	621	**Currency**	Australian dollar
Capital	West Island		

The Cocos Islands consist of numerous islands on two coral atolls in the eastern Indian Ocean between Sri Lanka and Australia. Most of the population lives on West Island or Home Island. Coconuts are the only cash crop, and the main export.

COMOROS
Union of the Comoros

Area Sq Km	1 862	**Languages**	Comorian, French, Arabic
Area Sq Miles	719	**Religions**	Sunni Muslim, Roman Catholic
Population	839 000	**Currency**	Comoros franc
Capital	Moroni	**Organizations**	UN

This state, in the Indian Ocean off the east African coast, comprises three volcanic islands of Njazidja (Grande Comore), Nzwani (Anjouan) and Mwali (Mohéli), and some coral atolls. These tropical islands are mountainous, with poor soil and few natural resources. Subsistence farming predominates. Vanilla, cloves and ylang-ylang (an essential oil) are exported, and the economy relies heavily on workers' remittances from abroad.

CONGO
Republic of the Congo

Area Sq Km	342 000	**Languages**	French, Kongo, Monokutuba, local languages
Area Sq Miles	132 047	**Religions**	Roman Catholic, Protestant, traditional beliefs, Sunni Muslim
Population	3 768 000	**Currency**	CFA franc
Capital	Brazzaville	**Organizations**	UN

Congo, in central Africa, is mostly a forest or savanna-covered plateau drained by the Ubangi-Congo river systems. Sand dunes and lagoons line the short Atlantic coast. The climate is hot and tropical. Most Congolese live in the southern third of the country. Half of the workforce are farmers, growing food and cash crops including sugar, coffee, cocoa and oil palms. Oil and timber are the mainstays of the economy, and oil generates over fifty per cent of the country's export revenues.

Cook Islands
New Zealand Overseas Territory

Area Sq Km	293	**Languages**	English, Maori
Area Sq Miles	113	**Religions**	Protestant, Roman Catholic
Population	13 000	**Currency**	New Zealand dollar
Capital	Avarua		

These consist of groups of coral atolls and volcanic islands in the southwest Pacific Ocean. The main island is Rarotonga. Distance from foreign markets and restricted natural resources hinder development.

COSTA RICA
Republic of Costa Rica

Area Sq Km	51 100	**Languages**	Spanish
Area Sq Miles	19 730	**Religions**	Roman Catholic, Protestant
Population	4 468 000	**Currency**	Costa Rican colón
Capital	San José	**Organizations**	UN

Costa Rica, in central America, has coastlines on the Caribbean Sea and Pacific Ocean. From tropical coastal plains, the land rises to mountains and a temperate central plateau, where most of the population lives. The economy depends on agriculture and tourism, with ecotourism becoming increasingly important. Main exports are textiles, coffee and bananas, and almost half of all trade is with the USA.

CÔTE D'IVOIRE (Ivory Coast)
Republic of Côte d'Ivoire

Area Sq Km	322 463	**Languages**	French, Creole, Akan, local languages
Area Sq Miles	124 504	**Religions**	Sunni Muslim, Roman Catholic, traditional beliefs, Protestant
Population	19 262 000	**Currency**	CFA franc
Capital	Yamoussoukro	**Organizations**	UN

Côte d'Ivoire (Ivory Coast) is in west Africa, on the Gulf of Guinea. In the north are plateaus and savanna; in the south are low undulating plains and rainforest, with sand-bars and lagoons on the coast. Temperatures are warm, and rainfall is heavier in the south. Most of the workforce is engaged in farming. Côte d'Ivoire is a major producer of cocoa and coffee, and agricultural products (also including cotton and timber) are the main exports. Oil and gas have begun to be exploited.

CROATIA
Republic of Croatia

Area Sq Km	56 538	**Languages**	Croatian, Serbian
Area Sq Miles	21 829	**Religions**	Roman Catholic, Serbian Orthodox, Sunni Muslim
Population	4 555 000	**Currency**	Kuna
Capital	Zagreb	**Organizations**	NATO, UN

The southern European state of Croatia has a long coastline on the Adriatic Sea, with many offshore islands. Coastal areas have a Mediterranean climate; inland is cooler and wetter. Croatia was once strong agriculturally and industrially, but conflict in the early 1990s, and associated loss of markets and a fall in tourist revenue, caused economic difficulties from which recovery has been slow.

CYPRUS
Republic of Cyprus

Area Sq Km	9 251	**Languages**	Greek, Turkish, English
Area Sq Miles	3 572	**Religions**	Greek Orthodox, Sunni Muslim
Population	855 000	**Currency**	Euro
Capital	Nicosia (Lefkosia)	**Organizations**	Comm., EU, UN

The eastern Mediterranean island of Cyprus has effectively been divided into two since 1974. The economy of the Greek-speaking south is based mainly on specialist agriculture and tourism, with shipping and offshore banking. The ethnically Turkish north depends on agriculture, tourism and aid from Turkey. The island has hot dry summers and mild winters. Cyprus joined the European Union in May 2004.

CZECH REPUBLIC

Area Sq Km	78 864	**Languages**	Czech, Moravian, Slovakian
Area Sq Miles	30 450	**Religions**	Roman Catholic, Protestant
Population	10 186 000	**Currency**	Czech koruna
Capital	Prague (Praha)	**Organizations**	EU, NATO, OECD, UN

The landlocked Czech Republic in central Europe consists of rolling countryside, wooded hills and fertile valleys. The climate is continental. The country has substantial reserves of coal and lignite, timber and some minerals, chiefly iron ore. It is highly industrialized, and major manufactured goods include industrial machinery, consumer goods, cars, iron and steel, chemicals and glass. Germany is the main trading partner. The Czech Republic joined the European Union in May 2004.

DENMARK
Kingdom of Denmark

Area Sq Km	43 075	**Languages**	Danish
Area Sq Miles	16 631	**Religions**	Protestant
Population	5 442 000	**Currency**	Danish krone
Capital	Copenhagen (København)	**Organizations**	EU, NATO, OECD, UN

northern Europe, Denmark occupies the Jutland (Jylland) peninsula
d nearly five hundred islands in and between the North and Baltic Seas.
he country is low-lying, with long, indented coastlines. The climate is
ol and temperate, with rainfall throughout the year. A fifth of the
pulation lives in and around the capital, Copenhagen (København), on
e largest of the islands, Zealand (Sjælland). The country's main natural
source is its agricultural potential: two-thirds of the total area is fertile
rmland or pasture. Agriculture is high-tech, and with forestry and
shing employs only around six per cent of the workforce. Denmark is
lf-sufficient in oil and natural gas, produced from fields in the North
ea. Manufacturing, largely based on imported raw materials, accounts for
er half of all exports, which include machinery, food, furniture and
harmaceuticals. The main trading partners are Germany and Sweden.

DJIBOUTI
epublic of Djibouti

ea Sq Km	23 200	Languages	Somali, Afar, French, Arabic
ea Sq Miles	8 958	Religions	Sunni Muslim, Christian
opulation	833 000	Currency	Djibouti franc
pital	Djibouti	Organizations	UN

jibouti lies in northeast Africa, on the Gulf of Aden at the entrance to the
ed Sea. Most of the country is semi-arid desert with high temperatures and
w rainfall. More than two-thirds of the population live in the capital. There
some camel, sheep and goat herding, but with few natural resources the
onomy is based on services and trade. Djibouti serves as a free trade zone
r northern Africa, and the capital's port is a major transhipment and
fuelling destination. It is linked by rail to Addis Ababa in Ethiopia.

DOMINICA
ommonwealth of Dominica

rea Sq Km	750	Languages	English, Creole
rea Sq Miles	290	Religions	Roman Catholic, Protestant
opulation	67 000	Currency	East Caribbean dollar
pital	Roseau	Organizations	CARICOM, Comm., UN

ominica is the most northerly of the Windward Islands, in the eastern
aribbean. It is very mountainous and forested, with a coastline of steep
iffs. The climate is tropical and rainfall is abundant. Approximately a
uarter of Dominicans live in the capital. The economy is based on
griculture, with bananas (the major export), coconuts and citrus fruits the
ost important crops. Tourism is a developing industry.

EAST TIMOR
emocratic Republic of Timor-Leste

rea Sq Km	14 874	Languages	Portuguese, Tetun, English
rea Sq Miles	5 743	Religions	Roman Catholic
opulation	1 155 000	Currency	United States dollar
pital	Dili	Organizations	UN

he island of Timor is part of the Indonesian archipelago, to the north of
estern Australia. East Timor occupies the eastern section of the island, and
small coastal enclave (Ocussi) to the west. A referendum in 1999 ended
ndonesia's occupation, after which the country was under UN transitional
dministration until full independence was achieved in 2002. The economy
s in a poor state and East Timor is heavily dependent on foreign aid.

EL SALVADOR
epublic of El Salvador

rea Sq Km	21 041	Languages	Spanish
rea Sq Miles	8 124	Religions	Roman Catholic, Protestant
opulation	6 857 000	Currency	El Salvador colón, United States dollar
apital	San Salvador	Organizations	UN

ocated on the Pacific coast of central America, El Salvador consists of a
oastal plain and volcanic mountain ranges which enclose a densely
opulated plateau area. The coast is hot, with heavy summer rainfall; the
ighlands are cooler. Coffee (the chief export), sugar and cotton are the
ain cash crops. The main trading partners are the USA and Guatemala.

EQUATORIAL GUINEA
epublic of Equatorial Guinea

rea Sq Km	28 051	Languages	Spanish, French, Fang
rea Sq Miles	10 831	Religions	Roman Catholic, traditional beliefs
opulation	507 000	Currency	CFA franc
apital	Malabo	Organizations	UN

he state consists of Rio Muni, an enclave on the Atlantic coast of central
frica, and the islands of Bioco, Annobón and the Corisco group. Most of the
opulation lives on the coastal plain and upland plateau of Rio Muni. The
apital city, Malabo, is on the fertile volcanic island of Bioco. The climate is
ot, humid and wet. Oil production started in 1992, and oil is now the main
xport, along with timber. The economy depends heavily on foreign aid.

ERITREA
tate of Eritrea

rea Sq Km	117 400	Languages	Tigrinya, Tigre
rea Sq Miles	45 328	Religions	Sunni Muslim, Coptic Christian
opulation	4 851 000	Currency	Nakfa
apital	Asmara	Organizations	UN

ritrea, on the Red Sea coast of northeast Africa, consists of a high plateau
n the north with a coastal plain which widens to the south. The coast is
ot; inland is cooler. Rainfall is unreliable. The agriculture-based economy
as suffered from over thirty years of war and occasional poor rains. Eritrea
s one of the least developed countries in the world.

ESTONIA
Republic of Estonia

Area Sq Km	45 200	Languages	Estonian, Russian
Area Sq Miles	17 452	Religions	Protestant, Estonian and Russian Orthodox
Population	1 335 000	Currency	Kroon
Capital	Tallinn	Organizations	EU, NATO, UN

Estonia is in northern Europe, on the Gulf of Finland and the Baltic Sea.
The land, over one-third of which is forested, is generally low-lying with
many lakes. Approximately one-third of Estonians live in the capital,
Tallinn. Exported goods include machinery, wood products, textiles and
food products. The main trading partners are the Russian Federation,
Finland and Sweden. Estonia joined the European Union in May 2004.

Falkland Islands
United Kingdom Overseas Territory

Area Sq Km	12 170	Languages	English
Area Sq Miles	4 699	Religions	Protestant, Roman Catholic
Population	3 000	Currency	Falkland Islands pound
Capital	Stanley		

Lying in the southwest Atlantic Ocean, northeast of Cape Horn, two main
islands, West Falkland and East Falkland and many smaller islands, form
the territory of the Falkland Islands. The economy is based on sheep
farming and the sale of fishing licences.

Faroe Islands
Self-governing Danish Territory

Area Sq Km	1 399	Languages	Faroese, Danish
Area Sq Miles	540	Religions	Protestant
Population	49 000	Currency	Danish krone
Capital	Tórshavn		

A self-governing territory, the Faroe Islands lie in the north Atlantic Ocean
between the UK and Iceland. The islands benefit from the North Atlantic
Drift ocean current, which has a moderating effect on the climate. The
economy is based on deep-sea fishing.

French Guiana
French Overseas Department

Area Sq Km	90 000	Languages	French, Creole
Area Sq Miles	34 749	Religions	Roman Catholic
Population	202 000	Currency	Euro
Capital	Cayenne		

French Guiana, on the north coast of South America, is densely forested.
The climate is tropical, with high rainfall. Most people live in the coastal
strip, and agriculture is mostly subsistence farming. Forestry and fishing
are important, but mineral resources are largely unexploited and industry
is limited. French Guiana depends on French aid. The main trading
partners are France and the USA.

French Polynesia
French Overseas Country

Area Sq Km	3 265	Languages	French, Tahitian, Polynesian languages
Area Sq Miles	1 261	Religions	Protestant, Roman Catholic
Population	263 000	Currency	CFP franc
Capital	Papeete		

Extending over a vast area of the southeast Pacific Ocean, French Polynesia
comprises more than one hundred and thirty islands and coral atolls. The
main island groups are the Marquesas Islands, the Tuamotu Archipelago
and the Society Islands. The capital, Papeete, is on Tahiti in the Society
Islands. The climate is subtropical, and the economy is based on tourism.
The main export is cultured pearls.

GABON
Gabonese Republic

Area Sq Km	267 667	Languages	French, Fang, local languages
Area Sq Miles	103 347	Religions	Roman Catholic, Protestant, traditional beliefs
Population	1 331 000		
Capital	Libreville	Currency	CFA franc
		Organizations	UN

Gabon, on the Atlantic coast of central Africa, consists of low plateaus and a
coastal plain lined by lagoons and mangrove swamps. The climate is
tropical and rainforests cover over three-quarters of the land area. Over
seventy per cent of the population lives in towns. The economy is heavily
dependent on oil, which accounts for around seventy-five per cent of
exports; manganese, uranium and timber are the other main exports.
Agriculture is mainly at subsistence level.

THE GAMBIA
Republic of the Gambia

Area Sq Km	11 295	Languages	English, Malinke, Fulani, Wolof
Area Sq Miles	4 361	Religions	Sunni Muslim, Protestant
Population	1 709 000	Currency	Dalasi
Capital	Banjul	Organizations	Comm., UN

The Gambia, on the coast of west Africa, occupies a strip of land along the
lower Gambia river. Sandy beaches are backed by mangrove swamps,
beyond which is savanna. The climate is tropical, with most rainfall in the
summer. Over seventy per cent of Gambians are farmers, growing chiefly
groundnuts (the main export), cotton, oil palms and food crops. Livestock
rearing and fishing are important, while manufacturing is limited. Re-
exports, mainly from Senegal, and tourism are major sources of income.

Gaza
Semi-autonomous region

Area Sq Km	363	Languages	Arabic
Area Sq Miles	140	Religions	Sunni Muslim, Shi'a Muslim
Population	1 586 008	Currency	Israeli shekel
Capital	Gaza		

Gaza is a narrow strip of land on the southeast corner of the
Mediterranean Sea, between Egypt and Israel. This Palestinian
territory has limited autonomy from Israel, but hostilities between
Israel and the indigenous Arab population continue to restrict its
economic development.

GEORGIA
Republic of Georgia

Area Sq Km	69 700	Languages	Georgian, Russian, Armenian, Azeri, Ossetian, Abkhaz
Area Sq Miles	26 911	Religions	Georgian Orthodox, Russian Orthodox, Sunni Muslim
Population	4 395 000		
Capital	T'bilisi	Currency	Lari
		Organizations	CIS, UN

Georgia is in the northwest Caucasus area of southwest Asia, on the
eastern coast of the Black Sea. Mountain ranges in the north and south
flank the Kura and Rioni valleys. The climate is generally mild, and
along the coast it is subtropical. Agriculture is important, with tea,
grapes, and citrus fruits the main crops. Mineral resources include
manganese ore and oil, and the main industries are steel, oil refining
and machine building. The main trading partners are the Russian
Federation and Turkey.

GHANA
Republic of Ghana

Area Sq Km	238 537	Languages	English, Hausa, Akan, local languages
Area Sq Miles	92 100	Religions	Christian, Sunni Muslim, traditional beliefs
Population	23 478 000		
Capital	Accra	Currency	Cedi
		Organizations	Comm., UN

A west African state on the Gulf of Guinea, Ghana is a land of plains
and low plateaus covered with savanna and rainforest. In the east is the
Volta basin and Lake Volta. The climate is tropical, with the highest
rainfall in the south, where most of the population lives. Agriculture
employs around sixty per cent of the workforce. Main exports are gold,
timber, cocoa, bauxite and manganese ore.

Gibraltar
United Kingdom Overseas Territory

Area Sq Km	7	Languages	English, Spanish
Area Sq Miles	3	Religions	Roman Catholic, Protestant, Sunni Muslim
Population	29 000		
Capital	Gibraltar	Currency	Gibraltar pound

Gibraltar lies on the south coast of Spain at the western entrance to the
Mediterranean Sea. The economy depends on tourism, offshore banking
and shipping services.

GREECE
Hellenic Republic

Area Sq Km	131 957	Languages	Greek
Area Sq Miles	50 949	Religions	Greek Orthodox, Sunni Muslim
Population	11 147 000	Currency	Euro
Capital	Athens (Athina)	Organizations	EU, NATO, OECD, UN

Greece comprises a mountainous peninsula in the Balkan region of
southeastern Europe and many islands in the Ionian, Aegean and
Mediterranean Seas. The islands make up over one-fifth of its area.
Mountains and hills cover much of the country. The main lowland
areas are the plains of Thessaly in the centre and around Thessaloniki
in the northeast. Summers are hot and dry while winters are mild and
wet, but colder in the north with heavy snowfalls in the mountains.
One-third of Greeks live in the Athens area. Employment in
agriculture accounts for approximately twenty per cent of the
workforce, and exports include citrus fruits, raisins, wine, olives and
olive oil. Aluminium and nickel are mined and a wide range of
manufactures are produced, including food products and tobacco,
textiles, clothing, and chemicals. Tourism is an important industry and
there is a large services sector. Most trade is with other European
Union countries.

GRENADA

Area Sq Km	378	Languages	English, Creole
Area Sq Miles	146	Religions	Roman Catholic, Protestant
Population	106 000	Currency	East Caribbean dollar
Capital	St George's	Organizations	CARICOM, Comm., UN

The Caribbean state comprises Grenada, the most southerly of the
Windward Islands, and the southern islands of the Grenadines. Grenada
has wooded hills, with beaches in the southwest. The climate is warm and
wet. Agriculture is the main activity, with bananas, nutmeg and cocoa the
main exports. Tourism is the main foreign exchange earner.

Guadeloupe

French Overseas Department

Area Sq Km	1 780	**Languages**	French, Creole
Area Sq Miles	687	**Religions**	Roman Catholic
Population	445 000	**Currency**	Euro
Capital	Basse-Terre		

Guadeloupe, in the Leeward Islands in the Caribbean, consists of two main islands (Basse-Terre and Grande-Terre, connected by a bridge), Marie-Galante, and a few outer islands. The climate is tropical, but moderated by trade winds. Bananas, sugar and rum are the main exports and tourism is a major source of income.

Guam

United States Unincorporated Territory

Area Sq Km	541	**Languages**	Chamorro, English, Tagalog
Area Sq Miles	209	**Religions**	Roman Catholic
Population	173 000	**Currency**	United States dollar
Capital	Hagåtña		

Lying at the south end of the Northern Mariana Islands in the western Pacific Ocean, Guam has a humid tropical climate. The island has a large US military base and the economy relies on that and on tourism.

GUATEMALA

Republic of Guatemala

Area Sq Km	108 890	**Languages**	Spanish, Mayan languages
Area Sq Miles	42 043	**Religions**	Roman Catholic, Protestant
Population	13 354 000	**Currency**	Quetzal, United States dollar
Capital	Guatemala City	**Organizations**	UN

The most populous country in Central America after Mexico, Guatemala has long Pacific and short Caribbean coasts separated by a mountain chain which includes several active volcanoes. The climate is hot tropical in the lowlands and cooler in the highlands, where most of the population lives. Farming is the main activity and coffee, sugar and bananas are the main exports. There is some manufacturing of clothing and textiles. The main trading partner is the USA.

Guernsey

United Kingdom Crown Dependency

Area Sq Km	78	**Languages**	English, French
Area Sq Miles	30	**Religions**	Protestant, Roman Catholic
Population	63 923	**Currency**	Pound sterling
Capital	St Peter Port		

Guernsey is one of the Channel Islands, lying off northern France. The dependency also includes the nearby islands of Alderney, Sark and Herm. Financial services are an important part of the island's economy.

GUINEA

Republic of Guinea

Area Sq Km	245 857	**Languages**	French, Fulani, Malinke, local languages
Area Sq Miles	94 926		
Population	9 370 000	**Religions**	Sunni Muslim, traditional beliefs, Christian
Capital	Conakry		
		Currency	Guinea franc
		Organizations	UN

Guinea is in west Africa, on the Atlantic Ocean. There are mangrove swamps along the coast, while inland are lowlands and the Fouta Djallon mountains and plateaus. To the east are savanna plains drained by the upper Niger river system. The southeast is hilly. The climate is tropical, with high coastal rainfall. Agriculture is the main activity, employing nearly eighty per cent of the workforce, with coffee, bananas and pineapples the chief cash crops. There are huge reserves of bauxite, which accounts for more than seventy per cent of exports. Other exports include aluminium oxide, gold, coffee and diamonds.

GUINEA-BISSAU

Republic of Guinea-Bissau

Area Sq Km	36 125	**Languages**	Portuguese, Crioulo, local languages
Area Sq Miles	13 948	**Religions**	Traditional beliefs, Sunni Muslim, Christian
Population	1 695 000		
Capital	Bissau	**Currency**	CFA franc
		Organizations	UN

Guinea-Bissau is on the Atlantic coast of west Africa. The mainland coast is swampy and contains many estuaries. Inland are forested plains, and to the east are savanna plateaus. The climate is tropical. The economy is based mainly on subsistence farming. There is little industry, and timber and mineral resources are largely unexploited. Cashews account for seventy per cent of exports. Guinea-Bissau is one of the least developed countries in the world.

GUYANA

Co-operative Republic of Guyana

Area Sq Km	214 969	**Languages**	English, Creole, Amerindian languages
Area Sq Miles	83 000	**Religions**	Protestant, Hindu, Roman Catholic, Sunni Muslim
Population	738 000		
Capital	Georgetown	**Currency**	Guyana dollar
		Organizations	CARICOM, Comm., UN

Guyana, on the northeast coast of South America, consists of highlands in the west and savanna uplands in the southwest. Most of the country is densely forested. A lowland coastal belt supports crops and most of the population. The generally hot, humid and wet conditions are modified along the coast by sea breezes. The economy is based on agriculture, bauxite, and forestry. Sugar, bauxite, gold, rice and timber are the main exports.

HAITI

Republic of Haiti

Area Sq Km	27 750	**Languages**	French, Creole
Area Sq Miles	10 714	**Religions**	Roman Catholic, Protestant, Voodoo
Population	9 598 000	**Currency**	Gourde
Capital	Port-au-Prince	**Organizations**	CARICOM, UN

Haiti, occupying the western third of the Caribbean island of Hispaniola, is a mountainous state with small coastal plains and a central valley. The Dominican Republic occupies the rest of the island. The climate is tropical, and is hottest in coastal areas. Haiti has few natural resources, is densely populated and relies on exports of local crafts and coffee, and remittances from workers abroad.

HONDURAS

Republic of Honduras

Area Sq Km	112 088	**Languages**	Spanish, Amerindian languages
Area Sq Miles	43 277	**Religions**	Roman Catholic, Protestant
Population	7 106 000	**Currency**	Lempira
Capital	Tegucigalpa	**Organizations**	UN

Honduras, in central America, is a mountainous and forested country with lowland areas along its long Caribbean and short Pacific coasts. Coastal areas are hot and humid with heavy summer rainfall; inland is cooler and drier. Most of the population lives in the central valleys. Coffee and bananas are the main exports, along with shellfish and zinc. Industry involves mainly agricultural processing.

HUNGARY

Republic of Hungary

Area Sq Km	93 030	**Languages**	Hungarian
Area Sq Miles	35 919	**Religions**	Roman Catholic, Protestant
Population	10 030 000	**Currency**	Forint
Capital	Budapest	**Organizations**	EU, NATO, OECD, UN

The Danube river flows north-south through central Hungary, a landlocked country in eastern Europe. In the east lies a great plain, flanked by highlands in the north. In the west low mountains and Lake Balaton separate a smaller plain and southern uplands. The climate is continental. Sixty per cent of the population lives in urban areas, and one-fifth lives in the capital, Budapest. Some minerals and energy resources are exploited, chiefly bauxite, coal and natural gas. Hungary has an industrial economy based on metals, machinery, transport equipment, chemicals and food products. The main trading partners are Germany and Austria. Hungary joined the European Union in May 2004.

ICELAND

Republic of Iceland

Area Sq Km	102 820	**Languages**	Icelandic
Area Sq Miles	39 699	**Religions**	Protestant
Population	301 000	**Currency**	Icelandic króna
Capital	Reykjavík	**Organizations**	NATO, OECD, UN

Iceland lies in the north Atlantic Ocean near the Arctic Circle, to the northwest of Scandinavia. The landscape is volcanic, with numerous hot springs, geysers, and approximately two hundred volcanoes. One-tenth of the country is covered by ice caps. Only coastal lowlands are cultivated and settled, and over half the population lives in the Reykjavik area. The climate is mild, moderated by the North Atlantic Drift ocean current and by southwesterly winds. The mainstays of the economy are fishing and fish processing, which account for seventy per cent of exports. Agriculture involves mainly sheep and dairy farming. Hydroelectric and geothermal energy resources are considerable. The main industries produce aluminium, ferro-silicon and fertilizers. Tourism, including ecotourism, is growing in importance.

IRAN

Islamic Republic of Iran

Area Sq Km	1 648 000	**Languages**	Farsi, Azeri, Kurdish, regional languages
Area Sq Miles	636 296		
Population	71 208 000	**Religions**	Shi'a Muslim, Sunni Muslim
Capital	Tehrān	**Currency**	Iranian rial
		Organizations	OPEC, UN

Iran is in southwest Asia, and has coasts on The Gulf, the Caspian Sea and the Gulf of Oman. In the east is a high plateau, with large salt pans and a vast sand desert. In the west the Zagros Mountains form a series of ridges, and to the north lie the Elburz Mountains. Most farming and settlement is on the narrow plain along the Caspian Sea and in the foothills of the north and west. The climate is one of extremes, with hot summers and very cold winters. Most of the light rainfall is in the winter months. Agriculture involves approximately one-third of the workforce. Wheat is the main crop, but fruit (especially dates) and pistachio nuts are grown for export. Petroleum (the main export) and natural gas are Iran's leading natural resources. Manufactured goods include carpets, clothing, food products and construction materials.

IRAQ

Republic of Iraq

Area Sq Km	438 317	**Languages**	Arabic, Kurdish, Turkmen
Area Sq Miles	169 235	**Religions**	Shi'a Muslim, Sunni Muslim, Christian
Population	28 993 000		
Capital	Baghdād	**Currency**	Iraqi dinar
		Organizations	OPEC, UN

Iraq, in southwest Asia, has at its heart the lowland valley of the Tigris and Euphrates rivers. In the southeast, where the two rivers join, are the Mesopotamian marshes and the Shaṭṭ al 'Arab waterway leading to The Gulf. The north is hilly, while the west is mostly desert. Summers are hot and dry, and winters are mild with light, unreliable rainfall. The Tigris-Euphrates valley contains most of the country's arable land. One in five of the population lives in the capital, Baghdad. The economy has suffered following the 1991 Gulf War and the invasion of US-led coalition forces in 2005. The latter resulted in the overthrow of the dictator Saddam Hussein, but there is continuing internal instability. Oil is normally the main expor

IRELAND

Republic of Ireland

Area Sq Km	70 282	**Languages**	English, Irish
Area Sq Miles	27 136	**Religions**	Roman Catholic, Protestant
Population	4 301 000	**Currency**	Euro
Capital	Dublin (Baile Átha Cliath)	**Organizations**	EU, OECD, UN

The Irish Republic occupies some eighty per cent of the island of Ireland, in northwest Europe. It is a lowland country of wide valleys, lakes and peat bogs with isolated mountain ranges around the coast. The west coast is rugged an indented with many bays. The climate is mild due to the modifying effect of the North Atlantic Drift ocean current and rainfall is plentiful, although highest in the west. Nearly sixty per cent of the population lives in urban areas, Dublin and Cork being the main cities. Resources include natural gas, peat, lead and zinc. Agriculture, the traditional mainstay, now employs less than ten per cent of the workforce, while industry employs nearly thirty per cent. The main industries are electronics, pharmaceuticals and engineering a well as food processing, brewing and textiles. Service industries are expanding, with tourism a major earner. The UK is the main trading partne

Isle of Man

United Kingdom Crown Dependency

Area Sq Km	572	**Languages**	English
Area Sq Miles	221	**Religions**	Protestant, Roman Catholic
Population	79 000	**Currency**	Pound sterling
Capital	Douglas		

The Isle of Man lies in the Irish Sea between England and Northern Irelan The island is self-governing, although the UK is responsible for its defence and foreign affairs. It is not part of the European Union, but has a special relationship with the EU which allows for free trade. Eighty per cent of the economy is based on the service sector, particularly financial services.

ISRAEL

State of Israel

Area Sq Km	20 770	**Languages**	Hebrew, Arabic
Area Sq Miles	8 019	**Religions**	Jewish, Sunni Muslim, Christian, Druze
Population	6 928 000		
Capital	Jerusalem (Yerushalayim) (El Quds) De facto capital. Disputed.	**Currency**	Shekel
		Organizations	UN

Israel lies on the Mediterranean coast of southwest Asia. Beyond the coasta Plain of Sharon are the hills and valleys of Samaria, with the Galilee highlands to the north. In the east is a rift valley, which extends from Lake Tiberias (Sea of Galilee) to the Gulf of Aqaba and contains the Jordan river and the Dead Sea. In the south is the Negev, a triangular semi-desert plateau. Most of the population lives on the coastal plain or in northern and central areas. Much of Israel has warm summers and mild, wet winters The south is hot and dry. Agricultural production was boosted by the occupation of the West Bank in 1967. Manufacturing makes the largest contribution to the economy, and tourism is also important. Israel's main exports are machinery and transport equipment, software, diamonds, clothing, fruit and vegetables. The country relies heavily on foreign aid. Security issues relating to territorial disputes over the West Bank and Gaza have still to be resolved.

Jammu and Kashmir

Disputed territory (India/Pakistan/China)

Area Sq Km	222 236	**Population**	13 000 000
Area Sq Miles	85 806	**Capital**	Srinagar

A disputed region in the north of the Indian subcontinent, to the west of the Karakoram and Himalaya mountains. The 'Line of Control' separates the northwestern, Pakistani-controlled area and the southeastern, Indian-controlled area. China occupies the Himalayan section known as the Aksai Chin, which is also claimed by India.

Jersey

United Kingdom Crown Dependency

Area Sq Km	116	**Languages**	English, French
Area Sq Miles	45	**Religions**	Protestant, Roman Catholic
Population	88 200	**Currency**	Pound sterling
Capital	St Helier		

One of the Channel Islands lying off the west coast of the Cherbourg peninsula in northern France. Financial services are the most important part of the economy.

JORDAN

Hashemite Kingdom of Jordan

Area Sq Km	89 206	**Languages**	Arabic
Area Sq Miles	34 443	**Religions**	Sunni Muslim, Christian
Population	5 924 000	**Currency**	Jordanian dinar
Capital	'Ammān	**Organizations**	UN

Jordan, in southwest Asia, is landlocked apart from a short coastline on the Gulf of Aqaba. Much of the country is rocky desert plateau. To the west of the mountains, the land falls below sea level to the Dead Sea and the ıan river. The climate is hot and dry. Most people live in the northwest. ›sphates, potash, pharmaceuticals, fruit and vegetables are the main orts. The tourist industry is important, and the economy relies on ·kers' remittances from abroad and foreign aid.

AZAKHSTAN

ɔublic of Kazakhstan

ı Sq Km	2 717 300	Languages	Kazakh, Russian, Ukrainian, German, Uzbek, Tatar
ı Sq Miles	1 049 155	Religions	Sunni Muslim, Russian Orthodox, Protestant
›ulation	15 422 000	Currency	Tenge
ital	Astana (Akmola)	Organizations	CIS, UN

›etching across central Asia, Kazakhstan covers a vast area of steppe land l semi-desert. The land is flat in the west, with large lowlands around Caspian Sea, rising to mountains in the southeast. The climate is ıtinental. Agriculture and livestock rearing are important, and cotton l tobacco are the main cash crops. Kazakhstan is very rich in minerals, luding coal, chromium, gold, molybdenum, lead and zinc, and has ›stantial reserves of oil and gas. Mining, metallurgy, machine building l food processing are major industries. Oil, gas and minerals are the ıin exports, and the Russian Federation is the dominant trading partner.

IRIBATI

ɔublic of Kiribati

a Sq Km	717	Languages	Gilbertese, English
a Sq Miles	277	Religions	Roman Catholic, Protestant
›ulation	95 000	Currency	Australian dollar
›ital	Bairiki	Organizations	Comm., UN

·ibati, in the Pacific Ocean, straddles the Equator and comprises coral ınds in the Gilbert, Phoenix and Line Island groups and the volcanic ınd of Banaba. Most people live on the Gilbert Islands, and the capital, ıriki, is on Tarawa island in this group. The climate is hot, and wetter in : north. Copra and fish are exported. Kiribati relies on remittances from ·rkers abroad and foreign aid.

OSOVO

public of Kosovo

a Sq Km	10 908	Languages	Albanian, Serbian
a Sq Miles	4 212	Religions	Sunni Muslim, Serbian Orthodox
pulation	2 069 989	Currency	Euro
pital	Prishtinë (Priština)		

›sovo, traditionally an autonomous southern province of Serbia, was the :us of ethnic conflict between Serbs and the majority ethnic Albanians in : 1990s until international intervention in 1999, after which it was ministered by the UN. Kosovo declared its independence from Serbia in bruary 2008. The landscape is largely hilly or mountainous, especially ɔng the southern and western borders.

UWAIT

ıte of Kuwait

ea Sq Km	17 818	Languages	Arabic
ea Sq Miles	6 880	Religions	Sunni Muslim, Shi'a Muslim, Christian, Hindu
pulation	2 851 000	Currency	Kuwaiti dinar
pital	Kuwait (Al Kuwayt)	Organizations	OPEC, UN

ıwait lies on the northwest shores of The Gulf in southwest Asia. It is ainly low-lying desert, with irrigated areas along the bay, Kuwait Jun, ıere most people live. Summers are hot and dry, and winters are cool with me rainfall. The oil industry, which accounts for eighty per cent of ports, has largely recovered from the damage caused by the Gulf War in 91. Income is also derived from extensive overseas investments. Japan and e USA are the main trading partners.

ʏRGYZSTAN

rgyz Republic

ea Sq Km	198 500	Languages	Kyrgyz, Russian, Uzbek
ea Sq Miles	76 641	Religions	Sunni Muslim, Russian Orthodox
pulation	5 317 000	Currency	Kyrgyz som
pital	Bishkek (Frunze)	Organizations	CIS, UN

landlocked central Asian state, Kyrgyzstan is rugged and mountainous, ıng to the west of the Tien Shan mountain range. Most of the population ·es in the valleys of the north and west. Summers are hot and winters ld. Agriculture (chiefly livestock farming) is the main activity. Some oil d gas, coal, gold, antimony and mercury are produced. Manufactured ›ods include machinery, metals and metal products, which are the main ports. Most trade is with Germany, the Russian Federation, Kazakhstan d Uzbekistan.

AOS

ıo People's Democratic Republic

ea Sq Km	236 800	Languages	Lao, local languages
ea Sq Miles	91 429	Religions	Buddhist, traditional beliefs
pulation	5 859 000	Currency	Kip
pital	Vientiane (Viangchan)	Organizations	ASEAN, UN

landlocked country in southeast Asia, Laos is a land of mostly forested ountains and plateaus. The climate is tropical monsoon. Most of the ›pulation lives in the Mekong valley and the low plateau in the south, ıere food crops, chiefly rice, are grown. Hydroelectricity from a plant on e Mekong river, timber, coffee and tin are exported. Laos relies heavily on reign aid.

LATVIA

Republic of Latvia

Area Sq Km	63 700	Languages	Latvian, Russian
Area Sq Miles	24 595	Religions	Protestant, Roman Catholic, Russian Orthodox
Population	2 277 000	Currency	Lats
Capital	Rīga	Organizations	EU, NATO, UN

Latvia is in northern Europe, on the Baltic Sea and the Gulf of Riga. The land is flat near the coast but hilly with woods and lakes inland. The country has a modified continental climate. One-third of the people live in the capital, Rīga. Crop and livestock farming are important. There are few natural resources. Industries and main exports include food products, transport equipment, wood and wood products and textiles. The main trading partners are the Russian Federation and Germany. Latvia joined the European Union in May 2004.

LEBANON

Republic of Lebanon

Area Sq Km	10 452	Languages	Arabic, Armenian, French
Area Sq Miles	4 036	Religions	Shi'a Muslim, Sunni Muslim, Christian
Population	4 099 000	Currency	Lebanese pound
Capital	Beirut (Beyrouth)	Organizations	UN

Lebanon lies on the Mediterranean coast of southwest Asia. Beyond the coastal strip, where most of the population lives, are two parallel mountain ranges, separated by the Bekaa Valley (El Beq'a). The economy and infrastructure have been recovering since the 1975–1991 civil war crippled the traditional sectors of financial services and tourism. Italy, France and the UAE are the main trading partners.

LESOTHO

Kingdom of Lesotho

Area Sq Km	30 355	Languages	Sesotho, English, Zulu
Area Sq Miles	11 720	Religions	Christian, traditional beliefs
Population	2 008 000	Currency	Loti, South African rand
Capital	Maseru	Organizations	Comm., SADC, UN

Lesotho is a landlocked state surrounded by the Republic of South Africa. It is a mountainous country lying within the Drakensberg mountain range. Farming and herding are the main activities. The economy depends heavily on South Africa for transport links and employment. A major hydroelectric plant completed in 1998 allows the sale of water to South Africa. Exports include manufactured goods (mainly clothing and road vehicles), food, live animals, wool and mohair.

LIBERIA

Republic of Liberia

Area Sq Km	111 369	Languages	English, Creole, local languages
Area Sq Miles	43 000	Religions	Traditional beliefs, Christian, Sunni Muslim
Population	3 750 000	Currency	Liberian dollar
Capital	Monrovia	Organizations	UN

Liberia is on the Atlantic coast of west Africa. Beyond the coastal belt of sandy beaches and mangrove swamps the land rises to a forested plateau and highlands along the Guinea border. A quarter of the population lives along the coast. The climate is hot with heavy rainfall. Liberia is rich in mineral resources and forests. The economy is based on the production and export of basic products. Exports include diamonds, iron ore, rubber and timber. Liberia has a huge international debt and relies heavily on foreign aid.

LIECHTENSTEIN

Principality of Liechtenstein

Area Sq Km	160	Languages	German
Area Sq Miles	62	Religions	Roman Catholic, Protestant
Population	35 000	Currency	Swiss franc
Capital	Vaduz	Organizations	UN

A landlocked state between Switzerland and Austria, Liechtenstein has an industrialized, free-enterprise economy. Low business taxes have attracted companies to establish offices which provide approximately one-third of state revenues. Banking is also important. Major products include precision instruments, ceramics and textiles.

LITHUANIA

Republic of Lithuania

Area Sq Km	65 200	Languages	Lithuanian, Russian, Polish
Area Sq Miles	25 174	Religions	Roman Catholic, Protestant, Russian Orthodox
Population	3 390 000	Currency	Litas
Capital	Vilnius	Organizations	EU, NATO, UN

Lithuania is in northern Europe on the eastern shores of the Baltic Sea. It is mainly lowland with many lakes, rivers and marshes. Agriculture, fishing and forestry are important, but manufacturing dominates the economy. The main exports are machinery, mineral products and chemicals. The Russian Federation and Germany are the main trading partners. Lithuania joined the European Union in May 2004.

LUXEMBOURG

Grand Duchy of Luxembourg

Area Sq Km	2 586	Languages	Letzeburgish, German, French
Area Sq Miles	998	Religions	Roman Catholic
Population	467 000	Currency	Euro
Capital	Luxembourg	Organizations	EU, NATO, OECD, UN

Luxembourg, a small landlocked country in western Europe, borders Belgium, France and Germany. The hills and forests of the Ardennes dominate the north, with rolling pasture to the south, where the main towns, farms and industries are found. The iron and steel industry is still important, but light industries (including textiles, chemicals and food products) are growing. Luxembourg is a major banking centre. Main trading partners are Belgium, Germany and France.

MACEDONIA (F.Y.R.O.M.)

Republic of Macedonia

Area Sq Km	25 713	Languages	Macedonian, Albanian, Turkish
Area Sq Miles	9 928	Religions	Macedonian Orthodox, Sunni Muslim
Population	2 038 000	Currency	Macedonian denar
Capital	Skopje	Organizations	NATO, UN

The Former Yugoslav Republic of Macedonia is a landlocked state in southern Europe. Lying within the southern Balkan Mountains, it is traversed northwest-southeast by the Vardar valley. The climate is continental. The economy is based on industry, mining and agriculture, but conflicts in the region have reduced trade and caused economic difficulties. Foreign aid and loans are now assisting in modernization and development of the country.

MADAGASCAR

Republic of Madagascar

Area Sq Km	587 041	Languages	Malagasy, French
Area Sq Miles	226 658	Religions	Traditional beliefs, Christian, Sunni Muslim
Population	19 683 000	Currency	Malagasy franc
Capital	Antananarivo	Organizations	SADC, UN

Madagascar lies off the east coast of southern Africa. The world's fourth largest island, it is mainly a high plateau, with a coastal strip to the east and scrubby plain to the west. The climate is tropical, with heavy rainfall in the north and east. Most of the population lives on the plateau. Although the amount of arable land is limited, the economy is based on agriculture. The main industries are agricultural processing, textile manufacturing and oil refining. Foreign aid is important. Exports include coffee, vanilla, cotton cloth, sugar and shrimps. France is the main trading partner.

MALAWI

Republic of Malawi

Area Sq Km	118 484	Languages	Chichewa, English, local languages
Area Sq Miles	45 747	Religions	Christian, traditional beliefs, Sunni Muslim
Population	13 925 000	Currency	Malawian kwacha
Capital	Lilongwe	Organizations	Comm., SADC, UN

Landlocked Malawi in central Africa is a narrow hilly country at the southern end of the Great Rift Valley. One-fifth is covered by Lake Nyasa. Most of the population lives in rural areas in the southern regions. The climate is mainly subtropical, with varying rainfall. The economy is predominantly agricultural, with tobacco, tea and sugar the main exports. Malawi is one of the world's least developed countries and relies heavily on foreign aid. South Africa is the main trading partner.

MALAYSIA

Federation of Malaysia

Area Sq Km	332 965	Languages	Malay, English, Chinese, Tamil, local languages
Area Sq Miles	128 559	Religions	Sunni Muslim, Buddhist, Hindu, Christian, traditional beliefs
Population	26 572 000	Currency	Ringgit
Capital	Kuala Lumpur/ Putrajaya	Organizations	APEC, ASEAN, Comm., UN

Malaysia, in southeast Asia, comprises two regions, separated by the South China Sea. The western region occupies the southern Malay Peninsula, which has a chain of mountains dividing the eastern coastal strip from wider plains to the west. East Malaysia, consisting of the states of Sabah and Sarawak in the north of the island of Borneo, is mainly rainforest-covered hills and mountains with mangrove swamps along the coast. Both regions have a tropical climate with heavy rainfall. About eighty per cent of the population lives in Peninsular Malaysia. The country is rich in natural resources and has reserves of minerals and fuels. It is an important producer of tin, oil, natural gas and tropical hardwoods. Agriculture remains a substantial part of the economy, but industry is the most important sector. The main exports are transport and electronic equipment, oil, chemicals, palm oil, wood and rubber. The main trading partners are Japan, the USA and Singapore.

MALDIVES

Republic of the Maldives

Area Sq Km	298	Languages	Divehi (Maldivian)
Area Sq Miles	115	Religions	Sunni Muslim
Population	306 000	Currency	Rufiyaa
Capital	Male	Organizations	Comm., UN

The Maldive archipelago comprises over a thousand coral atolls (around two hundred of which are inhabited), in the Indian Ocean, southwest of India. Over eighty per cent of the land area is less than one metre above sea level. The main atolls are North and South Male and Addu. The climate is hot, humid and monsoonal. There is little cultivation and almost all food is imported. Tourism has expanded rapidly and is the most important sector of the economy.

MALI
Republic of Mali

Area Sq Km	1 240 140	Languages	French, Bambara, local languages	
Area Sq Miles	478 821	Religions	Sunni Muslim, traditional beliefs, Christian	
Population	12 337 000	Currency	CFA franc	
Capital	Bamako	Organizations	UN	

A landlocked state in west Africa, Mali is low-lying, with a few rugged hills in the northeast. Northern regions lie within the Sahara desert. To the south, around the Niger river, are marshes and savanna grassland. Rainfall is unreliable. Most of the population lives along the Niger and Falémé rivers. Exports include cotton, livestock and gold. Mali is one of the least developed countries in the world and relies heavily on foreign aid.

MALTA
Republic of Malta

Area Sq Km	316	Languages	Maltese, English
Area Sq Miles	122	Religions	Roman Catholic
Population	407 000	Currency	Euro
Capital	Valletta	Organizations	Comm., EU, UN

The islands of Malta and Gozo lie in the Mediterranean Sea, off the coast of southern Italy. The islands have hot, dry summers and mild winters. The economy depends on foreign trade, tourism and the manufacture of electronics and textiles. Main trading partners are the USA, France and Italy. Malta joined the European Union in May 2004.

MARSHALL ISLANDS
Republic of the Marshall Islands

Area Sq Km	181	Languages	English, Marshallese
Area Sq Miles	70	Religions	Protestant, Roman Catholic
Population	59 000	Currency	United States dollar
Capital	Delap-Uliga-Djarrit	Organizations	UN

The Marshall Islands consist of over a thousand atolls, islands and islets, within two chains in the north Pacific Ocean. The main atolls are Majuro (home to half the population), Kwajalein, Jaluit, Enewetak and Bikini. The climate is tropical, with heavy autumn rainfall. About half the workforce is employed in farming or fishing. Tourism is a small source of foreign exchange and the islands depend heavily on aid from the USA.

Martinique
French Overseas Department

Area Sq Km	1 079	Languages	French, Creole
Area Sq Miles	417	Religions	Roman Catholic, traditional beliefs
Population	399 000	Currency	Euro
Capital	Fort-de-France		

Martinique, one of the Caribbean Windward Islands, has volcanic peaks in the north, a populous central plain, and hills and beaches in the south. Tourism is a major source of foreign exchange, and substantial aid is received from France. The main trading partners are France and Guadeloupe.

MAURITANIA
Islamic Arab and African Republic of Mauritania

Area Sq Km	1 030 700	Languages	Arabic, French, local languages
Area Sq Miles	397 955	Religions	Sunni Muslim
Population	3 124 000	Currency	Ouguiya
Capital	Nouakchott	Organizations	UN

Mauritania is on the Atlantic coast of northwest Africa and lies almost entirely within the Sahara desert. Oases and a fertile strip along the Senegal river to the south are the only areas suitable for cultivation. The climate is generally hot and dry. About a quarter of Mauritanians live in the capital, Nouakchott. Most of the workforce depends on livestock rearing and subsistence farming. There are large deposits of iron ore which account for more than half of total exports. Mauritania's coastal waters are among the richest fishing grounds in the world. The main trading partners are France, Japan and Italy.

MAURITIUS
Republic of Mauritius

Area Sq Km	2 040	Languages	English, Creole, Hindi, Bhojpuri, French
Area Sq Miles	788		
Population	1 262 000	Religions	Hindu, Roman Catholic, Sunni Muslim
Capital	Port Louis	Currency	Mauritius rupee
		Organizations	Comm., SADC, UN

The state comprises Mauritius, Rodrigues and some twenty small islands in the Indian Ocean, east of Madagascar. The main island of Mauritius is volcanic in origin and has a coral coast, rising to a central plateau. Most of the population lives on the north and west sides of the island. The climate is warm and humid. The economy is based on sugar production, light manufacturing (chiefly clothing) and tourism.

Mayotte
French Departmental Collectivity

Area Sq Km	373	Languages	French, Mahorian
Area Sq Miles	144	Religions	Sunni Muslim, Christian
Population	186 026	Currency	Euro
Capital	Dzaoudzi		

Lying in the Indian Ocean off the east coast of central Africa, Mayotte is geographically part of the Comoro archipelago. The economy is based on agriculture, but Mayotte depends heavily on aid from France.

MICRONESIA, FEDERATED STATES OF

Area Sq Km	701	Languages	English, Chuukese, Pohnpeian, local languages
Area Sq Miles	271		
Population	111 000	Religions	Roman Catholic, Protestant
Capital	Palikir	Currency	United States dollar
		Organizations	UN

Micronesia comprises over six hundred atolls and islands of the Caroline Islands in the north Pacific Ocean. A third of the population lives on Pohnpei. The climate is tropical, with heavy rainfall. Fishing and subsistence farming are the main activities. Fish, garments and bananas are the main exports. Income is also derived from tourism and the licensing of foreign fishing fleets. The islands depend heavily on aid from the USA.

MOLDOVA
Republic of Moldova

Area Sq Km	33 700	Languages	Romanian, Ukrainian, Gagauz, Russian
Area Sq Miles	13 012	Religions	Romanian Orthodox, Russian Orthodox
Population	3 794 000		
Capital	Chișinău (Kishinev)	Currency	Moldovan leu
		Organizations	CIS, UN

Moldova lies between Romania and Ukraine in eastern Europe. It consists of hilly steppe land, drained by the Prut and Dniester rivers. Moldova has no mineral resources, and the economy is mainly agricultural, with sugar beet, tobacco, wine and fruit the chief products. Food processing, machinery and textiles are the main industries. The Russian Federation is the main trading partner.

MONACO
Principality of Monaco

Area Sq Km	2	Languages	French, Monégasque, Italian
Area Sq Miles	1	Religions	Roman Catholic
Population	33 000	Currency	Euro
Capital	Monaco-Ville	Organizations	UN

The principality occupies a rocky peninsula and a strip of land on France's Mediterranean coast. Monaco's economy depends on service industries (chiefly tourism, banking and finance) and light industry.

MONTENEGRO

Area Sq Km	13 812	Languages	Serbian (Montenegrin), Albanian
Area Sq Miles	5 333	Religions	Montenegrin Orthodox, Sunni Muslim
Population	598 000	Currency	Euro
Capital	Podgorica	Organizations	UN

Montenegro, previously a constituent republic of the former Yugoslavia, became an independent nation in June 2006 when it opted to split from the state union of Serbia and Montenegro. Montenegro separates the much larger Serbia from the Adriatic coast. The landscape is rugged and mountainous, and the climate Mediterranean.

Montserrat
United Kingdom Overseas Territory

Area Sq Km	100	Languages	English
Area Sq Miles	39	Religions	Protestant, Roman Catholic
Population	6 000	Currency	East Caribbean dollar
Capital	Brades	Organizations	CARICOM

An island in the Leeward Islands group in the Lesser Antilles, in the Caribbean. From 1995 to 1997 the volcanoes in the Soufrière Hills erupted for the first time since 1630. Over sixty per cent of the island was covered in volcanic ash and Plymouth, the capital, was virtually destroyed. Many people emigrated, and the remaining population moved to the north of the island. Brades has replaced Plymouth as the temporary capital. Reconstruction is being funded by aid from the UK.

MOROCCO
Kingdom of Morocco

Area Sq Km	446 550	Languages	Arabic, Berber, French
Area Sq Miles	172 414	Religions	Sunni Muslim
Population	31 224 000	Currency	Moroccan dirham
Capital	Rabat	Organizations	UN

Lying in the northwest of Africa, Morocco has both Atlantic and Mediterranean coasts. The Atlas Mountains separate the arid south and disputed region of western Sahara from the fertile west and north, which have a milder climate. Most Moroccans live on the Atlantic coastal plain. The economy is based on agriculture, phosphate mining and tourism; the most important industries are food processing, textiles and chemicals.

MOZAMBIQUE
Republic of Mozambique

Area Sq Km	799 380	Languages	Portuguese, Makua, Tsonga, local languages
Area Sq Miles	308 642		
Population	21 397 000	Religions	Traditional beliefs, Roman Catholic, Sunni Muslim
Capital	Maputo	Currency	Metical
		Organizations	Comm., SADC, UN

Mozambique lies on the east coast of southern Africa. The land is mainly a savanna plateau drained by the Zambezi and Limpopo rivers, with highlands in the north. Most of the population lives on the coast or in the river valleys. In general the climate is tropical with winter rainfall, but droughts occur. The economy is based on subsistence agriculture. Exports include shrimps, cashews, cotton and sugar, but Mozambique relies heavily on aid, and remains one of the least developed countries in the world.

MYANMAR (Burma)
Union of Myanmar

Area Sq Km	676 577	Languages	Burmese, Shan, Karen, local languages
Area Sq Miles	261 228	Religions	Buddhist, Christian, Sunni Muslim
Population	48 798 000	Currency	Kyat
Capital	Rangoon (Yangôn)/ Nay Pyi Taw	Organizations	ASEAN, UN

Myanmar (Burma) is in southeast Asia, bordering the Bay of Bengal and th Andaman Sea. Most of the population lives in the valley and delta of the Irrawaddy river, which is flanked by mountains and high plateaus. The climate is hot and monsoonal, and rainforest covers much of the land. Most of the workforce is employed in agriculture. Myanmar is rich in minerals, including zinc, lead, copper and silver. Political and social unres and lack of foreign investment have affected economic development.

NAMIBIA
Republic of Namibia

Area Sq Km	824 292	Languages	English, Afrikaans, German, Ovambo, local languages
Area Sq Miles	318 261		
Population	2 074 000	Religions	Protestant, Roman Catholic
Capital	Windhoek	Currency	Namibian dollar
		Organizations	Comm., SADC, UN

Namibia lies on the southern Atlantic coast of Africa. Mountain ranges separate the coastal Namib Desert from the interior plateau, bordered to the south and east by the Kalahari Desert. The country is hot and dry, but some summer rain in the north supports crops and livestock. Employmen is in agriculture and fishing, although the economy is based on mineral extraction – diamonds, uranium, lead, zinc and silver. The economy is closely linked to the Republic of South Africa.

NAURU
Republic of Nauru

Area Sq Km	21	Languages	Nauruan, English
Area Sq Miles	8	Religions	Protestant, Roman Catholic
Population	10 000	Currency	Australian dollar
Capital	Yaren	Organizations	Comm., UN

Nauru is a coral island near the Equator in the Pacific Ocean. It has a ferti coastal strip and a barren central plateau. The climate is tropical. The economy is based on phosphate mining, but reserves are near exhaustion and replacement of this income is a serious long-term problem.

NEPAL

Area Sq Km	147 181	Languages	Nepali, Maithili, Bhojpuri, English, local languages
Area Sq Miles	56 827		
Population	28 196 000	Religions	Hindu, Buddhist, Sunni Muslim
Capital	Kathmandu	Currency	Nepalese rupee
		Organizations	UN

Nepal lies in the eastern Himalaya mountains between India and China. High mountains (including Everest) dominate the north. Most people live in the temperate central valleys and subtropical southern plains. The economy is based largely on agriculture and forestry. There is some manufacturing, chiefly of textiles and carpets, and tourism is important. Nepal relies heavily on foreign aid.

NETHERLANDS
Kingdom of the Netherlands

Area Sq Km	41 526	Languages	Dutch, Frisian
Area Sq Miles	16 033	Religions	Roman Catholic, Protestant, Sunni Muslim
Population	16 419 000		
Capital	Amsterdam/ The Hague	Currency	Euro
		Organizations	EU, NATO, OECD, UN

The Netherlands lies on the North Sea coast of western Europe. Apart from l hills in the far southeast, the land is flat and low-lying, much of it below sea level. The coastal region includes the delta of five rivers and polders (reclaim land), protected by sand dunes, dykes and canals. The climate is temperate, with cool summers and mild winters. Rainfall is spread evenly throughout th year. The Netherlands is a densely populated and highly urbanized country, with the majority of the population living in the cities of Amsterdam, Rotterdam and The Hague. Horticulture and dairy farming are important activities, although they employ less than four per cent of the workforce. The Netherlands ranks as the world's third agricultural exporter, and is a leading producer and exporter of natural gas from reserves in the North Sea. The economy is based mainly on international trade and manufacturing industry The main industries produce food products, chemicals, machinery, electrical and electronic goods and transport equipment. Germany is the main trading partner, followed by other European Union countries.

Netherlands Antilles
Self-governing Netherlands Territory (dissolved October 2010)

Area Sq Km	800	Languages	Dutch, Papiamento, English
Area Sq Miles	309	Religions	Roman Catholic, Protestant
Population	192 000	Currency	Netherlands Antilles guilder
Capital	Willemstad		

The territory comprised two island groups: Curaçao and Bonaire off the coast of Venezuela, and Saba, Sint Eustatius and Sint Maarten in the Lesser Antilles. Tourism, oil refining and offshore finance were the mainstays of the economy. The main trading partners were the USA, Venezuela and Mexico. Much delayed plans for the dissolution of the territory finally cam to fruition in October 2010. Under these plans, Curaçao and Sint Maarten became Self-governing Netherlands Territories, and Bonaire, Saba and Sint Eustatius are now governed directly from the Netherlands.

ew Caledonia

:nch Overseas Country

ea Sq Km	19 058	Languages	French, local languages
ea Sq Miles	7 358	Religions	Roman Catholic, Protestant, Sunni Muslim
oulation	242 000		
oital	Nouméa	Currency	CFP franc

ı island group lying in the southwest Pacific, with a sub-tropical climate. :w Caledonia has over one-fifth of the world's nickel reserves, and the ain economic activity is metal mining. Tourism is also important. New ıledonia relies on aid from France.

'IGER

public of Niger

ea Sq Km	1 267 000	Languages	French, Hausa, Fulani, local languages
ea Sq Miles	489 191	Religions	Sunni Muslim, traditional beliefs
oulation	14 226 000	Currency	CFA franc
oital	Niamey	Organizations	UN

landlocked state of west Africa, Niger lies mostly within the Sahara desert, t with savanna in the south and in the Niger valley area. The mountains the Massif de l'Aïr dominate central regions. Much of the country is hot d dry. The south has some summer rainfall, although droughts occur. ıe economy depends on subsistence farming and herding, and uranium ports, but Niger is one of the world's least developed countries and relies avily on foreign aid. France is the main trading partner.

IGERIA

deral Republic of Nigeria

ea Sq Km	923 768	Languages	English, Hausa, Yoruba, Ibo, Fulani, local languages
ea Sq Miles	356 669		
pulation	148 093 000	Religions	Sunni Muslim, Christian, traditional beliefs
oital	Abuja	Currency	Naira
		Organizations	Comm., OPEC, UN

geria is in west Africa, on the Gulf of Guinea, and is the most populous untry in Africa. The Niger delta dominates coastal areas, fringed with sandy aches, mangrove swamps and lagoons. Inland is a belt of rainforest which es way to woodland or savanna on high plateaus. The far north is the semi-sert edge of the Sahara. The climate is tropical, with heavy summer rainfall the south but low rainfall in the north. Most of the population lives in the astal lowlands or in the west. About half the workforce is involved in riculture, mainly growing subsistence crops. Agricultural production, wever, has failed to keep up with demand, and Nigeria is now a net porter of food. Cocoa and rubber are the only significant export crops. The onomy is heavily dependent on vast oil resources in the Niger delta and in allow offshore waters, and oil accounts for over ninety per cent of export rnings. Nigeria also has natural gas reserves and some mineral deposits, but ese are largely undeveloped. Industry involves mainly oil refining, emicals (chiefly fertilizers), agricultural processing, textiles, steel anufacture and vehicle assembly. Political instability in the past has left geria with heavy debts, poverty and unemployment.

Jiue

lf-governing New Zealand Territory

ea Sq Km	258	Languages	English, Nivean
ea Sq Miles	100	Religions	Christian
pulation	2 000	Currency	New Zealand dollar
pital	Alofi		

ue, one of the largest coral islands in the world, lies in the south Pacific ean about 500 kilometres (300 miles) east of Tonga. The economy pends on aid and remittances from New Zealand. The population is clining because of migration to New Zealand.

Jorfolk Island

ıstralian External Territory

ea Sq Km	35	Languages	English
ea Sq Miles	14	Religions	Protestant, Roman Catholic
pulation	2 523	Currency	Australian dollar
pital	Kingston		

the south Pacific Ocean, Norfolk Island lies between Vanuatu and New aland. Tourism has increased steadily and is the mainstay of the onomy and provides revenues for agricultural development.

Jorthern Mariana Islands

nited States Commonwealth

ea Sq Km	477	Languages	English, Chamorro, local languages
ea Sq Miles	184	Religions	Roman Catholic
pulation	84 000	Currency	United States dollar
pital	Capitol Hill		

chain of islands in the northwest Pacific Ocean, extending over 550 lometres (350 miles) north to south. The main island is Saipan. Tourism a major industry, employing approximately half the workforce.

ORWAY

ngdom of Norway

ea Sq Km	323 878	Languages	Norwegian
ea Sq Miles	125 050	Religions	Protestant, Roman Catholic
pulation	4 698 000	Currency	Norwegian krone
pital	Oslo	Organizations	NATO, OECD, UN

Norway stretches along the north and west coasts of Scandinavia, from the Arctic Ocean to the North Sea. Its extensive coastline is indented with fjords and fringed with many islands. Inland, the terrain is mountainous, with coniferous forests and lakes in the south. The only major lowland areas are along the southern North Sea and Skagerrak coasts, where most of the population lives. The climate is modified by the effect of the North Atlantic Drift ocean current. Norway has vast petroleum and natural gas resources in the North Sea. It is one of western Europe's leading producers of oil and gas, and exports of oil account for approximately half of total export earnings. Related industries include engineering (oil and gas platforms) and petrochemicals. More traditional industries process local raw materials, particularly fish, timber and minerals. Agriculture is limited, but fishing and fish farming are important. Norway is the world's leading exporter of farmed salmon. Merchant shipping and tourism are major sources of foreign exchange.

OMAN

Sultanate of Oman

Area Sq Km	309 500	Languages	Arabic, Baluchi, Indian languages
Area Sq Miles	119 499	Religions	Ibadhi Muslim, Sunni Muslim
Population	2 595 000	Currency	Omani riyal
Capital	Muscat (Masqaṭ)	Organizations	UN

In southwest Asia, Oman occupies the east and southeast coasts of the Arabian Peninsula and an enclave north of the United Arab Emirates. Most of the land is desert, with mountains in the north and south. The climate is hot and mainly dry. Most of the population lives on the coastal strip on the Gulf of Oman. The majority depend on farming and fishing, but the oil and gas industries dominate the economy with around eighty per cent of export revenues coming from oil.

PAKISTAN

Islamic Republic of Pakistan

Area Sq Km	803 940	Languages	Urdu, Punjabi, Sindhi, Pushtu, English
Area Sq Miles	310 403	Religions	Sunni Muslim, Shi'a Muslim, Christian, Hindu
Population	163 902 000		
Capital	Islamabad	Currency	Pakistani rupee
		Organizations	Comm., UN

Pakistan is in the northwest part of the Indian subcontinent in south Asia, on the Arabian Sea. The east and south are dominated by the great basin of the Indus river system. This is the main agricultural area and contains most of the predominantly rural population. To the north the land rises to the mountains of the Karakoram, Hindu Kush and Himalaya mountains. The west is semi-desert plateaus and mountain ranges. The climate ranges between dry desert, and arctic tundra on the mountain tops. Temperatures are generally warm and rainfall is monsoonal. Agriculture is the main sector of the economy, employing approximately half of the workforce, and is based on extensive irrigation schemes. Pakistan is one of the world's leading producers of cotton and a major exporter of rice. Pakistan produces natural gas and has a variety of mineral deposits including coal and gold, but they are little developed. The main industries are textiles and clothing manufacture and food processing, with fabrics and ready-made clothing the leading exports. Pakistan also produces leather goods, fertilizers, chemicals, paper and precision instruments. The country depends heavily on foreign aid and remittances from workers abroad.

PALAU

Republic of Palau

Area Sq Km	497	Languages	Palauan, English
Area Sq Miles	192	Religions	Roman Catholic, Protestant, traditional beliefs
Population	20 000		
Capital	Melekeok	Currency	United States dollar
		Organizations	UN

Palau comprises over three hundred islands in the western Caroline Islands, in the west Pacific Ocean. The climate is tropical. The economy is based on farming, fishing and tourism, but Palau is heavily dependent on aid from the USA.

Pitcairn Islands

United Kingdom Overseas Territory

Area Sq Km	45	Languages	English
Area Sq Miles	17	Religions	Protestant
Population	48	Currency	New Zealand dollar
Capital	Adamstown		

An island group in the southeast Pacific Ocean consisting of Pitcairn Island and three uninhabited islands. It was originally settled by mutineers from HMS Bounty in 1790.

POLAND

Polish Republic

Area Sq Km	312 683	Languages	Polish, German
Area Sq Miles	120 728	Religions	Roman Catholic, Polish Orthodox
Population	38 082 000	Currency	Złoty
Capital	Warsaw (Warszawa)	Organizations	EU, NATO, OECD, UN

Poland lies on the Baltic coast of eastern Europe. The Oder (Odra) and Vistula (Wisła) river deltas dominate the coast. Inland, much of the country is low-lying, with woods and lakes. In the south the land rises to the Sudeten Mountains and the western part of the Carpathian Mountains, which form the borders with the Czech Republic and Slovakia respectively. The climate is continental. Around a quarter of the workforce is involved in agriculture, and exports include livestock products and sugar. The economy is heavily industrialized, with mining and manufacturing accounting for forty per cent of national income. Poland is one of the world's major producers of coal, and also produces copper, zinc, lead, sulphur and natural gas. The main industries are machinery and transport equipment, shipbuilding, and metal and chemical production. Exports include machinery and transport equipment, manufactured goods, food and live animals. Germany is the main trading partner. Poland joined the European Union in May 2004.

PORTUGAL

Portuguese Republic

Area Sq Km	88 940	Languages	Portuguese
Area Sq Miles	34 340	Religions	Roman Catholic, Protestant
Population	10 623 000	Currency	Euro
Capital	Lisbon (Lisboa)	Organizations	EU, NATO, OECD, UN

Portugal lies in the western part of the Iberian peninsula in southwest Europe, has an Atlantic coastline and is bordered by Spain to the north and east. The island groups of the Azores and Madeira are parts of Portugal. On the mainland, the land north of the river Tagus (Tejo) is mostly highland, with extensive forests of pine and cork. South of the river is undulating lowland. The climate in the north is cool and moist; the south is warmer, with dry, mild winters. Most Portuguese live near the coast, and more than one-third of the total population lives around the capital, Lisbon (Lisboa). Agriculture, fishing and forestry involve approximately ten per cent of the workforce. Mining and manufacturing are the main sectors of the economy. Portugal produces kaolin, copper, tin, zinc, tungsten and salt. Exports include textiles, clothing and footwear, electrical machinery and transport equipment, cork and wood products, and chemicals. Service industries, chiefly tourism and banking, are important to the economy, as are remittances from workers abroad. Most trade is with other European Union countries.

Puerto Rico

United States Commonwealth

Area Sq Km	9 104	Languages	Spanish, English
Area Sq Miles	3 515	Religions	Roman Catholic, Protestant
Population	3 991 000	Currency	United States dollar
Capital	San Juan		

The Caribbean island of Puerto Rico has a forested, hilly interior, coastal plains and a tropical climate. Half of the population lives in the San Juan area. The economy is based on manufacturing (chiefly chemicals, electronics and food), tourism and agriculture. The USA is the main trading partner.

QATAR

State of Qatar

Area Sq Km	11 437	Languages	Arabic
Area Sq Miles	4 416	Religions	Sunni Muslim
Population	841 000	Currency	Qatari riyal
Capital	Doha (Ad Dawḥah)	Organizations	OPEC, UN

Qatar occupies a peninsula in southwest Asia that extends northwards from east-central Saudi Arabia into The Gulf. The land is flat and barren with sand dunes and salt pans. The climate is hot and mainly dry. Most people live in the area of the capital, Doha. The economy is heavily dependent on oil and natural gas production and the oil-refining industry. Income also comes from overseas investment. Japan is the largest trading partner.

Réunion

French Overseas Department

Area Sq Km	2 551	Languages	French, Creole
Area Sq Miles	985	Religions	Roman Catholic
Population	807 000	Currency	Euro
Capital	St-Denis		

The Indian Ocean island of Réunion is mountainous, with coastal lowlands and a warm climate. The economy depends on tourism, French aid, and exports of sugar. In 2005 France transferred the administration of various small uninhabited islands in the seas around Madagascar from Réunion to the French Southern and Antarctic Lands.

ROMANIA

Area Sq Km	237 500	Languages	Romanian, Hungarian
Area Sq Miles	91 699	Religions	Romanian Orthodox, Protestant, Roman Catholic
Population	21 438 000		
Capital	Bucharest (București)	Currency	Romanian leu
		Organizations	EU, NATO, UN

Romania lies in eastern Europe, on the northwest coast of the Black Sea. Mountains separate the Transylvanian Basin in the centre of the country from the populous plains of the east and south and from the Danube delta. The climate is continental. Romania has mineral resources (zinc, lead, silver and gold) and oil and natural gas reserves. Economic development has been slow and sporadic, but measures to accelerate change were introduced in 1999. Agriculture employs over one-third of the workforce. The main exports are textiles, mineral products, chemicals, machinery and footwear. The main trading partners are Germany and Italy.

RWANDA

Republic of Rwanda

Area Sq Km	26 338	**Languages**	Kinyarwanda, French, English
Area Sq Miles	10 169	**Religions**	Roman Catholic, traditional beliefs, Protestant
Population	9 725 000		
Capital	Kigali	**Currency**	Rwandan franc
		Organizations	Comm., UN

Rwanda, the most densely populated country in Africa, is situated in the mountains and plateaus to the east of the western branch of the Great Rift Valley in east Africa. The climate is warm with a summer dry season. Rwanda depends on subsistence farming, coffee and tea exports, light industry and foreign aid. The country is slowly recovering from serious internal conflict which caused devastation in the early 1990s.

St-Barthélemy

Area Sq Km	21	**Languages**	French
Area Sq Miles	8	**Religions**	Roman Catholic
Population	6 852	**Currency**	Euro
Capital	Gustavia		

An island in the Leeward Islands in the Lesser Antilles, in the Caribbean south of St-Martin. It was separated from Guadeloupe politically in 2007. Tourism is the main economic activity.

St Helena and Dependencies

United Kingdom Overseas Territory

Area Sq Km	307	**Languages**	English
Area Sq Miles	119	**Religions**	Protestant, Roman Catholic
Population	7 000	**Currency**	St Helena pound, Pound sterling
Capital	Jamestown		

St Helena and its dependencies Ascension and Tristan da Cunha are isolated island groups lying in the south Atlantic Ocean. St Helena is a rugged island of volcanic origin. The main activity is fishing, but the economy relies on financial aid from the UK. Main trading partners are the UK and South Africa.

ST KITTS AND NEVIS

Federation of St Kitts and Nevis

Area Sq Km	261	**Languages**	English, Creole
Area Sq Miles	101	**Religions**	Protestant, Roman Catholic
Population	50 000	**Currency**	East Caribbean dollar
Capital	Basseterre	**Organizations**	CARICOM, Comm., UN

St Kitts and Nevis are in the Leeward Islands, in the Caribbean. Both volcanic islands are mountainous and forested, with sandy beaches and a warm, wet climate. About three-quarters of the population lives on St Kitts. Agriculture is the main activity, with sugar the main product. Tourism and manufacturing (chiefly garments and electronic components) and offshore banking are important activities.

ST LUCIA

Area Sq Km	616	**Languages**	English, Creole
Area Sq Miles	238	**Religions**	Roman Catholic, Protestant
Population	165 000	**Currency**	East Caribbean dollar
Capital	Castries	**Organizations**	CARICOM, Comm., UN

St Lucia, one of the Windward Islands in the Caribbean Sea, is a volcanic island with forested mountains, hot springs, sandy beaches and a wet tropical climate. Agriculture is the main activity, with bananas accounting for approximately forty per cent of export earnings. Tourism, agricultural processing and light manufacturing are increasingly important.

St-Martin

Area Sq Km	54	**Languages**	French
Area Sq Miles	21	**Religions**	Roman Catholic
Population	33 102	**Currency**	Euro
Capital	Marigot		

The northern part of St-Martin, one of the Leeward Islands, in the Caribbean. The other part of the island is part of the Netherlands Antilles (Sint Maarten). It was separated from Guadeloupe politically in 2007. Tourism is the main source of income.

St Pierre and Miquelon

French Territorial Collectivity

Area Sq Km	242	**Languages**	French
Area Sq Miles	93	**Religions**	Roman Catholic
Population	6 000	**Currency**	Euro
Capital	St-Pierre		

A group of islands off the south coast of Newfoundland in eastern Canada. The islands are largely unsuitable for agriculture, and fishing and fish processing are the most important activities. The islands rely heavily on financial assistance from France.

ST VINCENT AND THE GRENADINES

Area Sq Km	389	**Languages**	English, Creole
Area Sq Miles	150	**Religions**	Protestant, Roman Catholic
Population	120 000	**Currency**	East Caribbean dollar
Capital	Kingstown	**Organizations**	CARICOM, Comm., UN

St Vincent, whose territory includes islets and cays in the Grenadines, is in the Windward Islands, in the Caribbean. St Vincent itself is forested and mountainous, with an active volcano, Soufrière. The climate is tropical and wet. The economy is based mainly on agriculture and tourism. Bananas account for approximately one-third of export earnings and arrowroot is also important. Most trade is with the USA and other CARICOM countries.

SAMOA

Independent State of Samoa

Area Sq Km	2 831	**Languages**	Samoan, English
Area Sq Miles	1 093	**Religions**	Protestant, Roman Catholic
Population	187 000	**Currency**	Tala
Capital	Apia	**Organizations**	Comm., UN

Samoa consists of two larger mountainous and forested islands, Savai'i and Upolu, and seven smaller islands, in the south Pacific Ocean. Over half the population lives on Upolu. The climate is tropical. The economy is based on agriculture, with some fishing and light manufacturing. Traditional exports are coconut products, fish and beer. Tourism is increasing, but the islands depend on workers' remittances and foreign aid.

SAN MARINO

Republic of San Marino

Area Sq Km	61	**Languages**	Italian
Area Sq Miles	24	**Religions**	Roman Catholic
Population	31 000	**Currency**	Euro
Capital	San Marino	**Organizations**	UN

Landlocked San Marino lies in northeast Italy. A third of the people live in the capital. There is some agriculture and light industry, but most income comes from tourism. Italy is the main trading partner.

SÃO TOMÉ AND PRÍNCIPE

Democratic Republic of São Tomé and Príncipe

Area Sq Km	964	**Languages**	Portuguese, Creole
Area Sq Miles	372	**Religions**	Roman Catholic, Protestant
Population	158 000	**Currency**	Dobra
Capital	São Tomé	**Organizations**	UN

The two main islands and adjacent islets lie off the coast of west Africa in the Gulf of Guinea. São Tomé is the larger island, with over ninety per cent of the population. Both São Tomé and Príncipe are mountainous and tree-covered, and have a hot and humid climate. The economy is heavily dependent on cocoa, which accounts for around ninety per cent of export earnings.

SENEGAL

Republic of Senegal

Area Sq Km	196 720	**Languages**	French, Wolof, Fulani, local languages
Area Sq Miles	75 954	**Religions**	Sunni Muslim, Roman Catholic, traditional beliefs
Population	12 379 000		
Capital	Dakar	**Currency**	CFA franc
		Organizations	UN

Senegal lies on the Atlantic coast of west Africa. The north is arid semi-desert, while the south is mainly fertile savanna bushland. The climate is tropical with summer rains, although droughts occur. One-fifth of the population lives in and around Dakar, the capital and main port. Fish, groundnuts and phosphates are the main exports. France is the main trading partner.

SERBIA

Republic of Serbia

Area Sq Km	77 453	**Languages**	Serbian, Hungarian
Area Sq Miles	29 904	**Religions**	Serbian Orthodox, Roman Catholic, Sunni Muslim
Population	7 788 448		
Capital	Belgrade (Beograd)	**Currency**	Serbian dinar
		Organizations	UN

Following ethnic conflict and the break-up of Yugoslavia through the 1990s, the state union of Serbia and Montenegro retained the name Yugoslavia until 2003. The two then became separate independent countries in 2006. The southern Serbian province of Kosovo declared its independence from Serbia in February 2008. The landscape is rugged, mountainous and forested in the south, while the north is low-lying and drained by the Danube river system.

SEYCHELLES

Republic of Seychelles

Area Sq Km	455	**Languages**	English, French, Creole
Area Sq Miles	176	**Religions**	Roman Catholic, Protestant
Population	87 000	**Currency**	Seychelles rupee
Capital	Victoria	**Organizations**	Comm., SADC, UN

The Seychelles comprises an archipelago of over one hundred granitic a coral islands in the western Indian Ocean. Over ninety per cent of the population lives on the main island, Mahé. The climate is hot and humi with heavy rainfall. The economy is based mainly on tourism, fishing an light manufacturing.

SIERRA LEONE

Republic of Sierra Leone

Area Sq Km	71 740	**Languages**	English, Creole, Mende, Temne, local languages
Area Sq Miles	27 699		
Population	5 866 000	**Religions**	Sunni Muslim, traditional beliefs
Capital	Freetown	**Currency**	Leone
		Organizations	Comm., UN

Sierra Leone lies on the Atlantic coast of west Africa. Its coastline is heavily indented and is lined with mangrove swamps. Inland is a foreste area rising to savanna plateaus, with mountains to the northeast. The climate is tropical and rainfall is heavy. Most of the workforce is involve in subsistence farming. Cocoa and coffee are the main cash crops. Diamonds and rutile (titanium ore) are the main exports. Sierra Leone i one of the world's poorest countries, and the economy relies on substantial foreign aid.

SINGAPORE

Republic of Singapore

Area Sq Km	639	**Languages**	Chinese, English, Malay, Tamil
Area Sq Miles	247	**Religions**	Buddhist, Taoist, Sunni Muslim, Christian, Hindu
Population	4 436 000		
Capital	Singapore	**Currency**	Singapore dollar
		Organizations	APEC, ASEAN, Comm., UN

The state comprises the main island of Singapore and over fifty other islands, lying off the southern tip of the Malay Peninsula in southeast As Singapore is generally low-lying and includes land reclaimed from swam and the sea. It is hot and humid, with heavy rainfall throughout the year. There are fish farms and vegetable gardens in the north and east of the island, but most food is imported. Singapore also lacks mineral and ener resources. Manufacturing industries and services are the main sectors of the economy. Their rapid development has fuelled the nation's impressiv economic growth during recent decades. Main industries include electronics, oil refining, chemicals, pharmaceuticals, ship repair, food processing and textiles. Singapore is also a major financial centre. Its por is one of the world's largest and busiest and acts as an entrepôt for neighbouring states. Tourism is also important. Japan, the USA and Malaysia are the main trading partners.

SLOVAKIA

Slovak Republic

Area Sq Km	49 035	**Languages**	Slovakian, Hungarian, Czech
Area Sq Miles	18 933	**Religions**	Roman Catholic, Protestant, Orthodox
Population	5 390 000	**Currency**	Slovakian koruna
Capital	Bratislava	**Organizations**	EU, NATO, OECD, UN

A landlocked country in central Europe, Slovakia is mountainous in the north, but low-lying in the southwest. The climate is continental. There a range of manufacturing industries, and the main exports are machine and transport equipment, but in recent years there have been economic difficulties and growth has been slow. Slovakia joined the European Union in May 2004. Most trade is with other EU countries, especially th Czech Republic.

SLOVENIA

Republic of Slovenia

Area Sq Km	20 251	**Languages**	Slovenian, Croatian, Serbian
Area Sq Miles	7 819	**Religions**	Roman Catholic, Protestant
Population	2 002 000	**Currency**	Euro
Capital	Ljubljana	**Organizations**	EU, NATO, UN

Slovenia lies in the northwest Balkan Mountains of southern Europe an has a short coastline on the Adriatic Sea. It is mountainous and hilly, wi lowlands on the coast and in the Sava and Drava river valleys. The clima is generally continental inland and Mediterranean nearer the coast. The main agricultural products are potatoes, grain and sugar beet; the main industries include metal processing, electronics and consumer goods. Trade has been re-orientated towards western markets and the main trading partners are Germany and Italy. Slovenia joined the European Union in May 2004.

SOLOMON ISLANDS

Area Sq Km	28 370	**Languages**	English, Creole, local languages
Area Sq Miles	10 954	**Religions**	Protestant, Roman Catholic
Population	496 000	**Currency**	Solomon Islands dollar
Capital	Honiara	**Organizations**	Comm., UN

The state consists of the Solomon, Santa Cruz and Shortland Islands in th southwest Pacific Ocean. The six main islands are volcanic, mountainous and forested, although Guadalcanal, the most populous, has a large lowlar area. The climate is generally hot and humid. Subsistence farming, forest and fishing predominate. Exports include timber products, fish, copra an palm oil. The islands depend on foreign aid.

OMALIA

mali Republic

ea Sq Km	637 657	Languages	Somali, Arabic
ea Sq Miles	246 201	Religions	Sunni Muslim
pulation	8 699 000	Currency	Somali shilling
pital	Mogadishu (Muqdisho)	Organizations	UN

malia is in northeast Africa, on the Gulf of Aden and Indian Ocean. It nsists of a dry scrubby plateau, rising to highlands in the north. The mate is hot and dry, but coastal areas and the Jubba and Webi Shabeelle ver valleys support crops and most of the population. Subsistence farming d livestock rearing are the main activities. Exports include livestock and nanas. Frequent drought and civil war have prevented economic velopment. Somalia is one of the poorest, most unstable and least veloped countries in the world.

RI LANKA

mocratic Socialist Republic of Sri Lanka

ea Sq Km	65 610	Languages	Sinhalese, Tamil, English
ea Sq Miles	25 332	Religions	Buddhist, Hindu, Sunni Muslim, Roman Catholic
pulation	19 299 000	Currency	Sri Lankan rupee
pital	Sri Jayewardenepura Kotte	Organizations	Comm., UN

i Lanka lies in the Indian Ocean off the southeast coast of India in south ia. It has rolling coastal plains, with mountains in the centre-south. The mate is hot and monsoonal. Most people live on the west coast. anufactures (chiefly textiles and clothing), tea, rubber, copra and gems are ported. The economy relies on foreign aid and workers' remittances. The SA and the UK are the main trading partners.

URINAME

public of Suriname

ea Sq Km	163 820	Languages	Dutch, Surinamese, English, Hindi
ea Sq Miles	63 251	Religions	Hindu, Roman Catholic, Protestant, Sunni Muslim
pulation	458 000	Currency	Suriname guilder
pital	Paramaribo	Organizations	CARICOM, UN

riname, on the Atlantic coast of northern South America, consists of a vampy coastal plain (where most of the population lives), central ateaus, and highlands in the south. The climate is tropical, and inforest covers much of the land. Bauxite mining is the main industry, d alumina and aluminium are the chief exports, with shrimps, rice, nanas and timber also exported. The main trading partners are the etherlands, Norway and the USA.

WAZILAND

ngdom of Swaziland

ea Sq Km	17 364	Languages	Swazi, English
ea Sq Miles	6 704	Religions	Christian, traditional beliefs
pulation	1 141 000	Currency	Emalangeni, South African rand
pital	Mbabane	Organizations	Comm., SADC, UN

ndlocked Swaziland in southern Africa lies between Mozambique and the public of South Africa. Savanna plateaus descend from mountains in the est towards hill country in the east. The climate is subtropical, but mperate in the mountains. Subsistence farming predominates. Asbestos d diamonds are mined. Exports include sugar, fruit and wood pulp. ourism and workers' remittances are important to the economy. Most ade is with South Africa.

WITZERLAND

viss Confederation

ea Sq Km	41 293	Languages	German, French, Italian, Romansch
ea Sq Miles	15 943	Religions	Roman Catholic, Protestant
pulation	7 484 000	Currency	Swiss franc
pital	Bern	Organizations	OECD, UN

vitzerland is a mountainous landlocked country in west central Europe. he southern regions lie within the Alps, while the northwest is dominated y the Jura mountains. The rest of the land is a high plateau, where most of ie population lives. The climate varies greatly, depending on altitude and lief, but in general summers are mild and winters are cold with heavy owfalls. Switzerland has one of the highest standards of living in the orld, yet it has few mineral resources, and most food and industrial raw aterials are imported. Manufacturing makes the largest contribution to ie economy. Engineering is the most important industry, producing recision instruments and heavy machinery. Other important industries e chemicals and pharmaceuticals. Banking and financial services are very nportant, and Zürich is one of the world's leading banking cities. ourism, and international organizations based in Switzerland, are also ajor foreign currency earners. Germany is the main trading partner.

YRIA

rian Arab Republic

ea Sq Km	185 180	Languages	Arabic, Kurdish, Armenian
ea Sq Miles	71 498	Religions	Sunni Muslim, Shi'a Muslim, Christian
pulation	19 929 000	Currency	Syrian pound
pital	Damascus (Dimashq)	Organizations	UN

Syria is in southwest Asia, has a short coastline on the Mediterranean Sea, and stretches inland to a plateau traversed northwest-southeast by the Euphrates river. Mountains flank the southwest borders with Lebanon and Israel. The climate is Mediterranean in coastal regions, hotter and drier inland. Most Syrians live on the coast or in the river valleys. Cotton, cereals and fruit are important products, but the main exports are petroleum and related products, and textiles.

TAIWAN

Republic of China

Area Sq Km	36 179	Languages	Mandarin, Min, Hakka, local languages
Area Sq Miles	13 969	Religions	Buddhist, Taoist, Confucian, Christian
Population	22 880 009	Currency	Taiwan dollar
Capital	T'aipei	Organizations	APEC

The east Asian state consists of the island of Taiwan, separated from mainland China by the Taiwan Strait, and several much smaller islands. Much of Taiwan is mountainous and forested. Densely populated coastal plains in the west contain the bulk of the population and most economic activity. Taiwan has a tropical monsoon climate, with warm, wet summers and mild winters. Agriculture is highly productive. The country is virtually self-sufficient in food and exports some products. Coal, oil and natural gas are produced and a few minerals are mined, but none of them are of great significance to the economy. Taiwan depends heavily on imports of raw materials and exports of manufactured goods. The main manufactures are electrical and electronic goods, including television sets, personal computers and calculators, textiles, fertilizers, clothing, footwear and toys. The main trading partners are the USA, Japan and Germany. The People's Republic of China claims Taiwan as its 23rd Province.

TAJIKISTAN

Republic of Tajikistan

Area Sq Km	143 100	Languages	Tajik, Uzbek, Russian
Area Sq Miles	55 251	Religions	Sunni Muslim
Population	6 736 000	Currency	Somoni
Capital	Dushanbe	Organizations	CIS, UN

Landlocked Tajikistan in central Asia is a mountainous country, dominated by the mountains of the Alai Range and the Pamir. In the less mountainous western areas summers are warm, although winters are cold. Agriculture is the main sector of the economy, chiefly cotton growing and cattle breeding. Mineral deposits include lead, zinc, and uranium. Processed metals, textiles and clothing are the main manufactured goods; the main exports are aluminium and cotton. Uzbekistan, Kazakhstan and the Russian Federation are the main trading partners.

TANZANIA

United Republic of Tanzania

Area Sq Km	945 087	Languages	Swahili, English, Nyamwezi, local languages
Area Sq Miles	364 900	Religions	Shi'a Muslim, Sunni Muslim, traditional beliefs, Christian
Population	40 454 000	Currency	Tanzanian shilling
Capital	Dodoma	Organizations	Comm., SADC, UN

Tanzania lies on the coast of east Africa and includes the island of Zanzibar in the Indian Ocean. Most of the mainland is a savanna plateau lying east of the Great Rift Valley. In the north, near the border with Kenya, is Kilimanjaro, the highest mountain in Africa. The climate is tropical. The economy is predominantly based on agriculture, which employs an estimated ninety per cent of the workforce. Agricultural processing and gold and diamond mining are the main industries, although tourism is growing. Coffee, cotton, cashew nuts and tobacco are the main exports, with cloves from Zanzibar. Most export trade is with India and the UK. Tanzania depends heavily on foreign aid.

THAILAND

Kingdom of Thailand

Area Sq Km	513 115	Languages	Thai, Lao, Chinese, Malay, Mon-Khmer languages
Area Sq Miles	198 115	Religions	Buddhist, Sunni Muslim
Population	63 884 000	Currency	Baht
Capital	Bangkok (Krung Thep)	Organizations	APEC, ASEAN, UN

The largest country in the Indo-China peninsula, Thailand has coastlines on the Gulf of Thailand and Andaman Sea. Central Thailand is dominated by the Chao Phraya river basin, which contains Bangkok, the capital city and centre of most economic activity. To the east is a dry plateau drained by tributaries of the Mekong river, while to the north, west and south, extending down most of the Malay peninsula, are forested hills and mountains. Many small islands line the coast. The climate is hot, humid and monsoonal. About half the workforce is involved in agriculture. Fishing and fish processing are important. Thailand produces natural gas, some oil and lignite, minerals (chiefly tin, tungsten and baryte) and gemstones. Manufacturing is the largest contributor to national income, with electronics, textiles, clothing and footwear, and food processing the main industries. With around seven million visitors a year, tourism is the major source of foreign exchange. Thailand is one of the world's leading exporters of rice and rubber, and a major exporter of maize and tapioca. Japan and the USA are the main trading partners.

TOGO

Republic of Togo

Area Sq Km	56 785	Languages	French, Ewe, Kabre, local languages
Area Sq Miles	21 925	Religions	Traditional beliefs, Christian, Sunni Muslim
Population	6 585 000	Currency	CFA franc
Capital	Lomé	Organizations	UN

Togo is a long narrow country in west Africa with a short coastline on the Gulf of Guinea. The interior consists of plateaus rising to mountainous areas. The climate is tropical, and is drier inland. Agriculture is the mainstay of the economy. Phosphate mining and food processing are the main industries. Cotton, phosphates, coffee and cocoa are the main exports. Lomé, the capital, is an entrepôt trade centre.

Tokelau

New Zealand Overseas Territory

Area Sq Km	10	Languages	English, Tokelauan
Area Sq Miles	4	Religions	Christian
Population	1 000	Currency	New Zealand dollar

Tokelau consists of three atolls, Atafu, Nukunonu and Fakaofa, lying in the Pacific Ocean north of Samoa. Subsistence agriculture is the main activity, and the islands rely on aid from New Zealand and remittances from workers overseas.

TONGA

Kingdom of Tonga

Area Sq Km	748	Languages	Tongan, English
Area Sq Miles	289	Religions	Protestant, Roman Catholic
Population	100 000	Currency	Pa'anga
Capital	Nuku'alofa	Organizations	Comm., UN

Tonga comprises some one hundred and seventy islands in the south Pacific Ocean, northeast of New Zealand. The three main groups are Tongatapu (where sixty per cent of Tongans live), Ha'apai and Vava'u. The climate is warm and wet, and the economy relies heavily on agriculture. Tourism and light industry are also important to the economy. Exports include squash, fish, vanilla beans and root crops. Most trade is with New Zealand, Japan and Australia.

TRINIDAD AND TOBAGO

Republic of Trinidad and Tobago

Area Sq Km	5 130	Languages	English, Creole, Hindi
Area Sq Miles	1 981	Religions	Roman Catholic, Hindu, Protestant, Sunni Muslim
Population	1 333 000	Currency	Trinidad and Tobago dollar
Capital	Port of Spain	Organizations	CARICOM, Comm., UN

Trinidad, the most southerly Caribbean island, lies off the Venezuelan coast. It is hilly in the north, with a central plain. Tobago, to the northeast, is smaller, more mountainous and less developed. The climate is tropical. The main crops are cocoa, sugar cane, coffee, fruit and vegetables. Oil and petrochemical industries dominate the economy. Tourism is also important. The USA is the main trading partner.

TUNISIA

Tunisian Republic

Area Sq Km	164 150	Languages	Arabic, French
Area Sq Miles	63 379	Religions	Sunni Muslim
Population	10 327 000	Currency	Tunisian dinar
Capital	Tunis	Organizations	UN

Tunisia is on the Mediterranean coast of north Africa. The north is mountainous with valleys and coastal plains, has a Mediterranean climate and is the most populous area. The south is hot and arid. Oil and phosphates are the main resources, and the main crops are olives and citrus fruit. Tourism is an important industry. Exports include petroleum products, textiles, fruit and phosphorus. Most trade is with European Union countries.

TURKEY

Republic of Turkey

Area Sq Km	779 452	Languages	Turkish, Kurdish
Area Sq Miles	300 948	Religions	Sunni Muslim, Shi'a Muslim
Population	74 877 000	Currency	Lira
Capital	Ankara	Organizations	NATO, OECD, UN

Turkey occupies a large peninsula of southwest Asia and has coastlines on the Black, Mediterranean and Aegean Seas. It includes eastern Thrace, which is in southeastern Europe and is separated from the rest of the country by the Bosporus, the Sea of Marmara and the Dardanelles. The Asian mainland consists of the semi-arid Anatolian plateau, flanked to the north, south and east by mountains. Over forty per cent of Turks live in central Anatolia and on the Marmara and Aegean coastal plains. The coast has a Mediterranean climate, but inland conditions are more extreme with hot, dry summers and cold, snowy winters. Agriculture involves about forty per cent of the workforce, and products include cotton, grain, tobacco, fruit, nuts and livestock. Turkey is a leading producer of chromium, iron ore, lead, tin, borate, and baryte while coal is also mined. The main manufactured goods are clothing, textiles, food products, steel and vehicles. Tourism is a major industry, with nine million visitors a year. Germany and the USA are the main trading partners. Remittances from workers abroad are important to the economy.

TURKMENISTAN
Republic of Turkmenistan

Area Sq Km	488 100	**Languages**	Turkmen, Uzbek, Russian
Area Sq Miles	188 456	**Religions**	Sunni Muslim, Russian Orthodox
Population	4 965 000	**Currency**	Turkmen manat
Capital	Aşgabat (Ashkhabad)	**Organizations**	UN

Turkmenistan, in central Asia, comprises the plains of the Karakum Desert, the foothills of the Kopet Dag mountains in the south, the Amudar'ya valley in the north and the Caspian Sea plains in the west. The climate is dry, with extreme temperatures. The economy is based mainly on irrigated agriculture (chiefly cotton growing), and natural gas and oil. Main exports are natural gas, oil and cotton fibre. Ukraine, Iran, Turkey and the Russian Federation are the main trading partners.

Turks and Caicos Islands
United Kingdom Overseas Territory

Area Sq Km	430	**Languages**	English
Area Sq Miles	166	**Religions**	Protestant
Population	26 000	**Currency**	United States dollar
Capital	Grand Turk (Cockburn Town)		

The state consists of over forty low-lying islands and cays in the northern Caribbean. Only eight islands are inhabited, and two-fifths of the people live on Grand Turk and Salt Cay. The climate is tropical, and the economy is based on tourism, fishing and offshore banking.

TUVALU

Area Sq Km	25	**Languages**	Tuvaluan, English
Area Sq Miles	10	**Religions**	Protestant
Population	11 000	**Currency**	Australian dollar
Capital	Vaiaku	**Organizations**	Comm., UN

Tuvalu comprises nine low-lying coral atolls in the south Pacific Ocean. One-third of the population lives on Funafuti, and most people depend on subsistence farming and fishing. The islands export copra, stamps and clothing, but rely heavily on foreign aid. Most trade is with Fiji, Australia and New Zealand.

UGANDA
Republic of Uganda

Area Sq Km	241 038	**Languages**	English, Swahili, Luganda, local languages
Area Sq Miles	93 065	**Religions**	Roman Catholic, Protestant, Sunni Muslim, traditional beliefs
Population	30 884 000	**Currency**	Ugandan shilling
Capital	Kampala	**Organizations**	Comm., UN

A landlocked country in east Africa, Uganda consists of a savanna plateau with mountains and lakes. The climate is warm and wet. Most people live in the southern half of the country. Agriculture employs around eighty per cent of the workforce and dominates the economy. Coffee, tea, fish and fish products are the main exports. Uganda relies heavily on aid.

UKRAINE

Area Sq Km	603 700	**Languages**	Ukrainian, Russian
Area Sq Miles	233 090	**Religions**	Ukrainian Orthodox, Ukrainian Catholic, Roman Catholic
Population	46 205 000	**Currency**	Hryvnia
Capital	Kiev (Kyiv)	**Organizations**	CIS, UN

The country lies on the Black Sea coast of eastern Europe. Much of the land is steppe, generally flat and treeless, but with rich black soil, and it is drained by the river Dnieper. Along the border with Belarus are forested, marshy plains. The only uplands are the Carpathian Mountains in the west and smaller ranges on the Crimean peninsula. Summers are warm and winters are cold, with milder conditions in the Crimea. About a quarter of the population lives in the mainly industrial areas around Donets'k, Kiev and Dnipropetrovs'k. The Ukraine is rich in natural resources: fertile soil, substantial mineral and natural gas deposits, and forests. Agriculture and livestock rearing are important, but mining and manufacturing are the dominant sectors of the economy. Coal, iron and manganese mining, steel and metal production, machinery, chemicals and food processing are the main industries. The Russian Federation is the main trading partner.

UNITED ARAB EMIRATES
Federation of Emirates

Area Sq Km	77 700	**Languages**	Arabic, English
Area Sq Miles	30 000	**Religions**	Sunni Muslim, Shi'a Muslim
Population	4 380 000	**Currency**	United Arab Emirates dirham
Capital	Abu Dhabi (Abū Ẓabī)	**Organizations**	OPEC, UN

The UAE lies on the Gulf coast of the Arabian Peninsula. Six emirates are on The Gulf, while the seventh, Fujairah, is on the Gulf of Oman. Most of the land is flat desert with sand dunes and salt pans. The only hilly area is in the northeast. Over eighty per cent of the population lives in three of the emirates - Abu Dhabi, Dubai and Sharjah. Summers are hot and winters are mild, with occasional rainfall in coastal areas. Fruit and vegetables are grown in oases and irrigated areas, but the Emirates' wealth is based on hydrocarbons found in Abu Dhabi, Dubai, Sharjah and Ras al Khaimah. The UAE is one of the major oil producers in the Middle East. Dubai is an important entrepôt trade centre The main trading partner is Japan.

UZBEKISTAN
Republic of Uzbekistan

Area Sq Km	447 400	**Languages**	Uzbek, Russian, Tajik, Kazakh
Area Sq Miles	172 742	**Religions**	Sunni Muslim, Russian Orthodox
Population	27 372 000	**Currency**	Uzbek som
Capital	Tashkent	**Organizations**	CIS, UN

A landlocked country of central Asia, Uzbekistan consists mainly of the flat Kyzylkum Desert. High mountains and valleys are found towards the southeast borders with Kyrgyzstan and Tajikistan. Most settlement is in the Fergana basin. The climate is hot and dry. The economy is based mainly on irrigated agriculture, chiefly cotton production. Uzbekistan is rich in minerals, including gold, copper, lead, zinc and uranium, and it has one of the largest gold mines in the world. Industry specializes in fertilizers and machinery for cotton harvesting and textile manufacture. The Russian Federation is the main trading partner.

VATICAN CITY
Vatican City State or Holy See

Area Sq Km	0.5	**Languages**	Italian
Area Sq Miles	0.2	**Religions**	Roman Catholic
Population	557	**Currency**	Euro
Capital	Vatican City		

The world's smallest sovereign state, the Vatican City occupies a hill to the west of the river Tiber within the Italian capital, Rome. It is the headquarters of the Roman Catholic church, and income comes from investments, voluntary contributions and tourism.

VENEZUELA
Republic of Venezuela

Area Sq Km	912 050	**Languages**	Spanish, Amerindian languages
Area Sq Miles	352 144	**Religions**	Roman Catholic, Protestant
Population	27 657 000	**Currency**	Bolívar fuerte
Capital	Caracas	**Organizations**	OPEC, UN

Venezuela is in northern South America, on the Caribbean. Its coast is much indented, with the oil-rich area of Lake Maracaibo at the western end, and the swampy Orinoco Delta to the east. Mountain ranges run parallel to the coast, and turn southwestwards to form a northern extension of the Andes. Central Venezuela is an area of lowland grasslands drained by the Orinoco river system. To the south are the Guiana Highlands, which contain the Angel Falls, the world's highest waterfall. Almost ninety per cent of the population lives in towns, mostly in the coastal mountain areas. The climate is tropical, with most rainfall in summer. Farming is important, particularly cattle ranching and dairy farming; coffee, maize, rice and sugar cane are the main crops. Venezuela is a major oil producer, and oil accounts for about seventy-five per cent of export earnings. Aluminium, iron ore, copper and gold are also mined, and manufactures include petrochemicals, aluminium, steel, textiles and food products. The USA and Puerto Rico are the main trading partners.

VIETNAM
Socialist Republic of Vietnam

Area Sq Km	329 565	**Languages**	Vietnamese, Thai, Khmer, Chinese, local languages
Area Sq Miles	127 246	**Religions**	Buddhist, Taoist, Roman Catholic, Cao Dai, Hoa Hao
Population	87 375 000	**Currency**	Dong
Capital	Ha Nôi	**Organizations**	APEC, ASEAN, UN

Vietnam lies in southeast Asia on the west coast of the South China Sea. The Red River delta lowlands in the north are separated from the huge Mekong delta in the south by long, narrow coastal plains backed by the mountainous and forested terrain of the Annam Highlands. Most of the population lives in the river deltas. The climate is tropical, with summer monsoon rains. Over three-quarters of the workforce is involved in agriculture, forestry and fishing. Coffee, tea and rubber are important cash crops, but Vietnam is the world's second largest rice exporter. Oil, coal and copper are produced, and other main industries are food processing, clothing and footwear, cement and fertilizers. Exports include oil, coffee, rice, clothing, fish and fish products. Japan and Singapore are the main trading partners.

Virgin Islands (U.K.)
United Kingdom Overseas Territory

Area Sq Km	153	**Languages**	English
Area Sq Miles	59	**Religions**	Protestant, Roman Catholic
Population	23 000	**Currency**	United States dollar
Capital	Road Town		

The Caribbean territory comprises four main islands and over thirty islets at the eastern end of the Virgin Islands group. Apart from the flat coral atoll of Anegada, the islands are volcanic in origin and hilly. The climate is subtropical, and tourism is the main industry.

Virgin Islands (U.S.A.)
United States Unincorporated Territory

Area Sq Km	352	**Languages**	English, Spanish
Area Sq Miles	136	**Religions**	Protestant, Roman Catholic
Population	111 000	**Currency**	United States dollar
Capital	Charlotte Amalie		

The territory consists of three main islands and over fifty islets in the Caribbean's western Virgin Islands. The islands are hilly, of volcanic origin, and the climate is subtropical. The economy is based on tourism, with some manufacturing, including a major oil refinery on St Croix.

Wallis and Futuna Islands
French Overseas Territory

Area Sq Km	274	**Languages**	French, Wallisian, Futunian
Area Sq Miles	106	**Religions**	Roman Catholic
Population	15 000	**Currency**	CFP franc
Capital	Matā'utu		

The south Pacific territory comprises the volcanic islands of the Wallis archipelago and the Hoorn Islands. The climate is tropical. The islands depend on subsistence farming, the sale of licences to foreign fishing fleets, workers' remittances from abroad and French aid.

West Bank
Disputed territory

Area Sq Km	5 860	**Languages**	Arabic, Hebrew
Area Sq Miles	2 263	**Religions**	Sunni Muslim, Jewish, Shi'a Muslim, Christian
Population	2 676 284	**Currency**	Jordanian dinar, Isreali shekel

The territory consists of the west bank of the river Jordan and parts of Judea and Samaria. The land was annexed by Israel in 1967, but some areas have been granted autonomy under agreements between Israel and the Palestinian Authority. Conflict between the Israelis and the Palestinians continues to restrict economic development.

Western Sahara
Disputed territory

Area Sq Km	266 000	**Languages**	Arabic
Area Sq Miles	102 703	**Religions**	Sunni Muslim
Population	480 000	**Currency**	Moroccan dirham
Capital	Laâyoune		

Situated on the northwest coast of Africa, the territory of the Western Sahara is now effectively controlled by Morocco. The land is low, flat desert with higher land in the northeast. There is little cultivation and only about twenty per cent of the land is pasture. Livestock herding, fishing and phosphate mining are the main activities. All trade is controlled by Morocco.

YEMEN
Republic of Yemen

Area Sq Km	527 968	**Languages**	Arabic
Area Sq Miles	203 850	**Religions**	Sunni Muslim, Shi'a Muslim
Population	22 389 000	**Currency**	Yemeni riyal
Capital	Şan'ā'	**Organizations**	UN

Yemen occupies the southwestern part of the Arabian Peninsula, on the Red Sea and the Gulf of Aden. Beyond the Red Sea coastal plain the land rises to a mountain range and then descends to desert plateaus. Much of the country is hot and arid, but there is more rainfall in the west, where most of the population lives. Farming and fishing are the main activities, with cotton the main cash crop. The main exports are crude oil, fish, coffee and dried fruit. Despite some oil resources Yemen is one of the poorest countries in the Arab world. Main trading partners are Thailand, China, South Korea and Saudi Arabia.

ZAMBIA
Republic of Zambia

Area Sq Km	752 614	**Languages**	English, Bemba, Nyanja, Tonga, local languages
Area Sq Miles	290 586	**Religions**	Christian, traditional beliefs
Population	11 922 000	**Currency**	Zambian kwacha
Capital	Lusaka	**Organizations**	Comm., SADC, UN

A landlocked state in south central Africa, Zambia consists principally of high savanna plateaus and is bordered by the Zambezi river in the south. Most people live in the Copperbelt area in the centre-north. The climate is tropical, with a rainy season from November to May. Agriculture employs approximately eighty per cent of the workforce, but is mainly at subsistence level. Copper mining is the mainstay of the economy, although reserves are declining. Copper and cobalt are the main exports. Most trade is with South Africa.

INTRODUCTION TO THE INDEX

The index includes all names shown on the reference maps in the atlas. Each entry includes the country or geographical area in which the feature is located, a page number and an alphanumeric reference. Additional entry details and aspects of the index are explained below.

REFERENCING

Names are referenced by page number and by grid reference. The grid reference relates to the alphanumeric values which appear in the margin of each map. These reflect the graticule on the map – the letter relates to longitude divisions, the number to latitude divisions.

Names are generally referenced to the largest scale map page on which they appear. For large geographical features, including countries, the reference is to the largest scale map on which the feature appears in its entirety, or on which the majority of it appears.

Rivers are referenced to their lowest downstream point – either their mouth or their confluence with another river. The river name will generally be positioned as close to this point as possible.

Entries relating to names appearing on insets are indicated by a small box symbol: ▫ followed by a grid reference if the inset has its own alphanumeric values.

ALTERNATIVE NAMES

Alternative names appear as cross-references and refer the user to the index entry for the form of the name used on the map.

For rivers with multiple names – for example those which flow through several countries – all alternative name forms are included within the main index entries, with details of the countries in which each form applies.

ADMINISTRATIVE QUALIFIERS

Administrative divisions are included in an entry to differentiate duplicate names – entries of exactly the same name and feature type within the one country – where these division names are shown on the maps. In such cases, duplicate names are alphabetized in the order of the administrative division names. Additional qualifiers are included for names within selected geographical areas, to indicate more clearly their location.

DESCRIPTORS

Entries, other than those for towns and cities, include a descriptor indicating the type of geographical feature. Descriptors are not included where the type of feature is implicit in the name itself, unless there is a town or city of exactly the same name.

NAME FORMS AND ALPHABETICAL ORDER

Name forms are as they appear on the maps, with additional alternative forms included as cross-references. Names appear in full in the index, although they may appear in abbreviated form on the maps.

The German character ß is alphabetized as 'ss'. Names beginning with Mac or Mc are alphabetized exactly as they appear. The terms Saint, Sainte, etc, are abbreviated to St, Ste, etc, but alphabetized as if in the full form.

NUMERICAL ENTRIES

Entries beginning with numerals appear at the beginning of the index, in numerical order. Elsewhere, numerals are alphabetized before 'a'.

PERMUTED TERMS

Names beginning with generic, geographical terms are permuted – the descriptive term is placed after, and the index alphabetized by, the main part of the name. For example, Lake Superior is indexed as Superior, Lake. This policy is applied to all languages. Permuting has not been applied to names of towns, cities or administrative divisions beginning with such geographical terms. These remain in their full form, for example, Lake Isabella, USA.

INDEX ABBREVIATIONS

admin. dist.	administrative district	IN	Indiana	Phil.	Philippines
admin. div.	administrative division	Indon.	Indonesia	plat.	plateau
admin. reg.	administrative region	is	islands	P.N.G.	Papua New Guinea
Afgh.	Afghanistan	Kazakh.	Kazakhstan	Port.	Portugal
AK	Alaska	KS	Kansas	prov.	province
AL	Alabama	KY	Kentucky	pt	point
Alg.	Algeria	Kyrg.	Kyrgyzstan	Qld	Queensland
Alta	Alberta	l.	lake	Que.	Québec
AR	Arkansas	LA	Louisiana	r.	river
Arg.	Argentina	lag.	lagoon	reg.	region
aut. comm.	autonomous community	Lith.	Lithuania	res.	reserve
aut. reg.	autonomous region	Lux.	Luxembourg	resr	reservoir
aut. rep.	autonomous republic	MA	Massachusetts	RI	Rhode Island
AZ	Arizona	Madag.	Madagascar	r. mouth	river mouth
Azer.	Azerbaijan	Man.	Manitoba	Rus. Fed.	Russian Federation
b.	bay	MD	Maryland	S.	South
Bangl.	Bangladesh	ME	Maine	S.A.	South Australia
B.C.	British Columbia	Mex.	Mexico	S. Africa	Republic of South Africa
Bol.	Bolivia	MI	Michigan	salt l.	salt lake
Bos.-Herz.	Bosnia-Herzegovina	MN	Minnesota	Sask.	Saskatchewan
Bulg.	Bulgaria	MO	Missouri	SC	South Carolina
c.	cape	Mont.	Montenegro	SD	South Dakota
CA	California	Moz.	Mozambique	sea chan.	sea channel
Cent. Afr. Rep.	Central African Republic	MS	Mississippi	Sing.	Singapore
CO	Colorado	MT	Montana	Switz.	Switzerland
Col.	Colombia	mt.	mountain	Tajik.	Tajikistan
CT	Connecticut	mts	mountains	Tanz.	Tanzania
Czech Rep.	Czech Republic	N.	North, Northern	Tas.	Tasmania
DC	District of Columbia	nat. park	national park	terr.	territory
DE	Delaware	N.B.	New Brunswick	Thai.	Thailand
Dem. Rep. Congo	Democratic Republic of the Congo	NC	North Carolina	TN	Tennessee
depr.	depression	ND	North Dakota	Trin. and Tob.	Trinidad and Tobago
des.	desert	NE	Nebraska	Turkm.	Turkmenistan
Dom. Rep.	Dominican Republic	Neth.	Netherlands	TX	Texas
Equat. Guinea	Equatorial Guinea	Neth. Antilles	Netherlands Antilles	U.A.E.	United Arab Emirates
esc.	escarpment	Nfld.	Newfoundland	U.K.	United Kingdom
est.	estuary	NH	New Hampshire	Ukr.	Ukraine
Eth.	Ethiopia	NJ	New Jersey	U.S.A.	United States of America
Fin.	Finland	NM	New Mexico	UT	Utah
FL	Florida	N.S.	Nova Scotia	Uzbek.	Uzbekistan
for.	forest	N.S.W.	New South Wales	VA	Virginia
Fr. Guiana	French Guiana	N.W.T.	Northwest Territories	Venez.	Venezuela
Fr. Polynesia	French Polynesia	N.Z.	New Zealand	Vic.	Victoria
g.	gulf	NV	Nevada	vol.	volcano
GA	Georgia	NY	New York	vol. crater	volcanic crater
Guat.	Guatemala	OH	Ohio	VT	Vermont
h.	hill	OK	Oklahoma	W.	Western
hd	headland	Ont.	Ontario	WA	Washington
HI	Hawaii	OR	Oregon	W.A.	Western Australia
Hond.	Honduras	PA	Pennsylvania	WI	Wisconsin
i.	island	Pak.	Pakistan	WV	West Virginia
IA	Iowa	Para.	Paraguay	WY	Wyoming
ID	Idaho	P.E.I.	Prince Edward Island		
IL	Illinois	pen.	peninsula		

Bangassou

108 C3 **Bangassou** Centr. Afr. Rep.
94 C2 **Banggai** Indon.
101 E7 **Banggai, Kepulauan** *is* Indon.
101 D6 **Banggi** *i.* Malaysia
Banghāzī Libya *see* **Benghazi**
101 C7 **Bangka** *i.* Indon.
101 C7 **Bangko** Indon.
99 I5 **Bangkok** Thai.
106 B4 **Bangolo** Côte d'Ivoire
113 M3 **Bangor** U.S.A.
108 B3 **Bangui** Centr. Afr. Rep.
109 C5 **Bangweulu, Lake** Zambia
109 D6 **Banhine, Parque Nacional de** *nat. park* Moz.
108 C3 **Bani** Centr. Afr. Rep.
108 B3 **Bania** Centr. Afr. Rep.
98 B4 **Banī Suwayf** Egypt
105 F5 **Banī Walīd** Libya
105 K4 **Bāniyās** Syria
105 G3 **Banja Luka** Bos.-Herz.
101 D7 **Banjarmasin** Indon.
106 A3 **Banjul** Gambia
106 B3 **Bankass** Mali
110 E4 **Banks Island** *B.C.* Canada
110 F2 **Banks Island** *N.W.T.* Canada
95 G3 **Banks Islands** Vanuatu
95 H6 **Banks Peninsula** N.Z.
104 B1 **Bantry** Ireland
107 D4 **Banyo** Cameroon
119 L6 **Banzare Seamount** *sea feature* Indian Ocean
Banzart Tunisia *see* **Bizerte**
100 D2 **Baochang** China
100 D3 **Baoding** China
100 C3 **Baoji** China
101 B4 **Baoshan** China
100 D2 **Baotou** China
98 C3 **Ba'qūbah** Iraq
Baquerizo Moreno Ecuador *see* **Puerto Baquerizo Moreno**
105 G3 **Bar** Montenegro
107 F3 **Bara** Sudan
108 E3 **Baraawe** Somalia
115 J4 **Baracoa** Cuba
115 J5 **Barahona** Dom. Rep.
107 F3 **Baraka** *watercourse* Eritrea/Sudan
103 L5 **Baranavichy** Belarus
97 R3 **Baranikha** Rus. Fed.
Baranovichi Belarus *see* **Baranavichy**
Baranowicze Belarus *see* **Baranavichy**
106 B3 **Baraouéli** Mali
101 E7 **Barat Daya, Kepulauan** *is* Indon.
117 J8 **Barbacena** Brazil
115 M6 **Barbados** *country* Caribbean Sea
104 D3 **Barbastro** Spain
115 L5 **Barbuda** *i.* Antigua and Barbuda
95 E4 **Barcaldine** Australia
Barce Libya *see* **Al Marj**
104 D3 **Barcelona** Spain
117 F1 **Barcelona** Venez.
117 F4 **Barcelos** Brazil
Barcino Spain *see* **Barcelona**
106 B4 **Barclayville** Liberia
102 D2 **Barðsneshorn** *pt* Iceland
99 F4 **Bareilly** India
96 C2 **Barentsburg** Svalbard
96 D2 **Barentsøya** *i.* Svalbard
103 N1 **Barents Sea** Arctic Ocean
108 D2 **Barentu** Eritrea
105 G3 **Bari** Italy
104 E4 **Barika** Alg.
116 D2 **Barinas** Venez.
101 C7 **Barisan, Pegunungan** *mts* Indon.
101 D7 **Barito** *r.* Indon.
117 F8 **Baritú, Parque Nacional** *nat. park* Arg.
Barium Italy *see* **Bari**
94 D3 **Barkly Tableland** *reg.* Australia
100 B2 **Barkol** China
94 B4 **Barlee, Lake** *salt flat* Australia
97 J4 **Barnaul** Rus. Fed.
111 K2 **Barnes Icecap** Canada
104 C1 **Barnstaple** U.K.
116 E1 **Barquisimeto** Venez.
117 J6 **Barra** Brazil
117 G6 **Barra do Bugres** Brazil
117 I5 **Barra do Corda** Brazil
117 H7 **Barra do Garças** Brazil
117 G5 **Barra do São Manuel** Brazil
116 C6 **Barranca** *Lima* Peru
116 C4 **Barranca** *Loreto* Peru
116 D2 **Barrancabermeja** Col.
117 F2 **Barrancas** Venez.
118 E3 **Barranqueras** Arg.
116 D1 **Barranquilla** Col.
117 J6 **Barreiras** Brazil
117 G4 **Barreirinha** Brazil
117 J4 **Barreirinhas** Brazil
117 K5 **Barreiros** Brazil
117 I8 **Barretos** Brazil
113 K3 **Barrie** Canada
95 E5 **Barrier Range** *hills* Australia
110 C2 **Barrow** U.S.A.
110 C2 **Barrow, Point** U.S.A.
94 D4 **Barrow Creek** Australia
94 B4 **Barrow Island** Australia
111 I2 **Barrow Strait** Canada
112 C5 **Barstow** U.S.A.
117 G2 **Bartica** Guyana
105 J3 **Bartın** Turkey
95 E3 **Bartle Frere, Mount** Australia
113 G4 **Bartlesville** U.S.A.
115 H7 **Barú, Volcán** *vol.* Panama
100 D2 **Baruun-Urt** Mongolia
95 E5 **Barwon** *r.* Australia
103 L5 **Barysaw** Belarus
103 P5 **Barysh** Rus. Fed.
108 B3 **Basankusu** Dem. Rep. Congo
102 H6 **Basel** Switz.
103 O5 **Bashmakovo** Rus. Fed.
101 E6 **Basilan** *i.* Phil.
113 K2 **Baskatong, Réservoir** *resr* Canada
105 J4 **Başkomutan Tarıhı Milli Parkı** *nat. park* Turkey
Basle Switz. *see* **Basel**
108 C3 **Basoko** Dem. Rep. Congo
98 C3 **Basra** Iraq
106 C4 **Bassar** Togo
109 D6 **Bassas da India** *rf* Indian Ocean
101 B5 **Bassein** Myanmar
106 A3 **Basse Santa Su** Gambia
115 L5 **Basse-Terre** Guadeloupe
115 L5 **Basseterre** St Kitts and Nevis
106 B3 **Bassikounou** Mauritania
106 C4 **Bassila** Benin
95 E5 **Bass Strait** Australia
98 D4 **Bastak** Iran
104 E3 **Bastia** France
113 H5 **Bastrop** U.S.A.
106 C4 **Bata** Equat. Guinea
115 H4 **Batabanó, Golfo de** *b.* Cuba
97 O3 **Batagay** Rus. Fed.
97 N3 **Batamay** Rus. Fed.
108 B3 **Batangafo** Centr. Afr. Rep.
101 E5 **Batangas** Phil.
101 E4 **Batan Islands** Phil.
Batavia Indon. *see* **Jakarta**
105 K2 **Bataysk** Rus. Fed.
101 F8 **Batchelor** Australia
101 C5 **Bătdâmbâng** Cambodia
95 F5 **Batemans Bay** Australia
113 M2 **Bathurst** Canada
111 H3 **Bathurst Inlet** Canada
111 H3 **Bathurst Inlet** *inlet* Canada
101 E8 **Bathurst Island** Australia
111 I2 **Bathurst Island** Canada
105 J4 **Batı Toroslar** *mts* Turkey
104 E4 **Batna** Alg.
113 H5 **Baton Rouge** U.S.A.
107 D4 **Batouri** Cameroon
99 G6 **Batticaloa** Sri Lanka
113 I3 **Battle Creek** U.S.A.
112 C3 **Battle Mountain** U.S.A.
101 B7 **Batu, Pulau-pulau** *is* Indon.
98 C2 **Bat'umi** Georgia
101 E7 **Baubau** Indon.
106 C3 **Bauchi** Nigeria
117 I8 **Bauru** Brazil
103 K4 **Bauska** Latvia
105 F1 **Bautzen** Germany
112 E6 **Bavispe** *r.* Mex.
101 D7 **Bawean** *i.* Indon.
106 B3 **Bawku** Ghana
115 I4 **Bayamo** Cuba
100 B3 **Bayan Har Shan** *mts* China
100 C2 **Bayanhongor** Mongolia
97 L6 **Bayan Hot** China
100 C2 **Bayan Obo** China
97 M5 **Bayan Ul Hot** China
97 M5 **Bayan-Uul** Mongolia
98 C2 **Bayburt** Turkey
113 J3 **Bay City** *MI* U.S.A.
113 G6 **Bay City** *TX* U.S.A.
96 H3 **Baydaratskaya Guba** Rus. Fed.
108 E3 **Baydhabo** Somalia
Baykal, Ozero *l.* Rus. Fed. *see* **Baikal, Lake**
100 C1 **Baykal'skiy Khrebet** *mts* Rus. Fed.
99 E2 **Baykonyr** Kazakh.
98 D1 **Baymak** Rus. Fed.
101 E5 **Bayombong** Phil.
Bayona Spain *see* **Baiona**
104 C3 **Bayonne** France
105 F2 **Bayreuth** Germany
105 G5 **Bayy al Kabīr, Wādī** *watercourse* Libya
109 D6 **Bazaruto, Ilha do** *i.* Moz.
109 E5 **Bé, Nosy** *i.* Madag.
118 C8 **Beagle, Canal** *sea chan.* Arg.
101 E8 **Beagle Gulf** Australia
109 E5 **Bealanana** Madag.
Béal an Átha Ireland *see* **Ballina**
113 I2 **Beardmore** Canada
115 J5 **Beata, Cabo** *c.* Dom. Rep.
115 J5 **Beata, Isla** *i.* Dom. Rep.
113 G3 **Beatrice** U.S.A.
118 E8 **Beauchene Island** Falkland Is
110 D2 **Beaufort Sea** Canada/U.S.A.
113 H5 **Beaumont** U.S.A.
104 D2 **Beaune** France
104 D2 **Beauvais** France
111 H4 **Beaver** *r.* Canada
110 D3 **Beaver Creek** Canada
113 I3 **Beaver Dam** U.S.A.
99 F4 **Beawar** India
118 C4 **Beazley** Arg.
117 I8 **Bebedouro** Brazil
104 C5 **Béchar** Alg.
113 J4 **Beckley** U.S.A.
108 D3 **Bedelē** Eth.
95 F4 **Beenleigh** Australia
98 B3 **Beersheba** Israel
Be'ér Sheva' Israel *see* **Beersheba**
113 G6 **Beeville** U.S.A.
108 C3 **Befale** Dem. Rep. Congo
109 E5 **Befandriana Avaratra** Madag.
95 E5 **Bega** Australia
117 H3 **Béhague, Pointe** Fr. Guiana
110 G3 **Behchokô** Canada
119 I3 **Behrendt Mountains** Antarctica
98 D3 **Behshahr** Iran
100 E2 **Bei'an** China
Beida Libya *see* **Al Bayḍā'**
101 C4 **Beihai** China
97 M6 **Beijing** China
109 D5 **Beira** Moz.
98 B3 **Beirut** Lebanon
109 C6 **Beitbridge** Zimbabwe
104 B4 **Beja** Port.
104 E4 **Béja** Tunisia
104 E4 **Bejaïa** Alg.
105 H2 **Békéscsaba** Hungary
109 E6 **Bekily** Madag.
106 B4 **Bekwai** Ghana
99 E4 **Bela** Pak.
107 D4 **Bélabo** Cameroon
103 L5 **Belarus** *country* Europe
109 D6 **Bela Vista** Moz.
97 S3 **Belaya** *r.* Rus. Fed.
Belaya Tserkva Ukr. *see* **Bila Tserkva**
111 J4 **Belcher Islands** Canada
108 E3 **Beledweyne** Somalia
117 I4 **Belém** Brazil
118 C3 **Belén** Arg.
112 E5 **Belen** U.S.A.
95 G3 **Belep, Îles** *is* New Caledonia
103 N5 **Belev** Rus. Fed.
102 E5 **Belfast** U.K.
104 E2 **Belfort** France
België *country* Europe *see* **Belgium**
Belgique *country* Europe *see* **Belgium**
102 G5 **Belgium** *country* Europe
105 K1 **Belgorod** Rus. Fed.
Belgorod-Dnestrovskyy Ukr. *see* **Bilhorod-Dnistrovs'kyy**
105 H3 **Belgrade** Serbia
119 J3 **Belgrano II** *research stn* Antarctica
101 C7 **Belinyu** Indon.
101 C7 **Belitung** *i.* Indon.
115 G5 **Belize** Belize
Beljak Austria *see* **Villach**
97 O2 **Bel'kovskiy, Ostrov** *i.* Rus. Fed.
104 D2 **Bellac** France
110 F4 **Bella Coola** Canada
99 F5 **Bellary** India
113 F3 **Belle Fourche** *r.* U.S.A.
104 C2 **Belle-Île** *i.* France
111 M4 **Belle Isle, Strait of** Canada
112 B2 **Bellingham** U.S.A.
119 L2 **Bellingshausen** *research stn* Antarctica
119 I3 **Bellingshausen Sea** Antarctica
104 E2 **Bellinzona** Switz.
116 C2 **Bello** Col.
105 F2 **Belluno** Italy
117 K7 **Belmonte** Brazil
115 G5 **Belmopan** Belize
100 E1 **Belogorsk** Rus. Fed.
109 E6 **Beloha** Madag.
117 J7 **Belo Horizonte** Brazil
113 I3 **Beloit** U.S.A.
103 M3 **Belomorsk** Rus. Fed.
96 G4 **Beloretsk** Rus. Fed.
Belorussia *country* Europe *see* **Belarus**
Belorusskaya S.S.R. *country* Europe *see* **Belarus**
109 E5 **Belo Tsiribihina** Madag.
103 N3 **Beloye, Ozero** *l.* Rus. Fed.
Beloye More *sea* Rus. Fed. *see* **White Sea**
103 N3 **Belozersk** Rus. Fed.
103 P2 **Belush'ye** Rus. Fed.
96 I2 **Belyy, Ostrov** *i.* Rus. Fed.
113 H2 **Bemidji** U.S.A.
109 C4 **Bena Dibele** Dem. Rep. Congo
112 B3 **Bend** U.S.A.
108 E3 **Bender-Bayla** Somalia
95 E5 **Bendigo** Australia
109 D5 **Bene** Moz.
109 E6 **Benenitra** Madag.
105 F2 **Benešov** Czech Rep.
105 F3 **Benevento** Italy
Beneventum Italy *see* **Benevento**
99 G5 **Bengal, Bay of** *sea* Asia
108 C3 **Bengamisa** Dem. Rep. Congo
100 D3 **Bengbu** China
105 H5 **Benghazi** Libya
101 C7 **Bengkulu** Indon.
109 B5 **Benguela** Angola
116 E6 **Beni** *r.* Bol.
108 C3 **Beni** Dem. Rep. Congo
104 C5 **Beni Abbès** Alg.
106 B1 **Beni Mellal** Morocco
106 C4 **Benin** *country* Africa
106 C4 **Benin, Bight of** *g.* Africa
106 C4 **Benin City** Nigeria
104 C4 **Beni Saf** Alg.
118 E5 **Benito Juárez** Arg.
116 E4 **Benjamim Constant** Brazil
112 D5 **Benjamín Hill** Mex.
94 D2 **Benjina** Indon.
97 P2 **Bennetta, Ostrov** *i.* Rus. Fed.
102 E4 **Ben Nevis** *mt.* U.K.
107 D4 **Bénoué, Parc National de la** *nat. park* Cameroon
101 E7 **Benteng** Indon.
94 D3 **Bentinck Island** Australia
107 D4 **Benue** *r.* Nigeria
100 E2 **Benxi** China
Beograd Serbia *see* **Belgrade**
106 B4 **Béoumi** Côte d'Ivoire
95 H3 **Beqa** *i.* Fiji
105 G3 **Berat** Albania
101 F7 **Berau, Teluk** *b.* Indon.
107 F3 **Berber** Sudan
108 E2 **Berbera** Somalia
108 B3 **Berbérati** Centr. Afr. Rep.
Berdichev Ukr. *see* **Berdychiv**
97 N3 **Berdigestyakh** Rus. Fed.
100 A1 **Berdsk** Rus. Fed.
103 N6 **Berdyans'k** Ukr.
103 L6 **Berdychiv** Ukr.
95 E2 **Bereina** P.N.G.
98 D3 **Bereket** Turkm.
Berenice Libya *see* **Benghazi**
113 G1 **Berens River** Canada
Bereza Belarus *see* **Byaroza**
103 M6 **Berezivka** Ukr.
96 F3 **Bereznik** Rus. Fed.
Berezovka Ukr. *see* **Berezivka**
96 H3 **Berezovo** Rus. Fed.
104 D3 **Berga** Spain
105 I4 **Bergama** Turkey
104 E2 **Bergamo** Italy
102 H3 **Bergen** Norway
Bergomum Italy *see* **Bergamo**
97 R4 **Beringa, Ostrov** *i.* Rus. Fed.
97 S3 **Beringovskiy** Rus. Fed.
97 S4 **Bering Sea** Pacific Ocean
110 B3 **Bering Strait** Rus. Fed./U.S.A.
112 B4 **Berkeley** U.S.A.
119 J3 **Berkner Island** Antarctica
105 F1 **Berlin** Germany
111 K5 **Berlin** U.S.A.
111 J2 **Berlinguet Inlet** Canada
118 D2 **Bermejo** *r.* Arg./Bol.
118 D2 **Bermejo** Bol.
115 M2 **Bermuda** *terr.* Atlantic Ocean
123 E4 **Bermuda Rise** *sea feature* N. Atlantic Ocean
102 H6 **Bern** Switz.
118 A7 **Bernardo O'Higgins, Parque Nacional** *nat. park* Chile
118 D5 **Bernasconi** Arg.
Berne Switz. *see* **Bern**
111 J2 **Bernier Bay** Canada
94 B4 **Bernier Island** Australia
Beroea Greece *see* **Veroia**
109 E6 **Beroroha** Madag.
104 D5 **Berriane** Alg.
113 K6 **Berry Islands** Bahamas
117 J5 **Bertolinía** Brazil
107 D4 **Bertoua** Cameroon
95 H2 **Beru** *atoll* Kiribati
117 F4 **Beruri** Brazil
102 F4 **Berwick-upon-Tweed** U.K.
109 E5 **Besalampy** Madag.
102 H6 **Besançon** France
Beskra Alg. *see* **Biskra**
113 I5 **Bessemer** U.S.A.
109 E6 **Betanty** Madag.
107 D4 **Bétaré Oya** Cameroon
110 B3 **Bethel** U.S.A.
109 E6 **Betioky** Madag.
99 F2 **Betpak-Dala** *plain* Kazakh.
109 E6 **Betroka** Madag.
113 M2 **Betsiamites** Canada
109 E5 **Betsiboka** *r.* Madag.
99 G4 **Bettiah** India
110 C4 **Beverley, Lake** U.S.A.
106 B4 **Beyla** Guinea
105 J3 **Beypazarı** Turkey
105 J4 **Beyşehir** Turkey
105 J4 **Beyşehir Gölü** *l.* Turkey
103 N4 **Bezhetsk** Rus. Fed.
104 D3 **Béziers** France
101 B4 **Bhamo** Myanmar
99 F4 **Bhilwara** India
99 F5 **Bhima** *r.* India
99 F4 **Bhopal** India
99 G4 **Bhubaneshwar** India
99 E4 **Bhuj** India
101 F7 **Biak** Indon.
101 F7 **Biak** *i.* Indon.
96 D4 **Białystok** Poland
Bianco, Monte *mt.* France/Italy *see* **Blanc, Mont**
106 B4 **Biankouma** Côte d'Ivoire
109 B5 **Bibala** Angola
94 D3 **Bickerton Island** Australia
109 B5 **Bicuari, Parque Nacional do** *nat. park* Angola
106 C4 **Bida** Nigeria
102 H6 **Biel** Switz.
104 E1 **Bielefeld** Germany
Bielitz Poland *see* **Bielsko-Biała**
103 J6 **Bielsko-Biała** Poland
101 C5 **Biên Hoa** Vietnam
Bienne Switz. *see* **Biel**
111 K4 **Bienville, Lac** *l.* Canada
109 B4 **Bifoun** Gabon
113 F6 **Big Bend National Park** U.S.A.
113 J6 **Big Cypress National Preserve** U.S.A.
112 E1 **Biggar** Canada
112 E2 **Bighorn** *r.* U.S.A.
112 E3 **Bighorn Mountains** U.S.A.
111 K3 **Big Island** Canada
106 A3 **Bignona** Senegal
113 F5 **Big Spring** U.S.A.
113 I1 **Big Trout Lake** Canada
111 J4 **Big Trout Lake** *l.* Canada
105 G3 **Bihać** Bos.-Herz.
99 G4 **Bihar** *state* India
106 A3 **Bijagós, Arquipélago dos** *is* Guinea-Bissau
96 F6 **Bījār** Iran
105 G3 **Bijelo Polje** Montenegro
100 F2 **Bikin** Rus. Fed.
120 G5 **Bikini** *atoll* Marshall Is
109 B4 **Bikoro** Dem. Rep. Congo
103 M6 **Bila Tserkva** Ukr.
104 C3 **Bilbao** Spain
Bilbo Spain *see* **Bilbao**
105 I3 **Bilecik** Turkey
109 D4 **Bilharamulo** Tanz.
105 J2 **Bilhorod-Dnistrovs'kyy** Ukr.
108 C3 **Bili** Dem. Rep. Congo
97 R3 **Bilibino** Rus. Fed.
123 J2 **Billingford** U.K.
112 E2 **Billings** U.S.A.
107 D3 **Bilma** Niger
107 D3 **Bilma, Grand Erg de** *des.* Niger
95 F4 **Biloela** Australia
113 I5 **Biloxi** U.S.A.
94 D4 **Bilpa Morea Claypan** *salt flat* Australia
107 E3 **Biltine** Chad
108 B3 **Bimbo** C.A.R.
113 K6 **Bimini Islands** Bahamas
101 E7 **Binaija, Gunung** *mt.* Indon.
109 B4 **Bindu** Dem. Rep. Congo
109 D5 **Bindura** Zimbabwe
106 B4 **Bingerville** Côte d'Ivoire
113 K3 **Binghamton** U.S.A.
101 C7 **Bintuhan** Indon.
101 D6 **Bintulu** Malaysia
118 B5 **Biobío** *r.* Chile
106 C4 **Bioco** *i.* Equat. Guinea
107 D2 **Birāk** Libya
108 C2 **Birao** Centr. Afr. Rep.
119 J1 **Bird Island** S. Georgia
94 D4 **Birdsville** Australia
107 E3 **Bir en Natrûn** *well* Sudan
101 B6 **Bireun** Indon.
108 D2 **Birhan** *mt.* Eth.
118 F2 **Birigüi** Brazil
98 D3 **Bīrjand** Iran
104 C1 **Birmingham** U.K.
113 I5 **Birmingham** U.S.A.
106 A2 **Bîr Mogreïn** Mauritania
106 C3 **Birnin-Kebbi** Nigeria
106 C3 **Birnin Konni** Niger
100 F2 **Birobidzhan** Rus. Fed.
112 E5 **Bisbee** U.S.A.
104 B2 **Biscay, Bay of** *sea* France/Spain
123 I3 **Biscay Abyssal Plain** *sea feature* N. Atlantic Ocean
113 J6 **Biscayne National Park** U.S.A.
119 I2 **Biscoe Islands** Antarctica
99 F2 **Bishkek** Kyrg.
100 E1 **Bishui** China
104 E5 **Biskra** Alg.
113 F2 **Bismarck** U.S.A.
95 E2 **Bismarck Archipelago** *is* P.N.G.
95 E2 **Bismarck Range** *mts* P.N.G.
95 E2 **Bismarck Sea** P.N.G.
106 A3 **Bissau** Guinea-Bissau
107 D4 **Bissaula** Nigeria
110 G4 **Bistcho Lake** Canada
105 H2 **Bistriţa** Romania
104 E2 **Bitburg** Germany
107 D3 **Bitkine** Chad
105 H3 **Bitola** Macedonia
Bitolj Macedonia *see* **Bitola**
112 C2 **Bitterroot Range** *mts* U.S.A.
107 D3 **Biu** Nigeria
108 E2 **Bīye K'obē** Eth.
97 J4 **Biysk** Rus. Fed.
Bizerta Tunisia *see* **Bizerte**
104 E4 **Bizerte** Tunisia
102 B2 **Bjargtangar** *hd* Iceland
96 C2 **Bjørnøya** *i.* Svalbard
106 B3 **Bla** Mali
95 E4 **Blackall** Australia
113 F3 **Black Hills** U.S.A.
111 H4 **Black Lake** *l.* Canada
104 C1 **Blackpool** U.K.
99 I4 **Black River** *r.* Vietnam
105 K3 **Black Sea** Asia/Europe
106 B4 **Black Volta** *r.* Africa
94 B5 **Blackwood** *r.* Australia
103 O6 **Blagodarnyy** Rus. Fed.
105 H3 **Blagoevgrad** Bulg.
100 E1 **Blagoveshchensk** Rus. Fed.
104 E2 **Blanc, Mont** *mt.* France/Italy
118 D5 **Blanca, Bahía** *b.* Arg.
94 D4 **Blanche, Lake** *salt flat* Australia
118 C4 **Blanco** *r.* Arg.
117 F6 **Blanco** *r.* Bol.
112 B3 **Blanco, Cape** U.S.A.
112 E4 **Blanding** U.S.A.
117 F1 **Blanquilla, Isla** *i.* Venez.
109 D5 **Blantyre** Malawi
95 H6 **Blenheim** N.Z.
104 D4 **Blida** Alg.
95 H3 **Bligh Water** *b.* Fiji
102 B2 **Blönduós** Iceland
113 I3 **Bloomington** *IL* U.S.A.
113 I4 **Bloomington** *IN* U.S.A.
111 P3 **Blosseville Kyst** *coastal area* Greenland
113 J4 **Bluefield** U.S.A.
115 H6 **Bluefields** Nicaragua
112 C2 **Blue Mountains** U.S.A.
107 F3 **Blue Nile** *r.* Sudan *alt.* **Ābay Wenz (Ethiopia),** *al* **Azraq, Bahr el (Sudan)**
107 F3 **Blue Nile** *r.* Sudan
110 G3 **Bluenose Lake** Canada
113 J4 **Blue Ridge** *mts* U.S.A.
112 D5 **Blythe** U.S.A.
106 A4 **Bo** Sierra Leone
101 E5 **Boac** Phil.
117 J5 **Boa Esperança, Açude** *resr* Brazil
108 B3 **Boali** Centr. Afr. Rep.
117 K5 **Boa Viagem** Brazil
117 F3 **Boa Vista** Brazil
106 □ **Boa Vista** *i.* Cape Verde
109 E5 **Bobaomby, Tanjona** *c.* Madag
106 B3 **Bobo-Dioulasso** Burkina
109 C6 **Bobonong** Botswana
Bobriki Rus. Fed. *see* **Novomoskovsk**
Bobruysk Belarus *see* **Babruysk**
109 E6 **Boby** *mt.* Madag.
115 L7 **Boca de Macareo** Venez.
116 E5 **Boca do Acre** Brazil
117 H4 **Boca do Jari** Brazil
108 B3 **Bocaranga** Centr. Afr. Rep.
115 H7 **Bocas del Toro** Panama
108 B3 **Boda** Centr. Afr. Rep.
100 D1 **Bodaybo** Rus. Fed.
107 D3 **Bodélé** *reg.* Chad
103 K2 **Boden** Sweden
Bodensee *l.* Germany/Switz. *see* **Constance, Lake**
102 I2 **Bodø** Norway
105 I4 **Bodrum** Turkey
109 C4 **Boende** Dem. Rep. Congo
106 A3 **Boffa** Guinea
106 B3 **Bogandé** Burkina
100 A2 **Bogda Shan** *mts* China
Boghari Alg. *see* **Ksar el Boukhari**
101 C7 **Bogor** Indon.
116 D3 **Bogotá** Col.
100 A1 **Bogotol** Rus. Fed.
97 K4 **Boguchany** Rus. Fed.
106 A3 **Bogué** Mauritania
100 D3 **Bo Hai** *g.* China
100 D3 **Bohai Wan** *b.* China
Bohemian Forest *mts* Germany *see* **Böhmer Wald**
103 I6 **Böhmer Wald** *mts* Germany
101 E6 **Bohol Sea** Phil.
99 G2 **Bohu** China
117 G4 **Boim** Brazil
117 K6 **Boipeba, Ilha** *i.* Brazil
110 F3 **Bois, Lac des** *l.* Canada
112 C3 **Boise** U.S.A.
98 D3 **Bojnūrd** Iran
109 B4 **Bokatola** Dem. Rep. Congo
106 A3 **Boké** Guinea
109 C4 **Bokele** Dem. Rep. Congo
102 H4 **Boknafjorden** *sea chan.* Norway
107 D3 **Bokoro** Chad
109 C4 **Bolaiti** Dem. Rep. Congo
106 A3 **Bolama** Guinea-Bissau
99 G2 **Bole** China
106 B4 **Bole** Ghana
109 B4 **Boleko** Dem. Rep. Congo
106 B3 **Bolgatanga** Ghana
Bolgrad Ukr. *see* **Bolhrad**
105 I2 **Bolhrad** Ukr.
109 B4 **Bolia** Dem. Rep. Congo
116 C5 **Bolívar** Peru
116 D2 **Bolívar, Pico** *mt.* Venez.
116 E7 **Bolivia** *country* S. America
103 J3 **Bollnäs** Sweden
103 I4 **Bolmen** *l.* Sweden
109 B4 **Bolobo** Dem. Rep. Congo
105 F3 **Bologna** Italy
103 M3 **Bologoye** Rus. Fed.
108 B3 **Bolomba** Dem. Rep. Congo
97 J4 **Bolotnoye** Rus. Fed.
97 L2 **Bol'shevik, Ostrov** *i.* Rus. Fed.
103 Q2 **Bol'shezemel'skaya Tundra** *lowland* Rus. Fed.
97 R3 **Bol'shoy Aluy** *r.* Rus. Fed.
Bol'shoy Tokmak Ukr. *see* **Tokmak**
113 F6 **Bolsón de Mapimí** *des.* Mex.
105 J3 **Bolu** Turkey
105 F2 **Bolzano** Italy
109 B4 **Boma** Dem. Rep. Congo
Bombay India *see* **Mumbai**
101 F7 **Bomberai, Semenanjung** *pen.* Indon.
116 E5 **Bom Comércio** Brazil
101 B4 **Bomdila** India
117 J6 **Bom Jesus da Lapa** Brazil
105 F4 **Bon, Cap** *c.* Tunisia
Bona Alg. *see* **Annaba**
115 K6 **Bonaire** *i.* Neth. Antilles
115 H6 **Bonanza** Nicaragua

Carrizal Bajo

94 C3 Bonaparte Archipelago is Australia
11 M5 Bonavista Bay Canada
08 C3 Bondo Dem. Rep. Congo
06 B4 Bondoukou Côte d'Ivoire
Bône Alg. see Annaba
01 E7 Bone, Teluk b. Indon.
01 E7 Bonerate, Kepulauan is Indon.
08 D3 Bonga Eth.
08 C3 Bongandanga Dem. Rep. Congo
08 C3 Bongo, Massif des mts Centr. Afr. Rep.
09 E5 Bongolava mts Madag.
07 D3 Bongor Chad
06 B4 Bongouanou Côte d'Ivoire
04 E3 Bonifacio France
Bonifacio, Bocche di str. France/Italy see Bonifacio, Strait of
Bonifacio, Bouches de str. France/Italy see Bonifacio, Strait of
04 E3 Bonifacio, Strait of France/Italy
01 G4 Bonin Islands Japan
02 H5 Bonn Germany
Bonna Germany see Bonn
94 B5 Bonnie Rock Australia
10 G4 Bonnyville Canada
Bononia Italy see Bologna
06 A4 Bonthe Sierra Leone
01 E5 Bontoc Phil.
01 D7 Bontosunggu Indon.
13 H4 Boonville U.S.A.
08 E2 Boosaaso Somalia
11 I2 Boothia, Gulf of Canada
11 I2 Boothia Peninsula Canada
06 A4 Bopolu Liberia
12 E6 Boquilla, Presa de la resr Mex.
07 F4 Bor Sudan
05 J4 Bor Turkey
09 F5 Boraha, Nosy i. Madag.
103 I4 Borås Sweden
98 D4 Borāzjān Iran
117 G4 Borba Brazil
117 K5 Borborema, Planalto da plat. Brazil
02 F7 Bordeaux France
10 G2 Borden Island Canada
111 J2 Borden Peninsula Canada
104 D4 Bordj Bou Arréridj Alg.
104 E5 Bordj Messaouda Alg.
106 C2 Bordj Omer Driss Alg.
102 B3 Borgarnes Iceland
105 L1 Borisoglebsk Rus. Fed.
Borisov Belarus see Barysaw
103 J3 Borlänge Sweden
01 D6 Borneo i. Asia
103 I4 Bornholm i. Denmark
97 J3 Borodino Rus. Fed.
97 O3 Borogontsy Rus. Fed.
106 B3 Boromo Burkina
103 M4 Borovichi Rus. Fed.
103 Q3 Borovoy Rus. Fed.
94 D3 Borroloola Australia
100 C2 Borshchovochnyy Khrebet mts Rus. Fed.
98 C3 Borūjerd Iran
100 D1 Borzya Rus. Fed.
101 C4 Bose China
Bosna i Hercegovina country Europe see Bosnia-Herzegovina
Bosna Saray Bos.-Herz. see Sarajevo
105 G3 Bosnia-Herzegovina country Europe
108 B3 Bosobolo Dem. Rep. Congo
108 B3 Bossangoa Centr. Afr. Rep.
108 B3 Bossembélé Centr. Afr. Rep.
100 A2 Bosten Hu l. China
113 L3 Boston U.S.A.
113 H4 Boston Mountains U.S.A.
95 F5 Botany Bay Australia
103 J3 Bothnia, Gulf of Fin./Sweden
105 I2 Botoșani Romania
109 C6 Botswana country Africa
106 B4 Bouaflé Côte d'Ivoire
106 B4 Bouaké Côte d'Ivoire
108 B3 Bouar Centr. Afr. Rep.
104 C5 Bouârfa Morocco
107 D4 Bouba Ndjida, Parc National de nat. park Cameroon
108 B3 Bouca Centr. Afr. Rep.
106 B3 Boucle du Baoulé, Parc National de la nat. park Mali
95 F2 Bougainville Island P.N.G.
Bougie Alg. see Bejaïa
106 B3 Bougouni Mali
104 D5 Bougtob Alg.
104 D4 Bouira Alg.
106 A2 Boujdour W. Sahara
112 E3 Boulder U.S.A.
112 D4 Boulder City U.S.A.
94 D4 Boulia Australia
Boulogne France see Boulogne-sur-Mer
102 G5 Boulogne-sur-Mer France
106 B3 Boulsa Burkina
109 B4 Boumango Gabon
107 D4 Boumba r. Cameroon
106 B4 Bouna Côte d'Ivoire
104 C5 Bou Naceur, Jbel mt. Morocco
106 B4 Boundiali Côte d'Ivoire
109 B4 Boundji Congo
95 H6 Bounty Islands N.Z.
120 G9 Bounty Trough sea feature S. Pacific Ocean
106 B3 Bourem Mali
104 E2 Bourg-en-Bresse France
102 G6 Bourges France
95 E5 Bourke Australia
104 C1 Bournemouth U.K.
104 D4 Bou Saâda Alg.
107 D3 Bousso Chad
106 A3 Boutilimit Mauritania
123 J9 Bouvetøya terr. Atlantic Ocean
112 D2 Bow r. Canada
95 E4 Bowen Australia
120 G2 Bowers Ridge sea feature Bering Sea
113 I4 Bowling Green U.S.A.
119 K6 Bowman Island Antarctica
105 J3 Boyabat Turkey
118 D2 Boyuibe Bol.
112 D2 Bozeman U.S.A.
Bozen Italy see Bolzano
108 B3 Bozoum Centr. Afr. Rep.
Bracara Port. see Braga
113 K2 Bracebridge Canada
115 L5 Brades Montserrat
113 G5 Brady U.S.A.
104 B3 Braga Port.
117 I4 Bragança Brazil
104 B3 Bragança Port.
99 G5 Brahmapur India
99 H4 Brahmaputra r. Asia
105 I2 Brăila Romania
109 B6 Brakwater Namibia
117 F4 Branco r. Brazil
113 G2 Brandon Canada
119 I2 Bransfield Strait Antarctica
111 L5 Bras d'Or Lake Canada
116 E6 Brasileia Brazil
117 I7 Brasília Brazil
117 G4 Brasília Legal Brazil
98 A2 Brașov Romania
103 J6 Bratislava Slovakia
100 C1 Bratsk Rus. Fed.
100 C1 Bratskoye Vodokhranilishche resr Rus. Fed.
105 F2 Braunau am Inn Austria
103 I5 Braunschweig Germany
106 □ Brava i. Cape Verde
112 C5 Brawley U.S.A.
117 H6 Brazil country S. America
123 H7 Brazil Basin sea feature S. Atlantic Ocean
90 Brazilian Highlands plat. Brazil
113 G6 Brazos r. U.S.A.
109 B4 Brazzaville Congo
113 G5 Breckenridge U.S.A.
105 G2 Břeclav Czech Rep.
104 D1 Breda Neth.
117 I6 Brejinho de Nazaré Brazil
104 E1 Bremen Germany
104 E1 Bremerhaven Germany
113 G5 Brenham U.S.A.
105 F2 Brescia Italy
Breslau Poland see Wrocław
105 F2 Bressanone Italy
96 D4 Brest Belarus
104 C2 Brest France
113 I6 Breton Sound b. U.S.A.
117 H4 Breves Brazil
95 E4 Brewarrina Australia
103 N4 Breytovo Rus. Fed.
108 C3 Bria Centr. Afr. Rep.
104 E3 Briançon France
113 L3 Bridgeport U.S.A.
115 M6 Bridgetown Barbados
111 L5 Bridgewater Canada
104 E2 Brig Switz.
112 D3 Brigham City U.S.A.
104 C1 Brighton U.K.
106 A3 Brikama Gambia
105 G3 Brindisi Italy
95 F4 Brisbane Australia
104 C1 Bristol U.K.
113 J4 Bristol U.S.A.
110 B4 Bristol Bay U.S.A.
119 K3 British Antarctic Territory reg. Antarctica
112 B1 British Columbia prov. Canada
111 J1 British Empire Range mts Canada
122 E5 British Isles N. Atlantic Ocean
104 D2 Brive-la-Gaillarde France
Brixia Italy see Brescia
103 J6 Brno Czech Rep.
113 J5 Broad r. U.S.A.
113 K1 Broadback r. Canada
111 H4 Brochet Canada
111 H4 Brochet, Lac l. Canada
110 G2 Brock Island Canada
113 L3 Brockton U.S.A.
111 J2 Brodeur Peninsula Canada
105 I1 Brody Ukr.
113 G4 Broken Arrow U.S.A.
95 E5 Broken Hill Australia
123 P8 Broken Plateau sea feature Indian Ocean
101 D6 Brooke's Point Phil.
113 H5 Brookhaven U.S.A.
113 G3 Brookings U.S.A.
112 D1 Brooks Canada
119 J3 Brooks, Cape Antarctica
110 D3 Brooks Range mts U.S.A.
94 C3 Broome Australia
Broughton Island Canada see Qikiqtarjuaq
113 F5 Brownfield U.S.A.
113 G6 Brownsville U.S.A.
113 G5 Brownwood U.S.A.
113 I2 Bruce Crossing U.S.A.
Bruges Belgium see Brugge
102 G5 Brugge Belgium
117 J6 Brumado Brazil
Brundisium Italy see Brindisi
101 D6 Brunei country Asia
Brünn Czech Rep. see Brno
Brunswick Germany see Braunschweig
113 J5 Brunswick GA U.S.A.
113 M3 Brunswick ME U.S.A.
118 B8 Brunswick, Península de pen. Chile
119 J3 Brunt Ice Shelf Antarctica
95 E6 Bruny Island Australia
Brussel Belgium see Brussels
102 G5 Brussels Belgium
Bruxelles Belgium see Brussels
113 G5 Bryan U.S.A.
105 J1 Bryansk Rus. Fed.
108 E3 Bu'aale Somalia
95 F2 Buala Solomon Is
106 A3 Buba Guinea-Bissau
105 J4 Bucak Turkey
116 D2 Bucaramanga Col.
106 A4 Buchanan Liberia
111 K2 Buchan Gulf Canada
98 A2 Bucharest Romania
112 D5 Buckeye U.S.A.
94 D3 Buckingham Bay Australia
95 E4 Buckland Tableland reg. Australia
119 I6 Buckle Island Antarctica
București Romania see Bucharest
103 J6 Budapest Hungary
Budweis Czech Rep. see České Budějovice
106 C4 Buea Cameroon
116 C3 Buenaventura Col.
114 C3 Buenaventura Mex.
118 E4 Buenos Aires Arg.
118 B7 Buenos Aires, Lago l. Arg./Chile
118 C7 Buen Pasto Arg.
113 K3 Buffalo U.S.A.
111 H4 Buffalo Narrows Canada
105 H1 Bug r. Poland
116 C3 Buga Col.
103 P2 Bugrino Rus. Fed.
109 D5 Buhera Zimbabwe
106 B4 Bui National Park Ghana
103 P5 Buinsk Rus. Fed.
100 D2 Buir Nur l. Mongolia
109 B6 Buitepos Namibia
109 C4 Bujumbura Burundi
100 D1 Bukachacha Rus. Fed.
95 F2 Buka Island P.N.G.
109 C4 Bukavu Dem. Rep. Congo
Bukhara Uzbek. see Buxoro
109 D4 Bukoba Tanz.
101 F7 Bula Indon.
109 C6 Bulawayo Zimbabwe
100 C2 Bulgan Mongolia
105 I3 Bulgaria country Europe
Bŭlgariya country Europe see Bulgaria
94 C2 Bulukumba Indon.
97 N2 Bulun Rus. Fed.
109 B4 Bulungu Bandundu Dem. Rep. Congo
109 C4 Bulungu Kasai-Occidental Dem. Rep. Congo
108 C3 Bumba Dem. Rep. Congo
109 B4 Buna Dem. Rep. Congo
108 D3 Buna Kenya
109 D4 Bunazi Tanz.
94 B5 Bunbury Australia
109 D4 Bunda Tanz.
95 F4 Bundaberg Australia
108 D3 Bunia Dem. Rep. Congo
109 C4 Bunianga Dem. Rep. Congo
107 D3 Buni-Yadi Nigeria
99 I5 Buôn Ma Thuôt Vietnam
Buôn Mê Thuôt Vietnam see Buôn Ma Thuôt
97 O2 Buorkhaya, Guba b. Rus. Fed.
109 D4 Bura Kenya
Burang China see Jirang
Burao Somalia see Burco
98 C4 Buraydah Saudi Arabia
98 C6 Burco Somalia
Burdigala France see Bordeaux
105 J4 Burdur Turkey
108 D2 Burē Eth.
100 F1 Bureinskiy Khrebet mts Rus. Fed.
105 I3 Burgas Bulg.
104 C3 Burgos Spain
100 B3 Burhan Budai Shan mts China
117 J5 Buriti Bravo Brazil
94 D3 Burketown Australia
106 B3 Burkina country Africa
112 D3 Burley U.S.A.
113 F4 Burlington CO U.S.A.
113 H3 Burlington IA U.S.A.
113 L3 Burlington VT U.S.A.
Burma country Asia see Myanmar
95 E6 Burnie Australia
112 C3 Burns U.S.A.
110 F4 Burns Lake Canada
97 J5 Burqin China
94 D5 Burra Australia
113 F6 Burro, Serranías del mts Mex.
98 A2 Bursa Turkey
107 F2 Būr Safājah Egypt
Būr Sa'īd Egypt see Port Said
111 K4 Burton, Lac l. Canada
101 E7 Buru i. Indon.
109 D4 Burundi country Africa
109 C4 Bururi Burundi
109 C4 Busanga Dem. Rep. Congo
98 D4 Būshehr Iran
109 D4 Bushenyi Uganda
108 C3 Businga Dem. Rep. Congo
94 B5 Busselton Australia
108 C3 Buta Dem. Rep. Congo
109 C4 Butare Rwanda
120 G6 Butaritari atoll Kiribati
101 E7 Buton i. Indon.
112 D2 Butte U.S.A.
101 C6 Butterworth Malaysia
111 I4 Button Bay Canada
101 E6 Butuan Phil.
105 L1 Buturlinovka Rus. Fed.
108 E3 Buulobarde Somalia
109 E4 Buur Gaabo Somalia
108 E3 Buurhabaka Somalia
96 H6 Buxoro Uzbek.
103 O4 Buy Rus. Fed.
103 P7 Buynaksk Rus. Fed.
105 I4 Büyükmenderes r. Turkey
105 I2 Buzău Romania
109 D5 Búzi Moz.
96 G4 Buzuluk Rus. Fed.
111 H2 Byam Martin Island Canada
103 K5 Byaroza Belarus
96 C4 Bydgoszcz Poland
Byelorussia country Europe see Belarus
103 P6 Bykovo Rus. Fed.
111 K2 Bylot Island Canada
95 F4 Byron Bay Australia
97 L2 Byrranga, Gory mts Rus. Fed.
97 O3 Bytantay r. Rus. Fed.

C

118 E3 Caacupé Para.
116 C6 Caballas Peru
116 D4 Caballococha Peru
101 E5 Cabanatuan Phil.
108 E2 Cabdul Qaadir Somalia
117 L5 Cabedelo Brazil
118 D1 Cabezas Bol.
116 D1 Cabimas Venez.
109 B4 Cabinda Angola
109 B4 Cabinda prov. Angola
Cabistra Turkey see Ereğli
117 J8 Cabo Frio Brazil
113 K2 Cabonga, Réservoir resr Canada
95 F4 Caboolture Australia
117 H3 Cabo Orange, Parque Nacional de nat. park Brazil
116 C4 Cabo Pantoja Peru
109 D5 Cabora Bassa, Lake resr Moz.
112 D5 Caborca Mex.
111 M5 Cabot Strait Canada
116 E2 Cabruta Venez.
118 F3 Caçador Brazil
118 F4 Caçapava do Sul Brazil
117 G7 Cáceres Brazil
104 B4 Cáceres Spain
106 A3 Cacheu Guinea-Bissau
118 C3 Cachi r. Arg.
118 C2 Cachi, Nevados de mts Arg.
117 H5 Cachimbo, Serra do hills Brazil
118 F4 Cachoeira do Sul Brazil
117 J8 Cachoeiro de Itapemirim Brazil
106 A3 Cacine Guinea-Bissau
117 H3 Caciporé, Cabo c. Brazil
109 B5 Cacolo Angola
109 B4 Cacongo Angola
113 I3 Cadillac U.S.A.
104 B4 Cádiz Spain
104 B4 Cádiz, Golfo de g. Spain
104 C2 Caen France
Caerdydd U.K. see Cardiff
Caerfyrddin U.K. see Carmarthen
Caergybi U.K. see Holyhead
Caesaraugusta Spain see Zaragoza
Caesarea Philippi Syria see Bāniyās
Caesarodunum France see Tours
118 C3 Cafayate Arg.
Caffa Ukr. see Feodosiya
101 E6 Cagayan de Oro Phil.
104 E4 Cagliari Italy
Cahora Bassa, Lago de resr Moz. see Cabora Bassa, Lake
104 D3 Cahors France
116 C5 Cahuapanas Peru
116 D4 Cahuinarí, Parque Nacional nat. park Col.
109 D5 Caia Moz.
117 G6 Caiabis, Serra dos hills Brazil
109 C5 Caianda Angola
117 H7 Caiapó, Serra do mts Brazil
115 I4 Caibarién Cuba
115 J4 Caicos Islands Turks and Caicos Is
95 E3 Cairns Australia
98 B3 Cairo Egypt
Caisleán an Bharraigh Ireland see Castlebar
109 B5 Caiundo Angola
116 C5 Cajamarca Peru
106 C4 Calabar Nigeria
116 E2 Calabozo Venez.
105 H3 Calafat Romania
118 B8 Calafate Arg.
109 B5 Calai Angola
104 D1 Calais France
113 M2 Calais U.S.A.
117 F5 Calama Brazil
118 C2 Calama Chile
116 D3 Calamar Guaviare Col.
101 D5 Calamian Group is Phil.
109 B4 Calandula Angola
101 E5 Calapan Phil.
105 I3 Călărași Romania
104 C3 Calatayud Spain
117 K5 Calcanhar, Ponta do pt Brazil
117 H3 Calçoene Brazil
118 B3 Caldera Chile
112 C3 Caldwell U.S.A.
118 C7 Caleta Olivia Arg.
112 D1 Calgary Canada
116 C3 Cali Col.
99 F5 Calicut India
112 D4 Caliente U.S.A.
112 B3 California state U.S.A.
California, Golfo de g. Mex. see California, Gulf of
112 D5 California, Gulf of Mex.
116 C6 Callao Peru
Callipolis Turkey see Gallipoli
105 F4 Caltanissetta Italy
109 B5 Calunga Angola
109 B5 Caluquembe Angola
108 F2 Caluula Somalia
104 E3 Calvi France
109 B5 Camacuio Angola
109 B5 Camacupa Angola
115 I4 Camagüey Cuba
115 I4 Camagüey, Archipiélago de is Cuba
116 D7 Camana Peru
109 C5 Camanongue Angola
114 E3 Camargo Mex.
118 C6 Camarones Arg.
118 C6 Camarones, Bahía b. Arg.
101 C6 Ca Mau Vietnam
101 C6 Ca Mau, Mui c. Vietnam
104 C1 Cambrian Mountains U.K.
104 D1 Cambridge U.K.
113 H2 Cambridge U.S.A.
113 H5 Camden U.S.A.
118 B8 Camden, Isla i. Chile
109 C5 Cameia, Parque Nacional da nat. park Angola
107 D4 Cameroon country Africa
107 D4 Cameroon Highlands slope Cameroon/Nigeria
106 C4 Cameroun, Mont vol. Cameroon
117 I4 Cametá Brazil
118 D2 Camiri Bol.
117 J4 Camocim Brazil
94 D3 Camooweal Australia
118 A7 Campana, Isla i. Chile
123 U9 Campbell Island N.Z.
123 U9 Campbell Plateau sea feature S. Pacific Ocean
112 A1 Campbell River Canada
102 E4 Campbeltown U.K.
115 F5 Campeche Mex.
115 F5 Campeche, Bahía de g. Mex.
117 K5 Campina Grande Brazil
117 I8 Campinas Brazil
106 C4 Campo Cameroon
105 F3 Campobasso Italy
117 I8 Campo Belo Brazil
117 H6 Campo de Diauarum Brazil
118 D3 Campo Gallo Arg.
118 F2 Campo Grande Brazil
117 J4 Campo Maior Brazil
118 F2 Campo Mourão Brazil
117 J8 Campos Brazil
105 I2 Câmpulung Moldovenesc Romania
Camulodunum U.K. see Colchester
105 I3 Çan Turkey
110 G3 Canada country N. America
124 O1 Canada Basin sea feature Arctic Ocean
113 F4 Canadian r. U.S.A.
91 Canadian Shield N. America
117 F2 Canaima, Parque Nacional nat. park Venez.
105 I3 Çanakkale Turkey
112 D5 Cananea Mex.
116 C4 Cañar Ecuador
Canarias, Islas terr. N. Atlantic Ocean see Canary Islands
106 A2 Canary Islands terr. N. Atlantic Ocean
113 J6 Canaveral, Cape U.S.A.
95 E5 Canberra Australia
115 G4 Cancún Mex.
Candia Greece see Iraklion
117 I4 Cândido Mendes Brazil
Canea Greece see Chania
118 E4 Canelones Uruguay
116 D6 Cangallo Peru
109 B5 Cangamba Angola
117 K5 Canguaretama Brazil
118 F4 Canguçu Brazil
111 L4 Caniapiscau r. Canada
111 K4 Caniapiscau, Réservoir de l. Canada
117 K4 Canindé Brazil
117 J5 Canindé r. Brazil
98 B2 Çankırı Turkey
104 E3 Cannes France
118 F3 Canoas Brazil
111 H4 Canoe Lake Canada
113 F1 Canora Canada
Cantabrian Mountains mts Spain see Cantábrica, Cordillera
104 C3 Cantábrica, Cordillera mts Spain
104 B3 Cantábrico, Mar sea Spain
95 H6 Canterbury Bight b. N.Z.
101 C5 Cân Thơ Vietnam
117 J5 Canto do Buriti Brazil
Canton China see Guangzhou
113 J3 Canton U.S.A.
117 G4 Canumã Brazil
117 F5 Canutama Brazil
113 F4 Canyon U.S.A.
101 C4 Cao Băng Vietnam
117 I4 Capanema Brazil
117 I8 Capão Bonito Brazil
95 E6 Cape Barren Island Australia
123 J8 Cape Basin sea feature S. Atlantic Ocean
111 L5 Cape Breton I. Canada
106 B4 Cape Coast Ghana
111 K3 Cape Dorset Canada
109 B4 Capenda-Camulemba Angola
122 F7 Cape Town S. Africa
123 H4 Cape Verde country N. Atlantic Ocean
123 G5 Cape Verde Basin sea feature N. Atlantic Ocean
123 G4 Cape Verde Plateau sea feature N. Atlantic Ocean
95 E3 Cape York Peninsula Australia
115 J5 Cap-Haïtien Haiti
117 I4 Capim r. Brazil
101 G5 Capitol Hill N. Mariana Is
104 E3 Capraia, Isola di i. Italy
105 F3 Capri, Isola di i. Italy
95 F4 Capricorn Channel Australia
109 C5 Caprivi Strip reg. Namibia
Capsa Tunisia see Gafsa
116 C3 Caquetá r. Col.
105 H3 Caracal Romania
116 E1 Caracas Venez.
117 J5 Caracol Brazil
118 B5 Carahue Chile
Carales Italy see Cagliari
Caralis Italy see Cagliari
105 H2 Caransebeș Romania
113 M2 Caraquet Canada
115 H5 Caratasca, Laguna de lag. Hond.
117 J7 Caratinga Brazil
116 E4 Carauari Brazil
118 F3 Carazinho Brazil
104 E4 Carbonara, Capo c. Italy
104 D3 Carcassonne France
114 E4 Cárdenas San Kuis Potosi Mex.
118 B7 Cardiel, Lago l. Arg.
102 F5 Cardiff U.K.
105 H2 Carei Romania
94 C4 Carey, Lake salt flat Australia
123 M7 Cargados Carajos Islands Mauritius
118 D5 Carhué Arg.
117 J8 Cariacica Brazil
115 I5 Caribbean Sea Atlantic Ocean
113 M2 Caribou U.S.A.
111 J4 Caribou Lake Canada
110 G4 Caribou Mountains Canada
117 J6 Carinhanha r. Brazil
117 F1 Caripito Venez.
113 K2 Carleton Place Canada
102 F5 Carlisle U.K.
Carlsbad Czech Rep. see Karlovy Vary
113 F5 Carlsbad U.S.A.
113 F5 Carlsbad Caverns National Park U.S.A.
123 M5 Carlsberg Ridge sea feature Indian Ocean
102 F5 Carmarthen U.K.
112 D6 Carmen, Isla i. Mex.
94 C4 Carnegie, Lake salt flat Australia
121 N6 Carnegie Ridge sea feature S. Pacific Ocean
119 I4 Carney Island Antarctica
108 B3 Carnot Centr. Afr. Rep.
94 D5 Carnot, Cape Australia
117 I5 Carolina Brazil
120 E5 Caroline Islands N. Pacific Ocean
103 J6 Carpathian Mountains Europe
Carpații mts Europe see Carpathian Mountains
94 D3 Carpentaria, Gulf of Australia
117 K5 Carpina Brazil
104 B1 Carrantuohill mt. Ireland
118 B5 Carranza, Cabo c. Chile
118 B3 Carrizal Bajo Chile

Carrizo Springs

113 G6 Carrizo Springs U.S.A.
113 H3 Carroll U.S.A.
112 C4 Carson City U.S.A.
116 C1 Cartagena Col.
104 C4 Cartagena Spain
115 H7 Cartago Costa Rica
113 H4 Carthage U.S.A.
Carthago Nova Spain see Cartagena
117 K5 Caruarú Brazil
117 F1 Carúpano Venez.
106 B1 Casablanca Morocco
112 D5 Casa Grande U.S.A.
112 E5 Casas Grandes Mex.
112 B3 Cascade Range mts U.S.A.
118 F2 Cascavel Brazil
119 K6 Casey research stn Antarctica
119 L4 Casey Bay Antarctica
Caseyr, Raas c. Somalia see Gwardafuy, Gees
95 F4 Casino Australia
116 C5 Casma Peru
Casnewydd U.K. see Newport
112 E3 Casper U.S.A.
98 C2 Caspian Lowland Kazakh./Rus. Fed.
96 F5 Caspian Sea l. Asia/Europe
109 C5 Cassai Angola
117 I4 Castanhal Brazil
118 C4 Castaño r. Arg.
Castellón Spain see Castellón de la Plana
104 C4 Castellón de la Plana Valencia Spain
104 B4 Castelo Branco Port.
105 F4 Castelvetrano Italy
102 E5 Castlebar Ireland
112 C2 Castlegar Canada
113 F4 Castle Rock U.S.A.
Castra Regina Germany see Regensburg
115 L6 Castries St Lucia
118 B6 Castro Chile
116 B5 Catacaos Peru
118 C3 Catamarca Arg.
Catana Italy see Catania
101 E5 Catanduanes i. Phil.
105 G4 Catania Italy
105 G4 Catanzaro Italy
101 E5 Catarman Phil.
116 D2 Catatumbo r. Venez.
101 E5 Catbalogan Phil.
Catherine, Mount mt. Egypt see Kātrīnā, Jabal
113 K7 Cat Island Bahamas
115 G4 Catoche, Cabo c. Mex.
95 F4 Cato Island and Bank rf Australia
118 D5 Catriló Arg.
113 L3 Catskill Mountains U.S.A.
116 D2 Cauca r. Col.
117 K4 Caucaia Brazil
116 C2 Caucasia Col.
118 B5 Cauquenes Chile
117 I6 Cavalcante Brazil
106 B4 Cavally r. Côte d'Ivoire
117 J4 Caxias Brazil
118 F3 Caxias do Sul Brazil
109 B4 Caxito Angola
117 H3 Cayenne Fr. Guiana
115 I5 Cayman Brac i. Cayman Is
115 H5 Cayman Islands terr. Caribbean Sea
123 D4 Cayman Trench sea feature Caribbean Sea
108 E3 Caynabo Somalia
109 C5 Cazombo Angola
Ceann a Deas na Hearadh pen. U.K. see South Harris
123 G6 Ceara Abyssal Plain sea feature S. Atlantic Ocean
101 E5 Cebu Phil.
105 F3 Cecina Italy
112 D4 Cedar City U.S.A.
113 H3 Cedar Falls U.S.A.
113 F1 Cedar Lake Canada
113 H3 Cedar Rapids U.S.A.
112 C6 Cedros, Isla i. Mex.
94 D5 Ceduna Australia
108 E3 Ceeldheere Somalia
108 E2 Ceerigaabo Somalia
105 F4 Cefalù Italy
114 D4 Celaya Mex.
94 C2 Celebes i. Indon.
101 E6 Celebes Sea Indon./Phil.
Celovec Austria see Klagenfurt
123 I2 Celtic Shelf sea feature N. Atlantic Ocean
101 F7 Cenderawasih, Teluk b. Indon.
116 C3 Central, Cordillera mts Col.
116 C5 Central, Cordillera mts Peru
107 D4 Central African Republic country Africa
99 E4 Central Brahui Ra. mts Pak.
112 B2 Centralia U.S.A.
108 D2 Central Island National Park Kenya
120 G5 Central Pacific Basin sea feature Pacific Ocean
95 E2 Central Range mts P.N.G.
96 E4 Central Russian Upland hills Rus. Fed.
97 L3 Central Siberian Plateau Rus. Fed.
Cephaloedium Italy see Cefalù
105 H4 Cephalonia i. Greece
Ceram Sea sea Indon. see Seram, Laut
118 D3 Ceres Arg.
105 G3 Cerignola Italy
Cerigo i. Greece see Kythira
Cernăuţi Ukr. see Chernivtsi
112 E7 Ceralvo, Isla i. Mex.
114 D4 Cerritos Mex.
116 C6 Cerro de Pasco Peru
116 B4 Cerros de Amotape, Parque Nacional nat. park Peru
103 L4 Cēsis Latvia
Česká Republika country Europe see Czech Republic
103 I6 České Budějovice Czech Rep.
Cetatea Albă Ukr. see Bilhorod-Dnistrovs'kyy
105 G3 Cetinje Montenegro
104 B4 Ceuta N. Africa
95 H4 Ceva-i-Ra rf Fiji
99 E4 Chābahār Iran
116 C5 Chachapoyas Peru
101 C5 Chachoengsao Thai.
107 D3 Chad country Africa
107 D3 Chad, Lake Africa
99 H1 Chadan Rus. Fed.
113 F3 Chadron U.S.A.
99 E3 Chaghcharān Afgh.
103 N4 Chagoda Rus. Fed.
123 N6 Chagos Archipelago is British Indian Ocean Terr.
123 N6 Chagos-Laccadive Ridge sea feature Indian Ocean
123 N6 Chagos Trench sea feature Indian Ocean
118 E4 Chajarí Arg.
116 D7 Chala Peru
115 G6 Chalatenango El Salvador
111 L5 Chaleur Bay inlet Canada
105 H4 Chalkida Greece
118 C1 Challapata Bol.
120 E5 Challenger Deep sea feature N. Pacific Ocean
102 G6 Châlons-en-Champagne France
Châlons-sur-Marne France see Châlons-en-Champagne
104 D2 Chalon-sur-Saône France
109 D5 Chama Zambia
99 E3 Chaman Pak.
104 E2 Chambéry France
109 D5 Chambeshi Zambia
104 E4 Chambi, Jebel mt. Tunisia
113 I3 Champaign U.S.A.
118 D4 Champaqui, Cerro mt. Arg.
113 L3 Champlain, Lake Canada/U.S.A.
115 F5 Champotón Mex.
Chanak Turkey see Çanakkale
118 B3 Chañaral Chile
110 D3 Chandalar r. U.S.A.
113 I6 Chandeleur Islands U.S.A.
99 F3 Chandigarh India
112 D5 Chandler U.S.A.
99 F5 Chandrapur India
109 D6 Changane r. Moz.
109 D5 Changara Moz.
100 E2 Changchun China
101 D4 Changde China
Chang Jiang r. China see Yangtze
101 D4 Changsha China
100 D3 Changzhou China
105 H4 Chania Greece
102 F6 Channel Islands English Chan.
112 C5 Channel Islands U.S.A.
111 M5 Channel-Port-aux-Basques Canada
101 C5 Chanthaburi Thai.
96 I4 Chany, Ozero salt l. Rus. Fed.
104 B4 Chaouèn Morocco
101 D4 Chaozhou China
117 I6 Chapada dos Veadeiros, Parque Nacional da nat. park Brazil
114 D4 Chapala, Laguna de l. Mex.
96 G4 Chapayevo Kazakh.
118 F3 Chapecó Brazil
118 F3 Chapecó r. Brazil
113 J2 Chapleau Canada
103 N5 Chaplygin Rus. Fed.
118 C1 Chaqui Bol.
119 I3 Charcot Island Antarctica
104 D5 Charef Alg.
104 C5 Charef, Oued watercourse Morocco
99 E3 Chārīkār Afgh.
103 Q2 Charkayuvom Rus. Fed.
104 D1 Charleroi Belgium
113 K4 Charles, Cape U.S.A.
113 H3 Charles City U.S.A.
113 K5 Charleston SC U.S.A.
113 J4 Charleston WV U.S.A.
112 C4 Charleston Peak U.S.A.
95 E4 Charleville Australia
104 D2 Charleville-Mézières France
119 J5 Charlie, Dome ice feature Antarctica
113 J4 Charlotte U.S.A.
113 J6 Charlotte Harbor b. U.S.A.
113 K4 Charlottesville U.S.A.
111 L5 Charlottetown Canada
113 K1 Charlton Island Canada
95 E4 Charters Towers Australia
104 D2 Chartres France
112 C1 Chase Canada
104 D2 Château-du-Loir France
104 D2 Châteauroux France
104 D2 Châtellerault France
95 I6 Chatham Islands N.Z.
121 H8 Chatham Rise sea feature S. Pacific Ocean
113 I4 Chattanooga U.S.A.
104 E2 Chaumont France
97 R3 Chaunskaya Guba b. Rus. Fed.
117 I4 Chaves Brazil
104 B3 Chaves Port.
105 F1 Cheb Czech Rep.
103 P4 Cheboksarskoye Vodokhranilishche resr Rus. Fed.
103 P4 Cheboksary Rus. Fed.
113 J2 Cheboygan U.S.A.
103 P7 Chechen', Ostrov i. Rus. Fed.
110 B3 Chefornak U.S.A.
106 B2 Chegga Mauritania
109 D5 Chegutu Zimbabwe
100 E3 Cheju do S. Korea
100 E3 Cheju-haehyŏp sea chan. S. Korea
96 D4 Chełm Poland
96 H4 Chelyabinsk Rus. Fed.
109 D5 Chemba Moz.
103 I5 Chemnitz Germany
106 B2 Chenachane Alg.
100 D2 Chengde China
100 C3 Chengdu China
101 D5 Chengmai China
99 G5 Chennai India
Chenstokhov Poland see Częstochowa
101 D4 Chenzhou China
116 C5 Chepén Peru
104 D2 Cher r. France
104 C2 Cherbourg France
100 C1 Cheremkhovo Rus. Fed.
103 N4 Cherepovets Rus. Fed.
104 C5 Chergui, Chott ech imp. l. Alg.
96 E5 Cherkasy Ukr.
96 F5 Cherkessk Rus. Fed.
109 C5 Chermenze Angola
96 E4 Chernihiv Ukr.
103 L6 Chernivtsi Ukr.
100 B1 Chernogorsk Rus. Fed.
Chernovtsy Ukr. see Chernivtsi
Chernoye More sea Asia/Europe see Black Sea
103 K5 Chernyakhovsk Rus. Fed.
97 M3 Chernyshevskiy Rus. Fed.
95 G3 Cherry Island Solomon Is
97 P3 Cherskogo, Khrebet mts Rus. Fed.
105 L2 Chertkovo Rus. Fed.
Chervonoarmiys'k Ukr. see Krasnoarmiys'k
Chervonograd Ukr. see Chervonohrad
103 K5 Chervonohrad Ukr.
113 K4 Chesapeake U.S.A.
113 K4 Chesapeake Bay U.S.A.
103 P2 Cheshskaya Guba b. Rus. Fed.
102 F5 Chester U.K.
95 F3 Chesterfield, Îles is New Caledonia
111 I3 Chesterfield Inlet Canada
111 I3 Chesterfield Inlet inlet Canada
115 G5 Chetumal Mex.
113 F3 Cheyenne U.S.A.
111 H5 Cheyenne r. U.S.A.
109 E4 Chiamboni Kenya
101 B5 Chiang Mai Thai.
101 B5 Chiang Rai Thai.
97 P6 Chiba Japan
109 B5 Chibia Angola
109 D6 Chiboma Moz.
113 L2 Chibougamau Canada
113 I3 Chicago U.S.A.
94 B4 Chichester Range mts Australia
113 G4 Chickasha U.S.A.
116 C5 Chiclayo Peru
118 C6 Chico r. Chubut Arg.
118 C7 Chico r. Santa Cruz Arg.
112 B4 Chico U.S.A.
113 L2 Chicoutimi Canada
100 D2 Chifeng China
117 J7 Chifre, Serra do mts Brazil
96 I5 Chiganak Kazakh.
109 D6 Chigubo Moz.
112 E6 Chihuahua Mex.
112 E6 Chihuahua state Mex.
99 F3 Chilas Pak.
113 F5 Childress U.S.A.
118 B5 Chile country S. America
123 D8 Chile Basin sea feature S. Pacific Ocean
118 C3 Chilecito Arg.
123 D8 Chile Rise sea feature S. Pacific Ocean
Chilia-Nouă Ukr. see Kiliya
109 C5 Chililabombwe Zambia
118 B5 Chillán Chile
113 H4 Chillicothe U.S.A.
112 B2 Chilliwack Canada
118 B6 Chiloé, Isla de i. Chile
114 E5 Chilpancingo Mex.
109 D4 Chimala Tanz.
118 C4 Chimbas Arg.
116 C4 Chimborazo mt. Ecuador
116 C5 Chimbote Peru
109 D5 Chimoio Moz.
100 B3 China country Asia
115 G6 Chinandega Nicaragua
116 C6 Chincha Alta Peru
110 G4 Chinchaga r. Canada
115 G5 Chinchorro, Banco sea feature Mex.
109 D5 Chinde Moz.
100 B3 Chindu China
101 B4 Chindwin r. Myanmar
109 C5 Chingola Zambia
109 B5 Chinguar Angola
109 D5 Chinhoyi Zimbabwe
108 C3 Chinko r. Centr. Afr. Rep.
112 E4 Chinle U.S.A.
121 H3 Chinook Trough sea feature N. Pacific Ocean
112 D5 Chino Valley U.S.A.
109 D5 Chinsali Zambia
105 F2 Chioggia Italy
105 I4 Chios Greece
105 I4 Chios i. Greece
109 D5 Chipata Zambia
118 C6 Chipchihua, Sierra de mts Arg.
109 B5 Chipindo Angola
109 D6 Chipinge Zimbabwe
99 F5 Chiplun India
115 G6 Chiquimula Guat.
116 D2 Chiquinquira Col.
109 D6 Chiredzi Zimbabwe
110 C4 Chirikof Island U.S.A.
115 H7 Chiriquí, Golfo de b. Panama
115 H7 Chirripo mt. Costa Rica
109 C5 Chirundu Zambia
111 K4 Chisasibi Canada
113 H2 Chisholm U.S.A.
96 D5 Chişinău Moldova
103 Q4 Chistopol' Rus. Fed.
100 D1 Chita Rus. Fed.
109 B5 Chitado Angola
109 D5 Chitambo Zambia
109 C4 Chitato Angola
109 B5 Chitembo Angola
109 D4 Chitipa Malawi
109 C5 Chitokoloki Zambia
99 F5 Chitradurga India
99 F3 Chitral Pak.
115 H7 Chitré Panama
101 B4 Chittagong Bangl.
109 D5 Chitungulu Zambia
109 D5 Chitungwiza Zimbabwe
109 C5 Chiume Angola
109 D5 Chivhu Zimbabwe
104 D4 Chlef Alg.
104 D4 Chlef, Oued r. Alg.
109 C5 Chobe National Park Botswana
118 C5 Choele Choel Arg.
95 F2 Choiseul i. Solomon Is
118 E8 Choiseul Sound sea chan. Falkland Is
105 G1 Chojnice Poland
108 D2 Ch'ok'ē Mountains Eth.
97 P2 Chokurdakh Rus. Fed.
109 D6 Chókwé Moz.
115 G6 Choluteca Hond.
109 C5 Choma Zambia
105 F1 Chomutov Czech Rep.
97 L3 Chona r. Rus. Fed.
100 E3 Ch'ŏnan S. Korea
101 C5 Chon Buri Thai.
116 B4 Chone Ecuador
100 E2 Ch'ŏngjin N. Korea
101 C4 Chongqing China
109 C5 Chongwe Zambia
100 E3 Chŏnju S. Korea
118 B7 Chonos, Archipiélago de los is Chile
105 J2 Chornomors'ke Ukr.
116 C5 Chota Peru
106 A2 Choûm Mauritania
100 D2 Choybalsan Mongolia
100 C2 Choyr Mongolia
95 H6 Christchurch N.Z.
111 L2 Christian, Cape Canada
Christianshåb Greenland see Qasigiannguit
101 C8 Christmas Island terr. Indian Ocean
96 H5 Chu r. Kazakh.
Chubarovka Ukr. see Polohy
118 C6 Chubut r. Arg.
103 M4 Chudovo Rus. Fed.
110 C4 Chugach Mountains U.S.A.
100 F1 Chukchagirskoye, Ozero l. Rus. Fed.
124 M1 Chukchi Plateau sea feature Arctic Ocean
97 U3 Chukchi Sea Rus. Fed./U.S.A.
110 A3 Chukotskiy Poluostrov pen. Rus. Fed.
97 J4 Chulym Rus. Fed.
118 C3 Chumbicha Arg.
100 F1 Chumikan Rus. Fed.
101 B5 Chumphon Thai.
97 K4 Chuna r. Rus. Fed.
100 E3 Ch'unch'ŏn S. Korea
97 L3 Chunya r. Rus. Fed.
116 D7 Chuquibamba Peru
118 C2 Chuquicamata Chile
102 H6 Chur Switz.
97 O3 Churapcha Rus. Fed.
111 L4 Churchill r. Nfld Canada
111 I4 Churchill r. Sask. Canada
111 I4 Churchill, Cape Canada
111 L4 Churchill Falls Canada
111 H4 Churchill Lake Canada
116 E1 Churuguara Venez.
Chust Ukr. see Khust
101 C4 Chuxiong China
105 H1 Ciechanów Poland
115 I4 Ciego de Ávila Cuba
116 D1 Ciénaga Col.
115 H4 Cienfuegos Cuba
105 J4 Cihanbeyli Turkey
101 C7 Cilacap Indon.
Cill Airne Ireland see Killarney
Cill Chainnigh Ireland see Kilkenny
Cill Mhantáin Ireland see Wicklow
105 F3 Cimone, Monte mt. Italy
Cîmpulung Moldovenesc Romania see Câmpulung Moldovenesc
116 E2 Cinaruco-Capanaparo, Parque Nacional nat. park Venez.
113 J4 Cincinnati U.S.A.
110 D3 Circle U.S.A.
101 C7 Cirebon Indon.
Cirta Alg. see Constantine
115 H5 Cisne, Islas del Hond.
113 F6 Ciudad Acuña Mex.
114 D5 Ciudad Altamirano Mex.
117 F2 Ciudad Bolívar Venez.
112 E6 Ciudad Camargo Mex.
112 D6 Ciudad Constitución Mex.
115 F5 Ciudad del Carmen Mex.
112 E6 Ciudad Delicias Mex.
114 E4 Ciudad de Valles Mex.
117 F2 Ciudad Guayana Venez.
114 D5 Ciudad Guzmán Mex.
114 E5 Ciudad Ixtepec Mex.
112 E5 Ciudad Juárez Mex.
113 F6 Ciudad Lerdo Mex.
114 E4 Ciudad Mante Mex.
112 E6 Ciudad Obregón Mex.
104 C4 Ciudad Real Spain
104 B3 Ciudad Rodrigo Spain
114 E4 Ciudad Victoria Mex.
105 F3 Civitanova Marche Italy
105 F3 Civitavecchia Italy
105 I4 Çivril Turkey
110 G4 Claire, Lake Canada
121 L4 Clarión, Isla i. Mex.
95 E6 Clarke Island Australia
112 D2 Clark Fork r. U.S.A.
113 J5 Clark Hill Reservoir U.S.A.
113 H5 Clarksdale U.S.A.
113 I4 Clarksville U.S.A.
118 F1 Claro r. Brazil
113 F4 Clayton U.S.A.
110 D4 Cleare, Cape U.S.A.
110 G4 Clearwater r. Canada
113 J6 Clearwater U.S.A.
95 E4 Clermont Australia
104 D2 Clermont-Ferrand France
113 H5 Cleveland MS U.S.A.
113 J3 Cleveland OH U.S.A.
113 J4 Cleveland TN U.S.A.
112 D2 Cleveland, Mount U.S.A.
112 E5 Clifton U.S.A.
113 H4 Clinton MO U.S.A.
113 G4 Clinton OK U.S.A.
114 C6 Clipperton, Île terr. Pacific Ocean
95 E4 Cloncurry Australia
112 E3 Cloud Peak U.S.A.
113 F5 Clovis U.S.A.
98 A2 Cluj-Napoca Romania
111 L2 Clyde River Canada
113 F6 Coahuila state Mex.
117 F4 Coari Brazil
117 F5 Coari r. Brazil
113 I5 Coastal Plain U.S.A.
110 F4 Coast Mountains Canada
112 B3 Coast Ranges mts U.S.A.
111 J3 Coats Island Canada
119 J3 Coats Land reg. Antarctica
115 F5 Coatzacoalcos Mex.
115 F5 Cobán Guat.
95 E5 Cobar Australia
116 E6 Cobija Bol.
Coblenz Germany see Koblenz
101 F8 Cobourg Peninsula Australia
116 C4 Coca Ecuador
116 E7 Cochabamba Bol.
99 F6 Cochin India
113 J2 Cochrane Canada
118 B7 Cochrane Chile
Cockburn Town Turks and Caicos Is see Grand Turk
115 G7 Coco, Isla de i. Col.
123 P5 Cocos Basin sea feature Indian Ocean
101 B8 Cocos Islands terr. Indian Ocean
121 N5 Cocos Ridge sea feature N. Pacific Ocean
116 D2 Cocuy, Sierra Nevada del mt. Col.
113 L3 Cod, Cape U.S.A.
117 F4 Codajás Brazil
111 L4 Cod Island Canada
117 J4 Codó Brazil
112 E3 Cody U.S.A.
95 E3 Coen Australia
112 C2 Coeur d'Alene U.S.A.
113 G4 Coffeyville U.S.A.
95 F5 Coffs Harbour Australia
106 C4 Cogo Equat. Guinea
115 H7 Coiba, Isla de i. Panama
115 H7 Coiba, Parque Nacional nat. park Panama
118 C8 Coig r. Arg.
118 B7 Coihaique Chile
99 F5 Coimbatore India
104 B3 Coimbra Port.
118 C1 Coipasa, Salar de salt flat Bo
Coire Switz. see Chur
95 E5 Colac Australia
117 J7 Colatina Brazil
113 F4 Colby U.S.A.
116 D7 Colca r. Peru
102 G5 Colchester U.K.
113 G5 Coleman U.S.A.
102 E4 Coleraine U.K.
114 D5 Colima Mex.
114 D5 Colima, Nevado de vol. Mex
94 C3 Collier Bay Australia
104 E2 Colmar France
102 H5 Cologne Germany
Colomb-Béchar Alg. see Béchar
123 D5 Colombian Basin sea feature S. Atlantic Ocean
99 F6 Colombo Sri Lanka
118 E4 Colón Arg.
115 H4 Colón Cuba
115 I7 Colón Panama
Colonia Agrippina Germany see Cologne
121 M5 Colon Ridge sea feature Pacific Ocean
118 D5 Colorado r. Arg.
113 G6 Colorado r. U.S.A.
112 D5 Colorado r. U.S.A.
112 E4 Colorado state U.S.A.
112 E4 Colorado Plateau U.S.A.
113 F4 Colorado Springs U.S.A.
112 B2 Columbia r. Canada/U.S.A.
113 H4 Columbia MO U.S.A.
113 J5 Columbia SC U.S.A.
113 I4 Columbia TN U.S.A.
111 K1 Columbia, Cape Canada
112 C1 Columbia, Mount Canada
113 J5 Columbus GA U.S.A.
113 I5 Columbus MS U.S.A.
113 G3 Columbus NE U.S.A.
113 J4 Columbus OH U.S.A.
110 C3 Colville r. U.S.A.
110 F3 Colville Lake Canada
105 F3 Comacchio Italy
119 L2 Comandante Ferraz research stn Antarctica
118 C4 Comandante Salas Arg.
118 B4 Combarbalá Chile
115 F5 Comitán de Domínguez Me
111 J3 Committee Bay Canada
119 I6 Commonwealth Bay Antarctica
104 E2 Como Italy
118 C7 Comodoro Rivadavia Arg.
106 B4 Comoé, Parc National de la nat. park Côte d'Ivoire
123 O5 Comorin, Cape India
109 E5 Comoros country Africa
114 D4 Compostela Mex.
105 I2 Comrat Moldova
106 A4 Conakry Guinea
117 K7 Conceição da Barra Brazil
117 I5 Conceição do Araguaia Braz
118 C3 Concepción Arg.
117 F7 Concepción Bol.
118 B5 Concepción Chile
Concepción Panama see La Concepción
118 E2 Concepción Para.
112 B5 Conception, Point U.S.A.
113 F4 Conchas Lake U.S.A.
113 G7 Conchos r. Mex.
112 E6 Conchos r. U.S.A.
112 B4 Concord CA U.S.A.
113 L3 Concord NH U.S.A.
119 J6 Concordia research stn Antarctica
118 E4 Concordia Arg.
113 G4 Concordia U.S.A.
95 F3 Conflict Group is P.N.G.
Confoederatio Helvetica countyry Europe see Switzerland
109 B4 Congo country Africa
108 B3 Congo r. Africa
109 C4 Congo, Democratic Republic of the country Africa
91 Congo Basin basin Africa
123 J6 Congo Cone sea feature S. Atlantic Ocean
113 L3 Connecticut r. U.S.A.
113 L3 Connecticut state U.S.A.
123 L9 Conrad Rise sea feature Southern Ocean
113 G5 Conroe U.S.A.
117 J8 Conselheiro Lafaiete Brazil
102 H6 Constance, Lake Germany/Switz.
117 F5 Constância dos Baetas Brazil
98 A2 Constanţa Romania
104 E4 Constantine Alg.
116 C5 Contamana Peru
117 K6 Contas r. Brazil
110 G3 Contwoyto Lake Canada
113 H4 Conway U.S.A.
94 D4 Coober Pedy Australia
95 G3 Cook, Grand Récif de rf New Caledonia

Drammen

103 I4 Drammen Norway
112 D1 Drayton Valley Canada
105 F1 Dresden Germany
105 H3 Drobeta-Turnu Severin Romania
Drogichin Belarus see Drahichyn
111 P2 Dronning Louise Land reg. Greenland
99 F3 Drosh Pak.
112 D1 Drumheller Canada
113 L2 Drummondville Canada
97 P3 Druzhina Rus. Fed.
113 H2 Dryden Canada
94 C3 Drysdale r. Australia
115 J5 Duarte, Pico mt. Dom. Rep.
98 B4 Ḍubā Saudi Arabia
98 D4 Dubai U.A.E.
111 H3 Dubawnt Lake Canada
Dubayy U.A.E. see Dubai
98 B4 Dubbagh, Jabal ad mt. Saudi Arabia
95 E5 Dubbo Australia
102 E5 Dublin Ireland
113 J5 Dublin U.S.A.
105 I1 Dubno Ukr.
106 A4 Dubréka Guinea
Dubris U.K. see Dover
105 G3 Dubrovnik Croatia
113 H3 Dubuque U.S.A.
121 J7 Duc de Gloucester, Îles du is Fr. Polynesia
121 K7 Ducie Island atoll Pitcairn Is
97 J3 Dudinka Rus. Fed.
106 B4 Duékoué Côte d'Ivoire
104 B3 Duero r. Spain
95 G2 Duff Islands Solomon Is
116 E3 Duida-Marahuaca, Parque Nacional Venez.
104 E1 Duisburg Germany
100 B3 Dulan China
Dulawan Phil. see Datu Piang
118 D3 Dulce r. Arg.
113 H2 Duluth U.S.A.
101 E6 Dumaguete Phil.
99 I6 Dumai Indon.
113 H5 Dumas AR U.S.A.
113 F4 Dumas TX U.S.A.
102 F4 Dumfries U.K.
119 J6 Dumont d'Urville research stn Antarctica
119 J6 Dumont d'Urville Sea Antarctica
98 B3 Dumyāṭ Egypt
113 G5 Duncan U.S.A.
102 E5 Dundalk Ireland
111 L2 Dundas Greenland
Dún Dealgan Ireland see Dundalk
102 F4 Dundee U.K.
95 H6 Dunedin N.Z.
118 C8 Dungeness, Punta pt Arg.
108 C3 Dungu Dem. Rep. Congo
101 C6 Dungun Malaysia
107 F2 Dungunab Sudan
97 N5 Dunhua China
100 B2 Dunhuang China
106 B4 Dunkwa Ghana
Duperré Alg. see Aïn Defla
94 C3 Durack r. Australia
114 D4 Durango Mex.
113 F7 Durango state Mex.
112 E4 Durango U.S.A.
113 G5 Durant U.S.A.
118 E4 Durazno Uruguay
Durazzo Albania see Durrës
122 G6 Durban S. Africa
113 K4 Durham U.S.A.
102 F4 Durness U.K.
Durocortorum France see Reims
105 G3 Durrës Albania
94 D2 D'Urville, Tanjung pt Indon.
99 E3 Dushanbe Tajik.
104 E1 Düsseldorf Germany
106 C3 Dutse Nigeria
101 C4 Duyun China
105 J3 Düzce Turkey
Dvina r. Europe see Zapadnaya Dvina
103 N2 Dvinskaya Guba g. Rus. Fed.
99 E4 Dwarka India
103 M5 Dyat'kovo Rus. Fed.
111 L3 Dyer, Cape Canada
113 I4 Dyersburg U.S.A.
Dyrrhachium Albania see Durrës
100 D2 Dzamīn Üüd Mongolia
109 E5 Dzaoudzi Africa
103 O4 Dzerzhinsk Rus. Fed.
100 E1 Dzhagdy, Khrebet mts Rus. Fed.
105 J2 Dzhankoy Ukr.
Dzhizak Uzbek. see Jizzax
Dzhokhar Ghala Rus. Fed. see Groznyy
100 F1 Dzhugdzhur, Khrebet mts Rus. Fed.
99 F2 Dzhungarskiy Alatau, Khrebet mts China/Kazakh.
96 H5 Dzhusaly Kazakh.
Dzungaria Basin basin China see Junggar Pendi
100 C2 Dzuunmod Mongolia

E

111 M4 Eagle r. Canada
113 H2 Eagle Lake l. Canada
113 F6 Eagle Pass U.S.A.
110 D3 Eagle Plain Canada
113 H1 Ear Falls Canada
119 K5 East Antarctica reg. Antarctica
95 H5 East Cape N.Z.
120 E5 East Caroline Basin sea feature N. Pacific Ocean
100 E3 East China Sea Asia
121 L7 Easter Island i. S. Pacific Ocean
105 J6 Eastern Desert Egypt
99 F5 Eastern Ghats mts India
118 E8 East Falkland i. Falkland Is
102 H5 East Frisian Islands Germany
123 P7 East Indiaman Ridge sea feature Indian Ocean
113 K1 Eastmain Canada
113 K1 Eastmain r. Canada
120 F5 East Mariana Basin sea feature Pacific Ocean
121 L8 East Pacific Ridge sea feature S. Pacific Ocean
121 L4 East Pacific Rise sea feature N. Pacific Ocean
97 Q2 East Siberian Sea Rus. Fed.
101 E7 East Timor country Asia
113 H3 Eau Claire U.S.A.
111 K4 Eau Claire, Lac à l' l. Canada
101 G6 Eauripik atoll Micronesia
120 E5 Eauripik Rise-New Guinea Rise sea feature N. Pacific Ocean
114 E4 Ebano Mex.
107 D4 Ebebiyin Equat. Guinea
105 F1 Eberswalde-Finow Germany
107 D4 Ebolowa Cameroon
Ebre r. Spain see Ebro
104 D3 Ebro r. Spain
Eburacum U.K. see York
Ebusus i. Spain see Ibiza
104 B4 Écija Spain
111 K2 Eclipse Sound sea chan. Canada
104 E3 Écrins, Massif des mt. France
116 C4 Ecuador country S. America
108 E2 Ed Eritrea
107 E3 Ed Da'ein Sudan
107 F3 Ed Damazin Sudan
107 F3 Ed Damer Sudan
107 F3 Ed Debba Sudan
107 F3 Ed Dueim Sudan
95 E6 Eddystone Point Australia
107 D4 Edéa Cameroon
95 E5 Eden Australia
105 H3 Edessa Greece
Edessa Turkey see Şanlıurfa
Édhessa Greece see Edessa
113 G6 Edinburg U.S.A.
102 F4 Edinburgh U.K.
105 I3 Edirne Turkey
112 D1 Edmonton Canada
113 M2 Edmundston Canada
105 I4 Edremit Turkey
110 G4 Edson Canada
109 C4 Edward, Lake Dem. Rep. Congo/Uganda
113 F5 Edwards Plateau U.S.A.
119 I5 Edward VII Peninsula Antarctica
Eesti country Europe see Estonia
95 G3 Éfaté i. Vanuatu
113 I4 Effingham U.S.A.
102 H4 Egersund Norway
105 J4 Eğirdir Turkey
105 J4 Eğirdir Gölü l. Turkey
110 F2 Eglinton Island Canada
Egmont, Mount vol. N.Z. see Taranaki, Mount
97 U3 Egvekinot Rus. Fed.
105 J6 Egypt country Africa
100 E3 Ehen Hudag China
99 F6 Eight Degree Channel India/Maldives
94 C3 Eighty Mile Beach Australia
105 J6 Eilat Israel
104 E1 Eindhoven Neth.
124 V3 Eirik Ridge sea feature N. Atlantic Ocean
116 E5 Eirunepé Brazil
109 C5 Eiseb watercourse Namibia
Eivissa Spain see Ibiza
Eivissa i. Spain see Ibiza
109 E6 Ejeda Madag.
103 K4 Ekenäs Fin.
99 F1 Ekibastuz Kazakh.
97 L3 Ekonda Rus. Fed.
103 M2 Ekostrovskaya Imandra, Ozero l. Rus. Fed.
109 C4 Ekuku Dem. Rep. Congo
113 J1 Ekwan r. Canada
El 'Âmirîya Egypt see Al 'Āmirīyah
El Araïche Morocco see Larache
104 C5 El Aricha Alg.
El 'Arîsh Egypt see Al 'Arīsh
El Asnam Alg. see Chlef
Elat Israel see Eilat
98 B3 Elazığ Turkey
105 F3 Elba, Isola d' i. Italy
100 F1 El'ban Rus. Fed.
116 D2 El Banco Col.
112 E5 El Barreal salt l. Mex.
105 H3 Elbasan Albania
116 E2 El Baúl Venez.
104 D5 El Bayadh Alg.
104 E1 Elbe r. Germany
112 E4 Elbert, Mount U.S.A.
105 K4 Elbistan Turkey
96 C4 Elbląg Poland
El Boulaïda Alg. see Blida
96 F5 El'brus mt. Rus. Fed.
98 C3 Elburz Mountains mts Iran
117 F2 El Callao Venez.
112 C5 El Centro U.S.A.
117 F7 El Cerro Bol.
Elche Spain see Elche-Elx
104 C4 Elche-Elx Spain
94 D3 Elcho Island Australia
97 O3 El'dikan Rus. Fed.
El Djezair country Africa see Algeria
El Djezair Alg. see Algiers
118 F3 Eldorado Arg.
114 C4 El Dorado Mex.
117 F2 El Dorado Venez.
108 D3 Eldoret Kenya
106 B2 El Eglab plat. Alg.
116 D4 El Encanto Col.
119 I2 Elephant Island Antarctica
104 E4 El Eulma Alg.
113 K6 Eleuthera i. Bahamas
107 E3 El Fasher Sudan
112 E6 El Fuerte Mex.
107 E3 El Geneina Sudan
107 F3 El Geteina Sudan
102 F4 Elgin U.K.
113 I3 Elgin U.S.A.
97 P3 El'ginskiy Rus. Fed.
104 D5 El Goléa Alg.
108 D3 Elgon, Mount Uganda
El Ḥammâm Egypt see Al Ḥammām
106 A2 El Hierro i. Canary Is
104 D6 El Homr Alg.
110 B3 Elim U.S.A.
Elimberrum France see Auch
El Iskandarîya Egypt see Alexandria
96 F5 Elista Rus. Fed.
113 L3 Elizabeth U.S.A.
106 B1 El Jadida Morocco
105 F4 El Jem Tunisia
103 K5 Ełk Poland
104 E4 El Kala Alg.
107 F3 El Kamlin Sudan
113 G4 Elk City U.S.A.
El Kef Tunisia see Le Kef
113 I3 Elkhart U.S.A.
106 B2 El Khnâchîch esc. Mali
112 C3 Elko U.S.A.
Ellas country Europe see Greece
111 H2 Ellef Ringnes Island Canada
112 B2 Ellensburg U.S.A.
111 J2 Ellesmere Island Canada
111 H3 Ellice r. Canada
119 I3 Ellsworth Land reg. Antarctica
119 I3 Ellsworth Mountains Antarctica
El Maghreb country Africa see Morocco
105 I4 Elmalı Turkey
104 E5 El Meghaïer Alg.
104 E4 El Milia Alg.
El Minya Egypt see Al Minyā
113 K3 Elmira U.S.A.
106 B2 El Mreyyé reg. Mauritania
107 E3 El Muglad Sudan
116 D3 El Nevado, Cerro mt. Col.
107 F3 El Obeid Sudan
104 E5 El Oued Alg.
112 E5 El Paso U.S.A.
115 G5 El Progreso Hond.
113 G4 El Reno U.S.A.
114 C4 El Salto Mex.
117 F2 El Tigre Venez.
116 E2 El Tocuyo Venez.
116 E2 El Tuparro, Parque Nacional nat. park Col.
El Ṭûr Egypt see Aṭ Ṭūr
118 B8 El Turbio Chile
116 D5 Elvira Brazil
108 E3 El Wak Kenya
Elx Spain see Elche-Elx
112 D4 Ely U.S.A.
95 G3 Émaé i. Vanuatu
117 H7 Emas, Parque Nacional das nat. park Brazil
98 D2 Emba Kazakh.
117 I7 Emborcação, Represa de resr Brazil
109 D4 Embu Kenya
102 H5 Emden Germany
95 E4 Emerald Australia
Emerita Augusta Spain see Mérida
107 D3 Emi Koussi mt. Chad
105 J4 Emirdağ Turkey
Emona Slovenia see Ljubljana
113 F6 Emory Peak U.S.A.
112 D6 Empalme Mex.
118 E3 Empedrado Arg.
120 G2 Emperor Seamount Chain sea feature N. Pacific Ocean
120 G2 Emperor Trough sea feature N. Pacific Ocean
101 F7 Enarotali Indon.
112 C5 Encantada, Cerro de la mt. Mex.
118 F4 Encantadas, Serra das hills Brazil
118 E3 Encarnación Para.
94 C2 Ende Indon.
95 E3 Endeavour Strait Australia
Endeh Indon. see Ende
123 L9 Enderby Abyssal Plain sea feature Southern Ocean
119 L4 Enderby Land reg. Antarctica
110 C3 Endicott Mountains U.S.A.
120 G6 Enewetak atoll Marshall Is
101 E5 Engaño, Cape Phil.
96 F4 Engel's Rus. Fed.
101 C7 Enggano i. Indon.
113 H1 English r. Canada
102 F6 English Channel France/U.K.
113 G4 Enid U.S.A.
103 J4 Enköping Sweden
111 H3 Ennadai Lake Canada
107 E3 En Nahud Sudan
107 E3 Ennedi, Massif mts Chad
102 E5 Ennis Ireland
102 E5 Enniskillen U.K.
103 K2 Enontekiö Fin.
104 E1 Enschede Neth.
112 C5 Ensenada Mex.
100 C3 Enshi China
118 D2 Entre Ríos Bol.
106 C4 Enugu Nigeria
110 A3 Enurmino Rus. Fed.
116 D5 Envira Brazil
116 D5 Envira r. Brazil
95 G3 Épi i. Vanuatu
Epidamnus Albania see Durrës
104 E2 Épinal France
102 F5 Epsom U.K.
106 C4 Equatorial Guinea country Africa
105 K4 Erciyes Dağı mt. Turkey
105 J4 Erdemli Turkey
107 E3 Erdi reg. Chad
119 I5 Erebus, Mount vol. Antarctica
118 F3 Erechim Brazil
100 D2 Ereentsav Mongolia
105 J4 Ereğli Konya Turkey
105 J3 Ereğli Zonguldak Turkey
100 D2 Erenhot China
105 F1 Erfurt Germany
106 B2 'Erg Chech des. Alg./Mali
113 J3 Erie U.S.A.
113 J3 Erie, Lake Canada/U.S.A.
108 D2 Eritrea country Africa
105 F2 Erlangen Germany
94 D4 Erldunda Australia
105 K4 Ermenek Turkey
105 H4 Ermoupoli Greece
99 F6 Ernakulam India
99 F5 Erode India
104 C5 Er Rachidia Morocco
107 F3 Er Rahad Sudan
104 C6 Er Raoui des. Alg.
109 D5 Errego Moz.
95 G3 Erromango i. Vanuatu
105 L1 Ertil' Rus. Fed.
103 I5 Erzgebirge mts Czech Rep./Germany
98 B3 Erzincan Turkey
98 C3 Erzurum Turkey
102 H4 Esbjerg Denmark
Esbo Fin. see Espoo
113 I2 Escanaba U.S.A.
115 F5 Escárcega Mex.
112 C5 Escondido U.S.A.
98 D3 Eşfahān Iran
109 C6 Esigodini Zimbabwe
103 J4 Eskilstuna Sweden
110 E3 Eskimo Lakes Canada
98 B3 Eskişehir Turkey
116 C3 Esmeraldas Ecuador
España country Europe see Spain
113 J2 Espanola Canada
112 E4 Espanola U.S.A.
116 □ Española, Isla i. Ecuador
94 C5 Esperance Australia
119 L2 Esperanza research stn Antarctica
114 C3 Esperanza Mex.
117 J7 Espinhaço, Serra do mts Brazil
117 J6 Espinosa Brazil
95 G3 Espíritu Santo i. Vanuatu
112 D7 Espíritu Santo, Isla i. Mex.
103 K3 Espoo Fin.
118 B6 Esquel Arg.
106 B1 Essaouira Morocco
106 A2 Es Semara W. Sahara
104 E1 Essen Germany
117 G3 Essequibo r. Guyana
97 Q4 Esso Rus. Fed.
113 F5 Estacado, Llano plain U.S.A.
118 D3 Estados, Isla de los i. Arg.
117 K6 Estância Brazil
118 D2 Esteros Para.
113 F2 Estevan Canada
103 L4 Estonia country Europe
Estonskaya S.S.R. country Europe see Estonia
117 I5 Estrondo, Serra hills Brazil
104 D2 Étampes France
108 D3 Ethiopia country Africa
Etna, Monte vol. Italy see Etna, Mount
105 G4 Etna, Mount vol. Italy
109 B5 Etosha National Park Namibia
109 B5 Etosha Pan salt pan Namibia
Euboea i. Greece see Evvoia
94 C5 Eucla Australia
117 K6 Euclides da Cunha Brazil
112 B3 Eugene U.S.A.
112 C6 Eugenia, Punta pt Mex.
98 B3 Euphrates r. Iraq/Syria
112 B3 Eureka U.S.A.
109 E6 Europa, Île i. Indian Ocean
122 E5 Europe CONTINENT
110 F4 Eutsuk Lake Canada
113 K1 Evans, Lac l. Canada
111 J3 Evans Strait Canada
112 D3 Evanston U.S.A.
113 I4 Evansville U.S.A.
97 Q3 Evensk Rus. Fed.
94 D4 Everard Range hills Australia
99 G4 Everest, Mount China
112 B2 Everett U.S.A.
113 J6 Everglades swamp U.S.A.
113 J6 Everglades National Park U.S.A.
107 D4 Evinayong Equat. Guinea
102 H4 Evje Norway
104 B4 Évora Port.
100 F1 Evoron, Ozero l. Rus. Fed.
104 D2 Évreux France
105 H4 Evvoia i. Greece
108 D3 Ewaso Ngiro r. Kenya
109 B4 Ewo Congo
116 E6 Exaltación Bol.
119 I4 Executive Committee Range mts Antarctica
104 C1 Exeter U.K.
104 C1 Exmoor hills U.K.
94 B4 Exmouth Gulf Australia
123 Q7 Exmouth Plateau sea feature Indian Ocean
113 K7 Exuma Cays sea chan. Bahamas
109 D4 Eyasi, Lake salt l. Tanz.
108 E3 Eyl Somalia
94 D4 Eyre (North), Lake salt flat Australia
94 D4 Eyre (South), Lake salt flat Australia
94 D5 Eyre Peninsula Australia
102 E3 Eysturoy i. Faroe Is
118 C5 Ezequiel Ramos Mexía, Embalse resr Arg.
105 I4 Ezine Turkey

F

107 D3 Fachi Niger
118 B7 Facundo Arg.
106 C3 Fada-N'Gourma Burkina
Faeroes terr. Atlantic Ocean see Faroe Islands
101 F7 Fafanlap Indon.
108 E3 Fafen Shet' watercourse Eth.
105 H2 Făgăraş Romania
103 J4 Fagersta Sweden
118 C8 Fagnano, Lago l. Arg./Chile
106 B3 Faguibine, Lac l. Mali
107 F4 Fagwir Sudan
110 D3 Fairbanks U.S.A.
102 F4 Fair Isle i. U.K.
113 H3 Fairmont U.S.A.
110 E4 Fairweather, Mount Canada/U.S.A.
101 G6 Fais i. Micronesia
99 F3 Faisalabad Pak.
95 I2 Fakaofo atoll Tokelau
101 F7 Fakfak Indon.
106 A4 Falaba Sierra Leone
113 G6 Falcon Lake Mex./U.S.A.
110 G4 Falher Canada
103 I4 Falkenberg Sweden
123 F9 Falkland Escarpment sea feature S. Atlantic Ocean
118 E8 Falkland Islands terr. Atlantic Ocean
123 F9 Falkland Plateau sea feature S. Atlantic Ocean
118 D8 Falkland Sound sea chan. Falkland Is
103 I4 Falköping Sweden
112 C4 Fallon U.S.A.
113 L3 Fall River U.S.A.
113 G3 Falls City U.S.A.
103 I5 Falster i. Denmark
103 J3 Falun Sweden
105 J4 Famagusta Cyprus
100 E2 Fangzheng China
108 C3 Faradje Dem. Rep. Congo
109 E6 Farafangana Madag.
107 E2 Farāfirah, Wāḥāt al oasis Egypt
Farafra Oasis oasis Egypt see Farāfirah, Wāḥāt al
99 E3 Farāh Afgh.
106 A3 Faranah Guinea
98 C5 Farasān, Jazā'ir is Saudi Arabia
101 G6 Faraulep atoll Micronesia
111 N4 Farewell, Cape Greenland
95 H6 Farewell, Cape N.Z.
113 G2 Fargo U.S.A.
96 I5 Farg'ona Uzbek.
113 H3 Faribault U.S.A.
106 A3 Farim Guinea-Bissau
112 E4 Farmington U.S.A.
117 G4 Faro Brazil
104 B4 Faro Port.
96 A3 Faroe Islands terr. Atlantic Ocean
122 H5 Farquhar Group is Seychelle
Farquhar Islands Seychelles see Farquhar Group
Farvel, Kap c. Greenland see Farewell, Cape
98 D4 Fāryāb Iran
105 G3 Fasano Italy
103 L5 Fastiv Ukr.
Fastov Ukr. see Fastiv
106 A3 Fatick Senegal
102 B3 Faxaflói b. Iceland
107 D3 Faya Chad
113 K4 Fayetteville U.S.A.
106 C4 Fazao Malfakassa, Parc National de nat. park Togo
106 A2 Fdérik Mauritania
113 K5 Fear, Cape U.S.A.
118 E4 Federal Arg.
116 D5 Feijó Brazil
117 K6 Feira de Santana Brazil
104 E2 Feldkirch Austria
Felsina Italy see Bologna
100 D2 Fengzhen China
95 F2 Feni Islands P.N.G.
109 E5 Fenoarivo Atsinanana Mada
105 K2 Feodosiya Ukr.
104 E4 Fer, Cap de c. Alg.
Fergana Uzbek. see Farg'ona
113 G2 Fergus Falls U.S.A.
95 F2 Fergusson Island P.N.G.
106 B4 Ferkessédougou Côte d'Ivoi
116 □ Fernandina, Isla i. Ecuador
118 B8 Fernando de Magallanes, Parque Nacional nat. park Chile
123 G6 Fernando de Noronha i. Bra
118 F2 Fernandópolis Brazil
105 F3 Ferrara Italy
Ferryville Tunisia see Menzel Bourguiba
104 C5 Fès Morocco
109 B4 Feshi Dem. Rep. Congo
105 I4 Fethiye Turkey
99 F3 Feyzābād Afgh.
Fez Morocco see Fès
109 E6 Fianarantsoa Madag.
108 D3 Fichē Eth.
104 D3 Figeac France
Figueras Spain see Figueres
104 D3 Figueres Spain
104 C5 Figuig Morocco
95 H3 Fiji country Pacific Ocean
118 D2 Filadelfia Para.
119 J3 Filchner Ice Shelf Antarctica
Filibe Bulg. see Plovdiv
119 K3 Fimbull Ice Shelf Antarctica
95 E6 Fingal Australia
109 D5 Fingoè Moz.
Finisterre, Cabo c. Spain see Finisterre, Cape
104 B3 Finisterre, Cape Spain
103 L3 Finland country Europe
103 K4 Finland, Gulf of Europe
110 F4 Finlay r. Canada
Firenze Italy see Florence
118 D4 Firmat Arg.
98 D4 Fīrūzābād Iran
109 B6 Fish watercourse Namibia
119 I6 Fisher Bay Antarctica
111 J3 Fisher Strait Canada
119 J3 Fiske, Cape Antarctica
Fisterra, Cabo c. Spain see Finisterre, Cape
118 C7 Fitz Roy Arg.
94 C3 Fitzroy Crossing Australia
Fiume Croatia see Rijeka
109 C4 Fizi Dem. Rep. Congo
112 D2 Flathead Lake U.S.A.
95 E3 Flattery, Cape Australia
112 B2 Flattery, Cape U.S.A.
102 H4 Flekkefjord Norway
123 G2 Flemish Cap sea feature N. Atlantic Ocean
104 E1 Flensburg Germany
95 E3 Flinders r. Australia
94 B5 Flinders Bay Australia
95 E5 Flinders Island Australia
94 D5 Flinders Ranges mts Australi
111 H4 Flin Flon Canada
113 J3 Flint U.S.A.
121 I5 Flint Island Kiribati
119 I4 Flood Range mts Antarctica
105 F3 Florence Italy
113 I5 Florence AL U.S.A.
112 D5 Florence AZ U.S.A.
113 K5 Florence SC U.S.A.
116 C3 Florencia Col.
Florentia Italy see Florence
118 C6 Florentino Ameghino, Embalse resr Arg.
118 E5 Flores r. Arg.
115 G5 Flores Guat.
101 E7 Flores i. Indon.
94 B2 Flores, Laut sea Indon.
Flores Sea sea Indon. see Flores, Laut
117 K5 Floresta Brazil
117 J5 Floriano Brazil
118 E4 Florida Uruguay
113 J5 Florida state U.S.A.

Greenland

13 J7 Florida, Straits of Bahamas/U.S.A.
95 G2 Florida Islands Solomon Is
13 J7 Florida Keys is U.S.A.
05 H3 Florina Greece
Flushing Neth. see Vlissingen
01 G7 Fly r. P.N.G.
05 G3 Foča Bos.-Herz.
05 I2 Focşani Romania
05 G3 Foggia Italy
06 □ Fogo i. Cape Verde
11 M5 Fogo Island Canada
04 D3 Foix France
03 O4 Fominskoye Rus. Fed.
11 H4 Fond-du-Lac Canada
13 I3 Fond du Lac U.S.A.
15 G6 Fonseca, Golfo de b. Central America
16 E4 Fonte Boa Brazil
02 D2 Fontur pt Iceland
95 E5 Forbes Australia
02 H3 Førde Norway
19 I4 Ford Range mts Antarctica
06 A4 Forécariah Guinea
05 F3 Forlì Italy
04 D4 Formentera i. Spain
Former Yugoslav Republic of Macedonia country Europe see Macedonia
18 E3 Formosa Arg.
17 I7 Formosa Brazil
17 G6 Formosa, Serra hills Brazil
13 H4 Forrest City U.S.A.
95 E3 Forsayth Australia
03 K3 Forssa Fin.
13 J1 Fort Albany Canada
17 K4 Fortaleza Brazil
10 G4 Fort Chipewyan Canada
15 L6 Fort-de-France Martinique
10 F3 Fort Good Hope Canada
02 F4 Forth, Firth of est. U.K.
18 D2 Fortín Capitán Demattei Para.
18 D2 Fortín General Mendoza Para.
18 E2 Fortín Madrejón Para.
18 D2 Fortín Pilcomayo Arg.
18 D1 Fortín Ravelo Bol.
18 D1 Fortín Suárez Arana Bol.
13 J6 Fort Lauderdale U.S.A.
10 F3 Fort Liard Canada
12 D2 Fort Macleod Canada
10 G4 Fort McMurray Canada
10 E3 Fort McPherson Canada
13 J6 Fort Myers U.S.A.
10 F4 Fort Nelson Canada
10 F4 Fort Nelson r. Canada
Fort Norman Canada see Tulita
13 I5 Fort Payne U.S.A.
12 E2 Fort Peck Reservoir U.S.A.
13 J6 Fort Pierce U.S.A.
10 G3 Fort Providence Canada
13 F1 Fort Qu'Appelle Canada
Fort Rupert Canada see Waskaganish
10 F4 Fort St James Canada
12 D1 Fort Saskatchewan Canada
13 H4 Fort Scott U.S.A.
11 J4 Fort Severn Canada
98 D2 Fort-Shevchenko Rus. Fed.
10 F3 Fort Simpson Canada
10 G3 Fort Smith Canada
13 H4 Fort Smith U.S.A.
13 F5 Fort Stockton U.S.A.
10 G4 Fort Vermilion Canada
13 I5 Fort Walton Beach U.S.A.
13 I3 Fort Wayne U.S.A.
02 E4 Fort William U.K.
13 G5 Fort Worth U.S.A.
10 D3 Fort Yukon U.S.A.
01 D4 Foshan China
04 E3 Fossano Italy
11 P2 Foster Bugt b. Greenland
07 D4 Foumban Cameroon
19 J4 Foundation Ice Stream glacier Antarctica
06 A3 Foundiougne Senegal
06 A3 Fouta Djallon reg. Guinea
95 G6 Foveaux Strait N.Z.
19 I3 Fowler Ice Rise Antarctica
94 D5 Fowlers Bay Australia
11 J3 Foxe Basin g. Canada
11 J3 Foxe Channel Canada
11 K3 Foxe Peninsula Canada
09 B5 Foz do Cunene Angola
18 F3 Foz do Iguaçu Brazil
17 I8 Franca Brazil
95 G3 Français, Récif des rf New Caledonia
02 G6 France country Europe
09 B4 Franceville Gabon
13 G3 Francis Case, Lake U.S.A.
09 C6 Francistown Botswana
13 J4 Frankfort U.S.A.
Frankfurt Germany see Frankfurt am Main
02 H5 Frankfurt am Main Germany
05 F1 Frankfurt an der Oder Germany
10 F3 Franklin Bay Canada
12 C2 Franklin D. Roosevelt Lake resr U.S.A.
10 F3 Franklin Mountains Canada
11 I2 Franklin Strait Canada
96 G2 Frantsa-Iosifa, Zemlya is Rus. Fed.
10 F4 Fraser r. Canada
102 F4 Fraserburgh U.K.
113 J2 Fraserdale Canada
95 F4 Fraser Island Australia
118 E4 Fray Bentos Uruguay
113 G5 Fredericksburg U.S.A.
110 E4 Frederick Sound sea chan. U.S.A.
113 M2 Fredericton Canada
Frederikshåb Greenland see Paamiut
103 I4 Frederikshavn Denmark
103 I4 Fredrikstad Norway
113 I3 Freeport IL U.S.A.
113 G6 Freeport TX U.S.A.
113 K6 Freeport City Bahamas
106 A4 Freetown Sierra Leone
119 L2 Frei (Chile) research stn Antarctica
Freiburg Switz. see Fribourg
104 E2 Freiburg im Breisgau Germany
94 B5 Fremantle Australia
117 H3 French Guiana terr. S. America
112 E2 Frenchman Creek r. U.S.A.
93 French Southern and Antarctic Lands terr. Indian Ocean
114 D4 Fresnillo Mex.
112 C4 Fresno U.S.A.
106 A3 Fria Guinea
118 C3 Frias Arg.
102 H6 Fribourg Switz.
104 E2 Friedrichshafen Germany
111 L3 Frobisher Bay Canada
103 O6 Frolovo Rus. Fed.
94 D5 Frome, Lake salt flat Australia
115 F5 Frontera Mex.
105 F3 Frosinone Italy
119 J6 Frost Glacier Antarctica
Frusino Italy see Frosinone
118 E2 Fuerte Olimpo Para.
106 A2 Fuerteventura i. Canary Is
98 D4 Fujairah U.A.E.
100 F3 Fukui Japan
100 F3 Fukuoka Japan
100 G3 Fukushima Japan
104 E1 Fulda Germany
95 H2 Funafuti atoll Tuvalu
106 A1 Funchal Madeira
111 L5 Fundy, Bay of g. Canada
Fünen i. Denmark see Fyn
Fünfkirchen Hungary see Pécs
109 D6 Funhalouro Moz.
106 C3 Funtua Nigeria
98 D4 Fürgun, Kūh-e mt. Iran
117 I8 Furnas, Represa resr Brazil
95 E6 Furneaux Group is Australia
111 J3 Fury and Hecla Strait Canada
100 E2 Fushun China
97 N5 Fusong China
95 H3 Futuna i. Vanuatu
Futuna islands is Wallis and Futuna Is see Hoorn, Îles de
100 D3 Fuyang China
100 E2 Fuyu China
101 D4 Fuzhou Fujian China
101 D4 Fuzhou Jiangxi China
103 I4 Fyn i. Denmark

G

108 E3 Gaalkacyo Somalia
109 B5 Gabela Angola
105 F5 Gabès Tunisia
105 F5 Gabès, Golfe de g. Tunisia
109 B4 Gabon country Africa
109 C6 Gaborone Botswana
105 I3 Gabrovo Bulg.
106 A3 Gabú Guinea-Bissau
Gades Spain see Cádiz
113 I5 Gadsden U.S.A.
Gadyach Ukr. see Hadyach
105 F3 Gaeta Italy
120 E5 Gaferut i. Micronesia
104 E5 Gafsa Tunisia
103 N4 Gagarin Rus. Fed.
106 B4 Gagnoa Côte d'Ivoire
111 L4 Gagnon Canada
Gaillimh Ireland see Galway
113 J6 Gainesville FL U.S.A.
113 G5 Gainesville TX U.S.A.
94 D5 Gairdner, Lake salt flat Australia
109 D4 Galana r. Kenya
121 N6 Galapagos Islands Pacific Ocean
121 M6 Galapagos Rise sea feature Pacific Ocean
105 I2 Galaţi Romania
102 H3 Galdhøpiggen mt. Norway
113 F7 Galeana Mex.
118 B6 Galera, Punta pt Chile
103 O4 Galich Rus. Fed.
103 O4 Galichskaya Vozvyshennost' hills Rus. Fed.
107 F3 Gallabat Sudan
99 G6 Galle Sri Lanka
121 L6 Gallego Rise sea feature Pacific Ocean
118 B8 Gallegos r. Arg.
Gallia country Europe see France
116 D1 Gallinas, Punta pt Col.
105 I3 Gallipoli Turkey
103 K2 Gällivare Sweden
112 E4 Gallup U.S.A.
106 A2 Galtat Zemmour W. Sahara
113 H6 Galveston U.S.A.
113 H6 Galveston Bay U.S.A.
102 E5 Galway Ireland
102 E5 Galway Bay Ireland
108 D3 Gambēla Eth.
108 D3 Gambēla National Park Eth.
110 A3 Gambell U.S.A.
106 A3 Gambia r. Gambia
106 A3 Gambia, The country Africa
121 K7 Gambier, Îles is Fr. Polynesia
109 B4 Gamboma Congo
112 E4 Ganado U.S.A.
98 C2 Gäncä Azer.
101 D7 Gandadiwata, Bukit mt. Indon.
109 C4 Gandajika Dem. Rep. Congo
111 M5 Gander Canada
99 F4 Gandhinagar India
104 C4 Gandía Spain
99 G4 Ganga, Mouths of the Bangl./India
118 C6 Gangán Arg.
99 F4 Ganganagar India
99 I3 Gangca China
99 G3 Gangdisê Shan mts China
123 O4 Ganges Cone sea feature Indian Ocean
99 G4 Gangtok India
112 E3 Gannett Peak U.S.A.
107 F4 Ganzi Sudan
106 B3 Gao Mali
106 B3 Gaoua Burkina
106 A3 Gaoual Guinea
100 D3 Gaoyou Hu l. China
104 E3 Gap France
99 G3 Gar China
96 G5 Garabogazköl Aýlagy b. Turkm.
108 C3 Garamba r. Dem. Rep. Congo
108 C3 Garamba, Parc National de la nat. park Dem. Rep. Congo
117 K5 Garanhuns Brazil
108 D3 Garba Tula Kenya
113 F4 Garden City U.S.A.
Gardez Afgh. see Gardēz
99 E3 Gardēz Afgh.
121 H4 Gardner Pinnacles is U.S.A.
109 D4 Garissa Kenya
Garmo, Qullai Tajik. see Ismoili Somoní, Qullai
95 E5 Garnpung Lake imp. l. Australia
104 C3 Garonne r. France
108 E3 Garoowe Somalia
107 D4 Garoua Cameroon
118 D5 Garré Arg.
111 H3 Garry Lake Canada
109 E4 Garsen Kenya
113 I3 Gary U.S.A.
100 B3 Garzê China
116 C3 Garzón Col.
Gascogne, Golfe de g. France see Gascony, Gulf of
104 C3 Gascony, Gulf of France
94 B4 Gascoyne r. Australia
107 D3 Gashua Nigeria
113 N2 Gaspé Canada
111 L5 Gaspésie, Péninsule de la pen. Canada
Gasteiz Spain see Vitoria-Gasteiz
113 J4 Gastonia U.S.A.
104 C4 Gata, Cabo de c. Spain
103 M4 Gatchina Rus. Fed.
113 K2 Gatineau r. Canada
95 H3 Gau i. Fiji
111 I4 Gauer Lake Canada
Gaul country Europe see France
105 H5 Gavdos i. Greece
117 J6 Gavião r. Brazil
103 J3 Gävle Sweden
105 D5 Gawler Australia
106 C3 Gaya Niger
103 Q3 Gayny Rus. Fed.
105 J5 Gaza terr. Asia
98 B3 Gaza Gaza
Gazandzhyk Turkm. see Bereket
Gaza Strip terr. Asia see Gaza
98 B3 Gazi Antep Turkey
Gazibenli Turkey see Yahyalı
Gazimağusa Cyprus see Famagusta
108 C3 Gbadolite Dem. Rep. Congo
106 A4 Gbangbatok Sierra Leone
106 B4 Gbarnga Liberia
106 C4 Gboko Nigeria
96 C4 Gdańsk Poland
103 J5 Gdańsk, Gulf of Poland/Rus. Fed.
Gdańska, Zatoka g. Poland/Rus. Fed. see Gdańsk, Gulf of
Gdingen Poland see Gdynia
103 L4 Gdov Rus. Fed.
103 J5 Gdynia Poland
107 F3 Gedaref Sudan
95 E5 Geelong Australia
107 D3 Geidam Nigeria
111 H4 Geikie r. Canada
102 H3 Geilo Norway
101 C4 Gejiu China
105 F4 Gela Italy
108 E3 Geladī Eth.
Gelibolu Turkey see Gallipoli
105 J4 Gelincik Dağı mt. Turkey
108 B3 Gemena Dem. Rep. Congo
105 I3 Gemlik Turkey
109 C6 Gemsbok National Park Botswana
108 E3 Genalē Wenz r. Eth.
118 D5 General Acha Arg.
118 C5 General Alvear Arg.
118 E5 General Belgrano Arg.
118 B7 General Carrera, Lago l. Chile
118 E5 General Juan Madariaga Arg.
118 D5 General Pico Arg.
118 C5 General Roca Arg.
101 E6 General Santos Phil.
102 H6 Geneva Switz.
102 H6 Geneva, Lake France/Switz.
Genève Switz. see Geneva
Genf Switz. see Geneva
104 E3 Genoa Italy
104 E3 Genoa, Gulf of Italy
Genova Italy see Genoa
Genova, Golfo di g. Italy see Genoa, Gulf of
Gent Belgium see Ghent
Genua Italy see Genoa
94 B5 Geographe Bay Australia
96 F2 George, Zemlya i. Rus. Fed.
111 L4 George r. Canada
113 J6 George, Lake U.S.A.
106 A3 Georgetown Gambia
117 G2 Georgetown Guyana
101 C6 George Town Malaysia
113 G5 Georgetown U.S.A.
119 J6 George V Land reg. Antarctica
113 J5 Georgia state U.S.A.
113 J2 Georgian Bay Canada
94 D4 Georgina watercourse Australia
Georgiu-Dezh Rus. Fed. see Liski
99 G2 Georgiyevka Kazakh.
105 F1 Gera Germany
117 I6 Geral de Goiás, Serra hills Brazil
94 B4 Geraldton Australia
105 J3 Gerede Turkey
Germania country Europe see Germany
103 I5 Germany country Europe
Gerona Spain see Girona
Géryville Alg. see El Bayadh
99 G3 Gêrzê China
Gesoriacum France see Boulogne-sur-Mer
108 E3 Gestro, Wabē r. Eth.
119 I4 Getz Ice Shelf Antarctica
Ghadamés Libya see Ghadāmis
104 E5 Ghadāmis Libya
99 G4 Ghaghara r. India
106 B4 Ghana country Africa
109 C6 Ghanzi Botswana
104 D5 Ghardaïa Alg.
Ghârib, Gebel mt. Egypt see Ghārib, Jabal
105 J6 Ghārib, Jabal mt. Egypt
Ghārib, Jabal mt. Egypt see Ḩamāţah, Jabal
105 F5 Gharyān Libya
107 D2 Ghāt Libya
107 D3 Ghazal, Bahr el watercourse Chad
104 C4 Ghazaouet Alg.
99 F4 Ghaziabad India
99 E3 Ghaznī Afgh.
102 G5 Ghent Belgium
Ghudamis Libya see Ghadāmis
104 B4 Gibraltar terr. Europe
104 B4 Gibraltar, Strait of Morocco/Spain
94 C4 Gibson Desert Australia
100 B2 Gichgeniyn Nuruu mts Mongolia
108 D3 Gīdolē Eth.
104 D2 Gien France
104 E1 Gießen Germany
97 O6 Gifu Japan
Gijón Spain see Gijón-Xixón
104 B3 Gijón-Xixón Spain
112 D5 Gila r. U.S.A.
95 E3 Gilbert r. Australia
95 H2 Gilbert Islands Kiribati
120 G6 Gilbert Ridge sea feature Pacific Ocean
117 I5 Gilbués Brazil
109 D4 Gilgil Kenya
99 F3 Gilgit Jammu and Kashmir
111 I4 Gillam Canada
112 E3 Gillette U.S.A.
111 K4 Gilmour Island Canada
107 E3 Gimbala, Jebel mt. Sudan
108 D3 Gīmbī Eth.
113 G1 Gimli Canada
116 E6 Ginebra, Laguna l. Bol.
108 E3 Gīnīr Eth.
105 K3 Giresun Turkey
Girgenti Italy see Agrigento
Girne Cyprus see Kyrenia
Giron Sweden see Kiruna
104 D3 Girona Spain
95 H5 Gisborne N.Z.
109 C4 Gitarama Rwanda
109 C4 Gitega Burundi
98 B4 Giza Egypt
97 R3 Gizhiga Rus. Fed.
105 H3 Gjirokastër Albania
Gjirokastra Albania see Gjirokastër
111 I3 Gjoa Haven Canada
103 I3 Gjøvik Norway
111 M5 Glace Bay Canada
112 B2 Glacier Peak vol. U.S.A.
95 F4 Gladstone Australia
102 F4 Glasgow U.K.
113 I4 Glasgow KY U.S.A.
112 E2 Glasgow MT U.S.A.
103 Q4 Glazov Rus. Fed.
Gleiwitz Poland see Gliwice
112 D5 Glendale U.S.A.
95 F4 Glen Innes Australia
110 D3 Glennallen U.S.A.
112 E4 Glenwood Springs U.S.A.
Glevum U.K. see Gloucester
103 J5 Gliwice Poland
112 D5 Globe U.S.A.
Glogau Poland see Głogów
103 J5 Głogów Poland
103 I4 Glomma r. Norway
109 E5 Glorieuses, Îles is Indian Ocean
102 F5 Gloucester U.K.
Glubokoye Belarus see Hlybokaye
99 G1 Glubokoye Kazakh.
99 F5 Goa state India
108 E3 Goba Eth.
109 B6 Gobabis Namibia
118 B7 Gobernador Gregores Arg.
100 C2 Gobi Desert Mongolia
109 B6 Gochas Namibia
99 F5 Godavari r. India
99 G5 Godavari, Mouths of the India
108 E3 Godere Eth.
111 I4 Gods r. Canada
111 I4 Gods Lake Canada
Godthåb Greenland see Nuuk
113 K2 Goéland, Lac au l. Canada
111 L4 Goélands, Lac aux l. Canada
117 L5 Goiana Brazil
117 I7 Goiânia Brazil
117 H7 Goiás Brazil
118 F2 Goio-Erê Brazil
105 I3 Gökçeada i. Turkey
109 C5 Gokwe Zimbabwe
102 H3 Gol Norway
95 F4 Gold Coast Australia
106 B4 Gold Coast coastal area Ghana
112 C1 Golden Canada
113 K4 Goldsboro U.S.A.
100 B3 Golmud China
Golyshi Rus. Fed. see Vetluzhskiy
107 D3 Gombe Nigeria
109 D4 Gombe r. Tanz.
107 D3 Gombi Nigeria
113 F6 Gómez Palacio Mex.
115 J5 Gonaïves Haiti
115 J5 Gonâve, Île de la i. Haiti
98 D3 Gonbad-e Kavus Iran
108 D2 Gonder Eth.
107 D3 Gongola r. Nigeria
119 J6 Goodenough, Cape Antarctica
95 F2 Goodenough Island P.N.G.
122 F7 Good Hope, Cape of S. Africa
95 F4 Goondiwindi Australia
112 B3 Goose Lake U.S.A.
99 G4 Gorakhpur India
95 E6 Gordon, Lake Australia
107 D4 Goré Chad
108 D3 Gorē Eth.
98 D3 Gorgān Iran
98 C2 Gori Georgia
Gor'kiy Rus. Fed. see Nizhniy Novgorod
105 F1 Görlitz Germany
Gorna Dzhumaya Bulg. see Blagoevgrad
100 A1 Gorno-Altaysk Rus. Fed.
99 G1 Gornyak Rus. Fed.
103 O4 Gorodets Rus. Fed.
95 E2 Goroka P.N.G.
106 B3 Gorom Gorom Burkina
109 D5 Gorongosa Moz.
101 E6 Gorontalo Indon.
103 J5 Gorzów Wielkopolski Poland
105 G3 Gospić Croatia
Göteborg Sweden see Gothenburg
Gotenhafen Poland see Gdynia
96 C4 Gothenburg Sweden
103 J4 Gotland i. Sweden
105 H3 Gotse Delchev Bulg.
104 E1 Göttingen Germany
106 A3 Goudiri Senegal
107 D3 Goudoumaria Niger
123 I8 Gough Island S. Atlantic Ocean
113 L2 Gouin, Réservoir resr Canada
95 E5 Goulburn Australia
101 F8 Goulburn Islands Australia
106 B3 Goundam Mali
107 D3 Gouré Niger
106 B3 Gourma-Rharous Mali
117 J7 Governador Valadares Brazil
100 B2 Govĭ Altayn Nuruu mts Mongolia
118 E3 Goya Arg.
105 J3 Göynük Turkey
104 Gozo i. Malta
106 B4 Grabo Côte d'Ivoire
95 F4 Grafton Australia
Graham Bell Island i. Rus. Fed. see Greem-Bell, Ostrov
110 E4 Graham Island B.C. Canada
111 I2 Graham Island Nunavut Canada
106 A4 Grain Coast Liberia
117 I5 Grajaú Brazil
105 H3 Grammos mt. Greece
102 F4 Grampian Mountains U.K.
115 G6 Granada Nicaragua
104 C4 Granada Spain
106 A2 Gran Canaria i. Canary Is
118 D3 Gran Chaco reg. Arg./Para.
Grand Atlas mts Morocco see Haut Atlas
113 K6 Grand Bahama i. Bahamas
111 M5 Grand Bank Canada
123 F3 Grand Banks of Newfoundland sea feature N. Atlantic Ocean
106 B4 Grand-Bassam Côte d'Ivoire
112 D4 Grand Canyon U.S.A.
112 D4 Grand Canyon gorge U.S.A.
115 H5 Grand Cayman i. Cayman Is
112 C2 Grand Coulee U.S.A.
118 C5 Grande r. Arg.
118 D1 Grande r. Bol.
117 I6 Grande r. Brazil
118 F2 Grande r. Brazil
118 C8 Grande, Bahía b. Arg.
111 K4 Grande 3, Réservoir de La resr Canada
Grande Comore i. Comoros see Njazidja
110 G4 Grande Prairie Canada
104 C5 Grand Erg Occidental des. Alg.
104 E6 Grand Erg Oriental des. Alg.
118 C4 Grandes, Salinas salt flat Arg.
113 M2 Grand Falls Canada
111 M5 Grand Falls-Windsor Canada
112 C2 Grand Forks Canada
113 G2 Grand Forks U.S.A.
113 G3 Grand Island U.S.A.
112 E4 Grand Junction U.S.A.
106 B4 Grand-Lahou Côte d'Ivoire
95 G3 Grand Passage New Caledonia
113 G1 Grand Rapids Canada
113 I3 Grand Rapids U.S.A.
112 D3 Grand Teton mt. U.S.A.
115 J4 Grand Turk Turks and Caicos Is
118 C6 Gran Laguna Salada l. Arg.
119 H4 Grant Island Antarctica
112 E4 Grants U.S.A.
112 B3 Grants Pass U.S.A.
111 H4 Granville Lake Canada
Graudenz Poland see Grudziądz
105 G2 Graz Austria
113 K6 Great Abaco i. Bahamas
94 C5 Great Australian Bight g. Australia
113 K6 Great Bahama Bank sea feature Bahamas
95 H5 Great Barrier Island N.Z.
95 E3 Great Barrier Reef Australia
112 C3 Great Basin U.S.A.
110 F3 Great Bear Lake Canada
103 I4 Great Belt sea chan. Denmark
113 G4 Great Bend U.S.A.
91 Great Britain Europe
95 E5 Great Dividing Range mts Australia
Great Eastern Erg des. Alg. see Grand Erg Oriental
115 H4 Greater Antilles is Caribbean Sea
101 B7 Greater Sunda Islands Indon.
113 K7 Great Exuma i. Bahamas
112 D2 Great Falls U.S.A.
115 J4 Great Inagua i. Bahamas
95 E6 Great Lake Australia
123 H4 Great Meteor Tablemount sea feature N. Atlantic Ocean
Great Oasis, The oasis Egypt see Khārijah, Wāḩāt al
113 F2 Great Plains Can./U.S.A.
108 D3 Great Rift Valley Africa
109 D4 Great Ruaha r. Tanz.
112 D3 Great Salt Lake U.S.A.
112 D3 Great Salt Lake Desert U.S.A.
107 E2 Great Sand Sea des. Egypt/Libya
94 C4 Great Sandy Desert Australia
95 H3 Great Sea Reef Fiji
110 G3 Great Slave Lake Canada
94 C4 Great Victoria Desert Australia
119 L2 Great Wall research stn Antarctica
Great Western Erg des. Alg. see Grand Erg Occidental
102 G5 Great Yarmouth U.K.
Grebenkovskiy Ukr. see Hrebinka
Grebyonka Ukr. see Hrebinka
105 H4 Greece country Europe
113 F3 Greeley U.S.A.
111 J1 Greely Fiord inlet Canada
96 H1 Greem-Bell, Ostrov i. Rus. Fed.
110 H6 Green r. U.S.A.
113 I3 Green Bay U.S.A.
113 I2 Green Bay b. U.S.A.
111 N2 Greenland terr. N. America

Greenland Basin

Kangal

09 A4 Iguéla Gabon
06 B2 Iguidi, Erg des. Alg./Mauritania
09 D4 Igunga Tanz.
09 E5 Iharaña Madag.
09 E6 Ihosy Madag.
03 L3 Iisalmi Fin.
04 E1 IJsselmeer l. Neth.
05 I4 Ikaria i. Greece
09 C4 Ikela Dem. Rep. Congo
06 C4 Ikom Nigeria
09 E6 Ikongo Madag.
09 D4 Ikungu Tanz.
01 E5 Ilagan Phil.
08 D3 Ilaisamis Kenya
98 C3 Īlām Iran
06 C4 Ilaro Nigeria
09 C4 Ilebo Dem. Rep. Congo
08 D3 Ileret Kenya
18 F2 Ilha Solteira, Represa resr Brazil
17 K6 Ilhéus Brazil
10 C4 Iliamna Lake U.S.A.
Ilici Spain see Elche-Elx
03 P3 Il'insko-Podomskoye Rus. Fed.
18 B4 Illapel Chile
16 E7 Illimani, Nevado de mt. Bol.
13 H4 Illinois r. U.S.A.
13 I4 Illinois state U.S.A.
06 C2 Illizi Alg.
03 M4 Il'men', Ozero l. Rus. Fed.
16 D7 Ilo Peru
01 E5 Iloilo Phil.
03 M3 Ilomantsi Fin.
06 C4 Ilorin Nigeria
03 O6 Ilovlya Rus. Fed.
11 M3 Ilulissat Greenland
Ilva i. Italy see Elba, Isola d'
03 O4 imeni Babushkina Rus. Fed.
08 E3 Īmī Eth.
17 I5 Imperatriz Brazil
08 B3 Impfondo Congo
01 B4 Imphal India
İmroz i. Turkey see Gökçeada
16 E6 Inambari r. Peru
06 C2 In Aménas Alg.
01 F7 Inanwatan Indon.
03 L2 Inarijärvi l. Fin.
05 J3 İnce Burun pt Turkey
00 E3 Inch'ŏn S. Korea
13 H4 Independence U.S.A.
98 D2 Inderborskiy Kazakh.
99 F4 India country Asia
13 I3 Indiana state U.S.A.
Indian-Antarctic Basin sea feature Southern Ocean see Australian-Antarctic Basin
23 Q9 Indian-Antarctic Ridge sea feature Southern Ocean
13 I4 Indianapolis U.S.A.
19 L7 Indian Ocean World
13 H3 Indianola IA U.S.A.
13 H5 Indianola MS U.S.A.
12 C4 Indian Springs U.S.A.
03 P2 Indiga Rus. Fed.
97 P2 Indigirka r. Rus. Fed.
12 C5 Indio U.S.A.
95 G3 Indispensable Reefs Solomon Is
01 D7 Indonesia country Asia
99 F4 Indore India
99 E4 Indus, Mouths of the Pak.
23 N4 Indus Cone sea feature Indian Ocean
05 J3 İnebolu Turkey
05 I3 İnegöl Turkey
Inevi Turkey see Cihanbeyli
14 D5 Infiernillo, Presa resr Mex.
18 C6 Ingeniero Jacobacci Arg.
11 K2 Inglefield Land reg. Greenland
05 F2 Ingolstadt Germany
09 D6 Inhambane Moz.
09 D5 Inhaminga Moz.
Inis Ireland see Ennis
105 F2 Inn r. Europe
111 L2 Innaanganeq c. Greenland
Inner Mongolia aut. reg. China see Nei Mongol Zizhiqu
95 E3 Innisfail Australia
105 F2 Innsbruck Austria
09 B4 Inongo Dem. Rep. Congo
103 J5 Inowrocław Poland
06 C2 In Salah Alg.
Insterburg Rus. Fed. see Chernyakhovsk
03 S2 Inta Rus. Fed.
Interamna Italy see Teramo
13 H2 International Falls U.S.A.
10 E3 Inuvik Canada
95 G6 Invercargill N.Z.
95 F4 Inverell Australia
02 F4 Inverness U.K.
123 P6 Investigator Ridge sea feature Indian Ocean
94 D5 Investigator Strait Australia
99 G1 Inya Rus. Fed.
109 D4 Inyonga Tanz.
103 P5 Inza Rus. Fed.
105 H4 Ioannina Greece
113 G4 Iola U.S.A.
105 G4 Ionian Islands Greece
105 G4 Ionian Sea Greece/Italy
Ionioi Nisoi is Greece see Ionian Islands
100 G1 Iony, Ostrov i. Rus. Fed.
105 I4 Ios i. Greece
101 G4 Iō-tō i. Japan
113 H3 Iowa state U.S.A.
113 H3 Iowa City U.S.A.
116 D5 Iparía Peru
117 J7 Ipatinga Brazil
103 O6 Ipatovo Rus. Fed.
116 C3 Ipiales Col.
117 K6 Ipiaú Brazil
101 C6 Ipoh Malaysia
117 K5 Ipojuca r. Brazil
117 H7 Iporá Brazil
108 C3 Ippy Centr. Afr. Rep.
104 D1 Ipswich U.K.
111 L3 Iqaluit Canada
118 B2 Iquique Chile
116 D4 Iquitos Peru
Irakleio Greece see Iraklion
105 I4 Iraklion Greece
98 D3 Iran country Asia
99 E4 Īrānshahr Iran
114 D4 Irapuato Mex.
107 G1 Iraq country Asia
118 F3 Irati Brazil
105 K5 Irbid Jordan
96 H4 Irbit Rus. Fed.
117 J6 Irecê Brazil
102 E5 Ireland country Europe
109 C4 Irema Dem. Rep. Congo
99 E2 Irgiz Kazakh.
101 F7 Irian Jaya Indon.
106 B3 Irîgui reg. Mali/Mauritania
109 D4 Iringa Tanz.
117 H4 Iriri r. Brazil
104 B1 Irish Sea Ireland/U.K.
117 I4 Irituia Brazil
100 C1 Irkutsk Rus. Fed.
124 V3 Irminger Basin sea feature N. Atlantic Ocean
113 I2 Iron Mountain U.S.A.
113 H2 Ironwood U.S.A.
101 E5 Irosin Phil.
101 B5 Irrawaddy r. China/Myanmar
101 B5 Irrawaddy, Mouths of the Myanmar
96 H3 Irtysh r. Kazakh./Rus. Fed.
108 C3 Irumu Dem. Rep. Congo
Iruña Spain see Pamplona
Iruñea Spain see Pamplona
101 E6 Isabela Phil.
116 □ Isabela, Isla i. Ecuador
115 G6 Isabelia, Cordillera mts Nicaragua
102 B2 Ísafjörður Iceland
109 E6 Isalo, Massif de l' mts Madag.
109 E6 Isalo, Parc National de l' nat. park Madag.
105 F3 Ischia, Isola d' i. Italy
108 C3 Isengi Dem. Rep. Congo
105 F3 Isernia Italy
106 C4 Iseyin Nigeria
100 G2 Ishikari-wan b. Japan
113 I2 Ishpeming U.S.A.
116 E7 Isiboro Sécure, Parque Nacional nat. park Bol.
96 I4 Isil'kul' Rus. Fed.
108 C3 Isiro Dem. Rep. Congo
105 K4 İskenderun Turkey
105 K4 İskenderun Körfezi b. Turkey
100 A1 Iskitim Rus. Fed.
99 F3 Islamabad Pak.
Ísland country Europe see Iceland
94 D5 Island Lagoon salt flat Australia
113 H1 Island Lake l. Canada
102 E4 Islay i. U.K.
Ismail Ukr. see Izmayil
96 A4 Ismoili Somoní, Qullai mt. Tajik.
109 D5 Isoka Zambia
105 J5 Israel country Asia
Isra'īl country Asia see Israel
106 B4 Issia Côte d'Ivoire
98 A2 İstanbul Turkey
Istra pen. Croatia see Istria
105 F2 Istria pen. Croatia
117 K6 Itabaianinha Brazil
117 J6 Itaberaba Brazil
117 K6 Itabuna Brazil
117 G4 Itacoatiara Brazil
117 G4 Itaituba Brazil
Italia country Europe see Italy
102 I7 Italy country Europe
117 K7 Itamaraju Brazil
117 J7 Itambé, Pico de mt. Brazil
109 E6 Itampolo Madag.
117 J8 Itapemirim Brazil
117 J7 Itapetinga Brazil
117 I8 Itapetininga Brazil
117 K6 Itapicuru r. Bahia Brazil
117 J5 Itapicuru r. Maranhão Brazil
117 J4 Itapicuru Mirim Brazil
117 K4 Itapipoca Brazil
117 I8 Itararé Brazil
113 K3 Ithaca U.S.A.
108 C3 Itimbiri r. Dem. Rep. Congo
117 H7 Itiquira Brazil
117 G7 Itiquira r. Brazil
116 D5 Ituí r. Brazil
109 C4 Itula Dem. Rep. Congo
117 I7 Itumbiara Brazil
117 G2 Ituni Guyana
117 I5 Itupiranga Brazil
118 F1 Iturama Brazil
100 G2 Iturup, Ostrov i. Rus. Fed.
116 E5 Ituxi r. Brazil
97 U3 Iul'tin Rus. Fed.
118 F2 Ivaí r. Brazil
103 L2 Ivalo Fin.
95 E5 Ivanhoe Australia
103 K6 Ivano-Frankivs'k Ukr.
Ivano-Frankovsk Ukr. see Ivano-Frankivs'k
103 O4 Ivanovo Rus. Fed.
Ivantsevichi Belarus see Ivatsevichy
103 L5 Ivatsevichy Belarus
96 H3 Ivdel' Rus. Fed.
118 F2 Ivinheima r. Brazil
111 N3 Ivittuut Greenland
Iviza i. Spain see Ibiza
109 E6 Ivohibe Madag.
Ivory Coast country Africa see Côte d'Ivoire
111 K3 Ivujivik Canada
106 C4 Iwo Nigeria
Iwo Jima i. Japan see Iō-tō
114 E4 Ixmiquilpán Mex.
115 G5 Izabal, Lago de l. Guat.
109 D4 Izazi Tanz.
96 G4 Izhevsk Rus. Fed.
103 Q2 Izhma Respublika Komi Rus. Fed.
Izhma Respublika Komi Rus. Fed. see Sosnogorsk
103 Q2 Izhma r. Rus. Fed.
Izmail Ukr. see Izmayil
105 I2 Izmayil Ukr.
98 A3 İzmir Turkey
105 I4 İzmit Turkey
118 D1 Izozog, Bañados del swamp Bol.
120 E3 Izu-Ogasawara Trench sea feature N. Pacific Ocean
105 K2 Izyum Ukr.

J

107 F3 Jabal, Bahr el r. Sudan/Uganda alt. Abiad, Bahr el, conv. White Nile
99 F4 Jabalpur India
101 F8 Jabiru Australia
117 L5 Jaboatão Brazil
117 J6 Jacaré r. Brazil
117 G5 Jacareacanga Brazil
117 I8 Jacareí Brazil
117 F5 Jaciparaná r. Brazil
113 J3 Jackson MI U.S.A.
113 H5 Jackson MS U.S.A.
113 I4 Jackson TN U.S.A.
119 I3 Jackson, Mount Antarctica
113 J5 Jacksonville FL U.S.A.
113 K5 Jacksonville NC U.S.A.
115 J5 Jacmel Haiti
117 J6 Jacobina Brazil
118 F4 Jacuí r. Brazil
117 K6 Jacuípe r. Brazil
117 I4 Jacunda Brazil
105 F5 Jādū Libya
116 C5 Jaén Peru
104 C4 Jaén Spain
94 D5 Jaffa, Cape Australia
99 F6 Jaffna Sri Lanka
99 G5 Jagdalpur India
98 D4 Jahrom Iran
99 F4 Jaipur India
105 G3 Jajce Bos.-Herz.
101 C7 Jakarta Indon.
Jakobshavn Greenland see Ilulissat
103 K3 Jakobstad Fin.
99 F3 Jalālābād Afgh.
99 F2 Jalal-Abad Kyrg.
99 F3 Jalandhar India
114 E5 Jalapa Mex.
99 F4 Jalgaon India
107 D4 Jalingo Nigeria
99 G4 Jalpaiguri India
107 E2 Jālū Libya
115 I5 Jamaica country Caribbean Sea
115 I5 Jamaica Channel Haiti/Jamaica
117 G5 Jamanxim r. Brazil
101 C7 Jambi Indon.
113 G2 James r. ND U.S.A.
113 K4 James r. VA U.S.A.
113 J1 James Bay Canada
111 P2 Jameson Land reg. Greenland
119 I2 James Ross Island Antarctica
111 I3 James Ross Strait Canada
94 D5 Jamestown Australia
113 G2 Jamestown ND U.S.A.
113 K3 Jamestown NY U.S.A.
99 F3 Jammu Jammu and Kashmir
99 F3 Jammu and Kashmir terr. Asia
103 L3 Jämsä Fin.
99 G4 Jamshedpur India
117 J7 Janaúba Brazil
113 I3 Janesville U.S.A.
124 X2 Jan Mayen terr. Arctic Ocean
117 J7 Januária Brazil
120 D3 Japan country Asia
100 F3 Japan, Sea of Asia
123 S3 Japan Basin sea feature Sea of Japan
120 E3 Japan Trench sea feature N. Pacific Ocean
116 E4 Japurá r. Brazil
118 E2 Jardim Brazil
115 I4 Jardines de la Reina, Archipiélago de los is Cuba
100 C3 Jartai China
117 F6 Jarú Brazil
98 D4 Jāsk Iran
118 D8 Jason Islands Falkland Is
119 I2 Jason Peninsula Antarctica
112 C1 Jasper Canada
117 H7 Jataí Brazil
117 G4 Jatapu r. Brazil
117 I8 Jaú Brazil
117 F4 Jaú r. Brazil
117 F4 Jaú, Parque Nacional do nat. park Brazil
117 F3 Jaua Sarisariñama, Parque Nacional nat. park Venez.
101 C7 Java i. Indon.
123 Q6 Java Ridge sea feature Indian Ocean
Java Sea sea Indon. see Jawa, Laut
Jawa i. Indon. see Java
101 D7 Jawa, Laut sea Indon.
108 E3 Jawhar Somalia
101 F7 Jaya, Puncak mt. Indon.
101 G7 Jayapura Indon.
98 D4 Jaz Mūrīān, Hāmūn-e salt marsh Iran
106 C4 Jebba Nigeria
107 E3 Jebel Abyad Plateau Sudan
98 B4 Jeddah Saudi Arabia
113 H4 Jefferson City U.S.A.
118 E2 Jejuí Guazú r. Para.
103 J5 Jelenia Góra Poland
103 K4 Jelgava Latvia
101 D7 Jember Indon.
105 F1 Jena Germany
104 E4 Jendouba Tunisia
113 H5 Jennings U.S.A.
117 J6 Jequié Brazil
117 J7 Jequitaí Brazil
117 K7 Jequitinhonha r. Brazil
105 F5 Jerba, Île de i. Tunisia
107 F4 Jerbar Sudan
115 J5 Jérémie Haiti
104 B4 Jerez de la Frontera Spain
104 E5 Jerid, Chott el salt l. Tunisia
104 C2 Jersey terr. Channel Is
117 J5 Jerumenha Brazil
98 B3 Jerusalem Israel/West Bank
113 J5 Jesup U.S.A.
115 F5 Jesús Carranza Mex.
118 D4 Jesús María Arg.
99 F4 Jhansi India
100 F2 Jiamusi China
101 D4 Ji'an Jiangxi China
100 E2 Ji'an Jilin China
101 D4 Jianyang China
100 E3 Jiaxing China
100 B3 Jiayuguan China
103 J2 Jiehkkevárri mt. Norway
100 C3 Jigzhi China
105 G2 Jihlava Czech Rep.
104 E4 Jijel Alg.
108 E3 Jijiga Eth.
107 E2 Jilf al Kabīr, Haḍabat al plat. Egypt
108 E3 Jilib Somalia
100 E2 Jilin China
108 D3 Jīma Eth.
113 F6 Jiménez Chihuahua Mex.
114 E4 Jiménez Tamaulipas Mex.
100 D3 Jinan China
101 D4 Jingdezhen China
101 C4 Jinghong China
100 D3 Jingmen China
100 C3 Jingtai China
100 C3 Jingyuan China
100 D3 Jingzhou China
101 D4 Jinhua China
100 D2 Jining Nei Mongol China
100 D3 Jining Shandong China
108 D3 Jinja Uganda
108 D3 Jinka Eth.
115 G6 Jinotepe Nicaragua
100 D3 Jinzhong China
100 E2 Jinzhou China
117 F6 Ji-Paraná Brazil
117 F5 Jiparaná r. Brazil
116 B4 Jipijapa Ecuador
99 G3 Jirang China
101 C4 Jishou China
99 E4 Jiwani Pak.
100 F2 Jixi China
98 C5 Jīzān Saudi Arabia
96 H5 Jizzax Uzbek.
117 L5 João Pessoa Brazil
117 I7 João Pinheiro Brazil
99 F4 Jodhpur India
103 L3 Joensuu Fin.
109 D6 Jofane Moz.
113 J4 Johnson City U.S.A.
121 H4 Johnston Atoll terr. N. Pacific Ocean
101 C6 Johor Bahru Malaysia
119 I2 Joinville Island Antarctica
103 J2 Jokkmokk Sweden
113 I3 Joliet U.S.A.
113 L2 Joliette Canada
101 E6 Jolo Phil.
101 E6 Jolo i. Phil.
113 H4 Jonesboro U.S.A.
111 J2 Jones Sound sea chan. Canada
107 F4 Jonglei Canal Sudan
103 I4 Jönköping Sweden
113 L2 Jonquière Canada
113 H4 Joplin U.S.A.
107 F1 Jordan country Asia
105 K5 Jordan r. Asia
101 B4 Jorhat India
106 C4 Jos Nigeria
118 B6 José de San Martín Arg.
94 C3 Joseph Bonaparte Gulf Australia
106 C4 Jos Plateau Nigeria
112 B2 Juan de Fuca, Strait of U.S.A.
109 E5 Juan de Nova i. Indian Ocean
123 D8 Juan Fernández, Archipiélago is S. Pacific Ocean
117 J5 Juàzeiro Brazil
117 K5 Juàzeiro do Norte Brazil
107 F4 Juba Sudan
119 L2 Jubany research stn Antarctica
108 E3 Jubba r. Somalia
114 E5 Juchitán Mex.
115 G6 Juigalpa Nicaragua
117 J8 Juiz de Fora Brazil
118 C2 Julaca Bol.
116 D7 Juliaca Peru
117 G3 Juliana Top mt. Suriname
Juliomagus France see Angers
116 C5 Jumbilla Peru
99 F4 Junagadh India
113 G4 Junction City U.S.A.
110 E4 Juneau U.S.A.
104 E2 Jungfrau mt. Switz.
97 J5 Junggar Pendi basin China
107 E4 Jur r. Sudan
104 E2 Jura mts France/Switz.
116 E4 Juruá r. Brazil
117 G6 Juruena r. Brazil
116 E4 Jutaí r. Brazil
115 G6 Jutiapa Guat.
115 G6 Juticalpa Hond.
102 H4 Jutland pen. Denmark
115 H4 Juventud, Isla de la i. Cuba
109 C6 Jwaneng Botswana
Jylland pen. Denmark see Jutland
103 L3 Jyväskylä Fin.

K

99 F3 K2 mt. China/Pakistan
118 D1 Kaa-Iya del Gran Chaco, Parque Nacional nat. park Bol.
94 C2 Kabaena i. Indon.
106 A4 Kabala Sierra Leone
109 C4 Kabale Uganda
109 C4 Kabalo Dem. Rep. Congo
109 C4 Kabambare Dem. Rep. Congo
109 C5 Kabangu Dem. Rep. Congo
109 C4 Kabare Dem. Rep. Congo
109 C4 Kabinda Dem. Rep. Congo
108 B3 Kabo Centr. Afr. Rep.
109 C5 Kabompo Zambia
109 C4 Kabongo Dem. Rep. Congo
99 E3 Kābul Afgh.
109 C5 Kabwe Zambia
99 E4 Kachchh, Gulf of India
99 F4 Kachchh, Rann of marsh India
100 C1 Kachug Rus. Fed.
95 H3 Kadavu i. Fiji
95 H3 Kadavu Passage Fiji
106 B4 Kade Ghana
98 A2 Kadıköy Turkey
106 B3 Kadiolo Mali
Kadiyevka Ukr. see Stakhanov
99 F5 Kadmat atoll India
109 C5 Kadoma Zimbabwe
107 E3 Kadugli Sudan
106 C3 Kaduna Nigeria
106 C3 Kaduna state Nigeria
103 N4 Kaduy Rus. Fed.
103 R3 Kadzherom Rus. Fed.
106 A3 Kaédi Mauritania
107 D3 Kaélé Cameroon
100 E3 Kaesŏng N. Korea
Kafa Ukr. see Feodosiya
109 C4 Kafakumba Dem. Rep. Congo
106 A3 Kaffrine Senegal
109 C5 Kafue Zambia
109 C5 Kafue r. Zambia
109 C5 Kafue National Park Zambia
108 B3 Kaga Bandoro Centr. Afr. Rep.
100 F3 Kagoshima Japan
109 D4 Kahama Tanz.
101 D7 Kahayan r. Indon.
109 B4 Kahemba Dem. Rep. Congo
103 K2 Kahperusvaarat mts Fin.
98 B3 Kahramanmaraş Turkey
109 C4 Kahuzi-Biega, Parc National du nat. park Dem. Rep. Congo
101 F7 Kai, Kepulauan is Indon.
106 C4 Kaiama Nigeria
101 F7 Kai Besar i. Indon.
100 D3 Kaifeng China
101 F7 Kai Kecil i. Indon.
106 A4 Kailahun Sierra Leone
94 D2 Kaimana Indon.
99 G4 Kaimur Range hills India
106 C3 Kainji Lake National Park Nigeria
106 C3 Kainji Reservoir Nigeria
95 H5 Kaipara Harbour N.Z.
105 F4 Kairouan Tunisia
94 C2 Kaiwatu Indon.
101 C4 Kaiyuan China
103 L3 Kajaani Fin.
95 E4 Kajabbi Australia
108 D3 Kakamega Kenya
106 A4 Kakata Liberia
109 C4 Kakenge Dem. Rep. Congo
105 J2 Kakhovs'ke Vodoskhovyshche resr Ukr.
99 G5 Kakinada India
109 C4 Kakoswa Dem. Rep. Congo
110 D2 Kaktovik U.S.A.
Kalaallit Nunaat terr. N. America see Greenland
101 E7 Kalabahi Indon.
109 C5 Kalabo Zambia
105 L1 Kalach Rus. Fed.
108 D3 Kalacha Dida Kenya
103 O6 Kalach-na-Donu Rus. Fed.
109 C6 Kalahari Desert Africa
109 B6 Kalahari Gemsbok National Park S. Africa
103 K3 Kalajoki Fin.
Kalámai Greece see Kalamata
105 H4 Kalamata Greece
113 I3 Kalamazoo U.S.A.
107 E2 Kalanshiyū ar Ramlī al Kabīr, Sarīr des. Libya
94 B4 Kalbarri Australia
105 J3 Kalecik Turkey
109 C4 Kalema Dem. Rep. Congo
109 C4 Kalemie Dem. Rep. Congo
103 M2 Kalevala Rus. Fed.
94 C5 Kalgoorlie Australia
109 C4 Kalima Dem. Rep. Congo
96 D4 Kaliningrad Rus. Fed.
96 D4 Kaliningradskaya Oblast' admin. div. Rus. Fed.
103 L5 Kalinkavichy Belarus
Kalinkovichi Belarus see Kalinkavichy
Kalisch Poland see Kalisz
112 D2 Kalispell U.S.A.
103 J5 Kalisz Poland
109 D4 Kaliua Tanz.
109 B6 Kalkfeld Namibia
103 L3 Kallavesi l. Fin.
103 J4 Kalmar Sweden
103 J4 Kalmarsund sea chan. Sweden
99 G6 Kalmunai Sri Lanka
109 C5 Kalomo Zambia
99 F5 Kalpeni atoll India
110 C3 Kaltag U.S.A.
103 N5 Kaluga Rus. Fed.
103 I4 Kalundborg Denmark
103 N4 Kalyazin Rus. Fed.
109 C4 Kama Dem. Rep. Congo
100 G3 Kamaishi Japan
105 J4 Kaman Turkey
109 B5 Kamanjab Namibia
94 C5 Kambalda Australia
109 C5 Kambove Dem. Rep. Congo
97 R4 Kamchatka r. Rus. Fed.
120 G2 Kamchatka Basin sea feature Bering Sea
97 Q4 Kamchatka Peninsula Rus. Fed.
Kamenets-Podol'skiy Ukr. see Kam"yanets'-Podil's'kyy
103 O2 Kamenka Arkhangel'skaya Oblast' Rus. Fed.
103 O5 Kamenka Penzenskaya Oblast' Rus. Fed.
99 G1 Kamen'-na-Obi Rus. Fed.
97 R3 Kamenskoye Rus. Fed.
Kamenskoye Ukr. see Dniprodzerzhyns'k
105 L2 Kamensk-Shakhtinskiy Rus. Fed.
96 H4 Kamensk-Ural'skiy Rus. Fed.
109 C4 Kamina Dem. Rep. Congo
111 I3 Kaminak Lake Canada
112 B1 Kamloops Canada
109 C4 Kamonia Dem. Rep. Congo
108 D3 Kampala Uganda
109 C4 Kampene Dem. Rep. Congo
101 C5 Kâmpóng Cham Cambodia
101 C5 Kâmpóng Chhnăng Cambodia
101 C5 Kâmpóng Spœ Cambodia
101 C5 Kâmpóng Thum Cambodia
101 C5 Kâmpôt Cambodia
101 F7 Kamrau, Teluk b. Indon.
96 G4 Kamskoye Vodokhranilishche resr Rus. Fed.
108 E3 Kamsuuma Somalia
108 D3 Kamuli Uganda
103 L6 Kam"yanets'-Podil's'kyy Ukr.
103 P5 Kamyshin Rus. Fed.
109 C4 Kananga Dem. Rep. Congo
103 P4 Kanash Rus. Fed.
113 J4 Kanawha r. U.S.A.
100 F3 Kanazawa Japan
99 F5 Kanchipuram India
99 E3 Kandahār Afgh.
103 M2 Kandalaksha Rus. Fed.
103 M2 Kandalakshskiy Zaliv g. Rus. Fed.
106 C3 Kandi Benin
109 E5 Kandreho Madag.
99 G6 Kandy Sri Lanka
98 D2 Kandyagash Kazakh.
111 L2 Kane Bassin b. Canada/Greenland
109 C6 Kang Botswana
111 K2 Kangaarsussuaq c. Greenland
111 M3 Kangaatsiaq Greenland
106 B3 Kangaba Mali
105 K4 Kangal Turkey

Kangān

98 D4 Kangān Iran
101 C6 Kangar Malaysia
94 D5 Kangaroo Island Australia
99 G4 Kangchenjunga mt. Nepal
101 D7 Kangean, Kepulauan is Indon.
111 L3 Kangeeak Point Canada
111 N3 Kangeq c. Greenland
111 M3 Kangerlussuaq inlet Greenland
111 O3 Kangerlussuaq inlet Greenland
111 N3 Kangerlussuatsiaq inlet Greenland
111 M2 Kangersuatsiaq Greenland
111 P2 Kangertittivaq sea chan. Greenland
111 O3 Kangertittivatsiaq inlet Greenland
100 E2 Kanggye N. Korea
111 K3 Kangiqsujuaq Canada
111 K3 Kangirsuk Canada
99 G4 Kangmar China
100 E3 Kangnŭng S. Korea
108 B3 Kango Gabon
109 C4 Kaniama Dem. Rep. Congo
103 O2 Kanin, Poluostrov pen. Rus. Fed.
103 O2 Kanin Nos, Mys c. Rus. Fed.
113 I3 Kankakee U.S.A.
106 B3 Kankan Guinea
113 J4 Kannapolis U.S.A.
106 C3 Kano Nigeria
99 G4 Kanpur India
112 H4 Kansas r. U.S.A.
113 G4 Kansas state U.S.A.
113 H4 Kansas City U.S.A.
100 B1 Kansk Rus. Fed.
106 C3 Kantchari Burkina
105 K2 Kantemirovka Rus. Fed.
95 I2 Kanton atoll Kiribati
109 C6 Kanye Botswana
101 E4 Kaohsiung Taiwan
109 B5 Kaokoveld plat. Namibia
106 A3 Kaolack Senegal
109 C5 Kaoma Zambia
109 C4 Kapanga Dem. Rep. Congo
99 F2 Kapchagay Kazakh.
120 F6 Kapingamarangi atoll Micronesia
120 F5 Kapingamarangi Rise sea feature N. Pacific Ocean
109 C5 Kapiri Mposhi Zambia
111 M3 Kapisillit Greenland
113 J1 Kapiskau r. Canada
107 F4 Kapoeta Sudan
105 G2 Kaposvár Hungary
108 D3 Kapsabet Kenya
Kapsukas Lith. see Marijampolė
101 D7 Kapuas r. Indon.
113 J2 Kapuskasing Canada
108 D3 Kaputir Kenya
106 C4 Kara Togo
99 E1 Karabalyk Kazakh.
Kara-Bogaz-Gol, Zaliv b. Turkm. see Garabogazköl Aýlagy
105 J3 Karabük Turkey
99 E2 Karabutak Kazakh.
99 E4 Karachi Pak.
Kara Deniz sea Asia/Europe see Black Sea
99 F2 Karaganda Kazakh.
99 F2 Karagayly Kazakh.
97 R4 Karaginskiy Zaliv b. Rus. Fed.
96 G6 Karaj Iran
Karak Jordan see Al Karak
101 E6 Karakelong i. Indon.
96 I5 Kara-Köl Kyrg.
99 F2 Karakol Kyrg.
99 F3 Karakoram Range mts Asia
108 D2 Kara K'orē Eth.
Karakum, Peski des. Kazakh. see Karakum Desert
98 D2 Karakum Desert des. Kazakh.
98 B3 Karaman Turkey
99 G2 Karamay China
95 H6 Karamea Bight b. N.Z.
105 J4 Karapınar Turkey
109 B6 Karasburg Namibia
96 I2 Kara Sea Rus. Fed.
Kárášjohka Norway see Karasjok
103 L2 Karasjok Norway
99 F1 Karasuk Rus. Fed.
99 F2 Karatau Kazakh.
99 E2 Karatau, Khrebet mts Kazakh.
105 H2 Karcag Hungary
Kardhítsa Greece see Karditsa
105 H4 Karditsa Greece
103 K4 Kärdla Estonia
107 F3 Kareima Sudan
103 M2 Karel'skiy Bereg coastal area Rus. Fed.
100 D1 Karenga r. Rus. Fed.
99 F3 Kargil India
103 N3 Kargopol' Rus. Fed.
109 C5 Kariba Zimbabwe
109 C5 Kariba, Lake resr Zambia/Zimbabwe
101 C7 Karimata, Selat str. Indon.
108 E2 Karin Somalia
95 E2 Karkar Island P.N.G.
105 J2 Karkinits'ka Zatoka g. Ukr.
Karl-Marx-Stadt Germany see Chemnitz
105 G2 Karlovac Croatia
103 I5 Karlovy Vary Czech Rep.
103 I4 Karlshamn Sweden
103 J4 Karlskrona Sweden
104 E2 Karlsruhe Germany
103 I4 Karlstad Sweden
Karmona Spain see Córdoba
102 H4 Karmøy i. Norway
99 F4 Karnal India
99 F5 Karnataka state India
105 I3 Karnobat Bulg.
109 C5 Karoi Zimbabwe
109 D4 Karonga Malawi
108 D2 Karora Eritrea
105 I4 Karpathos i. Greece
Karpaty mts Europe see Carpathian Mountains
105 H4 Karpenisi Greece
94 B4 Karratha Australia
98 C2 Kars Turkey
Karshi Uzbek. see Qarshi
96 G3 Karskiye Vorota, Proliv str. Rus. Fed.
Karskoye More sea Rus. Fed. see Kara Sea
99 E1 Kartaly Rus. Fed.
99 F5 Karwar India
100 D1 Karymskoye Rus. Fed.
105 I4 Kaş Turkey
109 B4 Kasaï r. Dem. Rep. Congo
109 C5 Kasaji Dem. Rep. Congo
109 D5 Kasama Zambia
109 C5 Kasane Botswana
109 B4 Kasangulu Dem. Rep. Congo
111 H3 Kasba Lake Canada
106 B1 Kasba Tadla Morocco
109 C5 Kasempa Zambia
109 C5 Kasenga Dem. Rep. Congo
109 C4 Kasese Dem. Rep. Congo
108 D3 Kasese Uganda
98 D3 Kāshān Iran
Kashgar China see Kashi
96 I6 Kashi China
103 N4 Kashin Rus. Fed.
98 D3 Kāshmar Iran
109 C4 Kashyukulu Dem. Rep. Congo
103 O5 Kasimov Rus. Fed.
103 K3 Kaskinen Fin.
Kaskö Fin. see Kaskinen
109 C4 Kasongo Dem. Rep. Congo
109 B4 Kasongo-Lunda Dem. Rep. Congo
Kassa Slovakia see Košice
107 F3 Kassala Sudan
104 E1 Kassel Germany
104 E4 Kasserine Tunisia
105 J3 Kastamonu Turkey
Kastéllion Greece see Kissamos
Kastellorizon i. Greece see Megisti
105 H3 Kastoria Greece
105 K1 Kastornoye Rus. Fed.
109 D4 Kasulu Tanz.
109 D5 Kasungu Malawi
113 M2 Katahdin, Mount U.S.A.
109 C4 Katako-Kombe Dem. Rep. Congo
94 B5 Katanning Australia
109 C4 Katea Dem. Rep. Congo
105 H3 Katerini Greece
110 E4 Kater's Needle mt. Canada/U.S.A.
109 D5 Katete Zambia
101 B4 Katha Myanmar
Katherîna, Gebel mt. Egypt see Kātrīnā, Jabal
94 D3 Katherine r. Australia
99 G4 Kathmandu Nepal
106 B3 Kati Mali
99 G4 Katihar India
109 C5 Katima Mulilo Namibia
106 B4 Katiola Côte d'Ivoire
103 J5 Katowice Poland
105 J6 Kātrīnā, Jabal mt. Egypt
103 J4 Katrineholm Sweden
106 C3 Katsina Nigeria
106 C4 Katsina-Ala Nigeria
Kattakurgan Uzbek. see Kattaqo'rg'on
96 H6 Kattaqo'rg'on Uzbek.
103 I4 Kattegat str. Denmark/Sweden
Kattowitz Poland see Katowice
121 I4 Kaua'i i. U.S.A.
Kauai i. U.S.A. see Kaua'i
96 D4 Kaunas Lith.
106 C3 Kaura-Namoda Nigeria
103 K2 Kautokeino Norway
105 H3 Kavala Greece
99 F5 Kavaratti atoll India
105 I3 Kavarna Bulg.
98 D3 Kavīr, Dasht-e des. Iran
109 C4 Kawambwa Zambia
106 B3 Kaya Burkina
109 C4 Kayanaza Burundi
109 C4 Kayembe-Mukulu Dem. Rep. Congo
112 D4 Kayenta U.S.A.
106 A3 Kayes Mali
106 A4 Kayima Sierra Leone
99 F2 Kaynar Kazakh.
98 B3 Kayseri Turkey
97 J3 Kayyerkan Rus. Fed.
97 O2 Kazach'ye Rus. Fed.
99 F1 Kazakhskiy Melkosopochnik plain Kazakh.
103 P4 Kazan' Rus. Fed.
105 I3 Kazanlŭk Bulg.
Kazan-rettō is Japan see Volcano Islands
Kazatin Ukr. see Kozyatyn
96 H3 Kazymskiy Mys Rus. Fed.
113 G3 Kearney U.S.A.
106 A3 Kébémèr Senegal
104 E5 Kebili Tunisia
107 E3 Kebkabiya Sudan
103 J2 Kebnekaise mt. Sweden
108 E3 K'ebrī Dehar Eth.
110 F4 Kechika r. Canada
105 G2 Kecskemét Hungary
103 K4 Kėdainiai Lith.
106 A3 Kédougou Senegal
Keeling Is terr. Indian Ocean see Cocos Islands
109 B6 Keetmanshoop Namibia
Kefallinía i. Greece see Cephalonia
Kefallonia i. Greece see Cephalonia
101 E7 Kefamenanu Indon.
Kefe Ukr. see Feodosiya
102 B3 Keflavík Iceland
99 F2 Kegen Kazakh.
99 F6 Kelai i. Maldives
103 L2 Kelloselkä Fin.
103 K4 Kelmė Lith.
107 D4 Kélo Chad
112 C2 Kelowna Canada
99 I6 Keluang Malaysia
103 M3 Kem' Rus. Fed.
100 A1 Kemerovo Rus. Fed.
103 K2 Kemi Fin.
103 L2 Kemijärvi Fin.
103 K2 Kemijoki r. Fin.
119 K5 Kemp Land pen. Antarctica
119 J3 Kemp Peninsula Antarctica
113 L2 Kempt, Lac l. Canada
105 F2 Kempten (Allgäu) Germany
110 C3 Kenai U.S.A.
110 C4 Kenai Mountains U.S.A.
102 F5 Kendal U.K.
101 E7 Kendari Indon.
107 D3 Kendégué Chad
106 A4 Kenema Sierra Leone
109 B4 Kenge Dem. Rep. Congo
101 B4 Kengtung Myanmar
106 A3 Kéniéba Mali
106 B1 Kenitra Morocco
113 M3 Kennebec r. U.S.A.
113 H2 Kenora Canada
113 I3 Kenosha U.S.A.
113 J4 Kentucky r. U.S.A.
113 J4 Kentucky state U.S.A.
113 I4 Kentucky Lake U.S.A.
108 D3 Kenya country Africa
108 D3 Kenya, Mount Kenya
113 H3 Keokuk U.S.A.
95 F4 Keppel Bay Australia
99 F5 Kerala state India
106 C4 Kéran, Parc National de la nat. park Togo
96 E5 Kerch Ukr.
95 E2 Kerema P.N.G.
108 D2 Keren Eritrea
122 I8 Kerguelen, Îles is Indian Ocean
119 L6 Kerguelen Plateau sea feature Indian Ocean
109 D4 Kericho Kenya
101 C7 Kerinci, Gunung vol. Indon.
105 F5 Kerkennah, Îles is Tunisia
Kerki Turkm. see Atamyrat
Kérkira i. Greece see Corfu
105 G4 Kerkyra Greece
Kerkyra i. Greece see Corfu
107 F3 Kerma Sudan
95 J5 Kermadec Islands S. Pacific Ocean
121 H8 Kermadec Trench sea feature S. Pacific Ocean
98 D3 Kermān Iran
98 C3 Kermānshāh Iran
106 B4 Kérouané Guinea
119 I5 Kerr, Cape Antarctica
Keryneia Cyprus see Kyrenia
113 J1 Kesagami Lake Canada
105 I3 Keşan Turkey
103 M3 Keskozero Rus. Fed.
97 J4 Ket' r. Rus. Fed.
106 C4 Keta Ghana
101 D7 Ketapang Indon.
113 I2 Keweenaw Peninsula U.S.A.
103 N2 Keyvy, Vozvyshennost' hills Rus. Fed.
113 J7 Key West U.S.A.
109 C5 Kezi Zimbabwe
109 C6 Kgalagadi Transfrontier National Park Botswana/S. Africa
103 Q2 Khabarikha Rus. Fed.
100 F2 Khabarovsk Rus. Fed.
99 E4 Khairpur Pak.
109 C6 Khakhea Botswana
98 D5 Khalīj Maşīrah b. Oman
Khalīj Surt g. Libya see Sirte, Gulf of
Khalkís Greece see Chalkida
100 C1 Khamar-Daban, Khrebet mts Rus. Fed.
99 F5 Khambhat, Gulf of India
97 M3 Khamra Rus. Fed.
99 E3 Khānābād Afgh.
97 O3 Khandyga Rus. Fed.
Khaniá Greece see Chania
100 F2 Khanka, Lake China/Rus. Fed.
99 F4 Khanpur Pak.
99 F2 Khantau Kazakh.
97 K3 Khantayskoye, Ozero l. Rus. Fed.
96 H3 Khanty-Mansiysk Rus. Fed.
107 F2 Khārijah, Wāḥāt al oasis Egypt
96 E5 Kharkiv Ukr.
103 N2 Kharlovka Rus. Fed.
103 O4 Kharovsk Rus. Fed.
107 F3 Khartoum Sudan
103 P7 Khasavyurt Rus. Fed.
99 E4 Khāsh Iran
105 I3 Khaskovo Bulg.
97 L2 Khatanga Rus. Fed.
97 L2 Khatangskiy Zaliv b. Rus. Fed.
97 S3 Khatyrka Rus. Fed.
104 E4 Khenchela Alg.
104 B5 Khenifra Morocco
105 J2 Kherson Ukr.
97 K2 Kheta r. Rus. Fed.
Khíos i. Greece see Chios
Khmel'nitskiy Ukr. see Khmel'nyts'kyy
103 L6 Khmel'nyts'kyy Ukr.
Khodzheyli Uzbek. see Xo'jayli
103 M4 Kholm Rus. Fed.
100 G2 Kholmsk Rus. Fed.
101 C5 Khon Kaen Thai.
97 P3 Khonuu Rus. Fed.
100 F2 Khor Rus. Fed.
100 F2 Khor r. Rus. Fed.
100 C1 Khorinsk Rus. Fed.
109 B6 Khorixas Namibia
98 C3 Khorramābād Iran
99 F3 Khorugh Tajik.
97 Q3 Khrebet Kolymskiy mts Rus. Fed.
97 P2 Khroma r. Rus. Fed.
98 D1 Khromtau Kazakh.
99 E2 Khŭjand Tajik.
99 G4 Khulna Bangl.
98 D3 Khunsar Iran
103 K6 Khust Ukr.
103 P5 Khvalynsk Rus. Fed.
103 M4 Khvoynaya Rus. Fed.
99 F3 Khyber Pass Afgh./Pak.
109 C4 Kiambi Dem. Rep. Congo
111 L2 Kiatassuaq i. Greenland
109 D4 Kibaya Tanz.
109 D4 Kibiti Tanz.
109 C4 Kibombo Dem. Rep. Congo
109 D4 Kibondo Tanz.
Kibris country Asia see Cyprus
103 P4 Kichmengskiy Gorodok Rus. Fed.
106 C3 Kidal Mali
108 D3 Kidepo Valley National Park Uganda
106 A3 Kidira Senegal
105 F1 Kiel Germany
105 H1 Kielce Poland
109 C5 Kienge Dem. Rep. Congo
96 E4 Kiev Ukr.
106 A3 Kiffa Mauritania
109 D4 Kigali Rwanda
109 C4 Kigoma Tanz.
105 H2 Kikinda Serbia
Kikládhes is Greece see Cyclades
109 C4 Kikondja Dem. Rep. Congo
95 E2 Kikori P.N.G.
95 E2 Kikori r. P.N.G.
109 B4 Kikwit Dem. Rep. Congo
109 B4 Kilembe Dem. Rep. Congo
Kilia Ukr. see Kiliya
109 D4 Kilifi Kenya
109 D4 Kilimanjaro vol. Tanz.
109 D4 Kilimanjaro National Park Tanz.
95 F2 Kilinailau Islands P.N.G.
109 D4 Kilindoni Tanz.
105 K4 Kilis Turkey
105 I2 Kiliya Ukr.
102 E5 Kilkenny Ireland
102 E5 Killarney Ireland
113 G5 Killeen U.S.A.
102 F4 Kilmarnock U.K.
103 Q4 Kil'mez' Rus. Fed.
109 D4 Kilosa Tanz.
99 F5 Kiltan atoll India
109 C4 Kilwa Dem. Rep. Congo
109 D4 Kilwa Masoko Tanz.
109 D4 Kimambi Tanz.
109 B4 Kimba Congo
95 F2 Kimbe P.N.G.
112 C2 Kimberley Canada
94 C3 Kimberley Plateau Australia
100 E2 Kimch'aek N. Korea
111 L3 Kimmirut Canada
109 B4 Kimpese Dem. Rep. Congo
103 N4 Kimry Rus. Fed.
109 B4 Kimvula Dem. Rep. Congo
101 D6 Kinabalu, Gunung mt. Malaysia
112 C1 Kinbasket Lake Canada
113 J3 Kincardine Canada
109 C4 Kinda Dem. Rep. Congo
112 E1 Kindersley Canada
106 A3 Kindia Guinea
109 C4 Kindu Dem. Rep. Congo
103 O4 Kineshma Rus. Fed.
95 F4 Kingaroy Australia
119 J1 King Edward Point research stn Antarctica
119 I2 King George Island Antarctica
111 K4 King George Islands Canada
103 L4 Kingisepp Rus. Fed.
95 E5 King Island Australia
Kingisseppa Estonia see Kuressaare
94 C3 King Leopold Ranges hills Australia
112 D4 Kingman U.S.A.
119 L2 King Sejong research stn Antarctica
102 G5 King's Lynn U.K.
95 H2 Kingsmill Group is Kiribati
94 C3 King Sound b. Australia
112 D3 Kings Peak U.S.A.
113 J4 Kingsport U.S.A.
113 K3 Kingston Canada
115 I5 Kingston Jamaica
102 F5 Kingston upon Hull U.K.
115 L6 Kingstown St Vincent
113 G6 Kingsville U.S.A.
111 I3 King William Island Canada
109 B4 Kinshasa Dem. Rep. Congo
113 K4 Kinston U.S.A.
106 B4 Kintampo Ghana
107 F4 Kinyeti mt. Sudan
Kiparissía Greece see Kyparissia
113 K2 Kipawa, Lac l. Canada
109 C5 Kipushi Dem. Rep. Congo
95 G3 Kirakira Solomon Is
101 C1 Kirenga r. Rus. Fed.
100 C1 Kirensk Rus. Fed.
105 J4 Kırıkkale Turkey
103 N4 Kirillov Rus. Fed.
Kirinyaga mt. Kenya see Kenya, Mount
102 F4 Kirkcaldy U.K.
103 M2 Kirkenes Norway
113 J2 Kirkland Lake Canada
105 I3 Kırklareli Turkey
119 J5 Kirkpatrick, Mount Antarctica
98 C3 Kirkūk Iraq
102 F4 Kirkwall U.K.
103 M5 Kirov Rus. Fed.
96 F4 Kirov Rus. Fed.
103 Q4 Kirovo-Chepetsk Rus. Fed.
96 E5 Kirovohrad Ukr.
103 M2 Kirovsk Rus. Fed.
103 Q4 Kirs Rus. Fed.
103 O5 Kirsanov Rus. Fed.
99 E4 Kirthar Range mts Pak.
103 K2 Kiruna Sweden
109 C4 Kirundu Dem. Rep. Congo
108 C3 Kisangani Dem. Rep. Congo
109 B4 Kisantu Dem. Rep. Congo
100 A1 Kiselevsk Rus. Fed.
106 C4 Kishi Nigeria
99 F1 Kishkenekol' Kazakh.
99 F3 Kishtwar Jammu and Kashmir
Kisi Nigeria see Kishi
109 D4 Kisii Kenya
109 E4 Kismaayo Somalia
105 H4 Kissamos Greece
106 A4 Kissidougou Guinea
113 J6 Kissimmee, Lake U.S.A.
109 D4 Kisumu Kenya
106 B3 Kita Mali
100 F3 Kita-Kyūshū Japan
108 D3 Kitale Kenya
100 G2 Kitami Japan
113 J3 Kitchener Canada
108 D3 Kitgum Uganda
Kíthira i. Greece see Kythira
110 F4 Kitimat Canada
109 B4 Kitona Dem. Rep. Congo
109 D4 Kitunda Tanz.
109 C5 Kitwe Zambia
109 C4 Kivu, Lake Dem. Rep. Congo/Rwanda
Kiyevskoye Vodokhranilishche resr Ukr. see Kyyivs'ke Vodoskhovyshche
96 G4 Kizel Rus. Fed.
103 O3 Kizema Rus. Fed.
105 K4 Kızıl Dağı mt. Turkey
105 K3 Kızılırmak r. Turkey
103 P7 Kizilyurt Rus. Fed.
103 P7 Kizlyar Rus. Fed.
105 F2 Klagenfurt Austria
96 D4 Klaipėda Lith.
112 B3 Klamath r. U.S.A.
112 B3 Klamath Falls U.S.A.
103 I4 Klarälven r. Sweden
103 N4 Klin Rus. Fed.
105 J1 Klintsy Rus. Fed.
105 G1 Kłodzko Poland
110 E3 Kluane Lake Canada
97 R4 Klyuchevskaya, Sopka vol. Rus. Fed.
111 I4 Knee Lake Canada
105 G3 Knin Croatia
119 I3 Knowles, Cape Antarctica
113 J4 Knoxville U.S.A.
111 M1 Knud Rasmussen Land reg. Greenland
100 F3 Kōbe Japan
København Denmark see Copenhagen
106 B3 Kobenni Mauritania
102 H5 Koblenz Germany
Kobrin Belarus see Kobryn
101 F7 Kobroör i. Indon.
103 K5 Kobryn Belarus
Kocaeli Turkey see İzmit
105 H3 Kočani Macedonia
103 Q4 Kochevo Rus. Fed.
100 F3 Kōchi Japan
110 C4 Kodiak U.S.A.
110 C4 Kodiak Island U.S.A.
107 F4 Kodok Sudan
109 B6 Koës Namibia
106 B4 Koforidua Ghana
100 F3 Kōfu Japan
99 F3 Kohat Pak.
101 B4 Kohima India
103 L4 Kohtla-Järve Estonia
Kokand Uzbek. see Qo'qon
96 D3 Kokkola Fin.
95 E2 Kokoda P.N.G.
113 I3 Kokomo U.S.A.
99 G2 Kokpekti Kazakh.
99 E1 Kokshetau Kazakh.
111 L4 Koksoak r. Canada
101 E7 Kolaka Indon.
96 E3 Kola Peninsula Rus. Fed.
103 K2 Kolari Fin.
Kolarovgrad Bulg. see Shum
Kolberg Poland see Kołobrz
103 N4 Kol'chugino Rus. Fed.
106 A3 Kolda Senegal
102 H4 Kolding Denmark
108 C3 Kole Haute-Zaïre Dem. Rep. Congo
109 C4 Kole Kasai-Oriental Dem. Rep. Congo
103 P2 Kolguyev, Ostrov i. Rus. Fed
99 G4 Kolkata India
Köln Germany see Cologne
103 J5 Kołobrzeg Poland
103 O4 Kologriv Rus. Fed.
106 B3 Kolokani Mali
95 F2 Kolombangara i. Solomon I
Kolomea Ukr. see Kolomyya
103 N4 Kolomna Rus. Fed.
Kołomyja Ukr. see Kolomyya
103 L6 Kolomyya Ukr.
106 B3 Kolondiéba Mali
94 C2 Kolonedale Indon.
97 J4 Kolpashevo Rus. Fed.
Kol'skiy Poluostrov pen. Rus. Fed. see Kola Peninsula
98 C5 Koluli Eritrea
109 C5 Kolwezi Dem. Rep. Congo
97 Q3 Kolyma r. Rus. Fed.
97 Q3 Kolymskaya Nizmennost' lo land Rus. Fed.
97 R4 Komandorskiye Ostrova is Rus. Fed.
109 C4 Kombe Dem. Rep. Congo
106 B3 Kombissiri Burkina
Kommunarsk Ukr. see Alchevs'k
109 B4 Komono Congo
105 I3 Komotini Greece
Komrat Moldova see Comra
97 K1 Komsomolets, Ostrov i. Rus. Fed.
100 F1 Komsomol'sk-na-Amure Rus. Fed.
109 D4 Kondoa Tanz.
103 M3 Kondopoga Rus. Fed.
111 O3 Kong Christian IX Land reg Greenland
111 N3 Kong Frederik VI Kyst coastal area Greenland
96 D2 Kong Karls Land is Svalbard
109 C4 Kongolo Dem. Rep. Congo
111 P2 Kong Oscars Fjord inlet Greenland
106 B3 Kongoussi Burkina
102 H4 Kongsberg Norway
103 I3 Kongsvinger Norway
109 D4 Kongwa Tanz.
111 P2 Kong Wilhelm Land reg. Greenland
100 F1 Konin r. Rus. Fed.
106 B3 Konna Mali
103 O3 Konosha Rus. Fed.
105 J1 Konotop Ukr.
Konstantinograd Ukr. see Krasnohrad
106 C3 Kontagora Nigeria
98 B3 Konya Turkey
112 C2 Kootenay Lake Canada
102 C2 Kópasker Iceland
105 F2 Koper Slovenia
103 J4 Kopparberg Sweden
105 G2 Koprivnica Croatia
105 J4 Köprülü Kanyon Milli Parkı nat. park Turkey
105 H3 Korçë Albania
100 E3 Korea Bay g. China/N. Korea
100 E3 Korea Strait Japan/S. Korea
105 I3 Körfez Turkey
119 J3 Korff Ice Rise Antarctica
106 B4 Korhogo Côte d'Ivoire
Korinthiakos Kolpos sea cha Greece see Corinth, Gulf of
Korinthos Greece see Corint
Koritsa Albania see Korçë
105 J4 Korkuteli Turkey
106 B4 Koro Côte d'Ivoire
95 H3 Koro i. Fiji
106 B3 Koro Mali
105 J3 Köroğlu Tepesi mt. Turkey
109 D4 Korogwe Tanz.
95 H3 Koro Sea Fiji
105 I1 Korosten' Ukr.
107 D3 Koro Toro Chad
100 G2 Korsakov Rus. Fed.
107 D4 Korup, Parc National de nat. park Cameroon

100 H1 Koryakskaya, Sopka vol. Rus. Fed.
97 R3 Koryakskiy Khrebet mts Rus. Fed.
103 P3 Koryazhma Rus. Fed.
103 Q4 Kosa Rus. Fed.
95 E5 Kosciuszko, Mount Australia
99 G2 Kosh-Agach Rus. Fed.
103 K6 Košice Slovakia
106 B4 Kossou, Lac de l. Côte d'Ivoire
99 E1 Kostanay Kazakh.
107 F3 Kosti Sudan
97 J3 Kostino Rus. Fed.
103 M3 Kostomuksha Rus. Fed.
103 O4 Kostroma Rus. Fed.
103 R2 Kos'yu Rus. Fed.
96 C4 Koszalin Poland
99 F4 Kota India
101 D7 Kotabaru Indon.
101 C6 Kota Bharu Malaysia
101 D6 Kota Kinabalu Malaysia
103 P4 Kotel'nich Rus. Fed.
103 O6 Kotel'nikovo Rus. Fed.
97 O2 Kotel'nyy, Ostrov i. Rus. Fed.
103 L3 Kotka Fin.
103 Q2 Kotkino Rus. Fed.
103 P3 Kotlas Rus. Fed.
110 B3 Kotlik U.S.A.
106 B4 Kotouba Côte d'Ivoire
103 O5 Kotovo Rus. Fed.
97 L2 Kotuy r. Rus. Fed.
110 B3 Kotzebue U.S.A.
110 B3 Kotzebue Sound sea chan. U.S.A.
106 A3 Koubia Guinea
106 B3 Koudougou Burkina
107 D3 Koufey Niger
109 B4 Koulamoutou Gabon
106 B3 Koulikoro Mali
95 G4 Koumac New Caledonia
106 A3 Koundâra Guinea
106 B3 Koupéla Burkina
117 H2 Kourou Fr. Guiana
106 B3 Kouroussa Guinea
107 D3 Kousséri Cameroon
106 B3 Koutiala Mali
103 M2 Kovdor Rus. Fed.
105 H1 Kovel' Ukr.
103 O4 Kovrov Rus. Fed.
103 O5 Kovylkino Rus. Fed.
103 Q3 Koygorodok Rus. Fed.
110 C3 Koyukuk r. U.S.A.
105 H3 Kozani Greece
105 J1 Kozelets' Ukr.
103 J6 Kozyatyn Ukr.
106 C4 Kpalimé Togo
101 B5 Kra, Isthmus of Thai.
101 B6 Krabi Thai.
101 C5 Krâchéh Cambodia
102 H4 Kragerø Norway
105 H3 Kragujevac Serbia
Krakau Poland see Kraków
103 J5 Kraków Poland
105 K2 Kramators'k Ukr.
103 J3 Kramfors Sweden
105 F2 Kranj Slovenia
103 P3 Krasavino Rus. Fed.
96 G2 Krasino Rus. Fed.
103 P5 Krasnoarmeysk Rus. Fed.
Krasnoarmeysk Ukr. see Krasnoarmiys'k
103 N6 Krasnoarmiys'k Ukr.
103 P3 Krasnoborsk Rus. Fed.
96 E5 Krasnodar Rus. Fed.
Krasnograd Ukr. see Krasnohrad
103 N6 Krasnohrad Ukr.
105 J2 Krasnoperekops'k Ukr.
103 O5 Krasnoslobodsk Rus. Fed.
100 B1 Krasnoyarsk Rus. Fed.
103 P4 Krasnyye Baki Rus. Fed.
103 N4 Krasnyy Kholm Rus. Fed.
103 P5 Krasnyy Kut Rus. Fed.
103 P7 Kraynovka Rus. Fed.
Kremenchug Ukr. see Kremenchuk
Kremenchugskoye Vodokhranilishche resr Ukr. see Kremenchuts'ka Vodoskhovyshche
103 M6 Kremenchuk Ukr.
103 M6 Kremenchuts'ka Vodoskhovyshche resr Ukr.
97 T3 Kresta, Zaliv g. Rus. Fed.
103 K4 Kretinga Lith.
106 C4 Kribi Cameroon
Krichev Belarus see Krychaw
99 F5 Krishna r. India
99 G5 Krishna, Mouths of the India
102 H4 Kristiansand Norway
103 I4 Kristianstad Sweden
102 H3 Kristiansund Norway
103 I4 Kristinehamn Sweden
Kristinopol' Ukr. see Chervonohrad
Kriti i. Greece see Crete
105 I4 Kritiko Pelagos sea Greece
Krivoy Rog Ukr. see Kryvyy Rih
111 O3 Kronprins Frederik Bjerge nunataks Greenland
105 L2 Kropotkin Rus. Fed.
105 H2 Krosno Poland
101 C7 Krui Indon.
Krung Thep Thai. see Bangkok
105 H3 Kruševac Serbia
103 M5 Krychaw Belarus
123 H4 Krylov Seamount sea feature N. Atlantic Ocean
96 E5 Krymsk Rus. Fed.
Kryms'kyy Pivostriv pen. Ukr. see Crimea
Krystynopol Ukr. see Chervonohrad
96 E5 Kryvyy Rih Ukr.
106 B2 Ksabi Alg.
104 D4 Ksar el Boukhari Alg.
104 B4 Ksar el Kebir Morocco
Ksar-es-Souk Morocco see Er Rachidia
103 R3 Ksenofontova Rus. Fed.
101 C6 Kuala Lumpur Malaysia
101 C6 Kuala Terengganu Malaysia
101 C6 Kuantan Malaysia
105 K2 Kuban' r. Rus. Fed.
101 D6 Kuching Malaysia
101 D6 Kudat Malaysia
111 J3 Kugaaruk Canada
110 G3 Kugluktuk Canada
110 E3 Kugmallit Bay Canada
103 L3 Kuhmo Fin.
109 B5 Kuito Angola
98 D2 Kulandy Kazakh.
97 O2 Kular Rus. Fed.
103 K4 Kuldīga Latvia
103 O4 Kulebaki Rus. Fed.
99 E3 Kŭlob Tajik.
98 D2 Kul'sary Kazakh.
99 F1 Kulunda Rus. Fed.
99 F1 Kulundinskoye, Ozero salt l. Rus. Fed.
100 F3 Kumamoto Japan
105 H3 Kumanovo Macedonia
106 B4 Kumasi Ghana
106 C4 Kumba Cameroon
103 P4 Kumeny Rus. Fed.
96 G4 Kumertau Rus. Fed.
107 D3 Kumo Nigeria
100 G2 Kunashir, Ostrov i. Rus. Fed.
109 B5 Kunene r. Angola/Namibia alt. Cunene
96 I5 Kungei Alatau mts Kazakh./Kyrg.
103 I4 Kungsbacka Sweden
108 B3 Kungu Dem. Rep. Congo
99 F3 Kunlun Shan mts China
101 C4 Kunming China
94 C3 Kununurra Australia
103 L3 Kuopio Fin.
101 E8 Kupang Indon.
105 K2 Kup"yans'k Ukr.
99 G2 Kuqa China
105 I3 Kŭrdzhali Bulg.
121 H4 Kure Atoll U.S.A.
103 K4 Kuressaare Estonia
96 H4 Kurgan Rus. Fed.
120 E2 Kuril Basin sea feature Sea of Okhotsk
97 P5 Kuril Islands Rus. Fed.
100 G2 Kuril'sk Rus. Fed.
Kuril'skiye Ostrova is Rus. Fed. see Kuril Islands
120 E3 Kuril Trench sea feature N. Pacific Ocean
107 F3 Kurmuk Sudan
99 F5 Kurnool India
105 K1 Kursk Rus. Fed.
100 A2 Kuruktag mts China
100 D1 Kurumkan Rus. Fed.
99 G6 Kurunegala Sri Lanka
107 F2 Kurush, Jebel hills Sudan
103 R3 Kur'ya Rus. Fed.
105 I4 Kuşadası Turkey
100 G2 Kushiro Japan
99 E1 Kushmurun Kazakh.
110 C3 Kuskokwim r. U.S.A.
110 B4 Kuskokwim Bay U.S.A.
110 C3 Kuskokwim Mountains U.S.A.
100 G2 Kussharo-ko l. Japan
98 A3 Kütahya Turkey
98 C2 K'ut'aisi Georgia
103 P7 Kutan Rus. Fed.
105 G1 Kutno Poland
109 B4 Kutu Dem. Rep. Congo
110 G2 Kuujjua r. Canada
103 L2 Kuusamo Fin.
109 B5 Kuvango Angola
98 C4 Kuwait country Asia
98 C4 Kuwait Kuwait
96 I4 Kuybyshev Rus. Fed.
Kuybyshev Rus. Fed. see Samara
96 F4 Kuybyshevskoye Vodokhranilishche resr Rus. Fed.
99 G2 Kuytun China
103 P5 Kuznetsk Rus. Fed.
110 C4 Kvichak Bay U.S.A.
120 G6 Kwajalein atoll Marshall Is
100 E3 Kwangju S. Korea
109 B4 Kwango r. Dem. Rep. Congo
109 D4 Kwangwazi Tanz.
109 C5 Kwekwe Zimbabwe
109 B4 Kwenge r. Dem. Rep. Congo
110 B4 Kwigillingok U.S.A.
95 E2 Kwikila P.N.G.
109 B4 Kwilu r. Angola/Dem. Rep. Congo
101 F7 Kwoka mt. Indon.
107 D4 Kyabé Chad
100 C1 Kyakhta Rus. Fed.
94 D5 Kyancutta Australia
101 B5 Kyaukpyu Myanmar
Kyiv Ukr. see Kiev
Kyklades is Greece see Cyclades
102 E4 Kyle of Lochalsh U.K.
108 D3 Kyoga, Lake Uganda
100 F3 Kyōto Japan
105 H4 Kyparissia Greece
Kypros country Asia see Cyprus
96 H4 Kypshak, Ozero salt l. Kazakh.
105 J4 Kyrenia Cyprus
103 R3 Kyrta Rus. Fed.
97 O3 Kytalyktakh Rus. Fed.
105 H4 Kythira i. Greece
100 F3 Kyūshū i. Japan
123 S4 Kyushu-Palau Ridge sea feature N. Pacific Ocean
105 H3 Kyustendil Bulg.
103 M5 Kyyivs'ke Vodoskhovyshche resr Ukr.
103 K3 Kyyjärvi Fin.
100 B1 Kyzyl Rus. Fed.
99 E2 Kyzylkum Desert Uzbek.
99 E2 Kyzylorda Kazakh.

L

115 F5 La Angostura, Presa de resr Mex.
108 E3 Laascaanood Somalia
115 G5 La Ascensión, Bahía de b. Mex.
108 E2 Laasgoray Somalia
117 F1 La Asunción Venez.
106 A2 Laâyoune W. Sahara
118 D3 La Banda Arg.
95 H3 Labasa Fiji
106 A3 Labé Guinea
118 D4 Laboulaye Arg.
111 L4 Labrador reg. Canada
111 M3 Labrador Sea Canada/Greenland
117 F5 Lábrea Brazil
101 E7 Labuna Indon.
96 H3 Labytnangi Rus. Fed.
La Calle Alg. see El Kala
99 F5 Laccadive Islands India
Lacedaemon Greece see Sparti
115 G5 La Ceiba Hond.
103 N3 Lacha, Ozero l. Rus. Fed.
95 E5 Lachlan r. Australia
115 I7 La Chorrera Panama
113 L2 Lachute Canada
110 G4 Lac La Biche Canada
115 H7 La Concepción Panama
La Coruña Spain see A Coruña
113 H3 La Crosse U.S.A.
99 E4 Lādīz Iran
96 E3 Ladoga, Lake Rus. Fed.
Ladozhskoye Ozero l. Rus. Fed. see Ladoga, Lake
111 J2 Lady Ann Strait Canada
95 E2 Lae P.N.G.
118 D2 La Esmeralda Bol.
103 I4 Læsø i. Denmark
113 I3 Lafayette IN U.S.A.
113 H5 Lafayette LA U.S.A.
106 C4 Lafia Nigeria
96 C4 Lagan Sweden
117 K6 Lagarto Brazil
106 C1 Laghouat Alg.
106 A2 La Gomera i. Canary Is
118 B7 Lago Posadas Arg.
106 C4 Lagos Nigeria
104 B4 Lagos Port.
114 D4 Lagos de Moreno Mex.
112 C2 La Grande U.S.A.
Lagrange Australia see La Grange
94 C3 La Grange Australia
113 I5 La Grange U.S.A.
117 F2 La Gran Sabana plat. Venez.
118 B5 Laguna de Laja, Parque Nacional nat. park Chile
116 C5 Lagunas Peru
118 A7 Laguna San Rafael, Parque Nacional nat. park Chile
La Habana Cuba see Havana
101 D6 Lahad Datu Malaysia
104 C2 La Hague, Cap de c. France
101 C7 Lahat Indon.
98 C5 Laḥij Yemen
99 F3 Lahore Pak.
103 L3 Lahti Fin.
107 D4 Laï Chad
Laibach Slovenia see Ljubljana
103 P4 Laishevo Rus. Fed.
100 E3 Laiyang China
100 D3 Laizhou Wan b. China
94 D3 Lajamanu Australia
117 K5 Lajes Rio Grande do Norte Brazil
118 F3 Lajes Santa Catarina Brazil
113 F4 La Junta U.S.A.
113 J5 Lake City U.S.A.
Lake Harbour Canada see Kimmirut
112 D5 Lake Havasu City U.S.A.
113 J6 Lakeland U.S.A.
112 B3 Lakeview U.S.A.
113 J6 Lake Worth U.S.A.
106 B4 Lakota Côte d'Ivoire
103 K1 Lakselv Norway
99 F5 Lakshadweep union terr. India
108 B3 Lalara Gabon
118 B4 La Ligua Chile
99 F4 Lalitpur India
111 H4 La Loche Canada
103 P3 Lal'sk Rus. Fed.
116 D3 La Macarena, Parque Nacional nat. park Col.
104 E3 La Maddalena Italy
La Manche str. France/U.K. see English Channel
113 F4 Lamar U.S.A.
104 E4 La Marmora, Punta mt. Italy
110 G3 La Martre, Lac l. Canada
109 B4 Lambaréné Gabon
116 C5 Lambayeque Peru
119 K5 Lambert Glacier Antarctica
116 C6 La Merced Peru
113 F5 Lamesa U.S.A.
105 H4 Lamia Greece
101 B5 Lampang Thai.
113 G5 Lampasas U.S.A.
114 D3 Lampazos Mex.
101 B5 Lamphun Thai.
109 E4 Lamu Kenya
100 B3 Lancang Jiang r. China conv. Mekong
112 C5 Lancaster CA U.S.A.
113 K3 Lancaster PA U.S.A.
111 J2 Lancaster Sound str. Canada
105 F2 Landeck Austria
112 E3 Lander U.S.A.
Landsberg Poland see Gorzów Wielkopolski
104 B1 Land's End pt U.K.
105 F2 Landshut Germany
104 E2 Langres France
101 B6 Langsa Indon.
101 C4 Lang Sơn Vietnam
118 B5 Lanín, Volcán vol. Arg.
113 J3 Lansing U.S.A.
107 F4 Lanya Sudan
106 A2 Lanzarote i. Canary Is
100 C3 Lanzhou China
101 E5 Laoag Phil.
101 C4 Lao Cai Vietnam
104 D2 Laon France
101 C5 Laos country Asia
106 A2 La Palma i. Canary Is
115 I7 La Palma Panama
117 F2 La Paragua Venez.
116 D3 La Paya, Parque Nacional nat. park Col.
116 E7 La Paz Bol.
112 D7 La Paz Mex.
116 E4 La Pedrera Col.
97 P5 La Pérouse Strait Japan/Rus. Fed.
118 E4 La Plata Arg.
116 B4 La Plata, Isla i. Ecuador
118 E4 La Plata, Río de sea chan. Arg./Uruguay
103 L3 Lappeenranta Fin.
103 J2 Lappland reg. Europe
97 M2 Laptev Sea Rus. Fed.
Laptevykh, More sea Rus. Fed. see Laptev Sea
Lapurdum France see Bayonne
118 C2 La Quiaca Arg.
105 F3 L'Aquila Italy
104 B4 Larache Morocco
112 E3 Laramie U.S.A.
112 E3 Laramie Mountains U.S.A.
118 F3 Laranjeiras do Sul Brazil
101 E7 Larantuka Indon.
101 F7 Larat i. Indon.
L'Ardenne, Plateau de plat. Belgium see Ardennes
118 C3 La Rioja Arg.
105 H4 Larisa Greece
Larissa Greece see Larisa
105 J5 Larnaca Cyprus
Larnaka Cyprus see Larnaca
104 C2 La Rochelle France
104 C2 La Roche-sur-Yon France
115 K5 La Romana Dom. Rep.
111 H4 La Ronge Canada
111 H4 La Ronge, Lac l. Canada
94 D3 Larrimah Australia
119 I2 Larsen Ice Shelf Antarctica
103 I4 Larvik Norway
113 K2 La Sarre Canada
112 E5 Las Cruces U.S.A.
115 J5 La Selle, Pic mt. Haiti
118 B3 La Serena Chile
118 E5 Las Flores Arg.
118 C4 Las Heras Arg.
101 B4 Lashio Myanmar
118 D2 Las Lomitas Arg.
118 C7 Las Martinetas Arg.
106 A2 Las Palmas de Gran Canaria Canary Is
104 E3 La Spezia Italy
118 C6 Las Plumas Arg.
115 H7 Las Tablas Panama
118 D3 Las Termas Arg.
112 E1 Last Mountain Lake Canada
118 C3 Las Tórtolas, Cerro mt. Chile
109 B4 Lastoursville Gabon
115 I4 Las Tunas Cuba
112 D5 Las Vegas NM U.S.A.
112 C4 Las Vegas NV U.S.A.
116 C4 Latacunga Ecuador
98 B3 Latakia Syria
105 F3 Latina Italy
116 E1 La Tortuga, Isla i. Venez.
113 L2 La Tuque Canada
103 K4 Latvia country Europe
Latvija country Europe see Latvia
Latviyskaya S.S.R. country Europe see Latvia
118 C1 Lauca, Parque Nacional nat. park Chile
111 L2 Lauge Koch Kyst pen. Greenland
95 E6 Launceston Australia
115 G6 La Unión El Salvador
95 E3 Laura Australia
113 I5 Laurel U.S.A.
104 E2 Lausanne Switz.
101 D7 Laut i. Indon.
95 H3 Lautoka Fiji
104 C2 Laval France
118 B5 Lavapié, Punta pt Chile
94 C4 Laverton Australia
117 J8 Lavras Brazil
106 B3 Lawra Ghana
113 G4 Lawrence U.S.A.
113 G5 Lawton U.S.A.
98 B4 Lawz, Jabal al mt. Saudi Arabia
103 I4 Laxå Sweden
121 H4 Laysan Island U.S.A.
114 D5 Lázaro Cárdenas Mex.
112 C5 Lázaro Cárdenas Mex.
112 E6 Lázaro Cárdenas, Presa resr Mex.
97 O3 Lazo Rus. Fed.
111 H4 Leaf Rapids Canada
105 K5 Lebanon country Asia
113 H4 Lebanon MO U.S.A.
113 L3 Lebanon NH U.S.A.
118 B5 Lebu Chile
105 G3 Lecce Italy
112 D1 Leduc Canada
104 C1 Leeds U.K.
113 H5 Leesville U.S.A.
102 H5 Leeuwarden Neth.
94 B5 Leeuwin, Cape Australia
115 L5 Leeward Islands Caribbean Sea
105 H4 Lefkada i. Greece
Lefkosia Cyprus see Nicosia
101 E5 Legaspi Phil.
Leghorn Italy see Livorno
103 J5 Legnica Poland
104 D2 Le Havre France
102 F5 Leicester U.K.
94 D3 Leichhardt r. Australia
105 F1 Leipzig Germany
104 B4 Leiria Port.
102 H4 Leirvik Norway
101 C4 Leizhou Bandao pen. China
109 B4 Lékana Congo
104 E4 Le Kef Tunisia
109 B4 Lékoni Gabon
106 A3 Lélouma Guinea
104 E1 Lelystad Neth.
118 C9 Le Maire, Estrecho de sea chan. Arg.
Léman, Lac l. France/Switz. see Geneva, Lake
104 D2 Le Mans France
Lemberg Ukr. see L'viv
Lemdiyya Alg. see Médéa
Lemesos Cyprus see Limassol
111 L3 Lemieux Islands Canada
Lemnos i. Greece see Limnos
103 R3 Lemtybozh Rus. Fed.
100 C1 Lena r. Rus. Fed.
117 J4 Lençóis Maranhenses, Parque Nacional dos nat. park Brazil
103 M3 Lendery Rus. Fed.
97 S3 Leningradskiy Rus. Fed.
103 P6 Leninsk Rus. Fed.
100 A1 Leninsk-Kuznetskiy Rus. Fed.
103 P4 Leninskoye Rus. Fed.
104 D1 Lens France
97 M3 Lensk Rus. Fed.
106 B3 Léo Burkina
105 G2 Leoben Austria
Leodhais, Eilean i. U.K. see Lewis, Isle of
114 D4 León Mex.
115 G6 León Nicaragua
104 B3 León Spain
109 B6 Leonardville Namibia
94 C4 Leonora Australia
Lepel' Belarus see Lyepyel'
109 C6 Lephepe Botswana
Le Puy France see Le Puy-en-Velay
104 D2 Le Puy-en-Velay France
107 D4 Léré Chad
116 D4 Lérida Col.
Lérida Spain see Lleida
102 F3 Lerwick U.K.
105 I4 Lesbos i. Greece
115 J5 Les Cayes Haiti
101 C4 Leshan China
103 P3 Leshukonskoye Rus. Fed.
105 H3 Leskovac Serbia
103 Q4 Lesnoy Rus. Fed.
97 K4 Lesosibirsk Rus. Fed.
115 K6 Lesser Antilles is Caribbean Sea
110 G4 Lesser Slave Lake Canada
101 D7 Lesser Sunda Islands Indon.
Lesvos i. Greece see Lesbos
103 J5 Leszno Poland
112 D2 Lethbridge Canada
117 G3 Lethem Guyana
101 E7 Leti, Kepulauan is Indon.
116 E4 Leticia Col.
103 M3 Letnerechenskiy Rus. Fed.
Lëtzebuerg country Europe see Luxembourg
103 P7 Levashi Rus. Fed.
94 C3 Lévêque, Cape Australia
104 E1 Leverkusen Germany
113 L2 Lévis Canada
Levkás i. Greece see Lefkada
102 E4 Lewis, Isle of i. U.K.
112 D2 Lewis Range mts U.S.A.
112 E2 Lewistown U.S.A.
113 J4 Lexington U.S.A.
Lezha Albania see Lezhë
105 G3 Lezhë Albania
105 K1 L'gov Rus. Fed.
99 H3 Lharigarbo China
101 B4 Lhasa China
99 G4 Lhazê China
100 E2 Liaodong Bandao pen. China
100 E2 Liaodong Wan b. China
Liban country Asia see Lebanon
108 B3 Libenge Dem. Rep. Congo
113 F4 Liberal U.S.A.
105 G1 Liberec Czech Rep.
106 B4 Liberia country Africa
115 G6 Liberia Costa Rica
108 A3 Libreville Gabon
105 G6 Libya country Africa
107 E2 Libyan Desert Egypt/Libya
105 I5 Libyan Plateau Egypt
109 D5 Lichinga Moz.
105 I1 Lida Belarus
103 I4 Lidköping Sweden
94 D4 Liebig, Mount Australia
104 E2 Liechtenstein country Europe
102 H5 Liège Belgium
Liegnitz Poland see Legnica
103 M3 Lieksa Fin.
108 C3 Lienart Dem. Rep. Congo
105 F2 Lienz Austria
96 D4 Liepāja Latvia
Lietuva country Europe see Lithuania
95 G4 Lifou i. New Caledonia
109 D5 Ligonha r. Moz.
Ligure, Mar sea France/Italy see Ligurian Sea
104 E3 Ligurian Sea France/Italy
Ligurienne, Mer sea France/Italy see Ligurian Sea
95 F2 Lihir Group is P.N.G.
109 C5 Likasi Dem. Rep. Congo
101 C6 Liku Indon.
104 D1 Lille France
103 I3 Lillehammer Norway
109 D5 Lilongwe Malawi
116 C6 Lima Peru
113 J3 Lima U.S.A.
105 J5 Limassol Cyprus
118 C5 Limay r. Arg.
106 C4 Limbe Cameroon
117 I8 Limeira Brazil
102 E5 Limerick Ireland
105 I4 Limnos i. Greece
104 D2 Limoges France
Limón Costa Rica see Puerto Limón
Limonum France see Poitiers
118 B5 Linares Chile
113 G7 Linares Mex.
104 C4 Linares Spain
101 C4 Lincang China
Linchuan China see Fuzhou
102 F5 Lincoln U.K.
113 I3 Lincoln IL U.S.A.
113 G3 Lincoln NE U.S.A.
117 G2 Linden Guyana
Lindenow Fjord inlet Greenland see Kangerlussuatsiaq
Líndhos Greece see Lindos
108 C3 Lindi r. Dem. Rep. Congo
109 D4 Lindi Tanz.
105 I4 Lindos Greece
Lindum U.K. see Lincoln
121 I5 Line Islands S. Pacific Ocean
100 D3 Linfen China
101 E5 Lingayen Phil.
101 C7 Lingga, Kepulauan is Indon.
108 C3 Lingomo Dem. Rep. Congo
106 A3 Linguère Senegal
117 J7 Linhares Brazil
97 L5 Linhe China
103 J4 Linköping Sweden
97 O5 Linkou China
117 I8 Lins Brazil
100 D2 Linxi China
100 C3 Linxia China
100 D3 Linyi China
105 F2 Linz Austria
104 D3 Lion, Golfe du g. France
Lions, Gulf of g. France see Lion, Golfe du
108 B3 Liouesso Congo
105 F4 Lipari, Isole is Italy
103 N5 Lipetsk Rus. Fed.
108 D3 Lira Uganda
109 B4 Liranga Congo
108 C3 Lisala Dem. Rep. Congo
Lisboa Port. see Lisbon
104 B4 Lisbon Port.
104 D2 Lisieux France
103 N5 Liski Rus. Fed.
Lissa Poland see Leszno

Litang

100 C3 Litang China
117 H3 Litani r. Fr. Guiana/Suriname
113 H2 Litchfield U.S.A.
95 F5 Lithgow Australia
103 K4 Lithuania country Europe
Litovskaya S.S.R. country Europe see Lithuania
113 K6 Little Abaco i. Bahamas
115 H5 Little Cayman i. Cayman Is
113 H2 Little Falls U.S.A.
102 E4 Little Minch sea chan. U.K.
113 H5 Little Rock U.S.A.
109 D5 Litunde Moz.
101 C4 Liuzhou China
105 H4 Livadeia Greece
94 C3 Liveringa Australia
111 L5 Liverpool Canada
104 C1 Liverpool U.K.
111 K2 Liverpool, Cape Canada
110 E3 Liverpool Bay Canada
109 C5 Livingstone Zambia
119 I2 Livingston Island Antarctica
113 J3 Livonia U.S.A.
105 F3 Livorno Italy
109 D4 Liwale Tanz.
Lixus Morocco see Larache
Ljouwert Neth. see Leeuwarden
105 F2 Ljubljana Slovenia
103 I4 Ljungby Sweden
103 J3 Ljusnan r. Sweden
118 B5 Llaima, Volcán vol. Chile
118 B6 Llanquihue, Lago l. Chile
104 D3 Lleida Spain
110 F4 Lloyd George, Mount Canada
111 H4 Lloyd Lake Canada
111 H4 Lloydminster Canada
118 C2 Llullaillaco, Volcán vol. Chile
118 C2 Loa r. Chile
109 C6 Lobatse Botswana
118 E5 Loberia Arg.
109 B5 Lobito Angola
118 E5 Lobos Arg.
Loch Garman Ireland see Wexford
113 G6 Lockhart U.S.A.
103 M3 Lodeynoye Pole Rus. Fed.
109 C4 Lodja Dem. Rep. Congo
108 D3 Lodwar Kenya
105 G1 Łódź Poland
102 I2 Lofoten is Norway
112 D3 Logan U.S.A.
110 D3 Logan, Mount Canada
104 C3 Logroño Spain
101 B5 Loikaw Myanmar
104 C2 Loire r. France
116 C4 Loja Ecuador
103 L2 Lokan tekojärvi l. Fin.
108 D3 Lokichar Kenya
108 D3 Lokichokio Kenya
103 M4 Loknya Rus. Fed.
106 C4 Lokoja Nigeria
106 C4 Lokossa Benin
111 L3 Loks Land i. Canada
106 B4 Lola Guinea
103 I5 Lolland i. Denmark
109 D4 Lollondo Tanz.
102 H3 Lom Norway
109 C4 Lomami r. Dem. Rep. Congo
118 E4 Lomas de Zamora Arg.
94 C2 Lomblen i. Indon.
101 D7 Lombok i. Indon.
101 D7 Lombok, Selat sea chan. Indon.
106 C4 Lomé Togo
109 C4 Lomela Dem. Rep. Congo
109 C4 Lomela r. Dem. Rep. Congo
124 M1 Lomonosov Ridge sea feature Arctic Ocean
101 D7 Lompobattang, Gunung mt. Indon.
105 H1 Łomża Poland
Londinium U.K. see London
113 J3 London Canada
102 F5 London U.K.
113 J4 London U.S.A.
102 E5 Londonderry U.K.
94 C3 Londonderry, Cape Australia
118 B9 Londonderry, Isla i. Chile
117 H8 Londrina Brazil
97 S2 Longa, Proliv sea chan. Rus. Fed.
113 K5 Long Bay U.S.A.
112 B5 Long Beach U.S.A.
102 E5 Longford Ireland
113 K7 Long Island Bahamas
111 K4 Long Island Canada
95 E2 Long Island P.N.G.
113 L3 Long Island U.S.A.
113 I2 Longlac Canada
111 M5 Long Range Mountains Canada
95 E4 Longreach Australia
113 H5 Longview TX U.S.A.
112 B2 Longview WA U.S.A.
101 C5 Long Xuyên Vietnam
101 D4 Longyan China
104 E2 Lons-le-Saunier France
113 K5 Lookout, Cape U.S.A.
100 G1 Lopatina, Gora mt. Rus. Fed.
101 C5 Lop Buri Thai.
109 D4 Lopé, Parc National de la nat. park Gabon
100 B2 Lop Nur salt flat China
108 C3 Lopori r. Dem. Rep. Congo
116 D2 Lora r. Venez.
113 J3 Lorain U.S.A.
104 C4 Lorca Spain
95 F5 Lord Howe Island Pacific Ocean
123 T7 Lord Howe Rise sea feature S. Pacific Ocean
112 E5 Lordsburg U.S.A.
101 F7 Lorentz r. Indon.
117 F7 Loreto Bol.
117 I5 Loreto Brazil
112 D6 Loreto Mex.
104 C2 Lorient France
111 I3 Lorillard r. Canada
118 B5 Los Ángeles Chile
112 C5 Los Angeles U.S.A.
118 D2 Los Blancos Arg.
118 B8 Los Glaciares, Parque Nacional nat. park Arg.
115 I7 Los Katios, Parque Nacional nat. park Col.
112 E6 Los Mochis Mex.
108 B3 Losombo Dem. Rep. Congo
116 E1 Los Roques, Islas Venez.
116 E1 Los Teques Venez.
117 F1 Los Testigos is Venez.
118 C3 Los Vientos Chile
118 B4 Los Vilos Chile
104 D3 Lot r. France
108 D3 Lotikipi Plain Kenya
109 C4 Loto Dem. Rep. Congo
Louang Namtha Laos see Louangnamtha
99 I4 Louangnamtha Laos
99 I5 Louangphabang Laos
Louangphrabang Laos see Louangphabang
109 B4 Loubomo Congo
109 B4 Loudima Congo
106 A3 Louga Senegal
95 F3 Louisiade Archipelago is P.N.G.
113 H5 Louisiana state U.S.A.
113 I4 Louisville U.S.A.
121 H8 Louisville Ridge sea feature S. Pacific Ocean
102 M2 Loukhi Rus. Fed.
111 K4 Loups Marins, Lacs des lakes Canada
105 H3 Lovech Bulg.
113 F5 Lovington U.S.A.
103 M2 Lovozero Rus. Fed.
109 C4 Lowa Dem. Rep. Congo
113 L3 Lowell U.S.A.
95 H6 Lower Hutt N.Z.
104 D1 Lowestoft U.K.
95 G4 Loyauté, Îs is New Caledonia
103 N6 Lozova Ukr.
Lozovaya Ukr. see Lozova
109 C5 Luacano Angola
109 B4 Luanda Angola
109 D5 Luangwa r. Zambia
109 C5 Luanshya Zambia
109 C4 Luanza Dem. Rep. Congo
109 C5 Luau Angola
109 B5 Lubango Angola
109 C4 Lubao Dem. Rep. Congo
113 F5 Lubbock U.S.A.
105 F1 Lübeck Germany
97 N5 Lubei China
109 C4 Lubero Dem. Rep. Congo
105 H1 Lublin Poland
Lubnān country Asia see Lebanon
105 J1 Lubny Ukr.
101 D6 Lubok Antu Malaysia
109 C4 Lubudi Dem. Rep. Congo
109 C4 Lubumbashi Dem. Rep. Congo
109 C5 Lubungu Zambia
109 C4 Lubutu Dem. Rep. Congo
109 B4 Lucala Angola
109 C4 Lucapa Angola
101 E5 Lucena Phil.
105 G2 Lučenec Slovakia
102 H6 Lucerne Switz.
109 B5 Lucira Angola
Łuck Ukr. see Luts'k
99 G4 Lucknow India
109 C5 Lucusse Angola
109 B6 Lüderitz Namibia
99 F3 Ludhiana India
103 J3 Ludvika Sweden
102 H6 Ludwigshafen am Rhein Germany
105 F1 Ludwigslust Germany
109 C4 Luebo Dem. Rep. Congo
109 B5 Luena Angola
113 H5 Lufkin U.S.A.
103 L4 Luga Rus. Fed.
104 E2 Lugano Switz.
Lugdunum France see Lyon
109 D5 Lugenda r. Moz.
104 B3 Lugo Spain
105 H2 Lugoj Romania
96 E5 Luhans'k Ukr.
109 D4 Luhombero Tanz.
109 C5 Luiana Angola
Luik Belgium see Liège
109 C4 Luilaka r. Dem. Rep. Congo
Luimneach Ireland see Limerick
109 C4 Luiza Dem. Rep. Congo
109 C4 Lukenie r. Dem. Rep. Congo
105 H1 Łuków Poland
109 C5 Lukulu Zambia
109 D4 Lukumburu Tanz.
103 K2 Luleå Sweden
100 D3 Lüliang Shan mts China
109 C5 Lumbala Kaquengue Angola
109 C5 Lumbala N'guimbo Angola
113 K5 Lumberton U.S.A.
103 I4 Lund Sweden
109 D5 Lundazi Zambia
105 F1 Lüneburg Germany
109 C5 Lunga r. Zambia
106 A4 Lungi Sierra Leone
99 H4 Lunglei India
109 C5 Lungwebungu r. Zambia
Luninets Belarus see Luninyets
103 L5 Luninyets Belarus
106 A4 Lunsar Sierra Leone
99 G2 Luntai China
100 D3 Luohe China
100 D3 Luoyang China
109 C5 Lupane Zimbabwe
101 C4 Lupanshui China
109 D5 Lupilichi Moz.
109 B4 Luremo Angola
109 E5 Lúrio Moz.
109 D5 Lurio r. Moz.
109 C5 Lusaka Zambia
109 C4 Lusambo Dem. Rep. Congo
95 F2 Lusancay Islands and Reefs P.N.G.
Lut, Bahrat salt l. Asia see Dead Sea
98 D3 Lut, Dasht-e des. Iran
Lutetia France see Paris
104 C1 Luton U.K.
103 L5 Luts'k Ukr.
119 L4 Lützow-Holm Bay Antarctica
108 E3 Luuq Somalia
109 C4 Luvua r. Dem. Rep. Congo
108 D3 Luwero Uganda
101 E7 Luwuk Indon.
102 H6 Luxembourg country Europe
104 E2 Luxembourg Lux.
Luxemburg country Europe see Luxembourg
98 B4 Luxor Egypt
103 P3 Luza Rus. Fed.
103 P3 Luza r. Rus. Fed.
Luzern Switz. see Lucerne
101 C4 Luzhou China
117 J4 Luzilândia Brazil
101 E5 Luzon i. Phil.
101 E4 Luzon Strait Phil.
103 K6 L'viv Ukr.
L'vov Ukr. see L'viv
Lwów Ukr. see L'viv
Lyck Poland see Ełk
103 J3 Lycksele Sweden
119 J3 Lyddan Island Antarctica
103 L5 Lyepyel' Belarus
113 K4 Lynchburg U.S.A.
Lynn U.K. see King's Lynn
111 H4 Lynn Lake Canada
111 H3 Lynx Lake Canada
104 D2 Lyon France
Lyons France see Lyon
95 F2 Lyra Reef P.N.G.
103 P4 Lyskovo Rus. Fed.
96 G4 Lys'va Rus. Fed.
103 O5 Lysyye Gory Rus. Fed.
103 N4 Lyubertsy Rus. Fed.

M

109 C5 Maamba Zambia
98 B3 Ma'ān Jordan
Ma'an Jordan see Ma'ān
109 D6 Mabalane Moz.
117 G2 Mabaruma Guyana
109 D6 Mabote Moz.
109 C6 Mabuasehube Game Reserve nature res. Botswana
118 B7 Macá, Monte mt. Chile
117 J8 Macaé Brazil
109 D5 Macaloge Moz.
111 H3 MacAlpine Lake Canada
101 D4 Macao China
117 H3 Macapá Brazil
116 C4 Macará Ecuador
116 C4 Macas Ecuador
Macassar Strait str. Indon. see Selat Makassar
117 K5 Macau Brazil
117 H6 Macaúba Brazil
94 C4 Macdonald, Lake salt flat Australia
94 D4 Macdonnell Ranges mts Australia
Macedon country Europe see Macedonia
105 H3 Macedonia country Europe
117 K5 Maceió Brazil
106 B4 Macenta Guinea
105 F3 Macerata Italy
94 D5 Macfarlane, Lake salt flat Australia
116 C4 Machachi Ecuador
109 D6 Machaila Moz.
109 D4 Machakos Kenya
116 C4 Machala Ecuador
109 D6 Machanga Moz.
116 D1 Machiques Venez.
116 D6 Machu Picchu tourist site Peru
106 B3 Macina Mali
95 E4 Mackay Australia
94 C4 Mackay, Lake salt flat Australia
110 G3 MacKay Lake Canada
110 F4 Mackenzie Canada
110 E3 Mackenzie r. Canada
119 L5 Mackenzie Bay Antarctica
110 E3 Mackenzie Bay Canada
110 G2 Mackenzie King Island Canada
110 E3 Mackenzie Mountains Canada
95 F5 Macksville Australia
94 B4 MacLeod, Lake dry lake Australia
104 E3 Macomer Italy
104 D2 Mâcon France
113 J5 Macon U.S.A.
109 C5 Macondo Angola
95 E5 Macquarie r. Australia
95 E6 Macquarie Harbour Australia
99 F7 Macquarie Island S. Pacific Ocean
123 T9 Macquarie Ridge sea feature S. Pacific Ocean
119 L5 Mac. Robertson Land reg. Antarctica
94 D4 Macumba watercourse Australia
116 D6 Macusani Peru
112 E6 Macuzari, Presa resr Mex.
109 E6 Madagascar country Africa
123 M7 Madagascar i. Africa
123 M7 Madagascar Basin sea feature Indian Ocean
123 L8 Madagascar Ridge sea feature Indian Ocean
107 D3 Madagali Nigeria
107 D2 Madama Niger
95 E2 Madang P.N.G.
106 C3 Madaoua Niger
106 A1 Madeira terr. Atlantic Ocean
117 F5 Madeira r. Brazil
123 H3 Madeira, Arquipélago da is Port.
111 L5 Madeleine, Îles de la is Canada
112 E6 Madera Mex.
99 F5 Madgaon India
99 F4 Madhya Pradesh state India
116 E6 Madidi r. Bol.
109 B4 Madingou Congo
Madini r. Bol. see Madidi
109 E5 Madirovalo Madag.
113 I4 Madison IN U.S.A.
113 I3 Madison WI U.S.A.
112 D2 Madison r. U.S.A.
108 D3 Mado Gashi Kenya
100 B3 Madoi China
103 L4 Madona Latvia
113 G6 Madre, Laguna lag. Mex.
116 D6 Madre de Dios r. Peru
118 A8 Madre de Dios, Isla i. Chile
114 D5 Madre del Sur, Sierra mts Mex.
112 E6 Madre Occidental, Sierra mts Mex.
113 F6 Madre Oriental, Sierra mts Mex.
104 C3 Madrid Spain
101 D7 Madura i. Indon.
99 F6 Madurai India
100 F3 Maebashi Japan
115 I5 Maestra, Sierra mts Cuba
109 E5 Maevatanana Madag.
95 G3 Maéwo i. Vanuatu
109 D4 Mafia Island Tanz.
109 D4 Mafinga Tanz.
Mafraq Jordan see Al Mafraq
97 Q4 Magadan Rus. Fed.
109 D4 Magadi Kenya
116 D2 Magangue Col.
99 F5 Magas Rus. Fed.
117 F6 Magdalena Bol.
112 D5 Magdalena Mex.
112 D7 Magdalena, Bahía b. Mex.
118 B6 Magdalena, Isla i. Chile
105 F1 Magdeburg Germany
118 B8 Magellan, Strait of Chile
120 E4 Magellan Seamounts sea feature N. Pacific Ocean
Maghâgha Egypt see Maghāghah
105 J6 Maghāghah Egypt
106 A3 Maghama Mauritania
119 L5 Magnet Bay Antarctica
95 E3 Magnetic Island Australia
98 D1 Magnitogorsk Rus. Fed.
Magosa Cyprus see Famagusta
113 N1 Magpie Lake Canada
106 A3 Magṭa' Laḥjar Mauritania
109 D4 Magu Tanz.
117 I4 Maguarinho, Cabo c. Brazil
101 B4 Magwe Myanmar
Magyar Köztársaság country Europe see Hungary
109 E6 Mahabo Madag.
109 D4 Mahagi Dem. Rep. Congo
109 E5 Mahajamba r. Madag.
109 E5 Mahajanga Madag.
109 C6 Mahalapye Botswana
109 E5 Mahalevona Madag.
109 E5 Mahanoro Madag.
99 F5 Maharashtra state India
101 C5 Maha Sarakham Thai.
109 E6 Mahatalaky Madag.
109 E5 Mahavanona Madag.
109 E5 Mahavavy r. Madag.
117 G2 Mahdia Guyana
105 F4 Mahdia Tunisia
95 H5 Mahia Peninsula N.Z.
96 E4 Mahilyow Belarus
104 D4 Mahón Spain
107 D3 Maiduguri Nigeria
109 C4 Maiko, Parc National de la nat. park Dem. Rep. Congo
109 B4 Mai-Ndombe, Lac l. Dem. Rep. Congo
113 M2 Maine state U.S.A.
107 D3 Maïné-Soroa Niger
109 E5 Maintirano Madag.
102 H5 Mainz Germany
106 □ Maio i. Cape Verde
116 E1 Maiquetía Venez.
109 C6 Maitengwe Botswana
119 K3 Maitri research stn Antarctica
115 H6 Maíz, Islas del Nicaragua
105 G3 Maja Jezercë mt. Albania
101 D7 Majene Indon.
108 D3 Majī Eth.
104 D4 Major, Puig mt. Spain
104 D4 Majorca i. Spain
Majuro atoll Marshall Is see Taongi
109 B4 Makabana Congo
101 D7 Makale Indon.
109 C4 Makamba Burundi
99 G2 Makanchi Kazakh.
124 M1 Makarov Basin sea feature Arctic Ocean
105 G3 Makarska Croatia
103 O4 Makar'yev Rus. Fed.
94 B2 Makassar Indon.
98 D2 Makat Kazakh.
Makedonija country Europe see Macedonia
106 A4 Makeni Sierra Leone
Makeyevka Ukr. see Makiyivka
109 C6 Makgadikgadi depr. Botswana
103 P7 Makhachkala Rus. Fed.
109 D4 Makindu Kenya
99 F1 Makinsk Kazakh.
103 N6 Makiyivka Ukr.
108 B3 Makokou Gabon
109 D4 Makongolosi Tanz.
109 B4 Makotipoko Congo
99 E4 Makran reg. Iran/Pak.
109 D4 Makumbako Tanz.
109 D5 Makunguwiro Tanz.
106 C4 Makurdi Nigeria
115 H7 Mala, Punta pt Panama
99 F5 Malabar Coast India
106 C4 Malabo Equat. Guinea
Malaca Spain see Málaga
101 B6 Malacca, Strait of Indon./Malaysia
103 L5 Maladzyechna Belarus
104 C4 Málaga Spain
95 G2 Malaita i. Solomon Is
107 F4 Malakal Sudan
95 G3 Malakula i. Vanuatu
101 E7 Malamala Indon.
101 D7 Malang Indon.
109 B4 Malanje Angola
103 J4 Mälaren l. Sweden
118 C5 Malargüe Arg.
98 B3 Malatya Turkey
109 D5 Malawi country Africa
Malawi, Lake l. Africa see Nyasa, Lake
103 M4 Malaya Vishera Rus. Fed.
122 K4 Malay Peninsula Asia
Malaysia, Semenanjung pen. Malaysia see Peninsular Malaysia
103 J5 Malbork Poland
122 I4 Maldives country Indian Ocean
118 F4 Maldonado Uruguay
105 H4 Maleas, Akrotirio pt Greece
99 F6 Male Atoll Maldives
109 B4 Malele Dem. Rep. Congo
109 D5 Malema Moz.
106 B3 Mali country Africa
109 C4 Mali Dem. Rep. Congo
106 A3 Mali Guinea
101 E7 Malili Indon.
109 E4 Malindi Kenya
102 E4 Malin Head Ireland
111 I3 Mallery Lake Canada
Mallorca i. Spain see Majorca
103 I4 Malmö Sweden
103 Q4 Malmyzh Rus. Fed.
95 G3 Malo i. Vanuatu
109 C5 Malonga Dem. Rep. Congo
103 N3 Maloshuyka Rus. Fed.
102 H3 Måløy Norway
103 N4 Maloyaroslavets Rus. Fed.
103 P2 Malozemel'skaya Tundra lowland Rus. Fed.
116 B3 Malpelo, Isla de i. Col.
105 F4 Malta country Europe
105 F4 Malta Channel Italy/Malta
109 B6 Maltahöhe Namibia
94 C2 Maluku, Laut sea Indon.
103 I3 Malung Sweden
95 G2 Malu'u Solomon Is
97 R3 Malyy Anyuy r. Rus. Fed.
97 P2 Malyy Lyakhovskiy, Ostrov i. Rus. Fed.
97 P3 Mama r. Rus. Fed.
103 Q4 Mamadysh Rus. Fed.
108 C3 Mambasa Dem. Rep. Congo
108 B3 Mambéré r. Centr. Afr. Rep.
106 C4 Mamfe Cameroon
Mamfé Cameroon see Mam
116 E6 Mamoré r. Bol./Brazil
106 A3 Mamou Guinea
109 E5 Mampikony Madag.
106 B4 Mampong Ghana
106 B4 Man Côte d'Ivoire
102 F5 Man, Isle of terr. Irish Sea
117 F4 Manacapuru Brazil
104 D4 Manacor Spain
101 E6 Manado Indon.
115 G6 Managua Nicaragua
115 G6 Managua, Lago de l. Nicaragua
109 E6 Manakara Madag.
98 D4 Manama Bahrain
95 E2 Manam Island P.N.G.
109 E6 Mananara r. Madag.
109 E5 Mananara, Parc National de nat. park Madag.
109 E5 Mananara Avaratra Madag.
109 E6 Mananjary Madag.
109 E5 Manarantsandry Madag.
100 A2 Manas Hu l. China
Manastir Macedonia see Bitola
101 E7 Manatuto East Timor
117 F4 Manaus Brazil
105 J4 Manavgat Turkey
104 C1 Manchester U.K.
113 L3 Manchester U.S.A.
91 Manchurian Plain plain Chi
109 E6 Mandabe Madag.
101 G7 Mandala, Puncak mt. Indon
101 B4 Mandalay Myanmar
100 C2 Mandalgovĭ Mongolia
107 D3 Mandara Mountains Cameroon/Nigeria
108 E3 Mandera Kenya
115 I5 Mandeville Jamaica
106 B3 Mandiana Guinea
109 D5 Mandié Moz.
109 D5 Mandimba Moz.
99 G4 Mandla India
109 E5 Mandritsara Madag.
99 F4 Mandsaur India
94 B5 Mandurah Australia
105 G3 Manfredonia, Golfo di g. Ita
117 J6 Manga Brazil
106 B3 Manga Burkina
109 B4 Mangai Dem. Rep. Congo
121 I7 Mangaia i. Cook Is
105 I3 Mangalia Romania
99 F5 Mangalore India
101 C7 Manggar Indon.
100 B3 Mangnai China
109 D5 Mangochi Malawi
101 E7 Mangole i. Indon.
107 D2 Manguéni, Plateau du Nige
100 E1 Mangui China
98 D2 Mangystau Kazakh.
109 D6 Manhica Moz.
117 J8 Manhuaçu Brazil
109 E5 Mania r. Madag.
117 F5 Manicoré Brazil
113 M1 Manicouagan r. Canada
113 M1 Manicouagan, Réservoir resr Canada
121 I6 Manihiki atoll Cook Is
101 E5 Manila Phil.
99 H4 Manipur state India
105 I4 Manisa Turkey
113 I3 Manistee U.S.A.
113 G1 Manitoba prov. Canada
113 G1 Manitoba, Lake Canada
113 J2 Manitoulin Island Canada
113 K2 Maniwaki Canada
116 C2 Manizales Col.
109 E6 Manja Madag.
113 H3 Mankato U.S.A.
106 B4 Mankono Côte d'Ivoire
122 J4 Mannar, Gulf of India/Sri Lanka
104 E2 Mannheim Germany
101 F7 Manokwari Indon.
109 C4 Manono Dem. Rep. Congo
113 L1 Manouane, Lac l. Canada
95 I2 Manra i. Kiribati
104 D3 Manresa Spain
109 C5 Mansa Zambia
106 A3 Mansa Konko Gambia
111 K3 Mansel Island Canada
113 J3 Mansfield U.S.A.
116 B4 Manta Ecuador
116 B4 Manta, Bahía de b. Ecuador
117 I8 Mantiqueira, Serra da mts Brazil
103 O4 Manturovo Rus. Fed.
116 D6 Manu, Parque Nacional nat. park Peru
121 I7 Manuae atoll Fr. Polynesia
Manua Islands American Samoa see Manu'a Islands
121 H6 Manu'a Islands American Samoa
117 H5 Manuelzinho Brazil
101 E7 Manui i. Indon.
95 H5 Manukau N.Z.
95 E2 Manus Island P.N.G.
103 O6 Manych-Gudilo, Ozero l. Rus. Fed.
109 D4 Manyoni Tanz.
115 I4 Manzanillo Cuba
114 D5 Manzanillo Mex.
100 D2 Manzhouli China

Monaco Basin

07 D3 **Mao** Chad
Maó Spain *see* **Mahón**
01 F7 **Maoke, Pegunungan** *mts* Indon.
09 D6 **Mapai** Moz.
99 G3 **Mapam Yumco** *l.* China
94 C2 **Mapane** Indon.
09 D6 **Mapinhane** Moz.
17 F2 **Mapire** Venez.
12 E2 **Maple Creek** Canada
20 G4 **Mapmakers Seamounts** *sea feature* N. Pacific Ocean
17 G4 **Mapuera** *r.* Brazil
09 D6 **Maputo** Moz.
09 B4 **Maquela do Zombo** Angola
18 C6 **Maquinchao** Arg.
16 E4 **Maraã** Brazil
17 I5 **Marabá** Brazil
17 H3 **Maracá, Ilha de** *i.* Brazil
16 D1 **Maracaibo** Venez.
Maracaibo, Lago de *inlet* Venez. *see* **Maracaibo, Lake**
16 D2 **Maracaibo, Lake** *inlet* Venez.
18 E2 **Maracaju, Serra de** *hills* Brazil
17 J6 **Maracás, Chapada de** *hills* Brazil
16 E1 **Maracay** Venez.
07 D2 **Marādah** Libya
06 C3 **Maradi** Niger
17 I4 **Marajó, Baía de** *est.* Brazil
17 I3 **Marajó, Ilha de** *i.* Brazil
08 D3 **Maralal** Kenya
94 D5 **Maralinga** Australia
95 G2 **Maramasike** *i.* Solomon Is
19 L2 **Marambio** *research stn* Antarctica
98 C3 **Marand** Iran
16 D4 **Marañón** *r.* Peru
13 I2 **Marathon** Canada
94 B4 **Marble Bar** Australia
Marburg Slovenia *see* **Maribor**
16 □ **Marchena, Isla** *i.* Ecuador
Mar Chiquita, Lago *l.* Arg. *see* **Mar Chiquita, Laguna**
18 D4 **Mar Chiquita, Laguna** *l.* Arg.
99 F3 **Mardan** Pak.
18 E5 **Mar del Plata** Arg.
98 C3 **Mardın** Turkey
95 G4 **Maré** *i.* New Caledonia
94 B5 **Margaret River** Australia
17 F1 **Margarita, Isla de** *i.* Venez.
08 C3 **Margherita Peak** Dem. Rep. Congo/Uganda
19 I2 **Marguerite Bay** Antarctica
04 C5 **Marhoum** Alg.
21 I7 **Maria** *atoll* Fr. Polynesia
18 C2 **María Elena** Chile
94 D3 **Maria Island** Australia
20 E4 **Mariana Ridge** *sea feature* N. Pacific Ocean
20 E5 **Mariana Trench** *sea feature* N. Pacific Ocean
Mariánica, Cordillera *mts* Spain *see* **Morena, Sierra**
113 I5 **Marianna** U.S.A.
114 C4 **Marías, Islas** Mex.
115 H7 **Mariato, Punta** *pt* Panama
95 H5 **Maria van Diemen, Cape** N.Z.
105 G2 **Maribor** Slovenia
107 E4 **Maridi** *watercourse* Sudan
119 I4 **Marie Byrd Land** *reg.* Antarctica
115 L5 **Marie-Galante** *i.* Guadeloupe
96 C3 **Mariehamn** Fin.
Marienburg Poland *see* **Malbork**
109 B6 **Mariental** Namibia
103 I4 **Mariestad** Sweden
100 G1 **Marii, Mys** *pt* Rus. Fed.
100 A1 **Mariinsk** Rus. Fed.
103 K5 **Marijampolė** Lith.
117 I8 **Marília** Brazil
Mar'ina Gorka Belarus *see* **Mar"ina Horka**
103 L5 **Mar"ina Horka** Belarus
118 F2 **Maringá** Brazil
113 J5 **Marion, Lake** U.S.A.
116 E2 **Maripa** Venez.
Mariscal Estigarribia Para. *see* **Mariscal José Félix Estigarribia**
117 F8 **Mariscal José Félix Estigarribia** Para.
96 E5 **Mariupol'** Ukr.
108 E3 **Marka** Somalia
97 M3 **Markha** *r.* Rus. Fed.
104 D3 **Marmande** France
105 I3 **Marmara, Sea of** *g.* Turkey
Marmara Denizi *g.* Turkey *see* **Marmara, Sea of**
105 I4 **Marmaris** Turkey
109 E5 **Maroantsetra** Madag.
Maroc *country* Africa *see* **Morocco**
109 E5 **Maromokotro** *mt.* Madag.
109 D5 **Marondera** Zimbabwe
117 H2 **Maroni** *r.* Fr. Guiana
107 D3 **Maroua** Cameroon
109 E5 **Marovoay** Madag.
121 J6 **Marquesas Islands** Fr. Polynesia
113 I2 **Marquette** U.S.A.
Marquises, Îles *is* Fr. Polynesia *see* **Marquesas Islands**
107 E3 **Marra, Jebel** Sudan
106 B1 **Marrakech** Morocco
Marra Plateau *plat.* Sudan *see* **Marra, Jebel**
109 D5 **Marromeu** Moz.
Marruecos *country* Africa *see* **Morocco**
109 D5 **Marrupa** Moz.
107 F2 **Marsá al 'Alam** Egypt
105 G5 **Marsa al Burayqah** Libya
108 D3 **Marsabit** Kenya
105 F4 **Marsala** Italy
105 I5 **Marsá Maṭrūḥ** Egypt
104 E3 **Marseille** France
Marseilles France *see* **Marseille**
113 H5 **Marshall** U.S.A.
120 F5 **Marshall Islands** *country* N. Pacific Ocean
113 H3 **Marshalltown** U.S.A.
113 H3 **Marshfield** U.S.A.
113 H6 **Marsh Island** U.S.A.
104 E2 **Martigny** Switz.
105 G2 **Martin** Slovakia
115 L6 **Martinique** *terr.* Caribbean Sea
119 I4 **Martin Peninsula** Antarctica
113 K4 **Martinsburg** U.S.A.
113 K4 **Martinsville** U.S.A.
123 H7 **Martin Vaz, Ilhas** *is* S. Atlantic Ocean
98 D1 **Martuk** Kazakh.
117 K6 **Maruim** Brazil
99 E3 **Mary** Turkm.
95 F4 **Maryborough** Australia
113 K4 **Maryland** *state* U.S.A.
113 H3 **Maryville** U.S.A.
109 D4 **Masaka** Uganda
94 C2 **Masamba** Indon.
100 E3 **Masan** S. Korea
109 D5 **Masasi** Tanz.
118 D1 **Masavi** Bol.
101 E5 **Masbate** *i.* Phil.
104 D4 **Mascara** Alg.
123 M7 **Mascarene Basin** *sea feature* Indian Ocean
123 M7 **Mascarene Plain** *sea feature* Indian Ocean
123 M6 **Mascarene Ridge** *sea feature* Indian Ocean
98 D3 **Mashhad** Iran
108 D3 **Masindi** Uganda
Masīrah *i.* Oman *see* **Maşīrah, Jazīrat**
98 D4 **Maşīrah, Jazīrat** *i.* Oman
109 F5 **Masoala, Tanjona** *c.* Madag.
113 H3 **Mason City** U.S.A.
Masqaṭ Oman *see* **Muscat**
113 L3 **Massachusetts** *state* U.S.A.
113 L3 **Massachusetts Bay** U.S.A.
107 D3 **Massakory** Chad
109 D6 **Massangena** Moz.
109 B4 **Massango** Angola
108 D2 **Massawa** Eritrea
113 L3 **Massena** U.S.A.
104 D2 **Massif Central** *mts* France
Massilia France *see* **Marseille**
109 D6 **Massinga** Moz.
109 D6 **Massingir** Moz.
95 H6 **Masterton** N.Z.
99 E4 **Mastung** Pak.
109 D6 **Masvingo** Zimbabwe
97 M5 **Matad** Mongolia
109 B4 **Matadi** Dem. Rep. Congo
115 G6 **Matagalpa** Nicaragua
113 K2 **Matagami** Canada
113 G6 **Matagorda Island** U.S.A.
109 B5 **Matala** Angola
106 A3 **Matam** Senegal
113 F6 **Matamoros** *Coahuila* Mex.
113 G6 **Matamoros** *Tamaulipas* Mex.
109 D4 **Matandu** *r.* Tanz.
113 M2 **Matane** Canada
115 H4 **Matanzas** Cuba
118 B5 **Mataquito** *r.* Chile
99 G6 **Matara** Sri Lanka
101 D7 **Mataram** Indon.
116 D7 **Matarani** Peru
94 D3 **Mataranka** Australia
95 J3 **Matā'utu** Wallis and Futuna Is
117 F6 **Mategua** Bol.
114 D4 **Matehuala** Mex.
109 D5 **Matemanga** Tanz.
105 G3 **Matera** Italy
99 F4 **Mathura** India
101 E6 **Mati** Phil.
114 E5 **Matías Romero** Mex.
117 G7 **Mato Grosso** Brazil
100 F3 **Matsue** Japan
100 F3 **Matsuyama** Japan
115 J4 **Matthew Town** Bahamas
95 H3 **Matuku** *i.* Fiji
117 F2 **Maturín** Venez.
119 L3 **Maud Seamount** *sea feature* S. Atlantic Ocean
117 G4 **Maués** Brazil
121 I4 **Maui** *i.* U.S.A.
118 B5 **Maule** *r.* Chile
118 B6 **Maullín** Chile
109 C5 **Maun** Botswana
110 F3 **Maunoir, Lac** *l.* Canada
94 D4 **Maurice, Lake** *salt flat* Australia
106 A3 **Mauritania** *country* Africa
123 M7 **Mauritius** *country* Indian Ocean
109 C5 **Mavinga** Angola
109 B4 **Mawanga** Dem. Rep. Congo
99 H5 **Mawlamyaing** Myanmar
119 L5 **Mawson** *research stn* Antarctica
119 K5 **Mawson Escarpment** Antarctica
119 I6 **Mawson Peninsula** Antarctica
100 F1 **Maya** *r.* Rus. Fed.
115 J4 **Mayaguana** *i.* Bahamas
115 K5 **Mayagüez** Puerto Rico
106 C3 **Mayahi** Niger
109 B4 **Mayama** Congo
115 G5 **Maya Mountains** Belize/Guat.
105 L3 **Maykop** Rus. Fed.
99 E3 **Maymanah** Afgh.
Maymyo Myanmar *see* **Pyin-U-Lwin**
103 P5 **Mayna** Rus. Fed.
100 B1 **Mayna** Rus. Fed.
110 E3 **Mayo** Canada
109 B4 **Mayoko** Congo
Mayor, Puig *mt.* Spain *see* **Major, Puig**
118 D1 **Mayor Pablo Lagerenza** Para.
109 E5 **Mayotte** *terr.* Africa
100 E1 **Mayskiy** Rus. Fed.
109 B4 **Mayumba** Gabon
109 C5 **Mazabuka** Zambia
Mazagan Morocco *see* **El Jadida**
117 H4 **Mazagão** Brazil
99 F3 **Mazar** China
99 E3 **Mazār-e Sharīf** Afgh.
114 C4 **Mazatlán** Mex.
103 K4 **Mažeikiai** Lith.
109 D4 **Mazomora** Tanz.
109 C6 **Mazunga** Zimbabwe
103 L5 **Mazyr** Belarus
106 B4 **Mbahiakro** Côte d'Ivoire
108 B3 **Mbaïki** Centr. Afr. Rep.
109 D4 **Mbala** Zambia
108 D3 **Mbale** Uganda
107 D4 **Mbalmayo** Cameroon
109 B4 **Mbandaka** Dem. Rep. Congo
106 C4 **Mbanga** Cameroon
109 B4 **M'banza Congo** Angola
109 D4 **Mbarara** Uganda
108 C3 **Mbari** *r.* Centr. Afr. Rep.
107 D4 **Mbengwi** Cameroon
109 D4 **Mbeya** Tanz.
109 D5 **Mbinga** Tanz.
109 D6 **Mbizi** Zimbabwe
108 B3 **Mbomo** Congo
107 D4 **Mbouda** Cameroon
106 A3 **Mbour** Senegal
106 A3 **Mbout** Mauritania
109 D4 **Mbozi** Tanz.
109 C4 **Mbuji-Mayi** Dem. Rep. Congo
109 D4 **Mbulu** Tanz.
109 D4 **Mbuyuni** Tanz.
113 G5 **McAlester** U.S.A.
111 H2 **McClintock Channel** Canada
111 G2 **McClure Strait** Canada
113 F3 **McCook** U.S.A.
123 N9 **McDonald Islands** Indian Ocean
112 D2 **McDonald Peak** U.S.A.
110 C3 **McGrath** U.S.A.
112 D2 **McGuire, Mount** U.S.A.
109 D4 **Mchinga** Tanz.
95 I2 **McKean** *i.* Kiribati
110 C3 **McKinley, Mount** U.S.A.
119 I5 **McMurdo** *research stn* Antarctica
112 D4 **Mead, Lake** *resr* U.S.A.
111 L4 **Mealy Mountains** Canada
109 B4 **Mebridege** *r.* Angola
104 C5 **Mecheria** Alg.
105 F1 **Mecklenburger Bucht** *b.* Germany
109 D5 **Mecula** Moz.
101 B6 **Medan** Indon.
118 C7 **Medanosa, Punta** *pt* Arg.
104 D4 **Médéa** Alg.
116 C2 **Medellín** Col.
105 F5 **Medenine** Tunisia
106 A3 **Mederdra** Mauritania
112 B3 **Medford** U.S.A.
112 E3 **Medicine Bow Mountains** U.S.A.
112 D1 **Medicine Hat** Canada
98 B4 **Medina** Saudi Arabia
104 C3 **Medinaceli** Spain
104 C3 **Medina del Campo** Spain
Mediolanum Italy *see* **Milan**
105 J5 **Mediterranean Sea**
98 D1 **Mednogorsk** Rus. Fed.
97 R2 **Medvezh'i, Ostrova** *is* Rus. Fed.
100 F2 **Medvezh'ya, Gora** *mt.* China/Rus. Fed.
103 M3 **Medvezh'yegorsk** Rus. Fed.
94 B4 **Meekatharra** Australia
99 F4 **Meerut** India
108 D3 **Mēga** Eth.
99 H4 **Meghalaya** *state* India
105 I4 **Megisti** *i.* Greece
103 L1 **Mehamn** Norway
94 B4 **Meharry, Mount** Australia
Mehdia Tunisia *see* **Mahdia**
117 I7 **Meia Ponte** *r.* Brazil
107 D4 **Meiganga** Cameroon
97 N5 **Meihekou** China
101 B4 **Meiktila** Myanmar
105 F1 **Meiningen** Germany
101 D4 **Meizhou** China
118 C3 **Mejicana** *mt.* Arg.
118 B2 **Mejillones** Chile
108 D2 **Mek'elē** Eth.
106 A3 **Mékhé** Senegal
104 B5 **Meknès** Morocco
101 C5 **Mekong** *r.* Asia
101 C6 **Mekong, Mouths of the** Vietnam
101 C6 **Melaka** Malaysia
95 G2 **Melanesia** *is* Oceania
120 F5 **Melanesian Basin** *sea feature* Pacific Ocean
95 E5 **Melbourne** Australia
113 J6 **Melbourne** U.S.A.
101 F6 **Melekeok** Palau
Melekess Rus. Fed. *see* **Dimitrovgrad**
111 K4 **Mélèzes, Rivière aux** *r.* Canada
107 D3 **Melfi** Chad
113 F1 **Melfort** Canada
103 I3 **Melhus** Norway
104 C4 **Melilla** N. Africa
Melitene Turkey *see* **Malatya**
105 K2 **Melitopol'** Ukr.
103 I4 **Mellerud** Sweden
Mellilia N. Africa *see* **Melilla**
118 F4 **Melo** Uruguay
104 E5 **Melrhir, Chott** *salt l.* Alg.
113 F1 **Melville** Canada
95 E3 **Melville, Cape** Australia
101 F8 **Melville Island** Australia
110 G2 **Melville Island** Canada
111 J3 **Melville Peninsula** Canada
101 F7 **Memberamo** *r.* Indon.
105 F2 **Memmingen** Germany
101 C6 **Mempawah** Indon.
113 H4 **Memphis** U.S.A.
105 J1 **Mena** Ukr.
106 C3 **Ménaka** Mali
104 D3 **Mende** France
108 D2 **Mendefera** Eritrea
124 M1 **Mendeleyev Ridge** *sea feature* Arctic Ocean
110 B4 **Mendenhall, Cape** U.S.A.
108 D3 **Mendī** Eth.
95 E2 **Mendi** P.N.G.
121 K3 **Mendocino, Cape** U.S.A.
118 C4 **Mendoza** Arg.
116 D1 **Mene de Mauroa** Venez.
101 C7 **Menggala** Indon.
95 E5 **Menindee, Lake** Australia
97 N3 **Menkere** Rus. Fed.
113 I2 **Menominee** U.S.A.
109 B5 **Menongue** Angola
Menorca *i.* Spain *see* **Minorca**
101 B7 **Mentawai, Kepulauan** *is* Indon.
104 E4 **Menzel Bourguiba** Tunisia
105 F4 **Menzel Temime** Tunisia
94 C4 **Menzies** Australia
119 K5 **Menzies, Mount** Antarctica
105 F2 **Merano** Italy
101 G7 **Merauke** Indon.
112 B4 **Merced** U.S.A.
118 E3 **Mercedes** Arg.
118 E4 **Mercedes** Uruguay
111 L3 **Mercy, Cape** Canada
105 K2 **Merefa** Ukr.
107 E3 **Merga Oasis** Sudan
Mergui Myanmar *see* **Myeik**
101 B5 **Mergui Archipelago** *is* Myanmar
115 G4 **Mérida** Mex.
104 B4 **Mérida** Spain
116 D2 **Mérida** Venez.
116 D2 **Mérida, Cordillera de** *mts* Venez.
113 I5 **Meridian** U.S.A.
107 F3 **Merowe** Sudan
94 B5 **Merredin** Australia
112 B1 **Merritt** Canada
108 E2 **Mersa Fatma** Eritrea
Mersa Maṭrûḥ Egypt *see* **Marsá Maṭrūḥ**
98 B3 **Mersin** Turkey
108 D3 **Merti** Kenya
119 J6 **Mertz Glacier** Antarctica
109 D4 **Meru** *vol.* Tanz.
105 K3 **Merzifon** Turkey
119 I3 **Merz Peninsula** Antarctica
105 H4 **Mesolongi** Greece
Mesolóngion Greece *see* **Mesolongi**
104 D5 **Messaad** Alg.
109 D5 **Messalo** *r.* Moz.
Messana Italy *see* **Messina**
105 G4 **Messina** Italy
111 P2 **Mesters Vig** *b.* Greenland
Mestghanem Alg. *see* **Mostaganem**
116 E2 **Meta** *r.* Col./Venez.
111 K3 **Meta Incognita Peninsula** Canada
118 C3 **Metán** Arg.
105 G3 **Metković** Croatia
104 E5 **Metlaoui** Tunisia
109 D5 **Metoro** Moz.
108 D3 **Metu** Eth.
104 E2 **Metz** France
112 C5 **Mexicali** Mex.
121 M4 **Mexico, Gulf of** Mex./U.S.A.
114 E5 **Mexico City** Mex.
103 O2 **Mezen'** Rus. Fed.
103 O2 **Mezen'** *r.* Rus. Fed.
100 A1 **Mezhdurechensk** *Kemerovskaya Oblast'* Rus. Fed.
103 P3 **Mezhdurechensk** *Respublika Komi* Rus. Fed.
96 G2 **Mezhdusharskiy, Ostrov** *i.* Rus. Fed.
114 C4 **Mezquital** *r.* Mex.
109 D5 **Mfuwe** Zambia
114 E5 **Miahuatlán** Mex.
113 J6 **Miami** *FL* U.S.A.
113 H4 **Miami** *OK* U.S.A.
113 J6 **Miami Beach** U.S.A.
109 E5 **Miandrivazo** Madag.
100 C3 **Mianyang** China
109 E5 **Miarinarivo** Madag.
96 H4 **Miass** Rus. Fed.
113 I2 **Michigan** *state* U.S.A.
113 I3 **Michigan, Lake** U.S.A.
113 I2 **Michipicoten Island** Canada
113 J2 **Michipicoten River** Canada
103 O5 **Michurinsk** Rus. Fed.
115 H6 **Mico** *r.* Nicaragua
120 E5 **Micronesia** *is* Pacific Ocean
123 F4 **Mid-Atlantic Ridge** *sea feature* Atlantic Ocean
123 H8 **Mid-Atlantic Ridge** *sea feature* Atlantic Ocean
123 C5 **Middle America Trench** *sea feature* N. Pacific Ocean
Middle Atlas *mts* Morocco *see* **Moyen Atlas**
113 J4 **Middlesboro** U.S.A.
102 F5 **Middlesbrough** U.K.
113 L3 **Middletown** *NY* U.S.A.
113 J4 **Middletown** *OH* U.S.A.
104 C5 **Midelt** Morocco
123 O6 **Mid-Indian Basin** *sea feature* Indian Ocean
123 N7 **Mid-Indian Ridge** *sea feature* Indian Ocean
113 F5 **Midland** U.S.A.
120 F4 **Mid-Pacific Mountains** *sea feature* N. Pacific Ocean
121 H4 **Midway Islands** *terr.* N. Pacific Ocean
109 D4 **Miembwe** Tanz.
105 I2 **Miercurea-Ciuc** Romania
108 E3 **Mī'ēso** Eth.
97 R3 **Mikhalkino** Rus. Fed.
Mikhaylovgrad Bulg. *see* **Montana**
119 L6 **Mikhaylov Island** Antarctica
105 L1 **Mikhaylovka** Rus. Fed.
99 F1 **Mikhaylovskiy** Rus. Fed.
103 L3 **Mikkeli** Fin.
109 D4 **Mikumi** Tanz.
103 Q3 **Mikun'** Rus. Fed.
99 F6 **Miladhunmadulu Atoll** Maldives
104 E2 **Milan** Italy
109 D5 **Milange** Moz.
Milano Italy *see* **Milan**
105 I4 **Milas** Turkey
95 E5 **Mildura** Australia
112 E2 **Miles City** U.S.A.
Milid Turkey *see* **Malatya**
112 E2 **Milk** *r.* Canada
107 E3 **Milk, Wadi el** *watercourse* Sudan
97 Q4 **Mil'kovo** Rus. Fed.
104 D3 **Millau** France
113 J5 **Milledgeville** U.S.A.
113 H2 **Mille Lacs** *lakes* U.S.A.
105 L2 **Millerovo** Rus. Fed.
119 K6 **Mill Island** Antarctica
105 H4 **Milos** *i.* Greece
113 I3 **Milwaukee** U.S.A.
123 E4 **Milwaukee Deep** *sea feature* Caribbean Sea
109 B4 **Mimongo** Gabon
98 D4 **Mīnāb** Iran
101 E6 **Minahasa, Semenanjung** *pen.* Indon.
101 C6 **Minas** Indon.
118 E4 **Minas** Uruguay
115 F5 **Minatitlán** Mex.
118 B6 **Minchinmávida** *vol.* Chile
101 E6 **Mindanao** *i.* Phil.
106 □ **Mindelo** Cape Verde
113 H5 **Minden** U.S.A.
101 E5 **Mindoro** *i.* Phil.
109 B4 **Mindouli** Congo
113 G5 **Mineral Wells** U.S.A.
99 G3 **Minfeng** China
109 C5 **Minga** Dem. Rep. Congo
98 C2 **Mingäçevir** Azer.
109 D5 **Mingoyo** Tanz.
100 E2 **Mingshui** China
99 F6 **Minicoy** *atoll* India
94 B4 **Minilya** Australia
111 L4 **Minipi Lake** Canada
108 B3 **Minkébé, Parc National de** *nat. park* Gabon
106 C4 **Minna** Nigeria
113 H3 **Minneapolis** U.S.A.
113 G1 **Minnedosa** Canada
113 G2 **Minnesota** *r.* U.S.A.
113 H2 **Minnesota** *state* U.S.A.
104 D3 **Minorca** *i.* Spain
113 F2 **Minot** U.S.A.
105 I1 **Minsk** Belarus
111 K4 **Minto, Lac** *l.* Canada
110 G2 **Minto Inlet** Canada
100 B1 **Minusinsk** Rus. Fed.
117 I5 **Miracema do Tocantins** Brazil
117 I5 **Mirador, Parque Nacional de** *nat. park* Brazil
118 E5 **Miramar** Arg.
113 M2 **Miramichi** Canada
118 E2 **Miranda** Brazil
118 E1 **Miranda** *r.* Brazil
104 C3 **Miranda de Ebro** Spain
98 D5 **Mirbāṭ** Oman
101 D6 **Miri** Malaysia
118 F4 **Mirim, Lagoa** *l.* Brazil
119 K6 **Mirny** *research stn* Antarctica
97 M3 **Mirnyy** Rus. Fed.
Mironovka Ukr. *see* **Myronivka**
95 F3 **Misima Island** P.N.G.
115 H6 **Miskitos, Cayos** *is* Nicaragua
105 H2 **Miskolc** Hungary
101 F7 **Misoöl** *i.* Indon.
Misr *country* Africa *see* **Egypt**
105 G5 **Mişrātah** Libya
113 J1 **Missinaibi** *r.* Canada
113 J2 **Missinaibi Lake** Canada
113 H5 **Mississippi** *r.* U.S.A.
113 I5 **Mississippi** *state* U.S.A.
113 I6 **Mississippi Delta** U.S.A.
Missolonghi Greece *see* **Mesolongi**
112 D2 **Missoula** U.S.A.
111 I5 **Missouri** *r.* U.S.A.
113 H4 **Missouri** *state* U.S.A.
113 L2 **Mistassibi** *r.* Canada
113 L1 **Mistassini, Lac** *l.* Canada
111 L4 **Mistastin Lake** Canada
113 L1 **Mistissini** Canada
Misuratah Libya *see* **Mişrātah**
95 E4 **Mitchell** Australia
95 E3 **Mitchell** *r.* Australia
113 G3 **Mitchell** U.S.A.
Mitilíni Greece *see* **Mytilini**
100 G3 **Mito** Japan
109 D4 **Mitole** Tanz.
95 H3 **Mitre Island** Solomon Is
116 D3 **Mitú** Col.
109 C5 **Mitumba, Chaîne des** *mts* Dem. Rep. Congo
109 C4 **Mitumba, Monts** *mts* Dem. Rep. Congo
108 B3 **Mitzic** Gabon
100 F3 **Miyake-jima** *i.* Japan
100 F3 **Miyazaki** Japan
108 D3 **Mīzan Teferī** Eth.
105 F5 **Mizdah** Libya
99 H4 **Mizoram** *state* India
103 J4 **Mjölby** Sweden
109 D4 **Mkata** Tanz.
109 D4 **Mkomazi** Tanz.
109 C5 **Mkushi** Zambia
105 H1 **Mława** Poland
112 E4 **Moab** U.S.A.
95 E3 **Moa Island** Australia
95 H3 **Moala** *i.* Fiji
109 C4 **Moba** Dem. Rep. Congo
108 C3 **Mobayi-Mbongo** Dem. Rep. Congo
113 H4 **Moberly** U.S.A.
113 I5 **Mobile** U.S.A.
113 I5 **Mobile Bay** U.S.A.
113 F2 **Mobridge** U.S.A.
117 I4 **Mocajuba** Brazil
109 E5 **Moçambique** Moz.
98 C5 **Mocha** Yemen
109 C6 **Mochudi** Botswana
109 E5 **Mocimboa da Praia** Moz.
116 C3 **Mocoa** Col.
109 D5 **Mocuba** Moz.
105 F3 **Modena** Italy
112 B4 **Modesto** U.S.A.
95 E5 **Moe** Australia
98 C6 **Mogadishu** Somalia
Mogilev Podol'skiy Ukr. *see* **Mohyliv Podil's'kyy**
100 D1 **Mogocha** Rus. Fed.
101 B4 **Mogok** Myanmar
Mogontiacum Germany *see* **Mainz**
113 L3 **Mohawk** *r.* U.S.A.
Moheli *i.* Comoros *see* **Mwali**
109 D4 **Mohoro** Tanz.
103 L6 **Mohyliv Podil's'kyy** Ukr.
102 I2 **Mo i Rana** Norway
112 C4 **Mojave Desert** U.S.A.
107 D3 **Mokolo** Cameroon
100 E3 **Mokp'o** S. Korea
103 O5 **Moksha** *r.* Rus. Fed.
Moldavia *country* Europe *see* **Moldova**
Moldavskaya S.S.R. *country* Europe *see* **Moldova**
102 H3 **Molde** Norway
103 L6 **Moldova** *country* Europe
106 B4 **Mole National Park** Ghana
109 C6 **Molepolole** Botswana
116 D7 **Mollendo** Peru
Molodechno Belarus *see* **Maladzyechna**
Molotovsk *Arkhangel'skaya Oblast'* Rus. Fed. *see* **Severodvinsk**
Molotovsk *Kirovskaya Oblast'* Rus. Fed. *see* **Nolinsk**
107 D4 **Moloundou** Cameroon
113 G1 **Molson Lake** Canada
94 C2 **Moluccas** *is* Indon.
Molucca Sea *sea* Indon. *see* **Maluku, Laut**
109 D5 **Moma** Moz.
109 D4 **Mombasa** Kenya
103 I4 **Møn** *i.* Denmark
115 K5 **Mona, Isla** *i.* Puerto Rico
104 E3 **Monaco** *country* Europe
123 H4 **Monaco Basin** *sea feature* N. Atlantic Ocean

Ounianga Kébir

98 B3 Nicosia Cyprus
115 H7 Nicoya, Golfo de b. Costa Rica
115 G7 Nicoya, Península de pen. Costa Rica
107 D4 Niefang Equat. Guinea
106 B3 Niellé Côte d'Ivoire
104 E1 Nienburg (Weser) Germany
117 G2 Nieuw Amsterdam Suriname
117 G2 Nieuw Nickerie Suriname
105 J4 Niğde Turkey
106 C3 Niger country Africa
106 C4 Niger r. Africa
106 C4 Niger, Mouths of the Nigeria
123 J5 Niger Cone sea feature S. Atlantic Ocean
106 C4 Nigeria country Africa
100 F3 Niigata Japan
102 H5 Nijmegen Neth.
103 M2 Nikel' Rus. Fed.
106 C4 Nikki Benin
103 P5 Nikolayevka Rus. Fed.
103 P5 Nikolayevsk Rus. Fed.
Nikolayevskiy Rus. Fed. see Nikol'sk
103 P4 Nikol'sk Rus. Fed.
97 R4 Nikol'skoye Rus. Fed.
105 J2 Nikopol' Ukr.
105 K3 Niksar Turkey
105 G3 Nikšić Montenegro
95 I2 Nikumaroro atoll Kiribati
95 H2 Nikunau i. Kiribati
108 F1 Nile r. Africa
104 D3 Nîmes France
119 J5 Nimrod Glacier Antarctica
107 F4 Nimule Sudan
Nimwegen Neth. see Nijmegen
99 F6 Nine Degree Channel India
123 O8 Ninetyeast Ridge sea feature Indian Ocean
101 E4 Ningbo China
100 B3 Ningjing Shan mts China
119 J6 Ninnis Glacier Antarctica
113 G3 Niobrara r. U.S.A.
106 A3 Niokolo Koba, Parc National du nat. park Senegal
106 B3 Niono Mali
106 B3 Nioro Mali
104 C2 Niort France
111 H4 Nipawin Canada
113 I2 Nipigon Canada
113 I2 Nipigon, Lake Canada
113 K2 Nipissing, Lake Canada
117 I6 Niquelândia Brazil
99 F5 Nirmal India
105 H3 Niš Serbia
Nistru r. Moldova see Dniester
117 J8 Niterói Brazil
95 I3 Niuatoputopu i. Tonga
95 J3 Niue terr. Pacific Ocean
95 H3 Niulakita i. Tuvalu
95 H2 Niutao i. Tuvalu
97 R3 Nizhnekolymsk Rus. Fed.
100 B1 Nizhneudinsk Rus. Fed.
96 I3 Nizhnevartovsk Rus. Fed.
97 O2 Nizhneyansk Rus. Fed.
103 O5 Nizhniy Lomov Rus. Fed.
96 F4 Nizhniy Novgorod Rus. Fed.
103 Q3 Nizhniy Odes Rus. Fed.
103 O2 Nizhnyaya Mola Rus. Fed.
100 C1 Nizhnyaya Tunguska r. Rus. Fed.
103 M5 Nizhyn Ukr.
Nizza France see Nice
109 E5 Njazidja i. Comoros
109 D4 Njinjo Tanz.
109 D4 Njombe Tanz.
107 D4 Nkambe Cameroon
106 B4 Nkawkaw Ghana
109 C5 Nkayi Zimbabwe
109 D5 Nkhata Bay Malawi
109 D5 Nkhotakota Malawi
106 C4 Nkongsamba Cameroon
109 B5 Nkurenkuru Namibia
100 F3 Nobeoka Japan
117 F6 Noel Kempff Mercado, Parque Nacional nat. park Bol.
112 D5 Nogales Mex.
112 D5 Nogales U.S.A.
103 N4 Noginsk Rus. Fed.
108 B3 Nola Centr. Afr. Rep.
103 P4 Nolinsk Rus. Fed.
110 B3 Nome U.S.A.
101 C5 Nong Khai Thai.
95 H2 Nonouti atoll Kiribati
96 H6 Norak Tajik.
113 K2 Noranda Canada
96 D2 Nordaustlandet i. Svalbard
97 K2 Nordenshel'da, Arkhipelag is Rus. Fed.
Nordfriesische Inseln is Germany see North Frisian Islands
Nord Kap c. Iceland see Horn
103 I3 Nordli Norway
102 E3 Norðoyar i. Faroe Is
Noreg country Europe see Norway
113 G3 Norfolk U.S.A.
95 G4 Norfolk Island terr. Pacific Ocean
120 G7 Norfolk Island Ridge sea feature Tasman Sea
Norge country Europe see Norway
97 J3 Noril'sk Rus. Fed.
113 G4 Norman U.S.A.
95 F2 Normanby Island P.N.G.
Normandes, Îles is English Chan. see Channel Islands
95 E3 Normanton Australia
118 B6 Ñorquinco Arg.
103 J4 Norrköping Sweden
103 J4 Norrtälje Sweden
94 C5 Norseman Australia
95 G3 Norsup Vanuatu
118 D6 Norte, Punta pt Arg.
118 E5 Norte, Punta pt Arg.
119 I6 North, Cape Antarctica
121 I6 North America
94 B4 Northampton Australia
104 C1 Northampton U.K.
123 Q6 North Australian Basin sea feature Indian Ocean
112 E1 North Battleford Canada
113 K2 North Bay Canada
111 K4 North Belcher Islands Canada
96 D2 North Cape Norway
95 H5 North Cape N.Z.
113 H1 North Caribou Lake Canada
113 K4 North Carolina state U.S.A.
113 J2 North Channel lake channel Canada
102 E4 North Channel U.K.
113 F2 North Dakota state U.S.A.
121 I4 Northeast Pacific Basin sea feature Pacific Ocean
111 I4 Northern Indian Lake Canada
101 G5 Northern Mariana Islands terr. Pacific Ocean
Northern Sporades is Greece see Voreies Sporades
94 D3 Northern Territory admin. div. Australia
113 H3 Northfield U.S.A.
102 H5 North Frisian Islands Germany
111 K2 North Geomagnetic Pole Can.
95 H5 North Island N.Z.
109 D5 North Luangwa National Park Zambia
124 P1 North Magnetic Pole Arctic Ocean
113 F3 North Platte U.S.A.
113 F3 North Platte r. U.S.A.
124 A1 North Pole Arctic Ocean
110 G4 North Saskatchewan r. Canada
102 G4 North Sea Europe
110 D3 North Slope plain U.S.A.
95 H5 North Taranaki Bight b. N.Z.
102 E4 North Uist i. U.K.
111 L5 Northumberland Strait Canada
123 F1 Northwest Atlantic Mid-Ocean Channel N. Atlantic Ocean
94 B4 North West Cape Australia
120 F3 Northwest Pacific Basin sea feature N. Pacific Ocean
111 H3 Northwest Territories admin. div. Canada
124 N1 Northwind Ridge sea feature Arctic Ocean
109 D5 Norton Zimbabwe
110 B3 Norton Sound sea chan. U.S.A.
119 K3 Norvegia, Cape Antarctica
103 I3 Norway country Europe
113 G1 Norway House Canada
124 X2 Norwegian Basin sea feature N. Atlantic Ocean
111 I2 Norwegian Bay Canada
102 H2 Norwegian Sea N. Atlantic Ocean
104 D1 Norwich U.K.
103 Q2 Nosovaya Rus. Fed.
109 E6 Nosy Varika Madag.
113 M2 Notre-Dame, Monts mts Canada
111 M5 Notre Dame Bay Canada
104 C1 Nottingham U.K.
106 A2 Nouâdhibou Mauritania
106 A3 Nouakchott Mauritania
106 A3 Nouâmghâr Mauritania
95 G4 Nouméa New Caledonia
106 B3 Nouna Burkina
95 G4 Nouvelle-Calédonie i. S. Pacific Ocean
117 J8 Nova Friburgo Brazil
117 J8 Nova Iguaçu Brazil
103 M6 Nova Kakhovka Ukr.
104 E2 Novara Italy
111 L5 Nova Scotia prov. Canada
Novaya Kakhovka Ukr. see Nova Kakhovka
103 M3 Novaya Ladoga Rus. Fed.
97 Q2 Novaya Sibir', Ostrov i. Rus. Fed.
96 G2 Novaya Zemlya is Rus. Fed.
105 G2 Nové Zámky Slovakia
Novgorod-Volynskiy Ukr. see Novohrad-Volyns'kyy
105 G2 Novi Sad Serbia
105 L1 Novoanninskiy Rus. Fed.
117 F5 Novo Aripuanã Brazil
103 P4 Novocheboksarsk Rus. Fed.
105 L2 Novocherkassk Rus. Fed.
96 F3 Novodvinsk Rus. Fed.
118 F3 Novo Hamburgo Brazil
103 L5 Novohrad-Volyns'kyy Ukr.
100 A1 Novokuznetsk Rus. Fed.
119 K3 Novolazarevskaya research stn Antarctica
105 G2 Novo Mesto Slovenia
103 N5 Novomoskovsk Rus. Fed.
105 J2 Novooleksiyivka Ukr.
105 K3 Novorossiysk Rus. Fed.
97 L2 Novorybnaya Rus. Fed.
105 K2 Novoshakhtinsk Rus. Fed.
97 J4 Novosibirsk Rus. Fed.
Novosibirskiye Ostrova is Rus. Fed. see New Siberia Islands
105 K1 Novyy Oskol Rus. Fed.
96 I3 Novyy Port Rus. Fed.
96 I3 Novyy Urengoy Rus. Fed.
100 F1 Novyy Urgal Rus. Fed.
95 F5 Nowra Australia
103 K6 Nowy Sącz Poland
96 I3 Noyabr'sk Rus. Fed.
97 L5 Noyon Mongolia
109 D5 Nsanje Malawi
109 B4 Ntandembele Dem. Rep. Congo
109 D4 Ntungamo Uganda
107 F3 Nuba Mountains Sudan
107 F2 Nubian Desert Sudan
116 D7 Nudo Coropuna mt. Peru
111 I3 Nueltin Lake Canada
118 B6 Nueva Lubecka Arg.
114 D3 Nueva Rosita Mex.
115 I4 Nuevitas Cuba
118 D6 Nuevo, G. Arg.
112 E5 Nuevo Casas Grandes Mex.
113 G6 Nuevo Laredo Mex.
113 G6 Nuevo León state Mex.
108 E3 Nugaal watercourse Somalia
95 F2 Nuguria Islands P.N.G.
95 H2 Nui atoll Tuvalu
Nu Jiang r. China see Salween
95 I4 Nuku'alofa Tonga
Nuku'alofa Tonga see Nuku'alofa
95 H2 Nukufetau atoll Tuvalu
121 J6 Nuku Hiva i. Fr. Polynesia
95 H2 Nukulaelae atoll Tuvalu
95 F2 Nukumanu Islands P.N.G.
Nukunono i. Pacific Ocean see Nukunonu
95 I2 Nukunonu atoll Pacific Ocean
98 D2 Nukus Uzbek.
94 C4 Nullagine Australia
94 C5 Nullarbor Plain Australia
107 D4 Numan Nigeria
101 F7 Numfoor i. Indon.
111 N3 Nunakuluut i. Greenland
Nunap Isua c. Greenland see Farewell, Cape
111 H3 Nunavut admin. div. Canada
110 B4 Nunivak Island U.S.A.
110 A3 Nunligran Rus. Fed.
104 E3 Nuoro Italy
95 G3 Nupani i. Solomon Is
98 C4 Nuqrah Saudi Arabia
103 I6 Nuremberg Germany
103 L3 Nurmes Fin.
Nürnberg Germany see Nuremberg
124 U2 Nuuk Greenland
111 M2 Nuussuaq Greenland
111 M2 Nuussuaq pen. Greenland
96 H3 Nyagan' Rus. Fed.
101 B4 Nyainqêntanglha Shan mts China
107 E3 Nyala Sudan
109 C5 Nyamandhiovu Zimbabwe
103 O3 Nyandoma Rus. Fed.
109 B4 Nyanga r. Gabon
109 D5 Nyanga Zimbabwe
109 D5 Nyasa, Lake Africa
103 J4 Nybro Sweden
111 M1 Nyeboe Land reg. Greenland
109 D4 Nyeri Kenya
99 G3 Nyima China
101 B4 Nyingchi China
105 H2 Nyíregyháza Hungary
105 F1 Nykøbing Denmark
103 J4 Nyköping Sweden
103 J4 Nynäshamn Sweden
96 G3 Nyrob Rus. Fed.
Nystad Fin. see Uusikaupunki
109 C4 Nyunzu Dem. Rep. Congo
97 M3 Nyurba Rus. Fed.
109 D4 Nzega Tanz.
106 B4 Nzérékoré Guinea
109 B4 N'zeto Angola
109 E5 Nzwani i. Comoros

O

113 F3 Oahe, Lake U.S.A.
121 I4 O'ahu i. U.S.A.
Oahu i. U.S.A. see O'ahu
113 H5 Oakdale U.S.A.
112 B4 Oakland U.S.A.
94 C4 Oakover r. Australia
95 H6 Oamaru N.Z.
119 I6 Oates Land reg. Antarctica
114 E5 Oaxaca Mex.
96 H3 Ob' r. Rus. Fed.
107 D4 Obala Cameroon
101 E7 Obi i. Indon.
117 G4 Óbidos Brazil
100 F2 Obluch'ye Rus. Fed.
108 C3 Obo Centr. Afr. Rep.
108 E2 Obock Djibouti
109 C4 Obokote Dem. Rep. Congo
105 K1 Oboyan' Rus. Fed.
103 O3 Obozerskiy Rus. Fed.
112 E6 Obregón, Presa resr Mex.
96 I2 Obskaya Guba sea chan. Rus. Fed.
106 B4 Obuasi Ghana
103 P3 Ob"yachevo Rus. Fed.
113 J6 Ocala U.S.A.
116 E7 Occidental, Cordillera mts Chile
116 C3 Occidental, Cordillera mts Col.
116 C6 Occidental, Cordillera mts Peru
110 F4 Ocean Falls Canada
112 C5 Oceanside U.S.A.
113 J5 Oconee r. U.S.A.
106 B4 Oda Ghana
102 H3 Odda Norway
Ödenburg Hungary see Sopron
103 I4 Odense Denmark
Odesa Ukr. see Odessa
105 J2 Odessa Ukr.
113 F5 Odessa U.S.A.
106 B4 Odienné Côte d'Ivoire
105 G2 Odra r. Germany/Pol.
Oea Libya see Tripoli
117 J5 Oeiras Brazil
102 H5 Offenbach am Main Germany
104 E2 Offenburg Germany
108 E3 Ogadēn reg. Eth.
Ogasawara-shotō is Japan see Bonin Islands
106 C4 Ogbomosho Nigeria
Ogbomoso Nigeria see Ogbomosho
112 D3 Ogden U.S.A.
113 K3 Ogdensburg U.S.A.
110 E3 Ogilvie r. Canada
110 E3 Ogilvie Mountains Canada
106 C4 Ogoja Nigeria
113 I1 Ogoki r. Canada
103 K4 Ogre Latvia
119 L2 O'Higgins (Chile) research stn Antarctica
118 B7 O'Higgins, Lago l. Chile
113 J4 Ohio r. U.S.A.
113 J3 Ohio state U.S.A.
105 H3 Ohrid Macedonia
117 H3 Oiapoque Brazil
104 D2 Oise r. France
100 F3 Ōita Japan
113 F6 Ojinaga Mex.
118 C3 Ojos del Salado, Nevado mt. Arg.
103 O4 Oka r. Rus. Fed.
109 B6 Okahandja Namibia
109 B6 Okakarara Namibia
112 C1 Okanagan Lake Canada
112 C2 Okanogan r. U.S.A.
108 C3 Okapi, Parc National de la nat. park Dem. Rep. Congo
109 B5 Okaukuejo Namibia
109 C5 Okavango r. Botswana/Namibia
109 C5 Okavango Delta swamp Botswana
113 J6 Okeechobee, Lake U.S.A.
113 J5 Okefenokee Swamp U.S.A.
106 C4 Okene Nigeria
100 G1 Okha Rus. Fed.
97 P3 Okhotka r. Rus. Fed.
97 P4 Okhotsk Rus. Fed.
97 P4 Okhotsk, Sea of Rus. Fed.
Okhotskoye More sea Rus. Fed. see Okhotsk, Sea of
103 M5 Okhtyrka Ukr.
101 E4 Okinawa i. Japan
Okinawa-guntō is Japan see Okinawa-shotō
101 E4 Okinawa-shotō is Japan
113 G4 Oklahoma state U.S.A.
113 G4 Oklahoma City U.S.A.
109 B4 Okondja Gabon
112 D1 Okotoks Canada
103 M5 Okovskiy Les for. Rus. Fed.
109 B4 Okoyo Congo
103 O3 Oktyabr'skiy Arkhangel'skaya Oblast' Rus. Fed.
100 H1 Oktyabr'skiy Kamchatskiy Kray Rus. Fed.
96 G4 Oktyabr'skiy Respublika Bashkortostan Rus. Fed.
96 H3 Oktyabr'skoye Rus. Fed.
97 K2 Oktyabr'skoy Revolyutsii, Ostrov i. Rus. Fed.
103 M4 Okulovka Rus. Fed.
100 F2 Okushiri-tō i. Japan
103 J4 Öland i. Sweden
118 D5 Olavarría Arg.
104 E3 Olbia Italy
110 E3 Old Crow Canada
104 E1 Oldenburg Germany
112 D2 Oldman r. Canada
112 E1 Old Wives Lake Canada
113 K3 Olean U.S.A.
97 N4 Olekma r. Rus. Fed.
97 N3 Olekminsk Rus. Fed.
103 M6 Oleksandriya Ukr.
103 M2 Olenegorsk Rus. Fed.
97 M3 Olenek Rus. Fed.
97 N2 Olenek r. Rus. Fed.
97 N2 Olenekskiy Zaliv b. Rus. Fed.
Olenya Rus. Fed. see Olenegorsk
105 I1 Olevs'k Ukr.
Olimbos mt. Greece see Olympus, Mount
105 J4 Olimpos Beydağları Milli Parkı nat. park Turkey
117 L5 Olinda Brazil
109 D5 Olinga Moz.
Olisipo Port. see Lisbon
118 C3 Oliva, Cordillera de mts Arg./Chile
118 C2 Ollagüe Chile
116 C5 Olmos Peru
Olmütz Czech Rep. see Olomouc
103 J6 Olomouc Czech Rep.
103 M3 Olonets Rus. Fed.
100 D1 Olovyannaya Rus. Fed.
96 D4 Olsztyn Poland
Ol'viopol' Ukr. see Pervomays'k
112 B2 Olympia U.S.A.
Olympos mt. Greece see Olympus, Mount
105 H3 Olympus, Mount Greece
112 B2 Olympus, Mount U.S.A.
97 S4 Olyutorskiy, Mys c. Rus. Fed.
97 R4 Olyutorskiy Zaliv b. Rus. Fed.
102 E5 Omagh U.K.
113 G3 Omaha U.S.A.
98 D4 Oman, Gulf of Asia
109 B6 Omaruru Namibia
109 B5 Omatako watercourse Namibia
116 D7 Omate Peru
109 A4 Omboué Gabon
107 F3 Omdurman Sudan
108 D2 Om Hajēr Eritrea
97 R3 Omolon Rus. Fed.
97 Q3 Omolon r. Rus. Fed.
108 D3 Omo National Park Eth.
96 I4 Omsk Rus. Fed.
97 Q3 Omsukchan Rus. Fed.
103 Q4 Omutninsk Rus. Fed.
109 B5 Oncócua Angola
109 B5 Ondangwa Namibia
109 B5 Ondjiva Angola
106 C4 Ondo Nigeria
100 D2 Öndörhaan Mongolia
103 N3 Onega Rus. Fed.
103 N3 Onega r. Rus. Fed.
Onega Bay g. Rus. Fed. see Onezhskaya Guba
100 H2 Onekotan, Ostrov i. Rus. Fed.
103 N3 Onezhskaya Guba g. Rus. Fed.
96 E3 Onezhskoye Ozero Rus. Fed.
109 B4 Onga Gabon
109 E6 Onilahy r. Madag.
106 C4 Onitsha Nigeria
95 I4 Ono-i-Lau i. Fiji
95 H2 Onotoa atoll Kiribati
94 B4 Onslow Australia
113 K5 Onslow Bay U.S.A.
113 H1 Ontario prov. Canada
113 K3 Ontario, Lake Canada/U.S.A.
95 F2 Ontong Java Atoll Solomon Is
94 D4 Oodnadatta Australia
Oostende Belgium see Ostend
110 F4 Ootsa Lake l. Canada
109 C4 Opala Dem. Rep. Congo
103 P4 Oparino Rus. Fed.
105 G2 Opava Czech Rep.
113 I5 Opelika U.S.A.
103 L4 Opochka Rus. Fed.
103 J5 Opole Poland
104 B3 Oporto Port.
Oppeln Poland see Opole
109 B5 Opuwo Namibia
103 K6 Oradea Romania
104 C4 Oran Alg.
118 D2 Orán Arg.
95 E5 Orange Australia
122 F6 Orange r. Namibia/S. Africa
113 H5 Orange U.S.A.
117 H3 Orange, Cabo c. Brazil
113 J5 Orangeburg U.S.A.
123 J8 Orange Cone sea feature S. Atlantic Ocean
115 G5 Orange Walk Belize
109 B6 Oranjemund Namibia
109 C6 Orapa Botswana
105 F3 Orbetello Italy
119 J2 Orcadas research stn S. Atlantic Ocean
116 E1 Orchila, Isla i. Venez.
94 C3 Ord r. Australia
94 C3 Ord, Mount h. Australia
105 K3 Ordu Turkey
103 J4 Örebro Sweden
112 B3 Oregon state U.S.A.
112 B2 Oregon City U.S.A.
103 N4 Orekhovo-Zuyevo Rus. Fed.
96 E4 Orel Rus. Fed.
100 F1 Orel', Ozero l. Rus. Fed.
Ore Mountains mts Czech Rep./Germany see Erzgebirge
98 D1 Orenburg Rus. Fed.
Orense Spain see Ourense
112 D5 Organ Pipe Cactus National Monument nat. park U.S.A.
116 E7 Oriental, Cordillera mts Bol.
116 D2 Oriental, Cordillera mts Col.
116 D6 Oriental, Cordillera mts Peru
113 K3 Orillia Canada
117 F2 Orinoco r. Col./Venez.
117 F2 Orinoco Delta Venez.
99 G4 Orissa state India
104 E4 Oristano Italy
117 G4 Oriximiná Brazil
114 E5 Orizaba Mex.
114 E5 Orizaba, Pico de vol. Mex.
102 F4 Orkney Islands U.K.
113 J6 Orlando U.S.A.
104 D2 Orléans France
Orléansville Alg. see Chlef
103 J3 Örnsköldsvik Sweden
116 D3 Orocué Col.
106 B3 Orodara Burkina
95 I2 Orona atoll Kiribati
101 E6 Oroquieta Phil.
117 K5 Orós, Açude resr Brazil
103 M5 Orsha Belarus
98 D1 Orsk Rus. Fed.
102 H3 Ørsta Norway
104 B3 Ortigueira Spain
97 N3 Orulgan, Khrebet mts Rus. Fed.
Orūmīyeh, Daryācheh-ye salt l. Iran see Urmia, Lake
116 E7 Oruro Bol.
115 H7 Osa, Península de pen. Costa Rica
100 F3 Ōsaka Japan
99 F2 Osh Kyrg.
109 B5 Oshakati Namibia
113 K3 Oshawa Canada
100 F2 Ō-shima i. Japan
113 I3 Oshkosh U.S.A.
106 C4 Oshogbo Nigeria
109 B4 Oshwe Dem. Rep. Congo
105 G2 Osijek Croatia
Osipenko Ukr. see Berdyans'k
Osipovichi Belarus see Asipovichy
103 J4 Oskarshamn Sweden
96 C4 Oslo Norway
105 J3 Osmancık Turkey
105 K4 Osmaniye Turkey
104 E1 Osnabrück Germany
118 B6 Osorno Chile
95 E3 Osprey Reef Coral Sea Is Terr.
95 E6 Ossa, Mount Australia
103 M4 Ostashkov Rus. Fed.
102 G5 Ostend Belgium
Ostende Belgium see Ostend
Österreich country Europe see Austria
103 I3 Östersund Sweden
Ostfriesische Inseln is Germany see East Frisian Islands
103 J3 Östhammar Sweden
105 G2 Ostrava Czech Rep.
105 G1 Ostróda Poland
103 L4 Ostrov Rus. Fed.
Ostrovets Poland see Ostrowiec Świętokrzyski
Ostrów Poland see Ostrów Wielkopolski
Ostrowiec Poland see Ostrowiec Świętokrzyski
103 K5 Ostrowiec Świętokrzyski Poland
105 H1 Ostrów Mazowiecka Poland
Ostrowo Poland see Ostrów Wielkopolski
103 J5 Ostrów Wielkopolski Poland
100 F3 Ōsumi-shotō is Japan
113 K3 Oswego U.S.A.
95 H6 Otago Peninsula N.Z.
100 G2 Otaru Japan
116 C3 Otavalo Ecuador
109 B5 Otavi Namibia
109 B6 Otjiwarongo Namibia
105 G3 Otranto, Strait of Albania/Italy
113 K2 Ottawa Canada
113 L2 Ottawa r. Canada
113 G4 Ottawa U.S.A.
111 J4 Ottawa Islands Canada
111 J1 Otto Fiord inlet Canada
113 H3 Ottumwa U.S.A.
106 C4 Otukpo Nigeria
118 D3 Otumpa Arg.
116 C5 Otuzco Peru
95 E5 Otway, Cape Australia
113 H5 Ouachita r. U.S.A.
113 H5 Ouachita, Lake U.S.A.
113 H5 Ouachita Mountains U.S.A.
106 A2 Ouadâne Mauritania
108 C3 Ouadda Centr. Afr. Rep.
107 E3 Ouaddaï reg. Chad
106 B3 Ouagadougou Burkina
106 B3 Ouahigouya Burkina
Ouahran Alg. see Oran
106 B3 Oualâta Mauritania
108 C3 Ouanda-Djallé Centr. Afr. Rep.
106 B2 Ouarâne reg. Mauritania
104 E5 Ouargla Alg.
106 B1 Ouarzazate Morocco
106 B1 Oued Zem Morocco
108 B3 Ouesso Congo
104 B5 Ouezzane Morocco
106 C4 Ouidah Benin
104 C5 Oujda Morocco
104 E5 Ouled Djellal Alg.
104 D5 Ouled Naïl, Monts des mts Alg.
96 D3 Oulu Fin.
103 L3 Oulujärvi l. Fin.
107 E3 Oum-Chalouba Chad
106 B4 Oumé Côte d'Ivoire
107 D3 Oum-Hadjer Chad
107 E3 Ounianga Kébir Chad

Ourense

104 B3 Ourense Spain
117 J5 Ouricurí Brazil
117 I8 Ourinhos Brazil
102 E4 Outer Hebrides is U.K.
109 B6 Outjo Namibia
112 E1 Outlook Canada
95 G4 Ouvéa atoll New Caledonia
95 H3 Ovalau i. Fiji
118 B4 Ovalle Chile
104 B3 Oviedo Spain
103 I3 Øvre Rendal Norway
105 I1 Ovruch Ukr.
109 B4 Owando Congo
113 I4 Owensboro U.S.A.
113 J3 Owen Sound Canada
95 E2 Owen Stanley Range mts P.N.G.
106 C4 Owerri Nigeria
106 C4 Owo Nigeria
112 C3 Owyhee r. U.S.A.
116 C6 Oxapampa Peru
104 C1 Oxford U.K.
113 I5 Oxford U.S.A.
112 C5 Oxnard U.S.A.
117 H3 Oyapock r. Brazil/Fr. Guiana
108 B3 Oyem Gabon
113 I5 Ozark U.S.A.
113 H4 Ozark Plateau U.S.A.
100 H1 Ozernovskiy Rus. Fed.

P

111 N3 Paamiut Greenland
99 E4 Pab Range mts Pak.
117 F6 Pacaás Novos, Parque Nacional nat. park Brazil
116 C5 Pacasmayo Peru
114 E4 Pachuca Mex.
121 I9 Pacific-Antarctic Ridge sea feature Pacific Ocean
119 H7 Pacific Ocean World
117 H4 Pacoval Brazil
101 C7 Padang Indon.
103 M3 Padany Rus. Fed.
118 D2 Padcaya Bol.
104 E1 Paderborn Germany
118 D1 Padilla Bol.
113 G6 Padre Island U.S.A.
105 F2 Padua Italy
113 I4 Paducah U.S.A.
Pafos Cyprus see Paphos
101 E6 Pagadian Phil.
101 C7 Pagai Utara i. Indon.
101 G5 Pagan i. N. Mariana Is
112 D4 Page U.S.A.
118 □ Paget, Mount Atlantic Ocean
103 L3 Päijänne l. Fin.
112 D4 Painted Desert U.S.A.
102 F4 Paisley U.K.
116 B5 Paita Peru
117 K5 Pajeú r. Brazil
117 F3 Pakaraima Mountains Brazil
117 F2 Pakaraima Mountains Guyana
97 R3 Pakhachi Rus. Fed.
101 C5 Pakxé Laos
107 D4 Pala Chad
101 C7 Palabuhanratu, Teluk b. Indon.
97 Q4 Palana Rus. Fed.
99 F4 Palanpur India
109 C6 Palapye Botswana
97 Q3 Palatka Rus. Fed.
101 F6 Palau country Pacific Ocean
120 D5 Palau Islands Palau
120 D5 Palau Trench sea feature N. Pacific Ocean
101 B5 Palaw Myanmar
101 D6 Palawan i. Phil.
123 Q5 Palawan Trough sea feature N. Pacific Ocean
103 K4 Paldiski Estonia
101 C7 Palembang Indon.
118 B6 Palena Chile
104 C3 Palencia Spain
115 F5 Palenque Mex.
105 F4 Palermo Italy
113 G5 Palestine U.S.A.
99 F4 Pali India
103 P5 Pallasovka Rus. Fed.
95 H6 Palliser, Cape N.Z.
104 D4 Palma de Mallorca Spain
117 I6 Palmas Brazil
106 B4 Palmas, Cape Liberia
117 K5 Palmeira dos Índios Brazil
117 J5 Palmeirais Brazil
119 L2 Palmer research stn Antarctica
110 D3 Palmer U.S.A.
91 Palmer Land pen. Antarctica
121 I7 Palmerston atoll Cook Is
95 H6 Palmerston North N.Z.
105 G4 Palmi Italy
116 C3 Palmira Col.
121 I5 Palmyra Atoll terr. N. Pacific Ocean
107 F3 Paloich Sudan
101 E7 Palopo Indon.
101 D7 Palu Indon.
97 S3 Palyavaam r. Rus. Fed.
Palyeskaya Nizina marsh Belarus/Ukr. see Pripet Marshes
113 K4 Pamlico Sound sea chan. U.S.A.
117 F7 Pampa Grande Bol.
Pampeluna Spain see Pamplona
104 C3 Pamplona Spain
99 F5 Panaji India
115 I7 Panamá, Canal de Panama
Panamá, Golfo de g. Panama see Panama, Gulf of
115 I7 Panama, Gulf of Panama
115 I7 Panama City Panama
113 I5 Panama City U.S.A.
101 E5 Panay i. Phil.
105 H3 Pančevo Serbia
Pancsova Serbia see Pančevo
Paneas Syria see Bāniyās
103 K4 Panevėžys Lith.
101 D7 Pangkalanbuun Indon.
101 B6 Pangkalansusu Indon.
101 C7 Pangkalpinang Indon.
101 E7 Pangkalsiang, Tanjung pt Indon.
111 L3 Pangnirtung Canada
96 I3 Pangody Rus. Fed.
109 C4 Pania-Mwanga Dem. Rep. Congo
99 E4 Panjgur Pak.
106 C4 Pankshin Nigeria
94 B4 Pannawonica Australia
Panormus Italy see Palermo
117 G7 Pantanal Matogrossense, Parque Nacional do nat. park Brazil
105 F4 Pantelleria, Isola di i. Italy
114 E4 Pánuco Mex.
101 C4 Panzhihua China
109 B4 Panzi Dem. Rep. Congo
108 B3 Paoua Centr. Afr. Rep.
105 G2 Pápa Hungary
114 E4 Papantla Mex.
105 J5 Paphos Cyprus
Paphus Cyprus see Paphos
95 E2 Papua, Gulf of P.N.G.
95 E2 Papua New Guinea country Oceania
Papun Myanmar see Hpapun
117 I4 Pará, Rio do r. Brazil
94 B4 Paraburdoo Australia
117 I7 Paracatu Brazil
101 D5 Paracel Islands S. China Sea
Paraetonium Egypt see Marsá Maţrūḩ
117 F6 Paragua r. Bol.
117 G7 Paraguai r. Brazil
118 E3 Paraguay r. Arg./Para.
118 E2 Paraguay country S. America
117 K5 Paraíba r. Brazil
106 C4 Parakou Benin
117 G2 Paramaribo Suriname
116 C2 Paramillo, Parque Nacional nat. park Col.
100 H1 Paramushir, Ostrov i. Rus. Fed.
118 D4 Paraná Arg.
117 I6 Paranã Brazil
117 I6 Paraná r. Brazil
118 E4 Paraná r. S. America
118 F1 Paranaíba Brazil
118 F2 Paranaíba r. Brazil
118 F2 Paranapanema r. Brazil
118 F2 Paranavaí Brazil
117 H7 Paraúna Brazil
117 K7 Pardo r. Brazil
118 F2 Pardo r. Brazil
105 G1 Pardubice Czech Rep.
99 G4 Pare Chu r. China
117 F6 Parecis, Serra dos hills Brazil
101 D7 Parepare Indon.
117 F1 Paria, Gulf of Trin. and Tob./Venez.
117 F3 Parima, Serra mts Brazil
117 F3 Parima-Tapirapecó, Parque Nacional nat. park Venez.
116 B4 Pariñas, Punta pt Peru
117 G4 Parintins Brazil
102 G6 Paris France
113 G5 Paris U.S.A.
103 K3 Parkano Fin.
95 E5 Parkes Australia
105 F3 Parma Italy
117 J4 Parnaíba Brazil
117 J4 Parnaíba r. Brazil
105 H4 Parnassus, Mount Greece
96 D4 Pärnu Estonia
105 I4 Paros i. Greece
113 F6 Parras Mex.
110 F2 Parry, Cape Canada
110 G2 Parry Islands Canada
113 J2 Parry Sound Canada
117 H4 Paru r. Brazil
112 C5 Pasadena U.S.A.
116 B4 Pasado, Cabo c. Ecuador
113 I5 Pascagoula U.S.A.
105 I2 Paşcani Romania
Pascua, Isla de i. S. Pacific Ocean see Easter Island
Pas de Calais str. France/U.K. see Dover, Strait of
111 H4 Pasfield Lake Canada
101 C6 Pasir Putih Malaysia
99 E4 Pasni Pak.
118 B7 Paso Río Mayo Arg.
105 F2 Passau Germany
118 F3 Passo Fundo Brazil
117 I8 Passos Brazil
103 L4 Pastavy Belarus
116 C4 Pastaza r. Peru
116 C3 Pasto Col.
118 B7 Patagonia reg. Arg.
Patavium Italy see Padua
113 L3 Paterson U.S.A.
112 E3 Pathfinder Reservoir U.S.A.
99 G4 Patna India
117 K5 Patos Brazil
118 F4 Patos, Lagoa dos l. Brazil
117 I7 Patos de Minas Brazil
118 C4 Patquía Arg.
Patra Greece see Patras
Patrae Greece see Patras
Pátrai Greece see Patras
105 H4 Patras Greece
117 I7 Patrocínio Brazil
114 D5 Pátzcuaro Mex.
104 C3 Pau France
117 J5 Paulistana Brazil
117 K5 Paulo Afonso Brazil
113 G5 Pauls Valley U.S.A.
99 F1 Pavlodar Kazakh.
Pavlograd Ukr. see Pavlohrad
103 N6 Pavlohrad Ukr.
105 L1 Pavlovsk Rus. Fed.
105 K2 Pavlovskaya Rus. Fed.
101 C7 Payakumbuh Indon.
96 H3 Pay-Khoy, Khrebet hills Rus. Fed.
111 K4 Payne, Lac l. Canada
118 E4 Paysandú Uruguay
110 G4 Peace r. Canada
110 G4 Peace River Canada
112 E4 Peale, Mount U.S.A.
113 I5 Pearl r. U.S.A.
111 H2 Peary Channel Canada
109 D5 Pebane Moz.
105 H3 Peć Kosovo
103 R2 Pechora Rus. Fed.
103 Q2 Pechora r. Rus. Fed.
113 F5 Pecos U.S.A.
113 F5 Pecos r. U.S.A.
105 G2 Pécs Hungary
117 J4 Pedreiras Brazil
117 I5 Pedro Afonso Brazil
118 C2 Pedro de Valdivia Chile
117 J4 Pedro II Brazil
118 E2 Pedro Juan Caballero Para.
Pedro Segundo Brazil see Pedro II
113 K5 Pee Dee r. U.S.A.
110 E3 Peel r. Canada
95 H6 Pegasus Bay N.Z.
101 B5 Pegu Myanmar
118 D5 Pehuajó Arg.
96 D4 Peipus, Lake Estonia/Rus. Fed.
Peiraias Greece see Piraeus
117 I6 Peixe Brazil
Pejë Kosovo see Peć
Peking China see Beijing
101 E7 Peleng i. Indon.
95 E2 Pelleluhu Islands P.N.G.
Pelly Bay Canada see Kugaaruk
110 E3 Pelly Mountains Canada
118 F4 Pelotas Brazil
118 F3 Pelotas, Rio das r. Brazil
101 C6 Pemangkat Indon.
109 E5 Pemba Moz.
109 C5 Pemba Zambia
109 D4 Pemba Island Tanz.
113 K2 Pembroke Canada
Peña Cerredo mt. Spain see Torrecerredo
114 E4 Peña Nevada, Co mt. Mex.
118 A7 Penas, Golfo de g. Chile
119 K6 Penck, Cape Antarctica
106 C3 Pendjari, Parc National de la nat. park Benin
112 C2 Pendleton U.S.A.
109 C4 Penge Dem. Rep. Congo
101 C6 Peninsular Malaysia Malaysia
102 F5 Pennines hills U.K.
113 K3 Pennsylvania state U.S.A.
111 L3 Penny Icecap Canada
113 M3 Penobscot r. U.S.A.
94 D5 Penong Australia
121 I6 Penrhyn atoll Cook Is
121 I6 Penrhyn Basin sea feature Pacific Ocean
113 I5 Pensacola U.S.A.
119 J4 Pensacola Mountains Antarctica
95 G3 Pentecost Island Vanuatu
112 C2 Penticton Canada
103 P5 Penza Rus. Fed.
104 B1 Penzance U.K.
97 R3 Penzhinskaya Guba b. Rus. Fed.
113 I3 Peoria U.S.A.
95 F4 Percy Isles Australia
96 H3 Peregrebnoye Rus. Fed.
116 C3 Pereira Col.
118 D4 Pergamino Arg.
118 C2 Perico Arg.
104 D2 Périgueux France
116 D2 Perija, Sierra de mts Venez.
118 B7 Perito Moreno Arg.
115 H6 Perlas, Punta de pt Nicaragua
96 G4 Perm' Rus. Fed.
Pernambuco Abyssal Plain sea feature S. Atlantic Ocean see Pernambuco Plain
122 C5 Pernambuco Plain sea feature S. Atlantic Ocean
105 H3 Pernik Bulg.
104 D3 Perpignan France
113 F4 Perryton U.S.A.
Persia country Asia see Iran
94 B5 Perth Australia
102 F4 Perth U.K.
123 Q7 Perth Basin sea feature Indian Ocean
103 N3 Pertominsk Rus. Fed.
116 C5 Peru country S. America
123 D6 Peru Basin sea feature S. Pacific Ocean
121 N6 Peru-Chile Trench sea feature S. Pacific Ocean
105 F3 Perugia Italy
Perusia Italy see Perugia
103 O5 Pervomaysk Rus. Fed.
103 M6 Pervomays'k Ukr.
97 R3 Pervorechenskiy Rus. Fed.
105 F3 Pesaro Italy
105 F3 Pescara Italy
105 L2 Peschanokopskoye Rus. Fed.
99 F3 Peshawar Pak.
103 N4 Pestovo Rus. Fed.
114 D5 Petatlán Mex.
109 D5 Petauke Zambia
113 K3 Peterborough Canada
104 C1 Peterborough U.K.
119 I3 Peter I Island Antarctica
111 I3 Peter Lake Canada
94 C4 Petermann Ranges mts Australia
111 H4 Peter Pond Lake Canada
113 K4 Petersburg U.S.A.
Petitjean Morocco see Sidi Kacem
111 L4 Petit Mécatina r. Canada
115 G4 Peto Mex.
113 J2 Petoskey U.S.A.
100 F2 Petra Velikogo, Zaliv b. Rus. Fed.
Petrikau Poland see Piotrków Trybunalski
Petrokov Poland see Piotrków Trybunalski
117 J5 Petrolina Brazil
96 H4 Petropavlovsk Kazakh.
100 H1 Petropavlovsk-Kamchatskiy Rus. Fed.
103 P5 Petrovsk Rus. Fed.
Petrovskoye Rus. Fed. see Svetlograd
100 C1 Petrovsk-Zabaykal'skiy Rus. Fed.
103 M3 Petrozavodsk Rus. Fed.
96 H4 Petukhovo Rus. Fed.
97 S3 Pevek Rus. Fed.
103 O2 Peza r. Rus. Fed.
104 E2 Pforzheim Germany
101 B6 Phangnga Thai.
101 C5 Phanom Dong Rak, Thiu Khao mts Cambodia/Thai.
Phan Rang Vietnam see Phan Rang-Thap Cham
99 I5 Phan Rang-Thap Cham Vietnam
101 C5 Phan Thiêt Vietnam
101 C6 Phatthalung Thai.
101 B5 Phayao Thai.
111 H4 Phelps Lake Canada
113 I5 Phenix City U.S.A.
101 B5 Phet Buri Thai.
Philadelphia Jordan see 'Ammān
Philadelphia Turkey see Alaşehir
113 K4 Philadelphia U.S.A.
Philippeville Alg. see Skikda
123 R4 Philippine Basin sea feature N. Pacific Ocean
120 D4 Philippines country Asia
123 R4 Philippine Trench sea feature N. Pacific Ocean
Philippopolis Bulg. see Plovdiv
110 D3 Philip Smith Mountains U.S.A.
111 I1 Phillips Inlet Canada
Philomelium Turkey see Akşehir
101 C5 Phitsanulok Thai.
101 C5 Phnom Penh Cambodia
Phnum Pénh Cambodia see Phnom Penh
112 D5 Phoenix U.S.A.
95 I2 Phoenix Islands Pacific Ocean
101 C4 Phôngsali Laos
101 C5 Phônsavan Laos
101 C5 Phrae Thai.
101 B6 Phuket Thai.
117 I5 Piaca Brazil
104 E2 Piacenza Italy
105 I2 Piatra Neamţ Romania
117 J5 Piauí r. Brazil
107 F4 Pibor r. Sudan
107 F4 Pibor Post Sudan
118 D2 Pichanal Arg.
118 B4 Pichilemu Chile
112 D7 Pichilingue Mex.
116 E3 Pico da Neblina, Parque Nacional do nat. park Brazil
117 J5 Picos Brazil
118 C7 Pico Truncado Arg.
118 E5 Piedras, Punta pt Arg.
116 D6 Piedras, Río de las r. Peru
113 F6 Piedras Negras Mex.
103 L3 Pielinen l. Fin.
113 F3 Pierre U.S.A.
Pietersaari Fin. see Jakobstad
Pietersburg S. Africa see Polokwane
105 H2 Pietrosa mt. Romania
118 D5 Pigüé Arg.
103 L3 Pihtipudas Fin.
115 F5 Pijijiapan Mex.
113 F4 Pikes Peak U.S.A.
113 J4 Pikeville U.S.A.
103 J5 Piła Poland
118 E4 Pilar Arg.
118 E3 Pilar Para.
118 E2 Pilcomayo r. Bol./Para.
Pillau Rus. Fed. see Baltiysk
Pílos Greece see Pylos
Pilsen Czech Rep. see Plzeň
117 F6 Pimenta Bueno Brazil
118 E5 Pinamar Arg.
101 C6 Pinang i. Malaysia
105 K4 Pınarbaşı Turkey
115 H4 Pinar del Río Cuba
117 I4 Pindaré r. Brazil
Píndhos Óros mts Greece see Pindus Mountains
Pindos mts Greece see Pindus Mountains
105 H4 Pindus Mountains Greece
113 H5 Pine Bluff U.S.A.
101 F8 Pine Creek Australia
103 O3 Pinega Rus. Fed.
103 O3 Pinega r. Rus. Fed.
119 I3 Pine Island Bay Antarctica
110 G3 Pine Point (abandoned) Canada
100 D3 Pingdingshan China
101 C4 Pingxiang Guangxi China
101 D4 Pingxiang Jiangxi China
117 I4 Pinheiro Brazil
114 E5 Pinotepa Nacional Mex.
95 G4 Pins, Île des i. New Caledonia
105 I1 Pinsk Belarus
116 □ Pinta, Isla i. Ecuador
112 D4 Pioche U.S.A.
109 C4 Piodi Dem. Rep. Congo
97 J1 Pioner, Ostrov i. Rus. Fed.
117 F4 Piorini, Lago l. Brazil
103 J5 Piotrków Trybunalski Poland
113 L2 Pipmuacan, Réservoir resr Canada
118 F2 Piquiri r. Brazil
117 I8 Piracicaba Brazil
117 J4 Piracuruca Brazil
105 H4 Piraeus Greece
Piráievs Greece see Piraeus
117 I8 Pirajuí Brazil
117 K5 Piranhas r. Brazil
Pírgos Greece see Pyrgos
Pirineos mts Europe see Pyrenees
117 J4 Piripiri Brazil
101 E7 Piru Indon.
105 F3 Pisa Italy
Pisae Italy see Pisa
118 B1 Pisagua Chile
Pisaurum Italy see Pesaro
116 C6 Pisco Peru
116 C6 Pisco, Bahía de b. Peru
105 F2 Písek Czech Rep.
118 C3 Pissis, Cerro mt. Arg.
112 B3 Pit r. U.S.A.
106 A3 Pita Guinea
121 K7 Pitcairn Island S. Pacific Ocean
103 K2 Piteå Sweden
105 H3 Pitești Romania
103 M3 Pitkyaranta Rus. Fed.
95 I6 Pitt Island Pacific Ocean
113 K3 Pittsburgh U.S.A.
116 B5 Piura Peru
Placentia Italy see Piacenza
115 I4 Placetas Cuba
113 F5 Plainview U.S.A.
97 U4 Platinum U.S.A.
116 D2 Plato Col.
113 G3 Platte r. U.S.A.
105 F1 Plauen Germany
103 N5 Plavsk Rus. Fed.
116 B4 Playas Ecuador
118 C5 Plaza Huincul Arg.
113 G6 Pleasanton U.S.A.
95 H5 Plenty, Bay of g. N.Z.
103 O3 Plesetsk Rus. Fed.
113 L1 Plétipi, Lac l. Canada
105 H3 Pleven Bulg.
Plevna Bulg. see Pleven
103 J5 Płock Poland
98 A2 Ploiești Romania
105 H3 Plovdiv Bulg.
Plozk Poland see Płock
104 C1 Plymouth U.K.
103 I6 Plzeň Czech Rep.
106 B3 Pô Burkina
106 B3 Pô, Parc National de nat. park Burkina
123 P10 Pobeda Ice Island Antarctica
97 J5 Pobeda Peak China/Kyrg.
113 H4 Pocahontas U.S.A.
112 D3 Pocatello U.S.A.
105 J1 Pochep Rus. Fed.
117 G7 Poconé Brazil
117 I8 Poços de Caldas Brazil
105 G3 Podgorica Montenegro
97 J4 Podgornoye Rus. Fed.
97 K3 Podkamennaya Tunguska r. Rus. Fed.
116 C4 Podocarpus, Parque Nacion nat. park Ecuador
103 N4 Podol'sk Rus. Fed.
103 M3 Podporozh'ye Rus. Fed.
109 C4 Poie Dem. Rep. Congo
119 K6 Poinsett, Cape Antarctica
115 L5 Pointe-à-Pitre Guadeloupe
109 B4 Pointe-Noire Congo
110 B3 Point Hope U.S.A.
110 G3 Point Lake Canada
102 G6 Poitiers France
99 F4 Pokaran India
103 R3 Pokcha Rus. Fed.
108 C3 Poko Dem. Rep. Congo
97 N3 Pokrovsk Rus. Fed.
Pola Croatia see Pula
103 J5 Poland country Europe
119 J4 Polar Plateau Antarctica
103 L4 Polatsk Belarus
99 E3 Pol-e Khomrī Afgh.
Poles'ye marsh Belarus/Ukr. see Pripet Marshes
94 B2 Polewali Indon.
107 D4 Poli Cameroon
Poli Cyprus see Polis
101 E5 Polillo Islands Phil.
105 J4 Polis Cyprus
Políyiros Greece see Polygyro
105 G4 Pollino, Monte mt. Italy
Pologi Ukr. see Polohy
103 N6 Polohy Ukr.
109 C6 Polokwane S. Africa
Polotsk Belarus see Polatsk
Polska country Europe see Poland
105 J2 Poltava Ukr.
Polyanovgrad Bulg. see Karnobat
97 S3 Polyarnyy Chukotskiy Avtonomnyy Okrug Rus. Fed.
103 M2 Polyarnyy Murmanskaya Oblast' Rus. Fed.
103 M2 Polyarnyye Zori Rus. Fed.
105 H3 Polygyros Greece
95 F2 Pomio P.N.G.
113 G4 Ponca City U.S.A.
115 K5 Ponce Puerto Rico
111 K2 Pond Inlet Canada
104 B3 Ponferrada Spain
107 E4 Pongo watercourse Sudan
106 □ Ponta do Sol Cape Verde
118 F3 Ponta Grossa Brazil
117 G7 Pontes-e-Lacerda Brazil
101 C7 Pontianak Indon.
Poona India see Pune
118 C1 Poopó, Lago de l. Bol.
116 C3 Popayán Col.
97 L2 Popigay r. Rus. Fed.
113 G1 Poplar r. Canada
113 H4 Poplar Bluff U.S.A.
114 E5 Popocatépetl, Volcán vol. Me
109 B4 Popokabaka Dem. Rep. Cong
105 H2 Poprad Slovakia
117 I6 Porangatu Brazil
99 E4 Porbandar India
110 E3 Porcupine r. Canada/U.S.A.
123 H2 Porcupine Abyssal Plain sea feature N. Atlantic Ocean
103 P4 Poretskoye Rus. Fed.
96 D3 Pori Fin.
103 L4 Porkhov Rus. Fed.
117 F1 Porlamar Venez.
100 G2 Poronaysk Rus. Fed.
103 M3 Porosozero Rus. Fed.
102 H4 Porsgrunn Norway
113 G2 Portage la Prairie Canada
112 B2 Port Alberni Canada
104 B4 Portalegre Port.
113 F5 Portales U.S.A.
112 B2 Port Angeles U.S.A.
95 E6 Port Arthur Australia
113 H6 Port Arthur U.S.A.
94 D5 Port Augusta Australia
115 J5 Port-au-Prince Haiti
99 H5 Port Blair India
113 J6 Port Charlotte U.S.A.
115 J5 Port-de-Paix Haiti
117 H4 Portel Brazil
109 A4 Port-Gentil Gabon
106 C4 Port Harcourt Nigeria
112 A1 Port Hardy Canada
94 B4 Port Hedland Australia
117 G2 Port Kaituma Guyana
Port Láirge Ireland see Waterford
95 E5 Portland Australia
113 L3 Portland ME U.S.A.
112 B2 Portland OR U.S.A.
104 B1 Portlaoise Ireland
113 G6 Port Lavaca U.S.A.
94 D5 Port Lincoln Australia
106 A4 Port Loko Sierra Leone
Port-Lyautey Morocco see Kenitra
95 F5 Port Macquarie Australia
110 B4 Port Moller b. U.S.A.
95 E2 Port Moresby P.N.G.
Porto Port. see Oporto
116 E5 Porto Acre Brazil
118 F4 Porto Alegre Brazil
117 G6 Porto Artur Brazil
117 G6 Porto dos Gaúchos Óbidos Brazil
117 G7 Porto Esperidião Brazil
117 I5 Porto Franco Brazil
117 F1 Port of Spain Trin. and Tob.

Q

R

S

South East Cape

99 F2 Sarkand Kazakh.
05 I3 Şarköy Turkey
01 F7 Sarmi Indon.
13 J3 Sarnia Canada
05 I1 Sarny Ukr.
99 F2 Saryozek Kazakh.
99 F2 Saryshagan Kazakh.
99 F3 Sary-Tash Kyrg.
00 E3 Sasebo Japan
12 E1 Saskatchewan prov. Canada
13 F1 Saskatchewan r. Canada
12 E1 Saskatoon Canada
97 M2 Saskylakh Rus. Fed.
03 O5 Sasovo Rus. Fed.
06 B4 Sassandra Côte d'Ivoire
04 E3 Sassari Italy
05 F1 Sassnitz Germany
06 A3 Satadougou Mali
99 F4 Satpura Range mts India
05 H2 Satu Mare Romania
02 H4 Sauda Norway
13 J2 Sault Sainte Marie Canada
11 J5 Sault Sainte Marie U.S.A.
99 E1 Saumalkol' Kazakh.
01 F7 Saumlakki Indon.
04 C2 Saumur France
09 C4 Saurimo Angola
95 I3 Savai'i i. Samoa
06 C4 Savalou Benin
13 J5 Savannah U.S.A.
13 J5 Savannah r. U.S.A.
01 C5 Savannakhét Laos
15 I5 Savanna-la-Mar Jamaica
06 C4 Savè Benin
09 D6 Save r. Moz.
03 O3 Savinskiy Rus. Fed.
04 E3 Savona Italy
03 L3 Savonlinna Fin.
Savu Sea sea Indon. see Sawu, Laut
12 E4 Sawatch Range mts U.S.A.
94 C2 Sawu, Laut sea Indon.
00 B1 Sayano-Shushenskoye Vodokhranilishche resr Rus. Fed.
Şaydā Lebanon see Sidon
98 D5 Sayḩūt Yemen
Sāylac Somalia see Saylac
98 C5 Saylac Somalia
00 D2 Saynshand Mongolia
06 B2 Sbaa Alg.
06 C1 Sbeitla Tunisia
02 F5 Scafell Pike h. U.K.
91 Scandinavia Europe
13 K3 Scarborough Canada
17 F1 Scarborough Trin. and Tob.
04 C1 Scarborough U.K.
Scarpanto i. Greece see Karpathos
11 L4 Schefferville Canada
13 L3 Schenectady U.S.A.
Schneidemühl Poland see Piła
95 E2 Schouten Islands P.N.G.
Schröttersburg Poland see Płock
05 F1 Schwedt an der Oder Germany
Schweiz country Europe see Switzerland
05 F1 Schwerin Germany
04 E2 Schwyz Switz.
05 F4 Sciacca Italy
04 B2 Scilly, Isles of U.K.
13 J3 Scioto r. U.S.A.
Scodra Albania see Shkodër
11 P2 Scoresby Land reg. Greenland
19 J2 Scotia Ridge sea feature S. Atlantic Ocean
22 B9 Scotia Ridge sea feature S. Atlantic Ocean
19 J1 Scotia Sea S. Atlantic Ocean
19 I5 Scott Base research stn Antarctica
19 I5 Scott Coast Antarctica
11 K2 Scott Inlet Canada
19 H6 Scott Island Antarctica
19 L4 Scott Mountains Antarctica
13 F3 Scottsbluff U.S.A.
13 K3 Scranton U.S.A.
Scupi Macedonia see Skopje
Scutari Albania see Shkodër
11 I4 Seal r. Canada
13 H4 Searcy U.S.A.
12 B2 Seattle U.S.A.
12 D6 Sebastián Vizcaíno, Bahía b. Mex.
Sebenico Croatia see Šibenik
05 H2 Sebeș Romania
05 K3 Şebinkarahisar Turkey
Sebta N. Africa see Ceuta
16 B5 Sechura Peru
16 B5 Sechura, Bahía de b. Peru
06 □ Secos, Ilhéus is Cape Verde
99 F5 Secunderabad India
06 A3 Sédhiou Senegal
09 B6 Seeheim Namibia
19 I4 Seelig, Mount Antarctica
06 A4 Sefadu Sierra Leone
01 C6 Segamat Malaysia
03 M3 Segezha Rus. Fed.
06 B3 Ségou Mali
04 C3 Segovia Spain
03 M3 Segozerskoye, Ozero resr Rus. Fed.
07 D2 Séguédine Niger
06 B4 Séguéla Côte d'Ivoire
113 G6 Seguin U.S.A.
109 C6 Sehithwa Botswana
103 K3 Seinäjoki Fin.
104 D2 Seine r. France
101 C7 Sekayu Indon.
106 B4 Sekondi Ghana
101 F7 Selaru i. Indon.
101 D7 Selatan, Tanjung pt Indon.
101 D7 Selat Makassar str. Indon.
110 B3 Selawik U.S.A.
109 C6 Selebi-Phikwe Botswana
100 F1 Selemdzhinskiy Khrebet mts Rus. Fed.
100 C1 Selenga r. Rus. Fed.
Seleucia Turkey see Silifke
106 A3 Sélibabi Mauritania
107 E2 Selîma Oasis Sudan
102 H4 Seljord Norway
113 G1 Selkirk Canada
103 Q4 Selty Rus. Fed.
116 D5 Selvas reg. Brazil
111 H3 Selwyn Lake Canada
110 E3 Selwyn Mountains Canada
94 D4 Selwyn Range hills Australia
101 D7 Semarang Indon.
108 B3 Sembé Congo
103 M5 Semenivka Ukr.
103 O4 Semenov Rus. Fed.
Semenovka Ukr. see Semenivka
112 E3 Seminoe Reservoir U.S.A.
113 F5 Seminole U.S.A.
113 J5 Seminole, Lake U.S.A.
99 G1 Semipalatinsk Kazakh.
98 D3 Semnān Iran
101 D6 Semporna Malaysia
116 E5 Sena Madureira Brazil
109 C5 Senanga Zambia
100 G3 Sendai Japan
106 A3 Senegal country Africa
106 A3 Sénégal r. Mauritania/Senegal
109 D4 Sengerema Tanz.
103 P5 Sengiley Rus. Fed.
117 J6 Senhor do Bonfim Brazil
103 J2 Senja i. Norway
113 K2 Senneterre Canada
104 D2 Sens France
115 G6 Sensuntepeque El Salvador
97 N6 Seoul S. Korea
101 G7 Sepik r. P.N.G.
113 M1 Sept-Îles Canada
105 L2 Serafimovich Rus. Fed.
101 E7 Seram i. Indon.
94 D2 Seram, Laut sea Indon.
101 C7 Serang Indon.
96 G6 Serdar Turkm.
Serdica Bulg. see Sofia
108 E2 Serdo Eth.
105 J4 Şereflikoçhisar Turkey
101 C6 Seremban Malaysia
109 D4 Serengeti National Park Tanz.
109 D5 Serenje Zambia
103 N4 Sergiyev Posad Rus. Fed.
Sergo Ukr. see Stakhanov
101 D6 Serian Malaysia
105 J4 Serik Turkey
101 E7 Sermata, Kepulauan is Indon.
111 M2 Sermersuaq glacier Greenland
103 P4 Sernur Rus. Fed.
96 H4 Serov Rus. Fed.
109 C6 Serowe Botswana
103 N5 Serpukhov Rus. Fed.
117 H3 Serra do Navio Brazil
Sérrai Greece see Serres
116 E3 Serranía de la Neblina, Parque Nacional nat. park Venez.
105 H3 Serres Greece
117 K6 Serrinha Brazil
101 D7 Seruyan r. Indon.
100 B3 Sêrxü China
109 B5 Sesfontein Namibia
109 C5 Sesheke Zambia
117 J7 Sete Lagoas Brazil
104 E4 Sétif Alg.
106 B1 Settat Morocco
104 B4 Setúbal Port.
113 H1 Seul, Lac l. Canada
98 C2 Sevan, Lake Armenia
Sevana Lich l. Armenia see Sevan, Lake
98 B2 Sevastopol' Ukr.
113 H1 Severn r. Canada
96 F3 Severnaya Dvina r. Rus. Fed.
97 L1 Severnaya Zemlya is Rus. Fed.
96 H3 Severnyy Rus. Fed.
100 D1 Severo-Baykal'skoye Nagor'ye mts Rus. Fed.
103 N3 Severodvinsk Rus. Fed.
97 Q4 Severo-Kuril'sk Rus. Fed.
103 M2 Severomorsk Rus. Fed.
103 N3 Severoonezhsk Rus. Fed.
97 K3 Severo-Yeniseyskiy Rus. Fed.
112 D4 Sevier Lake U.S.A.
116 C3 Sevilla Col.
Sevilla Spain see Seville
104 B4 Seville Spain
110 D3 Seward U.S.A.
110 B3 Seward Peninsula U.S.A.
112 E6 Sextín r. Mex.
96 I2 Seyakha Rus. Fed.
123 M6 Seychelles country Indian Ocean
102 D2 Seyðisfjörður Iceland
105 J4 Seyhan r. Turkey
97 Q3 Seymchan Rus. Fed.
105 I2 Sfântu Gheorghe Romania
105 F5 Sfax Tunisia
Sfintu Gheorghe Romania see Sfântu Gheorghe
's-Gravenhage Neth. see The Hague
109 C4 Shabunda Dem. Rep. Congo
99 F3 Shache China
119 J5 Shackleton Coast Antarctica
119 K6 Shackleton Ice Shelf Antarctica
119 J3 Shackleton Range mts Antarctica
119 I5 Shafer Peak Antarctica
110 C3 Shageluk U.S.A.
119 J1 Shag Rocks is S. Georgia
99 G4 Shahdol India
98 D3 Shahr-e Kord Iran
99 E3 Shahrisabz Uzbek.
103 N4 Shakhovskaya Rus. Fed.
Shakhrisabz Uzbek. see Shahrisabz
105 L2 Shakhty Rus. Fed.
103 P4 Shakhun'ya Rus. Fed.
98 D2 Shalkar Kazakh.
100 B3 Shaluli Shan mts China
109 D5 Shamva Zimbabwe
100 C3 Shandan China
100 E3 Shandong Bandao pen. China
109 C5 Shangani r. Zimbabwe
100 E3 Shanghai China
101 D4 Shangrao China
100 E2 Shangzhi China
102 E5 Shannon r. Ireland
101 D4 Shaoyang China
98 C4 Shaqrā' Saudi Arabia
98 D4 Sharjah U.A.E.
94 B4 Shark Bay Australia
105 J6 Sharm ash Shaykh Egypt
Sharm el Sheikh Egypt see Sharm ash Shaykh
103 P4 Shar'ya Rus. Fed.
109 C6 Shashe r. Botswana/Zimbabwe
108 D3 Shashemenē Eth.
112 B3 Shasta, Mount vol. U.S.A.
112 B3 Shasta Lake U.S.A.
103 O5 Shatsk Rus. Fed.
113 I3 Shawano U.S.A.
113 L2 Shawinigan Canada
113 G4 Shawnee U.S.A.
94 C4 Shay Gap (abandoned) Australia
103 Q2 Shchel'yayur Rus. Fed.
105 K1 Shchigry Rus. Fed.
98 C6 Shebelē Wenz, Wabē r. Eth.
108 E3 Shebelē Wenz, Wabē r. Somalia
99 E3 Sheberghān Afgh.
111 J5 Sheboygan U.S.A.
107 D4 Shebshi Mountains Nigeria
104 C1 Sheffield U.K.
97 S2 Shelagskiy, Mys pt Rus. Fed.
112 D2 Shelby U.S.A.
97 Q3 Shelikhova, Zaliv g. Rus. Fed.
110 C4 Shelikof Strait U.S.A.
106 C4 Shendam Nigeria
103 O3 Shenkursk Rus. Fed.
100 E2 Shenyang China
103 L5 Shepetivka Ukr.
Shepetovka Ukr. see Shepetivka
95 G3 Shepherd Islands Vanuatu
95 E5 Shepparton Australia
113 L2 Sherbrooke Canada
107 F3 Shereiq Sudan
112 E3 Sheridan U.S.A.
113 G5 Sherman U.S.A.
102 F3 Shetland Islands U.K.
98 D2 Shetpe Kazakh.
113 I2 Sheyenne r. U.S.A.
100 H2 Shiashkotan, Ostrov i. Rus. Fed.
98 C5 Shibām Yemen
99 G2 Shihezi China
100 D3 Shijiazhuang China
100 F3 Shikoku i. Japan
103 O3 Shilega Rus. Fed.
99 G4 Shiliguri India
99 H4 Shillong India
103 O5 Shilovo Rus. Fed.
100 E1 Shimanovsk Rus. Fed.
99 F5 Shimoga India
109 D4 Shimoni Kenya
97 O6 Shimonoseki Japan
109 D4 Shinyanga Tanz.
112 E4 Shiprock U.S.A.
100 F3 Shirane-san mt. Japan
119 L4 Shirase Glacier Antarctica
98 D4 Shīrāz Iran
97 R4 Shiveluch, Sopka vol. Rus. Fed.
99 F4 Shivpuri India
100 D3 Shiyan China
100 C3 Shizuishan China
105 G3 Shkodër Albania
Shkodra Albania see Shkodër
97 J1 Shmidta, Ostrov i. Rus. Fed.
123 J9 Shona Ridge sea feature S. Atlantic Ocean
105 J1 Shostka Ukr.
112 D5 Show Low U.S.A.
105 J2 Shpola Ukr.
Shqipëria country Europe see Albania
113 H5 Shreveport U.S.A.
104 C1 Shrewsbury U.K.
99 F2 Shu Kazakh.
98 D2 Shubarkuduk Kazakh.
99 B4 Shubrā al Khaymah Egypt
109 C5 Shumba Zimbabwe
105 I3 Shumen Bulg.
110 C3 Shungnak U.S.A.
98 C5 Shuqrah Yemen
109 D5 Shurugwi Zimbabwe
112 C1 Shuswap Lake Canada
103 O4 Shuya Rus. Fed.
103 O4 Shuyskoye Rus. Fed.
99 E2 Shymkent Kazakh.
101 F7 Sia Indon.
99 E4 Siahan Range mts Pak.
103 K4 Šiauliai Lith.
119 I5 Sibbald, Cape Antarctica
105 G3 Šibenik Croatia
97 M3 Siberia reg. Rus. Fed.
101 B7 Siberut i. Indon.
108 D3 Sibiloi National Park Kenya
Sibir' reg. Rus. Fed. see Siberia
109 B4 Sibiti Congo
105 H2 Sibiu Romania
101 B6 Sibolga Indon.
101 D6 Sibu Malaysia
108 B3 Sibut Centr. Afr. Rep.
Sicca Veneria Tunisia see Le Kef
101 C4 Sichuan Pendi basin China
Sicilia i. Italy see Sicily
105 F4 Sicilian Channel Italy/Tunisia
105 F4 Sicily i. Italy
116 D6 Sicuani Peru
104 C4 Sidi Bel Abbès Alg.
Sidi Bou Sa'id Tunisia see Sidi Bouzid
104 E4 Sidi Bouzid Tunisia
106 A2 Sidi Ifni Morocco
104 B5 Sidi Kacem Morocco
104 D5 Sidi Khaled Alg.
119 I4 Sidley, Mount Antarctica
113 F2 Sidney MT U.S.A.
113 F3 Sidney NE U.S.A.
113 J5 Sidney Lanier, Lake U.S.A.
98 B3 Sidon Lebanon
105 F3 Siena Italy
118 C6 Sierra Grande Arg.
106 A4 Sierra Leone country Africa
123 H5 Sierra Leone Basin sea feature N. Atlantic Ocean
123 H5 Sierra Leone Rise sea feature N. Atlantic Ocean
116 D2 Sierra Nevada, Parque Nacional nat. park Venez.
116 D1 Sierra Nevada de Santa Marta, Parque Nacional nat. park Col.
112 D5 Sierra Vista U.S.A.
111 M2 Sigguup Nunaa pen. Greenland
105 H2 Sighetu Marmației Romania
101 B6 Sigli Indon.
102 C2 Siglufjörður Iceland
123 C4 Sigsbee Deep sea feature G. of Mexico
106 B3 Siguiri Guinea
101 C5 Sihanoukville Cambodia
98 C3 Siirt Turkey
101 C7 Sijunjung Indon.
99 F4 Sikar India
106 B3 Sikasso Mali
113 I4 Sikeston U.S.A.
100 F2 Sikhote-Alin' mts Rus. Fed.
99 G4 Sikkim state India
114 D4 Silao Mex.
99 F1 Siletiteniz, Ozero salt l. Kazakh.
104 E4 Siliana Tunisia
105 J4 Silifke Turkey
99 G3 Siling Co salt l. China
103 I3 Siljan l. Sweden
103 K4 Šilutė Lith.
112 E5 Silver City U.S.A.
105 I4 Simav Turkey
108 C3 Simba Dem. Rep. Congo
98 B5 Simēn mts Eth.
Simēn Mountains Eth. see Simēn
99 H6 Simeulue i. Indon.
Simeuluë i. Indon. see Simeulue
105 J3 Simferopol' Ukr.
94 D4 Simpson Desert Australia
103 I4 Simrishamn Sweden
100 H2 Simushir, Ostrov i. Rus. Fed.
Sīnā', Shibh Jazīrat pen. Egypt see Sinai
98 B4 Sinai pen. Egypt
112 E6 Sinaloa state Mex.
116 C2 Sincelejo Col.
103 Q3 Sindor Rus. Fed.
104 B4 Sines Port.
106 B4 Sinfra Côte d'Ivoire
107 F3 Singa Sudan
101 C6 Singapore Sing.
109 D4 Singida Tanz.
Singidunum Serbia see Belgrade
94 C2 Singkang Indon.
101 C6 Singkawang Indon.
104 E3 Siniscola Italy
94 C2 Sinjai Indon.
107 F3 Sinkat Sudan
Sinkiang aut. reg. China see Xinjiang Uygur Zizhiqu
117 H2 Sinnamary Fr. Guiana
98 B2 Sinop Turkey
115 L5 Sint Eustatius i. Neth. Antilles
115 L5 Sint Maarten i. Neth. Antilles
113 G6 Sinton U.S.A.
100 E2 Sinŭiju N. Korea
113 G3 Sioux City U.S.A.
113 G3 Sioux Falls U.S.A.
113 H1 Sioux Lookout Canada
100 E2 Siping China
101 B7 Sipura i. Indon.
115 H6 Siquia r. Nicaragua
Siracusa Italy see Syracuse
94 D3 Sir Edward Pellew Group is Australia
98 D4 Sīrjān Iran
Síros i. Greece see Syros
99 F4 Sirsa India
105 G5 Sirte Libya
105 G5 Sirte, Gulf of Libya
105 G2 Sisak Croatia
Siscia Croatia see Sisak
101 C5 Sisŏphŏn Cambodia
105 I4 Siteia Greece
Sitía Greece see Siteia
117 I6 Sítio da Abadia Brazil
110 E4 Sitka U.S.A.
101 B4 Sittwe Myanmar
98 B3 Sivas Turkey
103 S2 Sivomaskinskiy Rus. Fed.
105 J4 Sivrihisar Turkey
107 E2 Sīwah Egypt
105 I6 Sīwah, Wāḥāt oasis Egypt
Siwa Oasis oasis Egypt see Sīwah, Wāḥāt
Sjælland i. Denmark see Zealand
105 J2 Skadovs'k Ukr.
103 I4 Skagen Denmark
102 H4 Skagerrak str. Denmark/Norway
110 E4 Skagway U.S.A.
104 D1 Skegness U.K.
103 K3 Skellefteå Sweden
102 H4 Skien Norway
104 E4 Skikda Alg.
Skíros i. Greece see Skyros
105 H3 Skopje Macedonia
Skoplje Macedonia see Skopje
103 I4 Skövde Sweden
102 E4 Skye i. U.K.
105 H4 Skyros i. Greece
105 H3 Slatina Romania
110 G4 Slave r. Canada
106 C4 Slave Coast Africa
110 G4 Slave Lake Canada
Slavgorod Belarus see Slawharad
99 F1 Slavgorod Rus. Fed.
105 G2 Slavonski Brod Croatia
Slavyansk Ukr. see Slov"yans'k
103 M5 Slawharad Belarus
119 J3 Slessor Glacier Antarctica
Sligeach Ireland see Sligo
102 E5 Sligo Ireland
105 I3 Sliven Bulg.
103 Q4 Slobodskoy Rus. Fed.
105 I3 Slobozia Romania
103 J6 Slovakia country Europe
105 F2 Slovenia country Europe
Slovenija country Europe see Slovenia
Slovensko country Europe see Slovakia
103 N6 Slov"yans'k Ukr.
105 I1 Sluch r. Ukr.
96 C4 Słupsk Poland
105 I1 Slutsk Belarus
97 L4 Slyudyanka Rus. Fed.
111 L4 Smallwood Reservoir Canada
Smalyenskaya Wzwyshsha hills Belarus/Rus. Fed. see Smolensko-Moskovskaya Vozvyshennost'
103 L5 Smarhon' Belarus
Smela Ukr. see Smila
103 M6 Smila Ukr.
110 C2 Smith Bay U.S.A.
110 F4 Smithers Canada
113 K3 Smiths Falls Canada
111 K2 Smith Sound sea chan. Canada/Greenland
113 G4 Smoky Hills U.S.A.
103 M5 Smolensk Rus. Fed.
Smolensk-Moscow Upland hills Belarus/Rus. Fed. see Smolensko-Moskovskaya Vozvyshennost'
103 M5 Smolensko-Moskovskaya Vozvyshennost' hills Belarus/Rus. Fed.
105 H3 Smolyan Bulg.
113 J2 Smooth Rock Falls Canada
Smorgon' Belarus see Smarhon'
112 C2 Snake r. U.S.A.
112 D3 Snake River Plain U.S.A.
95 G6 Snares Islands N.Z.
97 J3 Snezhnogorsk Rus. Fed.
102 F5 Snowdon mt. U.K.
111 I4 Snow Lake Canada
113 F5 Snyder U.S.A.
109 E5 Soalala Madag.
109 E5 Soanierana-Ivongo Madag.
107 F4 Sobat r. Sudan
101 G7 Sobger r. Indon.
117 J6 Sobradinho, Barragem de resr Brazil
117 J4 Sobral Brazil
105 K3 Sochi Rus. Fed.
Société, Archipel de la is Fr. Polynesia see Society Islands
121 I7 Society Islands Fr. Polynesia
116 D2 Socorro Col.
114 B5 Socorro, Isla i. Mex.
98 D5 Socotra i. Yemen
103 L2 Sodankylä Fin.
103 J3 Söderhamn Sweden
103 J4 Södertälje Sweden
107 E3 Sodiri Sudan
108 D3 Sodo Eth.
103 J3 Södra Kvarken str. Fin./Sweden
105 H3 Sofia Bulg.
Sofiya Bulg. see Sofia
103 M2 Sofporog Rus. Fed.
100 B3 Sog China
102 H3 Sognefjorden inlet Norway
95 F2 Sohano P.N.G.
104 D2 Soissons France
105 I4 Söke Turkey
96 F5 Sokhumi Georgia
106 C4 Sokodé Togo
103 O4 Sokol Rus. Fed.
106 B3 Sokolo Mali
106 C3 Sokoto Nigeria
106 C3 Sokoto r. Nigeria
99 F5 Solapur India
103 O4 Soligalich Rus. Fed.
Soligorsk Belarus see Salihorsk
96 G4 Solikamsk Rus. Fed.
98 D1 Sol'-Iletsk Rus. Fed.
95 G2 Solomon Islands country Pacific Ocean
95 F2 Solomon Sea P.N.G./Solomon Is
101 E7 Solor, Kepulauan is Indon.
103 M4 Sol'tsy Rus. Fed.
109 C5 Solwezi Zambia
105 I4 Soma Turkey
108 E3 Somalia country Africa
123 M6 Somali Basin sea feature Indian Ocean
109 C4 Sombo Angola
113 J4 Somerset U.S.A.
111 I2 Somerset Island Canada
104 E1 Sønderborg Denmark
104 E2 Sondrio Italy
109 D5 Songea Tanz.
101 C6 Songkhla Thai.
109 B4 Songo Angola
109 D5 Songo Moz.
100 E2 Songyuan China
101 C4 Sơn La Vietnam
117 I6 Sono r. Brazil
112 D6 Sonora r. Mex.
112 D6 Sonora state Mex.
115 G6 Sonsonate El Salvador
107 E4 Sopo watercourse Sudan
103 J6 Sopron Hungary
113 L2 Sorel Canada
95 E6 Sorell Australia
104 C3 Soria Spain
96 C2 Sørkappøya i. Svalbard
103 L6 Soroca Moldova
98 D1 Sorochinsk Rus. Fed.
Soroki Moldova see Soroca
101 G6 Sorol atoll Micronesia
101 F7 Sorong Indon.
108 D3 Soroti Uganda
103 K1 Sørøya i. Norway
109 B6 Sorris Sorris Namibia
103 J2 Sorsele Sweden
101 E5 Sorsogon Phil.
103 M3 Sortavala Rus. Fed.
118 C4 Sosneado mt. Arg.
103 Q3 Sosnogorsk Rus. Fed.
103 K5 Sosnovka Kaliningradskaya Oblast' Rus. Fed.
96 F3 Sosnovka Murmanskaya Oblast' Rus. Fed.
103 O5 Sosnovka Tambovskaya Oblast' Rus. Fed.
103 L4 Sosnovyy Bor Rus. Fed.
103 J5 Sosnowiec Poland
Sosnowitz Poland see Sosnowiec
114 E4 Soto la Marina Mex.
108 B3 Souanké Congo
106 B4 Soubré Côte d'Ivoire
104 E4 Souk Ahras Alg.
104 B5 Souk el Arbaâ du Rharb Morocco
Sŏul S. Korea see Seoul
Soûr Lebanon see Tyre
113 F2 Souris r. Canada
Souriya country Asia see Syria
117 K5 Sousa Brazil
105 F4 Sousse Tunisia
123 J6 South America
102 F5 Southampton U.K.
111 J3 Southampton Island Canada
94 D5 South Australia state Australia
123 Q8 South Australian Basin sea feature Indian Ocean
113 I3 South Bend U.S.A.
113 J5 South Carolina state U.S.A.
101 D5 South China Sea Pacific Ocean
113 F3 South Dakota state U.S.A.
95 E6 South East Cape Australia

T

Umuarama

117 G5 Teles Pires r. Brazil
106 A3 Télimélé Guinea
Tell Atlas mts Alg. see Atlas Tellien
110 B3 Teller U.S.A.
Telo Martius France see Toulon
103 R3 Telpoziz, Gora mt. Rus. Fed.
118 C6 Telsen Arg.
97 K3 Tembenchi r. Rus. Fed.
109 B4 Tembo Aluma Angola
101 C6 Temerluh Malaysia
99 F1 Temirtau Kazakh.
113 G5 Temple U.S.A.
105 K2 Temryuk Rus. Fed.
118 B5 Temuco Chile
116 C4 Tena Ecuador
99 G5 Tenali India
101 B5 Tenasserim Myanmar
108 E2 Tendaho Eth.
99 H6 Ten Degree Channel India
106 B3 Ténenkou Mali
107 D3 Ténéré reg. Niger
107 D3 Ténéré, Erg du des. Niger
107 D2 Ténéré du Tafassâsset des. Niger
106 A2 Tenerife i. Canary Is
104 D4 Ténès Alg.
101 D7 Tengah, Kepulauan is Indon.
100 C3 Tengger Shamo des. China
99 E1 Tengiz, Ozero salt l. Kazakh.
106 B3 Tengréla Côte d'Ivoire
109 C5 Tenke Dem. Rep. Congo
97 P2 Tenkeli Rus. Fed.
106 B3 Tenkodogo Burkina
94 D3 Tennant Creek Australia
113 I4 Tennessee r. U.S.A.
113 I4 Tennessee state U.S.A.
115 F5 Tenosique Mex.
94 C2 Tenteno Indon.
117 J7 Teófilo Otôni Brazil
114 D4 Tepatitlán Mex.
112 E6 Tepehuanes Mex.
114 D4 Tepic Mex.
105 F1 Teplice Czech Rep.
105 F3 Teramo Italy
117 J5 Teresina Brazil
Tergeste Italy see Trieste
Termez Uzbek. see Termiz
115 F5 Términos, Laguna de lag. Mex.
96 H6 Termiz Uzbek.
105 F3 Termoli Italy
101 E6 Ternate Indon.
105 F3 Terni Italy
96 D5 Ternopil' Ukr.
100 G2 Terpeniya, Mys c. Rus. Fed.
100 G2 Terpeniya, Zaliv g. Rus. Fed.
110 F4 Terrace Canada
113 I2 Terrace Bay Canada
113 I4 Terre Haute U.S.A.
104 C3 Teruel Spain
108 D2 Teseney Eritrea
110 C2 Teshekpuk Lake U.S.A.
110 E3 Teslin Canada
110 E3 Teslin Lake Canada
106 C3 Tessaoua Niger
118 B2 Tetas, Punta pt Chile
109 D5 Tete Moz.
104 B4 Tétouan Morocco
105 H3 Tetovo Macedonia
Tetuán Morocco see Tétouan
103 P5 Tetyushi Rus. Fed.
118 D2 Teuco r. Arg.
95 F4 Tewantin Australia
113 H5 Texarkana U.S.A.
113 G5 Texas state U.S.A.
113 H6 Texas City U.S.A.
113 G5 Texoma, Lake U.S.A.
101 B4 Tezu India
101 C4 Thai Binh Vietnam
101 C5 Thailand, Gulf of Asia
101 C4 Thai Nguyên Vietnam
99 I5 Thakèk Laos
99 F3 Thal Desert Pak.
99 H5 Thandwè Myanmar
101 C5 Thanh Hoa Vietnam
99 E4 Thar Desert India/Pak.
105 H3 Thasos i. Greece
101 B5 Thaton Myanmar
101 B5 Thayetmyo Myanmar
113 K7 The Bahamas country Caribbean Sea
106 A3 The Gambia country Africa
98 D4 The Gulf Asia
102 G5 The Hague Neth.
111 H3 Thelon r. Canada
102 E4 The Minch sea chan. U.K.
117 F5 Theodore Roosevelt r. Brazil
Theodosia Ukr. see Feodosiya
113 F1 The Pas Canada
105 I4 Thera i. Greece
105 H3 Thermaïkos Kolpos g. Greece
110 F2 Thesiger Bay Canada
Thessalonica Greece see Thessaloniki
105 H3 Thessaloniki Greece
113 L2 Thetford Mines Canada
Theveste Alg. see Tébessa
119 J4 Thiel Mountains Antarctica
106 A3 Thiès Senegal
109 D4 Thika Kenya
Thiladhunmathee Atoll Maldives see Thiladhunmathi Atoll
99 F6 Thiladhunmathi Atoll Maldives
99 G4 Thimphu Bhutan
111 I4 Thompson Canada
112 H4 Thompson r. U.S.A.
119 K4 Thorshavnheiane reg. Antarctica
105 H3 Thrakiko Pelagos sea Greece
100 C3 Three Gorges Reservoir resr China
95 H5 Three Kings Islands N.Z.
106 B4 Three Points, Cape Ghana
111 L2 Thule Greenland
109 C6 Thuli Zimbabwe
102 H6 Thun Switz.
113 I2 Thunder Bay Canada
102 F4 Thurso U.K.
119 H3 Thurston Island Antarctica
Thyatira Turkey see Akhisar
117 J4 Tianguá Brazil
100 D3 Tianjin China
100 B3 Tianjun China
100 C3 Tianshui China
104 D4 Tiaret Alg.
106 B4 Tiassalé Côte d'Ivoire
118 F2 Tibagi r. Brazil
107 D4 Tibati Cameroon
107 D2 Tibesti mts Chad
99 G3 Tibet, Plateau of China
Tibet Aut. Region aut. reg. China see Xizang Zizhiqu
95 E4 Tibooburra Australia
112 D6 Tiburón, Isla i. Mex.
106 B3 Tîchît Mauritania
106 A2 Tichla W. Sahara
115 G4 Ticul Mex.
106 C2 Tidikelt, Plaine du Alg.
106 A3 Tidjikja Mauritania
97 N5 Tieling China
106 B4 Tiémé Côte d'Ivoire
99 F2 Tien Shan mts China/Kyrg.
114 E5 Tierra Blanca Mex.
118 C8 Tierra del Fuego, Isla Grande de i. Arg./Chile
113 J5 Tifton U.S.A.
98 A2 Tighina Moldova
107 D4 Tignère Cameroon
116 C4 Tigre r. Ecuador/Peru
117 F2 Tigre r. Venez.
98 C5 Tihāmat 'Asīr reg. Saudi Arabia
112 C5 Tijuana Mex.
105 L2 Tikhoretsk Rus. Fed.
103 M4 Tikhvin Rus. Fed.
121 K7 Tiki Basin sea feature Pacific Ocean
95 G3 Tikopia i. Solomon Is
98 C3 Tikrīt Iraq
97 N2 Tiksi Rus. Fed.
118 C2 Tilcara Arg.
Tilimsen Alg. see Tlemcen
106 C3 Tillabéri Niger
Tilsit Rus. Fed. see Sovetsk
103 P2 Timanskiy Kryazh ridge Rus. Fed.
95 H6 Timaru N.Z.
103 N6 Timashevsk Rus. Fed.
Timashevskaya Rus. Fed. see Timashevsk
106 B3 Timbedgha Mauritania
94 D3 Timber Creek Australia
106 B3 Timbuktu Mali
106 B3 Timétrine reg. Mali
106 C2 Timimoun Alg.
105 H2 Timişoara Romania
113 J2 Timmins Canada
117 J5 Timon Brazil
101 E7 Timor i. Indon.
101 E8 Timor Sea Australia/Indon.
106 B2 Tindouf Alg.
Tingis Morocco see Tangier
99 G4 Tingri China
117 K6 Tinharé, Ilha de i. Brazil
101 G5 Tinian i. N. Mariana Is
118 C3 Tinogasta Arg.
105 I4 Tinos i. Greece
106 C2 Tinrhert, Hamada de Alg.
104 D4 Tipasa Alg.
117 I4 Tiracambu, Serra do hills Brazil
105 G3 Tirana Albania
Tiranë Albania see Tirana
105 I2 Tiraspol Moldova
Tîrgu Jiu Romania see Târgu Jiu
Tirreno, Mare sea France/Italy see Tyrrhenian Sea
99 F5 Tiruchchirappalli India
104 D4 Tissemsilt Alg.
119 J4 Titan Dome ice feature Antarctica
97 N2 Tit-Ary Rus. Fed.
Titawin Morocco see Tétouan
Titicaca, Lago l. Bol./Peru see Titicaca, Lake
116 E7 Titicaca, Lake Bol./Peru
Titograd Montenegro see Podgorica
Titovo Užice Serbia see Užice
Titov Veles Macedonia see Veles
113 J6 Titusville U.S.A.
115 G4 Tizimín Mex.
104 D4 Tizi Ouzou Alg.
106 B2 Tiznit Morocco
114 E5 Tlaxcala Mex.
104 C5 Tlemcen Alg.
109 E5 Toamasina Madag.
117 F1 Tobago i. Trin. and Tob.
101 E6 Tobelo Indon.
113 J2 Tobermory Canada
101 C7 Toboali Indon.
96 H4 Tobol r. Kazakh./Rus. Fed.
Tobruk Libya see Tubruq
103 Q2 Tobseda Rus. Fed.
117 I5 Tocantinópolis Brazil
117 I4 Tocantins r. Brazil
118 B2 Tocopilla Chile
116 E7 Todos Santos Bol.
95 I3 Tofua i. Tonga
101 E7 Togian, Kepulauan is Indon.
106 C4 Togo country Africa
110 D3 Tok U.S.A.
107 F3 Tokar Sudan
101 E4 Tokara-rettō is Japan
95 I2 Tokelau terr. Pacific Ocean
103 N6 Tokmak Ukr.
99 F2 Tokmok Kyrg.
95 H5 Tokoroa N.Z.
97 J5 Toksun China
100 F3 Tokushima Japan
100 F3 Tōkyō Japan
109 E6 Tôlañaro Madag.
Tolbukhin Bulg. see Dobrich
104 C4 Toledo Spain
113 J3 Toledo U.S.A.
113 H5 Toledo Bend Reservoir U.S.A.
Toletum Spain see Toledo
109 E6 Toliara Madag.
101 E6 Tolitoli Indon.
97 J3 Tol'ka Rus. Fed.
Tolosa France see Toulouse
114 E5 Toluca Mex.
96 F4 Tol'yatti Rus. Fed.
113 H3 Tomah U.S.A.
95 H3 Tomanivi mt. Fiji
117 F4 Tomar Brazil
113 I5 Tombigbee r. U.S.A.
109 B4 Tomboco Angola
Tombouctou Mali see Timbuktu
109 B5 Tombua Angola
101 E7 Tomini, Teluk g. Indon.
106 B3 Tominian Mali
97 N4 Tommot Rus. Fed.
97 O3 Tompo Rus. Fed.
94 B4 Tom Price Australia
100 A1 Tomsk Rus. Fed.
97 P3 Tomtor Rus. Fed.
115 F5 Tonalá Mex.
116 E4 Tonantins Brazil
101 E6 Tondano Indon.
95 I4 Tonga country Pacific Ocean
95 I4 Tongatapu Group is Tonga
121 H7 Tonga Trench sea feature S. Pacific Ocean
100 C3 Tongchuan China
101 C4 Tongking, Gulf of China/Vietnam
100 E2 Tongliao China
100 D3 Tongling China
100 E2 Tongyu China
99 F4 Tonk India
Tônlé Sab l. Cambodia see Tonle Sap
99 I5 Tonle Sap l. Cambodia
112 C4 Tonopah U.S.A.
109 C6 Tonota Botswana
112 D3 Tooele U.S.A.
95 F4 Toowoomba Australia
113 G4 Topeka U.S.A.
114 C3 Topolobampo Mex.
103 M2 Topozero, Ozero l. Rus. Fed.
108 D3 Tor Eth.
98 D3 Torbat-e Heydarīyeh Iran
99 E3 Torbat-e Jām Iran
Torino Italy see Turin
100 G3 Tori-shima i. Japan
107 F4 Torit Sudan
Torneå Fin. see Tornio
103 K2 Torneälven r. Sweden
111 L4 Torngat Mts Canada
103 K2 Tornio Fin.
118 D5 Tornquist Arg.
100 F1 Torom r. Rus. Fed.
113 K3 Toronto Canada
103 M4 Toropets Rus. Fed.
108 D3 Tororo Uganda
Toros Dağları mts Turkey see Taurus Mountains
104 C1 Torquay U.K.
104 B3 Torre mt. Port.
104 C3 Torrecerredo mt. Spain
94 D5 Torrens, Lake imp. l. Australia
113 F6 Torreón Mex.
95 G3 Torres Islands Vanuatu
95 E2 Torres Strait Australia
96 A3 Tórshavn Faroe Is
104 D3 Tortosa Spain
96 C4 Toruń Poland
103 M4 Torzhok Rus. Fed.
99 E2 Toshkent Uzbek.
103 M4 Tosno Rus. Fed.
118 D3 Tostado Arg.
105 J3 Tosya Turkey
103 O4 Tot'ma Rus. Fed.
100 F3 Tottori Japan
106 B4 Touba Côte d'Ivoire
106 A3 Touba Senegal
106 B1 Toubkal, Jbel mt. Morocco
106 B3 Tougan Burkina
104 E5 Touggourt Alg.
106 A3 Tougué Guinea
104 E3 Toulon France
104 D3 Toulouse France
106 B4 Toumodi Côte d'Ivoire
106 B2 Tounassine, Hamada des. Alg.
Toungoo Myanmar see Taung-ngu
117 K5 Touros Brazil
102 G6 Tours France
95 E3 Townsville Australia
101 E7 Towori, Teluk b. Indon.
100 F3 Toyama Japan
104 E5 Tozeur Tunisia
Trâblous Lebanon see Tripoli
98 B2 Trabzon Turkey
Trajectum Neth. see Utrecht
102 E5 Tralee Ireland
Trá Li Ireland see Tralee
118 C3 Trancas Arg.
101 F7 Trangan i. Indon.
119 I5 Transantarctic Mountains Antarctica
98 A2 Transylvanian Alps mts Romania
105 F4 Trapani Italy
113 I3 Traverse City U.S.A.
95 F2 Treasury Islands Solomon Is
118 F4 Treinta y Tres Uruguay
118 C6 Trelew Arg.
105 G2 Trenčín Slovakia
118 D5 Trenque Lauquén Arg.
Trent Italy see Trento
105 F2 Trento Italy
113 K3 Trenton Canada
113 H3 Trenton MO U.S.A.
113 L3 Trenton NJ U.S.A.
118 D5 Tres Arroyos Arg.
Tres Forcas, Cabo c. Morocco see Trois Fourches, Cap des
118 F2 Três Lagoas Brazil
118 B7 Tres Lagos Arg.
118 D5 Tres Picos, Cerro mt. Arg.
118 C7 Tres Puntas, Cabo c. Arg.
117 J8 Três Rios Brazil
Treves Germany see Trier
105 F2 Treviso Italy
Tridentum Italy see Trento
102 H6 Trier Germany
105 F2 Trieste Italy
105 H4 Trikala Greece
Tríkkala Greece see Trikala
101 F7 Trikora, Puncak mt. Indon.
99 G6 Trincomalee Sri Lanka
123 H7 Trindade, Ilha da i. S. Atlantic Ocean
117 F6 Trinidad Bol.
115 I4 Trinidad Cuba
117 F1 Trinidad i. Trin. and Tob.
118 E4 Trinidad Uruguay
113 F4 Trinidad U.S.A.
111 M5 Trinity Bay Canada
110 C4 Trinity Islands U.S.A.
105 H4 Tripoli Greece
98 B3 Tripoli Lebanon
105 F5 Tripoli Libya
Trípolis Greece see Tripoli
99 H4 Tripura state India
123 I8 Tristan da Cunha i. S. Atlantic Ocean
99 F6 Trivandrum India
105 G2 Trnava Slovakia
95 F2 Trobriand Islands P.N.G.
104 C4 Trois Fourches, Cap des c. Morocco
113 L2 Trois-Rivières Canada
103 R3 Troitsko-Pechorsk Rus. Fed.
119 K3 Troll research stn Antarctica
117 G3 Trombetas r. Brazil
123 M7 Tromelin, Île i. Indian Ocean
103 J2 Tromsø Norway
118 B6 Tronador, Monte mt. Arg.
103 I3 Trondheim Norway
105 J5 Troödos, Mount Cyprus
110 F3 Trout Lake l. N.W.T. Canada
113 H1 Trout Lake l. Ont. Canada
113 I5 Troy AL U.S.A.
113 L3 Troy NY U.S.A.
104 D2 Troyes France
115 G5 Trujillo Hond.
116 C5 Trujillo Peru
116 D2 Trujillo Venez.
111 L5 Truro Canada
112 E5 Truth or Consequences U.S.A.
103 I3 Trysil Norway
100 A2 Tsagaannuur Mongolia
109 E5 Tsaratanana, Massif du mts Madag.
109 D4 Tsavo East National Park Kenya
109 B6 Tses Namibia
109 C6 Tsetseng Botswana
97 K5 Tsetserleg Mongolia
100 C2 Tsetserleg Mongolia
109 C6 Tshabong Botswana
109 C6 Tshane Botswana
109 B4 Tshela Dem. Rep. Congo
109 C4 Tshibala Dem. Rep. Congo
109 C4 Tshikapa Dem. Rep. Congo
109 C4 Tshikapa r. Dem. Rep. Congo
109 C4 Tshitanzu Dem. Rep. Congo
109 C4 Tshofa Dem. Rep. Congo
109 C4 Tshuapa r. Dem. Rep. Congo
Tshwane S. Africa see Pretoria
103 O6 Tsimlyansk Rus. Fed.
103 O6 Tsimlyanskoye Vodokhranilishche resr Rus. Fed.
Tsingtao China see Qingdao
109 E6 Tsiombe Madag.
109 E5 Tsiroanomandidy Madag.
103 O5 Tsna r. Rus. Fed.
109 B5 Tsumeb Namibia
109 B6 Tsumis Park Namibia
109 C5 Tsumkwe Namibia
101 F7 Tual Indon.
121 J6 Tuamotu Islands Fr. Polynesia
105 K3 Tuapse Rus. Fed.
112 D4 Tuba City U.S.A.
106 A4 Tubmanburg Liberia
105 H5 Tubruq Libya
121 J7 Tubuai i. Fr. Polynesia
121 I7 Tubuai Islands Fr. Polynesia
117 K6 Tucano Brazil
118 E1 Tucavaca Bol.
112 D5 Tucson U.S.A.
113 F4 Tucumcari U.S.A.
117 F2 Tucupita Venez.
117 I4 Tucuruí Brazil
117 I4 Tucuruí, Represa resr Brazil
104 C3 Tudela Spain
121 J2 Tufts Abyssal Plain sea feature N. Pacific Ocean
101 E5 Tuguegarao Phil.
97 O4 Tugur Rus. Fed.
101 E7 Tukangbesi, Kepulauan is Indon.
110 E3 Tuktoyaktuk Canada
103 N5 Tula Rus. Fed.
114 E4 Tulancingo Mex.
116 C3 Tulcán Ecuador
111 I3 Tulemalu Lake Canada
110 F3 Tulita Canada
95 E3 Tully Australia
113 G4 Tulsa U.S.A.
116 C3 Tuluá Col.
110 B3 Tuluksak U.S.A.
100 C1 Tulun Rus. Fed.
116 C3 Tumaco Col.
109 B4 Tumba, Lac l. Dem. Rep. Congo
116 B4 Tumbes Peru
100 E2 Tumen China
117 F2 Tumereng Guyana
100 G2 Tumnin r. Rus. Fed.
106 B3 Tumu Ghana
117 G3 Tumucumaque, Serra hills Brazil
95 E5 Tumut Australia
109 D5 Tunduru Tanz.
Tunes Tunisia see Tunis
Tūnis country Africa see Tunisia
105 F4 Tunis Tunisia
104 E5 Tunisia country Africa
116 D2 Tunja Col.
112 B4 Tuolumne r. U.S.A.
118 F3 Tupanciretã Brazil
113 I5 Tupelo U.S.A.
118 C2 Tupiza Bol.
97 L3 Tura Rus. Fed.
98 C4 Turabah Saudi Arabia
100 F1 Turana, Khrebet mts Rus. Fed.
116 C2 Turbo Col.
Turfan China see Turpan
99 E2 Turgay Kazakh.
105 K3 Turhal Turkey
104 E2 Turin Italy
108 D3 Turkana, Lake salt l. Eth./Kenya
99 E2 Turkestan Kazakh.
105 J4 Turkey country Asia/Europe
Türkiye country Asia/Europe see Turkey
Turkmenabat Turkm. see Türkmenabat
96 H6 Türkmenabat Turkm.
Turkmenbashi Turkm. see Türkmenbaşy
96 G6 Türkmenbaşy Turkm.
115 J4 Turks and Caicos Islands terr. Caribbean Sea
115 J4 Turks Islands Turks and Caicos Is
96 D3 Turku Fin.
108 D3 Turkwel watercourse Kenya
115 G5 Turneffe Islands atoll Belize
Tŭrnovo Bulg. see Veliko Tŭrnovo
Turnu Severin Romania see Drobeta-Turnu Severin
Turones France see Tours
97 J5 Turpan China
100 A2 Turpan Pendi depr. China
115 I4 Turquino, Pico mt. Cuba
Turris Libisonis Italy see Porto Torres
99 F2 Turugart Pass China/Kyrg.
113 I5 Tuscaloosa U.S.A.
Tutera Spain see Tudela
99 F6 Tuticorin India
111 P2 Tuttut Nunaat reg. Greenland
95 I3 Tutuila i. Pacific Ocean
109 C6 Tutume Botswana
95 H2 Tuvalu country Pacific Ocean
114 E4 Tuxpan Mex.
115 F5 Tuxtla Gutiérrez Mex.
101 C5 Tuy Hoa Vietnam
98 B3 Tuz, Lake salt l. Turkey
Tuz Gölü salt l. Turkey see Tuz, Lake
103 P4 Tuzha Rus. Fed.
105 G3 Tuzla Bos.-Herz.
96 E4 Tver' Rus. Fed.
112 D3 Twin Falls U.S.A.
100 E1 Tygda Rus. Fed.
113 G5 Tyler U.S.A.
100 E1 Tynda Rus. Fed.
103 I3 Tynset Norway
Tyr Lebanon see Tyre
Tyras Ukr. see Bilhorod-Dnistrovs'kyy
105 K5 Tyre Lebanon
119 I3 Tyree, Mount Antarctica
95 E5 Tyrrell, Lake dry lake Australia
105 F3 Tyrrhenian Sea France/Italy
Tyrus Lebanon see Tyre
97 P3 Tyubelyakh Rus. Fed.
96 I4 Tyukalinsk Rus. Fed.
96 H4 Tyumen' Rus. Fed.
97 M3 Tyung r. Rus. Fed.

U

109 C5 Uamanda Angola
Uarc, Ras c. Morocco see Trois Fourches, Cap des
117 K5 Uauá Brazil
116 E4 Uaupés Brazil
117 J8 Ubá Brazil
117 K6 Ubaitaba Brazil
108 B3 Ubangi r. Centr. Afr. Rep./Dem. Rep. Congo
117 I7 Uberaba Brazil
117 G7 Uberaba, Lagoa l. Bol./Brazil
117 I7 Uberlândia Brazil
101 C5 Ubon Ratchathani Thai.
109 C4 Ubundu Dem. Rep. Congo
116 D5 Ucayali r. Peru
99 G2 Ucharal Kazakh.
100 F1 Uchur r. Rus. Fed.
97 O4 Uda r. Rus. Fed.
97 M3 Udachnyy Rus. Fed.
99 F4 Udaipur India
103 I4 Uddevalla Sweden
105 F2 Udine Italy
101 C5 Udon Thani Thai.
100 F1 Udskaya Guba b. Rus. Fed.
99 F5 Udupi India
100 F1 Udyl', Ozero l. Rus. Fed.
94 C2 Uekuli Indon.
108 C3 Uele r. Dem. Rep. Congo
110 B3 Uelen Rus. Fed.
105 F1 Uelzen Germany
108 C3 Uere r. Dem. Rep. Congo
96 G4 Ufa Rus. Fed.
109 B6 Ugab watercourse Namibia
109 D4 Ugalla r. Tanz.
108 D3 Uganda country Africa
100 G2 Uglegorsk Rus. Fed.
97 P3 Ugol'noye Rus. Fed.
97 S3 Ugol'nyye Kopi Rus. Fed.
Uibhist a' Deas i. U.K. see South Uist
Uibhist a' Tuath i. U.K. see North Uist
109 B4 Uíge Angola
110 G5 Uinta Mountains U.S.A.
109 B6 Uis Mine Namibia
99 F4 Ujjain India
Ujung Pandang Indon. see Makassar
Újvidék Serbia see Novi Sad
Ukhta Respublika Kareliya Rus. Fed. see Kalevala
103 Q3 Ukhta Respublika Komi Rus. Fed.
112 B4 Ukiah U.S.A.
111 M2 Ukkusissat Greenland
103 K4 Ukmergė Lith.
103 M6 Ukraine country Europe
Ukrainskaya S.S.R. country Europe see Ukraine
Ukrayina country Europe see Ukraine
Ulaanbaatar Mongolia see Ulan Bator
100 B2 Ulaangom Mongolia
97 L5 Ulan Bator Mongolia
100 E2 Ulanhot China
96 F5 Ulan-Khol Rus. Fed.
100 C1 Ulan-Ude Rus. Fed.
95 G2 Ulawa Island Solomon Is
100 D2 Uliastai China
100 B2 Uliastay Mongolia
101 F6 Ulithi atoll Micronesia
102 E4 Ullapool U.K.
104 E2 Ulm Germany
105 I3 Uludağ mt. Turkey
110 G2 Ulukhaktok Canada
100 A2 Ulungur Hu l. China
94 D4 Uluṟu h. Australia
96 F4 Ul'yanovsk Rus. Fed.
113 F4 Ulysses U.S.A.
105 J2 Uman' Ukr.
96 E3 Umba Rus. Fed.
95 E2 Umboi i. P.N.G.
103 K3 Umeå Sweden
103 K3 Umeälven r. Sweden
111 N3 Umiiviip Kangertiva inlet Greenland
111 H3 Umingmaktok Canada
107 E3 Umm Keddada Sudan
107 F3 Umm Ruwaba Sudan
105 I5 Umm Sa'ad Libya
109 B5 Umpulo Angola
106 C4 Umuahia Nigeria
118 F2 Umuarama Brazil

Zyryanka

13 H4 **West Memphis** U.S.A.
13 J4 **Weston** U.S.A.
13 J6 **West Palm Beach** U.S.A.
13 H4 **West Plains** U.S.A.
95 H6 **Westport** N.Z.
97 J3 **West Siberian Plain** Rus. Fed.
13 J4 **West Virginia** *state* U.S.A.
01 E7 **Wetar** *i.* Indon.
12 D1 **Wetaskiwin** Canada
95 E2 **Wewak** P.N.G.
02 E5 **Wexford** Ireland
13 F2 **Weyburn** Canada
11 I3 **Whale Cove** Canada
95 H5 **Whangarei** N.Z.
12 E4 **Wheeler Peak** *NM* U.S.A.
12 D4 **Wheeler Peak** *NV* U.S.A.
13 H4 **White** *r.* U.S.A.
94 C4 **White, Lake** *salt flat* Australia
11 M5 **White Bay** Canada
10 G4 **Whitecourt** Canada
10 E3 **Whitehorse** Canada
13 H6 **White Lake** U.S.A.
12 C4 **White Mountain Peak** U.S.A.
07 F3 **White Nile** *r.* Sudan/Uganda *alt.* **Abiad, Bahr el**, *alt.* **Jabal, Bahr el**
White Russia *country* Europe *see* **Belarus**
12 E5 **White Sands National Monument** *nat. park* U.S.A.
96 E3 **White Sea** Rus. Fed.
06 B4 **White Volta** *r.* Ghana
12 C4 **Whitney, Mount** U.S.A.
95 E4 **Whitsunday Island** Australia
94 D5 **Whyalla** Australia
13 G4 **Wichita** U.S.A.
13 G5 **Wichita Falls** U.S.A.
02 F4 **Wick** U.K.
12 D5 **Wickenburg** U.S.A.
02 E5 **Wicklow** Ireland
05 G1 **Wieluń** Poland
Wien Austria *see* **Vienna**
05 G2 **Wiener Neustadt** Austria
04 C1 **Wight, Isle of** *i.* U.K.
95 E5 **Wilcannia** Australia
95 E2 **Wilhelm, Mount** P.N.G.
04 E1 **Wilhelmshaven** Germany
19 J6 **Wilkes Land** *reg.* Antarctica
19 I3 **Wilkins Ice Shelf** Antarctica
15 K6 **Willemstad** Neth. Antilles
95 E5 **William, Mount** Australia
12 B1 **Williams Lake** Canada
113 J4 **Williamson** U.S.A.
113 K3 **Williamsport** U.S.A.
113 F2 **Williston** U.S.A.
110 F4 **Williston Lake** Canada
94 C4 **Wills, Lake** *salt flat* Australia
113 K4 **Wilmington** *DE* U.S.A.
113 K5 **Wilmington** *NC* U.S.A.
113 K4 **Wilson** U.S.A.
95 E5 **Wilson's Promontory** *pen.* Australia
94 C4 **Wiluna** Australia
110 E3 **Wind** *r.* Canada
109 B6 **Windhoek** Namibia
95 E4 **Windorah** Australia
112 E3 **Wind River Range** *mts* U.S.A.
115 L5 **Windward Islands** Caribbean Sea
115 J5 **Windward Passage** Cuba/Haiti
113 G4 **Winfield** U.S.A.
111 J4 **Winisk** *r.* Canada
111 J4 **Winisk (abandoned)** Canada
113 I1 **Winisk Lake** Canada
106 B4 **Winneba** Ghana
112 C3 **Winnemucca** U.S.A.
113 H5 **Winnfield** U.S.A.
113 G2 **Winnipeg** Canada
113 G1 **Winnipeg** *r.* Canada
113 G1 **Winnipeg, Lake** Canada
113 F1 **Winnipegosis, Lake** Canada
113 H3 **Winona** *MN* U.S.A.
113 I5 **Winona** *MS* U.S.A.
112 D4 **Winslow** U.S.A.
113 J4 **Winston-Salem** U.S.A.
113 J6 **Winter Haven** U.S.A.
95 E4 **Winton** Australia
113 H3 **Wisconsin** *r.* U.S.A.
113 I3 **Wisconsin** *state* U.S.A.
Wisła *r.* Poland *see* **Vistula**
105 F1 **Wismar** Germany
105 F1 **Wittenberge** Germany
95 E2 **Witu Islands** P.N.G.
109 B6 **Witvlei** Namibia
103 J5 **Włocławek** Poland
101 F7 **Wokam** *i.* Indon.
116 □ **Wolf, Volcán** *vol.* Ecuador
105 F2 **Wolfsberg** Austria
105 F1 **Wolfsburg** Germany
118 C9 **Wollaston, Islas** Chile
111 H4 **Wollaston Lake** *l.* Canada
110 G3 **Wollaston Peninsula** Canada
95 F5 **Wollongong** Australia
100 E3 **Wŏnsan** N. Korea
94 D3 **Woodah, Isle** *i.* Australia
95 F2 **Woodlark Island** P.N.G.
94 D4 **Woodroffe, Mount** Australia
94 D3 **Woods, Lake** *salt flat* Australia
113 G2 **Woods, Lake of the** Canada/U.S.A.
113 M2 **Woodstock** Canada
113 G4 **Woodward** U.S.A.
94 D5 **Woomera** Australia
113 L3 **Worcester** U.S.A.
112 E3 **Worland** U.S.A.
120 G6 **Wotje** *atoll* Marshall Is
101 E7 **Wotu** Indon.
101 E7 **Wowoni** *i.* Indon.
97 T4 **Wrangel Island** Rus. Fed.
110 C4 **Wrangell Mountains** U.S.A.
110 D3 **Wrangell-St Elias National Park and Preserve** U.S.A.
102 E4 **Wrath, Cape** U.K.
Wrecsam U.K. *see* **Wrexham**
102 F5 **Wrexham** U.K.
110 F3 **Wrigley** Canada
103 J5 **Wrocław** Poland
100 C3 **Wuhai** China
100 D3 **Wuhan** China
100 D3 **Wuhu** China
106 C4 **Wukari** Nigeria
101 C4 **Wuliang Shan** *mts* China
101 F7 **Wuliaru** *i.* Indon.
99 I4 **Wumeng Shan** *mts* China
101 B4 **Wuntho** Myanmar
104 E2 **Würzburg** Germany
95 E2 **Wuvulu Island** P.N.G.
100 C3 **Wuwei** China
100 E3 **Wuxi** China
100 E2 **Wuyiling** China
101 D4 **Wuyi Shan** *mts* China
100 C2 **Wuyuan** China
100 C3 **Wuzhong** China
101 D4 **Wuzhou** China
94 C3 **Wyndham** Australia
110 G2 **Wynniatt Bay** Canada
113 F1 **Wynyard** Canada
112 E3 **Wyoming** *state* U.S.A.

X

108 F2 **Xaafuun** Somalia
109 D6 **Xai-Xai** Moz.
Xam Hua Laos *see* **Xam Nua**
99 I4 **Xam Nua** Laos
109 C6 **Xanagas** Botswana
109 B5 **Xangongo** Angola
96 F6 **Xankändi** Azer.
105 H3 **Xanthi** Greece
116 E6 **Xapuri** Brazil
109 C6 **Xau, Lake** Botswana
117 I6 **Xavantes, Serra dos** *hills* Brazil
101 D4 **Xiamen** China
100 C3 **Xi'an** China
100 D3 **Xiangfan** China
99 H4 **Xianggelila** China
101 D4 **Xiangtan** China
100 C3 **Xianyang** China
100 E1 **Xiao Hinggan Ling** *mts* China
101 C4 **Xichang** China
99 G4 **Xigazê** China
100 D2 **Xilinhot** China
100 D2 **Xin Bulag** China
99 H3 **Xinghai** China
117 H4 **Xingu** *r.* Brazil
117 H6 **Xingu, Parque Indígena do** *res.* Brazil
101 C4 **Xingyi** China
100 C3 **Xining** China
99 F2 **Xinjiang Uygur Zizhiqu** *aut. reg.* China
100 D3 **Xintai** China
100 D3 **Xinxiang** China
100 D3 **Xinyang** China
100 D3 **Xinzhou** China
100 C3 **Xiqing Shan** *mts* China
117 J6 **Xique Xique** Brazil
100 C2 **Xishanzui** China
Xi Ujimqin Qi China *see* **Bayan Ul Hot**
99 G4 **Xixabangma Feng** *mt.* China
Xixón Spain *see* **Gijón-Xixón**
99 G3 **Xizang Zizhiqu** *aut. reg.* China
96 G5 **Xo'jayli** Uzbek.
101 C4 **Xuanwei** China
108 E3 **Xuddur** Somalia
101 D4 **Xun Jiang** *r.* China
100 D3 **Xuzhou** China

Y

100 C3 **Ya'an** China
106 C4 **Yabassi** Cameroon
108 D3 **Yabēlo** Eth.
100 C1 **Yablonovyy Khrebet** *mts* Rus. Fed.
116 E6 **Yacuma** *r.* Bol.
113 J4 **Yadkin** *r.* U.S.A.
107 D1 **Yafran** Libya
Yağda Turkey *see* **Erdemli**
119 I1 **Yaghan Basin** *sea feature* S. Atlantic Ocean
107 D3 **Yagoua** Cameroon
105 K4 **Yahyalı** Turkey
112 B2 **Yakima** U.S.A.
106 B3 **Yako** Burkina
110 E4 **Yakutat** U.S.A.
110 D4 **Yakutat Bay** U.S.A.
97 N3 **Yakutsk** Rus. Fed.
101 C6 **Yala** Thai.
100 G3 **Yamagata** Japan
Yamal, Poluostrov *pen.* Rus. Fed. *see* **Yamal Peninsula**
96 H2 **Yamal Peninsula** Rus. Fed.
107 E4 **Yambio** Sudan
105 I3 **Yambol** Bulg.
96 I3 **Yamburg** Rus. Fed.
106 B4 **Yamoussoukro** Côte d'Ivoire
99 G4 **Yamuna** *r.* India
101 B4 **Yamzho Yumco** *l.* China
97 O3 **Yana** *r.* Rus. Fed.
100 C3 **Yan'an** China
116 D6 **Yanaoca** Peru
98 B4 **Yanbu' al Baḩr** Saudi Arabia
94 B5 **Yanchep** Australia
106 B3 **Yanfolila** Mali
Yangôn Myanmar *see* **Rangoon**
99 I3 **Yangtze** *r.* China
108 E2 **Yangudi Rassa National Park** Eth.
100 E2 **Yanji** China
106 C4 **Yankara National Park** Nigeria
113 G3 **Yankton** U.S.A.
Yannina Greece *see* **Ioannina**
97 O2 **Yano-Indigirskaya Nizmennost'** *lowland* Rus. Fed.
97 O2 **Yanskiy Zaliv** *g.* Rus. Fed.
100 E3 **Yantai** China
107 D4 **Yaoundé** Cameroon
101 F6 **Yap** *i.* Micronesia
101 F7 **Yapen** *i.* Indon.
101 F7 **Yapen, Selat** *sea chan.* Indon.
120 E5 **Yap Trench** *sea feature* N. Pacific Ocean
112 D6 **Yaqui** *r.* Mex.
103 Q4 **Yar** Rus. Fed.
95 E4 **Yaraka** Australia
103 P4 **Yaransk** Rus. Fed.
95 G2 **Yaren** Nauru
103 P3 **Yarensk** Rus. Fed.
116 D4 **Yarí** *r.* Col.
Yarımca Turkey *see* **Körfez**
Yarlung Zangbo *r.* Asia *see* **Brahmaputra**
111 L5 **Yarmouth** Canada
Yarmouth U.K. *see* **Great Yarmouth**
103 N4 **Yaroslavl'** Rus. Fed.
97 J3 **Yartsevo** *Krasnoyarskiy Kray* Rus. Fed.
103 M4 **Yartsevo** *Smolenskaya Oblast'* Rus. Fed.
116 C2 **Yarumal** Col.
95 H3 **Yasawa Group** *is* Fiji
95 E5 **Yass** Australia
105 I4 **Yatağan** Turkey
95 G4 **Yaté** New Caledonia
111 I3 **Yathkyed Lake** Canada
116 D5 **Yavari** *r.* Brazil/Peru
99 F3 **Yavatmal** India
116 E2 **Yaví, Cerro** *mt.* Venez.
98 D3 **Yazd** Iran
113 H5 **Yazoo City** U.S.A.
99 F3 **Yecheng** China
103 N3 **Yefremov** Rus. Fed.
103 N4 **Yegor'yevsk** Rus. Fed.
107 F4 **Yei** Sudan
96 H4 **Yekaterinburg** Rus. Fed.
105 L4 **Yelan'** Rus. Fed.
105 K1 **Yelets** Rus. Fed.
106 A3 **Yélimané** Mali
Yellow *r.* China *see* **Yellow River**
110 G3 **Yellowknife** Canada
100 D3 **Yellow River** *r.* China
100 E3 **Yellow Sea** Pacific Ocean
112 E2 **Yellowstone** *r.* U.S.A.
112 D3 **Yellowstone Lake** U.S.A.
111 J1 **Yelverton Bay** Canada
108 C7 **Yemen** *country* Asia
103 Q3 **Yemva** Rus. Fed.
106 C4 **Yenagoa** Nigeria
103 N6 **Yenakiyeve** Ukr.
Yenakiyevo Ukr. *see* **Yenakiyeve**
106 B4 **Yendi** Ghana
109 B4 **Yénéganou** Congo
Yenihan Turkey *see* **Yıldızeli**
Yenişehir Greece *see* **Larisa**
99 H1 **Yenisey** *r.* Rus. Fed.
97 K4 **Yeniseysk** Rus. Fed.
97 K4 **Yeniseyskiy Kryazh** *ridge* Rus. Fed.
96 I2 **Yeniseyskiy Zaliv** *inlet* Rus. Fed.
95 F4 **Yeppoon** Australia
97 L3 **Yerbogachen** Rus. Fed.
98 C2 **Yerevan** Armenia
99 F1 **Yereymentau** Kazakh.
124 A1 **Yermak Plateau** *sea feature* Arctic Ocean
96 F4 **Yershov** Rus. Fed.
99 E1 **Yesil'** Kazakh.
97 L3 **Yessey** Rus. Fed.
101 B4 **Ye-U** Myanmar
Yeu Myanmar *see* **Ye-U**
105 J2 **Yevpatoriya** Ukr.
105 K2 **Yeysk** Rus. Fed.
101 C4 **Yibin** China
100 E2 **Yichun** China
105 K4 **Yıldızeli** Turkey
100 C3 **Yinchuan** China
101 D4 **Yingtan** China
99 G2 **Yining** China
108 D3 **Yirga Alem** Eth.
100 B2 **Yiwu** China
101 D4 **Yiyang** China
Yizra'el *country* Asia *see* **Israel**
Ynys Môn *i.* U.K. *see* **nglesey**
101 D7 **Yogyakarta** Indon.
107 D4 **Yokadouma** Cameroon
107 D4 **Yoko** Cameroon
100 F3 **Yokohama** Japan
107 D4 **Yola** Nigeria
106 B4 **Yomou** Guinea
101 D4 **Yong'an** China
116 D2 **Yopal** Col.
94 B5 **York** Australia
102 F5 **York** U.K.
95 E3 **York, Cape** Australia
94 D5 **Yorke Peninsula** Australia
113 F1 **Yorkton** Canada
106 B3 **Yorosso** Mali
103 P4 **Yoshkar-Ola** Rus. Fed.
119 I6 **Young Island** Antarctica
113 J3 **Youngstown** U.S.A.
106 B3 **Youvarou** Mali
105 J4 **Yozgat** Turkey
112 B3 **Yreka** U.S.A.
Yr Wyddfa *mt.* U.K. *see* **Snowdon**
99 F2 **Ysyk-Köl** *salt l.* Kyrg.
97 O3 **Ytyk-Kyuyel'** Rus. Fed.
112 B4 **Yuba City** U.S.A.
115 F5 **Yucatán** *pen.* Mex.
115 G4 **Yucatan Channel** Cuba/Mex.
97 O4 **Yudoma** *r.* Rus. Fed.
94 D4 **Yuendumu** Australia
96 H3 **Yugorsk** Rus. Fed.
97 Q3 **Yukagirskoye Ploskogor'ye** *plat.* Rus. Fed.
109 B4 **Yuki** Dem. Rep. Congo
110 C3 **Yukon** *r.* Canada/U.S.A.
110 E3 **Yukon Territory** *admin. div.* Canada
101 D4 **Yulin** *Guangxi* China
100 C3 **Yulin** *Shaanxi* China
112 D5 **Yuma** U.S.A.
100 B3 **Yumen** China
105 J4 **Yunak** Turkey
100 A1 **Yurga** Rus. Fed.
116 C5 **Yurimaguas** Peru
103 P4 **Yur'ya** Rus. Fed.
103 O4 **Yur'yevets** Rus. Fed.
103 M3 **Yushkozero** Rus. Fed.
100 B3 **Yushu** China
103 Q4 **Yus'va** Rus. Fed.
99 G3 **Yutian** China
101 C4 **Yuxi** China
103 O4 **Yuzha** Rus. Fed.
100 D1 **Yuzhno-Muyskiy Khrebet** *mts* Rus. Fed.
100 G2 **Yuzhno-Sakhalinsk** Rus. Fed.
103 P7 **Yuzhno-Sukhokumsk** Rus. Fed.

Z

100 D2 **Zabaykal'sk** Rus. Fed.
98 C5 **Zabīd** Yemen
99 E3 **Zābol** Iran
115 G5 **Zacapa** Guat.
114 D5 **Zacapu** Mex.
114 D4 **Zacatecas** Mex.
Zacynthus *i.* Greece *see* **Zakynthos**
105 G3 **Zadar** Croatia
Za'farâna Egypt *see* **Za'farānah**
105 J6 **Za'farānah** Egypt
Zafer Burnu *c.* Cyprus *see* **Apostolos Andreas, Cape**
104 B4 **Zafra** Spain
105 F4 **Zaghouan** Tunisia
Zagorsk Rus. Fed. *see* **Sergiyev Posad**
105 G2 **Zagreb** Croatia
98 D3 **Zagros Mountains** Iran
99 E4 **Zāhedān** Iran
98 B3 **Zahlé** Lebanon
Zaïre *country* Africa *see* **Congo, Democratic Republic of the**
105 H3 **Zaječar** Serbia
Zakhodnyaya Dzvina *r.* Europe *see* **Zapadnaya Dvina**
Zákinthos *i.* Greece *see* **Zakynthos**
107 D3 **Zakouma, Parc National de** *nat. park* Chad
105 H4 **Zakynthos** Greece
105 H4 **Zakynthos** *i.* Greece
105 G2 **Zalaegerszeg** Hungary
105 H2 **Zalău** Romania
107 E3 **Zalingei** Sudan
109 C5 **Zambeze** *r.* Angola *alt.* **Zambezi**
109 D5 **Zambezi** *r.* Africa *alt.* **Zambeze (Angola)**
109 C5 **Zambezi** Zambia
109 C5 **Zambia** *country* Africa
101 E6 **Zamboanga** Phil.
116 C4 **Zamora** Ecuador
104 B3 **Zamora** Spain
114 D5 **Zamora de Hidalgo** Mex.
96 D4 **Zamość** Poland
Zancle Italy *see* **Messina**
98 C3 **Zanjān** Iran
Zante *i.* Greece *see* **Zakynthos**
109 D4 **Zanzibar** Tanz.
109 D4 **Zanzibar Island** Tanz.
106 C2 **Zaouatallaz** Alg.
100 B1 **Zaozernyy** Rus. Fed.
100 D3 **Zaozhuang** China
103 M4 **Zapadnaya Dvina** *r.* Europe
103 M4 **Zapadnaya Dvina** Rus. Fed.
Zapadno-Sibirskaya Ravnina *plain* Rus. Fed. *see* **West Siberian Plain**
99 G1 **Zapadnyy Sayan** *reg.* Rus. Fed.
113 G6 **Zapata** U.S.A.
116 D2 **Zapatoza, Ciénaga de** *l.* Col.
103 M2 **Zapolyarnyy** Rus. Fed.
96 E5 **Zaporizhzhya** Ukr.
Zara Croatia *see* **Zadar**
105 K4 **Zara** Turkey
104 C3 **Zaragoza** Spain
98 D3 **Zarand** Iran
99 E3 **Zaranj** Afgh.
118 E4 **Zárate** Arg.
116 E2 **Zaraza** Venez.
106 C3 **Zaria** Nigeria
Zarqā' Jordan *see* **Az Zarqā'**
105 F5 **Zarzis** Tunisia
100 E1 **Zavitinsk** Rus. Fed.
99 G2 **Zaysan, Lake** Kazakh.
Zaysan, Ozero *l.* Kazakh. *see* **Zaysan, Lake**
Zayü China *see* **Gyigang**
103 I4 **Zealand** *i.* Denmark
94 D4 **Zeil, Mount** Australia
103 P4 **Zelenodol'sk** Rus. Fed.
103 L3 **Zelenogorsk** Rus. Fed.
103 N4 **Zelenograd** Rus. Fed.
108 C3 **Zémio** Centr. Afr. Rep.
105 G3 **Zenica** Bos.-Herz.
103 O6 **Zernograd** Rus. Fed.
Zernovoy Rus. Fed. *see* **Zernograd**
100 E1 **Zeya** Rus. Fed.
100 E1 **Zeya** *r.* Rus. Fed.
100 E1 **Zeyskoye Vodokhranilishche** *resr* Rus. Fed.
99 E1 **Zhaltyr** Kazakh.
98 D2 **Zhanaozen** Kazakh.
100 E2 **Zhangguangcai Ling** *mts* China
100 D2 **Zhangjiakou** China
101 D4 **Zhangping** China
100 C3 **Zhangye** China
101 D4 **Zhanjiang** China
101 C4 **Zhaotong** China
99 G3 **Zhari Namco** *salt l.* China
99 G2 **Zharkent** Kazakh.
99 G2 **Zharma** Kazakh.
103 M6 **Zhashkiv** Ukr.
Zhashkov Ukr. *see* **Zhashkiv**
Zhayyq *r.* Kazakh./Rus. Fed. *see* **Ural**
96 H2 **Zhelaniya, Mys** *c.* Rus. Fed.
Zheleznodorozhnyy Rus. Fed. *see* **Yemva**
105 K1 **Zheleznogorsk** Rus. Fed.
Zheltyye Vody Ukr. *see* **Zhovti Vody**
99 J3 **Zhengzhou** China
103 P3 **Zheshart** Rus. Fed.
99 E2 **Zhezkazgan** Kazakh.
99 E2 **Zhezkazgan** Kazakh.
97 N3 **Zhigansk** Rus. Fed.
99 E1 **Zhitikara** Kazakh.
Zhitkovichi Belarus *see* **Zhytkavichy**
105 J1 **Zhlobin** Belarus
Zhmerinka Ukr. *see* **Zhmerynka**
103 L6 **Zhmerynka** Ukr.
99 E3 **Zhob** Pak.
97 Q2 **Zhokhova, Ostrov** *i.* Rus. Fed.
99 G4 **Zhongba** China
Zhongdian China *see* **Xianggelila**
119 L5 **Zhongshan** *research stn* Antarctica
100 C3 **Zhongwei** China
103 M6 **Zhovti Vody** Ukr.
100 D3 **Zhucheng** China
101 D4 **Zhuzhou** China
103 L5 **Zhytkavichy** Belarus
96 D4 **Zhytomyr** Ukr.
100 D3 **Zibo** China
103 J5 **Zielona Góra** Poland
101 C4 **Zigong** China
106 A3 **Ziguinchor** Senegal
105 G2 **Žilina** Slovakia
100 C1 **Zima** Rus. Fed.
114 E4 **Zimapán** Mex.
109 C5 **Zimba** Zambia
109 C5 **Zimbabwe** *country* Africa
106 A4 **Zimmi** Sierra Leone
103 N2 **Zimniy Bereg** *coastal area* Rus. Fed.
106 C3 **Zinder** Niger
106 B3 **Ziniaré** Burkina
101 B4 **Ziro** India
114 D5 **Zitácuaro** Mex.
104 C5 **Ziz, Oued** *watercourse* Morocco
105 K1 **Zmiyevka** Rus. Fed.
Znamenka Ukr. *see* **Znam"yanka**
103 M6 **Znam"yanka** Ukr.
109 D5 **Zomba** Malawi
105 J3 **Zonguldak** Turkey
106 B3 **Zorgho** Burkina
106 B4 **Zorzor** Liberia
107 D2 **Zouar** Chad
106 A2 **Zouérat** Mauritania
104 C5 **Zousfana, Oued** *watercourse* Alg.
105 H2 **Zrenjanin** Serbia
103 O5 **Zubova Polyana** Rus. Fed.
106 B4 **Zuénoula** Côte d'Ivoire
Zuider Zee *l.* Neth. *see* **IJsselmeer**
109 D5 **Zumbo** Moz.
106 C4 **Zungeru** Nigeria
112 E4 **Zuni Mountains** U.S.A.
101 C4 **Zunyi** China
104 E2 **Zürich** Switz.
105 F5 **Zuwārah** Libya
103 Q4 **Zuyevka** Rus. Fed.
109 D6 **Zvishavane** Zimbabwe
105 G2 **Zvolen** Slovakia
105 G3 **Zvornik** Bos.-Herz.
106 B4 **Zwedru** Liberia
105 F1 **Zwickau** Germany
104 E1 **Zwolle** Neth.
97 Q3 **Zyryanka** Rus. Fed.

ACKNOWLEDGEMENTS
ATLAS OF THE WORLD

Maps, design and origination by Collins Geo, HarperCollins Publishers, Glasgow
Illustrations created by HarperCollins Publishers unless otherwise stated.

Pages 5–22 IMAGES

6–7

Blue Marble: Next Generation. NASA's Earth Observatory

8–9

Data courtesy Marc Imhoff of NASA GSFC and Christopher Elvidge of NOAA. Image Craig Mayhew and Robert Simmon, NASA GSFC

10–11

NASA/Goddard Space Flight Center Scientific Visualization Studio

12–13

NASA image created by Jesse Allen, using data provided courtesy of NASA/GSFC/METI/ERSDAC/JAROS, and U.S./Japan ASTER Science Team

14–15

NASA/ISS Crew Earth Observations experiment and Image Science & Analysis Laboratory, Johnson Space Center

16–17

NASA image by Norman Kuring, Ocean Color Team

18–19

NASA

20–21

NASA/ISS Crew Earth Observations experiment and Image Science & Analysis Laboratory, Johnson Space Center

22

NASA/JPL/USGS

Pages 23–62 THEMES

24

Dr Tim Hawarden, Royal Observatory, Edinburgh, UK

26–27

The Sun: Jisas/Lockheed/Science Photo Library
Asteroid: NASA/Science Photo Library
Mercury: NASA/Science Photo Library
Venus: NASA/Science Photo Library
Earth: Photo Library International/Science Photo Library
Mars: US Geological Survey/Science Photo Library
Jupiter: NASA/Science Photo Library
Saturn: Space Telescope Science Institute/NASA/Science Photo Library
Uranus: NASA/Science Photo Library
Neptune: NASA/Science Photo Library
Pluto and Charon: Space Telescope Science Institute/NASA/Science Photo Library

28

MODIS/NASA

30–31

Lhoknga 10 Jan: IKONOS image © CRISP 2004
Lhoknga 29 Dec: IKONOS image © CRISP 2004
Mount Bromo: Michael Pitts/naturepl.com

32–33

Seafloor Topography: WHF Smith, US National Oceanic and Atmospheric Administration (NOAA), USA
Sea Surface Height: CLS/DOS, Ramonville St–Agne, France. TOPEX/POSEIDON
Global Ocean Conveyor Belt: Science Photo Library

34–35

Nenets Herders: Bryan and Cherry Alexander
Arctic Peoples: Geo-Innovations, Llandudno, UK.
Cruise Ship: Bryan and Cherry Alexander
Novaya Zemlya: NASA
Antarctica: NRSC Ltd/Science Photo Library

36–37

Köppen classification map: Kottek, M., J. Grieser, C. Beck, B. Rudolf, and F. Rubel, 2006: World Map of the Köppen-Geiger climate classification updated. Meteorol. Z., 15, 259–263.
http://koeppen-geiger.vu-wien.ac.at
Image courtesy Lawrence Ong, EO-1 Mission Science Office, NASA GSFC
Nargis: MODIS/NASA

38

Male: Shahee Ilyas
McCarty Glacier 1909: NSIDC/Ulysses S. Grant
McCarty Glacier 2004: NSIDC/Bruce F. Molina

40–41

Land cover map: © ESA / ESA GlobCover Project, led by MEDIAS-France. Olivier Arino, Patrice Bicheron, Frederic Achard, John Latham, Ron Witt, Jean-Louis Weber, November 2008, GLOBCOVER. The most detailed portrait of Earth. ESA Bulletin 136, pp25–31.
Available at www.esa.int/esapub/bulletin/bulletin136/bul136d_arino.pdf
Ecological footprint: Global Footprint Network
Global Fresh water: Adapted with permission from maps by Philippe Rekacwicz, Le Monde diplomatique, Paris
Hamoun 1976: NASA Earth Observatory
Hamoun 2001: Image courtesy of UNEP

42

Gulf Oil Spill: NASA image by Jeff Schmaltz, MODIS Rapid Response Team
Itaipu dams: Image courtesy of UNEP

43

Campbell, Robert Wellman, ed. 1998. "Chernobyl, Ukraine: 1986, 1992." Earthshots: Satellite Images of Environmental Change. U.S. Geological Survey. http://earthshots.usgs.gov.
Great Barrier Reef: Provided by the SeaWiFS Project, NASA/Goddard Space Flight Center, and OrbImage

44–45

Global Biodiversity: UNEP-WCMC
Living Planet Index: WWF and ZSL, 2006 *Living Planet Report 2006*
Biodiversity under threat: LandScanTM Global Population Database. Oak Ridge, TN: Oak Ridge National Laboratory Modified and updated from: 2004 IUCN *Red List of Threatened Species: A Global Species Assessment*
Protected areas of the World: UNEP-WCMC and World Database on Protected Areas for terrestrial ecoregions as identified by the World Wide Fund for Nature (WWF). www.unep-wcmc.org/wdpa
Sea Around Us Project (L. Wood, 2007), University of British Columbia Fisheries Centre, in collaboration with UNEP-WCMC and WWF, for large marine ecosystems. www.mpaglobal.org

46

Justin Guariglia/Getty Images

48

Hector Conesa/Shutterstock

50

Population map: 2005. Gridded Population of the World Version 3 (GPWv3). Palisades, NY: Socioeconomic Data and Applications Center (SEDAC), Columbia University.
Available at: http://sedac.ciesin.columbia.edu/gpw
http://www.ciesin.columbia.edu
Tōkyō:USGS EROS DATA CENTER

52

Edgar Cleijne/Still Pictures

54

David Vaughan/Science Photo Library

56

IKONOS image courtesy of GeoEye

58

Babylonian Clay Map: © British Museum, London, UK
Ptolemaic World map: The British Library, London, UK
London Extract: Guildhall Library, Corporation of London/Bridgeman Art Library

59

Carte Pisane: PhotoJosse
Mappa Mundi: Hereford Cathedral/Bridgeman Art Library

60

Swiss Topo Map: Reproduced with the permission of the Director of Library Services and Keeper of the Hunterian Books and Manuscripts, Glasgow University Library, Glasgow, UK
Blaeu Map: The British Library, London, UK (also p64–65)
Carte de France: Reproduced by permission of the Trustees of the National Library of Scotland, Edinburgh, UK

61

Smith Geological Map: © The Natural History Museum, London, UK
Huang He: Image reproduced by kind permission of UNEP
Venice: IKONOS image courtesy of GeoEye

62

Garmin Streetpilot: Courtesy of Garmin Ltd www.Garmin.com

Pages 87–124 REFERENCE MAPPING

90

Great Barrier Reef: Provided by the SeaWiFS Project, NASA/Goddard Space Flight Center, and OrbImage
Kamchatka Peninsula: NASA/MODIS
Sand Dunes, Sahara: Jose Fuste Raga/CORBIS
Plains of North America: Robert Holmes/CORBIS

92

Joseph Sohm/Visions of America/CORBIS

124

National Oceanic and Atmospheric Administration (NOAA)

GeoEye   www.geoeye.com
NASA   earthobservatory.nasa.gov
NASA   rapidfire.sci.gsfc.nasa.gov
NASA   asterweb.jpl.nasa.gov/index.asp
NOAA   www.noaa.gov
United Nations Environment Programme   www.na.unep.net